Brett was one of my best friends growing up from when I was ten years old. We both loved cartoons and doodled a lot, and I'll never forget in our early days, when our friendship was still fairly new, he drew a cartoon of me in a matter of three minutes. I realized that day what an amazing gift and talent he had. Remembering back, it was always fun to see what we were thinking through his cartoons during our grade school, college, and post-college years. He really knew how to express ridiculous situations that surrounded us in his drawings. When Brett started his comic *Free for All* and I saw that he was using Johnny Jenkins as a character, I felt honored.

The last few years, we had a falling-out, but I always thought we would reconnect again, and I thought it would be soon. Now that day will never come because a coward decided to end my friend's life early. What I've learned is to try to forgive the ones you love the most right away, because you never know when an event might change your life forever.

I love you, Brett, and I hope you are in an amazing place right now, and I miss you. Thank you, Randy, Debbie, and Melanie and everyone else who loved Brett, for making this book happen and keeping Brett's memory and spirit alive.

—John Gohringer

THE BEST OF FREE FOR ALL

Brett Merhar

The Best of Free for All

iUniverse books may be ordered through booksellers or by contacting:

iUniverse
1663 Liberty Drive
Bloomington, IN 47403
www.iuniverse.com
1-800-Authors (1-800-288-4677)

Because of the dynamic nature of the Internet, any web addresses or links contained in this book may have changed since publication and may no longer be valid. The views expressed in this work are solely those of the author and do not necessarily reflect the views of the publisher, and the publisher hereby disclaims any responsibility for them.

Any people depicted in stock imagery provided by Thinkstock are models, and such images are being used for illustrative purposes only.
Certain stock imagery © Thinkstock.

ISBN: 978-1-5320-1811-4 (sc)
ISBN: 978-1-5320-1812-1 (e)

Library of Congress Control Number: 2017902846

Print information available on the last page.

iUniverse rev. date: 03/07/2017

This book is dedicated to the memory of our beloved son, Brett Merhar, by his parents Randall and Debra Merhar, so he can be remembered by his many fans and friends for his very popular comic strip, *Free for All.*

May he forever rest in peace. He will be missed.

Brett Merhar
June 16, 1970–July 28, 2016

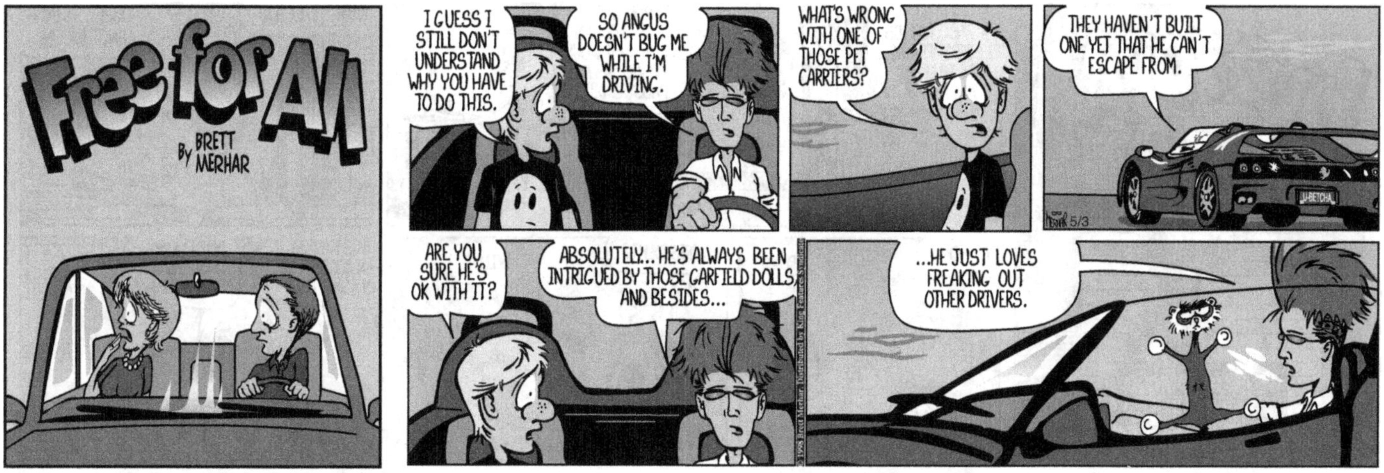
Free for All
By BRETT MERHAR
I GUESS I STILL DON'T UNDERSTAND WHY YOU HAVE TO DO THIS.
SO ANGUS DOESN'T BUG ME WHILE I'M DRIVING.
WHAT'S WRONG WITH ONE OF THOSE PET CARRIERS?
THEY HAVEN'T BUILT ONE YET THAT HE CAN'T ESCAPE FROM.
U-BETCHA
5/3
ARE YOU SURE HE'S OK WITH IT?
ABSOLUTELY... HE'S ALWAYS BEEN INTRIGUED BY THOSE GARFIELD DOLLS AND BESIDES...
...HE JUST LOVES FREAKING OUT OTHER DRIVERS.

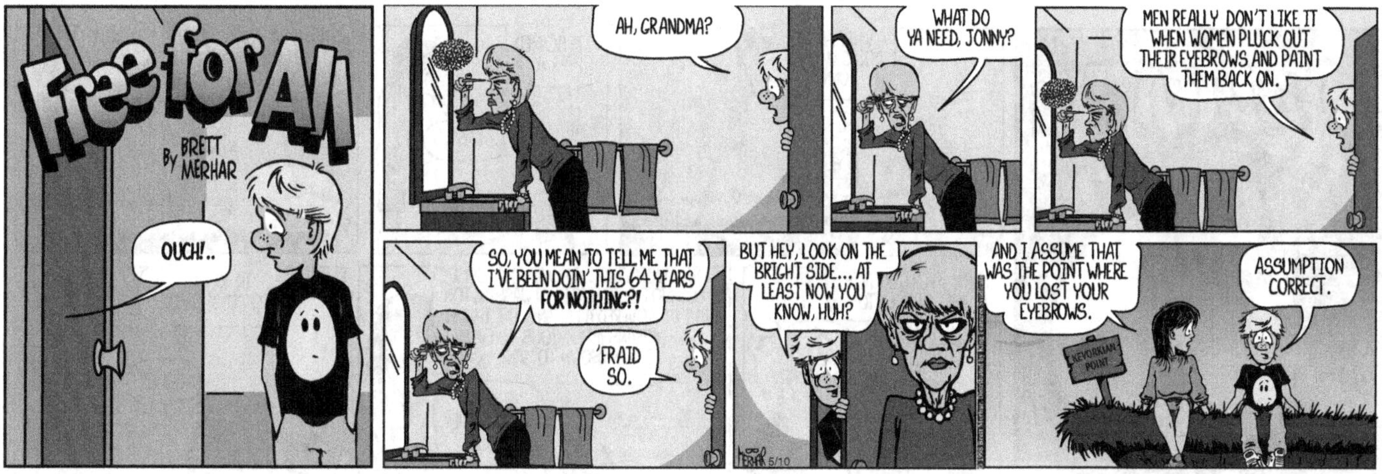
Free for All
By BRETT MERHAR
OUCH!..
AH, GRANDMA?
WHAT DO YA NEED, JONNY?
MEN REALLY DON'T LIKE IT WHEN WOMEN PLUCK OUT THEIR EYEBROWS AND PAINT THEM BACK ON.
SO, YOU MEAN TO TELL ME THAT I'VE BEEN DOIN' THIS 64 YEARS FOR NOTHING?!
'FRAID SO.
5/10
BUT HEY, LOOK ON THE BRIGHT SIDE... AT LEAST NOW YOU KNOW, HUH?
AND I ASSUME THAT WAS THE POINT WHERE YOU LOST YOUR EYEBROWS.
ASSUMPTION CORRECT.
KEVORKIAN POINT

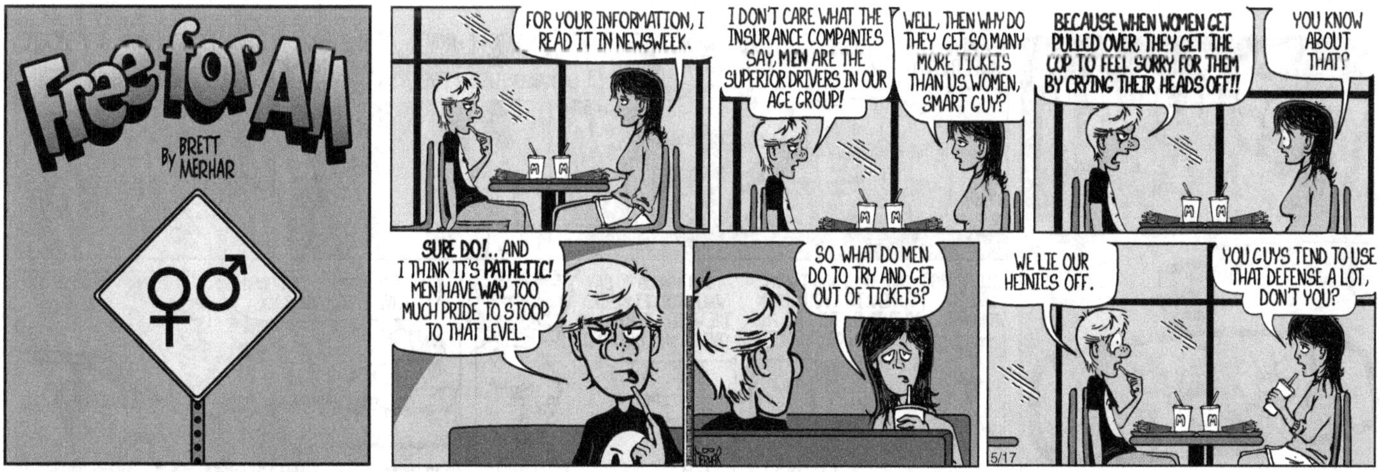
Free for All
By BRETT MERHAR
♀♂
FOR YOUR INFORMATION, I READ IT IN NEWSWEEK.
I DON'T CARE WHAT THE INSURANCE COMPANIES SAY, MEN ARE THE SUPERIOR DRIVERS IN OUR AGE GROUP!
WELL, THEN WHY DO THEY GET SO MANY MORE TICKETS THAN US WOMEN, SMART GUY?
BECAUSE WHEN WOMEN GET PULLED OVER, THEY GET THE COP TO FEEL SORRY FOR THEM BY CRYING THEIR HEADS OFF!!
YOU KNOW ABOUT THAT?
SURE DO!.. AND I THINK IT'S PATHETIC! MEN HAVE WAY TOO MUCH PRIDE TO STOOP TO THAT LEVEL.
SO WHAT DO MEN DO TO TRY AND GET OUT OF TICKETS?
WE LIE OUR HEINIES OFF.
YOU GUYS TEND TO USE THAT DEFENSE A LOT, DON'T YOU?
5/17

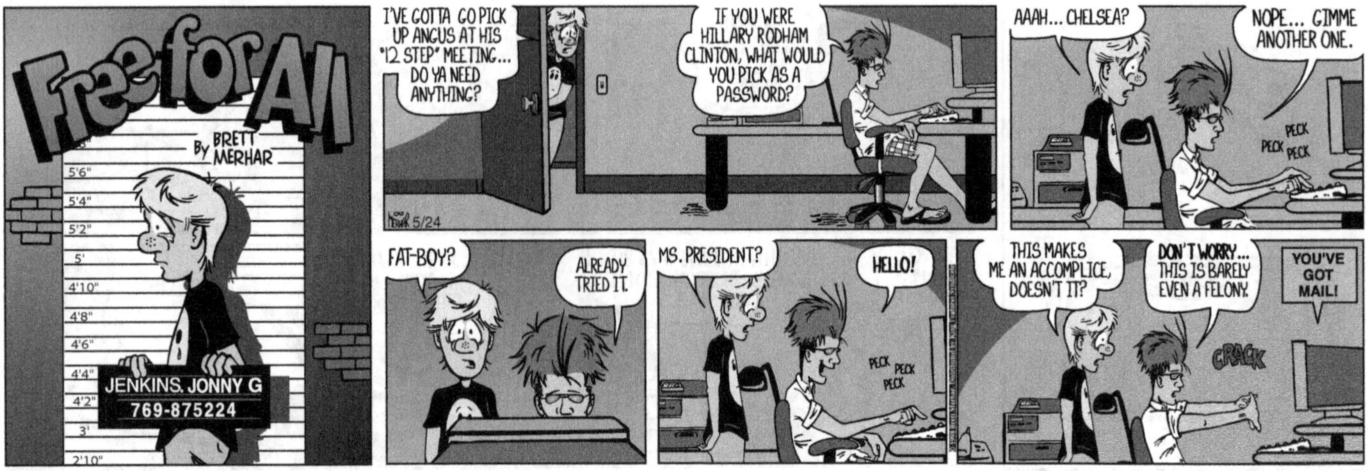
Free for All
By BRETT MERHAR
JENKINS, JONNY G
769-875224
I'VE GOTTA GO PICK UP ANGUS AT HIS "12 STEP" MEETING... DO YA NEED ANYTHING?
IF YOU WERE HILLARY RODHAM CLINTON, WHAT WOULD YOU PICK AS A PASSWORD?
5/24
AAAH... CHELSEA?
NOPE... GIMME ANOTHER ONE.
PECK PECK PECK
FAT-BOY?
ALREADY TRIED IT.
MS. PRESIDENT?
HELLO!
PECK PECK PECK
THIS MAKES ME AN ACCOMPLICE, DOESN'T IT?
DON'T WORRY... THIS IS BARELY EVEN A FELONY.
YOU'VE GOT MAIL!
CRACK

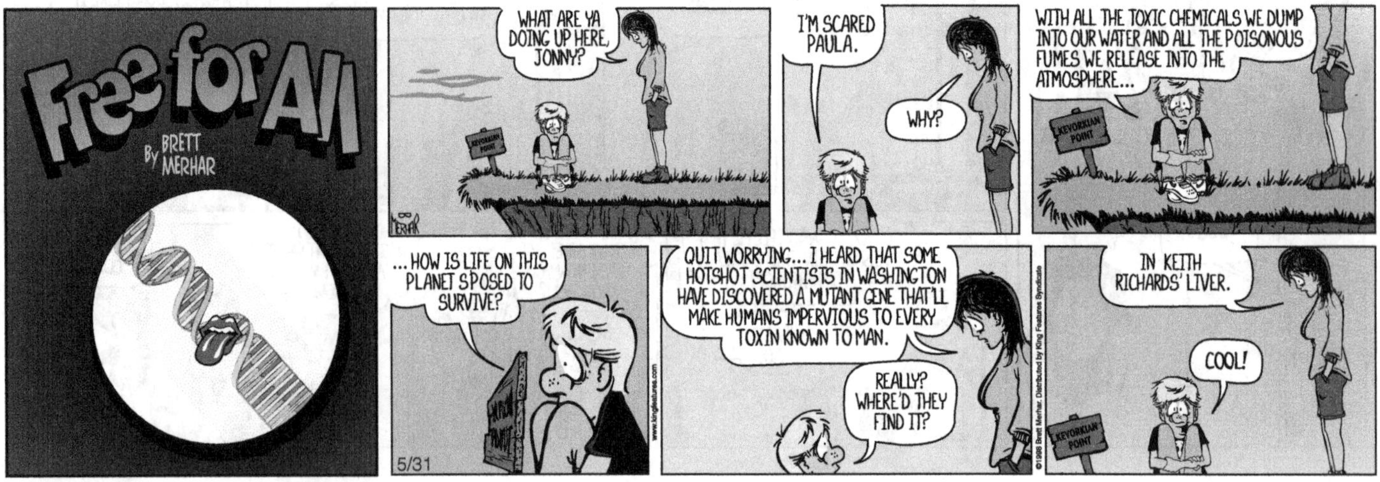
Free for All
By BRETT MERHAR
WHAT ARE YA DOING UP HERE, JONNY?
KEVORKIAN POINT
I'M SCARED PAULA.
WHY?
WITH ALL THE TOXIC CHEMICALS WE DUMP INTO OUR WATER AND ALL THE POISONOUS FUMES WE RELEASE INTO THE ATMOSPHERE...
...HOW IS LIFE ON THIS PLANET S'POSED TO SURVIVE?
5/31
QUIT WORRYING... I HEARD THAT SOME HOTSHOT SCIENTISTS IN WASHINGTON HAVE DISCOVERED A MUTANT GENE THAT'LL MAKE HUMANS IMPERVIOUS TO EVERY TOXIN KNOWN TO MAN.
REALLY? WHERE'D THEY FIND IT?
IN KEITH RICHARDS' LIVER.
COOL!
KEVORKIAN POINT

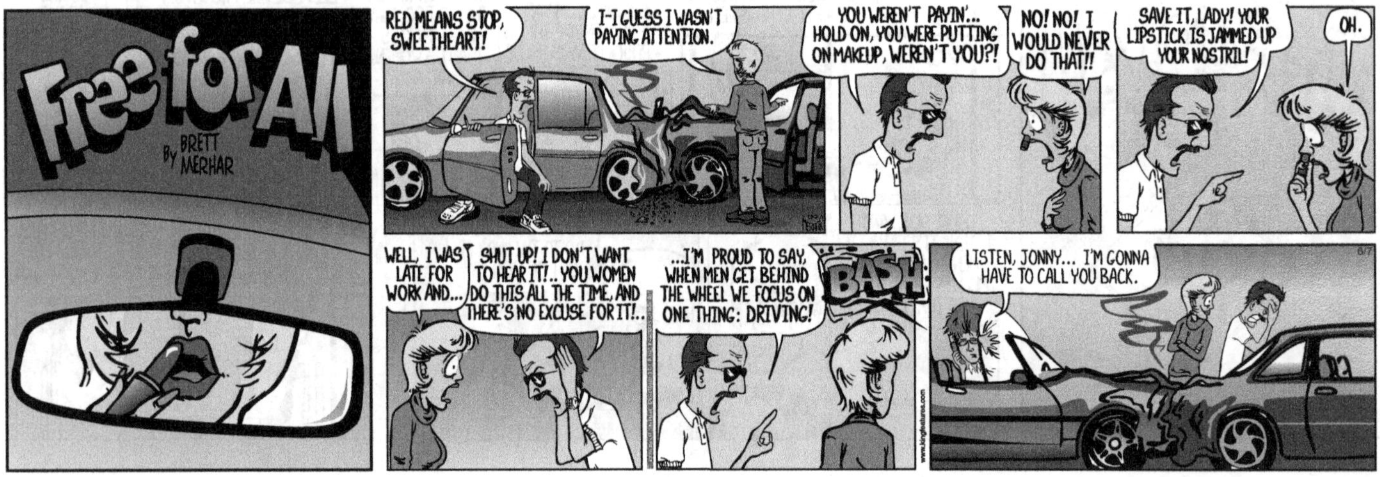
Free for All
By BRETT MERHAR
RED MEANS STOP, SWEETHEART!
I-I GUESS I WASN'T PAYING ATTENTION.
YOU WEREN'T PAYIN'... HOLD ON, YOU WERE PUTTING ON MAKEUP, WEREN'T YOU?!
NO! NO! I WOULD NEVER DO THAT!!
SAVE IT, LADY! YOUR LIPSTICK IS JAMMED UP YOUR NOSTRIL!
OH.
WELL, I WAS LATE FOR WORK AND...
SHUT UP! I DON'T WANT TO HEAR IT!.. YOU WOMEN DO THIS ALL THE TIME, AND THERE'S NO EXCUSE FOR IT!..
...I'M PROUD TO SAY, WHEN MEN GET BEHIND THE WHEEL WE FOCUS ON ONE THING: DRIVING!
BASH
LISTEN, JONNY... I'M GONNA HAVE TO CALL YOU BACK.

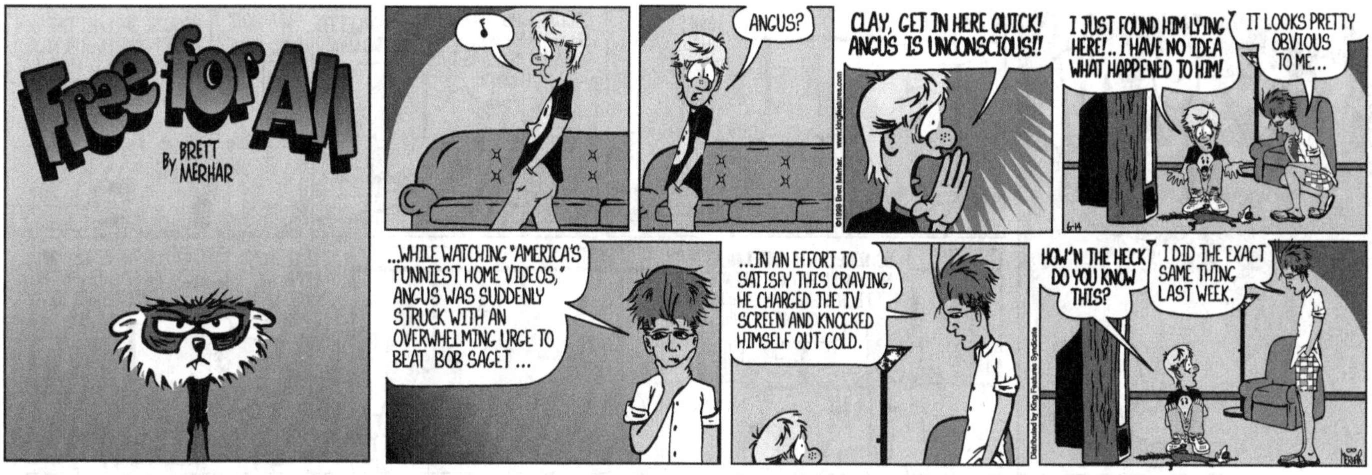

Free for All
By BRETT MERHAR
?
ANGUS?
CLAY, GET IN HERE QUICK! ANGUS IS UNCONSCIOUS!!
I JUST FOUND HIM LYING HERE!.. I HAVE NO IDEA WHAT HAPPENED TO HIM!
IT LOOKS PRETTY OBVIOUS TO ME...
...WHILE WATCHING "AMERICA'S FUNNIEST HOME VIDEOS," ANGUS WAS SUDDENLY STRUCK WITH AN OVERWHELMING URGE TO BEAT BOB SAGET...
...IN AN EFFORT TO SATISFY THIS CRAVING, HE CHARGED THE TV SCREEN AND KNOCKED HIMSELF OUT COLD.
HOW'N THE HECK DO YOU KNOW THIS?
I DID THE EXACT SAME THING LAST WEEK.

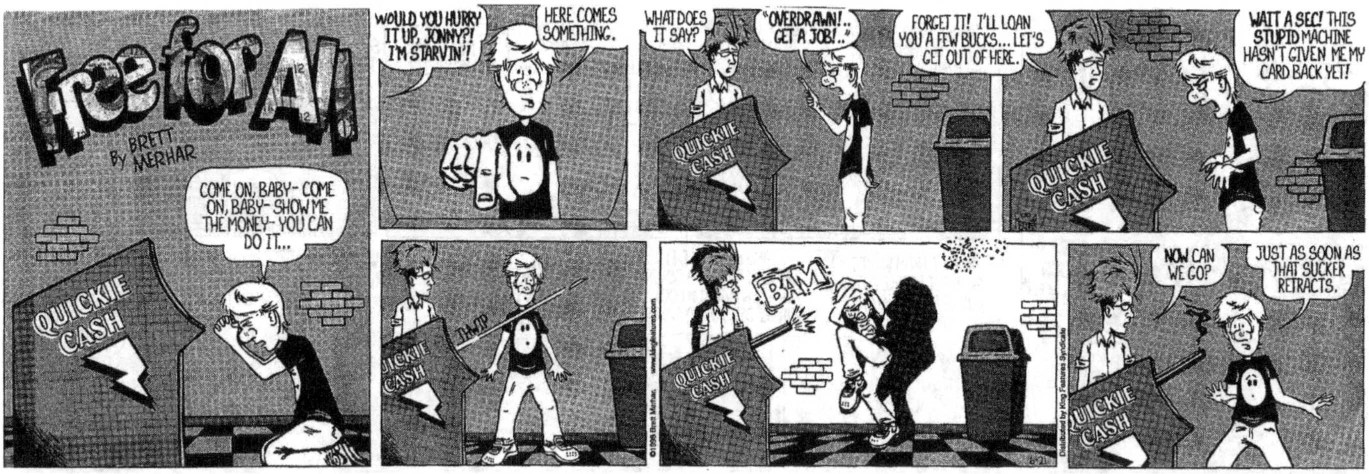

Free for All
BY BRETT MERHAR
COME ON, BABY- COME ON, BABY- SHOW ME THE MONEY- YOU CAN DO IT...
QUICKIE CASH
WOULD YOU HURRY IT UP, JONNY?! I'M STARVIN'!
HERE COMES SOMETHING.
WHAT DOES IT SAY?
"OVERDRAWN!.. GET A JOB!.."
FORGET IT! I'LL LOAN YOU A FEW BUCKS... LET'S GET OUT OF HERE.
WAIT A SEC! THIS STUPID MACHINE HASN'T GIVEN ME MY CARD BACK YET!
THWIP
BAM
NOW CAN WE GO?
JUST AS SOON AS THAT SUCKER RETRACTS.

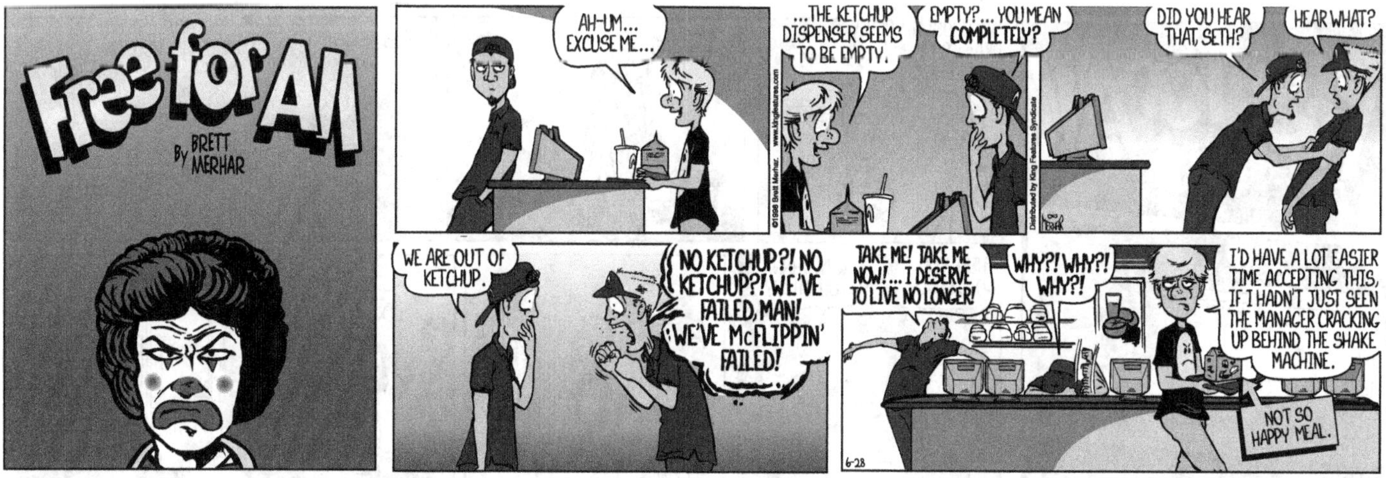

Free for All
BY BRETT MERHAR
AH-UM... EXCUSE ME...
...THE KETCHUP DISPENSER SEEMS TO BE EMPTY.
EMPTY?... YOU MEAN COMPLETELY?
DID YOU HEAR THAT, SETH?
HEAR WHAT?
WE ARE OUT OF KETCHUP.
NO KETCHUP?! NO KETCHUP?! WE'VE FAILED, MAN! WE'VE McFLIPPIN' FAILED!
TAKE ME! TAKE ME NOW!... I DESERVE TO LIVE NO LONGER!
WHY?! WHY?! WHY?!
I'D HAVE A LOT EASIER TIME ACCEPTING THIS, IF I HADN'T JUST SEEN THE MANAGER CRACKING UP BEHIND THE SHAKE MACHINE.
NOT SO HAPPY MEAL.

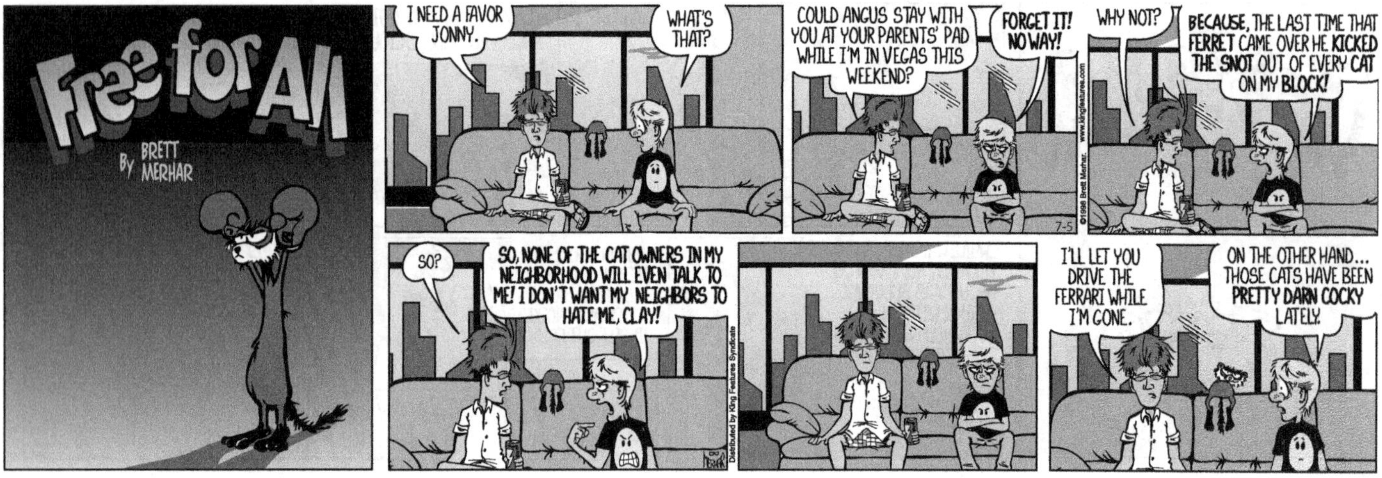

Free for All
By BRETT MERHAR
I NEED A FAVOR JONNY.
WHAT'S THAT?
COULD ANGUS STAY WITH YOU AT YOUR PARENTS' PAD WHILE I'M IN VEGAS THIS WEEKEND?
FORGET IT! NO WAY!
WHY NOT?
BECAUSE, THE LAST TIME THAT FERRET CAME OVER HE KICKED THE SNOT OUT OF EVERY CAT ON MY BLOCK!
SO?
SO, NONE OF THE CAT OWNERS IN MY NEIGHBORHOOD WILL EVEN TALK TO ME! I DON'T WANT MY NEIGHBORS TO HATE ME, CLAY!
I'LL LET YOU DRIVE THE FERRARI WHILE I'M GONE.
ON THE OTHER HAND... THOSE CATS HAVE BEEN PRETTY DARN COCKY LATELY.
7-5
©1998 Brett Merhar. www.kingfeatures.com
Distributed by King Features Syndicate

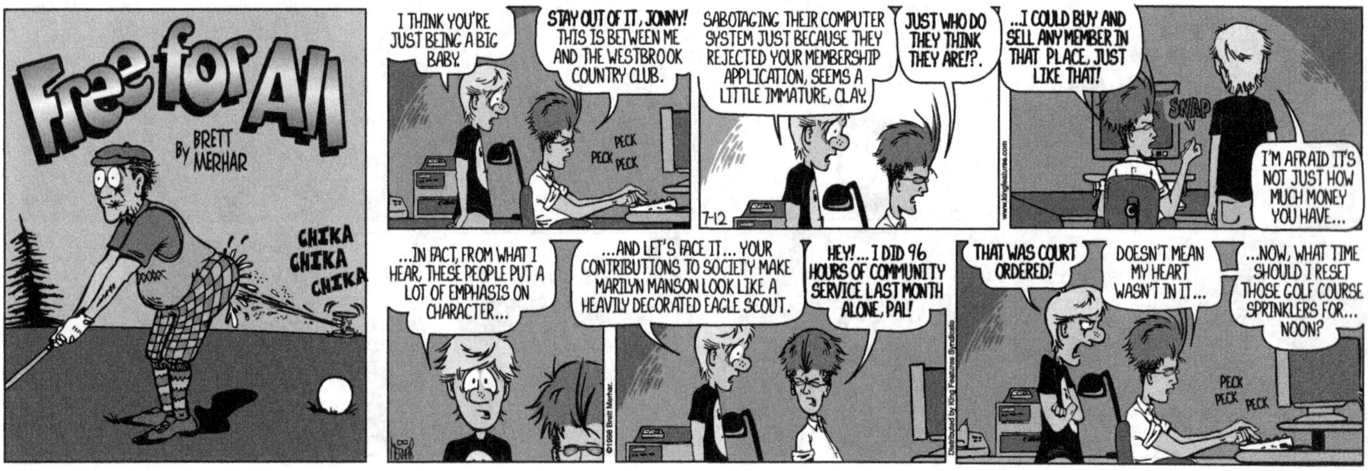

Free for All
By BRETT MERHAR
CHIKA CHIKA CHIKA
I THINK YOU'RE JUST BEING A BIG BABY.
STAY OUT OF IT, JONNY! THIS IS BETWEEN ME AND THE WESTBROOK COUNTRY CLUB.
PECK PECK PECK
SABOTAGING THEIR COMPUTER SYSTEM JUST BECAUSE THEY REJECTED YOUR MEMBERSHIP APPLICATION, SEEMS A LITTLE IMMATURE, CLAY.
JUST WHO DO THEY THINK THEY ARE!?.
...I COULD BUY AND SELL ANY MEMBER IN THAT PLACE, JUST LIKE THAT!
SNAP
I'M AFRAID IT'S NOT JUST HOW MUCH MONEY YOU HAVE...
7-12
www.kingfeatures.com
...IN FACT, FROM WHAT I HEAR, THESE PEOPLE PUT A LOT OF EMPHASIS ON CHARACTER...
...AND LET'S FACE IT... YOUR CONTRIBUTIONS TO SOCIETY MAKE MARILYN MANSON LOOK LIKE A HEAVILY DECORATED EAGLE SCOUT.
HEY!... I DID 96 HOURS OF COMMUNITY SERVICE LAST MONTH ALONE, PAL!
THAT WAS COURT ORDERED!
DOESN'T MEAN MY HEART WASN'T IN IT...
...NOW, WHAT TIME SHOULD I RESET THOSE GOLF COURSE SPRINKLERS FOR... NOON?
PECK PECK PECK
©1998 Brett Merhar.
Distributed by King Features Syndicate

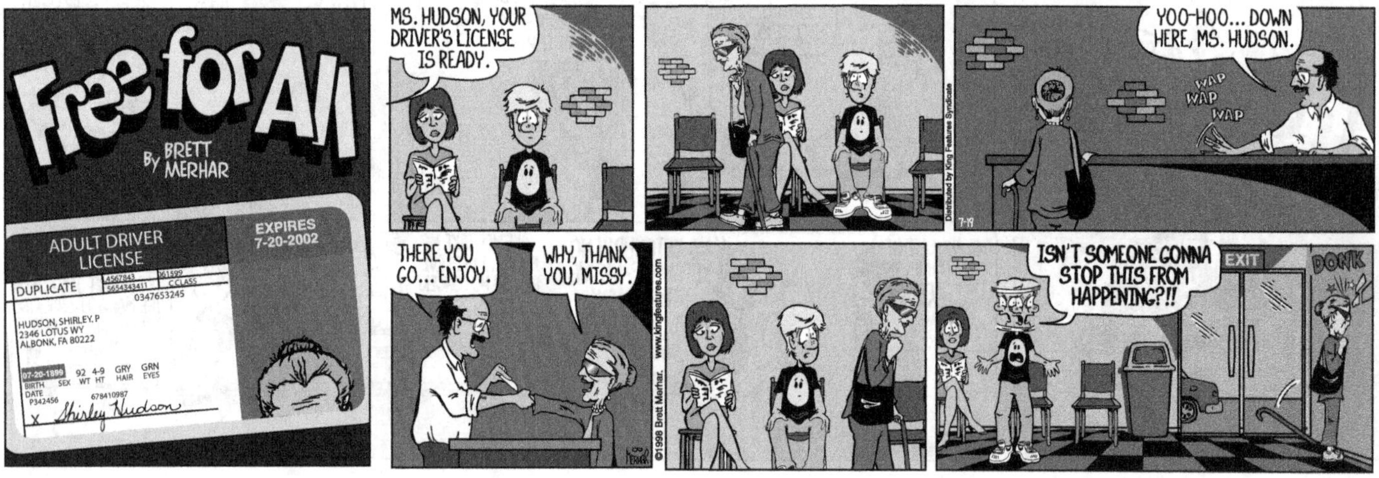

Free for All
By BRETT MERHAR
ADULT DRIVER LICENSE
EXPIRES 7-20-2002
DUPLICATE
HUDSON, SHIRLEY P
2346 LOTUS WY
ALBONK, FA 80222
Shirley Hudson
MS. HUDSON, YOUR DRIVER'S LICENSE IS READY.
YOO-HOO... DOWN HERE, MS. HUDSON.
WAP WAP WAP
7-19
Distributed by King Features Syndicate
THERE YOU GO... ENJOY.
WHY, THANK YOU, MISSY.
©1998 Brett Merhar. www.kingfeatures.com
ISN'T SOMEONE GONNA STOP THIS FROM HAPPENING?!!
EXIT
DONK

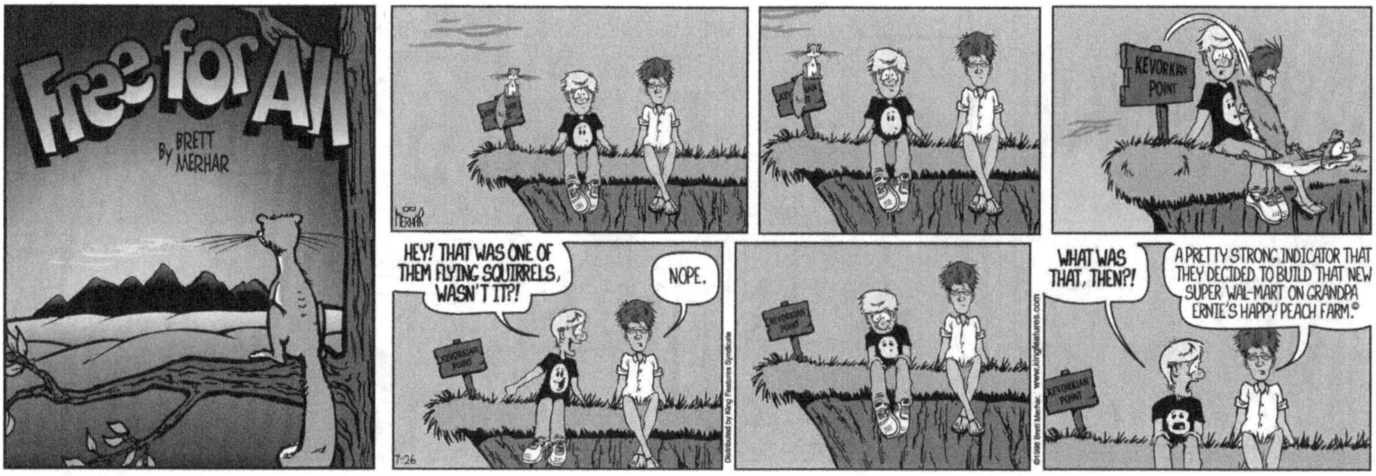
Free for All
By BRETT MERHAR
7-26
KEVORKIAN POINT
HEY! THAT WAS ONE OF THEM FLYING SQUIRRELS, WASN'T IT?!
NOPE.
Distributed by King Features Syndicate
©1998 Brett Merhar. www.kingfeatures.com
WHAT WAS THAT, THEN?!
A PRETTY STRONG INDICATOR THAT THEY DECIDED TO BUILD THAT NEW SUPER WAL-MART ON GRANDPA ERNIE'S HAPPY PEACH FARM.

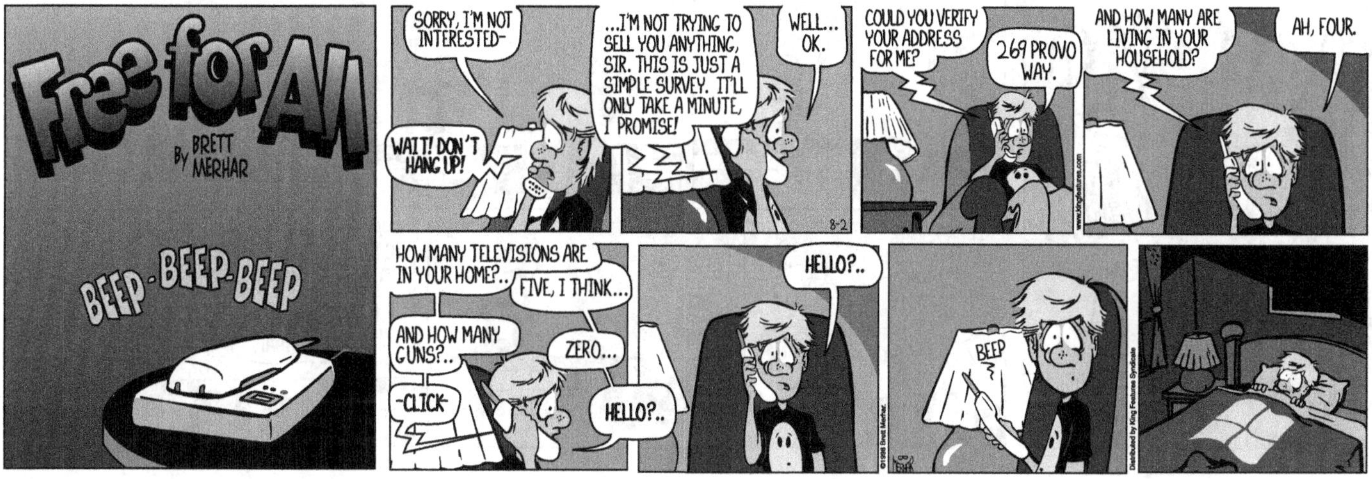
Free for All
By BRETT MERHAR
BEEP-BEEP-BEEP
SORRY, I'M NOT INTERESTED-
WAIT! DON'T HANG UP!
...I'M NOT TRYING TO SELL YOU ANYTHING, SIR. THIS IS JUST A SIMPLE SURVEY. IT'LL ONLY TAKE A MINUTE, I PROMISE!
WELL... OK.
8-2
COULD YOU VERIFY YOUR ADDRESS FOR ME?
269 PROVO WAY.
www.kingfeatures.com
AND HOW MANY ARE LIVING IN YOUR HOUSEHOLD?
AH, FOUR.
HOW MANY TELEVISIONS ARE IN YOUR HOME?..
FIVE, I THINK...
AND HOW MANY GUNS?..
ZERO...
-CLICK-
HELLO?..
HELLO?..
©1998 Brett Merhar.
BEEP
Distributed by King Features Syndicate

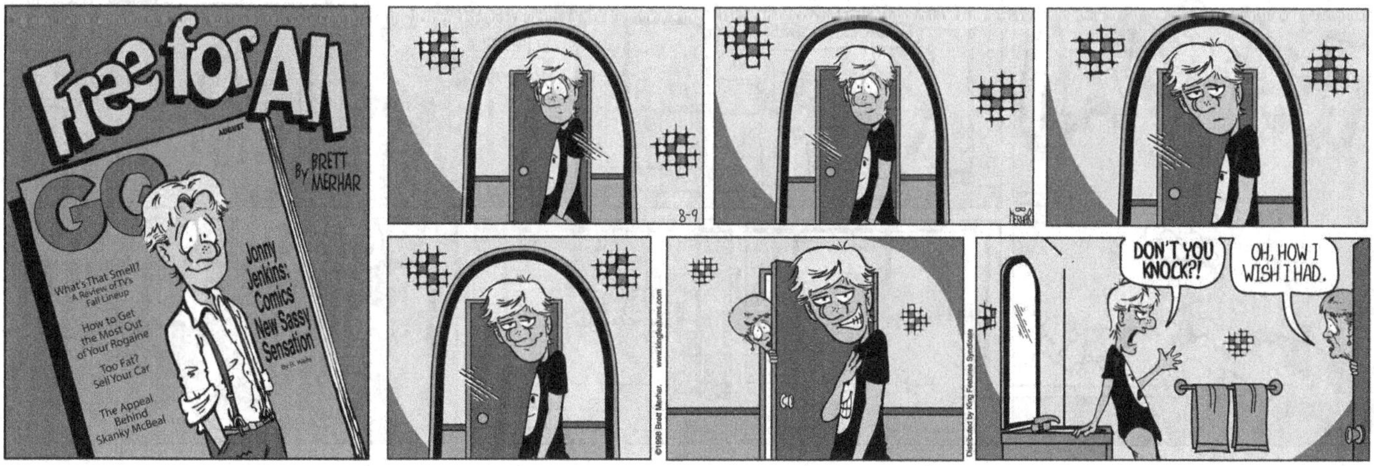
Free for All
By BRETT MERHAR
AUGUST
GQ
What's That Smell? A Review of TV's Fall Lineup
How to Get the Most Out of Your Rogaine
Too Fat? Sell Your Car
The Appeal Behind Skanky McBeal
Jonny Jenkins: Comics' New Sassy Sensation
8-9
©1998 Brett Merhar. www.kingfeatures.com
Distributed by King Features Syndicate
DON'T YOU KNOCK?!
OH, HOW I WISH I HAD.

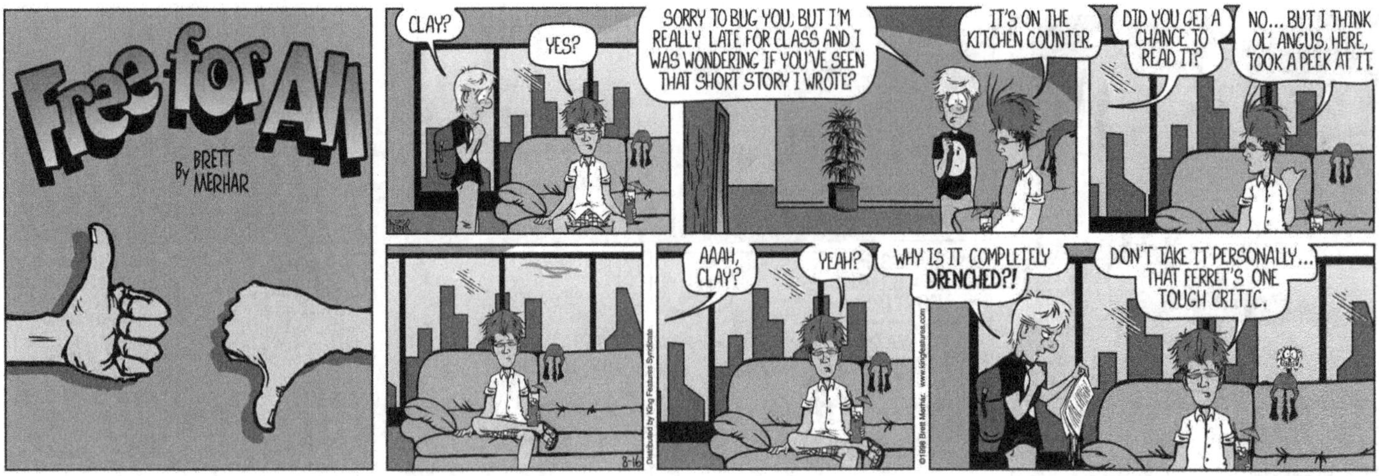
Free for All
By BRETT MERHAR
CLAY?
YES?
SORRY TO BUG YOU, BUT I'M REALLY LATE FOR CLASS AND I WAS WONDERING IF YOU'VE SEEN THAT SHORT STORY I WROTE?
IT'S ON THE KITCHEN COUNTER.
DID YOU GET A CHANCE TO READ IT?
NO... BUT I THINK OL' ANGUS, HERE, TOOK A PEEK AT IT.
8-16
Distributed by King Features Syndicate
AAAH, CLAY?
YEAH?
©1998 Brett Merhar. www.kingfeatures.com
WHY IS IT COMPLETELY DRENCHED?!
DON'T TAKE IT PERSONALLY... THAT FERRET'S ONE TOUGH CRITIC.

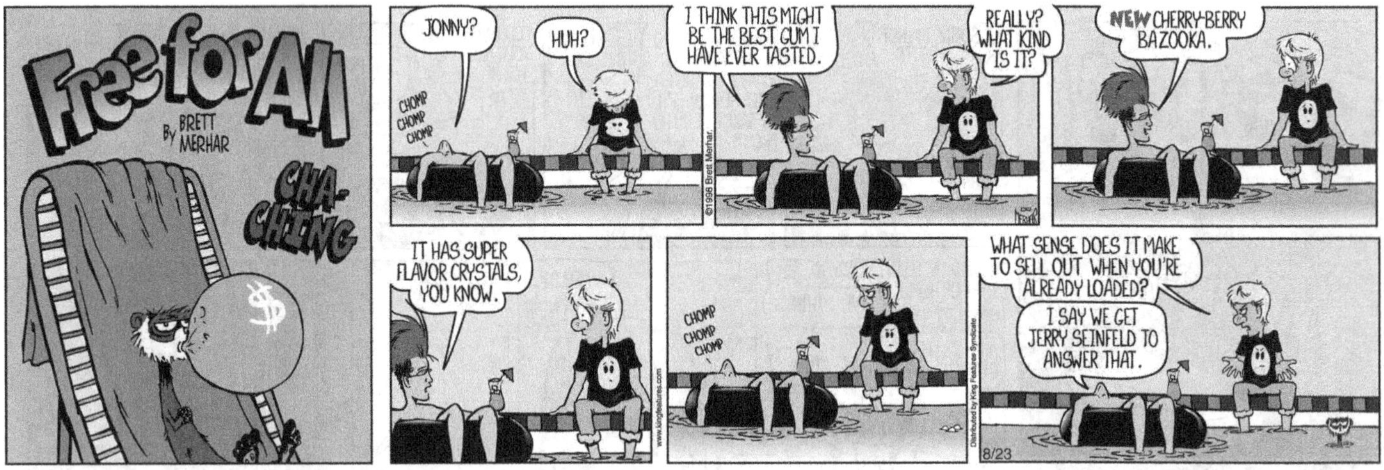
Free for All
By BRETT MERHAR
CHA-CHING
JONNY?
CHOMP CHOMP CHOMP
HUH?
©1998 Brett Merhar.
I THINK THIS MIGHT BE THE BEST GUM I HAVE EVER TASTED.
REALLY? WHAT KIND IS IT?
NEW CHERRY-BERRY BAZOOKA.
IT HAS SUPER FLAVOR CRYSTALS, YOU KNOW.
www.kingfeatures.com
CHOMP CHOMP CHOMP
Distributed by King Features Syndicate
WHAT SENSE DOES IT MAKE TO SELL OUT WHEN YOU'RE ALREADY LOADED?
I SAY WE GET JERRY SEINFELD TO ANSWER THAT.
8/23

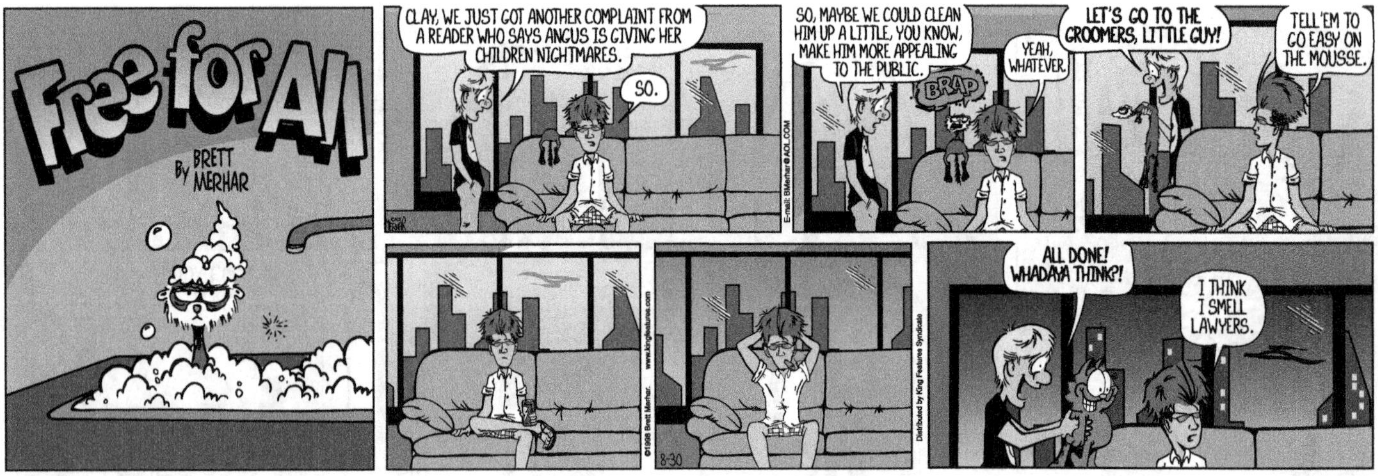
Free for All
By BRETT MERHAR
CLAY, WE JUST GOT ANOTHER COMPLAINT FROM A READER WHO SAYS ANGUS IS GIVING HER CHILDREN NIGHTMARES.
SO.
E-mail: BMerhar@AOL.COM
SO, MAYBE WE COULD CLEAN HIM UP A LITTLE, YOU KNOW, MAKE HIM MORE APPEALING TO THE PUBLIC.
BRAP
YEAH, WHATEVER.
LET'S GO TO THE GROOMERS, LITTLE GUY!
TELL 'EM TO GO EASY ON THE MOUSSE.
©1998 Brett Merhar. www.kingfeatures.com
8-30
Distributed by King Features Syndicate
ALL DONE! WHADAYA THINK?!
I THINK I SMELL LAWYERS.

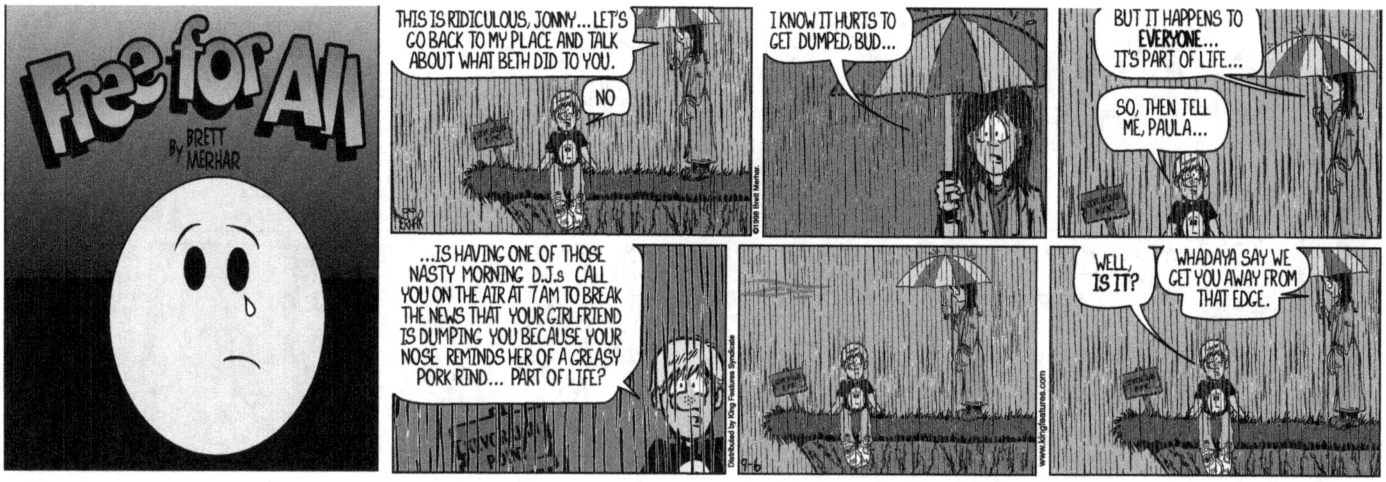
Free for All
By Brett Merhar
THIS IS RIDICULOUS, JONNY... LET'S GO BACK TO MY PLACE AND TALK ABOUT WHAT BETH DID TO YOU.
NO
I KNOW IT HURTS TO GET DUMPED, BUD...
BUT IT HAPPENS TO EVERYONE... IT'S PART OF LIFE...
SO, THEN TELL ME, PAULA...
...IS HAVING ONE OF THOSE NASTY MORNING D.J.s CALL YOU ON THE AIR AT 7 AM TO BREAK THE NEWS THAT YOUR GIRLFRIEND IS DUMPING YOU BECAUSE YOUR NOSE REMINDS HER OF A GREASY PORK RIND... PART OF LIFE?
WELL, IS IT?
WHADAYA SAY WE GET YOU AWAY FROM THAT EDGE.
©1998 Brett Merhar
Distributed by King Features Syndicate
www.kingfeatures.com
9-6

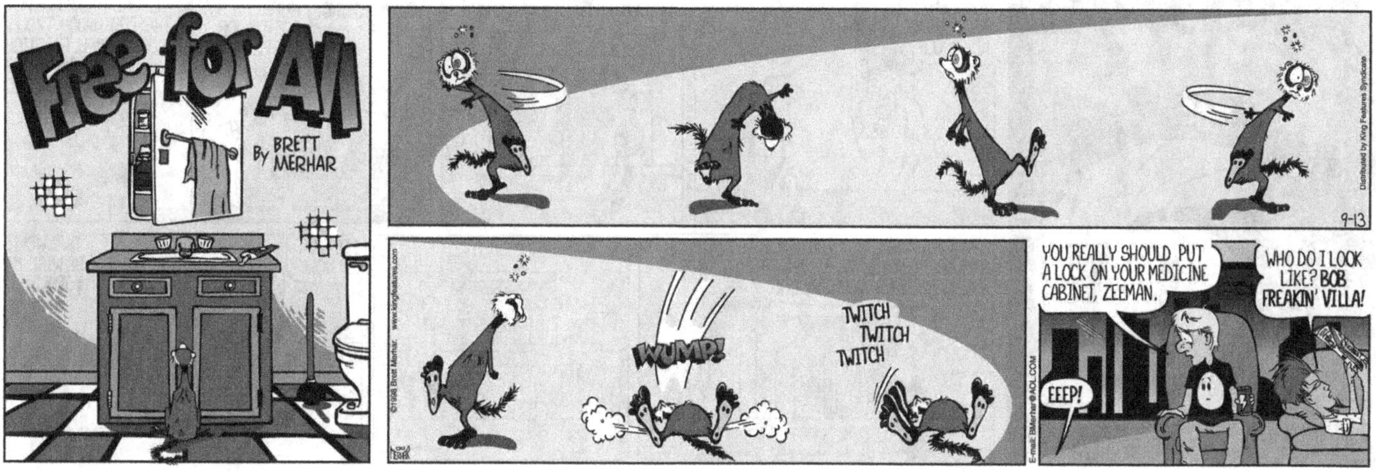
Free for All
By Brett Merhar
9-13
Distributed by King Features Syndicate
WUMP!
TWITCH
TWITCH
TWITCH
YOU REALLY SHOULD PUT A LOCK ON YOUR MEDICINE CABINET, ZEEMAN.
WHO DO I LOOK LIKE? BOB FREAKIN' VILLA!
EEEP!
©1998 Brett Merhar
www.kingfeatures.com
E-mail: BMerhar@AOL.COM

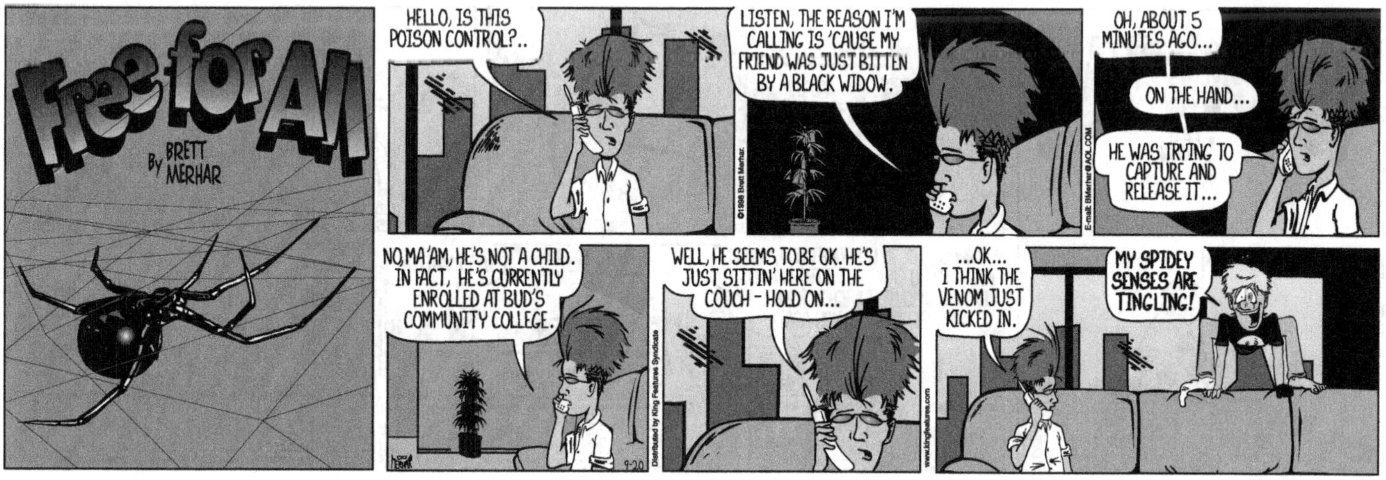
Free for All
By Brett Merhar
HELLO, IS THIS POISON CONTROL?..
LISTEN, THE REASON I'M CALLING IS 'CAUSE MY FRIEND WAS JUST BITTEN BY A BLACK WIDOW.
OH, ABOUT 5 MINUTES AGO...
ON THE HAND...
HE WAS TRYING TO CAPTURE AND RELEASE IT...
NO, MA'AM, HE'S NOT A CHILD. IN FACT, HE'S CURRENTLY ENROLLED AT BUD'S COMMUNITY COLLEGE.
WELL, HE SEEMS TO BE OK. HE'S JUST SITTIN' HERE ON THE COUCH - HOLD ON...
...OK... I THINK THE VENOM JUST KICKED IN.
MY SPIDEY SENSES ARE TINGLING!
©1998 Brett Merhar
E-mail: BMerhar@AOL.COM
Distributed by King Features Syndicate
www.kingfeatures.com
9-20

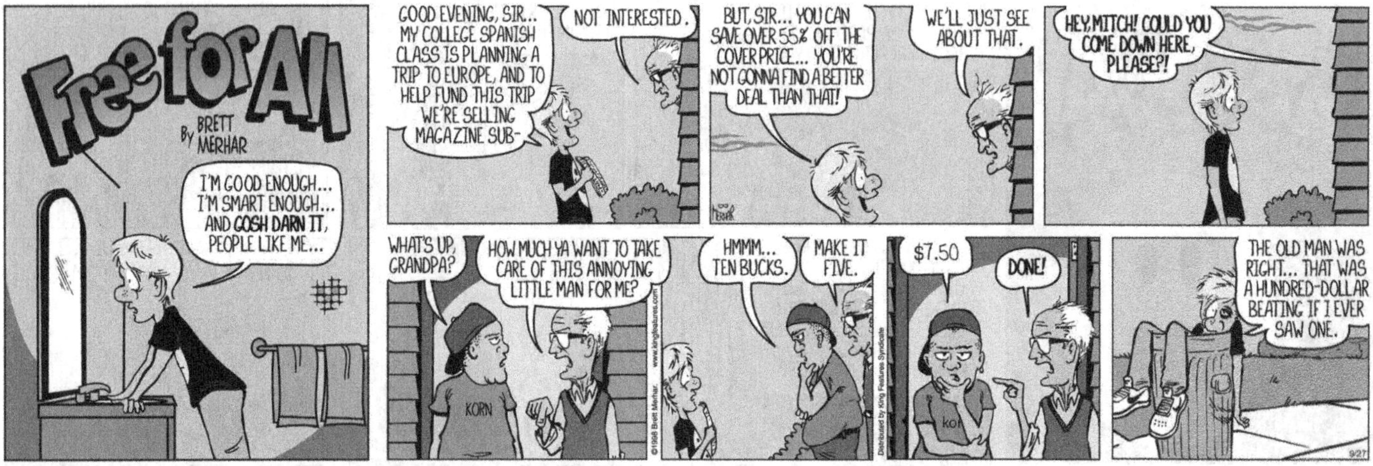
Free for All
By BRETT MERHAR
I'M GOOD ENOUGH... I'M SMART ENOUGH... AND GOSH DARN IT, PEOPLE LIKE ME...
GOOD EVENING, SIR... MY COLLEGE SPANISH CLASS IS PLANNING A TRIP TO EUROPE, AND TO HELP FUND THIS TRIP WE'RE SELLING MAGAZINE SUB-
NOT INTERESTED.
BUT, SIR... YOU CAN SAVE OVER 55% OFF THE COVER PRICE... YOU'RE NOT GONNA FIND A BETTER DEAL THAN THAT!
WE'LL JUST SEE ABOUT THAT.
HEY, MITCH! COULD YOU COME DOWN HERE, PLEASE?!
WHAT'S UP, GRANDPA?
HOW MUCH YA WANT TO TAKE CARE OF THIS ANNOYING LITTLE MAN FOR ME?
HMMM... TEN BUCKS.
MAKE IT FIVE.
$7.50
DONE!
THE OLD MAN WAS RIGHT... THAT WAS A HUNDRED-DOLLAR BEATING IF I EVER SAW ONE.
KORN
9/27

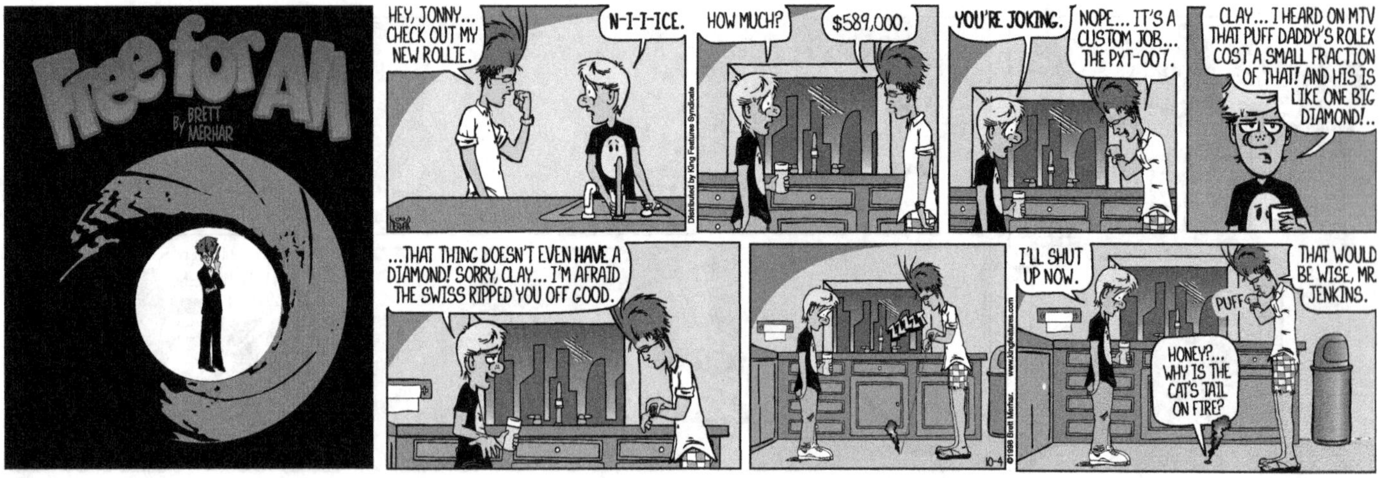
Free for All
By BRETT MERHAR
HEY, JONNY... CHECK OUT MY NEW ROLLIE.
N-I-I-ICE.
HOW MUCH?
$589,000.
YOU'RE JOKING.
NOPE... IT'S A CUSTOM JOB... THE PXT-007.
CLAY... I HEARD ON MTV THAT PUFF DADDY'S ROLEX COST A SMALL FRACTION OF THAT! AND HIS IS LIKE ONE BIG DIAMOND!..
...THAT THING DOESN'T EVEN HAVE A DIAMOND! SORRY, CLAY... I'M AFRAID THE SWISS RIPPED YOU OFF GOOD.
I'LL SHUT UP NOW.
THAT WOULD BE WISE, MR. JENKINS.
PUFF
HONEY?... WHY IS THE CAT'S TAIL ON FIRE?
10-4

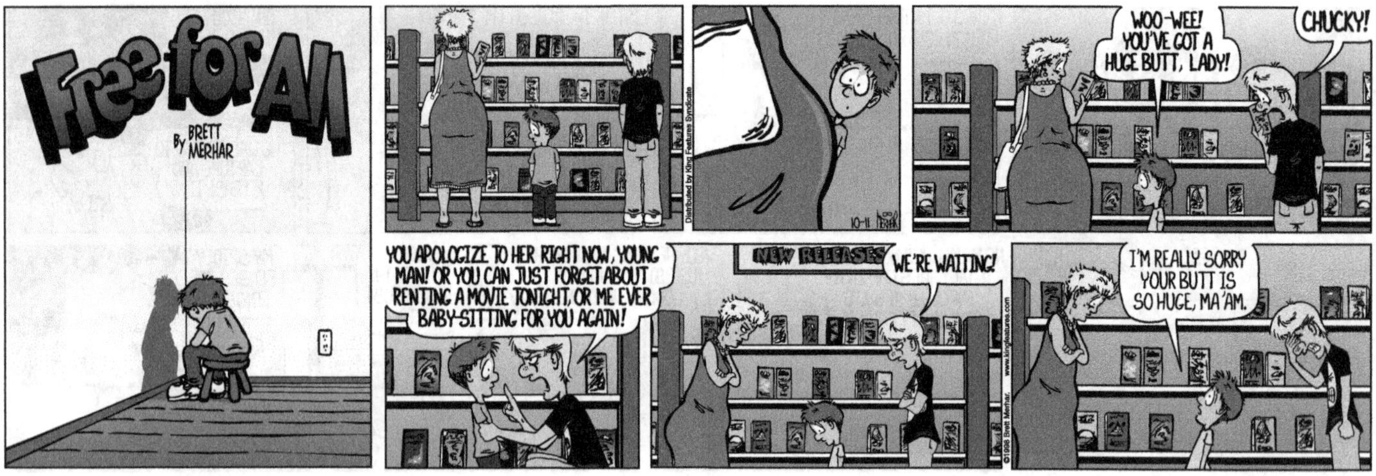
Free for All
By BRETT MERHAR
WOO-WEE! YOU'VE GOT A HUGE BUTT, LADY!
CHUCKY!
YOU APOLOGIZE TO HER RIGHT NOW, YOUNG MAN! OR YOU CAN JUST FORGET ABOUT RENTING A MOVIE TONIGHT, OR ME EVER BABY-SITTING FOR YOU AGAIN!
NEW RELEASES
WE'RE WAITING!
I'M REALLY SORRY YOUR BUTT IS SO HUGE, MA'AM.
10-11

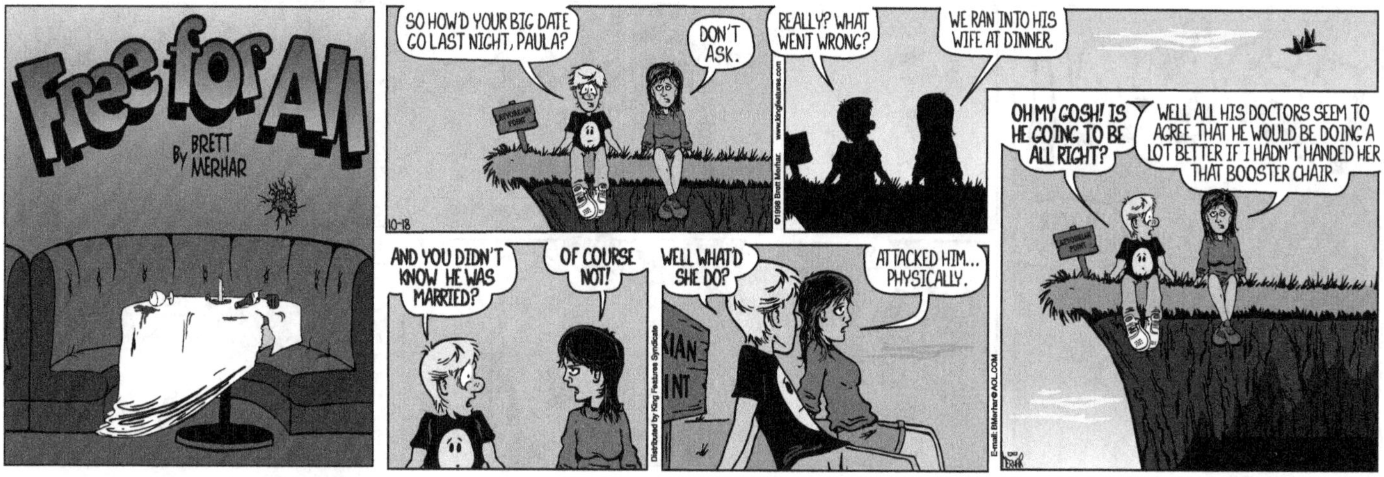
Free for All
BY BRETT MERHAR
SO HOW'D YOUR BIG DATE GO LAST NIGHT, PAULA?
DON'T ASK.
REALLY? WHAT WENT WRONG?
WE RAN INTO HIS WIFE AT DINNER.
AND YOU DIDN'T KNOW HE WAS MARRIED?
OF COURSE NOT!
WELL WHAT'D SHE DO?
ATTACKED HIM... PHYSICALLY.
OH MY GOSH! IS HE GOING TO BE ALL RIGHT?
WELL ALL HIS DOCTORS SEEM TO AGREE THAT HE WOULD BE DOING A LOT BETTER IF I HADN'T HANDED HER THAT BOOSTER CHAIR.

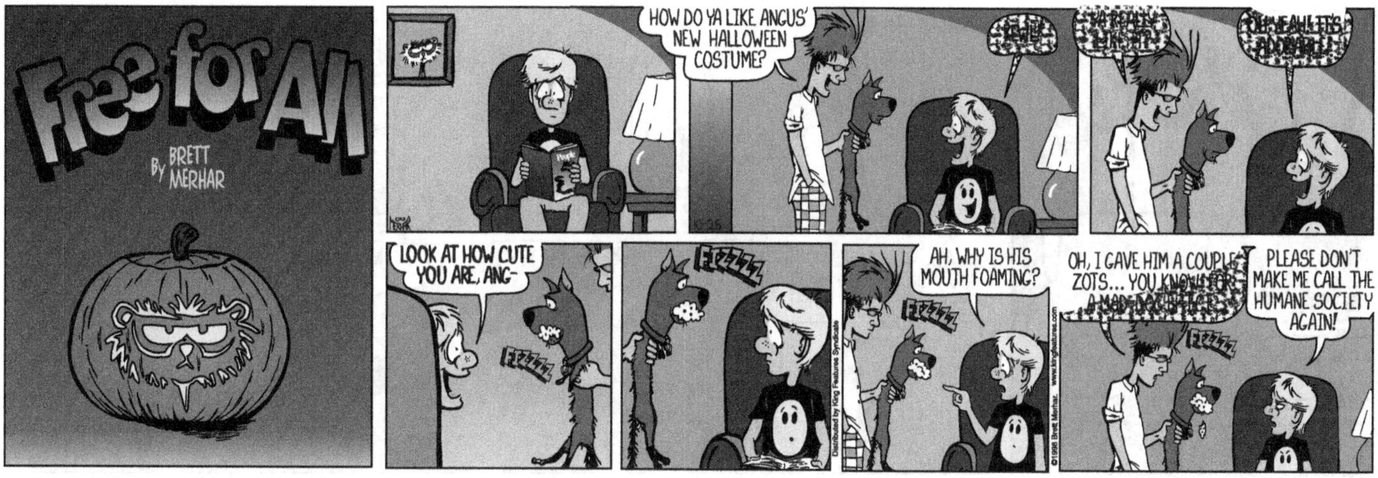
Free for All
BY BRETT MERHAR
HOW DO YA LIKE ANGUS' NEW HALLOWEEN COSTUME?
LOOK AT HOW CUTE YOU ARE, ANG-
FZZZZZ
AH, WHY IS HIS MOUTH FOAMING?
OH, I GAVE HIM A COUPL
ZOTS... YOU KNOW, FOR
PLEASE DON'T MAKE ME CALL THE HUMANE SOCIETY AGAIN!

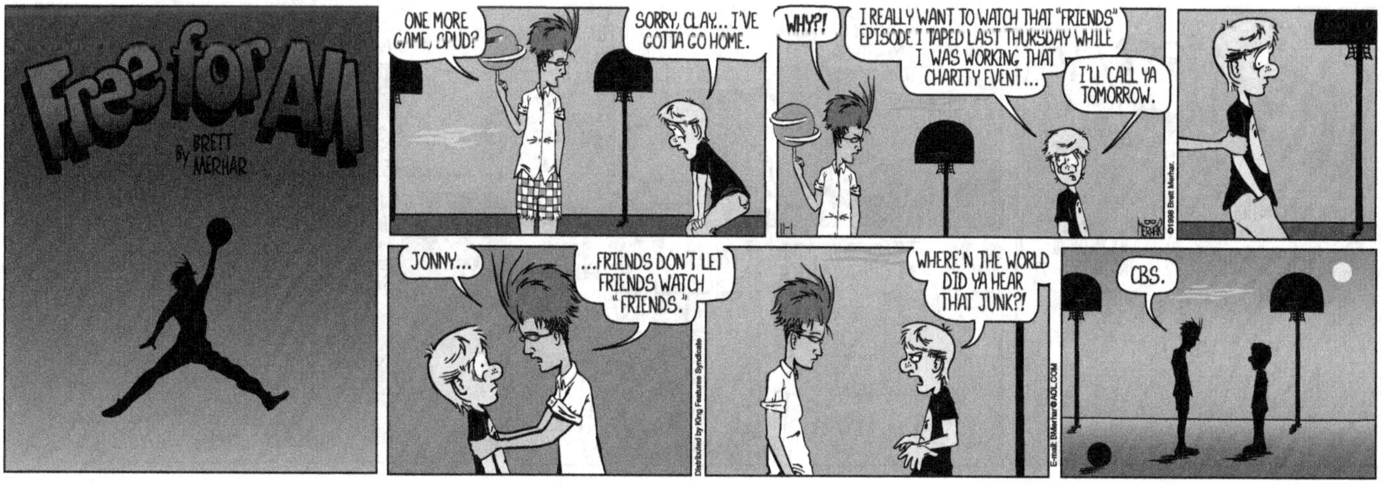
Free for All
BY BRETT MERHAR
ONE MORE GAME, SPUD?
SORRY, CLAY... I'VE GOTTA GO HOME.
WHY?!
I REALLY WANT TO WATCH THAT "FRIENDS" EPISODE I TAPED LAST THURSDAY WHILE I WAS WORKING THAT CHARITY EVENT...
I'LL CALL YA TOMORROW.
JONNY...
...FRIENDS DON'T LET FRIENDS WATCH "FRIENDS."
WHERE'N THE WORLD DID YA HEAR THAT JUNK?!
CBS.

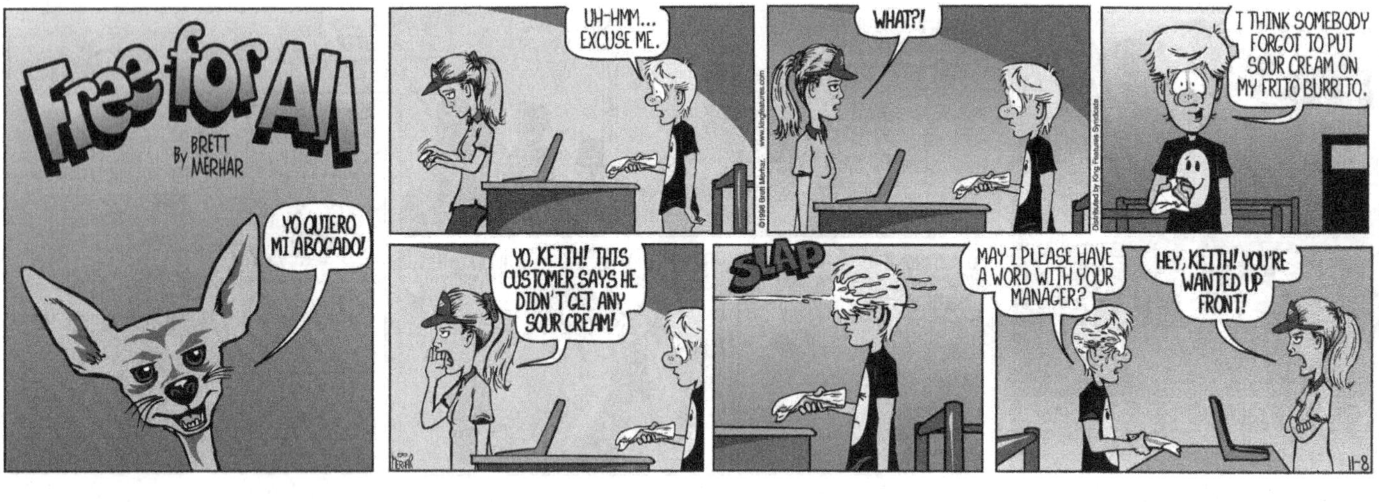
Free for All
By BRETT MERHAR
YO QUIERO MI ABOGADO!
UH-HMM... EXCUSE ME.
WHAT?!
I THINK SOMEBODY FORGOT TO PUT SOUR CREAM ON MY FRITO BURRITO.
YO, KEITH! THIS CUSTOMER SAYS HE DIDN'T GET ANY SOUR CREAM!
SLAP
MAY I PLEASE HAVE A WORD WITH YOUR MANAGER?
HEY, KEITH! YOU'RE WANTED UP FRONT!
©1998 Brett Merhar.
www.kingfeatures.com
Distributed by King Features Syndicate
11-8

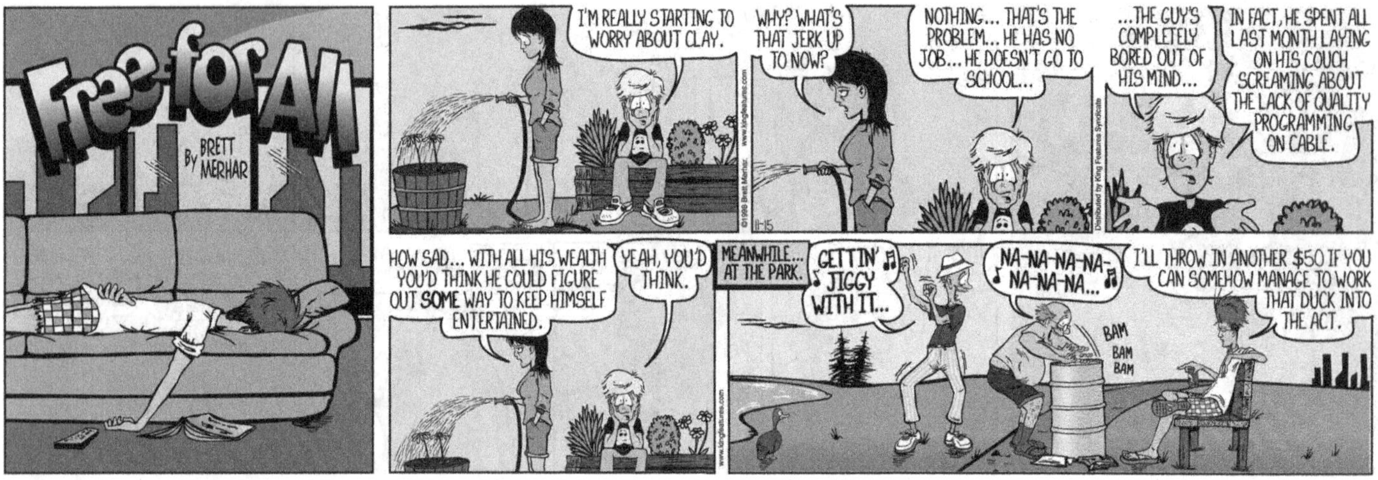
Free for All
By BRETT MERHAR
I'M REALLY STARTING TO WORRY ABOUT CLAY.
WHY? WHAT'S THAT JERK UP TO NOW?
NOTHING... THAT'S THE PROBLEM... HE HAS NO JOB... HE DOESN'T GO TO SCHOOL...
...THE GUY'S COMPLETELY BORED OUT OF HIS MIND...
IN FACT, HE SPENT ALL LAST MONTH LAYING ON HIS COUCH SCREAMING ABOUT THE LACK OF QUALITY PROGRAMMING ON CABLE.
HOW SAD... WITH ALL HIS WEALTH YOU'D THINK HE COULD FIGURE OUT SOME WAY TO KEEP HIMSELF ENTERTAINED.
YEAH, YOU'D THINK.
MEANWHILE... AT THE PARK.
GETTIN' JIGGY WITH IT...
NA-NA-NA-NA-NA-NA-NA...
BAM BAM BAM
I'LL THROW IN ANOTHER $50 IF YOU CAN SOMEHOW MANAGE TO WORK THAT DUCK INTO THE ACT.
11-15

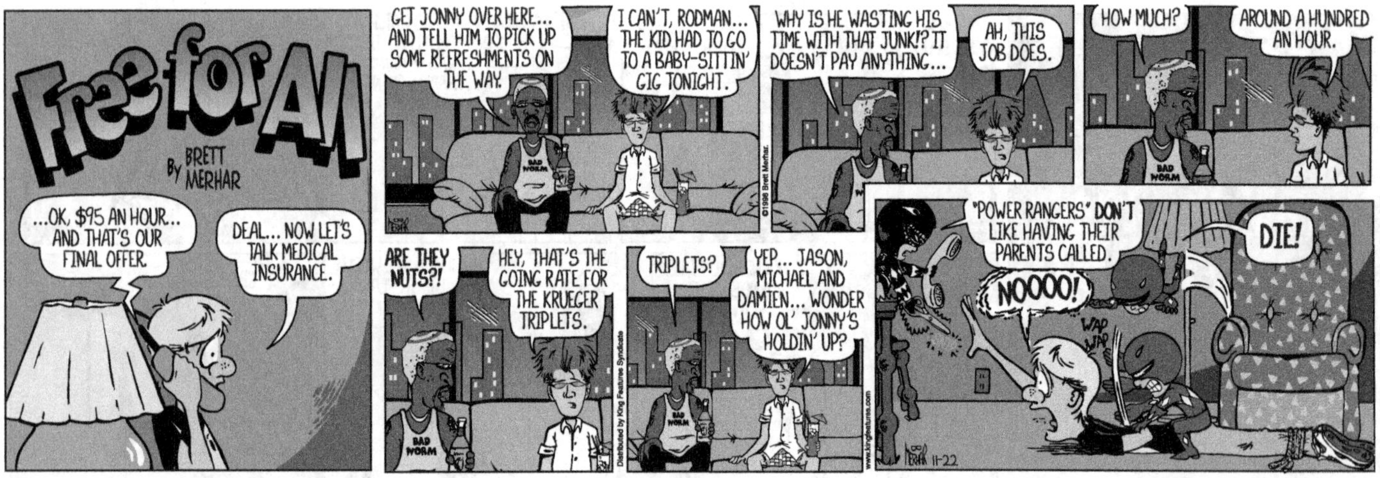
Free for All
By BRETT MERHAR
...OK, $95 AN HOUR... AND THAT'S OUR FINAL OFFER.
DEAL... NOW LET'S TALK MEDICAL INSURANCE.
GET JONNY OVER HERE... AND TELL HIM TO PICK UP SOME REFRESHMENTS ON THE WAY.
I CAN'T, RODMAN... THE KID HAD TO GO TO A BABY-SITTIN' GIG TONIGHT.
WHY IS HE WASTING HIS TIME WITH THAT JUNK!? IT DOESN'T PAY ANYTHING...
AH, THIS JOB DOES.
HOW MUCH?
AROUND A HUNDRED AN HOUR.
ARE THEY NUTS?!
HEY, THAT'S THE GOING RATE FOR THE KRUEGER TRIPLETS.
TRIPLETS?
YEP... JASON, MICHAEL AND DAMIEN... WONDER HOW OL' JONNY'S HOLDIN' UP?
"POWER RANGERS" DON'T LIKE HAVING THEIR PARENTS CALLED.
DIE!
NOOOO!
BAD WORM
11-22

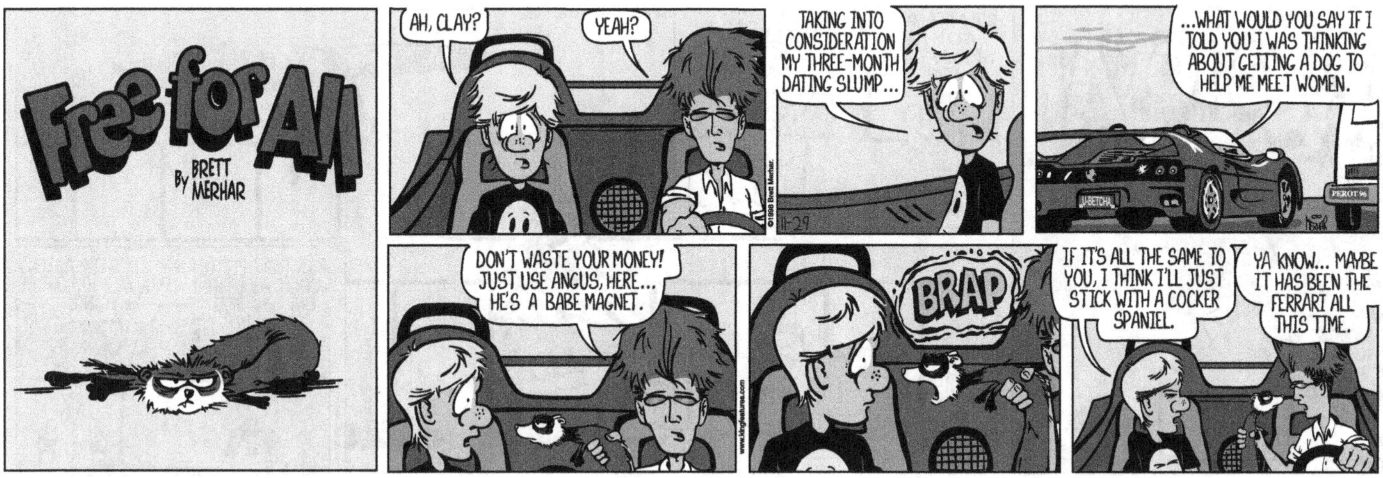
Free for All
By BRETT MERHAR
AH, CLAY?
YEAH?
TAKING INTO CONSIDERATION MY THREE-MONTH DATING SLUMP...
...WHAT WOULD YOU SAY IF I TOLD YOU I WAS THINKING ABOUT GETTING A DOG TO HELP ME MEET WOMEN.
PEROT 96
11-29
DON'T WASTE YOUR MONEY! JUST USE ANGUS, HERE... HE'S A BABE MAGNET.
BRAP
IF IT'S ALL THE SAME TO YOU, I THINK I'LL JUST STICK WITH A COCKER SPANIEL.
YA KNOW... MAYBE IT HAS BEEN THE FERRARI ALL THIS TIME.

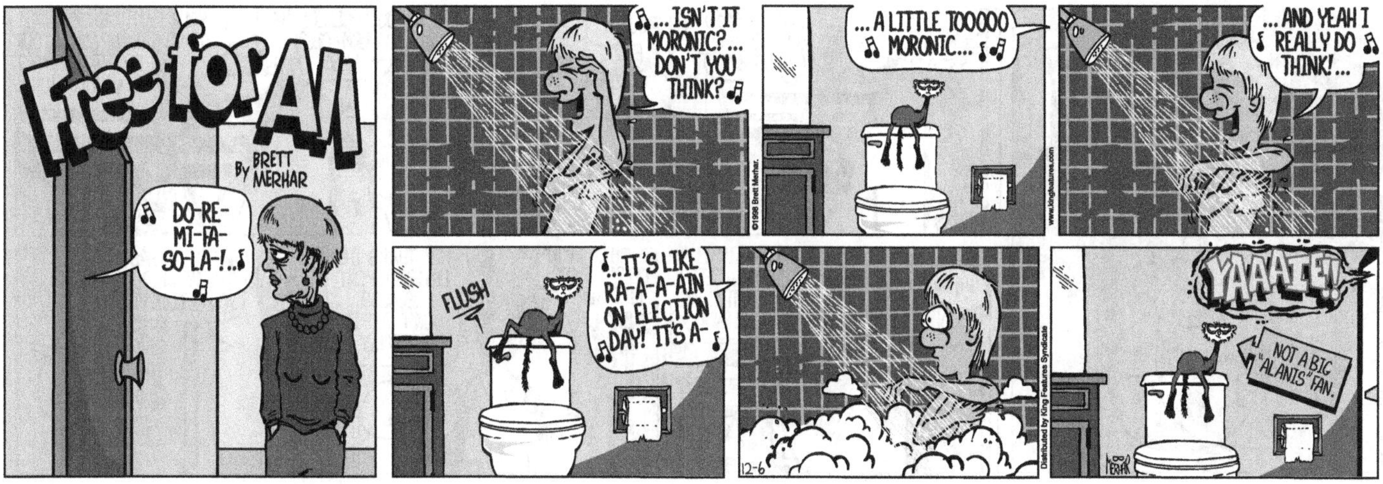
Free for All
By BRETT MERHAR
DO-RE-MI-FA-SO-LA-!..
...ISN'T IT MORONIC?... DON'T YOU THINK?
...A LITTLE TOOOOO MORONIC...
...AND YEAH I REALLY DO THINK!...
FLUSH
...IT'S LIKE RA-A-A-AIN ON ELECTION DAY! IT'S A-
12-6
YAAAIE!!
NOT A BIG "ALANIS" FAN.

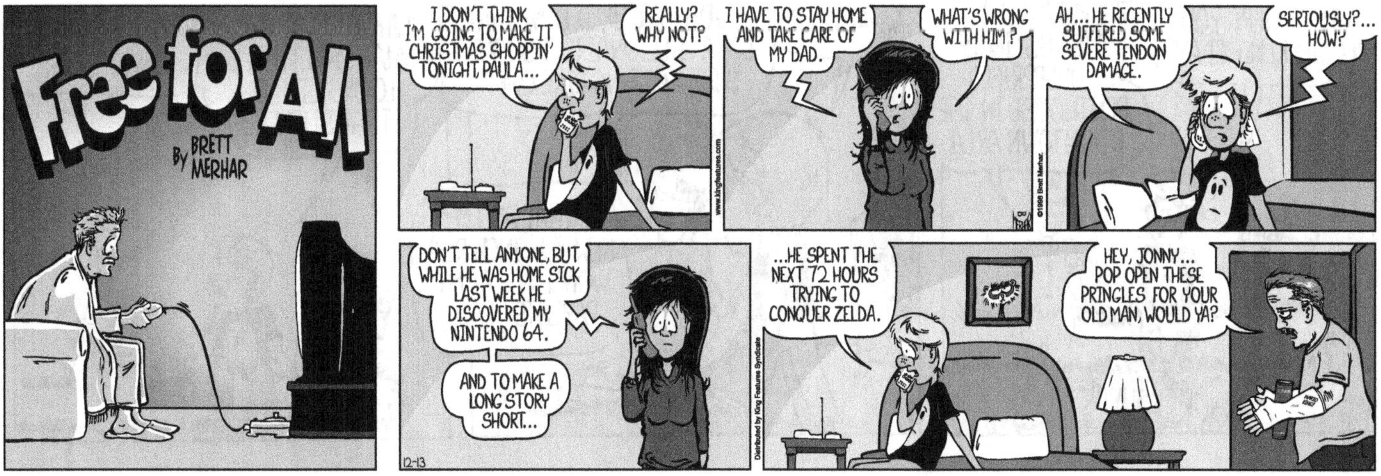
Free for All
By BRETT MERHAR
I DON'T THINK I'M GOING TO MAKE IT CHRISTMAS SHOPPIN' TONIGHT, PAULA...
REALLY? WHY NOT?
I HAVE TO STAY HOME AND TAKE CARE OF MY DAD.
WHAT'S WRONG WITH HIM?
AH... HE RECENTLY SUFFERED SOME SEVERE TENDON DAMAGE.
SERIOUSLY?... HOW?
DON'T TELL ANYONE, BUT WHILE HE WAS HOME SICK LAST WEEK HE DISCOVERED MY NINTENDO 64.
AND TO MAKE A LONG STORY SHORT...
12-13
...HE SPENT THE NEXT 72 HOURS TRYING TO CONQUER ZELDA.
HEY, JONNY... POP OPEN THESE PRINGLES FOR YOUR OLD MAN, WOULD YA?

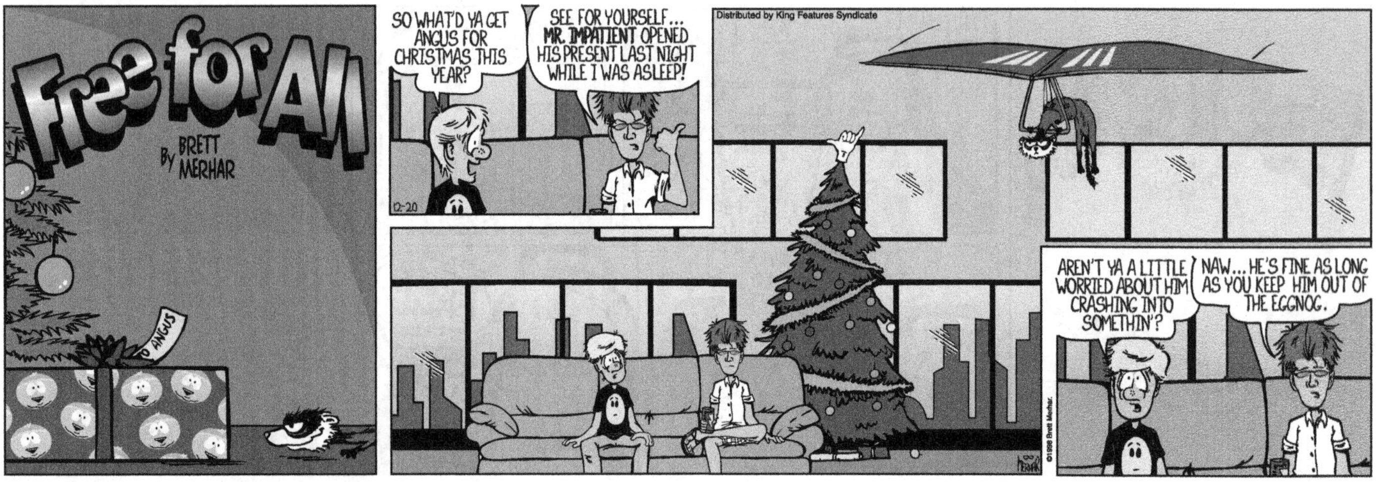
Free for All
By BRETT MERHAR
TO ANGUS
SO WHAT'D YA GET ANGUS FOR CHRISTMAS THIS YEAR?
SEE FOR YOURSELF... MR. IMPATIENT OPENED HIS PRESENT LAST NIGHT WHILE I WAS ASLEEP!
12-20
Distributed by King Features Syndicate
AREN'T YA A LITTLE WORRIED ABOUT HIM CRASHING INTO SOMETHIN'?
NAW... HE'S FINE AS LONG AS YOU KEEP HIM OUT OF THE EGGNOG.
©1998 Brett Merhar
MERHAR

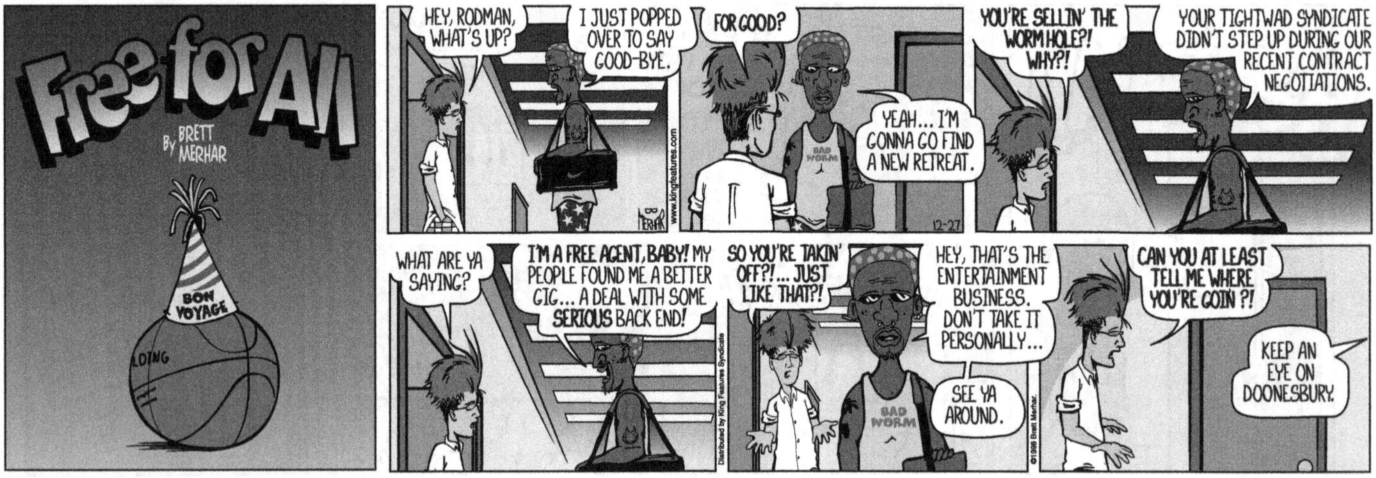
Free for All
By BRETT MERHAR
BON VOYAGE
HEY, RODMAN, WHAT'S UP?
I JUST POPPED OVER TO SAY GOOD-BYE.
www.kingfeatures.com
MERHAR
FOR GOOD?
YEAH... I'M GONNA GO FIND A NEW RETREAT.
BAD WORM
12-27
YOU'RE SELLIN' THE WORM HOLE?! WHY?!
YOUR TIGHTWAD SYNDICATE DIDN'T STEP UP DURING OUR RECENT CONTRACT NEGOTIATIONS.
WHAT ARE YA SAYING?
I'M A FREE AGENT, BABY! MY PEOPLE FOUND ME A BETTER GIG... A DEAL WITH SOME SERIOUS BACK END!
Distributed by King Features Syndicate
SO YOU'RE TAKIN' OFF?!... JUST LIKE THAT?!
HEY, THAT'S THE ENTERTAINMENT BUSINESS. DON'T TAKE IT PERSONALLY...
SEE YA AROUND.
©1998 Brett Merhar
CAN YOU AT LEAST TELL ME WHERE YOU'RE GOIN'?!
KEEP AN EYE ON DOONESBURY.

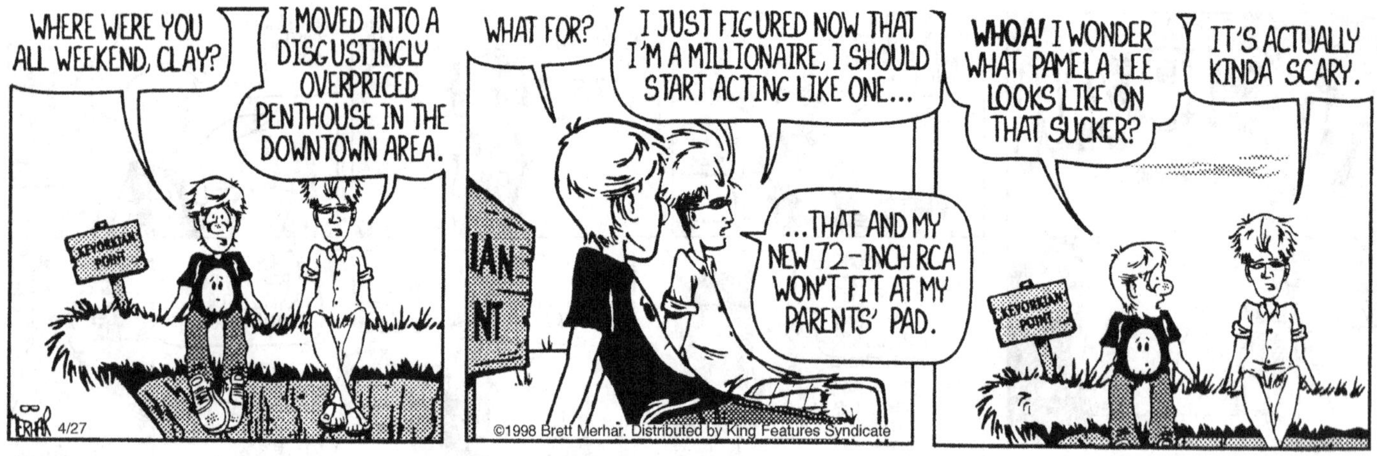
WHERE WERE YOU ALL WEEKEND, CLAY?
I MOVED INTO A DISGUSTINGLY OVERPRICED PENTHOUSE IN THE DOWNTOWN AREA.
KEVORKIAN POINT
MERHAR 4/27
WHAT FOR?
I JUST FIGURED NOW THAT I'M A MILLIONAIRE, I SHOULD START ACTING LIKE ONE...
...THAT AND MY NEW 72-INCH RCA WON'T FIT AT MY PARENTS' PAD.
©1998 Brett Merhar. Distributed by King Features Syndicate
WHOA! I WONDER WHAT PAMELA LEE LOOKS LIKE ON THAT SUCKER?
IT'S ACTUALLY KINDA SCARY.
KEVORKIAN POINT

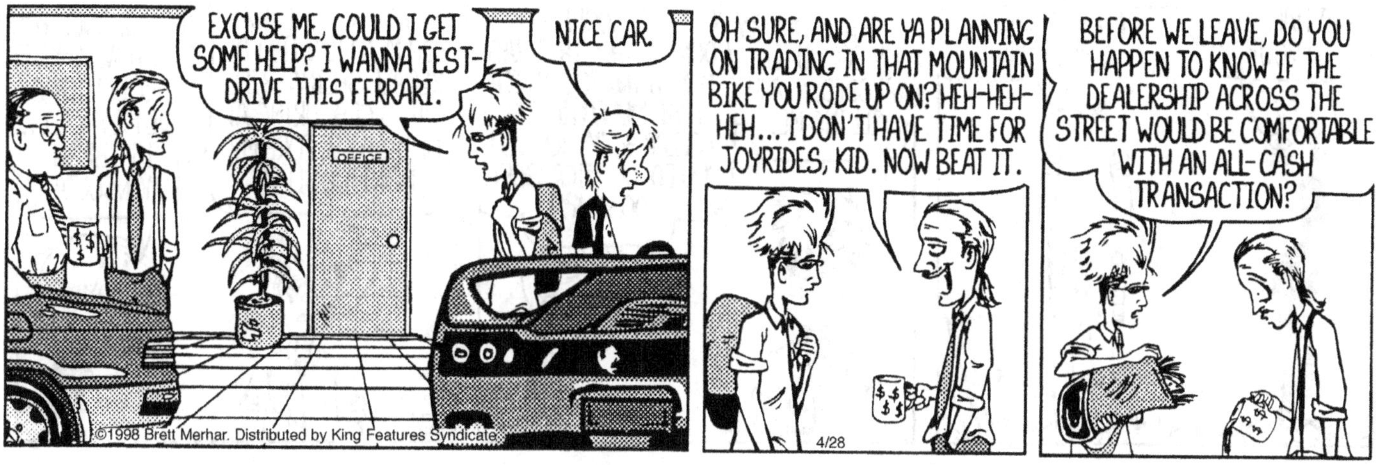
EXCUSE ME, COULD I GET SOME HELP? I WANNA TEST-DRIVE THIS FERRARI.
NICE CAR.
OFFICE
©1998 Brett Merhar. Distributed by King Features Syndicate
OH SURE, AND ARE YA PLANNING ON TRADING IN THAT MOUNTAIN BIKE YOU RODE UP ON? HEH-HEH-HEH... I DON'T HAVE TIME FOR JOYRIDES, KID. NOW BEAT IT.
4/28
BEFORE WE LEAVE, DO YOU HAPPEN TO KNOW IF THE DEALERSHIP ACROSS THE STREET WOULD BE COMFORTABLE WITH AN ALL-CASH TRANSACTION?

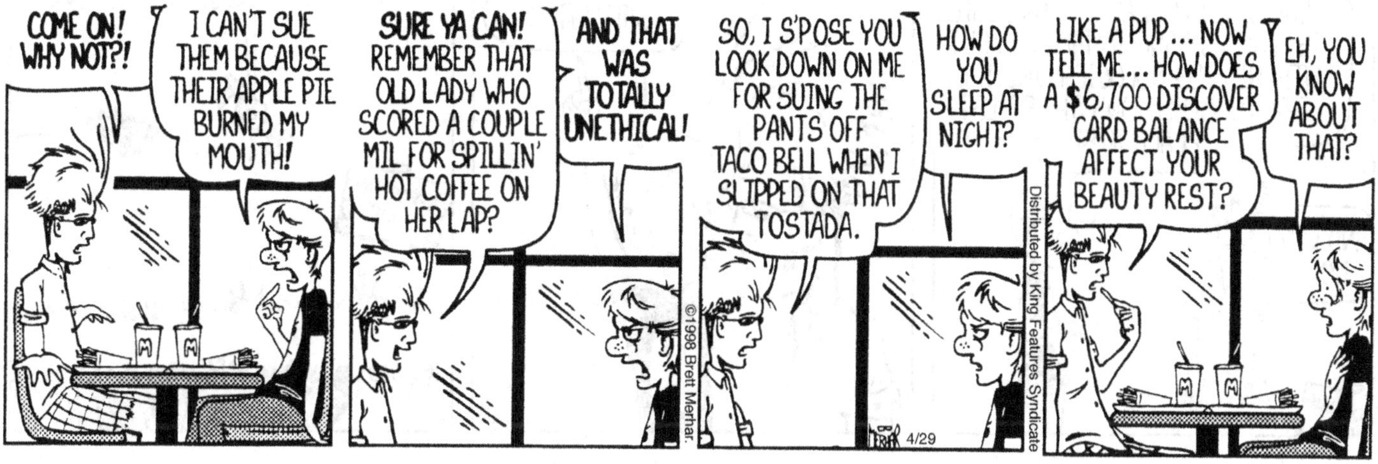
COME ON! WHY NOT?!
I CAN'T SUE THEM BECAUSE THEIR APPLE PIE BURNED MY MOUTH!
SURE YA CAN! REMEMBER THAT OLD LADY WHO SCORED A COUPLE MIL FOR SPILLIN' HOT COFFEE ON HER LAP?
AND THAT WAS TOTALLY UNETHICAL!
©1998 Brett Merhar.
SO, I S'POSE YOU LOOK DOWN ON ME FOR SUING THE PANTS OFF TACO BELL WHEN I SLIPPED ON THAT TOSTADA.
HOW DO YOU SLEEP AT NIGHT?
MERHAR 4/29
Distributed by King Features Syndicate
LIKE A PUP... NOW TELL ME... HOW DOES A $6,700 DISCOVER CARD BALANCE AFFECT YOUR BEAUTY REST?
EH, YOU KNOW ABOUT THAT?

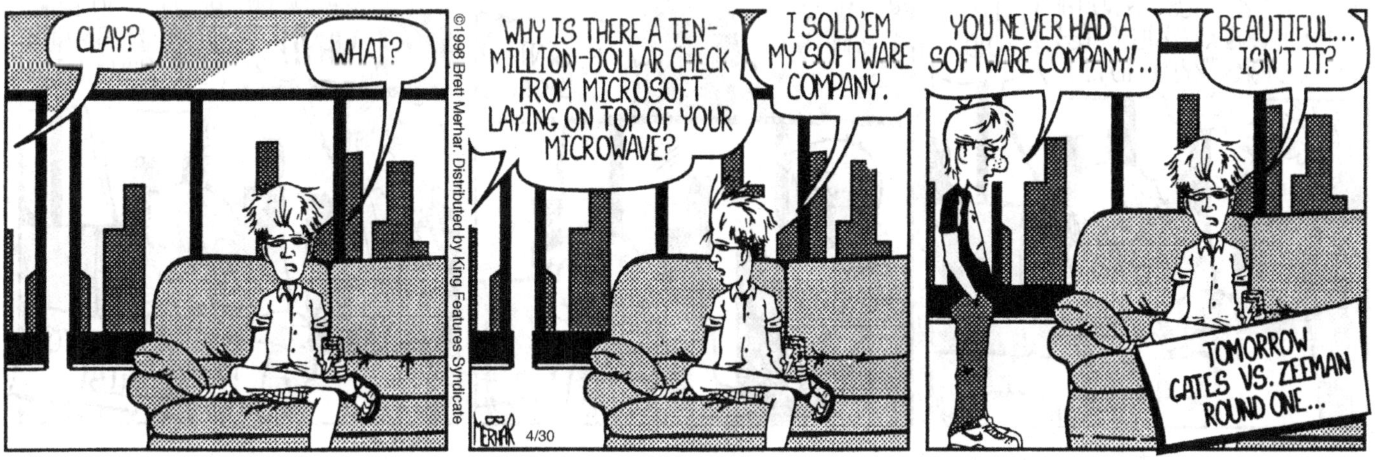
CLAY?
WHAT?
©1998 Brett Merhar. Distributed by King Features Syndicate
WHY IS THERE A TEN-MILLION-DOLLAR CHECK FROM MICROSOFT LAYING ON TOP OF YOUR MICROWAVE?
I SOLD 'EM MY SOFTWARE COMPANY.
MERHAR 4/30
YOU NEVER HAD A SOFTWARE COMPANY!..
BEAUTIFUL... ISN'T IT?
TOMORROW GATES VS. ZEEMAN ROUND ONE...

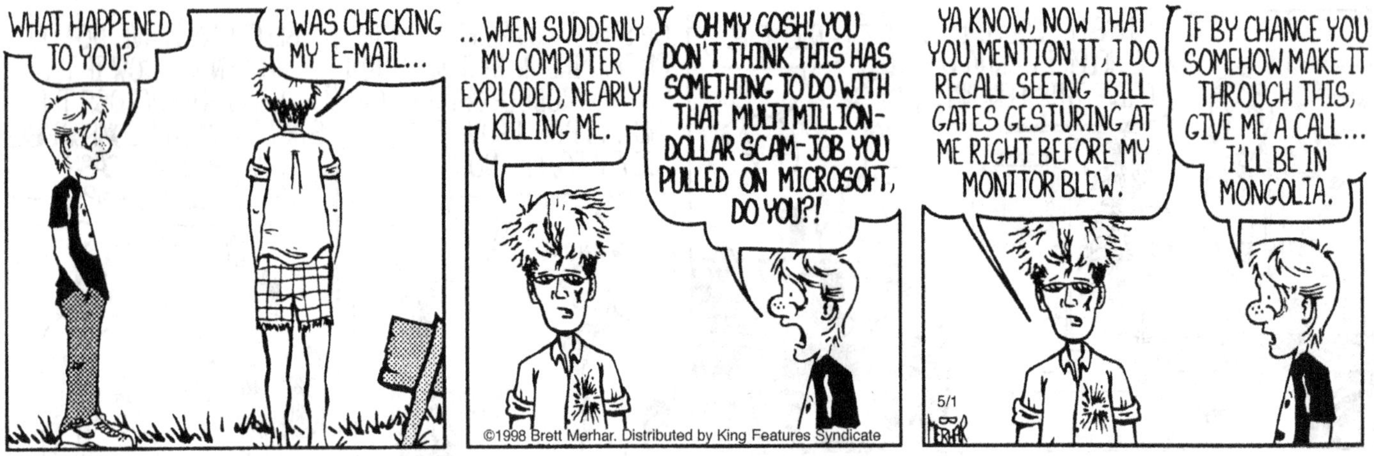
WHAT HAPPENED TO YOU?
I WAS CHECKING MY E-MAIL...
...WHEN SUDDENLY MY COMPUTER EXPLODED, NEARLY KILLING ME.
OH MY GOSH! YOU DON'T THINK THIS HAS SOMETHING TO DO WITH THAT MULTIMILLION-DOLLAR SCAM-JOB YOU PULLED ON MICROSOFT, DO YOU?!
YA KNOW, NOW THAT YOU MENTION IT, I DO RECALL SEEING BILL GATES GESTURING AT ME RIGHT BEFORE MY MONITOR BLEW.
IF BY CHANCE YOU SOMEHOW MAKE IT THROUGH THIS, GIVE ME A CALL... I'LL BE IN MONGOLIA.
©1998 Brett Merhar. Distributed by King Features Syndicate
5/1
MERHAR

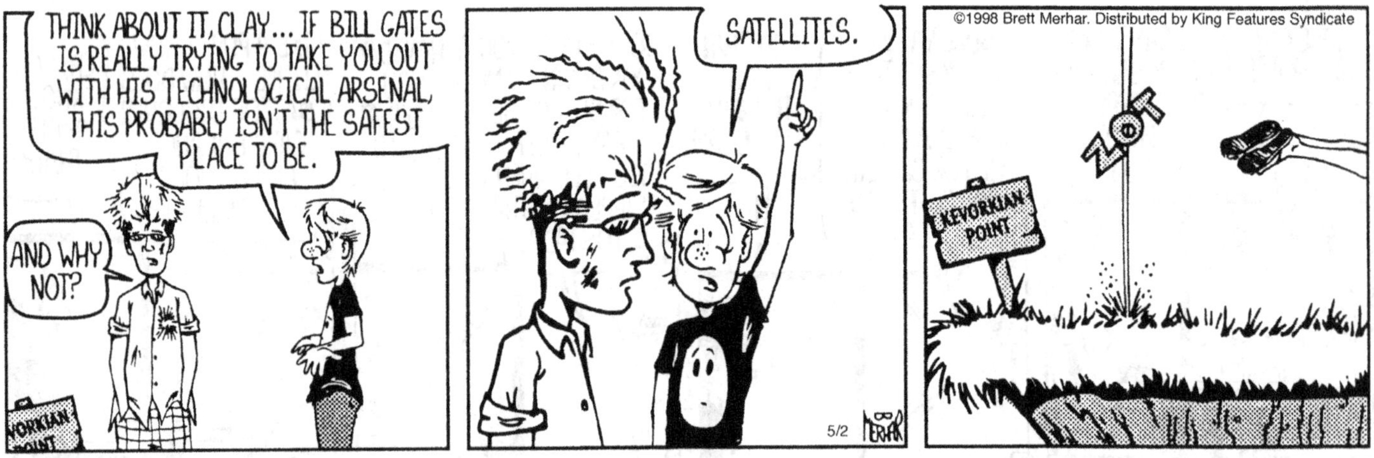
THINK ABOUT IT, CLAY... IF BILL GATES IS REALLY TRYING TO TAKE YOU OUT WITH HIS TECHNOLOGICAL ARSENAL, THIS PROBABLY ISN'T THE SAFEST PLACE TO BE.
AND WHY NOT?
SATELLITES.
5/2
MERHAR
©1998 Brett Merhar. Distributed by King Features Syndicate
ZOT
KEVORKIAN POINT

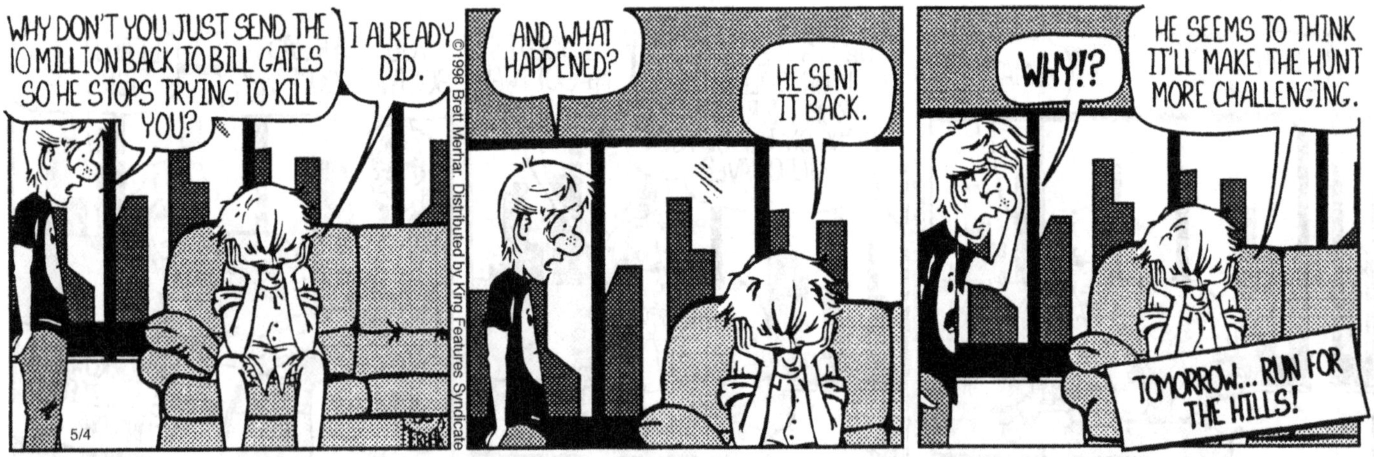
WHY DON'T YOU JUST SEND THE 10 MILLION BACK TO BILL GATES SO HE STOPS TRYING TO KILL YOU?
I ALREADY DID.
©1998 Brett Merhar. Distributed by King Features Syndicate
5/4
AND WHAT HAPPENED?
HE SENT IT BACK.
WHY!?
HE SEEMS TO THINK IT'LL MAKE THE HUNT MORE CHALLENGING.
TOMORROW... RUN FOR THE HILLS!

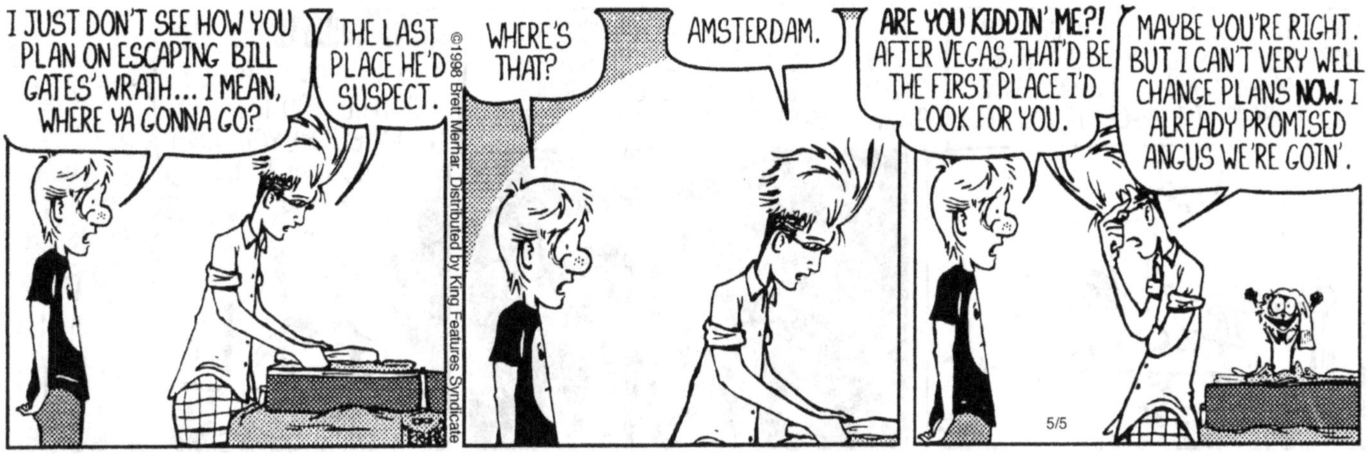
I JUST DON'T SEE HOW YOU PLAN ON ESCAPING BILL GATES' WRATH... I MEAN, WHERE YA GONNA GO?
THE LAST PLACE HE'D SUSPECT.
©1998 Brett Merhar. Distributed by King Features Syndicate
WHERE'S THAT?
AMSTERDAM.
ARE YOU KIDDIN' ME?! AFTER VEGAS, THAT'D BE THE FIRST PLACE I'D LOOK FOR YOU.
MAYBE YOU'RE RIGHT. BUT I CAN'T VERY WELL CHANGE PLANS NOW. I ALREADY PROMISED ANGUS WE'RE GOIN'.
5/5

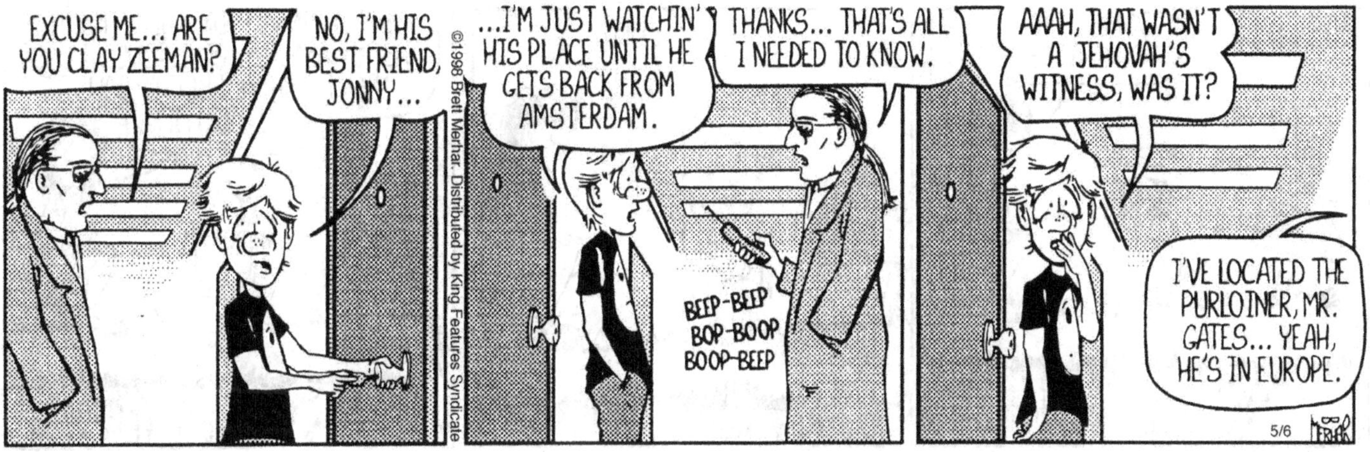
EXCUSE ME... ARE YOU CLAY ZEEMAN?
NO, I'M HIS BEST FRIEND, JONNY...
©1998 Brett Merhar. Distributed by King Features Syndicate
...I'M JUST WATCHIN' HIS PLACE UNTIL HE GETS BACK FROM AMSTERDAM.
THANKS... THAT'S ALL I NEEDED TO KNOW.
BEEP-BEEP
BOP-BOOP
BOOP-BEEP
AAAH, THAT WASN'T A JEHOVAH'S WITNESS, WAS IT?
I'VE LOCATED THE PURLOINER, MR. GATES... YEAH, HE'S IN EUROPE.
5/6
MERHAR

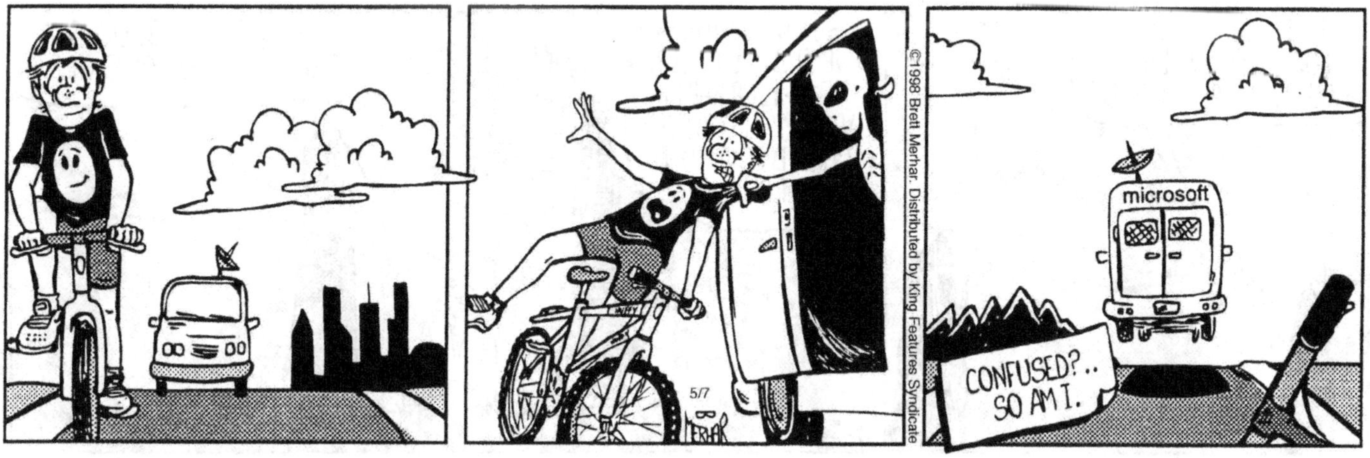
5/7
MERHAR
©1998 Brett Merhar. Distributed by King Features Syndicate
microsoft
CONFUSED?.. SO AM I.

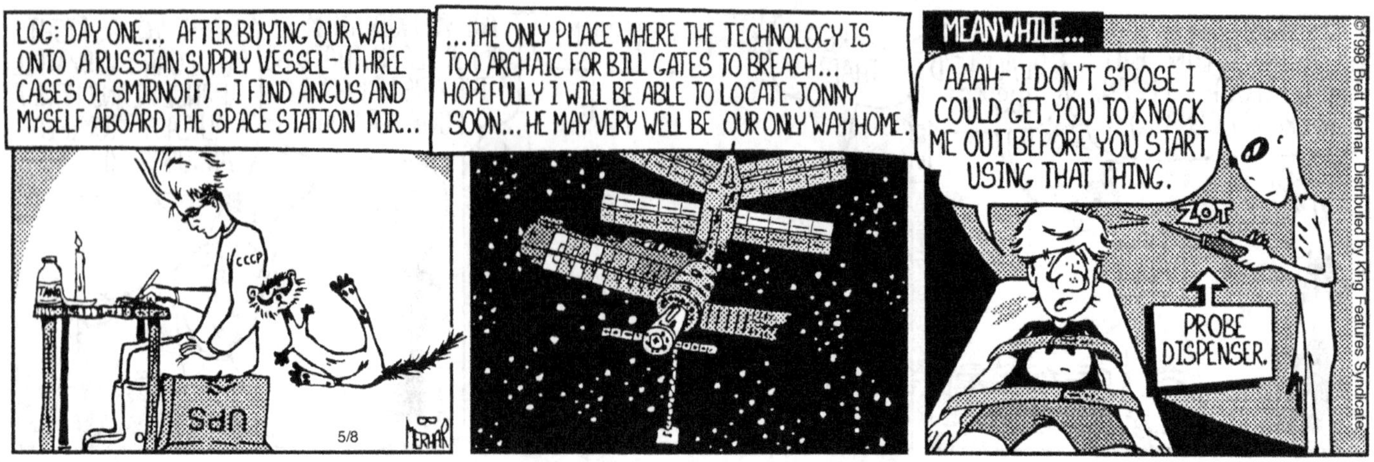
LOG: DAY ONE... AFTER BUYING OUR WAY ONTO A RUSSIAN SUPPLY VESSEL- (THREE CASES OF SMIRNOFF) - I FIND ANGUS AND MYSELF ABOARD THE SPACE STATION MIR...
...THE ONLY PLACE WHERE THE TECHNOLOGY IS TOO ARCHAIC FOR BILL GATES TO BREACH... HOPEFULLY I WILL BE ABLE TO LOCATE JONNY SOON... HE MAY VERY WELL BE OUR ONLY WAY HOME.
CCCP
5/8
MERHAR
MEANWHILE...
AAAH- I DON'T S'POSE I COULD GET YOU TO KNOCK ME OUT BEFORE YOU START USING THAT THING.
ZOT
PROBE DISPENSER.
©1998 Brett Merhar. Distributed by King Features Syndicate

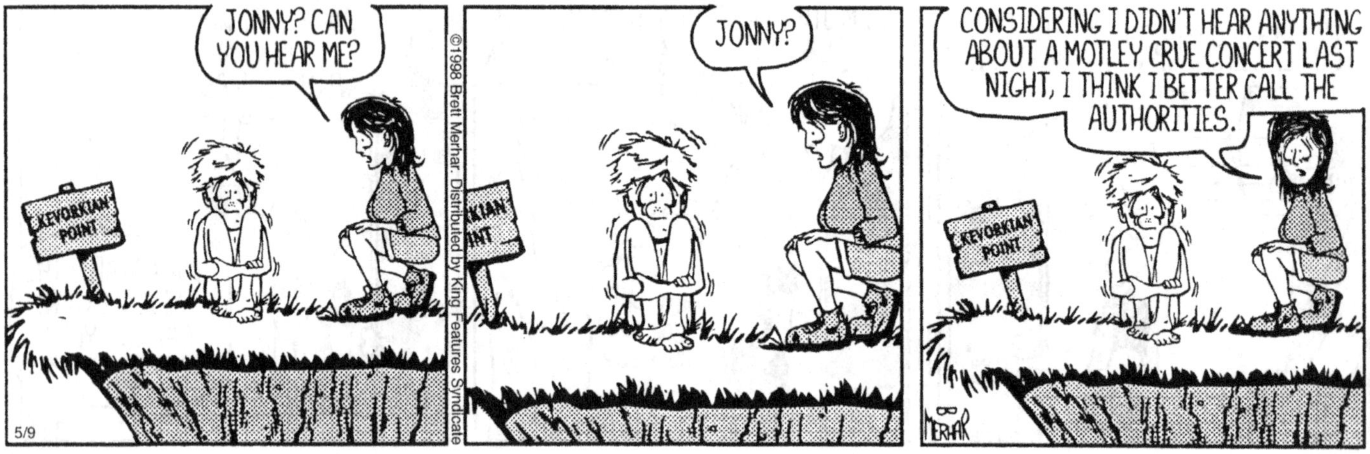
JONNY? CAN YOU HEAR ME?
KEVORKIAN POINT
5/9
©1998 Brett Merhar. Distributed by King Features Syndicate
JONNY?
CONSIDERING I DIDN'T HEAR ANYTHING ABOUT A MOTLEY CRUE CONCERT LAST NIGHT, I THINK I BETTER CALL THE AUTHORITIES.
KEVORKIAN POINT
MERHAR

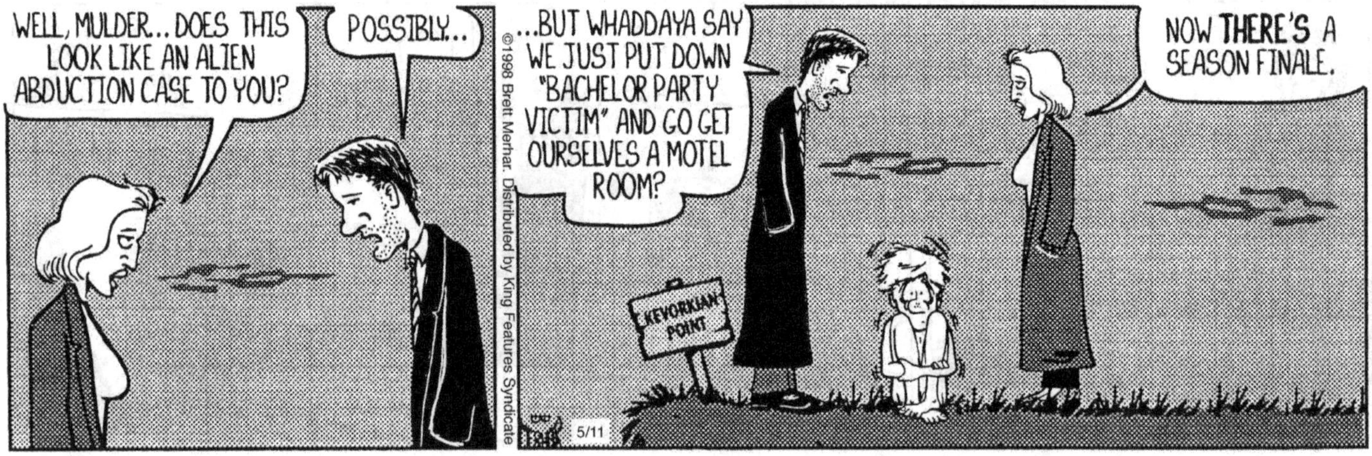
WELL, MULDER... DOES THIS LOOK LIKE AN ALIEN ABDUCTION CASE TO YOU?
POSSIBLY...
©1998 Brett Merhar. Distributed by King Features Syndicate
...BUT WHADDAYA SAY WE JUST PUT DOWN "BACHELOR PARTY VICTIM" AND GO GET OURSELVES A MOTEL ROOM?
NOW **THERE'S** A SEASON FINALE.
KEVORKIAN POINT
5/11

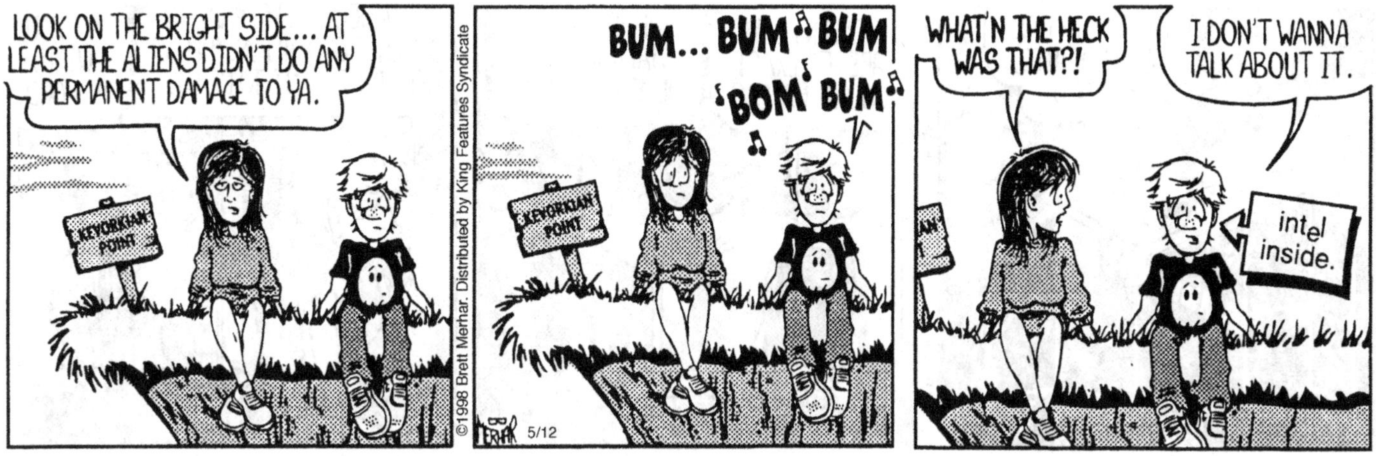
LOOK ON THE BRIGHT SIDE... AT LEAST THE ALIENS DIDN'T DO ANY PERMANENT DAMAGE TO YA.
KEVORKIAN POINT
©1998 Brett Merhar. Distributed by King Features Syndicate
BUM... BUM BUM
BOM BUM
MERHAR 5/12
WHAT'N THE HECK WAS THAT?!
I DON'T WANNA TALK ABOUT IT.
intel inside.

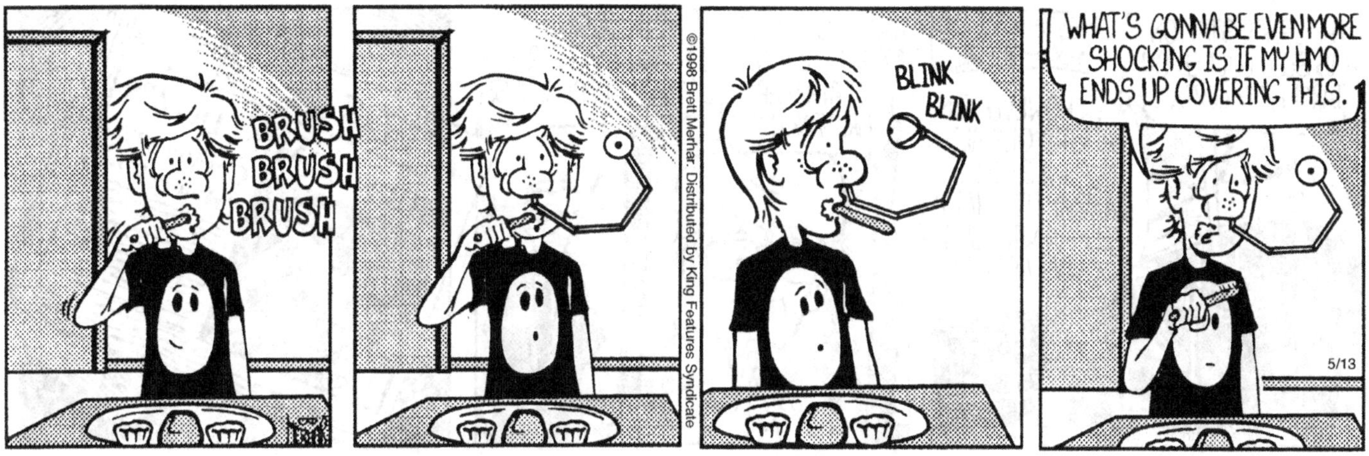
BRUSH
BRUSH
BRUSH
©1998 Brett Merhar. Distributed by King Features Syndicate
BLINK
BLINK
WHAT'S GONNA BE EVEN MORE SHOCKING IS IF MY HMO ENDS UP COVERING THIS.
5/13

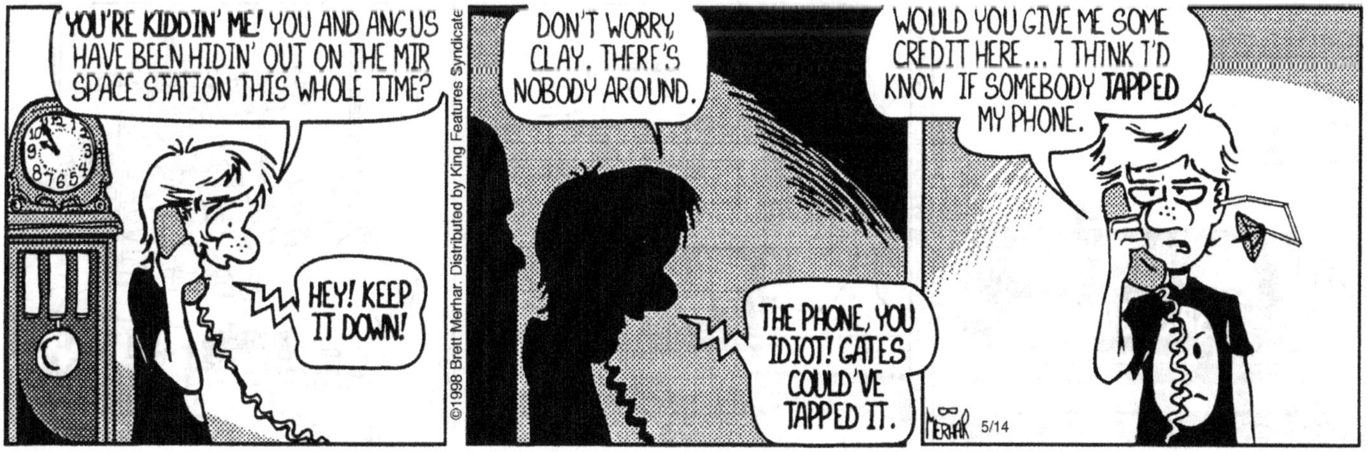
YOU'RE KIDDIN' ME! YOU AND ANGUS HAVE BEEN HIDIN' OUT ON THE MIR SPACE STATION THIS WHOLE TIME?
HEY! KEEP IT DOWN!
©1998 Brett Merhar. Distributed by King Features Syndicate
DON'T WORRY, CLAY. THERE'S NOBODY AROUND.
THE PHONE, YOU IDIOT! GATES COULD'VE TAPPED IT.
WOULD YOU GIVE ME SOME CREDIT HERE... I THINK I'D KNOW IF SOMEBODY TAPPED MY PHONE.
MERHAR 5/14

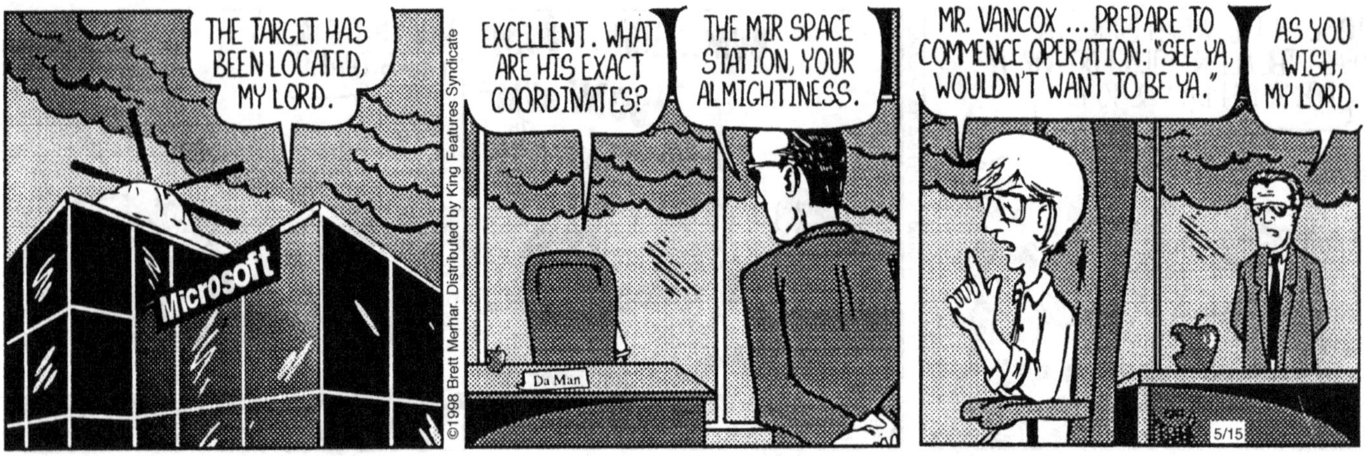
THE TARGET HAS BEEN LOCATED, MY LORD.
Microsoft
©1998 Brett Merhar. Distributed by King Features Syndicate
EXCELLENT. WHAT ARE HIS EXACT COORDINATES?
Da Man
THE MIR SPACE STATION, YOUR ALMIGHTINESS.
MR. VANCOX ... PREPARE TO COMMENCE OPERATION: "SEE YA, WOULDN'T WANT TO BE YA."
AS YOU WISH, MY LORD.
5/15

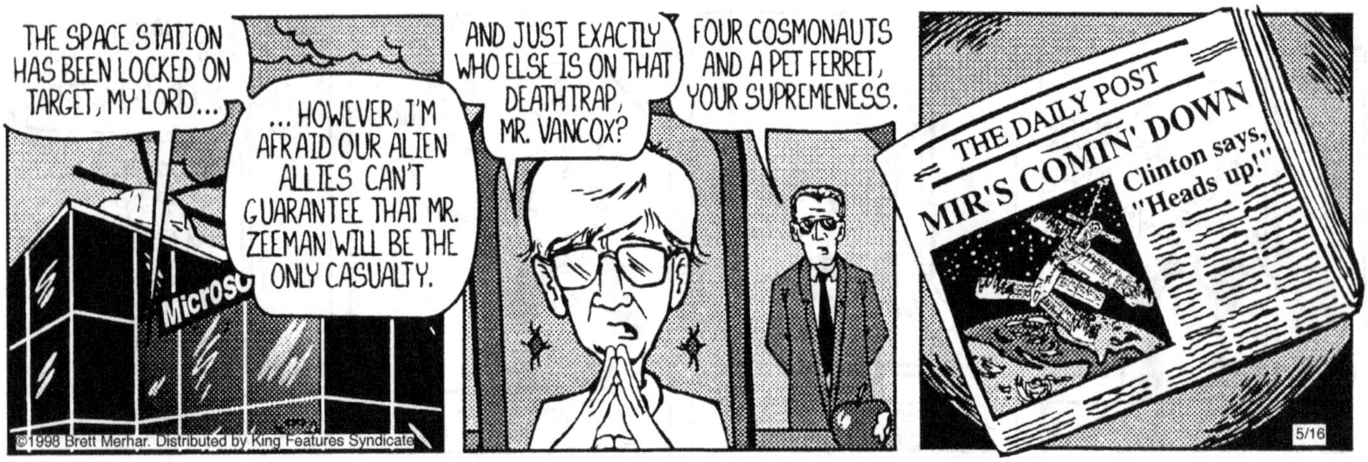
THE SPACE STATION HAS BEEN LOCKED ON TARGET, MY LORD...
... HOWEVER, I'M AFRAID OUR ALIEN ALLIES CAN'T GUARANTEE THAT MR. ZEEMAN WILL BE THE ONLY CASUALTY.
©1998 Brett Merhar. Distributed by King Features Syndicate
AND JUST EXACTLY WHO ELSE IS ON THAT DEATHTRAP, MR. VANCOX?
FOUR COSMONAUTS AND A PET FERRET, YOUR SUPREMENESS.
THE DAILY POST
MIR'S COMIN' DOWN
Clinton says, "Heads up!"
5/16

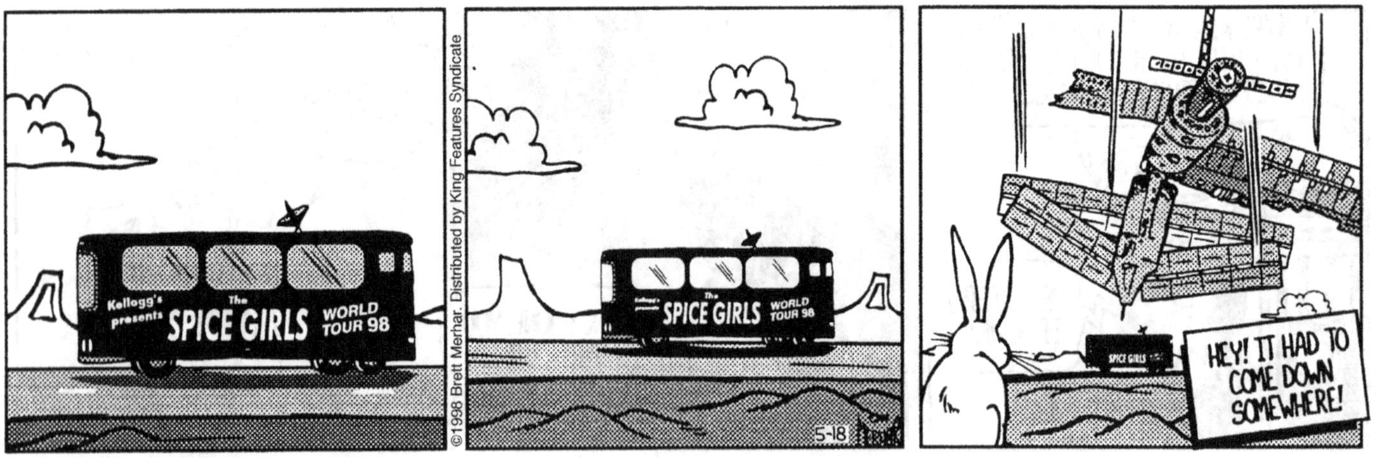
Kellogg's presents The SPICE GIRLS WORLD TOUR 98
©1998 Brett Merhar. Distributed by King Features Syndicate
The SPICE GIRLS WORLD TOUR 98
5-18
SPICE GIRLS
HEY! IT HAD TO COME DOWN SOMEWHERE!

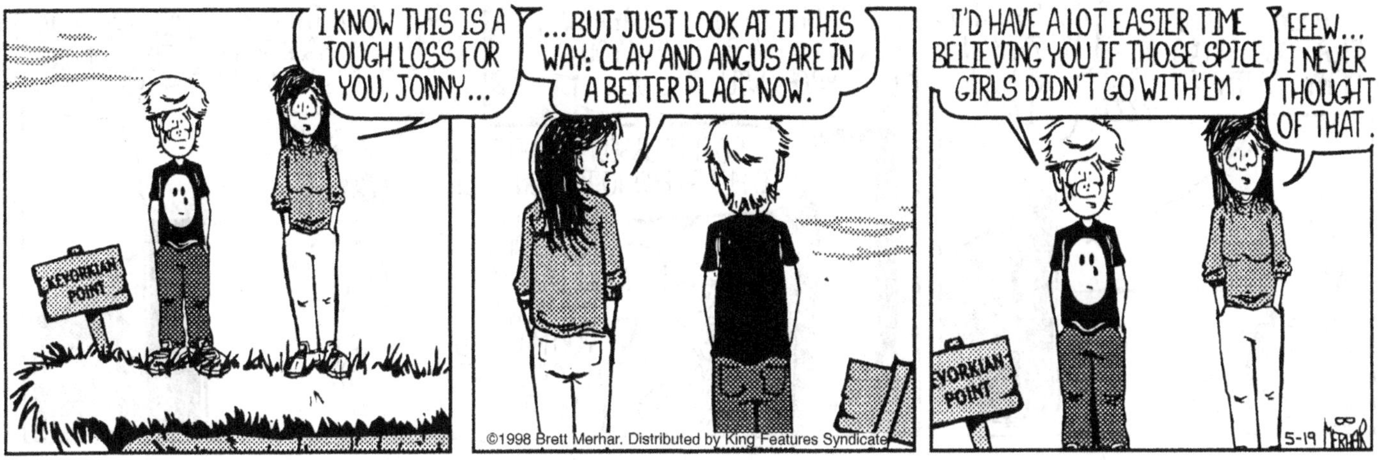
I KNOW THIS IS A TOUGH LOSS FOR YOU, JONNY...
...BUT JUST LOOK AT IT THIS WAY: CLAY AND ANGUS ARE IN A BETTER PLACE NOW.
I'D HAVE A LOT EASIER TIME BELIEVING YOU IF THOSE SPICE GIRLS DIDN'T GO WITH'EM.
EEEW... I NEVER THOUGHT OF THAT.
KEVORKIAN POINT
©1998 Brett Merhar. Distributed by King Features Syndicate
5-19 MERHAR

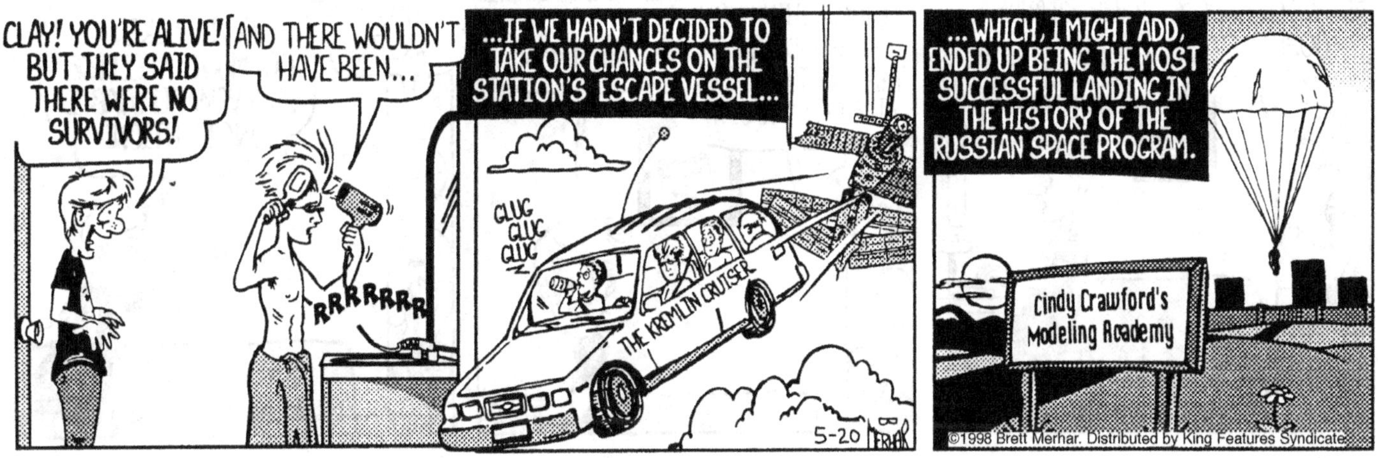
CLAY! YOU'RE ALIVE! BUT THEY SAID THERE WERE NO SURVIVORS!
AND THERE WOULDN'T HAVE BEEN...
RRRRRRRR
...IF WE HADN'T DECIDED TO TAKE OUR CHANCES ON THE STATION'S ESCAPE VESSEL...
GLUG GLUG GLUG
THE KREMLIN CRUISER
5-20 MERHAR
...WHICH, I MIGHT ADD, ENDED UP BEING THE MOST SUCCESSFUL LANDING IN THE HISTORY OF THE RUSSIAN SPACE PROGRAM.
Cindy Crawford's Modeling Academy
©1998 Brett Merhar. Distributed by King Features Syndicate

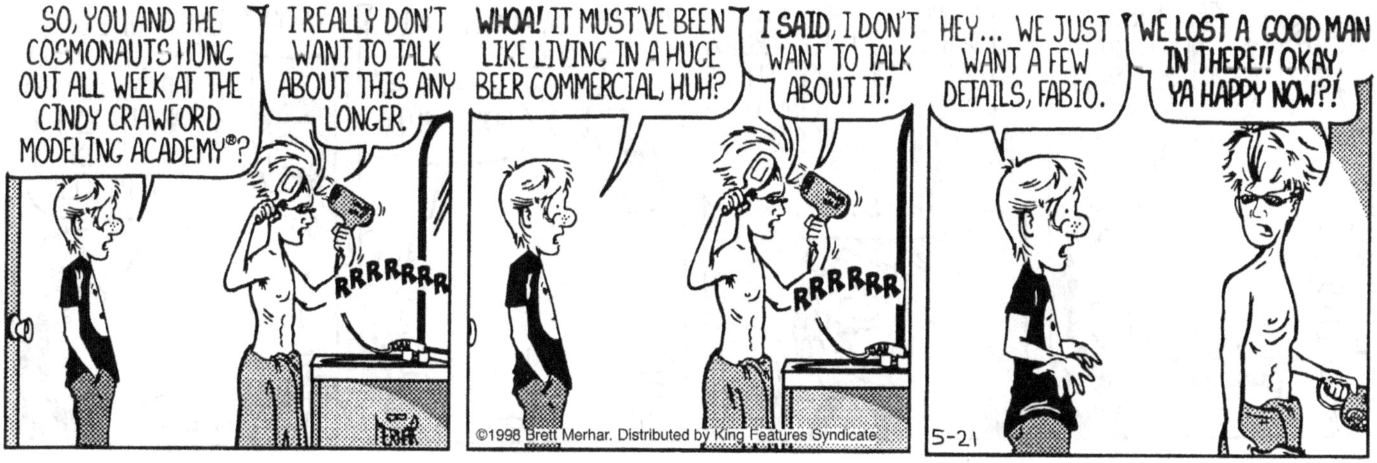
SO, YOU AND THE COSMONAUTS HUNG OUT ALL WEEK AT THE CINDY CRAWFORD MODELING ACADEMY®?
I REALLY DON'T WANT TO TALK ABOUT THIS ANY LONGER.
RRRRRRRR
WHOA! IT MUST'VE BEEN LIKE LIVING IN A HUGE BEER COMMERCIAL, HUH?
I SAID, I DON'T WANT TO TALK ABOUT IT!
RRRRRR
©1998 Brett Merhar. Distributed by King Features Syndicate
HEY... WE JUST WANT A FEW DETAILS, FABIO.
WE LOST A GOOD MAN IN THERE!! OKAY, YA HAPPY NOW?!
5-21

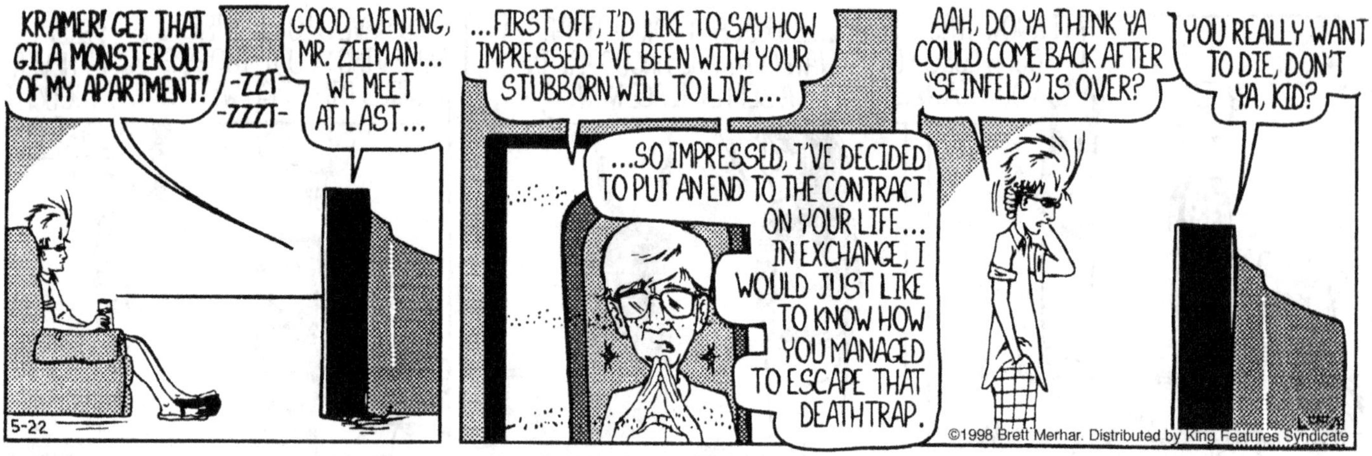
KRAMER! GET THAT GILA MONSTER OUT OF MY APARTMENT!
-ZZT- -ZZZT-
GOOD EVENING, MR. ZEEMAN... WE MEET AT LAST...
5-22
...FIRST OFF, I'D LIKE TO SAY HOW IMPRESSED I'VE BEEN WITH YOUR STUBBORN WILL TO LIVE...
...SO IMPRESSED, I'VE DECIDED TO PUT AN END TO THE CONTRACT ON YOUR LIFE... IN EXCHANGE, I WOULD JUST LIKE TO KNOW HOW YOU MANAGED TO ESCAPE THAT DEATHTRAP.
AAH, DO YA THINK YA COULD COME BACK AFTER "SEINFELD" IS OVER?
YOU REALLY WANT TO DIE, DON'T YA, KID?
©1998 Brett Merhar. Distributed by King Features Syndicate

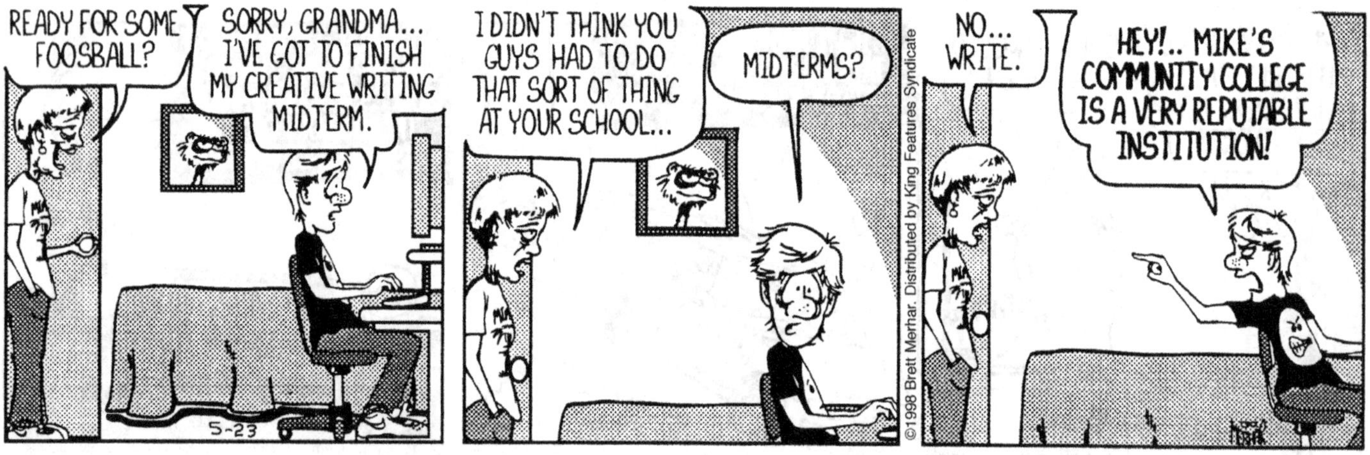
READY FOR SOME FOOSBALL?
SORRY, GRANDMA... I'VE GOT TO FINISH MY CREATIVE WRITING MIDTERM.
5-23
I DIDN'T THINK YOU GUYS HAD TO DO THAT SORT OF THING AT YOUR SCHOOL...
MIDTERMS?
©1998 Brett Merhar. Distributed by King Features Syndicate
NO... WRITE.
HEY!.. MIKE'S COMMUNITY COLLEGE IS A VERY REPUTABLE INSTITUTION!

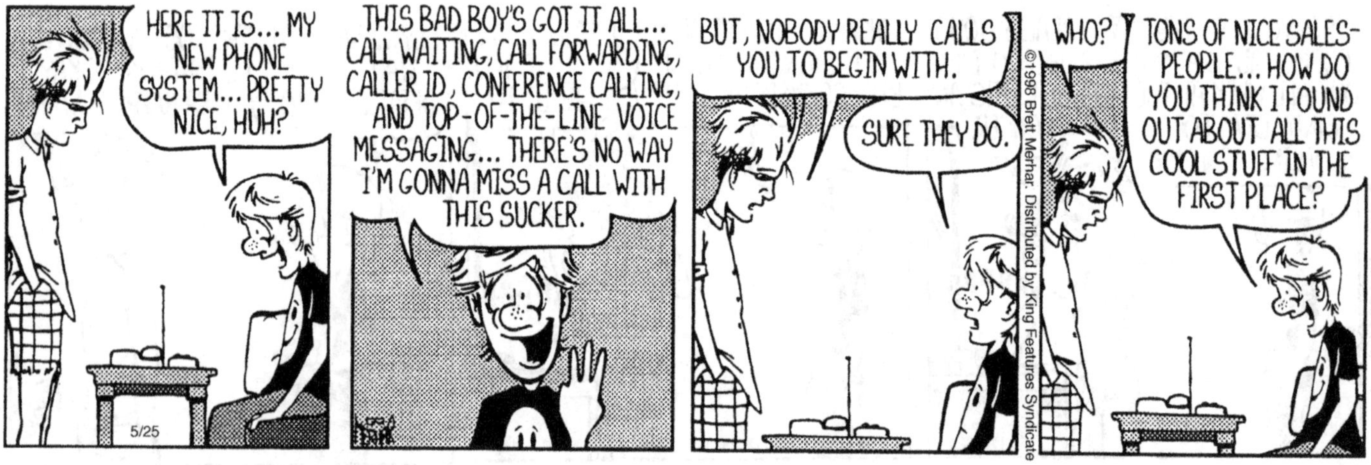
HERE IT IS... MY NEW PHONE SYSTEM... PRETTY NICE, HUH?
5/25
THIS BAD BOY'S GOT IT ALL... CALL WAITING, CALL FORWARDING, CALLER ID, CONFERENCE CALLING, AND TOP-OF-THE-LINE VOICE MESSAGING... THERE'S NO WAY I'M GONNA MISS A CALL WITH THIS SUCKER.
BUT, NOBODY REALLY CALLS YOU TO BEGIN WITH.
SURE THEY DO.
©1998 Brett Merhar. Distributed by King Features Syndicate
WHO?
TONS OF NICE SALES-PEOPLE... HOW DO YOU THINK I FOUND OUT ABOUT ALL THIS COOL STUFF IN THE FIRST PLACE?

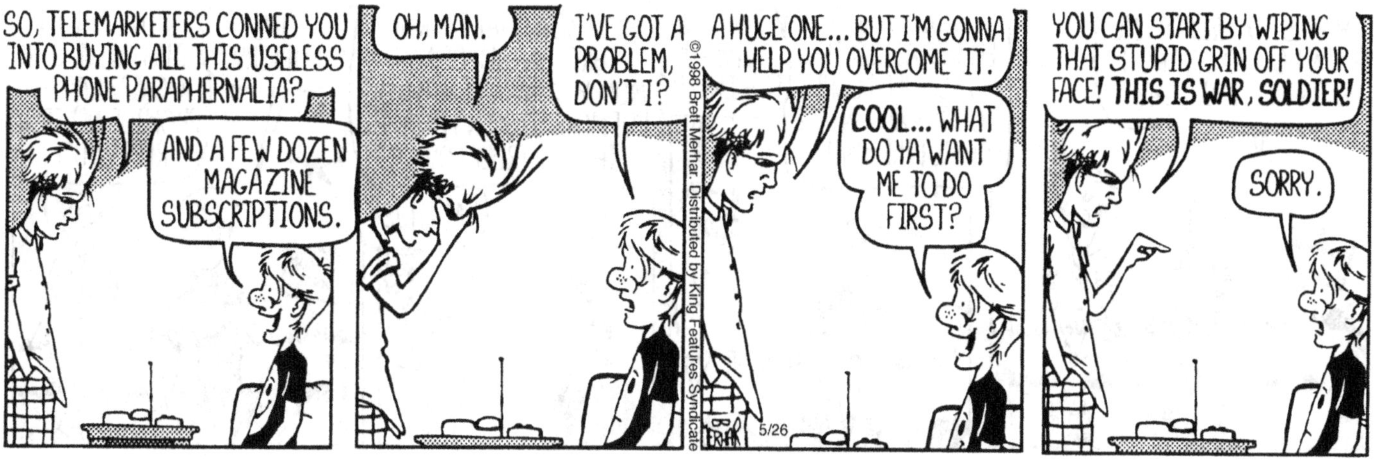
SO, TELEMARKETERS CONNED YOU INTO BUYING ALL THIS USELESS PHONE PARAPHERNALIA?
AND A FEW DOZEN MAGAZINE SUBSCRIPTIONS.
OH, MAN.
I'VE GOT A PROBLEM, DON'T I?
©1998 Brett Merhar. Distributed by King Features Syndicate
A HUGE ONE... BUT I'M GONNA HELP YOU OVERCOME IT.
COOL... WHAT DO YA WANT ME TO DO FIRST?
5/26
YOU CAN START BY WIPING THAT STUPID GRIN OFF YOUR FACE! THIS IS WAR, SOLDIER!
SORRY.

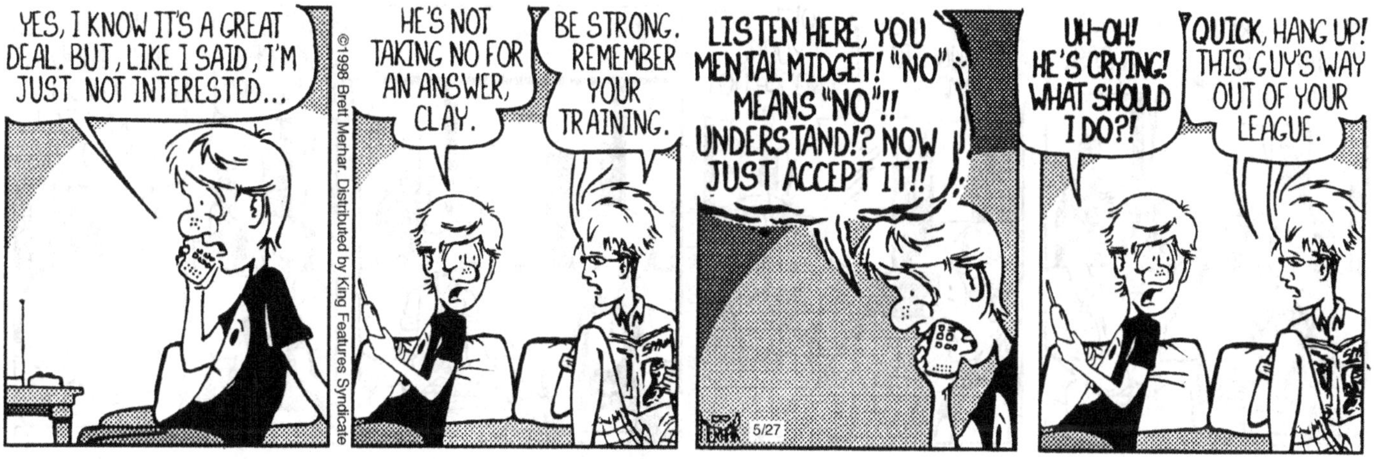
YES, I KNOW IT'S A GREAT DEAL. BUT, LIKE I SAID, I'M JUST NOT INTERESTED...
©1998 Brett Merhar. Distributed by King Features Syndicate
HE'S NOT TAKING NO FOR AN ANSWER, CLAY.
BE STRONG. REMEMBER YOUR TRAINING.
LISTEN HERE, YOU MENTAL MIDGET! "NO" MEANS "NO"!! UNDERSTAND!? NOW JUST ACCEPT IT!!
5/27
UH-OH! HE'S CRYING! WHAT SHOULD I DO?!
QUICK, HANG UP! THIS GUY'S WAY OUT OF YOUR LEAGUE.

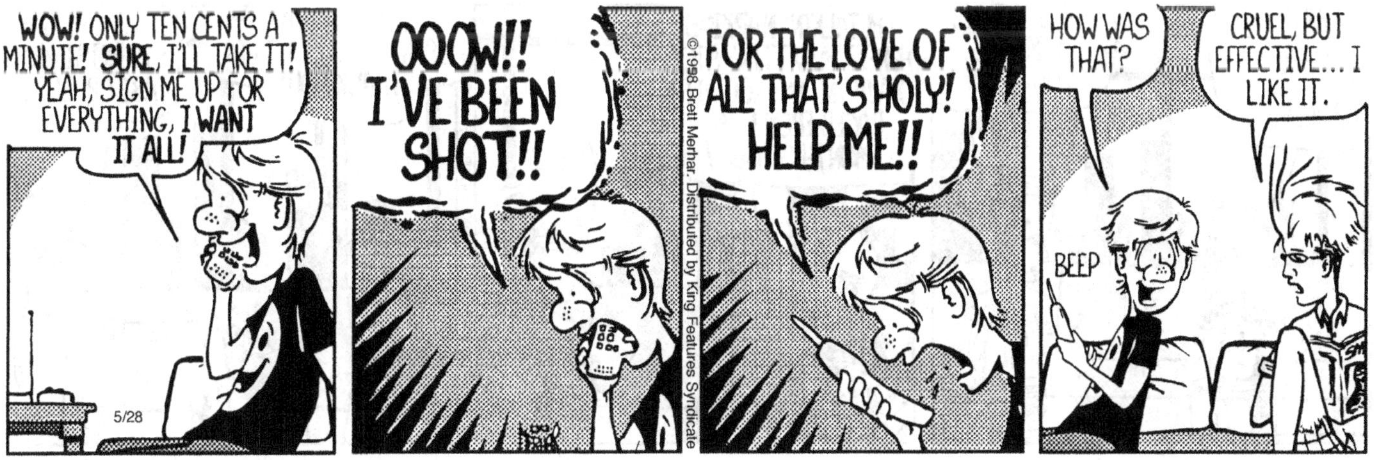
WOW! ONLY TEN CENTS A MINUTE! SURE, I'LL TAKE IT! YEAH, SIGN ME UP FOR EVERYTHING, I WANT IT ALL!
5/28
OOOW!! I'VE BEEN SHOT!!
©1998 Brett Merhar. Distributed by King Features Syndicate
FOR THE LOVE OF ALL THAT'S HOLY! HELP ME!!
HOW WAS THAT?
BEEP
CRUEL, BUT EFFECTIVE... I LIKE IT.

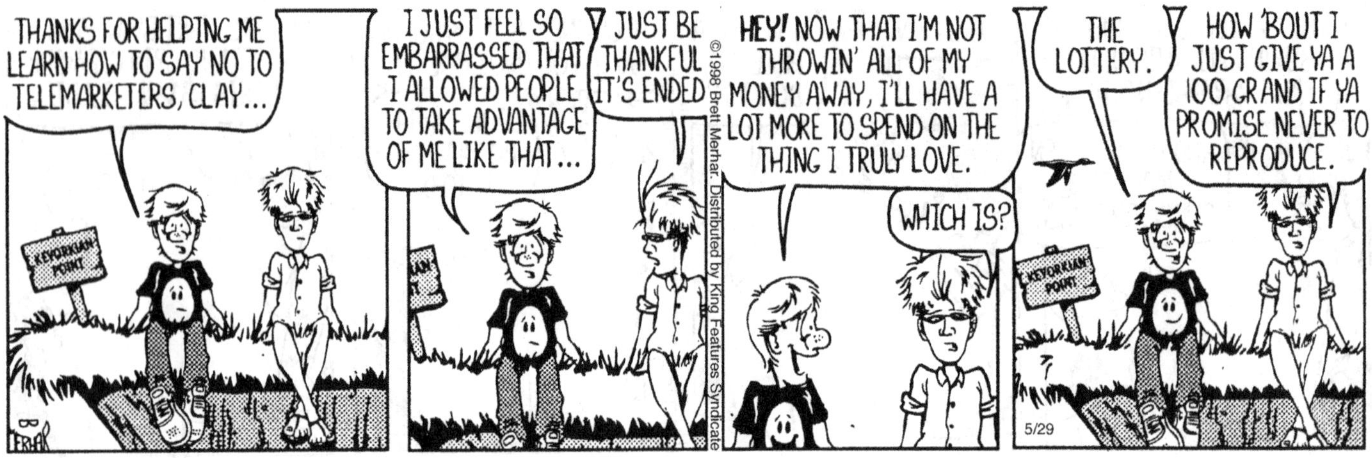
THANKS FOR HELPING ME LEARN HOW TO SAY NO TO TELEMARKETERS, CLAY...
KEVORKIAN POINT
I JUST FEEL SO EMBARRASSED THAT I ALLOWED PEOPLE TO TAKE ADVANTAGE OF ME LIKE THAT...
JUST BE THANKFUL IT'S ENDED
©1998 Brett Merhar. Distributed by King Features Syndicate
HEY! NOW THAT I'M NOT THROWIN' ALL OF MY MONEY AWAY, I'LL HAVE A LOT MORE TO SPEND ON THE THING I TRULY LOVE.
WHICH IS?
THE LOTTERY.
HOW 'BOUT I JUST GIVE YA A 100 GRAND IF YA PROMISE NEVER TO REPRODUCE.
KEVORKIAN POINT
5/29

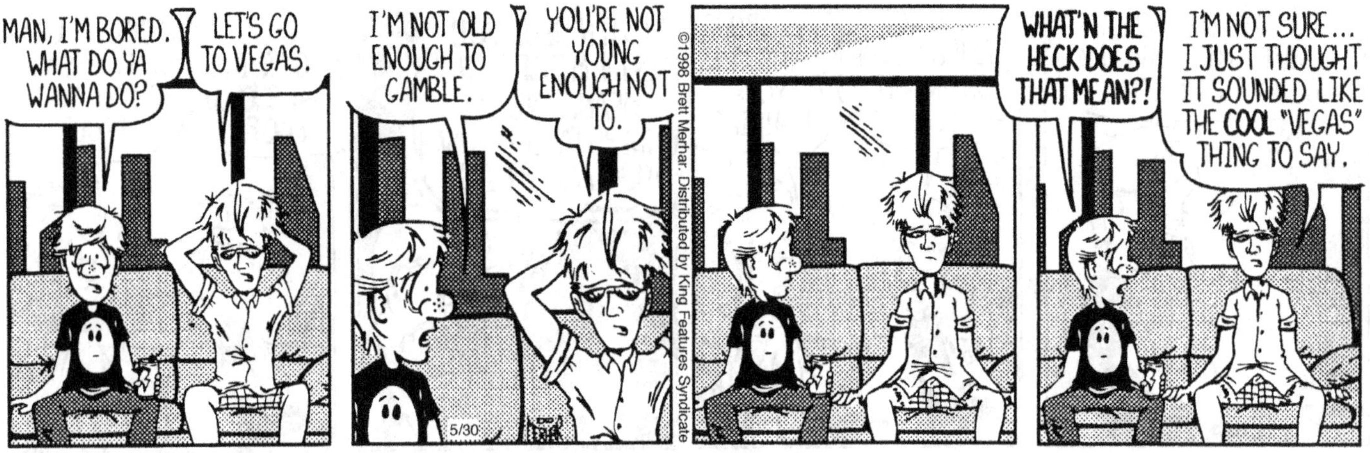
MAN, I'M BORED. WHAT DO YA WANNA DO?
LET'S GO TO VEGAS.
I'M NOT OLD ENOUGH TO GAMBLE.
YOU'RE NOT YOUNG ENOUGH NOT TO.
©1998 Brett Merhar. Distributed by King Features Syndicate
5/30
WHAT'N THE HECK DOES THAT MEAN?!
I'M NOT SURE... I JUST THOUGHT IT SOUNDED LIKE THE COOL "VEGAS" THING TO SAY.

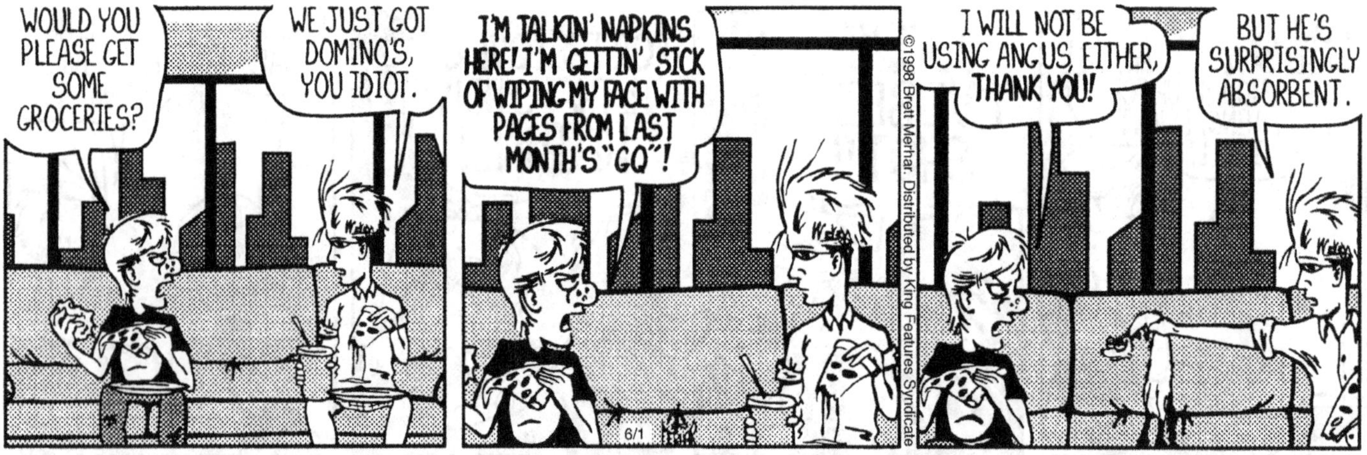
WOULD YOU PLEASE GET SOME GROCERIES?
WE JUST GOT DOMINO'S, YOU IDIOT.
I'M TALKIN' NAPKINS HERE! I'M GETTIN' SICK OF WIPING MY FACE WITH PAGES FROM LAST MONTH'S "GQ"!
6/1
©1998 Brett Merhar. Distributed by King Features Syndicate
I WILL NOT BE USING ANGUS, EITHER, THANK YOU!
BUT HE'S SURPRISINGLY ABSORBENT.

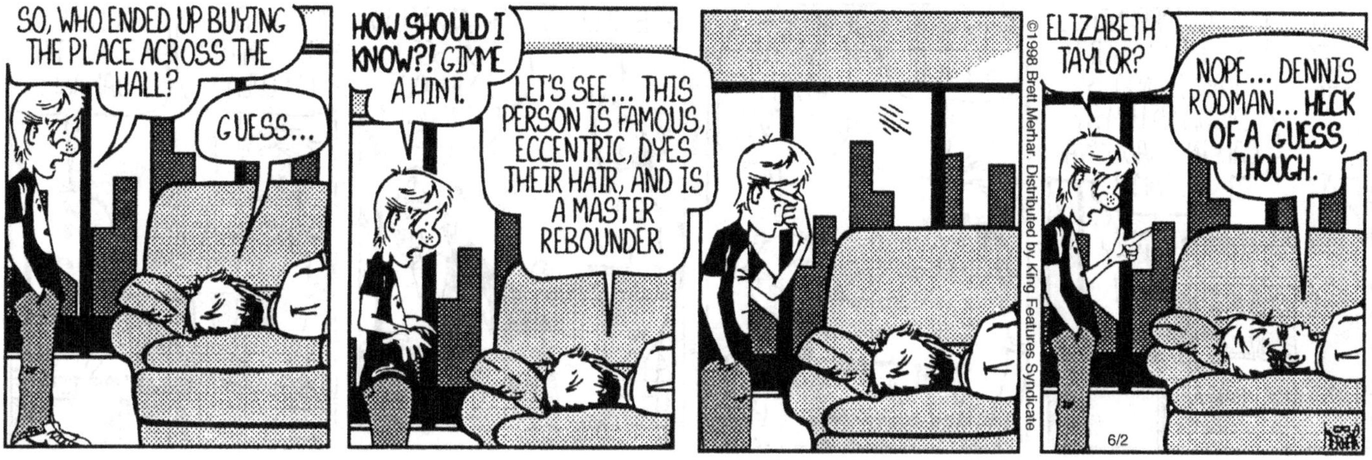
SO, WHO ENDED UP BUYING THE PLACE ACROSS THE HALL?
GUESS...
HOW SHOULD I KNOW?! GIMME A HINT.
LET'S SEE... THIS PERSON IS FAMOUS, ECCENTRIC, DYES THEIR HAIR, AND IS A MASTER REBOUNDER.
©1998 Brett Merhar. Distributed by King Features Syndicate
ELIZABETH TAYLOR?
NOPE... DENNIS RODMAN... HECK OF A GUESS, THOUGH.
6/2

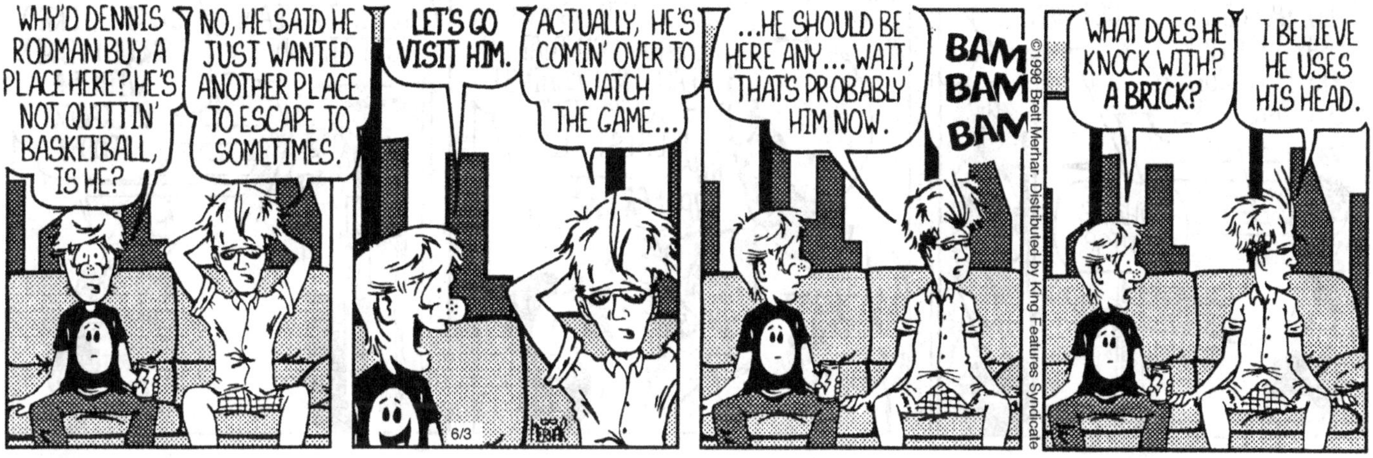
WHY'D DENNIS RODMAN BUY A PLACE HERE? HE'S NOT QUITTIN' BASKETBALL, IS HE?
NO, HE SAID HE JUST WANTED ANOTHER PLACE TO ESCAPE TO SOMETIMES.
LET'S GO VISIT HIM.
ACTUALLY, HE'S COMIN' OVER TO WATCH THE GAME...
6/3
...HE SHOULD BE HERE ANY... WAIT, THAT'S PROBABLY HIM NOW.
BAM BAM BAM
©1998 Brett Merhar. Distributed by King Features Syndicate
WHAT DOES HE KNOCK WITH? A BRICK?
I BELIEVE HE USES HIS HEAD.

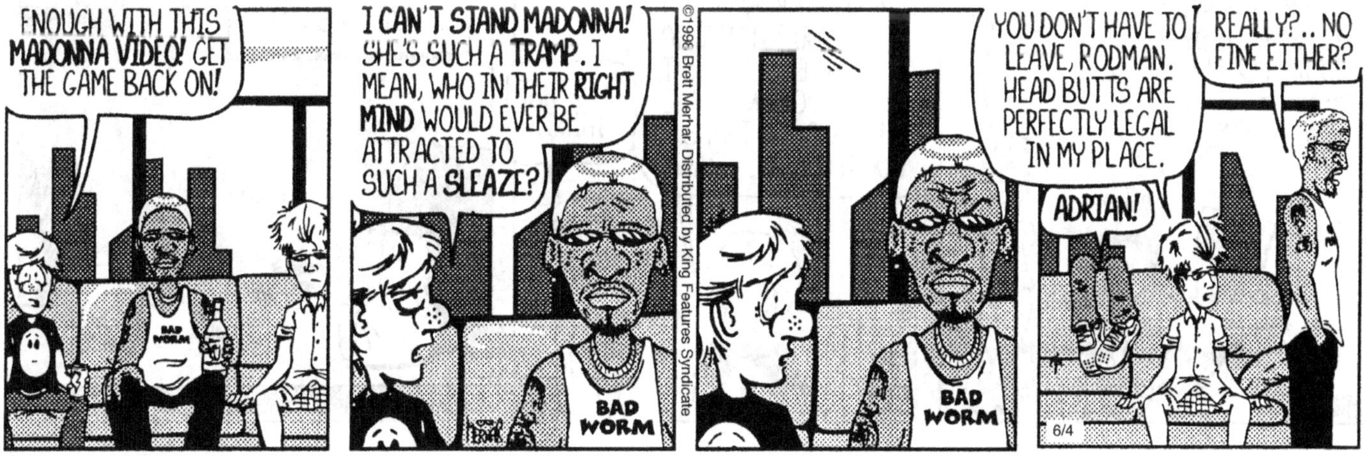
ENOUGH WITH THIS MADONNA VIDEO! GET THE GAME BACK ON!
BAD WORM
I CAN'T STAND MADONNA! SHE'S SUCH A TRAMP. I MEAN, WHO IN THEIR RIGHT MIND WOULD EVER BE ATTRACTED TO SUCH A SLEAZE?
BAD WORM
©1998 Brett Merhar. Distributed by King Features Syndicate
BAD WORM
YOU DON'T HAVE TO LEAVE, RODMAN. HEAD BUTTS ARE PERFECTLY LEGAL IN MY PLACE.
ADRIAN!
REALLY?.. NO FINE EITHER?
6/4

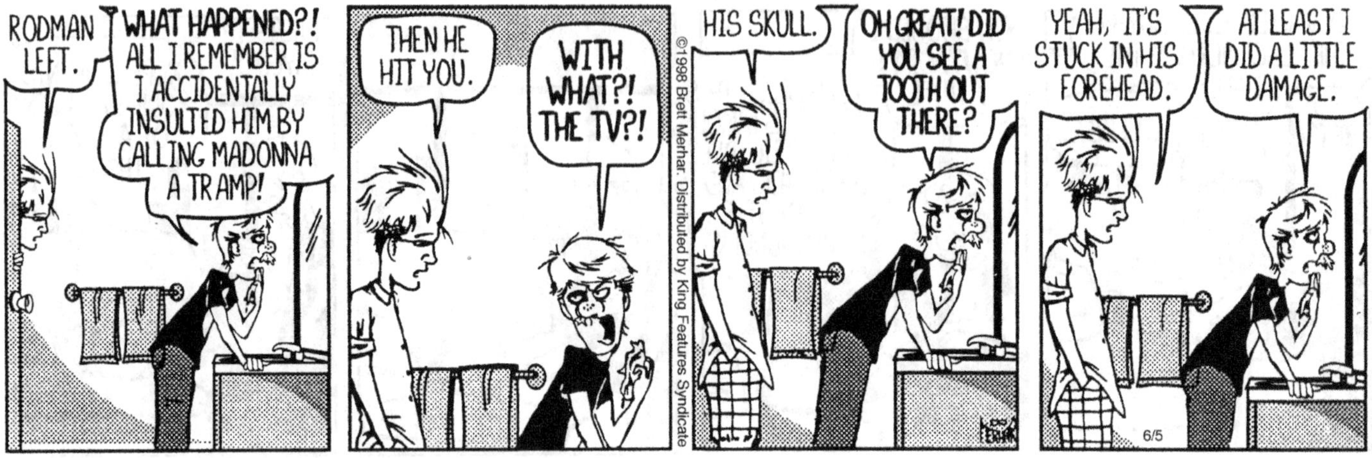
RODMAN LEFT.
WHAT HAPPENED?! ALL I REMEMBER IS I ACCIDENTALLY INSULTED HIM BY CALLING MADONNA A TRAMP!
THEN HE HIT YOU.
WITH WHAT?! THE TV?!
©1998 Brett Merhar. Distributed by King Features Syndicate
HIS SKULL.
OH GREAT! DID YOU SEE A TOOTH OUT THERE?
MERHAR
YEAH, IT'S STUCK IN HIS FOREHEAD.
AT LEAST I DID A LITTLE DAMAGE.
6/5

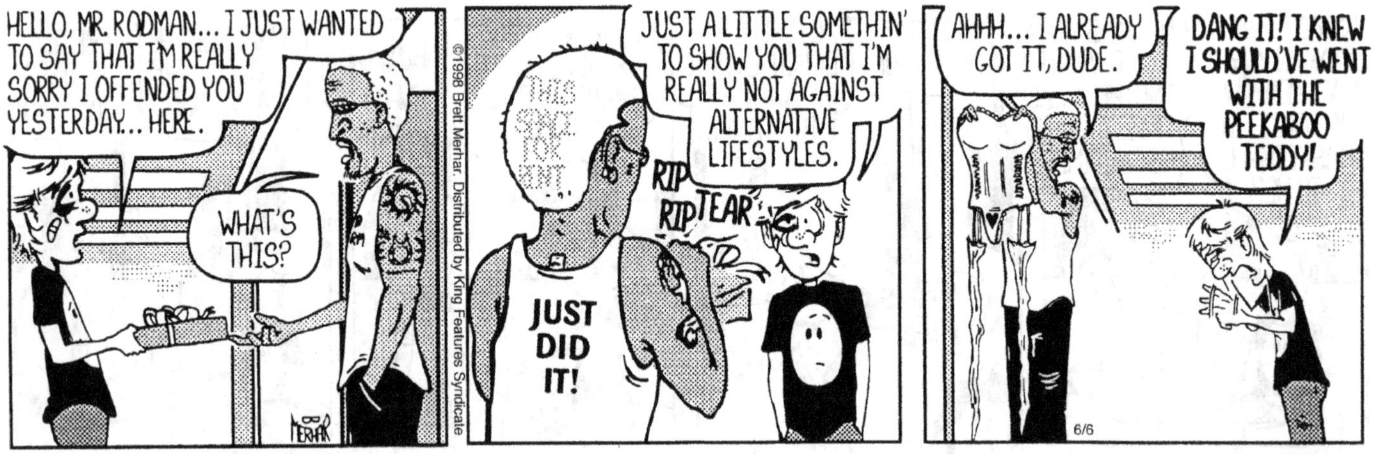
HELLO, MR. RODMAN... I JUST WANTED TO SAY THAT I'M REALLY SORRY I OFFENDED YOU YESTERDAY... HERE.
WHAT'S THIS?
MERHAR
©1998 Brett Merhar. Distributed by King Features Syndicate
JUST A LITTLE SOMETHIN' TO SHOW YOU THAT I'M REALLY NOT AGAINST ALTERNATIVE LIFESTYLES.
RIP
RIP
TEAR
JUST DID IT!
AHHH... I ALREADY GOT IT, DUDE.
DANG IT! I KNEW I SHOULD'VE WENT WITH THE PEEKABOO TEDDY!
6/6

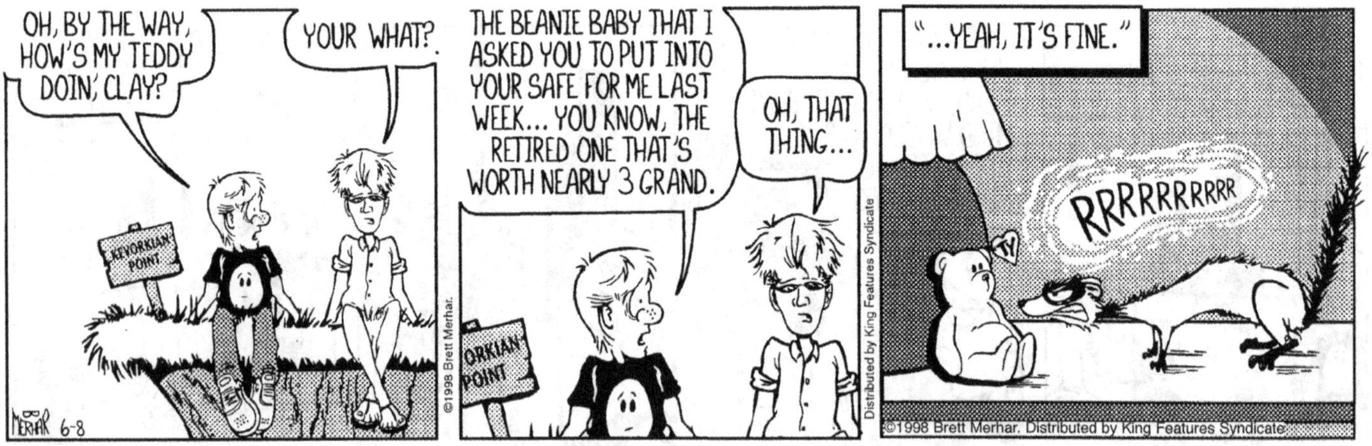
OH, BY THE WAY, HOW'S MY TEDDY DOIN,' CLAY?
YOUR WHAT?
KEVORKIAN POINT
MERHAR 6-8
©1998 Brett Merhar.
THE BEANIE BABY THAT I ASKED YOU TO PUT INTO YOUR SAFE FOR ME LAST WEEK... YOU KNOW, THE RETIRED ONE THAT'S WORTH NEARLY 3 GRAND.
OH, THAT THING...
ORKIAN POINT
Distributed by King Features Syndicate
"...YEAH, IT'S FINE."
TY
RRRRRRRRRR
©1998 Brett Merhar. Distributed by King Features Syndicate

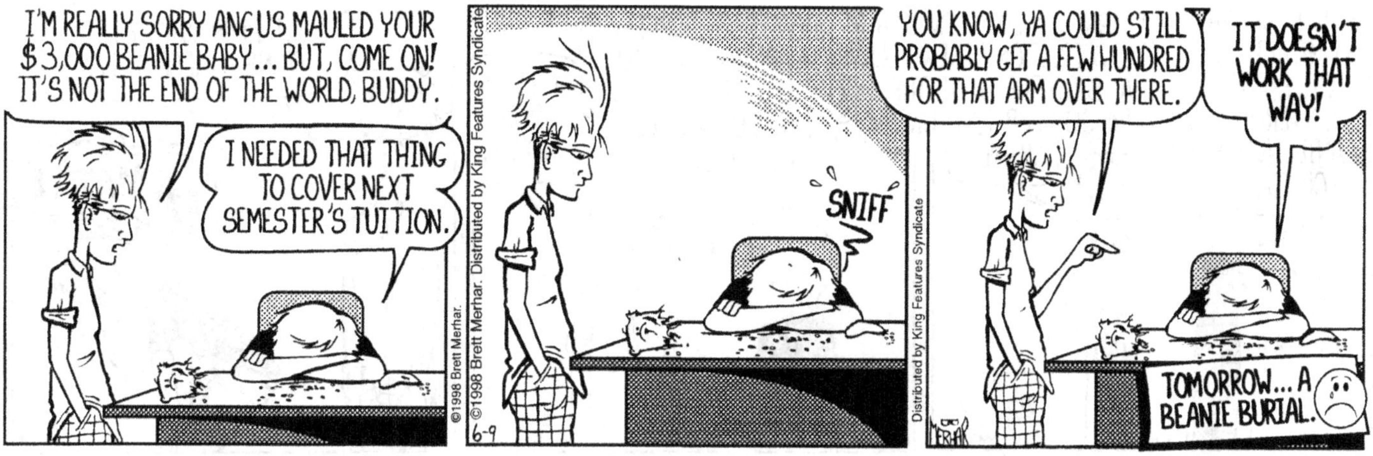
I'M REALLY SORRY ANGUS MAULED YOUR $3,000 BEANIE BABY... BUT, COME ON! IT'S NOT THE END OF THE WORLD, BUDDY.
I NEEDED THAT THING TO COVER NEXT SEMESTER'S TUITION.
©1998 Brett Merhar.
©1998 Brett Merhar. Distributed by King Features Syndicate
6-9
SNIFF
YOU KNOW, YA COULD STILL PROBABLY GET A FEW HUNDRED FOR THAT ARM OVER THERE.
IT DOESN'T WORK THAT WAY!
Distributed by King Features Syndicate
TOMORROW... A BEANIE BURIAL.
MERHAR

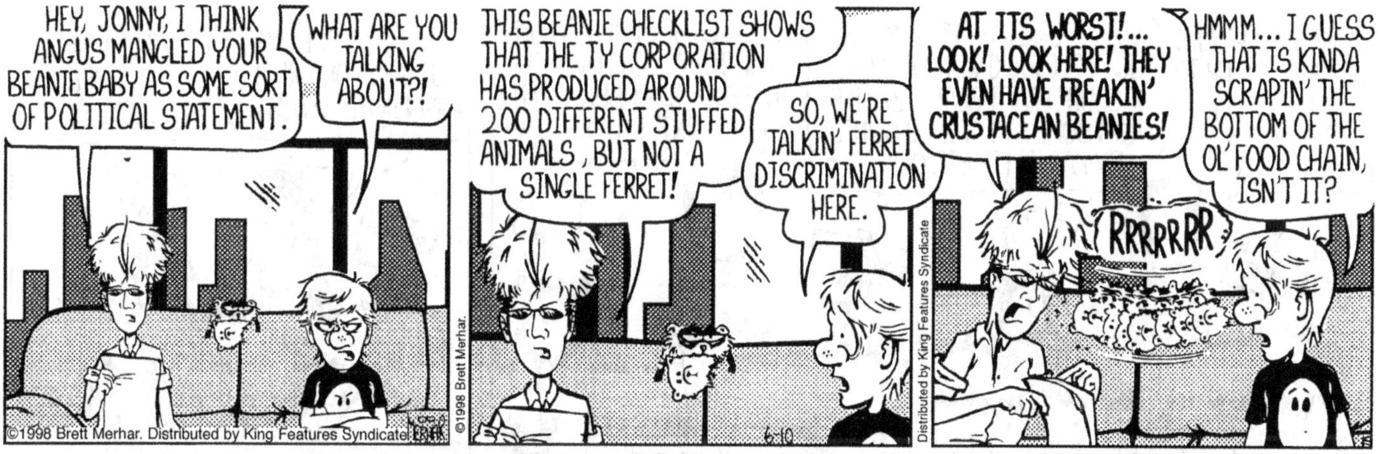
HEY, JONNY, I THINK ANGUS MANGLED YOUR BEANIE BABY AS SOME SORT OF POLITICAL STATEMENT.
WHAT ARE YOU TALKING ABOUT?!
©1998 Brett Merhar. Distributed by King Features Syndicate
THIS BEANIE CHECKLIST SHOWS THAT THE TY CORPORATION HAS PRODUCED AROUND 200 DIFFERENT STUFFED ANIMALS, BUT NOT A SINGLE FERRET!
SO, WE'RE TALKIN' FERRET DISCRIMINATION HERE.
©1998 Brett Merhar.
6-10
AT ITS WORST!... LOOK! LOOK HERE! THEY EVEN HAVE FREAKIN' CRUSTACEAN BEANIES!
HMMM... I GUESS THAT IS KINDA SCRAPIN' THE BOTTOM OF THE OL' FOOD CHAIN, ISN'T IT?
RRRRRRR
Distributed by King Features Syndicate

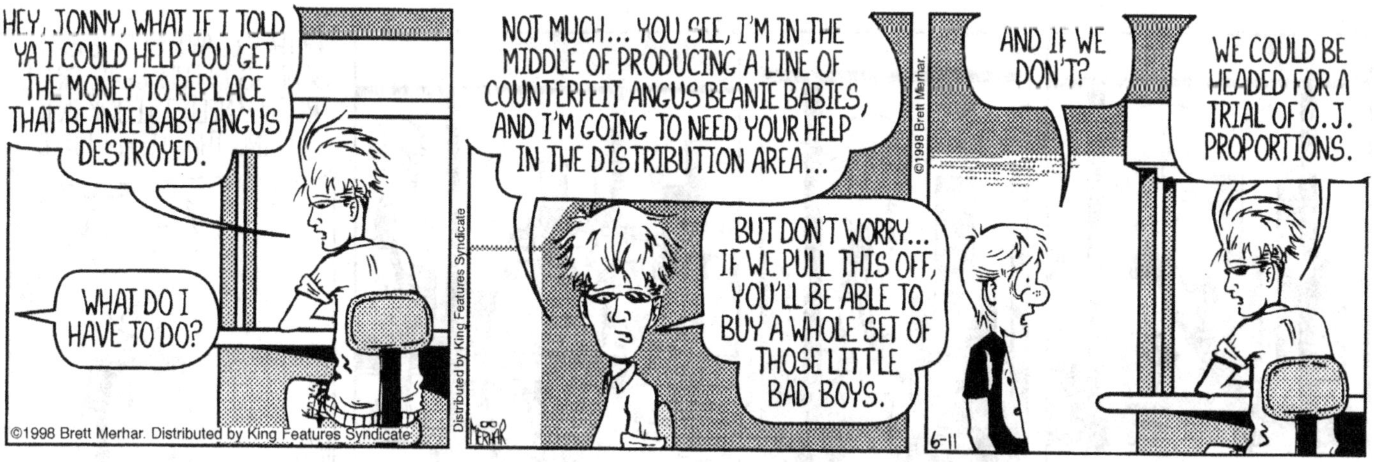
HEY, JONNY, WHAT IF I TOLD YA I COULD HELP YOU GET THE MONEY TO REPLACE THAT BEANIE BABY ANGUS DESTROYED.
WHAT DO I HAVE TO DO?
©1998 Brett Merhar. Distributed by King Features Syndicate
NOT MUCH... YOU SEE, I'M IN THE MIDDLE OF PRODUCING A LINE OF COUNTERFEIT ANGUS BEANIE BABIES, AND I'M GOING TO NEED YOUR HELP IN THE DISTRIBUTION AREA...
BUT DON'T WORRY... IF WE PULL THIS OFF, YOU'LL BE ABLE TO BUY A WHOLE SET OF THOSE LITTLE BAD BOYS.
Distributed by King Features Syndicate
MERHAR
©1998 Brett Merhar.
AND IF WE DON'T?
WE COULD BE HEADED FOR A TRIAL OF O.J. PROPORTIONS.
6-11

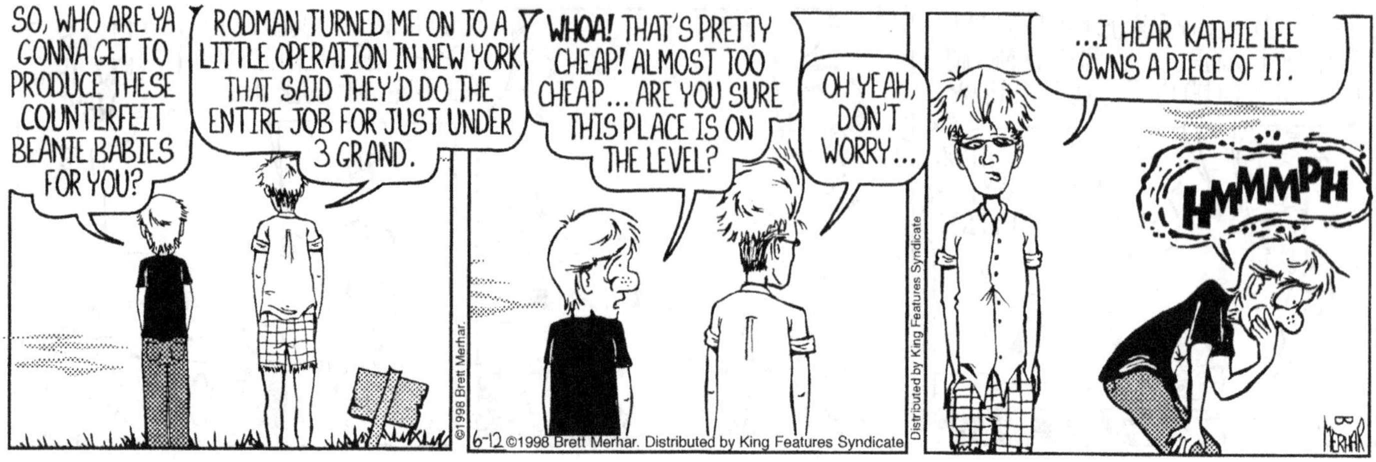
SO, WHO ARE YA GONNA GET TO PRODUCE THESE COUNTERFEIT BEANIE BABIES FOR YOU?
RODMAN TURNED ME ON TO A LITTLE OPERATION IN NEW YORK THAT SAID THEY'D DO THE ENTIRE JOB FOR JUST UNDER 3 GRAND.
WHOA! THAT'S PRETTY CHEAP! ALMOST TOO CHEAP... ARE YOU SURE THIS PLACE IS ON THE LEVEL?
OH YEAH, DON'T WORRY...
...I HEAR KATHIE LEE OWNS A PIECE OF IT.
HMMMPH
©1998 Brett Merhar.
6-12 ©1998 Brett Merhar. Distributed by King Features Syndicate
Distributed by King Features Syndicate
MERHAR

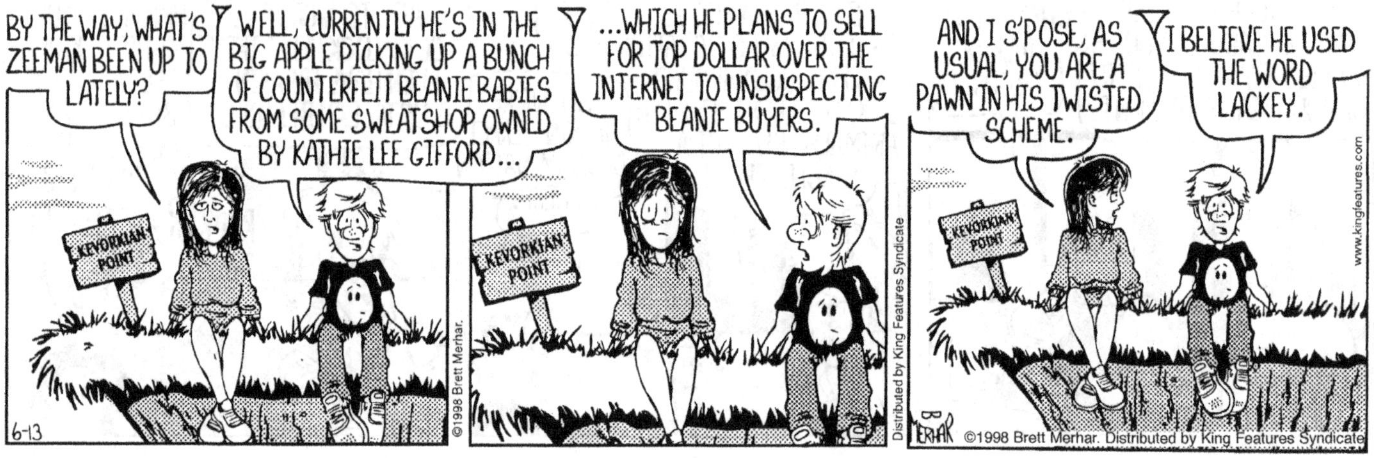
BY THE WAY, WHAT'S ZEEMAN BEEN UP TO LATELY?
WELL, CURRENTLY HE'S IN THE BIG APPLE PICKING UP A BUNCH OF COUNTERFEIT BEANIE BABIES FROM SOME SWEATSHOP OWNED BY KATHIE LEE GIFFORD...
...WHICH HE PLANS TO SELL FOR TOP DOLLAR OVER THE INTERNET TO UNSUSPECTING BEANIE BUYERS.
AND I S'POSE, AS USUAL, YOU ARE A PAWN IN HIS TWISTED SCHEME.
I BELIEVE HE USED THE WORD LACKEY.
KEVORKIAN POINT
6-13
©1998 Brett Merhar.
Distributed by King Features Syndicate
MERHAR ©1998 Brett Merhar. Distributed by King Features Syndicate
www.kingfeatures.com

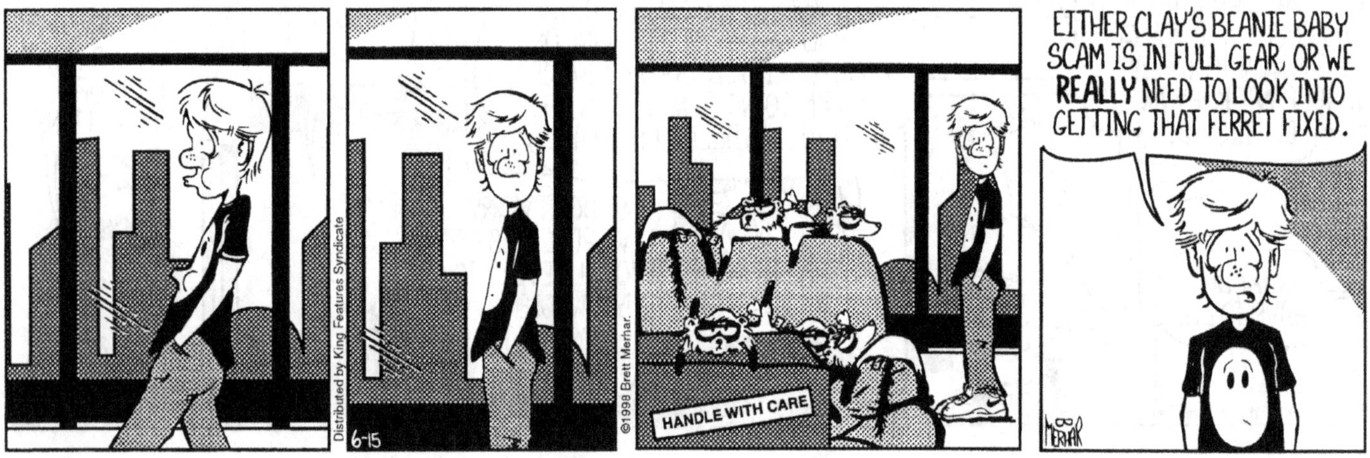
HANDLE WITH CARE
EITHER CLAY'S BEANIE BABY SCAM IS IN FULL GEAR, OR WE REALLY NEED TO LOOK INTO GETTING THAT FERRET FIXED.
Distributed by King Features Syndicate
6-15
©1998 Brett Merhar.
MERHAR

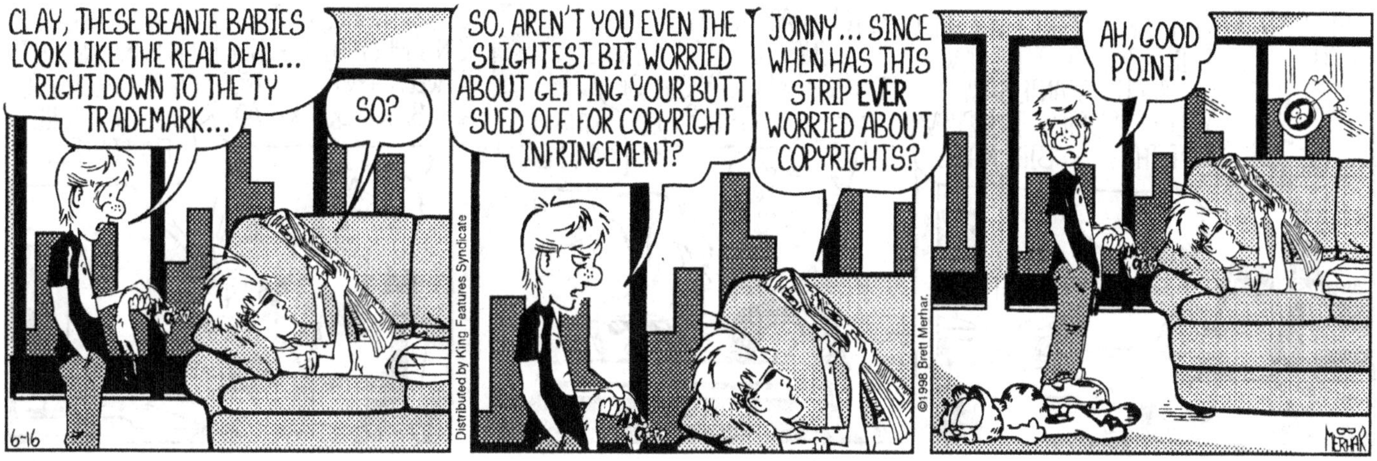
CLAY, THESE BEANIE BABIES LOOK LIKE THE REAL DEAL... RIGHT DOWN TO THE TY TRADEMARK...
SO?
SO, AREN'T YOU EVEN THE SLIGHTEST BIT WORRIED ABOUT GETTING YOUR BUTT SUED OFF FOR COPYRIGHT INFRINGEMENT?
JONNY... SINCE WHEN HAS THIS STRIP **EVER** WORRIED ABOUT COPYRIGHTS?
AH, GOOD POINT.
6-16
Distributed by King Features Syndicate
©1998 Brett Merhar.
MERHAR

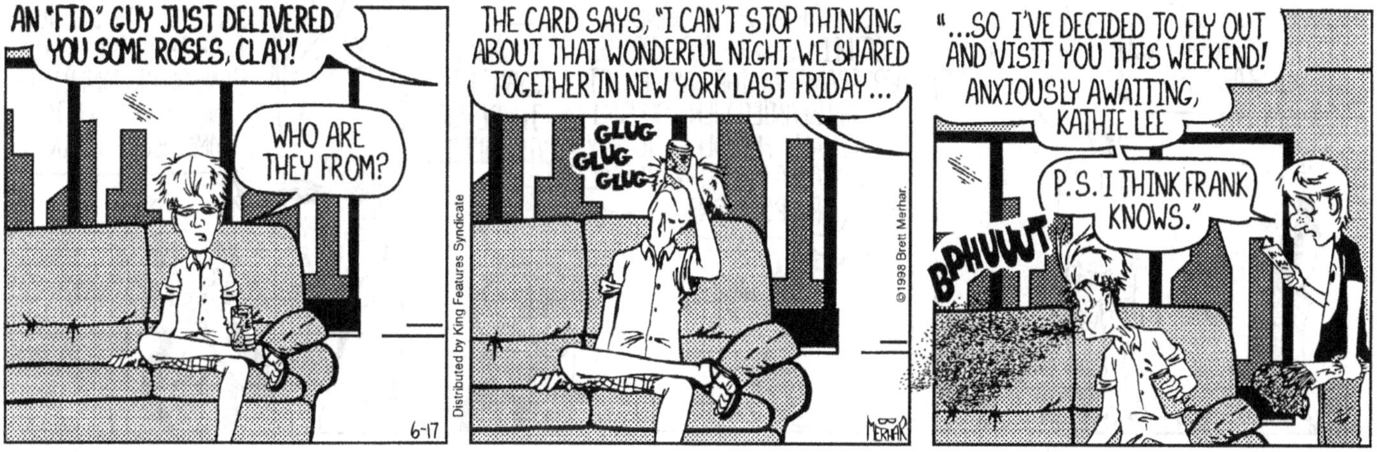
AN "FTD" GUY JUST DELIVERED YOU SOME ROSES, CLAY!
WHO ARE THEY FROM?
6-17
THE CARD SAYS, "I CAN'T STOP THINKING ABOUT THAT WONDERFUL NIGHT WE SHARED TOGETHER IN NEW YORK LAST FRIDAY...
GLUG GLUG GLUG
Distributed by King Features Syndicate
©1998 Brett Merhar.
MERHAR
"...SO I'VE DECIDED TO FLY OUT AND VISIT YOU THIS WEEKEND! ANXIOUSLY AWAITING, KATHIE LEE
P.S. I THINK FRANK KNOWS."
BPHUUUT

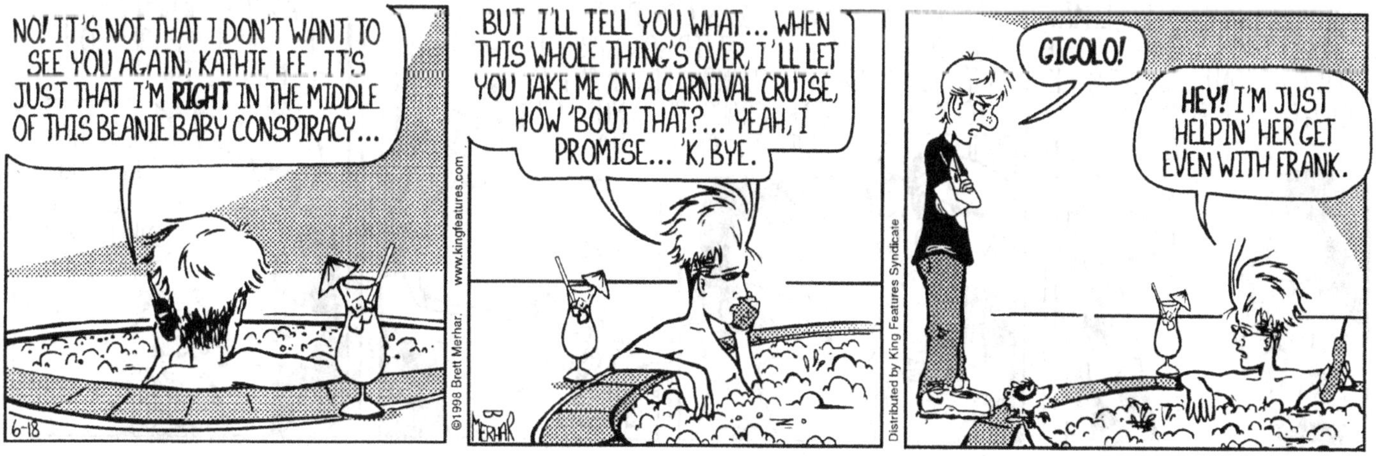
NO! IT'S NOT THAT I DON'T WANT TO SEE YOU AGAIN, KATHIE LEE. IT'S JUST THAT I'M **RIGHT** IN THE MIDDLE OF THIS BEANIE BABY CONSPIRACY...
6-18
©1998 Brett Merhar. www.kingfeatures.com
.BUT I'LL TELL YOU WHAT... WHEN THIS WHOLE THING'S OVER, I'LL LET YOU TAKE ME ON A CARNIVAL CRUISE, HOW 'BOUT THAT?... YEAH, I PROMISE... 'K, BYE.
MERHAR
Distributed by King Features Syndicate
GIGOLO!
HEY! I'M JUST HELPIN' HER GET EVEN WITH FRANK.

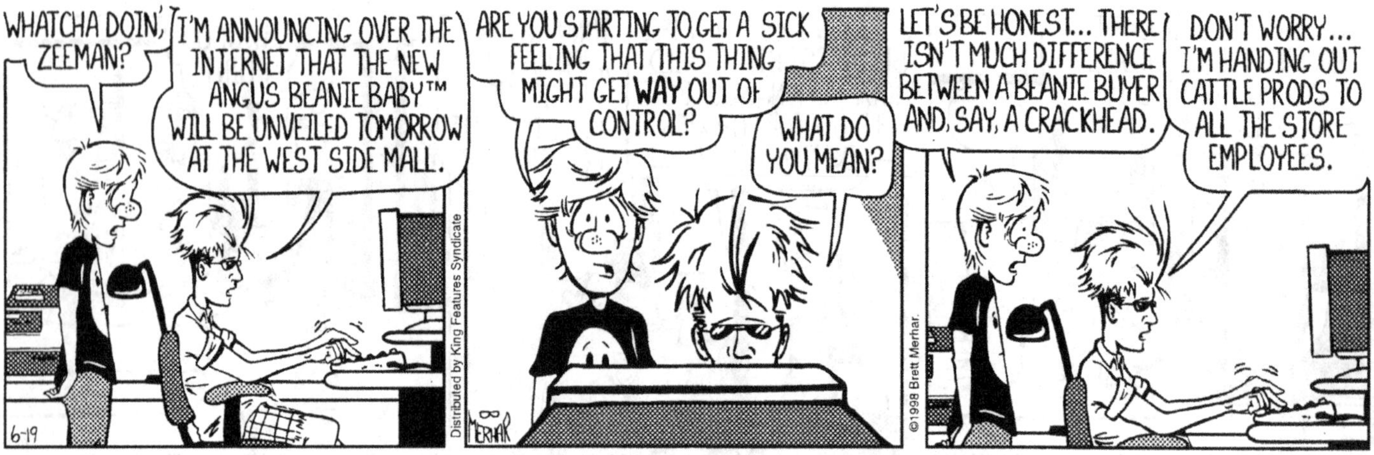
WHATCHA DOIN', ZEEMAN?
I'M ANNOUNCING OVER THE INTERNET THAT THE NEW ANGUS BEANIE BABY™ WILL BE UNVEILED TOMORROW AT THE WEST SIDE MALL.
6-19
Distributed by King Features Syndicate
MERHAR
ARE YOU STARTING TO GET A SICK FEELING THAT THIS THING MIGHT GET **WAY** OUT OF CONTROL?
WHAT DO YOU MEAN?
©1998 Brett Merhar.
LET'S BE HONEST... THERE ISN'T MUCH DIFFERENCE BETWEEN A BEANIE BUYER AND, SAY, A CRACKHEAD.
DON'T WORRY... I'M HANDING OUT CATTLE PRODS TO ALL THE STORE EMPLOYEES.

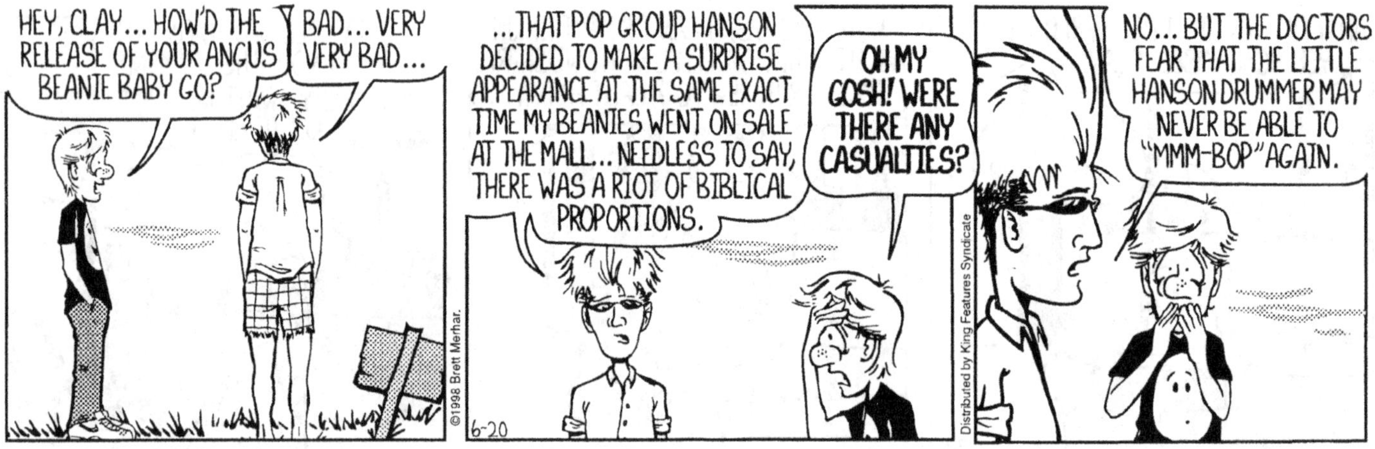
HEY, CLAY... HOW'D THE RELEASE OF YOUR ANGUS BEANIE BABY GO?
BAD... VERY VERY BAD...
©1998 Brett Merhar.
6-20
...THAT POP GROUP HANSON DECIDED TO MAKE A SURPRISE APPEARANCE AT THE SAME EXACT TIME MY BEANIES WENT ON SALE AT THE MALL... NEEDLESS TO SAY, THERE WAS A RIOT OF BIBLICAL PROPORTIONS.
OH MY GOSH! WERE THERE ANY CASUALTIES?
Distributed by King Features Syndicate
NO... BUT THE DOCTORS FEAR THAT THE LITTLE HANSON DRUMMER MAY NEVER BE ABLE TO "MMM-BOP" AGAIN.

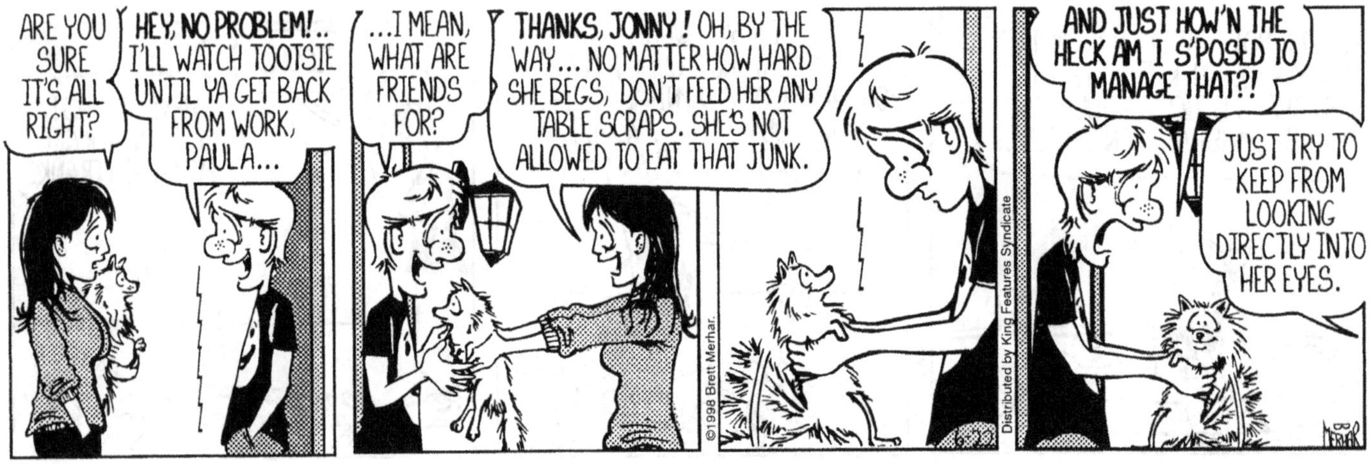
ARE YOU SURE IT'S ALL RIGHT?
HEY, NO PROBLEM!.. I'LL WATCH TOOTSIE UNTIL YA GET BACK FROM WORK, PAULA...
...I MEAN, WHAT ARE FRIENDS FOR?
THANKS, JONNY! OH, BY THE WAY... NO MATTER HOW HARD SHE BEGS, DON'T FEED HER ANY TABLE SCRAPS. SHE'S NOT ALLOWED TO EAT THAT JUNK.
©1998 Brett Merhar.
Distributed by King Features Syndicate
AND JUST HOW'N THE HECK AM I S'POSED TO MANAGE THAT?!
JUST TRY TO KEEP FROM LOOKING DIRECTLY INTO HER EYES.
MERHAR

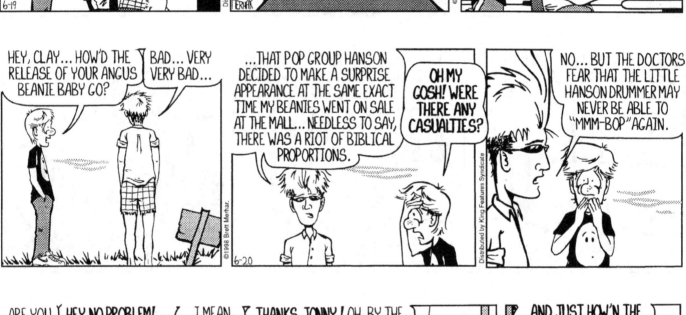

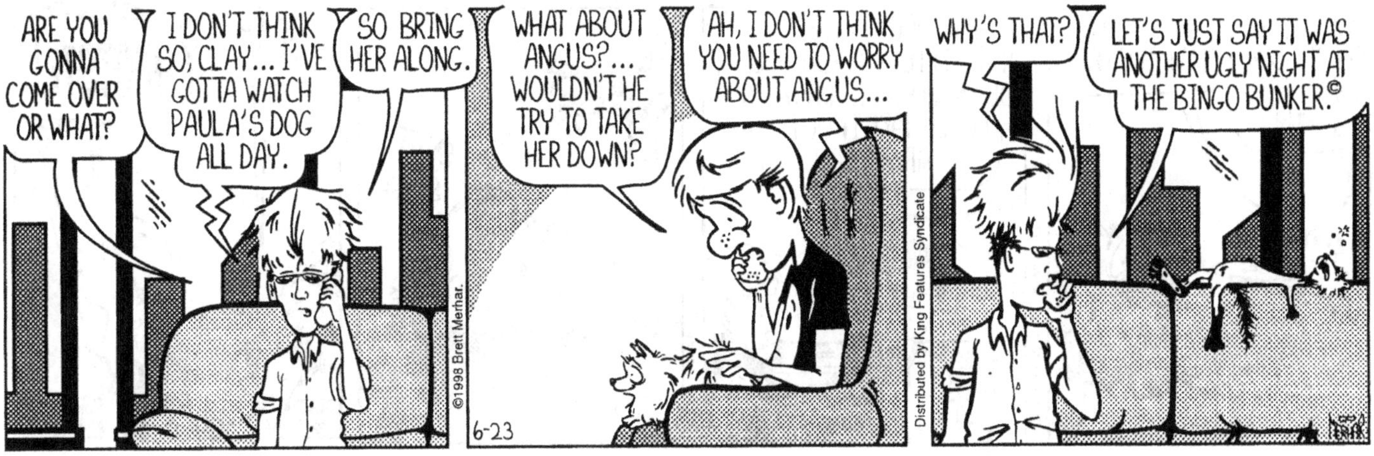
ARE YOU GONNA COME OVER OR WHAT?
I DON'T THINK SO, CLAY... I'VE GOTTA WATCH PAULA'S DOG ALL DAY.
SO BRING HER ALONG.
©1998 Brett Merhar.
6-23
WHAT ABOUT ANGUS?... WOULDN'T HE TRY TO TAKE HER DOWN?
AH, I DON'T THINK YOU NEED TO WORRY ABOUT ANGUS...
Distributed by King Features Syndicate
WHY'S THAT?
LET'S JUST SAY IT WAS ANOTHER UGLY NIGHT AT THE BINGO BUNKER.©

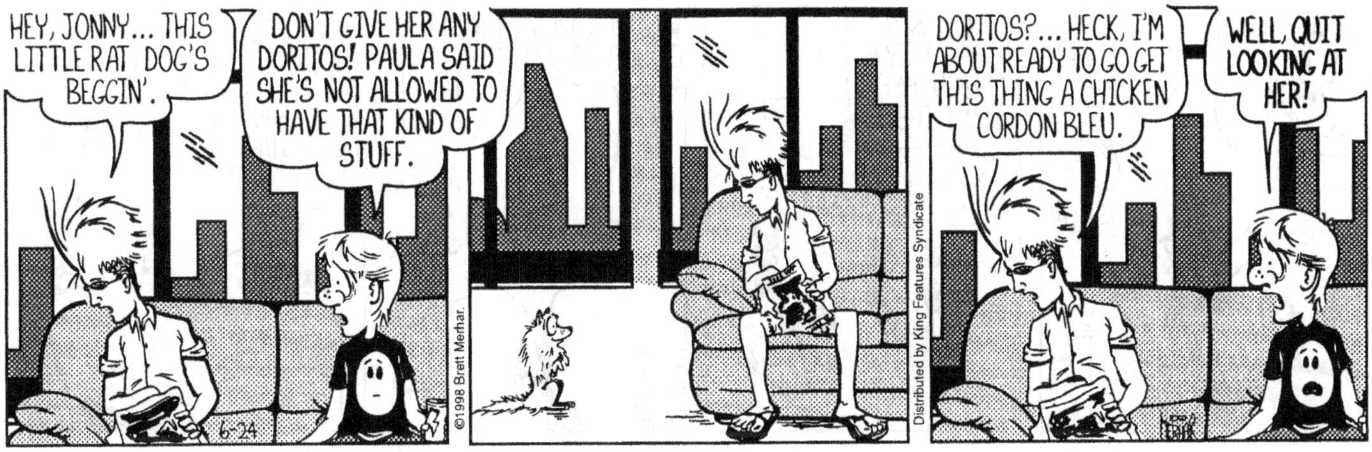
HEY, JONNY... THIS LITTLE RAT DOG'S BEGGIN'.
DON'T GIVE HER ANY DORITOS! PAULA SAID SHE'S NOT ALLOWED TO HAVE THAT KIND OF STUFF.
6-24
©1998 Brett Merhar.
Distributed by King Features Syndicate
DORITOS?... HECK, I'M ABOUT READY TO GO GET THIS THING A CHICKEN CORDON BLEU.
WELL, QUIT LOOKING AT HER!

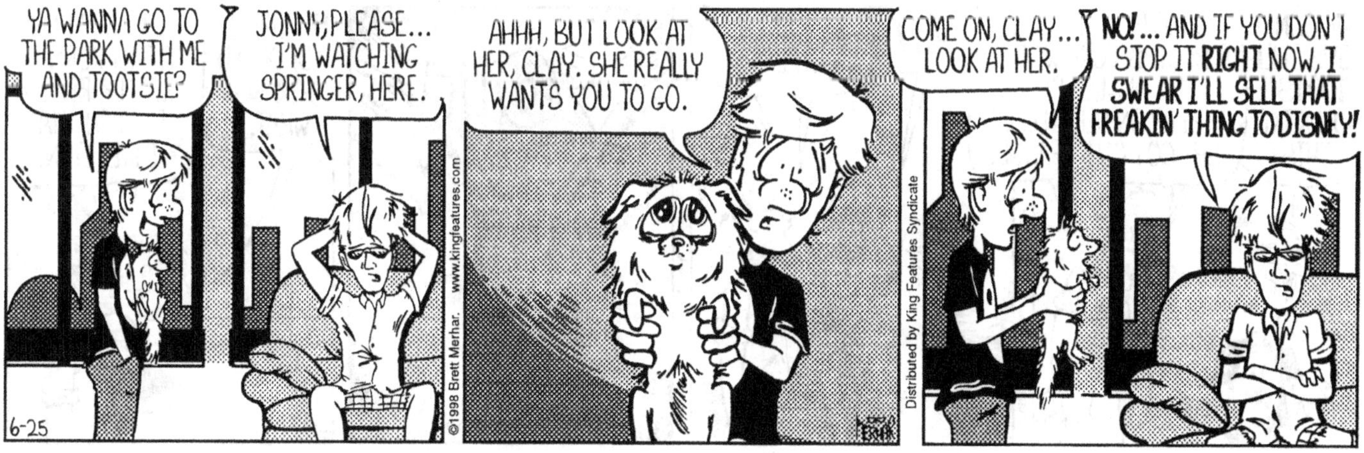
YA WANNA GO TO THE PARK WITH ME AND TOOTSIE?
JONNY, PLEASE... I'M WATCHING SPRINGER, HERE.
6-25
©1998 Brett Merhar. www.kingfeatures.com
AHHH, BUT LOOK AT HER, CLAY. SHE REALLY WANTS YOU TO GO.
Distributed by King Features Syndicate
COME ON, CLAY... LOOK AT HER.
NO!... AND IF YOU DON'T STOP IT RIGHT NOW, I SWEAR I'LL SELL THAT FREAKIN' THING TO DISNEY!

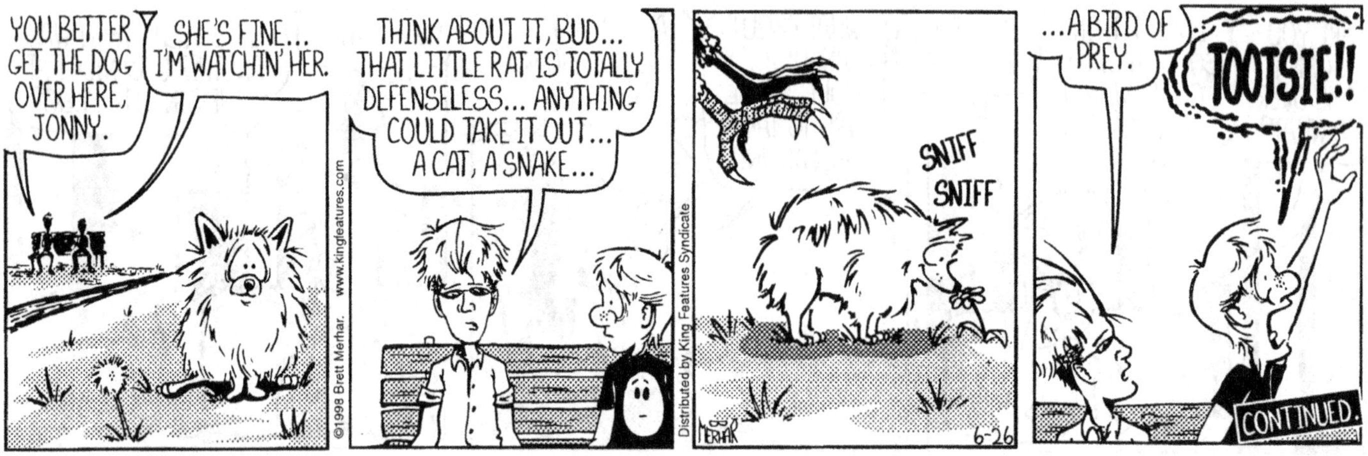
YOU BETTER GET THE DOG OVER HERE, JONNY.
SHE'S FINE... I'M WATCHIN' HER.
©1998 Brett Merhar. www.kingfeatures.com
THINK ABOUT IT, BUD... THAT LITTLE RAT IS TOTALLY DEFENSELESS... ANYTHING COULD TAKE IT OUT... A CAT, A SNAKE...
Distributed by King Features Syndicate
SNIFF
SNIFF
MERHAR
6-26
...A BIRD OF PREY.
TOOTSIE!!
CONTINUED.

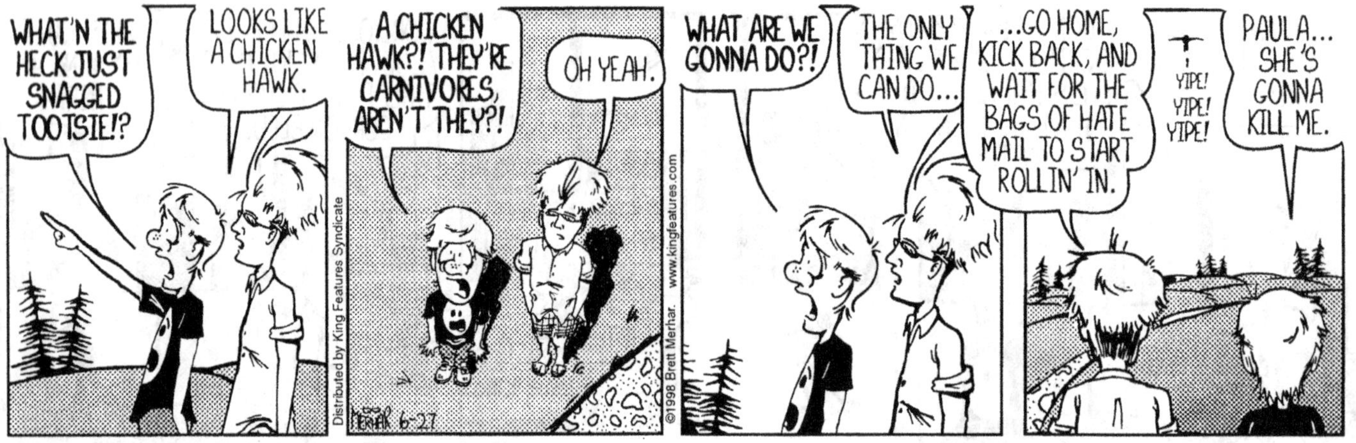
WHAT'N THE HECK JUST SNAGGED TOOTSIE!?
LOOKS LIKE A CHICKEN HAWK.
Distributed by King Features Syndicate
A CHICKEN HAWK?! THEY'RE CARNIVORES, AREN'T THEY?!
OH YEAH.
MERHAR 6-27
©1998 Brett Merhar. www.kingfeatures.com
WHAT ARE WE GONNA DO?!
THE ONLY THING WE CAN DO...
...GO HOME, KICK BACK, AND WAIT FOR THE BAGS OF HATE MAIL TO START ROLLIN' IN.
YIPE! YIPE! YIPE!
PAULA... SHE'S GONNA KILL ME.

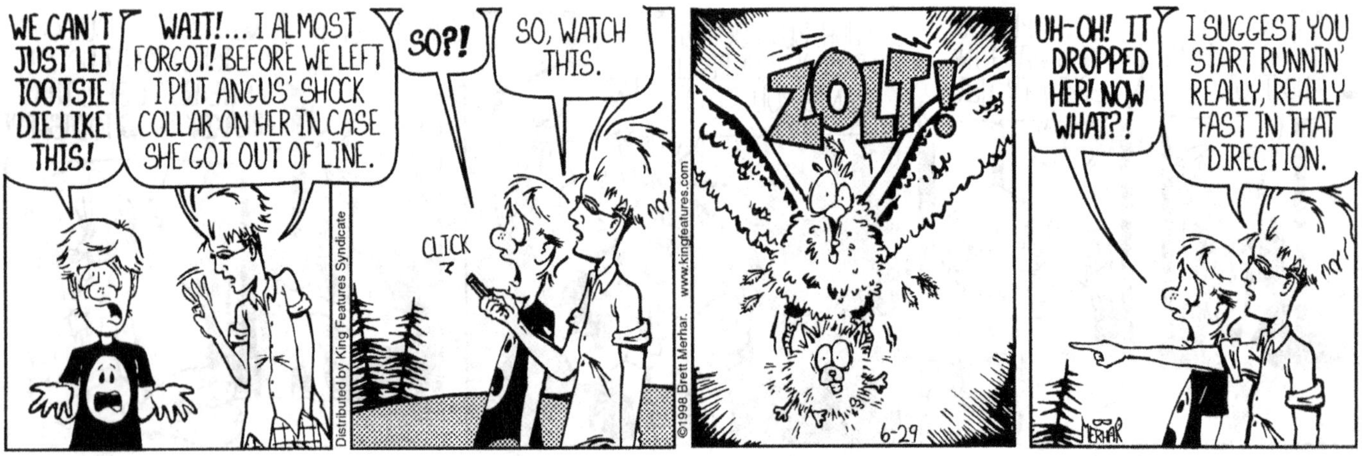
WE CAN'T JUST LET TOOTSIE DIE LIKE THIS!
WAIT!... I ALMOST FORGOT! BEFORE WE LEFT I PUT ANGUS' SHOCK COLLAR ON HER IN CASE SHE GOT OUT OF LINE.
Distributed by King Features Syndicate
SO?!
SO, WATCH THIS.
CLICK
©1998 Brett Merhar. www.kingfeatures.com
ZOLT!
6-29
UH-OH! IT DROPPED HER! NOW WHAT?!
I SUGGEST YOU START RUNNIN' REALLY, REALLY FAST IN THAT DIRECTION.
MERHAR

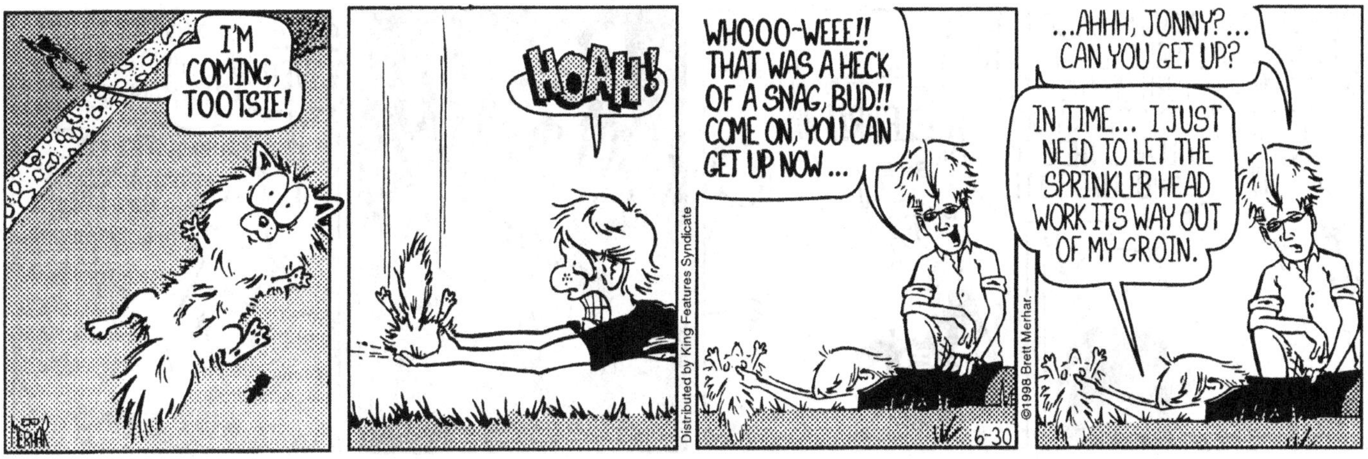
I'M COMING, TOOTSIE!
MERHAR
HOAH!
Distributed by King Features Syndicate
WHOOO-WEEE!! THAT WAS A HECK OF A SNAG, BUD!! COME ON, YOU CAN GET UP NOW ...
6-30
©1998 Brett Merhar.
...AHHH, JONNY?... CAN YOU GET UP?
IN TIME... I JUST NEED TO LET THE SPRINKLER HEAD WORK ITS WAY OUT OF MY GROIN.

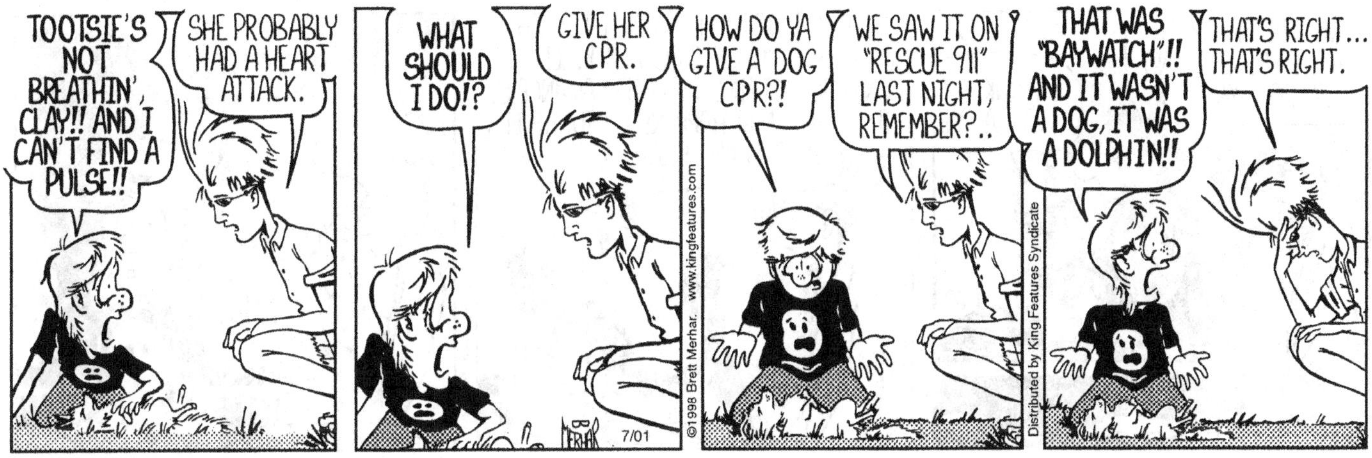
TOOTSIE'S NOT BREATHIN', CLAY!! AND I CAN'T FIND A PULSE!!
SHE PROBABLY HAD A HEART ATTACK.
WHAT SHOULD I DO!?
GIVE HER CPR.
MERHAR
7/01
©1998 Brett Merhar. www.kingfeatures.com
HOW DO YA GIVE A DOG CPR?!
WE SAW IT ON "RESCUE 911" LAST NIGHT, REMEMBER?..
Distributed by King Features Syndicate
THAT WAS "BAYWATCH"!! AND IT WASN'T A DOG, IT WAS A DOLPHIN!!
THAT'S RIGHT... THAT'S RIGHT.

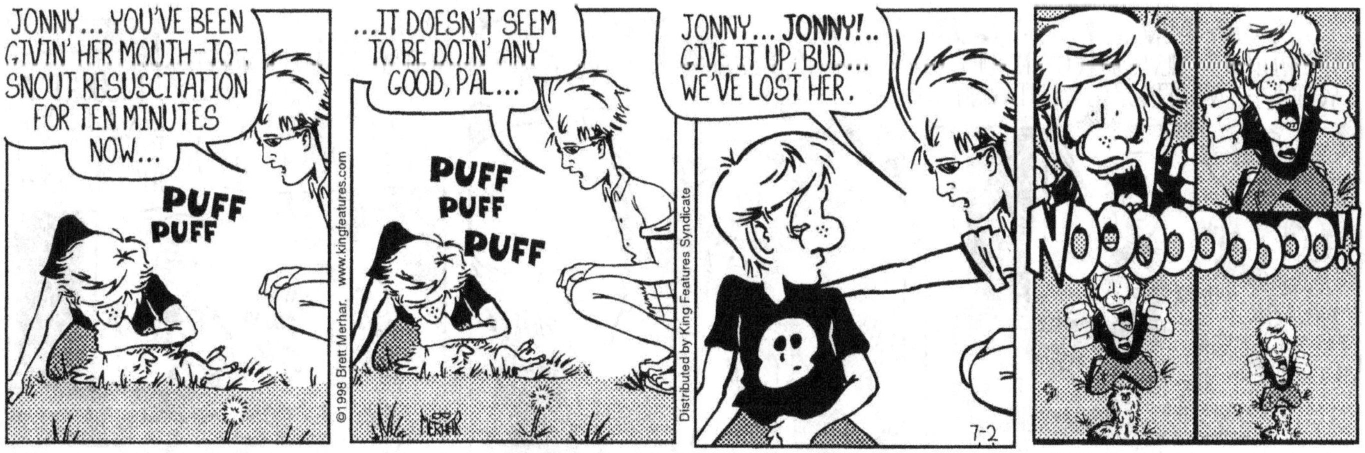
JONNY... YOU'VE BEEN GIVIN' HER MOUTH-TO-SNOUT RESUSCITATION FOR TEN MINUTES NOW...
PUFF PUFF
©1998 Brett Merhar. www.kingfeatures.com
...IT DOESN'T SEEM TO BE DOIN' ANY GOOD, PAL...
PUFF PUFF PUFF
MERHAR
Distributed by King Features Syndicate
JONNY... JONNY!.. GIVE IT UP, BUD... WE'VE LOST HER.
7-2
NOOOOOOOOO!!

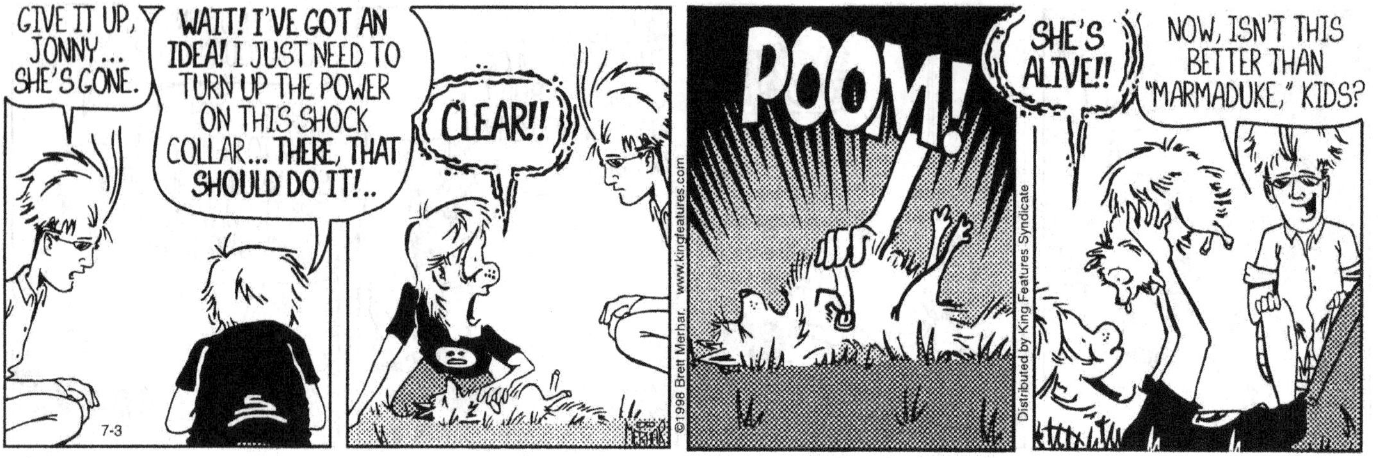
GIVE IT UP, JONNY... SHE'S GONE.
WAIT! I'VE GOT AN IDEA! I JUST NEED TO TURN UP THE POWER ON THIS SHOCK COLLAR... THERE, THAT SHOULD DO IT!..
7-3
CLEAR!!
©1998 Brett Merhar. www.kingfeatures.com
POOM!
Distributed by King Features Syndicate
SHE'S ALIVE!!
NOW, ISN'T THIS BETTER THAN "MARMADUKE," KIDS?

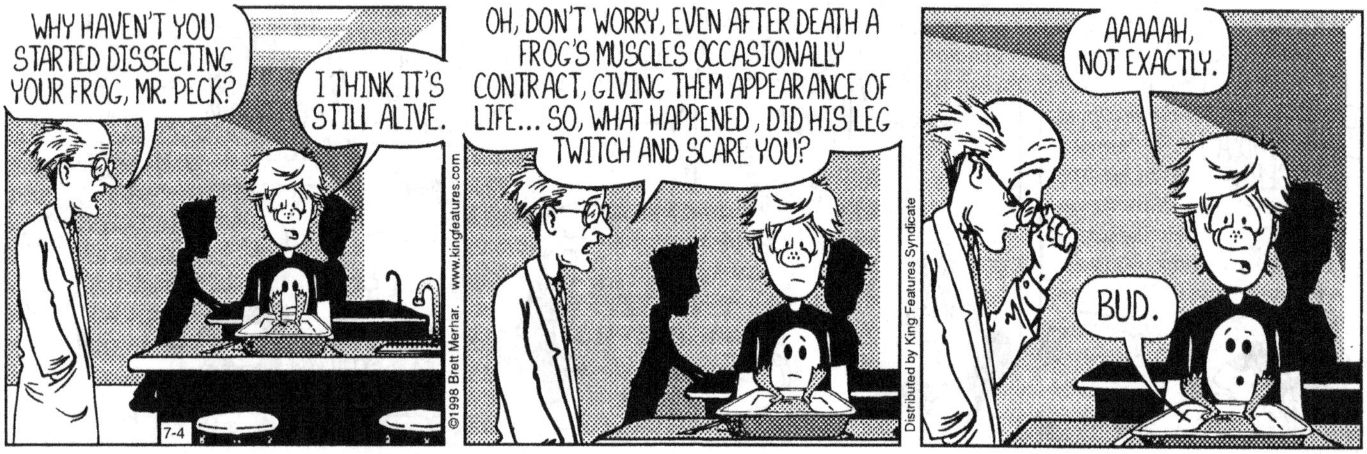
WHY HAVEN'T YOU STARTED DISSECTING YOUR FROG, MR. PECK?
I THINK IT'S STILL ALIVE.
7-4
©1998 Brett Merhar. www.kingfeatures.com
OH, DON'T WORRY, EVEN AFTER DEATH A FROG'S MUSCLES OCCASIONALLY CONTRACT, GIVING THEM APPEARANCE OF LIFE... SO, WHAT HAPPENED, DID HIS LEG TWITCH AND SCARE YOU?
Distributed by King Features Syndicate
AAAAAH, NOT EXACTLY.
BUD.

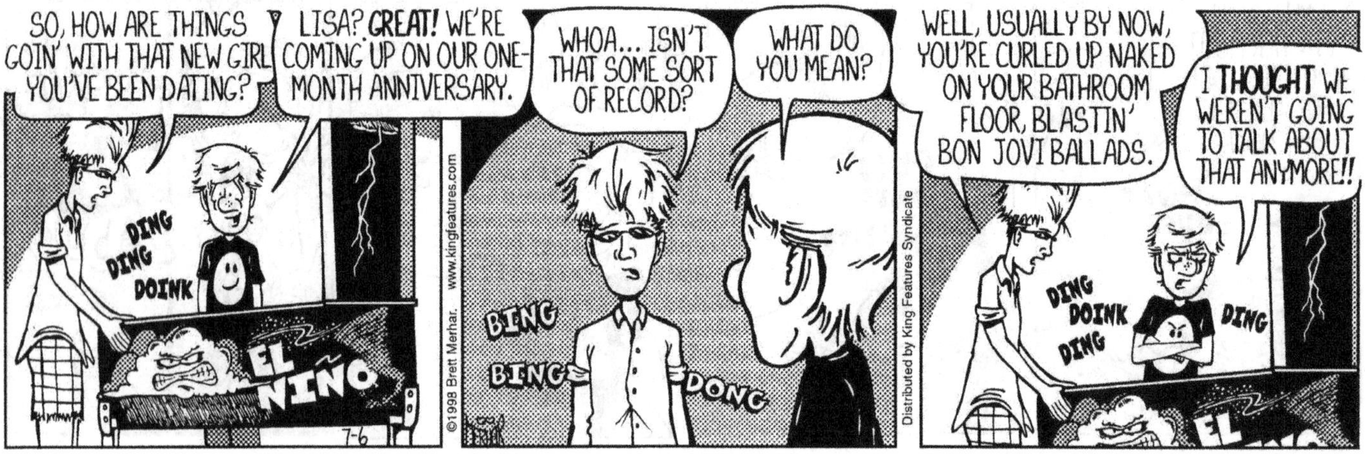
SO, HOW ARE THINGS GOIN' WITH THAT NEW GIRL YOU'VE BEEN DATING?
LISA? GREAT! WE'RE COMING UP ON OUR ONE-MONTH ANNIVERSARY.
DING
DING
DOINK
EL NIÑO
7-6
©1998 Brett Merhar. www.kingfeatures.com
WHOA... ISN'T THAT SOME SORT OF RECORD?
WHAT DO YOU MEAN?
BING
BING
DONG
Distributed by King Features Syndicate
WELL, USUALLY BY NOW, YOU'RE CURLED UP NAKED ON YOUR BATHROOM FLOOR, BLASTIN' BON JOVI BALLADS.
I THOUGHT WE WEREN'T GOING TO TALK ABOUT THAT ANYMORE!!
DING
DOINK
DING
DING
EL

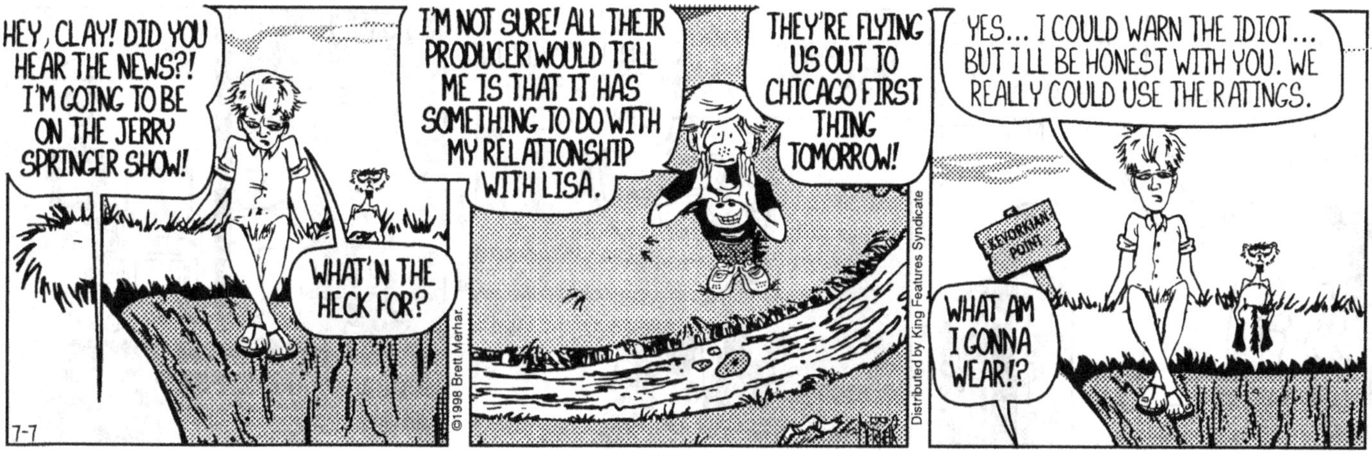
HEY, CLAY! DID YOU HEAR THE NEWS?! I'M GOING TO BE ON THE JERRY SPRINGER SHOW!
WHAT'N THE HECK FOR?
I'M NOT SURE! ALL THEIR PRODUCER WOULD TELL ME IS THAT IT HAS SOMETHING TO DO WITH MY RELATIONSHIP WITH LISA.
THEY'RE FLYING US OUT TO CHICAGO FIRST THING TOMORROW!
YES... I COULD WARN THE IDIOT... BUT I'LL BE HONEST WITH YOU. WE REALLY COULD USE THE RATINGS.
KEVORKIAN POINT
WHAT AM I GONNA WEAR!?
7-7
©1998 Brett Merhar.
Distributed by King Features Syndicate

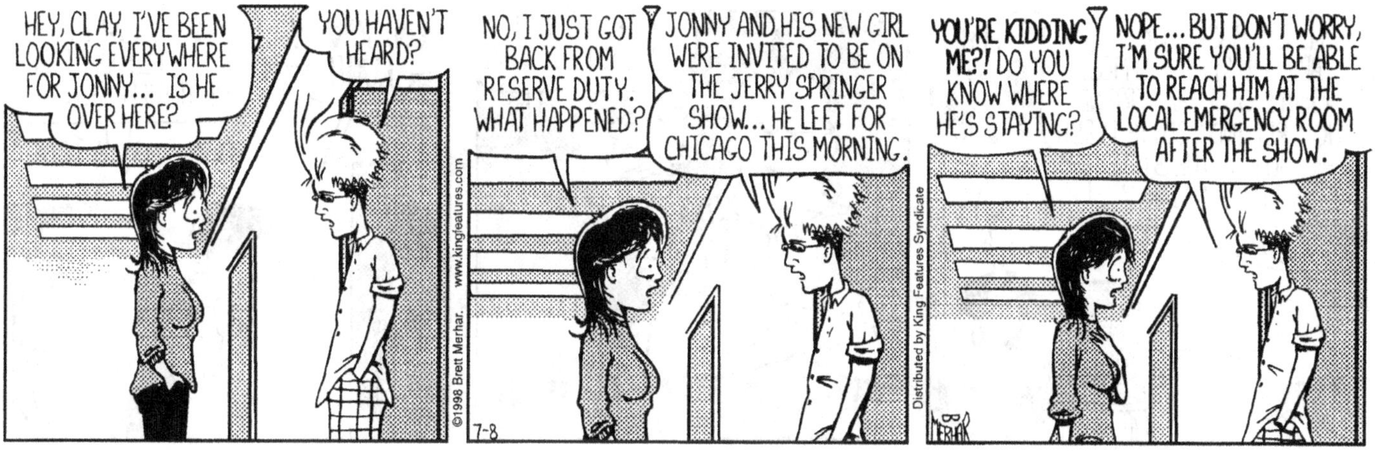
HEY, CLAY, I'VE BEEN LOOKING EVERYWHERE FOR JONNY... IS HE OVER HERE?
YOU HAVEN'T HEARD?
NO, I JUST GOT BACK FROM RESERVE DUTY. WHAT HAPPENED?
JONNY AND HIS NEW GIRL WERE INVITED TO BE ON THE JERRY SPRINGER SHOW... HE LEFT FOR CHICAGO THIS MORNING.
YOU'RE KIDDING ME?! DO YOU KNOW WHERE HE'S STAYING?
NOPE... BUT DON'T WORRY, I'M SURE YOU'LL BE ABLE TO REACH HIM AT THE LOCAL EMERGENCY ROOM AFTER THE SHOW.
7-8
©1998 Brett Merhar. www.kingfeatures.com
Distributed by King Features Syndicate

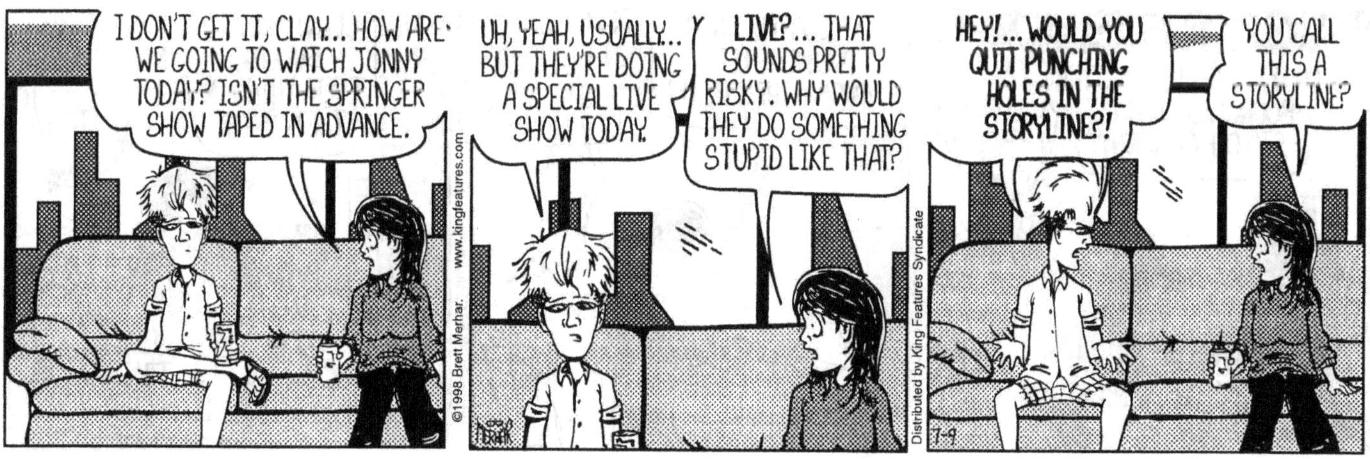
I DON'T GET IT, CLAY... HOW ARE WE GOING TO WATCH JONNY TODAY? ISN'T THE SPRINGER SHOW TAPED IN ADVANCE.
UH, YEAH, USUALLY... BUT THEY'RE DOING A SPECIAL LIVE SHOW TODAY.
LIVE?... THAT SOUNDS PRETTY RISKY. WHY WOULD THEY DO SOMETHING STUPID LIKE THAT?
HEY!... WOULD YOU QUIT PUNCHING HOLES IN THE STORYLINE?!
YOU CALL THIS A STORYLINE?
7-9
©1998 Brett Merhar. www.kingfeatures.com
Distributed by King Features Syndicate

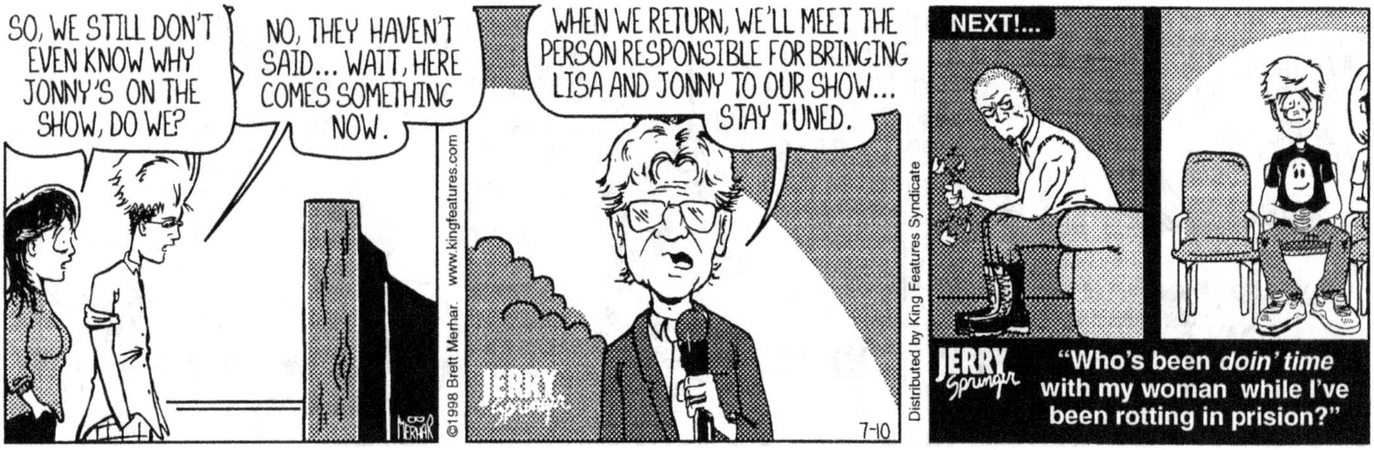
SO, WE STILL DON'T EVEN KNOW WHY JONNY'S ON THE SHOW, DO WE?
NO, THEY HAVEN'T SAID... WAIT, HERE COMES SOMETHING NOW.
©1998 Brett Merhar. www.kingfeatures.com
WHEN WE RETURN, WE'LL MEET THE PERSON RESPONSIBLE FOR BRINGING LISA AND JONNY TO OUR SHOW... STAY TUNED.
JERRY Springer
7-10
Distributed by King Features Syndicate
NEXT!...
JERRY Springer
"Who's been *doin' time* with my woman while I've been rotting in prision?"

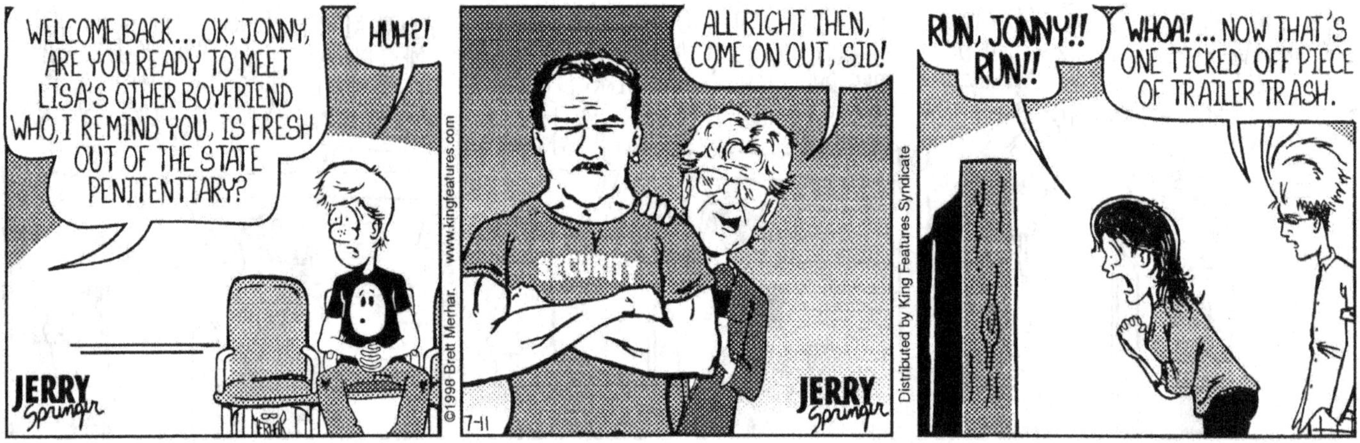
WELCOME BACK... OK, JONNY, ARE YOU READY TO MEET LISA'S OTHER BOYFRIEND WHO, I REMIND YOU, IS FRESH OUT OF THE STATE PENITENTIARY?
HUH?!
JERRY Springer
©1998 Brett Merhar. www.kingfeatures.com
ALL RIGHT THEN, COME ON OUT, SID!
SECURITY
7-11
JERRY Springer
Distributed by King Features Syndicate
RUN, JONNY!! RUN!!
WHOA!... NOW THAT'S ONE TICKED OFF PIECE OF TRAILER TRASH.

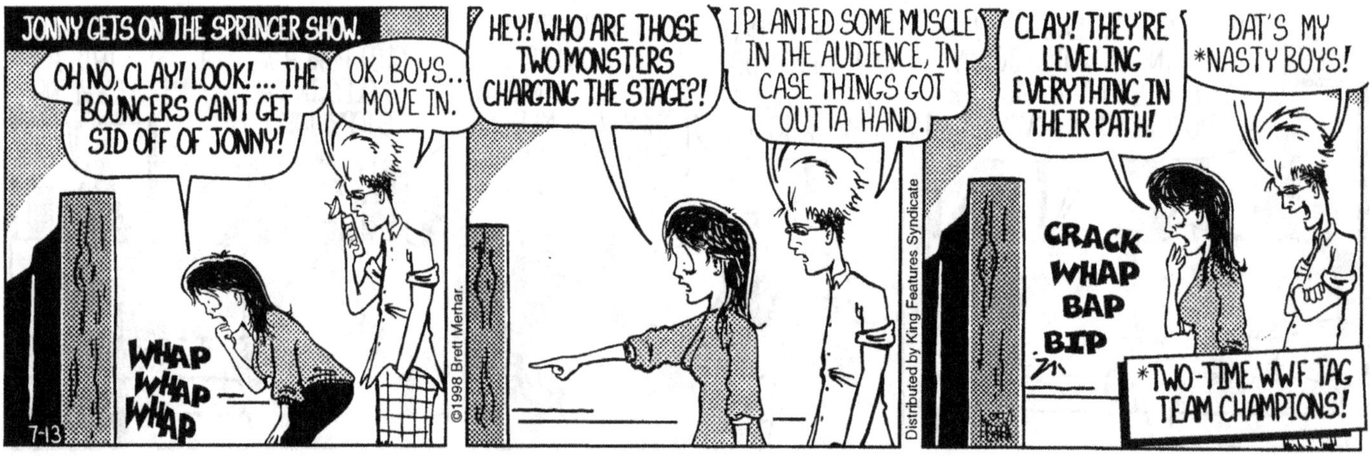
JONNY GETS ON THE SPRINGER SHOW.
OH NO, CLAY! LOOK!... THE BOUNCERS CANT GET SID OFF OF JONNY!
OK, BOYS.. MOVE IN.
WHAP WHAP WHAP
7-13
©1998 Brett Merhar.
HEY! WHO ARE THOSE TWO MONSTERS CHARGING THE STAGE?!
I PLANTED SOME MUSCLE IN THE AUDIENCE, IN CASE THINGS GOT OUTTA HAND.
Distributed by King Features Syndicate
CLAY! THEY'RE LEVELING EVERYTHING IN THEIR PATH!
DAT'S MY *NASTY BOYS!
CRACK WHAP BAP BIP
*TWO-TIME WWF TAG TEAM CHAMPIONS!

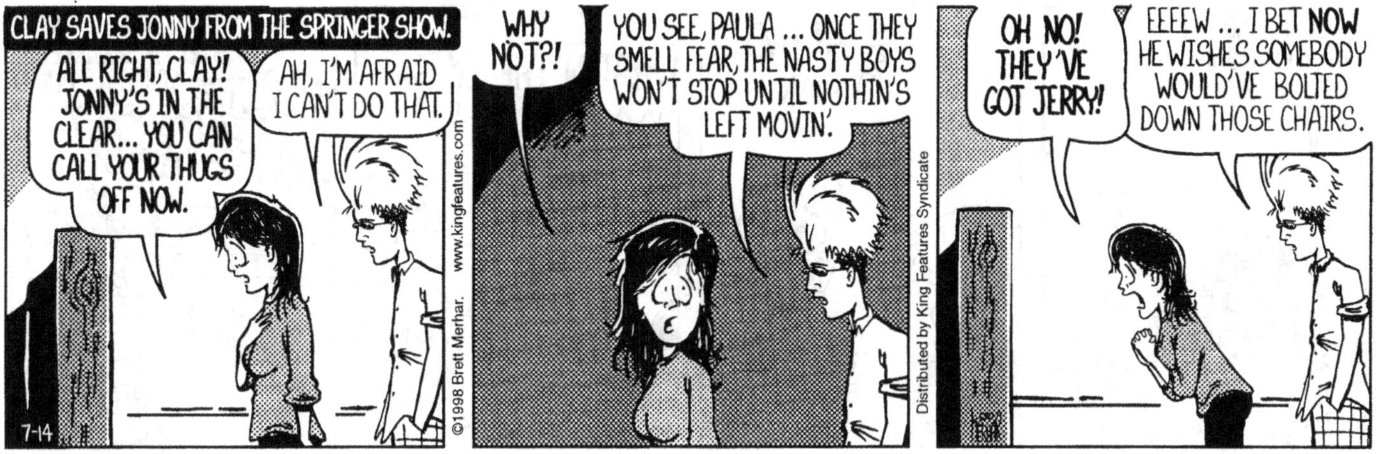
CLAY SAVES JONNY FROM THE SPRINGER SHOW.
ALL RIGHT, CLAY! JONNY'S IN THE CLEAR... YOU CAN CALL YOUR THUGS OFF NOW.
AH, I'M AFRAID I CAN'T DO THAT.
7-14
©1998 Brett Merhar. www.kingfeatures.com
WHY NOT?!
YOU SEE, PAULA ... ONCE THEY SMELL FEAR, THE NASTY BOYS WON'T STOP UNTIL NOTHIN'S LEFT MOVIN'.
OH NO! THEY'VE GOT JERRY!
EEEEW ... I BET NOW HE WISHES SOMEBODY WOULD'VE BOLTED DOWN THOSE CHAIRS.
Distributed by King Features Syndicate

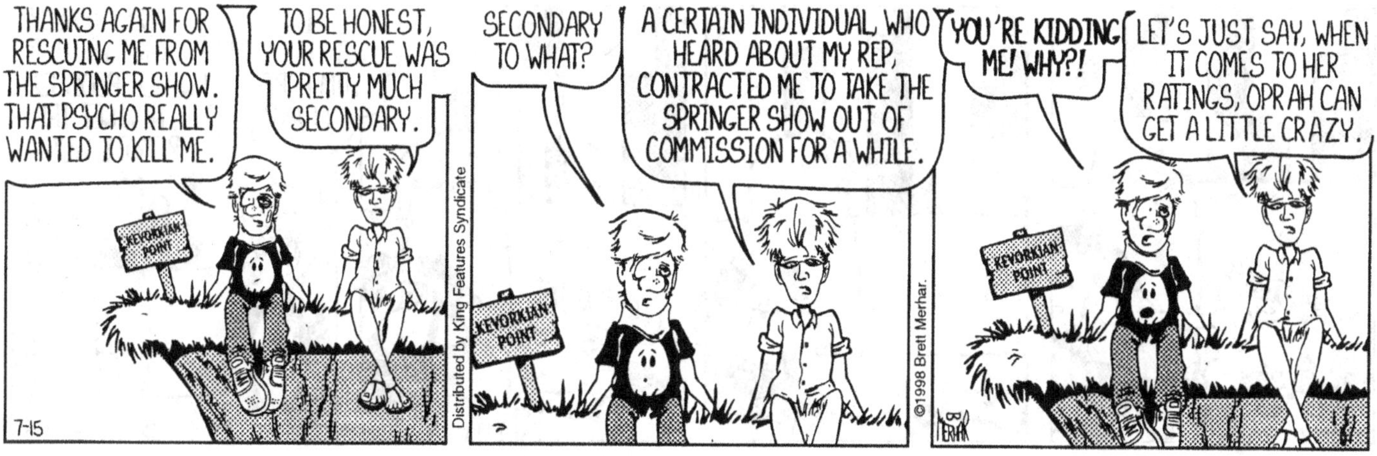
THANKS AGAIN FOR RESCUING ME FROM THE SPRINGER SHOW. THAT PSYCHO REALLY WANTED TO KILL ME.
TO BE HONEST, YOUR RESCUE WAS PRETTY MUCH SECONDARY.
KEVORKIAN POINT
7-15
Distributed by King Features Syndicate
SECONDARY TO WHAT?
A CERTAIN INDIVIDUAL, WHO HEARD ABOUT MY REP, CONTRACTED ME TO TAKE THE SPRINGER SHOW OUT OF COMMISSION FOR A WHILE.
©1998 Brett Merhar.
YOU'RE KIDDING ME! WHY?!
LET'S JUST SAY, WHEN IT COMES TO HER RATINGS, OPRAH CAN GET A LITTLE CRAZY.

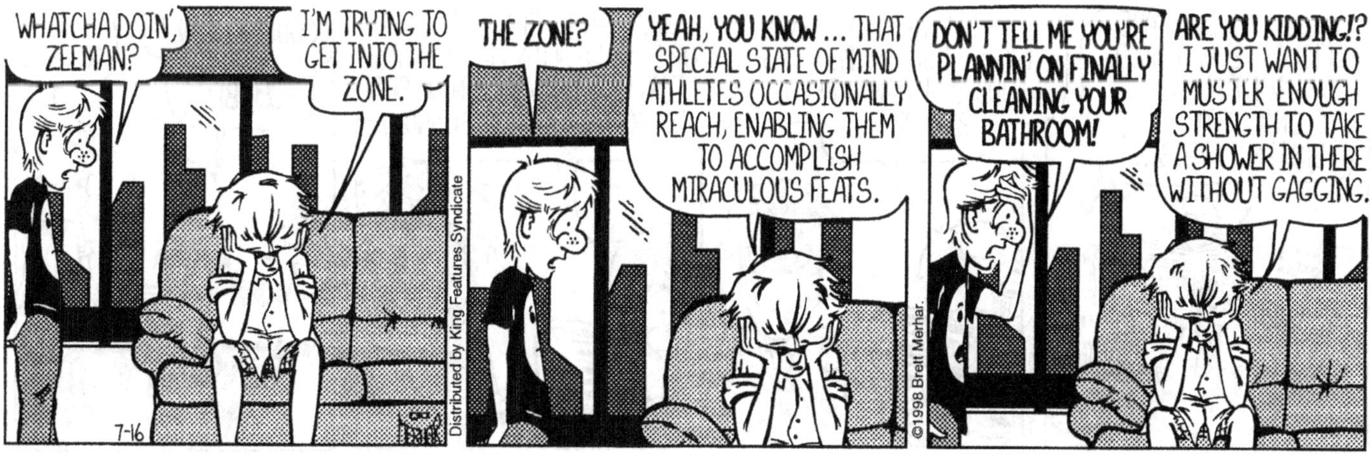
WHATCHA DOIN', ZEEMAN?
I'M TRYING TO GET INTO THE ZONE.
7-16
Distributed by King Features Syndicate
THE ZONE?
YEAH, YOU KNOW ... THAT SPECIAL STATE OF MIND ATHLETES OCCASIONALLY REACH, ENABLING THEM TO ACCOMPLISH MIRACULOUS FEATS.
©1998 Brett Merhar.
DON'T TELL ME YOU'RE PLANNIN' ON FINALLY CLEANING YOUR BATHROOM!
ARE YOU KIDDING!? I JUST WANT TO MUSTER ENOUGH STRENGTH TO TAKE A SHOWER IN THERE WITHOUT GAGGING.

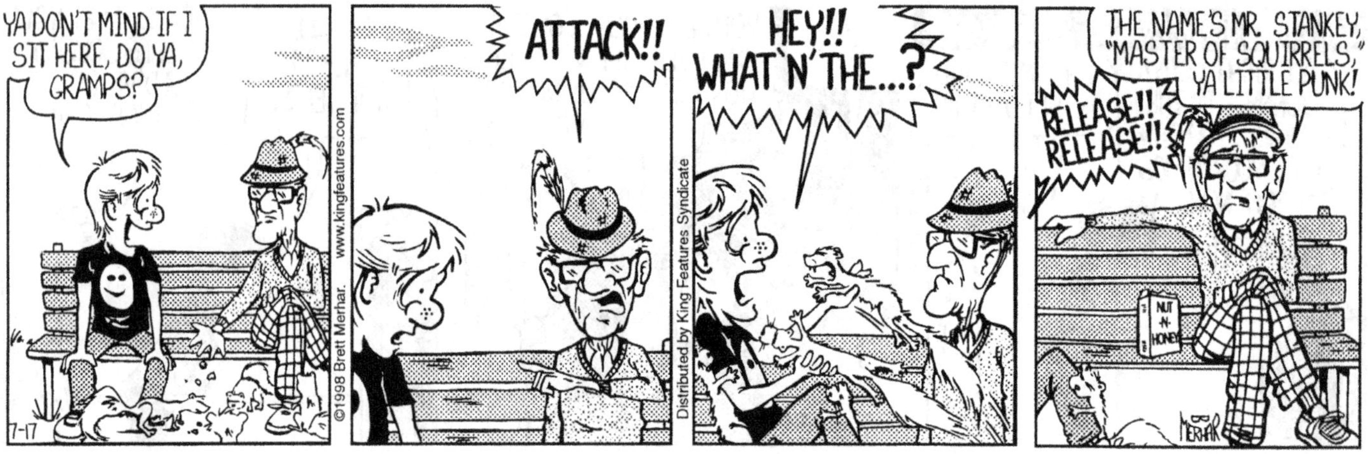
YA DON'T MIND IF I SIT HERE, DO YA, GRAMPS?
ATTACK!!
HEY!! WHAT'N'THE...?
RELEASE!! RELEASE!!
THE NAME'S MR. STANKEY, "MASTER OF SQUIRRELS," YA LITTLE PUNK!
NUT-N-HONEY
7-17
©1998 Brett Merhar. www.kingfeatures.com
Distributed by King Features Syndicate
MERHAR

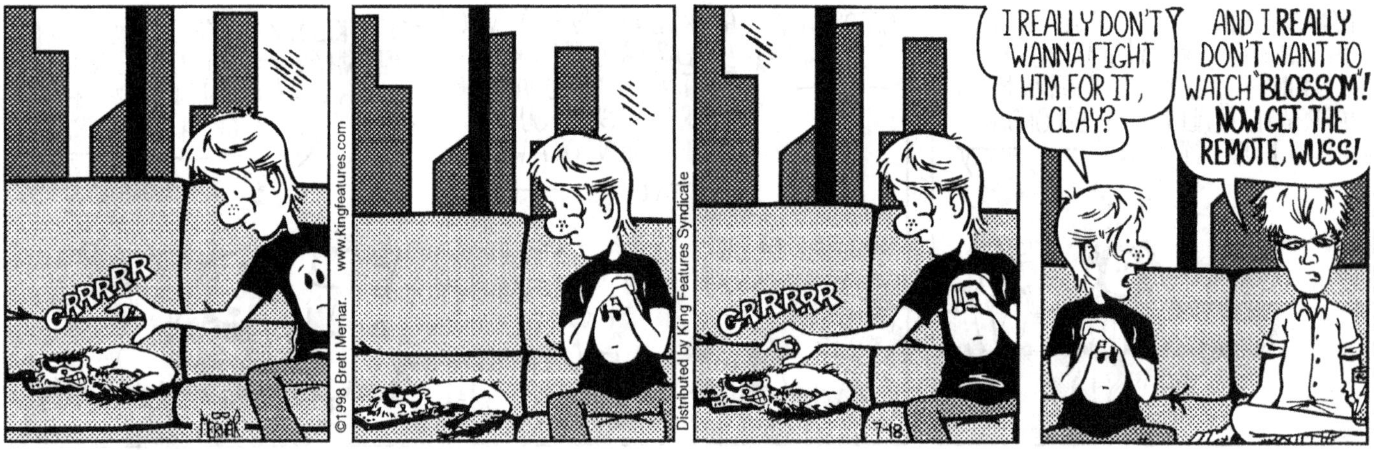
GRRRRR
GRRRRR
I REALLY DON'T WANNA FIGHT HIM FOR IT, CLAY?
AND I REALLY DON'T WANT TO WATCH "BLOSSOM"! NOW GET THE REMOTE, WUSS!
©1998 Brett Merhar. www.kingfeatures.com
Distributed by King Features Syndicate
MERHAR
7-18

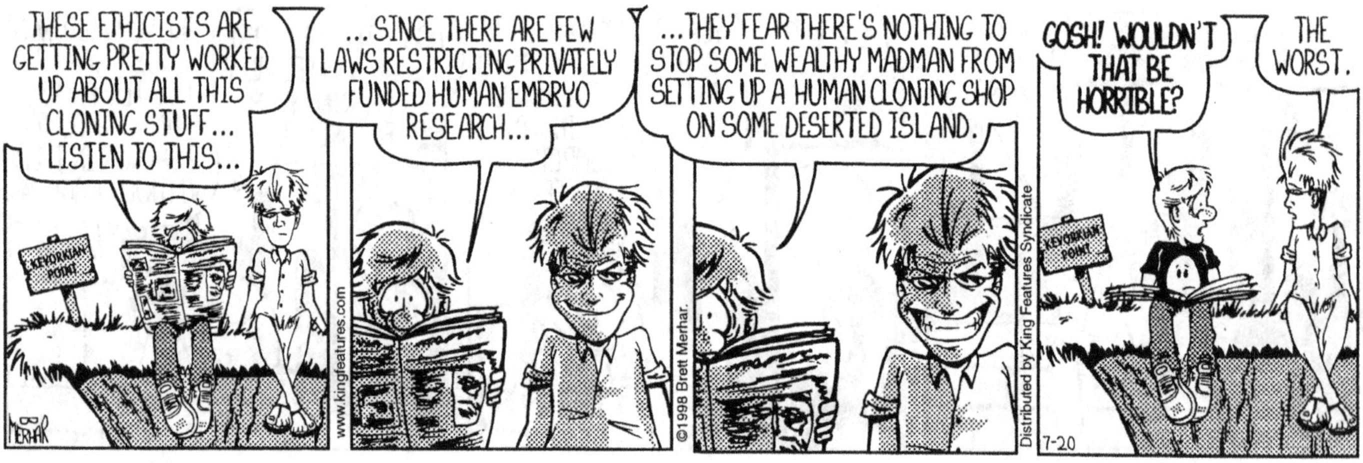
THESE ETHICISTS ARE GETTING PRETTY WORKED UP ABOUT ALL THIS CLONING STUFF... LISTEN TO THIS...
...SINCE THERE ARE FEW LAWS RESTRICTING PRIVATELY FUNDED HUMAN EMBRYO RESEARCH...
...THEY FEAR THERE'S NOTHING TO STOP SOME WEALTHY MADMAN FROM SETTING UP A HUMAN CLONING SHOP ON SOME DESERTED ISLAND.
GOSH! WOULDN'T THAT BE HORRIBLE?
THE WORST.
KEVORKIAN POINT
www.kingfeatures.com
©1998 Brett Merhar.
Distributed by King Features Syndicate
MERHAR
7-20

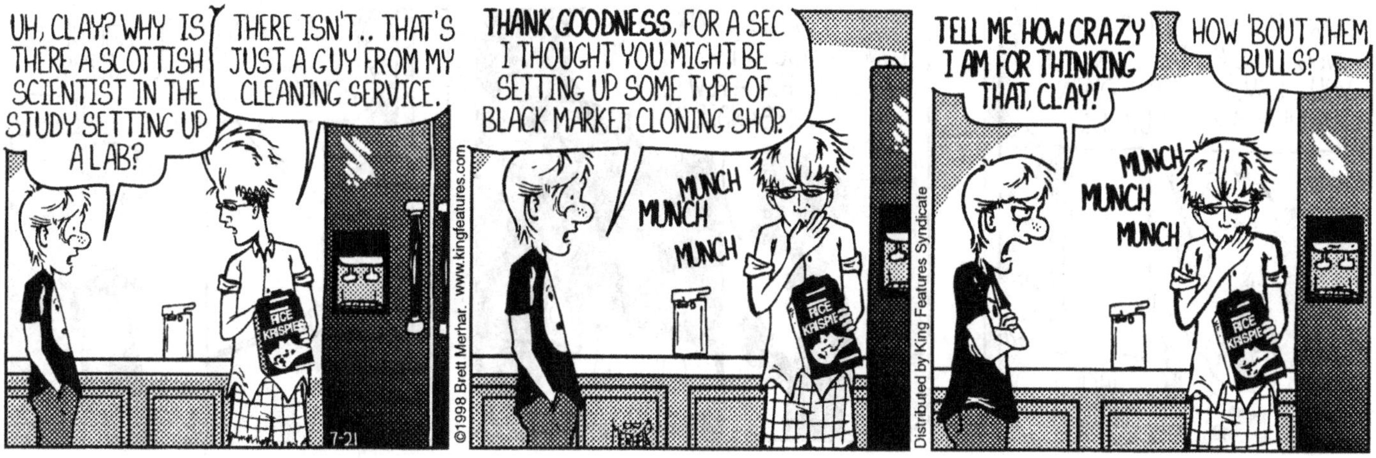
UH, CLAY? WHY IS THERE A SCOTTISH SCIENTIST IN THE STUDY SETTING UP A LAB?
THERE ISN'T.. THAT'S JUST A GUY FROM MY CLEANING SERVICE.
RICE KRISPIES
7-21
©1998 Brett Merhar. www.kingfeatures.com
THANK GOODNESS, FOR A SEC I THOUGHT YOU MIGHT BE SETTING UP SOME TYPE OF BLACK MARKET CLONING SHOP.
MUNCH MUNCH MUNCH
Distributed by King Features Syndicate
TELL ME HOW CRAZY I AM FOR THINKING THAT, CLAY!
HOW 'BOUT THEM BULLS?
MUNCH MUNCH MUNCH

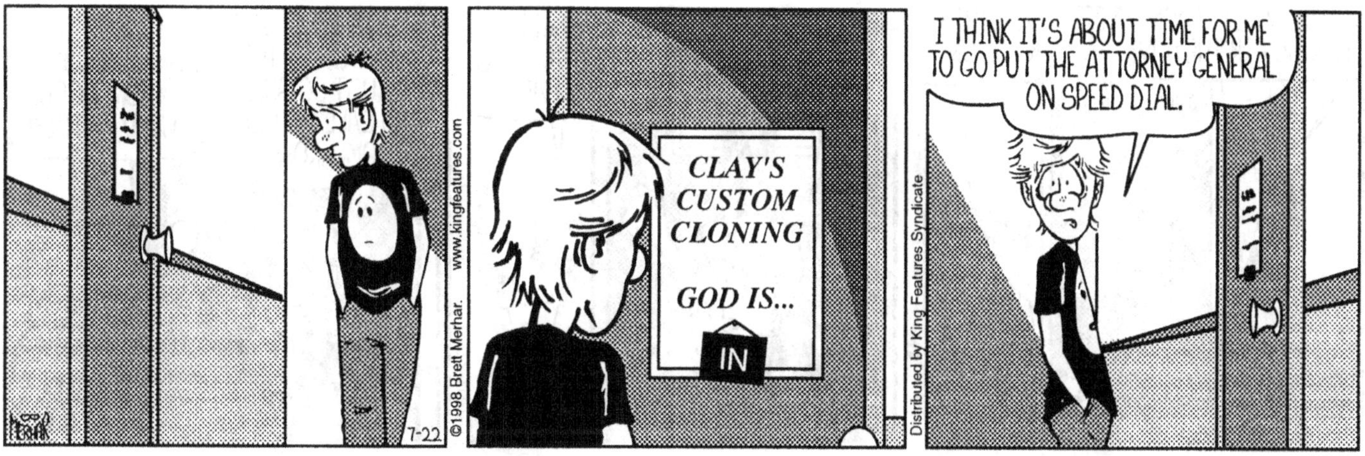
MERHAR
7-22
©1998 Brett Merhar. www.kingfeatures.com
CLAY'S CUSTOM CLONING
GOD IS...
IN
Distributed by King Features Syndicate
I THINK IT'S ABOUT TIME FOR ME TO GO PUT THE ATTORNEY GENERAL ON SPEED DIAL.

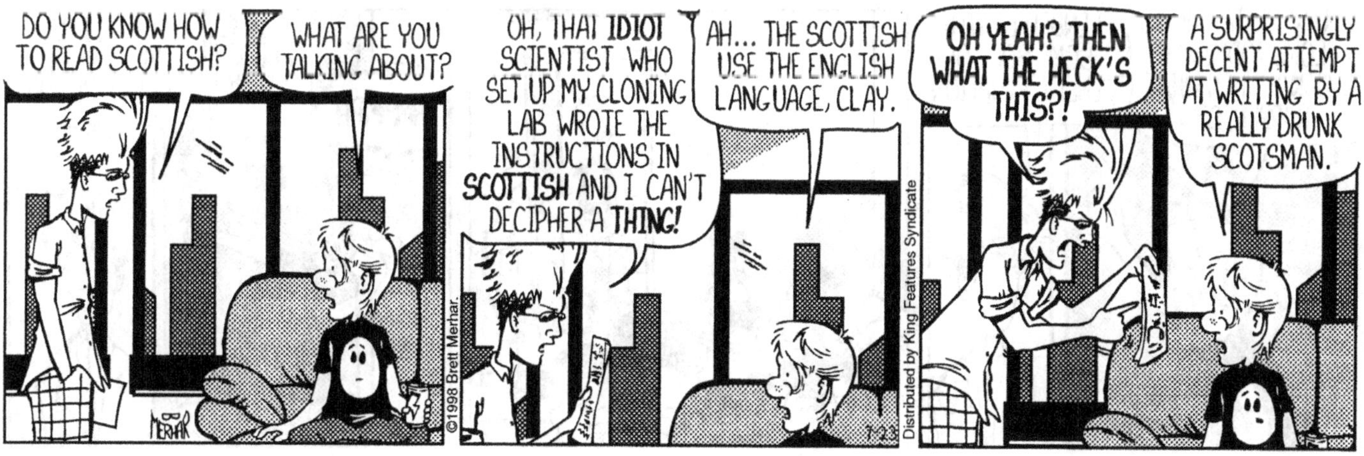
DO YOU KNOW HOW TO READ SCOTTISH?
WHAT ARE YOU TALKING ABOUT?
MERHAR
©1998 Brett Merhar.
OH, THAT IDIOT SCIENTIST WHO SET UP MY CLONING LAB WROTE THE INSTRUCTIONS IN SCOTTISH AND I CAN'T DECIPHER A THING!
AH... THE SCOTTISH USE THE ENGLISH LANGUAGE, CLAY.
7-23
Distributed by King Features Syndicate
OH YEAH? THEN WHAT THE HECK'S THIS?!
A SURPRISINGLY DECENT ATTEMPT AT WRITING BY A REALLY DRUNK SCOTSMAN.

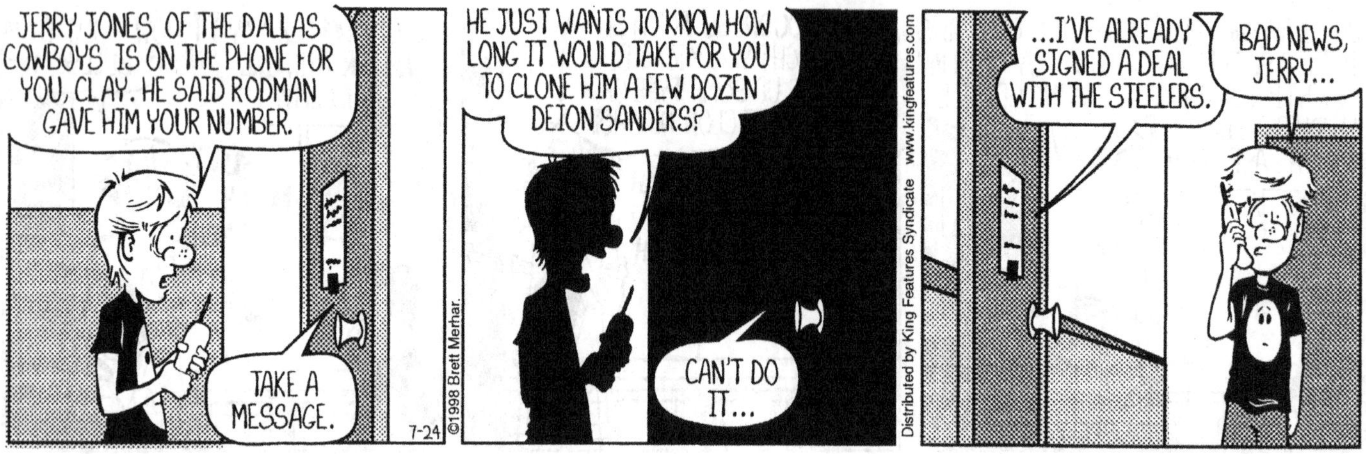
JERRY JONES OF THE DALLAS COWBOYS IS ON THE PHONE FOR YOU, CLAY. HE SAID RODMAN GAVE HIM YOUR NUMBER.
TAKE A MESSAGE.
7-24
©1998 Brett Merhar. www.kingfeatures.com
HE JUST WANTS TO KNOW HOW LONG IT WOULD TAKE FOR YOU TO CLONE HIM A FEW DOZEN DEION SANDERS?
CAN'T DO IT...
Distributed by King Features Syndicate
BAD NEWS, JERRY...
...I'VE ALREADY SIGNED A DEAL WITH THE STEELERS.

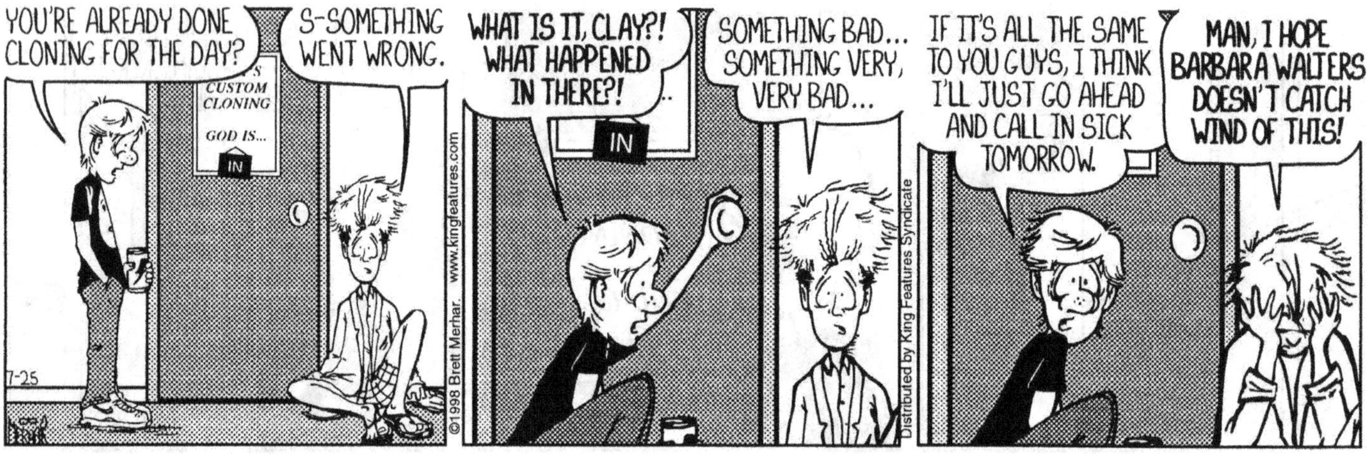
YOU'RE ALREADY DONE CLONING FOR THE DAY?
S-SOMETHING WENT WRONG.
CUSTOM CLONING
GOD IS...
IN
7-25
©1998 Brett Merhar. www.kingfeatures.com
WHAT IS IT, CLAY?! WHAT HAPPENED IN THERE?!
SOMETHING BAD... SOMETHING VERY, VERY BAD...
IN
Distributed by King Features Syndicate
IF IT'S ALL THE SAME TO YOU GUYS, I THINK I'LL JUST GO AHEAD AND CALL IN SICK TOMORROW.
MAN, I HOPE BARBARA WALTERS DOESN'T CATCH WIND OF THIS!

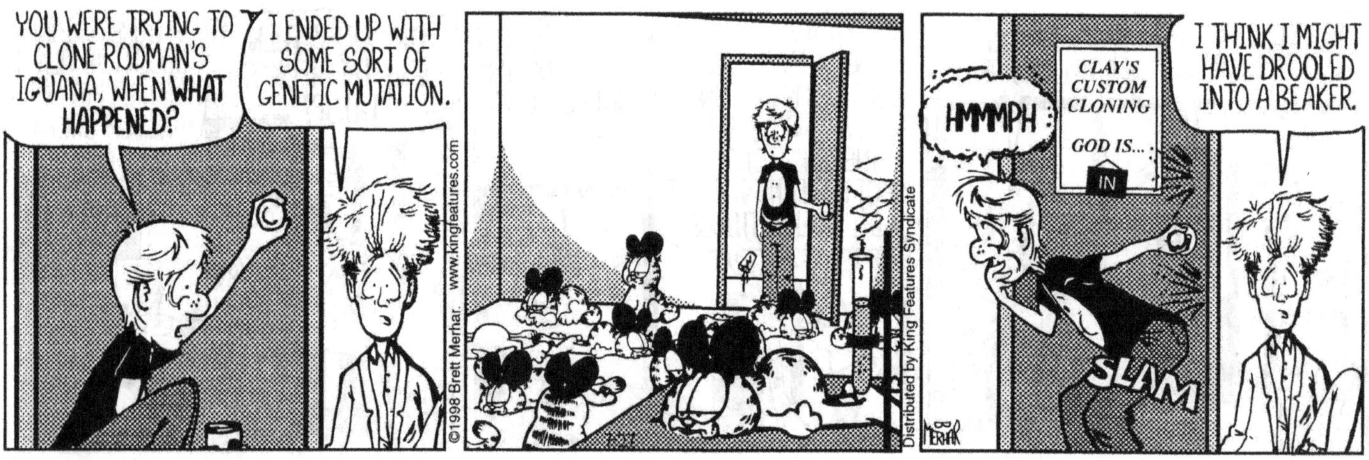
YOU WERE TRYING TO CLONE RODMAN'S IGUANA, WHEN WHAT HAPPENED?
I ENDED UP WITH SOME SORT OF GENETIC MUTATION.
©1998 Brett Merhar. www.kingfeatures.com
Distributed by King Features Syndicate
HMMMPH
CLAY'S CUSTOM CLONING
GOD IS...
IN
SLAM
MERHAR
I THINK I MIGHT HAVE DROOLED INTO A BEAKER.

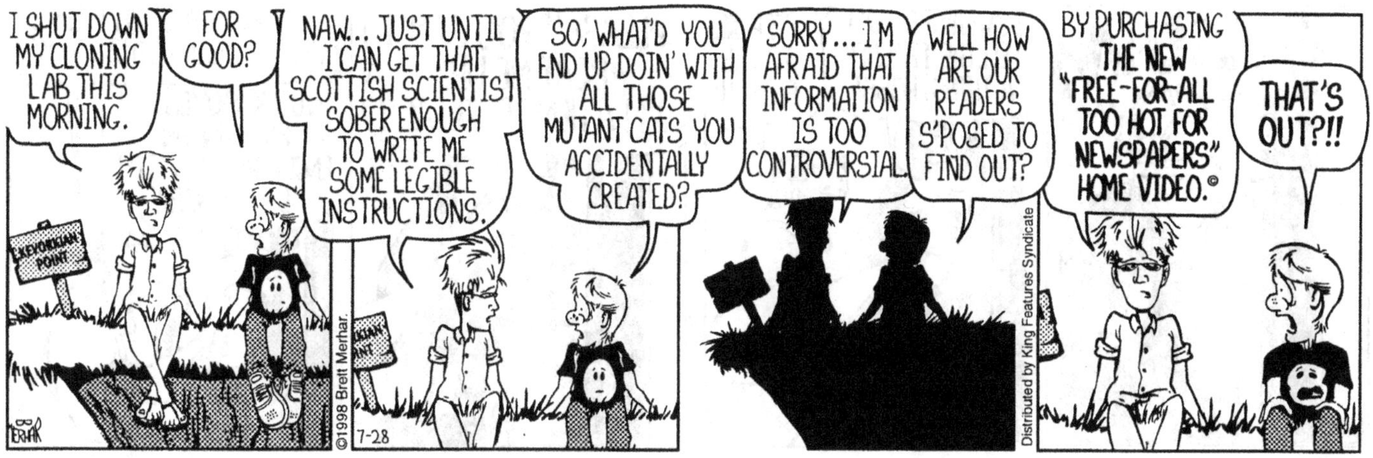
I SHUT DOWN MY CLONING LAB THIS MORNING.
FOR GOOD?
KEVORKIAN POINT
NAW... JUST UNTIL I CAN GET THAT SCOTTISH SCIENTIST SOBER ENOUGH TO WRITE ME SOME LEGIBLE INSTRUCTIONS.
SO, WHAT'D YOU END UP DOIN' WITH ALL THOSE MUTANT CATS YOU ACCIDENTALLY CREATED?
©1998 Brett Merhar.
7-28
SORRY... I'M AFRAID THAT INFORMATION IS TOO CONTROVERSIAL.
WELL HOW ARE OUR READERS S'POSED TO FIND OUT?
Distributed by King Features Syndicate
BY PURCHASING THE NEW "FREE-FOR-ALL TOO HOT FOR NEWSPAPERS" HOME VIDEO.©
THAT'S OUT?!!

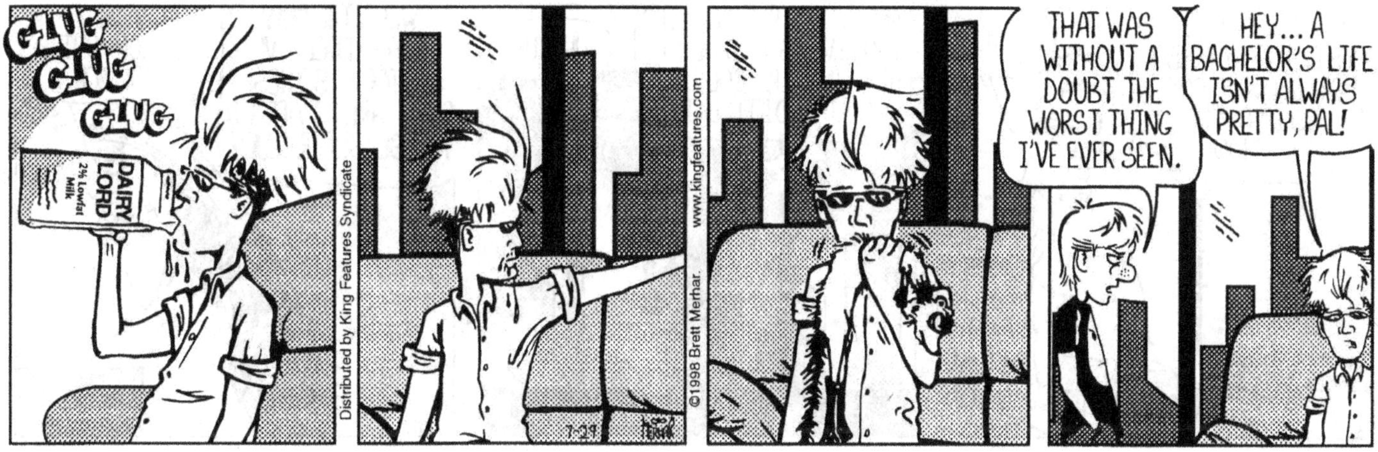
GLUG GLUG GLUG
DAIRY LORD
2% Lowfat Milk
Distributed by King Features Syndicate
7-29
www.kingfeatures.com
©1998 Brett Merhar.
THAT WAS WITHOUT A DOUBT THE WORST THING I'VE EVER SEEN.
HEY... A BACHELOR'S LIFE ISN'T ALWAYS PRETTY, PAL!

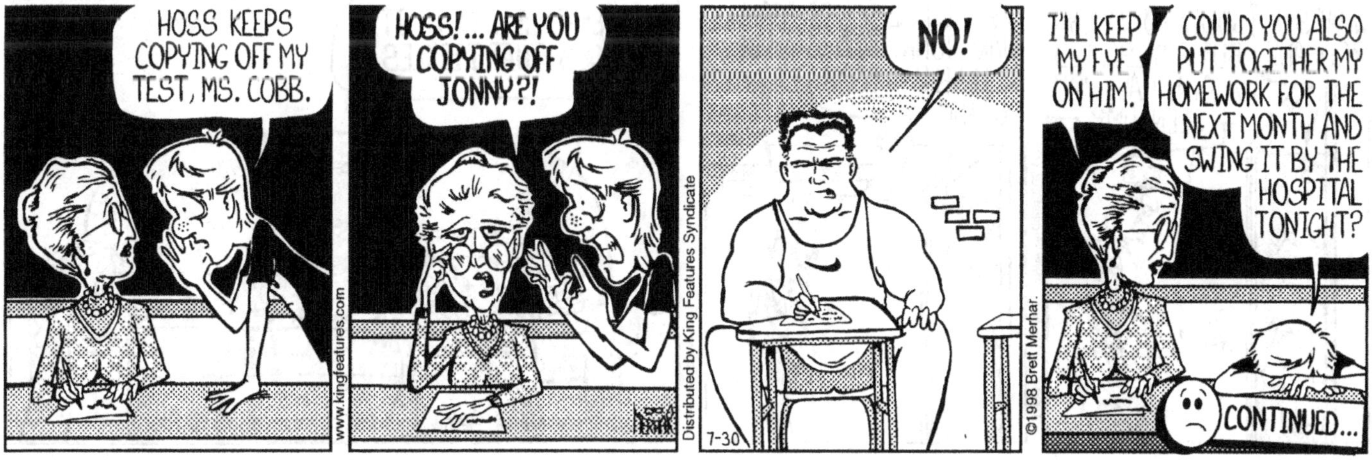
HOSS KEEPS COPYING OFF MY TEST, MS. COBB.
www.kingfeatures.com
HOSS!... ARE YOU COPYING OFF JONNY?!
Distributed by King Features Syndicate
NO!
7-30
©1998 Brett Merhar.
I'LL KEEP MY EYE ON HIM.
COULD YOU ALSO PUT TOGETHER MY HOMEWORK FOR THE NEXT MONTH AND SWING IT BY THE HOSPITAL TONIGHT?
CONTINUED...

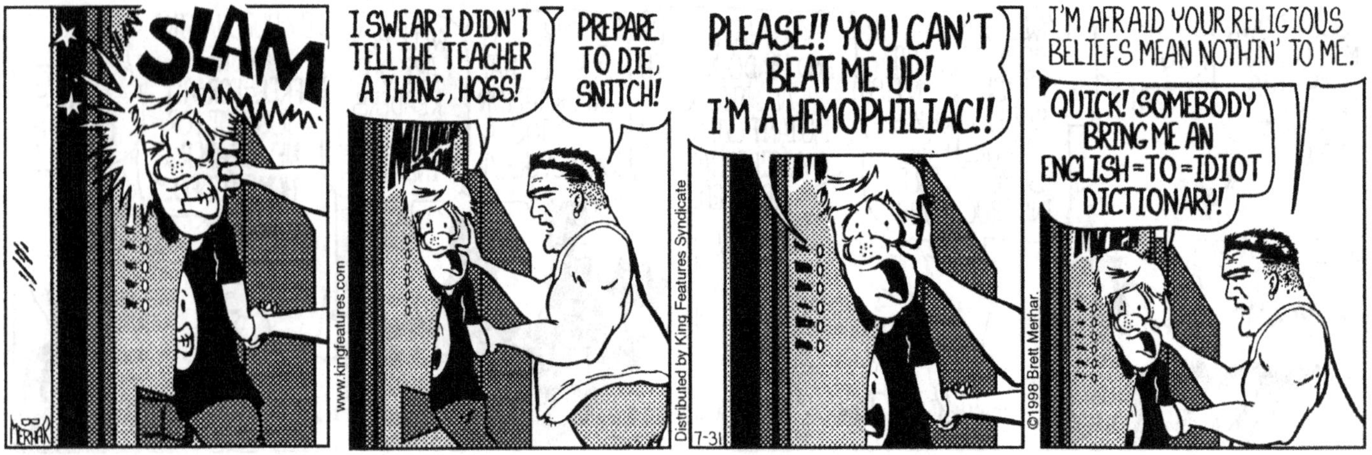
SLAM
MERHAR
www.kingfeatures.com
I SWEAR I DIDN'T TELL THE TEACHER A THING, HOSS!
PREPARE TO DIE, SNITCH!
Distributed by King Features Syndicate
7-31
PLEASE!! YOU CAN'T BEAT ME UP! I'M A HEMOPHILIAC!!
©1998 Brett Merhar.
I'M AFRAID YOUR RELIGIOUS BELIEFS MEAN NOTHIN' TO ME.
QUICK! SOMEBODY BRING ME AN ENGLISH=TO=IDIOT DICTIONARY!

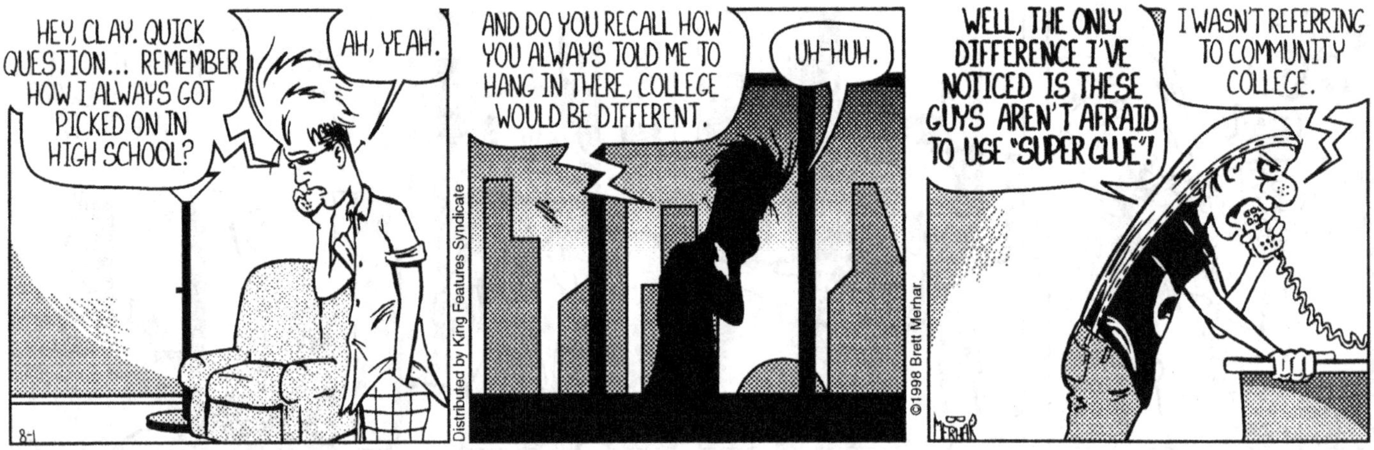
HEY, CLAY. QUICK QUESTION... REMEMBER HOW I ALWAYS GOT PICKED ON IN HIGH SCHOOL?
AH, YEAH.
8-1
Distributed by King Features Syndicate
AND DO YOU RECALL HOW YOU ALWAYS TOLD ME TO HANG IN THERE, COLLEGE WOULD BE DIFFERENT.
UH-HUH.
©1998 Brett Merhar.
WELL, THE ONLY DIFFERENCE I'VE NOTICED IS THESE GUYS AREN'T AFRAID TO USE "SUPER GLUE"!
I WASN'T REFERRING TO COMMUNITY COLLEGE.
MERHAR

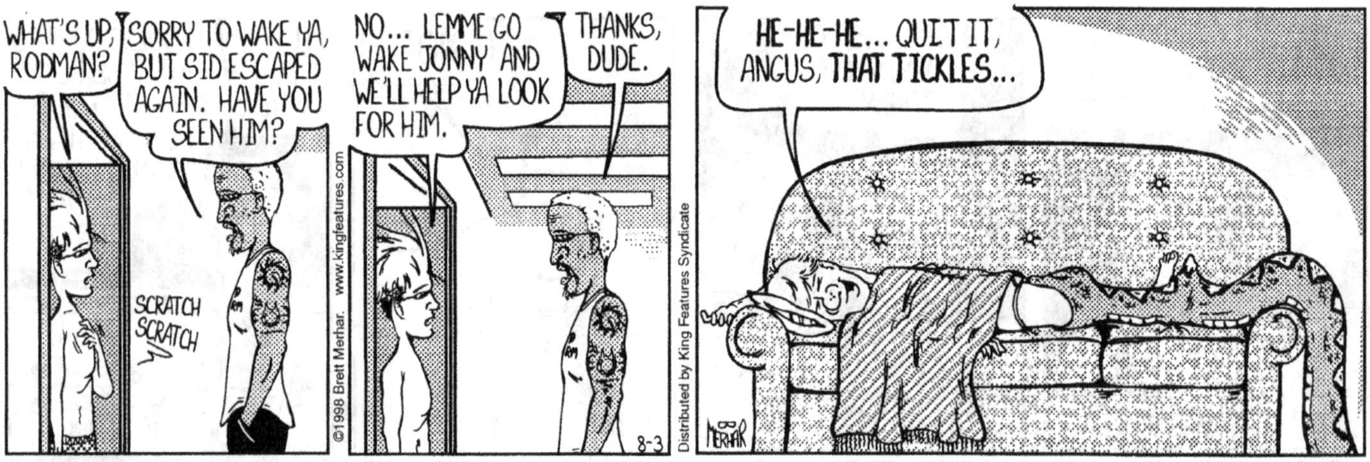
WHAT'S UP, RODMAN?
SORRY TO WAKE YA, BUT SID ESCAPED AGAIN. HAVE YOU SEEN HIM?
SCRATCH SCRATCH
©1998 Brett Merhar. www.kingfeatures.com
NO... LEMME GO WAKE JONNY AND WE'LL HELP YA LOOK FOR HIM.
THANKS, DUDE.
8-3
Distributed by King Features Syndicate
HE-HE-HE... QUIT IT, ANGUS, THAT TICKLES...
MERHAR

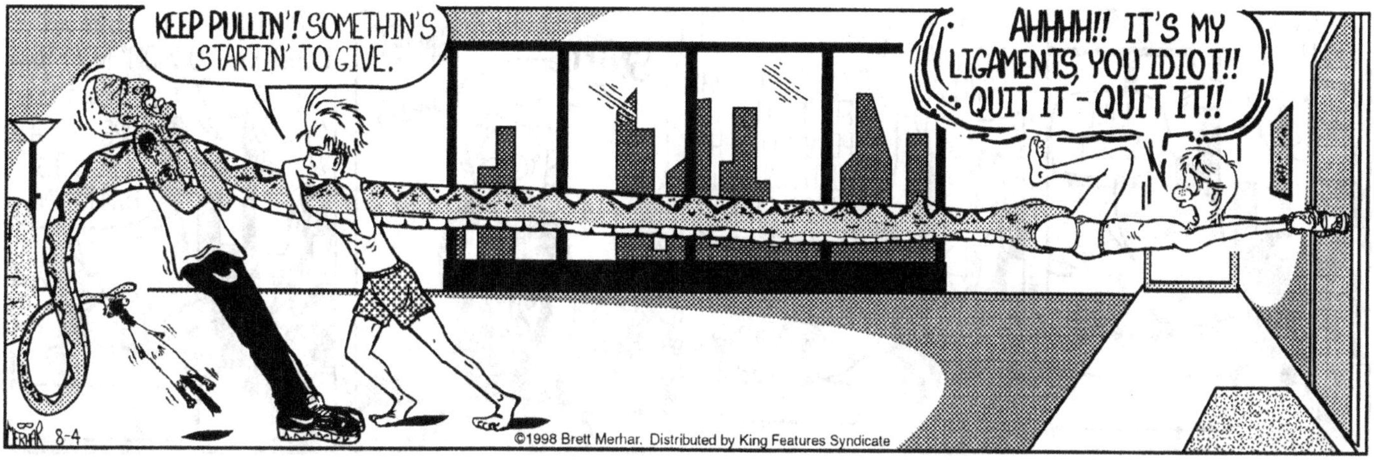
KEEP PULLIN'! SOMETHIN'S STARTIN' TO GIVE.
AHHHH!! IT'S MY LIGAMENTS, YOU IDIOT!! QUIT IT - QUIT IT!!
MERHAR 8-4
©1998 Brett Merhar. Distributed by King Features Syndicate

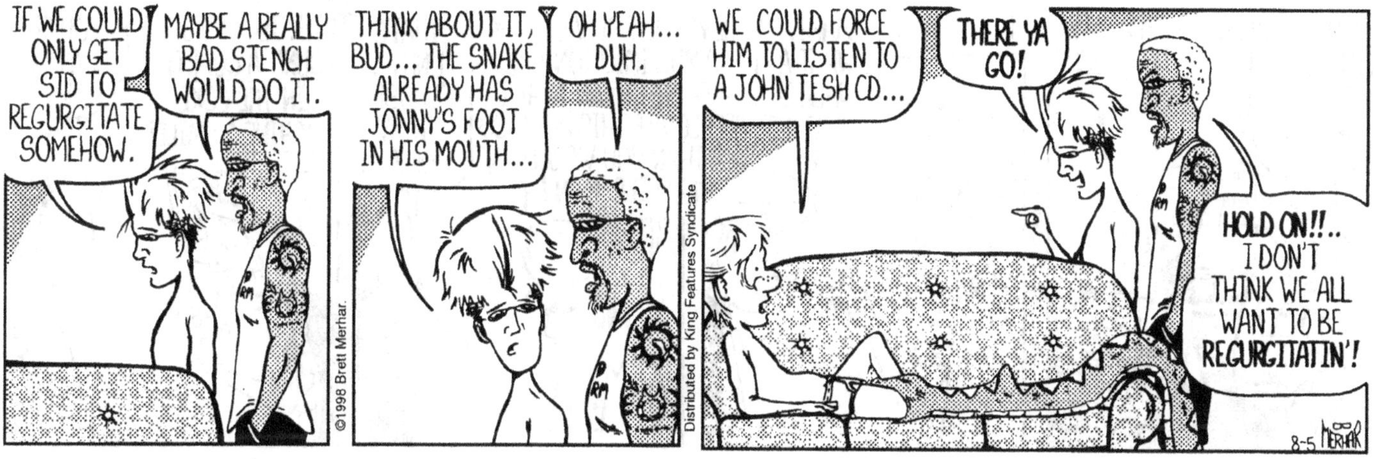
IF WE COULD ONLY GET SID TO REGURGITATE SOMEHOW.
MAYBE A REALLY BAD STENCH WOULD DO IT.
©1998 Brett Merhar.
THINK ABOUT IT, BUD... THE SNAKE ALREADY HAS JONNY'S FOOT IN HIS MOUTH...
OH YEAH... DUH.
Distributed by King Features Syndicate
WE COULD FORCE HIM TO LISTEN TO A JOHN TESH CD...
THERE YA GO!
HOLD ON!!.. I DON'T THINK WE ALL WANT TO BE REGURGITATIN'!
8-5 MERHAR

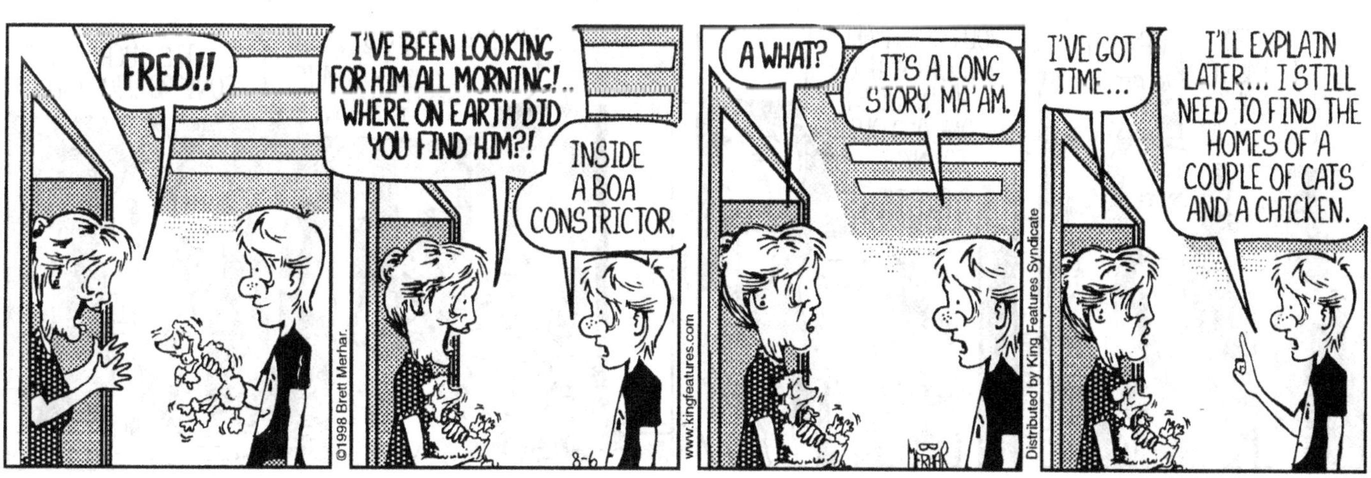
FRED!!
©1998 Brett Merhar.
I'VE BEEN LOOKING FOR HIM ALL MORNING!.. WHERE ON EARTH DID YOU FIND HIM?!
INSIDE A BOA CONSTRICTOR.
8-6
www.kingfeatures.com
A WHAT?
IT'S A LONG STORY, MA'AM.
MERHAR
Distributed by King Features Syndicate
I'VE GOT TIME...
I'LL EXPLAIN LATER... I STILL NEED TO FIND THE HOMES OF A COUPLE OF CATS AND A CHICKEN.

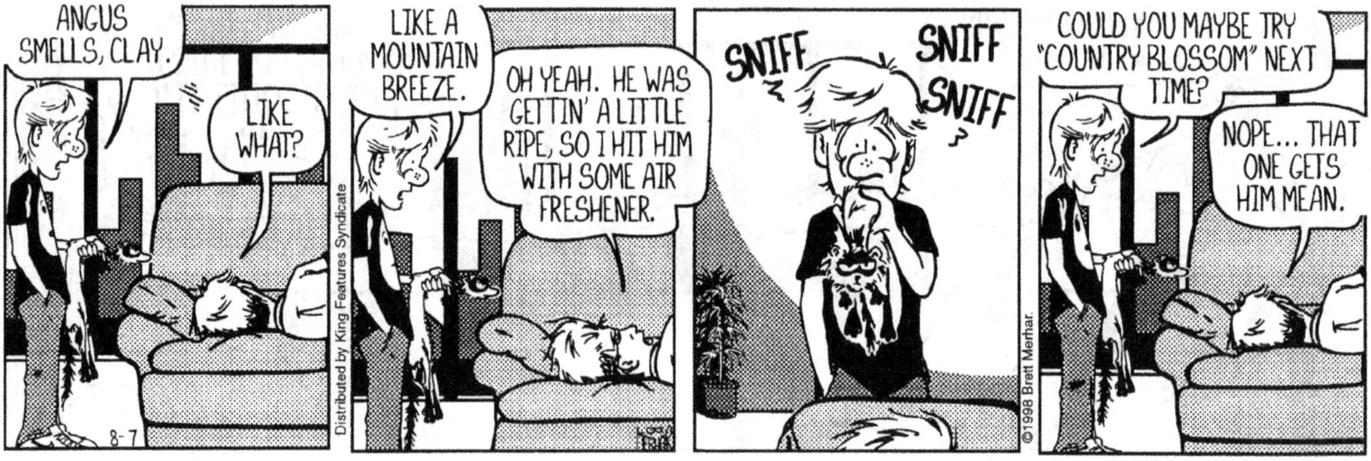
ANGUS SMELLS, CLAY.
LIKE WHAT?
8-7
Distributed by King Features Syndicate
LIKE A MOUNTAIN BREEZE.
OH YEAH. HE WAS GETTIN' A LITTLE RIPE, SO I HIT HIM WITH SOME AIR FRESHENER.
SNIFF
SNIFF
SNIFF
©1998 Brett Merhar.
COULD YOU MAYBE TRY "COUNTRY BLOSSOM" NEXT TIME?
NOPE... THAT ONE GETS HIM MEAN.

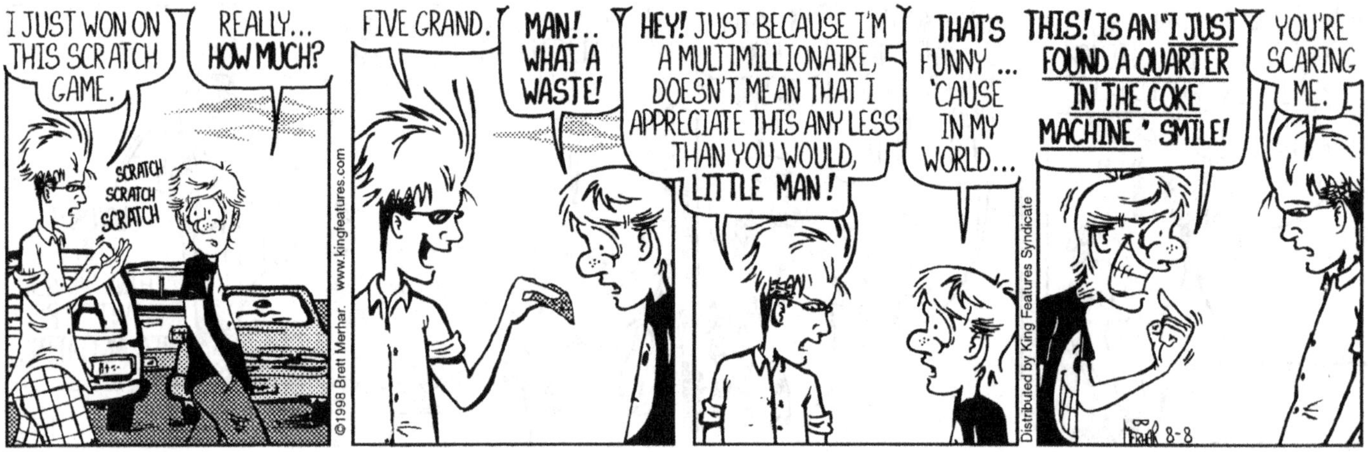
I JUST WON ON THIS SCRATCH GAME.
REALLY... HOW MUCH?
SCRATCH SCRATCH SCRATCH
©1998 Brett Merhar. www.kingfeatures.com
FIVE GRAND.
MAN!.. WHAT A WASTE!
HEY! JUST BECAUSE I'M A MULTIMILLIONAIRE, DOESN'T MEAN THAT I APPRECIATE THIS ANY LESS THAN YOU WOULD, LITTLE MAN!
THAT'S FUNNY ... 'CAUSE IN MY WORLD...
Distributed by King Features Syndicate
THIS! IS AN "I JUST FOUND A QUARTER IN THE COKE MACHINE" SMILE!
YOU'RE SCARING ME.
8-8

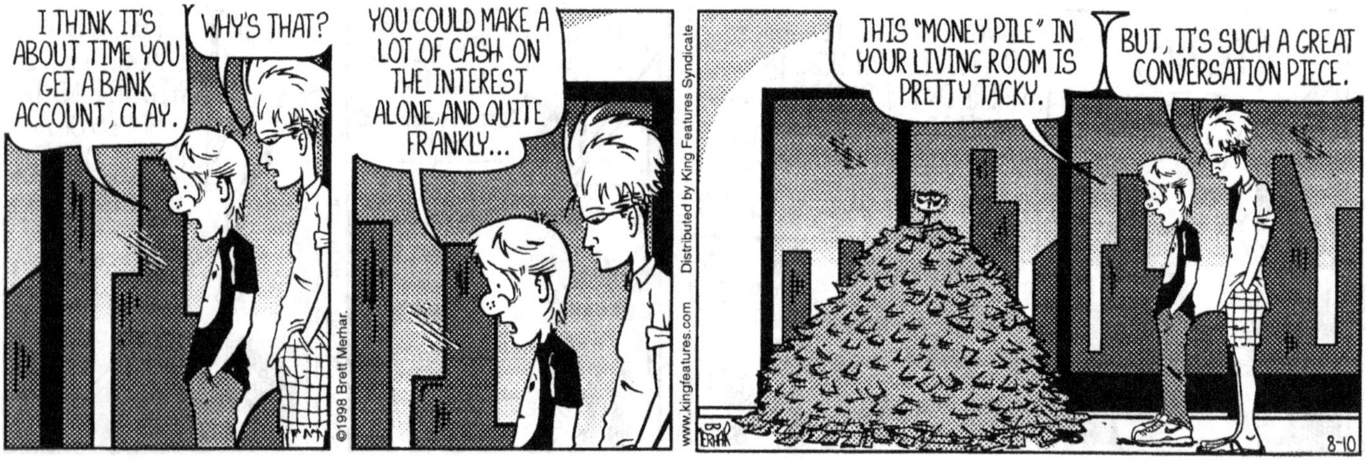
I THINK IT'S ABOUT TIME YOU GET A BANK ACCOUNT, CLAY.
WHY'S THAT?
©1998 Brett Merhar.
YOU COULD MAKE A LOT OF CASH ON THE INTEREST ALONE, AND QUITE FRANKLY...
Distributed by King Features Syndicate www.kingfeatures.com
THIS "MONEY PILE" IN YOUR LIVING ROOM IS PRETTY TACKY.
BUT, IT'S SUCH A GREAT CONVERSATION PIECE.
8-10

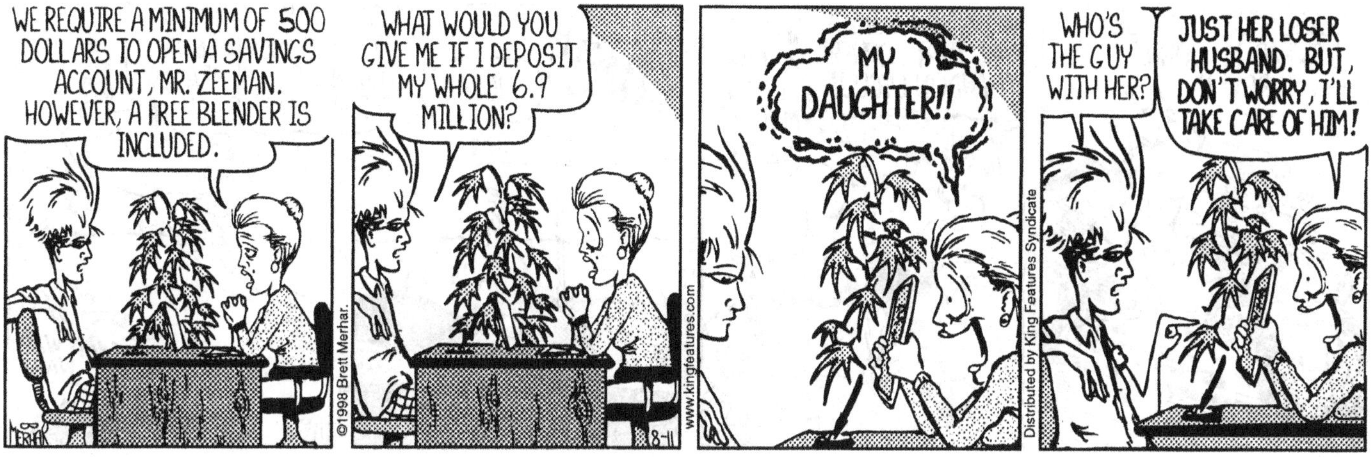
WE REQUIRE A MINIMUM OF 500 DOLLARS TO OPEN A SAVINGS ACCOUNT, MR. ZEEMAN. HOWEVER, A FREE BLENDER IS INCLUDED.
WHAT WOULD YOU GIVE ME IF I DEPOSIT MY WHOLE 6.9 MILLION?
MY DAUGHTER!!
WHO'S THE GUY WITH HER?
JUST HER LOSER HUSBAND. BUT, DON'T WORRY, I'LL TAKE CARE OF HIM!
MERHAR
©1998 Brett Merhar.
www.kingfeatures.com
8-11
Distributed by King Features Syndicate

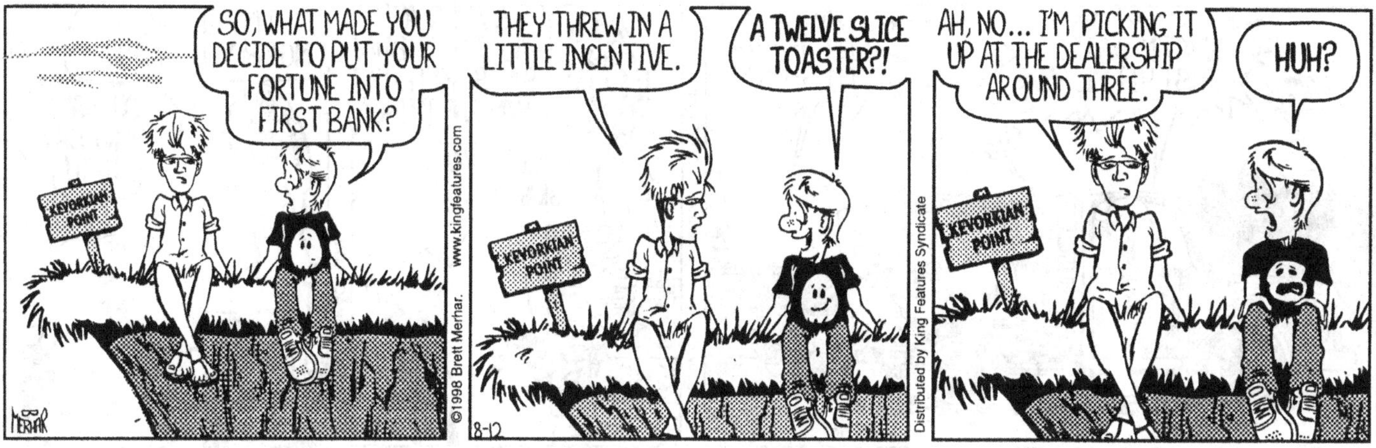
SO, WHAT MADE YOU DECIDE TO PUT YOUR FORTUNE INTO FIRST BANK?
KEVORKIAN POINT
THEY THREW IN A LITTLE INCENTIVE.
A TWELVE SLICE TOASTER?!
AH, NO... I'M PICKING IT UP AT THE DEALERSHIP AROUND THREE.
HUH?
MERHAR
©1998 Brett Merhar.
www.kingfeatures.com
8-12
Distributed by King Features Syndicate

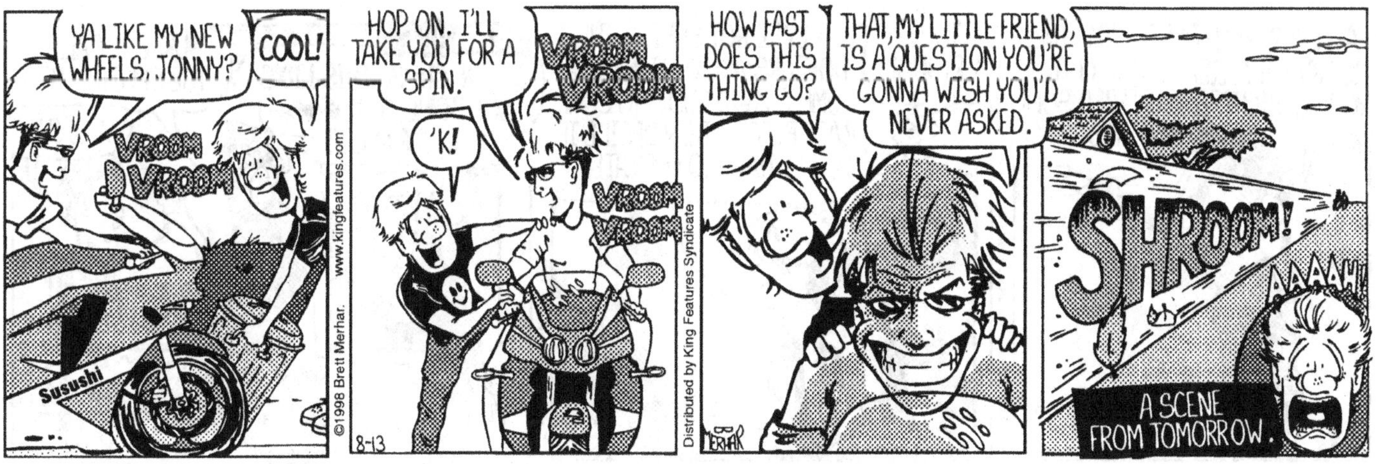
YA LIKE MY NEW WHEELS, JONNY?
COOL!
VROOM VROOM
Susushi
HOP ON. I'LL TAKE YOU FOR A SPIN.
'K!
VROOM VROOM
VROOM VROOM
HOW FAST DOES THIS THING GO?
THAT, MY LITTLE FRIEND, IS A QUESTION YOU'RE GONNA WISH YOU'D NEVER ASKED.
SHROOM!
AAAAH!
A SCENE FROM TOMORROW.
MERHAR
©1998 Brett Merhar.
www.kingfeatures.com
8-13
Distributed by King Features Syndicate

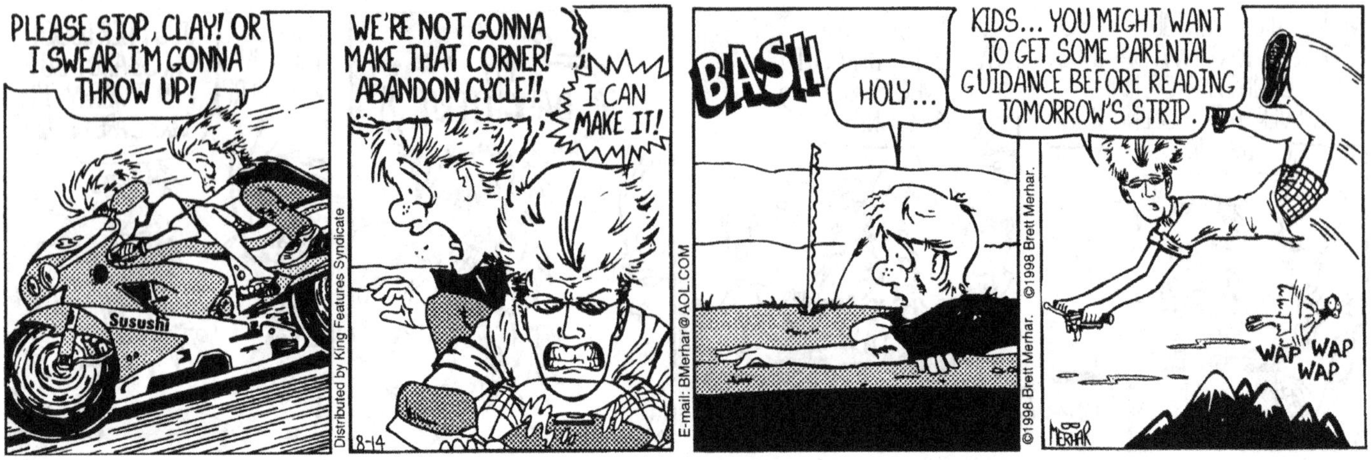
PLEASE STOP, CLAY! OR I SWEAR I'M GONNA THROW UP!
Sushi
Distributed by King Features Syndicate
WE'RE NOT GONNA MAKE THAT CORNER! ABANDON CYCLE!!
I CAN MAKE IT!
8-14
E-mail: BMerhar@AOL.COM
BASH
HOLY...
©1998 Brett Merhar.
KIDS... YOU MIGHT WANT TO GET SOME PARENTAL GUIDANCE BEFORE READING TOMORROW'S STRIP.
WAP WAP WAP
©1998 Brett Merhar.
MERHAR

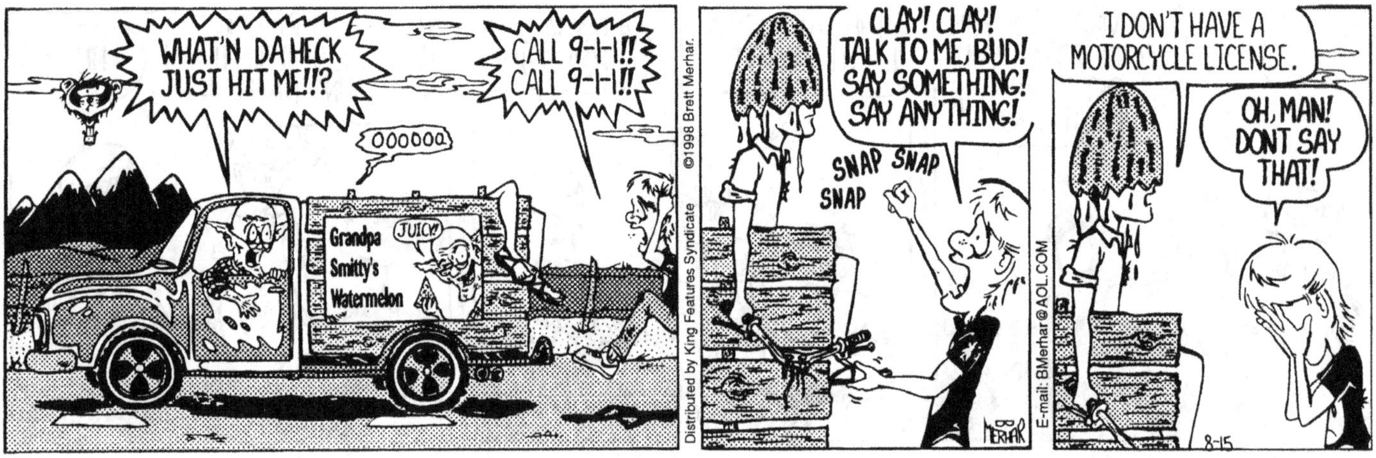
WHAT'N DA HECK JUST HIT ME!!?
CALL 9-1-1!! CALL 9-1-1!!
OOOOOO
Grandpa Smitty's Watermelon
JUICY!
©1998 Brett Merhar.
Distributed by King Features Syndicate
CLAY! CLAY! TALK TO ME, BUD! SAY SOMETHING! SAY ANYTHING!
SNAP SNAP SNAP
MERHAR
E-mail: BMerhar@AOL.COM
I DON'T HAVE A MOTORCYCLE LICENSE.
OH, MAN! DONT SAY THAT!
8-15

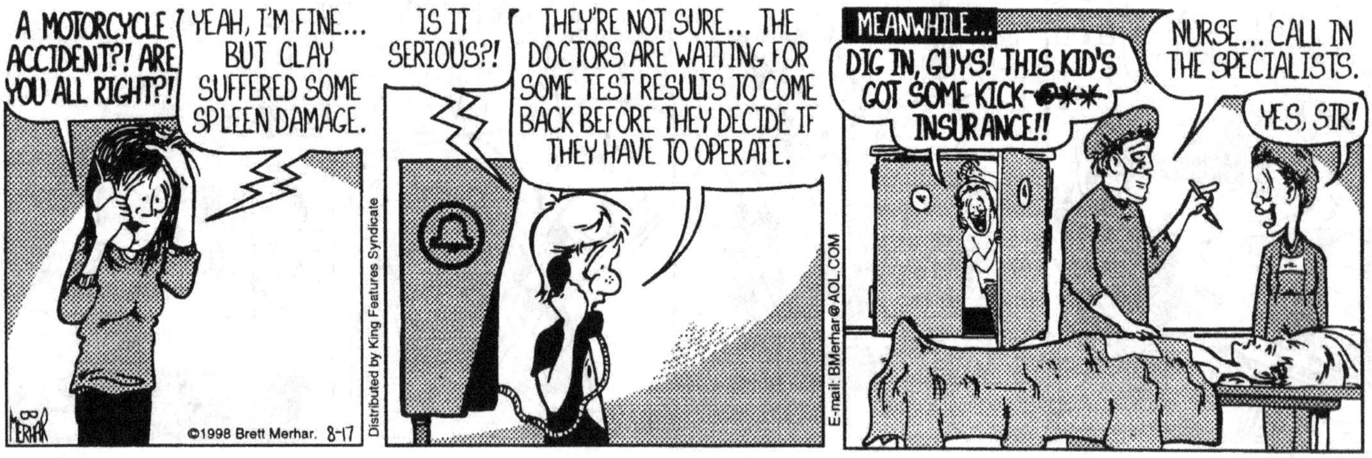
A MOTORCYCLE ACCIDENT?! ARE YOU ALL RIGHT?!
YEAH, I'M FINE... BUT CLAY SUFFERED SOME SPLEEN DAMAGE.
MERHAR
©1998 Brett Merhar. 8-17
Distributed by King Features Syndicate
IS IT SERIOUS?!
THEY'RE NOT SURE... THE DOCTORS ARE WAITING FOR SOME TEST RESULTS TO COME BACK BEFORE THEY DECIDE IF THEY HAVE TO OPERATE.
E-mail: BMerhar@AOL.COM
MEANWHILE...
DIG IN, GUYS! THIS KID'S GOT SOME KICK-@*** INSURANCE!!
NURSE... CALL IN THE SPECIALISTS.
YES, SIR!

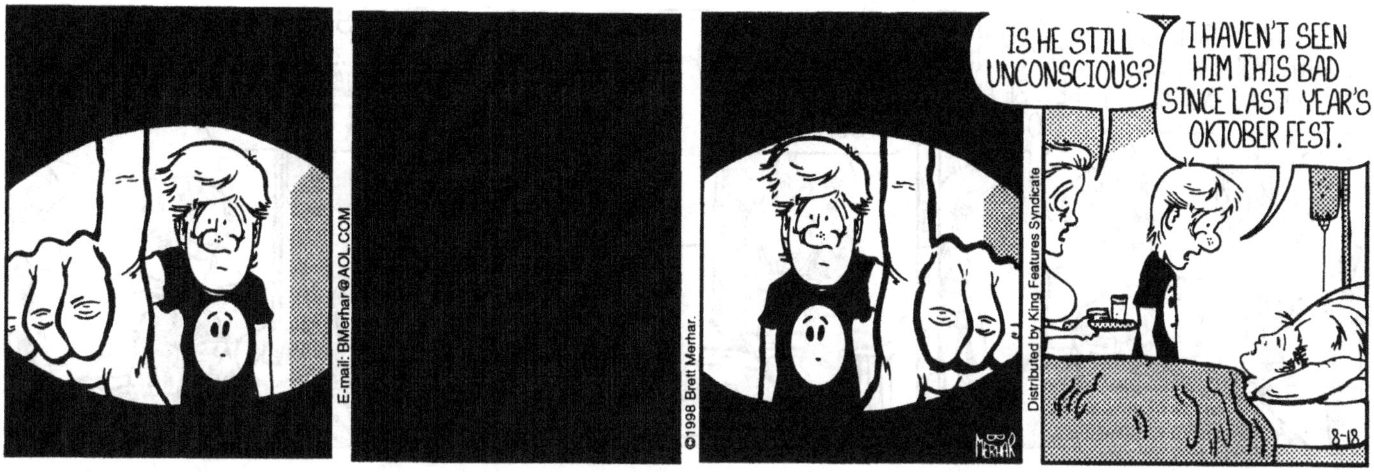
E-mail: BMerhar@AOL.COM
©1998 Brett Merhar.
Distributed by King Features Syndicate
IS HE STILL UNCONSCIOUS?
I HAVEN'T SEEN HIM THIS BAD SINCE LAST YEAR'S OKTOBER FEST.
MERHAR
8-18

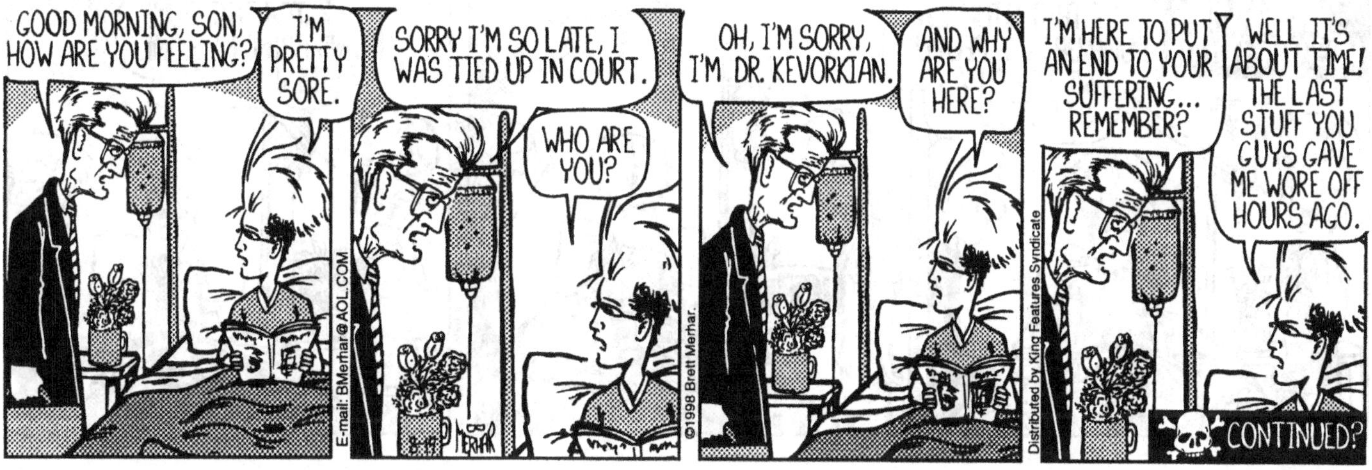
GOOD MORNING, SON, HOW ARE YOU FEELING?
I'M PRETTY SORE.
E-mail: BMerhar@AOL.COM
SORRY I'M SO LATE, I WAS TIED UP IN COURT.
WHO ARE YOU?
MERHAR
©1998 Brett Merhar.
OH, I'M SORRY, I'M DR. KEVORKIAN.
AND WHY ARE YOU HERE?
Distributed by King Features Syndicate
I'M HERE TO PUT AN END TO YOUR SUFFERING... REMEMBER?
WELL IT'S ABOUT TIME! THE LAST STUFF YOU GUYS GAVE ME WORE OFF HOURS AGO.
CONTINUED?

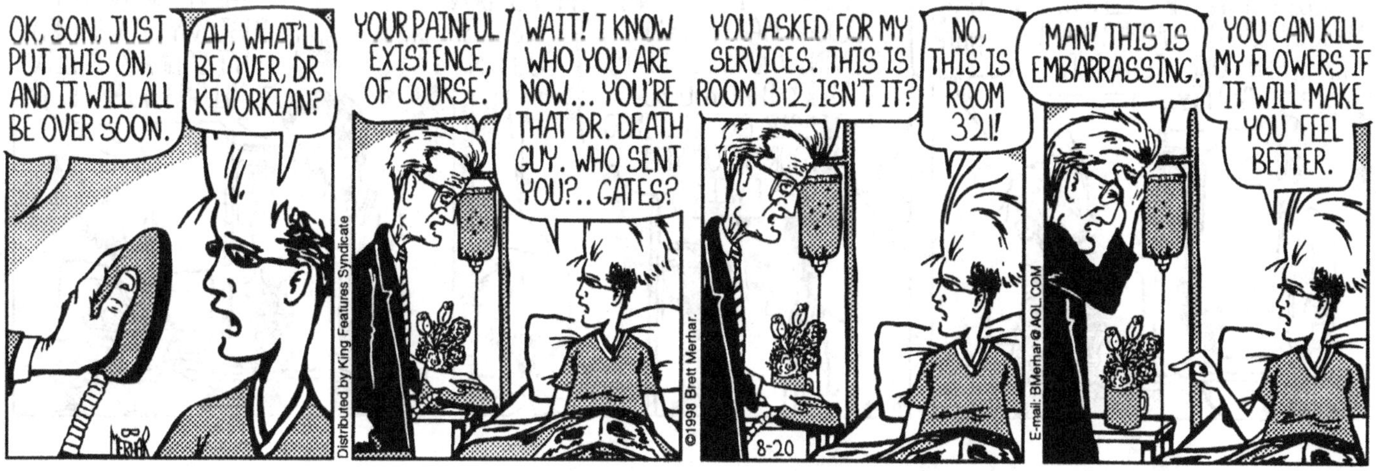
OK, SON, JUST PUT THIS ON, AND IT WILL ALL BE OVER SOON.
AH, WHAT'LL BE OVER, DR. KEVORKIAN?
MERHAR
Distributed by King Features Syndicate
YOUR PAINFUL EXISTENCE, OF COURSE.
WAIT! I KNOW WHO YOU ARE NOW... YOU'RE THAT DR. DEATH GUY. WHO SENT YOU?.. GATES?
©1998 Brett Merhar.
YOU ASKED FOR MY SERVICES. THIS IS ROOM 312, ISN'T IT?
NO, THIS IS ROOM 321!
8-20
E-mail: BMerhar@AOL.COM
MAN! THIS IS EMBARRASSING.
YOU CAN KILL MY FLOWERS IF IT WILL MAKE YOU FEEL BETTER.

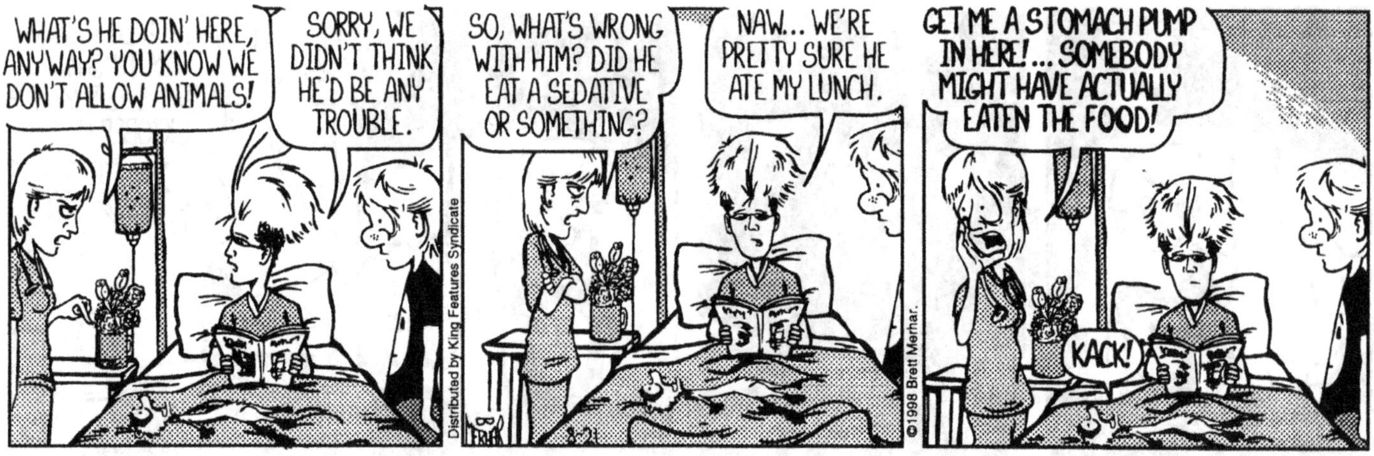
WHAT'S HE DOIN' HERE, ANYWAY? YOU KNOW WE DON'T ALLOW ANIMALS!
SORRY, WE DIDN'T THINK HE'D BE ANY TROUBLE.
Distributed by King Features Syndicate
SO, WHAT'S WRONG WITH HIM? DID HE EAT A SEDATIVE OR SOMETHING?
NAW... WE'RE PRETTY SURE HE ATE MY LUNCH.
8-21
©1998 Brett Merhar.
GET ME A STOMACH PUMP IN HERE!... SOMEBODY MIGHT HAVE ACTUALLY EATEN THE FOOD!
KACK!

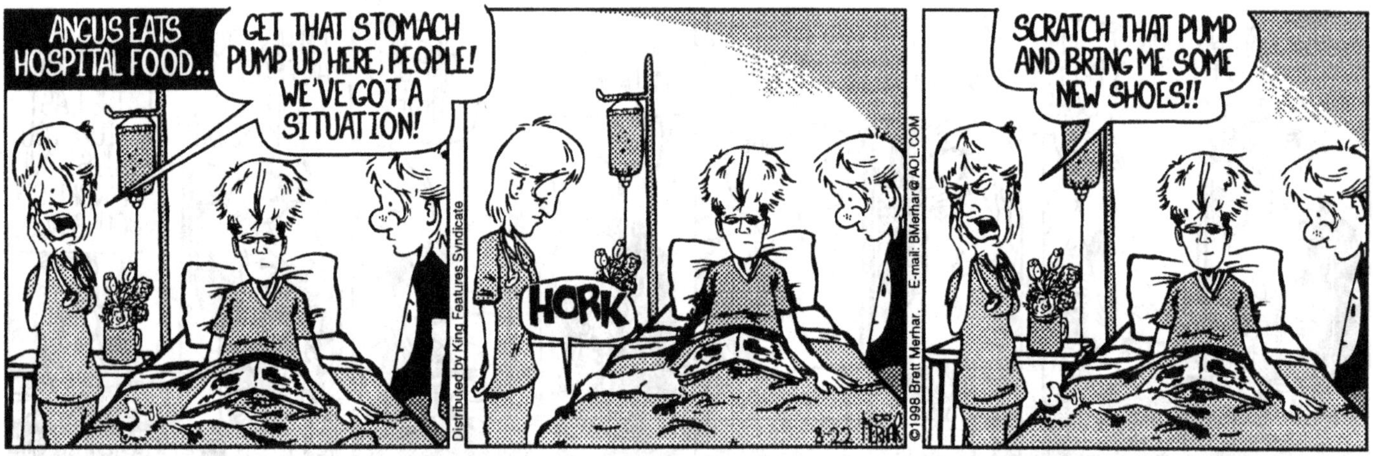
ANGUS EATS HOSPITAL FOOD..
GET THAT STOMACH PUMP UP HERE, PEOPLE! WE'VE GOT A SITUATION!
Distributed by King Features Syndicate
HORK
8-22
©1998 Brett Merhar. E-mail: BMerhar@AOL.COM
SCRATCH THAT PUMP AND BRING ME SOME NEW SHOES!!

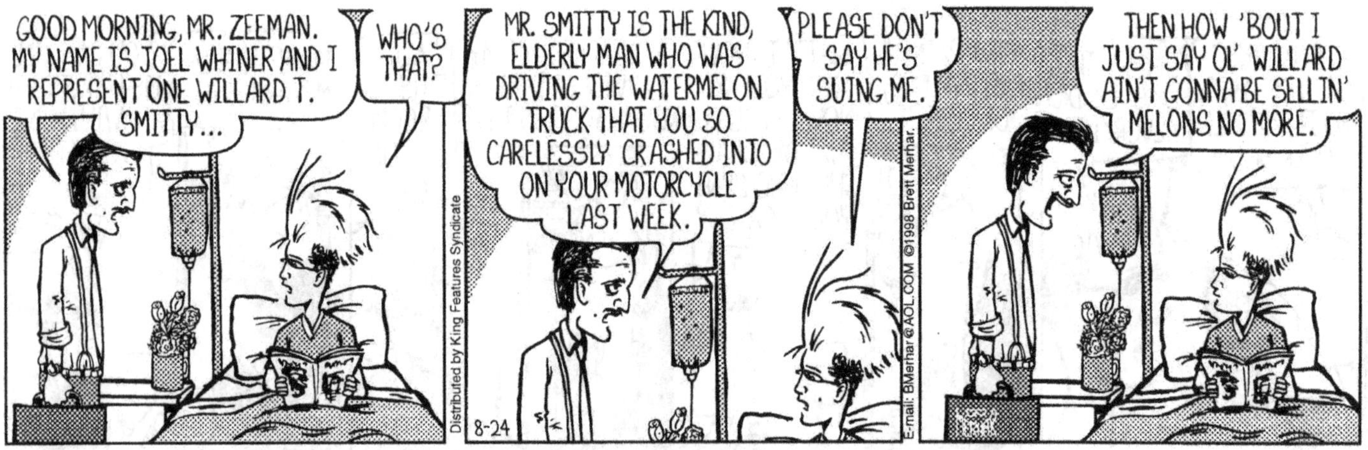
GOOD MORNING, MR. ZEEMAN. MY NAME IS JOEL WHINER AND I REPRESENT ONE WILLARD T. SMITTY...
WHO'S THAT?
Distributed by King Features Syndicate
MR. SMITTY IS THE KIND, ELDERLY MAN WHO WAS DRIVING THE WATERMELON TRUCK THAT YOU SO CARELESSLY CRASHED INTO ON YOUR MOTORCYCLE LAST WEEK.
PLEASE DON'T SAY HE'S SUING ME.
8-24
E-mail: BMerhar@AOL.COM ©1998 Brett Merhar.
THEN HOW 'BOUT I JUST SAY OL' WILLARD AIN'T GONNA BE SELLIN' MELONS NO MORE.

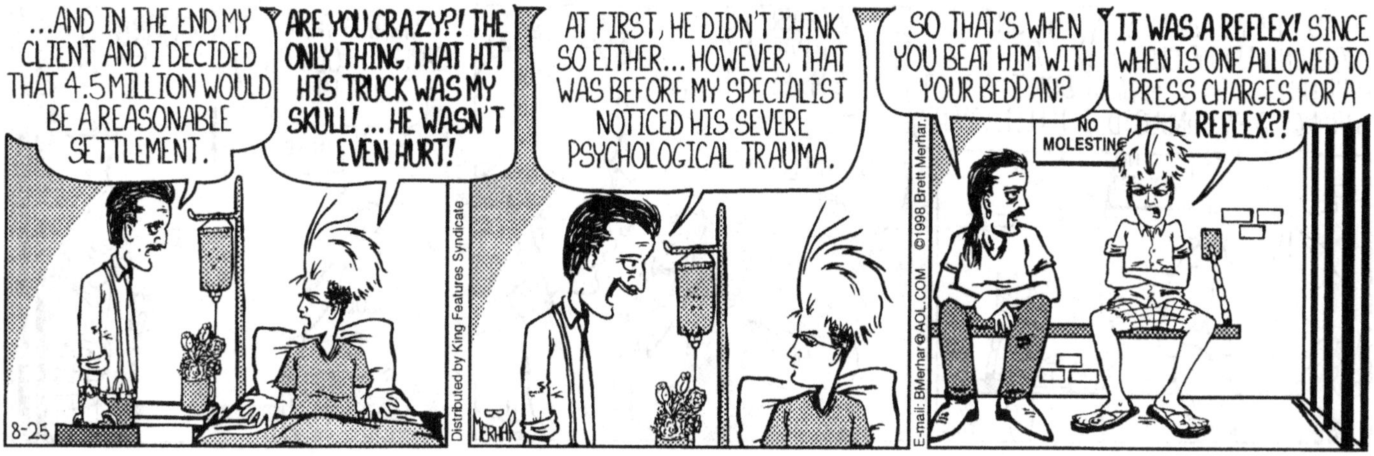
...AND IN THE END MY CLIENT AND I DECIDED THAT 4.5 MILLION WOULD BE A REASONABLE SETTLEMENT.
ARE YOU CRAZY?! THE ONLY THING THAT HIT HIS TRUCK WAS MY SKULL! ... HE WASN'T EVEN HURT!
8-25
Distributed by King Features Syndicate
MERHAR
AT FIRST, HE DIDN'T THINK SO EITHER... HOWEVER, THAT WAS BEFORE MY SPECIALIST NOTICED HIS SEVERE PSYCHOLOGICAL TRAUMA.
E-mail: BMerhar@AOL.COM ©1998 Brett Merhar.
SO THAT'S WHEN YOU BEAT HIM WITH YOUR BEDPAN?
NO MOLESTING
IT WAS A REFLEX! SINCE WHEN IS ONE ALLOWED TO PRESS CHARGES FOR A REFLEX?!

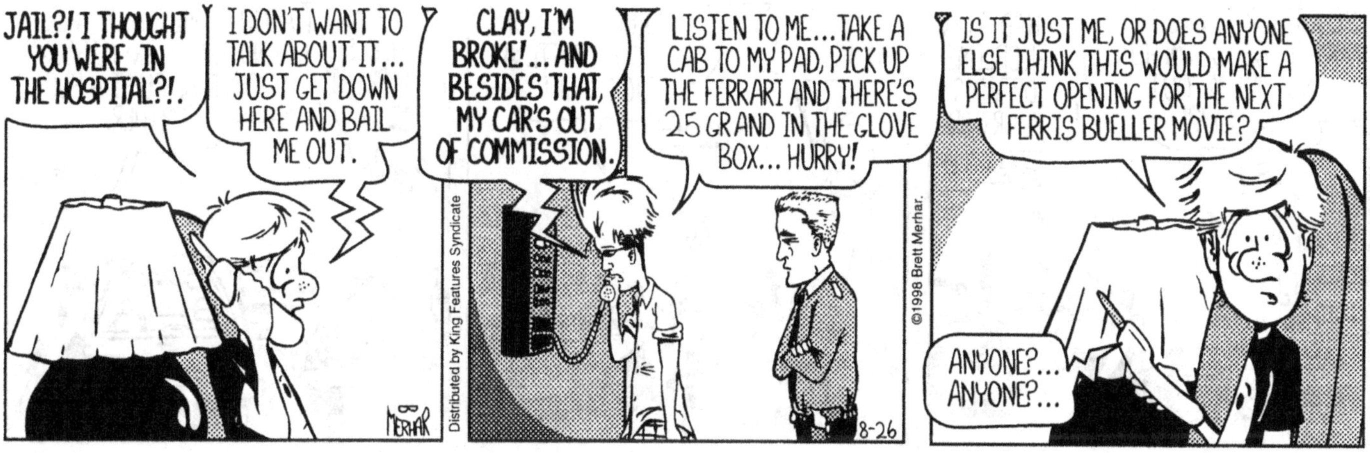
JAIL?! I THOUGHT YOU WERE IN THE HOSPITAL?!.
I DON'T WANT TO TALK ABOUT IT... JUST GET DOWN HERE AND BAIL ME OUT.
MERHAR
Distributed by King Features Syndicate
CLAY, I'M BROKE!... AND BESIDES THAT, MY CAR'S OUT OF COMMISSION.
LISTEN TO ME... TAKE A CAB TO MY PAD, PICK UP THE FERRARI AND THERE'S 25 GRAND IN THE GLOVE BOX... HURRY!
8-26
©1998 Brett Merhar.
IS IT JUST ME, OR DOES ANYONE ELSE THINK THIS WOULD MAKE A PERFECT OPENING FOR THE NEXT FERRIS BUELLER MOVIE?
ANYONE?... ANYONE?...

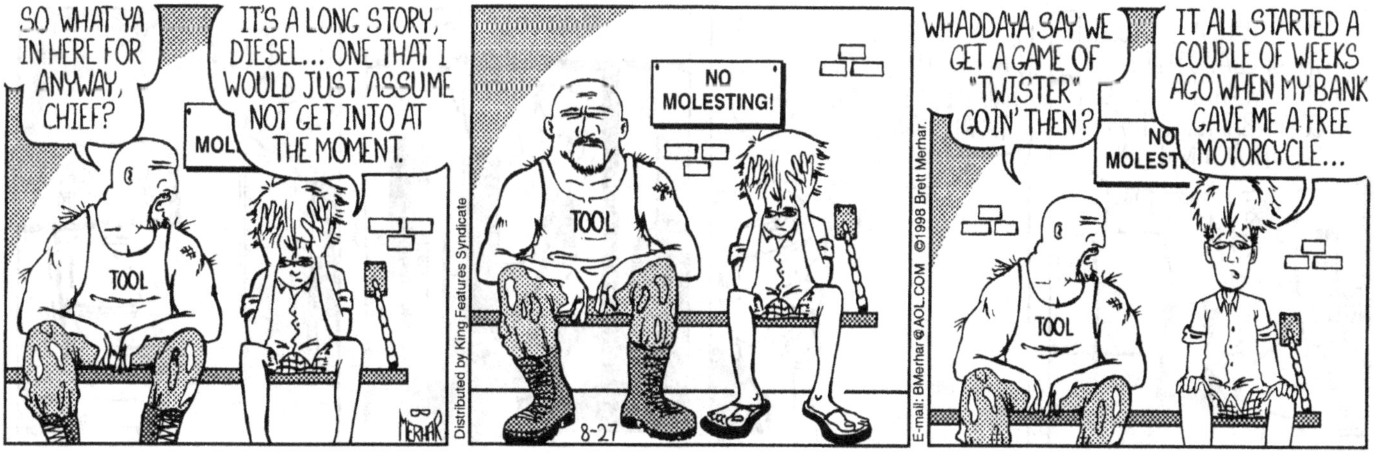
SO WHAT YA IN HERE FOR ANYWAY, CHIEF?
IT'S A LONG STORY, DIESEL... ONE THAT I WOULD JUST ASSUME NOT GET INTO AT THE MOMENT.
TOOL
MERHAR
Distributed by King Features Syndicate
NO MOLESTING!
TOOL
8-27
E-mail: BMerhar@AOL.COM ©1998 Brett Merhar.
WHADDAYA SAY WE GET A GAME OF "TWISTER" GOIN' THEN?
IT ALL STARTED A COUPLE OF WEEKS AGO WHEN MY BANK GAVE ME A FREE MOTORCYCLE...
TOOL

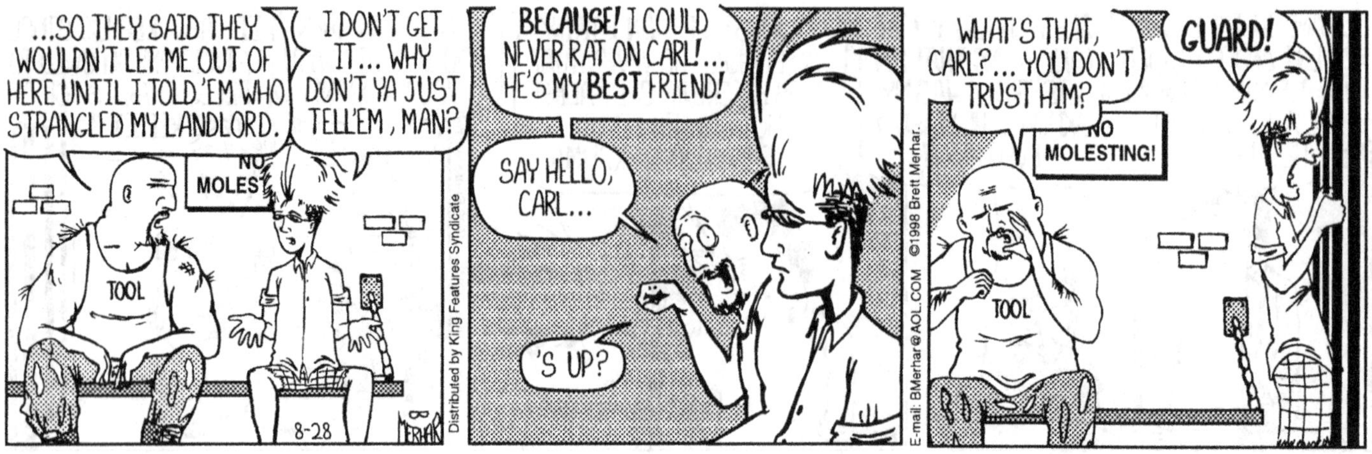
...SO THEY SAID THEY WOULDN'T LET ME OUT OF HERE UNTIL I TOLD 'EM WHO STRANGLED MY LANDLORD.
I DON'T GET IT... WHY DON'T YA JUST TELL'EM, MAN?
NO MOLES
TOOL
8-28
MERHAR
Distributed by King Features Syndicate
BECAUSE! I COULD NEVER RAT ON CARL!... HE'S MY BEST FRIEND!
SAY HELLO, CARL...
'S UP?
E-mail: BMerhar@AOL.COM ©1998 Brett Merhar.
WHAT'S THAT, CARL?... YOU DON'T TRUST HIM?
GUARD!
NO MOLESTING!
TOOL

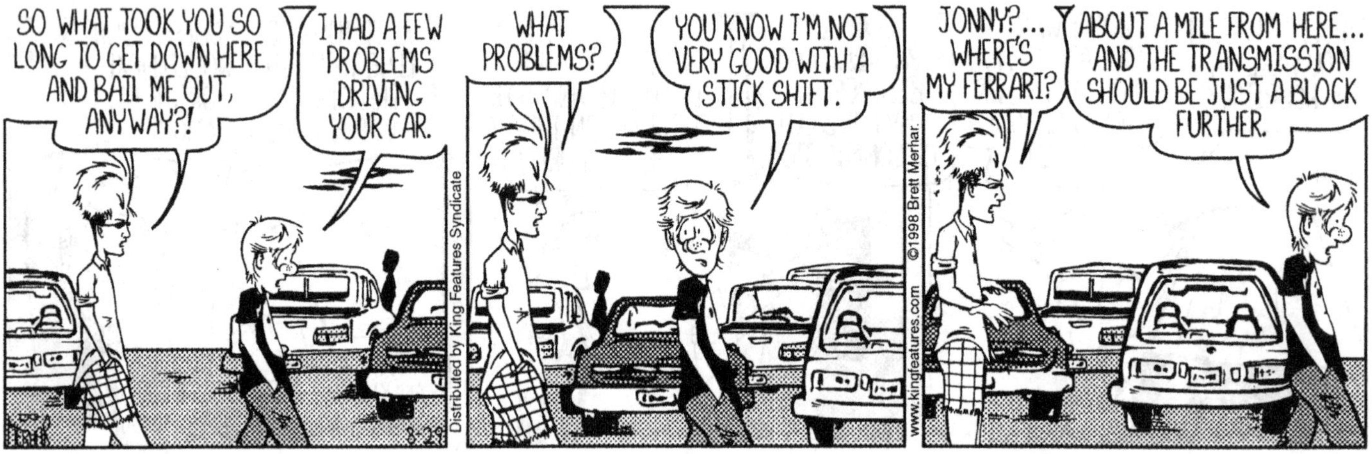
SO WHAT TOOK YOU SO LONG TO GET DOWN HERE AND BAIL ME OUT, ANYWAY?!
I HAD A FEW PROBLEMS DRIVING YOUR CAR.
8-29
Distributed by King Features Syndicate
WHAT PROBLEMS?
YOU KNOW I'M NOT VERY GOOD WITH A STICK SHIFT.
www.kingfeatures.com ©1998 Brett Merhar.
JONNY?... WHERE'S MY FERRARI?
ABOUT A MILE FROM HERE... AND THE TRANSMISSION SHOULD BE JUST A BLOCK FURTHER.

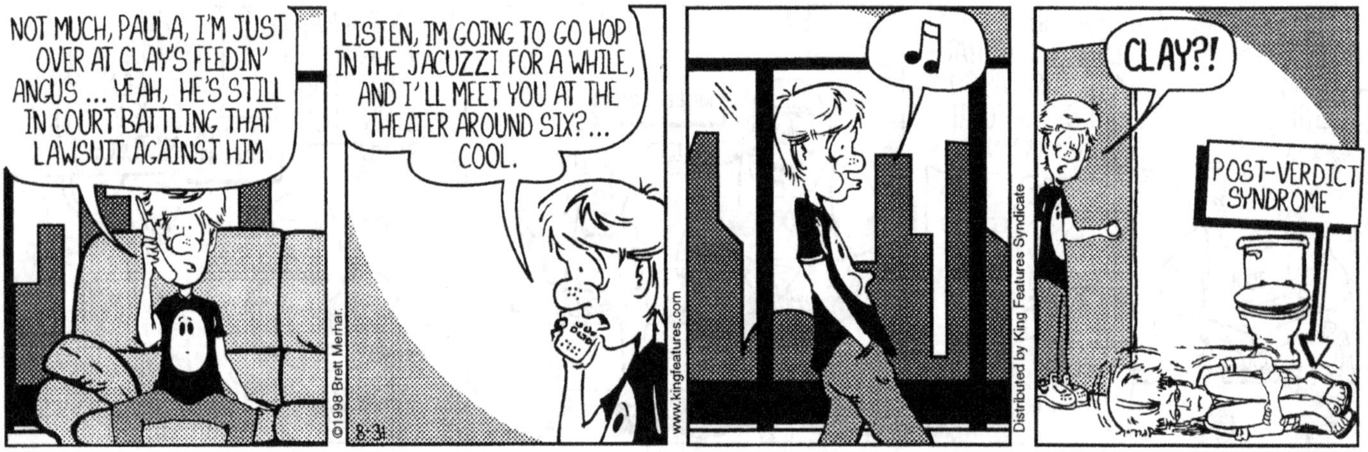
NOT MUCH, PAULA, I'M JUST OVER AT CLAY'S FEEDIN' ANGUS ... YEAH, HE'S STILL IN COURT BATTLING THAT LAWSUIT AGAINST HIM
©1998 Brett Merhar.
8-31
LISTEN, IM GOING TO GO HOP IN THE JACUZZI FOR A WHILE, AND I'LL MEET YOU AT THE THEATER AROUND SIX?... COOL.
www.kingfeatures.com
Distributed by King Features Syndicate
CLAY?!
POST-VERDICT SYNDROME

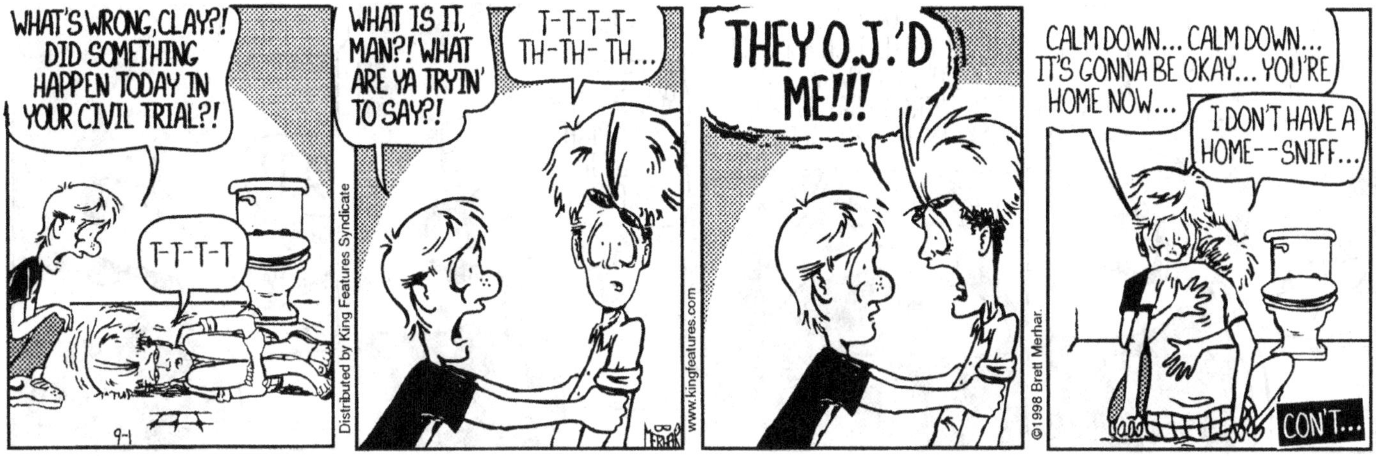
WHAT'S WRONG, CLAY?! DID SOMETHING HAPPEN TODAY IN YOUR CIVIL TRIAL?!
T-T-T-T
9-1
Distributed by King Features Syndicate
WHAT IS IT, MAN?! WHAT ARE YA TRYIN' TO SAY?!
T-T-T-T- TH-TH- TH...
MERHAR
www.kingfeatures.com
THEY O.J.'D ME!!!
©1998 Brett Merhar.
CALM DOWN... CALM DOWN... IT'S GONNA BE OKAY... YOU'RE HOME NOW...
I DON'T HAVE A HOME--SNIFF...
CON'T...

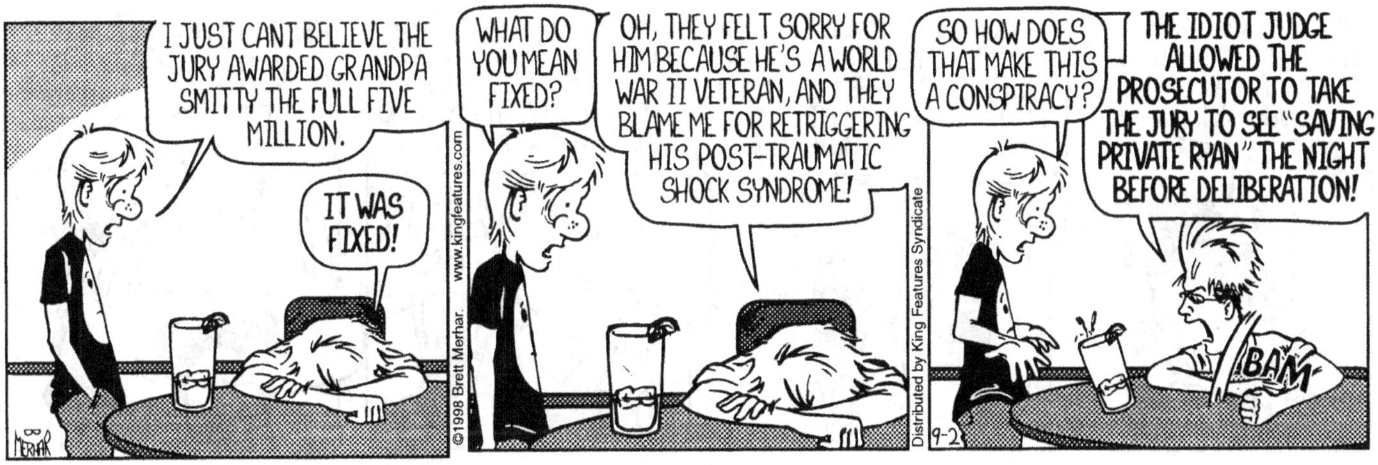
I JUST CANT BELIEVE THE JURY AWARDED GRANDPA SMITTY THE FULL FIVE MILLION.
IT WAS FIXED!
MERHAR
www.kingfeatures.com
©1998 Brett Merhar.
WHAT DO YOU MEAN FIXED?
OH, THEY FELT SORRY FOR HIM BECAUSE HE'S A WORLD WAR II VETERAN, AND THEY BLAME ME FOR RETRIGGERING HIS POST-TRAUMATIC SHOCK SYNDROME!
Distributed by King Features Syndicate
SO HOW DOES THAT MAKE THIS A CONSPIRACY?
THE IDIOT JUDGE ALLOWED THE PROSECUTOR TO TAKE THE JURY TO SEE "SAVING PRIVATE RYAN" THE NIGHT BEFORE DELIBERATION!
BAM
9-2

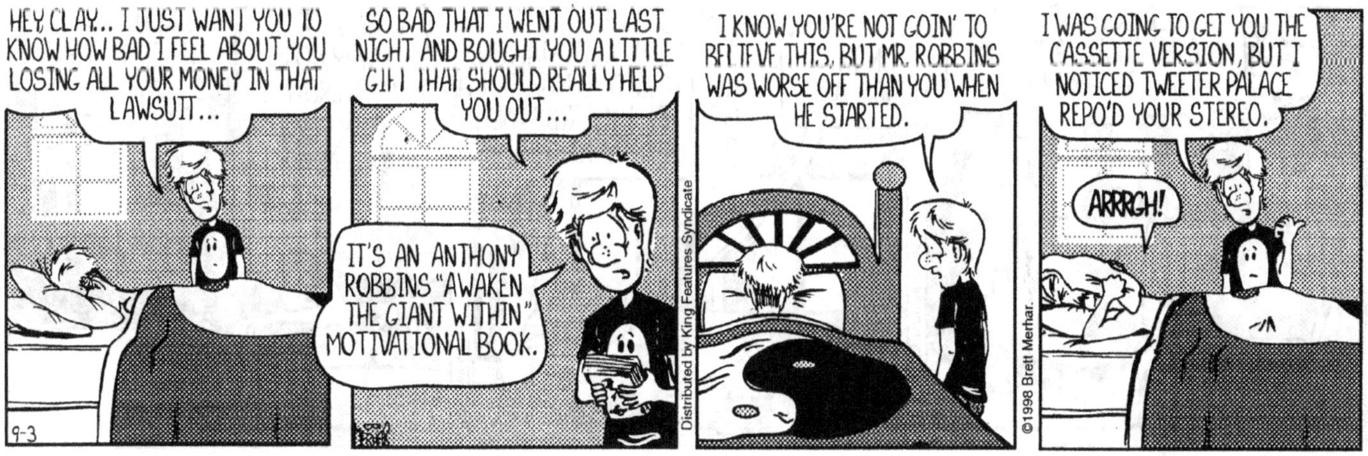
HEY, CLAY... I JUST WANT YOU TO KNOW HOW BAD I FEEL ABOUT YOU LOSING ALL YOUR MONEY IN THAT LAWSUIT...
9-3
SO BAD THAT I WENT OUT LAST NIGHT AND BOUGHT YOU A LITTLE GIFT THAT SHOULD REALLY HELP YOU OUT...
IT'S AN ANTHONY ROBBINS "AWAKEN THE GIANT WITHIN" MOTIVATIONAL BOOK.
Distributed by King Features Syndicate
I KNOW YOU'RE NOT GOIN' TO BELIEVE THIS, BUT MR. ROBBINS WAS WORSE OFF THAN YOU WHEN HE STARTED.
©1998 Brett Merhar.
I WAS GOING TO GET YOU THE CASSETTE VERSION, BUT I NOTICED TWEETER PALACE REPO'D YOUR STEREO.
ARRRGH!

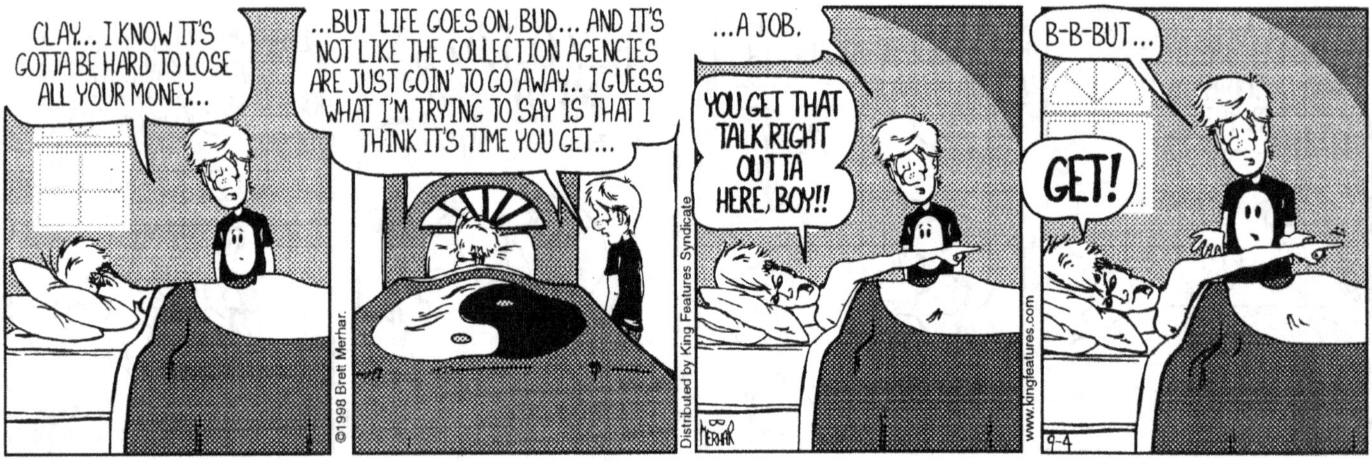
CLAY... I KNOW IT'S GOTTA BE HARD TO LOSE ALL YOUR MONEY...
©1998 Brett Merhar.
...BUT LIFE GOES ON, BUD... AND IT'S NOT LIKE THE COLLECTION AGENCIES ARE JUST GOIN' TO GO AWAY... I GUESS WHAT I'M TRYING TO SAY IS THAT I THINK IT'S TIME YOU GET...
Distributed by King Features Syndicate
...A JOB.
YOU GET THAT TALK RIGHT OUTTA HERE, BOY!!
MERHAR
B-B-BUT...
GET!
www.kingfeatures.com
9-4

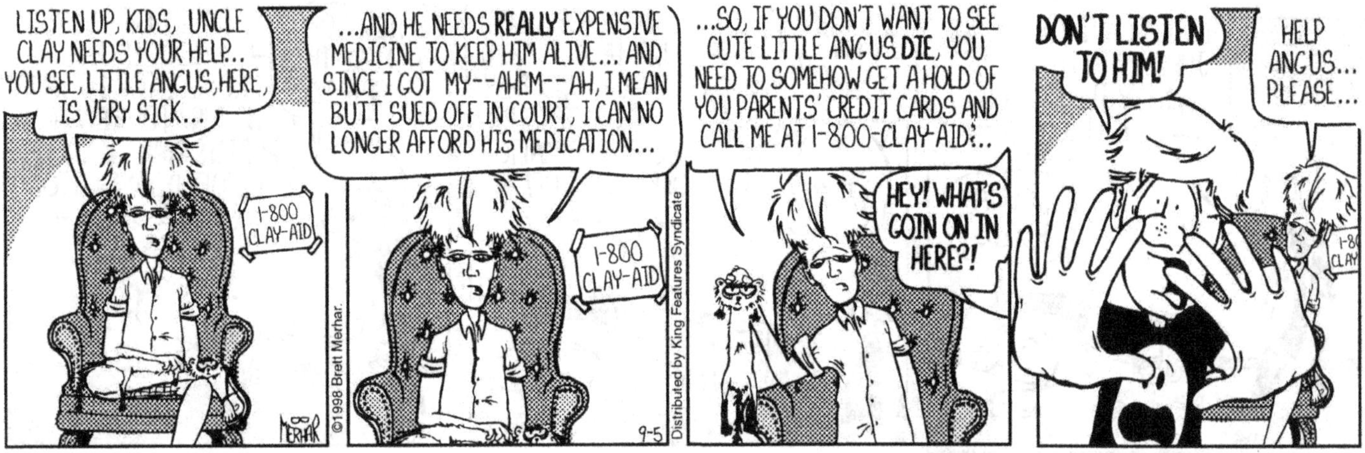
LISTEN UP, KIDS, UNCLE CLAY NEEDS YOUR HELP... YOU SEE, LITTLE ANGUS, HERE, IS VERY SICK...
1-800 CLAY-AID
MERHAR
©1998 Brett Merhar.
...AND HE NEEDS REALLY EXPENSIVE MEDICINE TO KEEP HIM ALIVE... AND SINCE I GOT MY--AHEM--AH, I MEAN BUTT SUED OFF IN COURT, I CAN NO LONGER AFFORD HIS MEDICATION...
1-800 CLAY-AID
9-5
Distributed by King Features Syndicate
...SO, IF YOU DON'T WANT TO SEE CUTE LITTLE ANGUS DIE, YOU NEED TO SOMEHOW GET A HOLD OF YOU PARENTS' CREDIT CARDS AND CALL ME AT 1-800-CLAY-AID!...
HEY! WHAT'S GOIN ON IN HERE?!
DON'T LISTEN TO HIM!
HELP ANGUS... PLEASE...

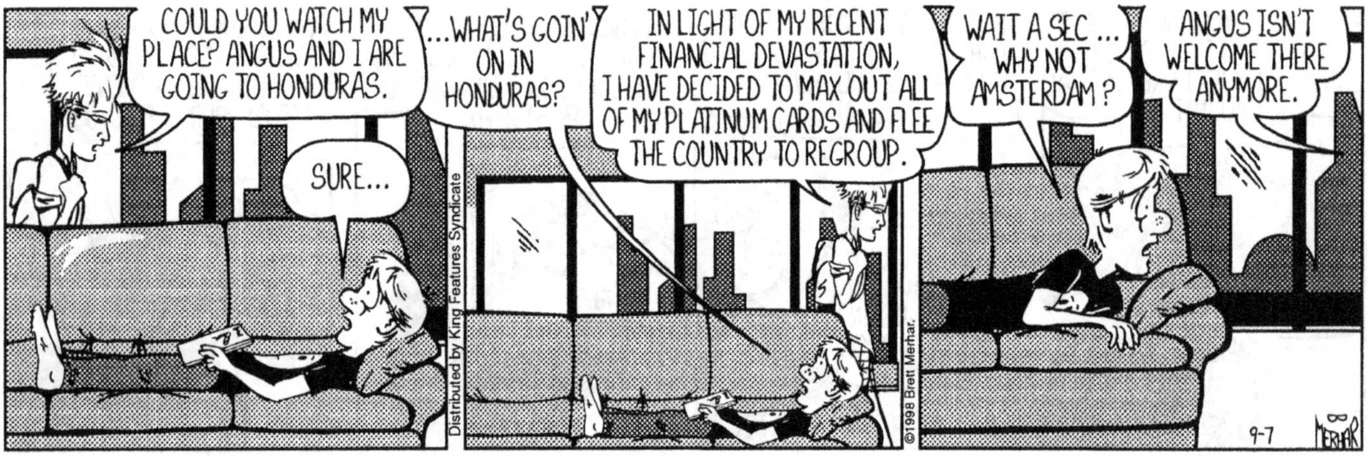
COULD YOU WATCH MY PLACE? ANGUS AND I ARE GOING TO HONDURAS.
SURE...
Distributed by King Features Syndicate
...WHAT'S GOIN' ON IN HONDURAS?
IN LIGHT OF MY RECENT FINANCIAL DEVASTATION, I HAVE DECIDED TO MAX OUT ALL OF MY PLATINUM CARDS AND FLEE THE COUNTRY TO REGROUP.
©1998 Brett Merhar.
WAIT A SEC... WHY NOT AMSTERDAM?
ANGUS ISN'T WELCOME THERE ANYMORE.
9-7
MERHAR

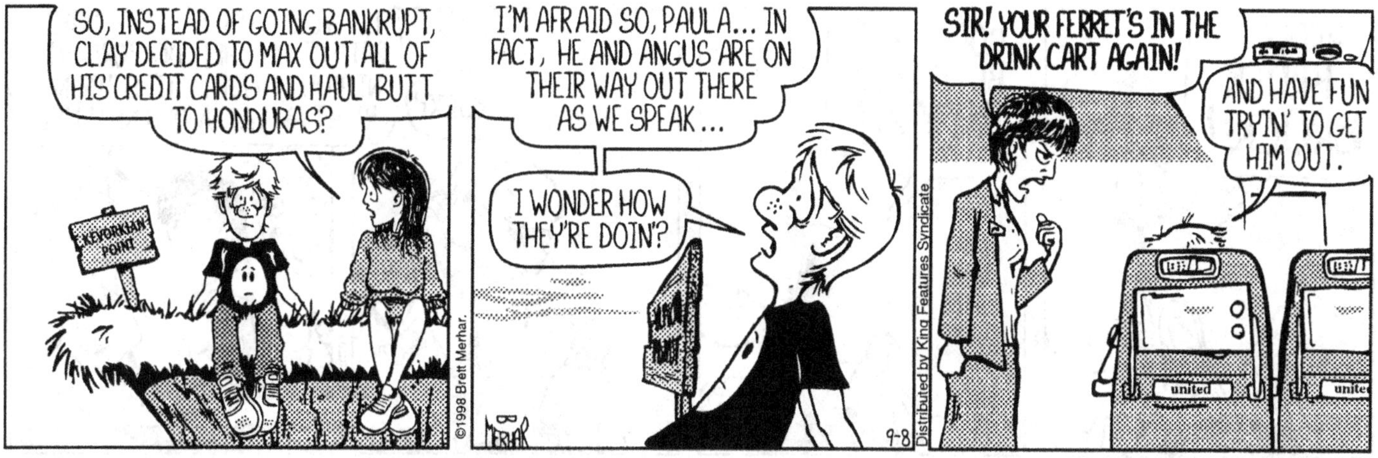
SO, INSTEAD OF GOING BANKRUPT, CLAY DECIDED TO MAX OUT ALL OF HIS CREDIT CARDS AND HAUL BUTT TO HONDURAS?
KEVORKIAN POINT
©1998 Brett Merhar.
I'M AFRAID SO, PAULA... IN FACT, HE AND ANGUS ARE ON THEIR WAY OUT THERE AS WE SPEAK...
I WONDER HOW THEY'RE DOIN'?
MERHAR
9-8
Distributed by King Features Syndicate
SIR! YOUR FERRET'S IN THE DRINK CART AGAIN!
AND HAVE FUN TRYIN' TO GET HIM OUT.
united

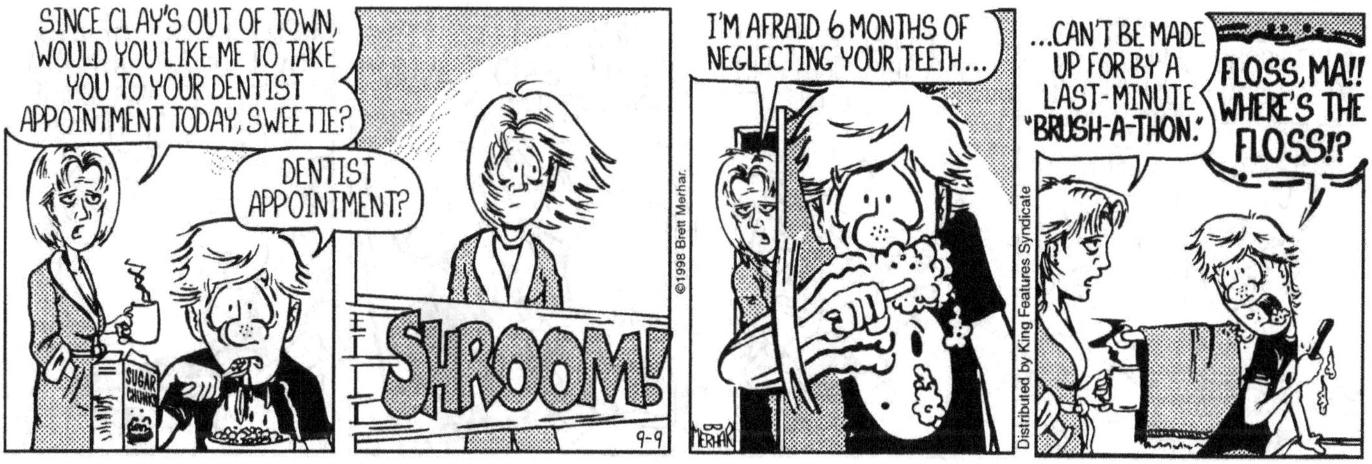
SINCE CLAY'S OUT OF TOWN, WOULD YOU LIKE ME TO TAKE YOU TO YOUR DENTIST APPOINTMENT TODAY, SWEETIE?
DENTIST APPOINTMENT?
SUGAR CHUNKS
SHROOM!
9-9
©1998 Brett Merhar.
I'M AFRAID 6 MONTHS OF NEGLECTING YOUR TEETH...
MERHAR
Distributed by King Features Syndicate
...CAN'T BE MADE UP FOR BY A LAST-MINUTE "BRUSH-A-THON."
FLOSS, MA!! WHERE'S THE FLOSS!?

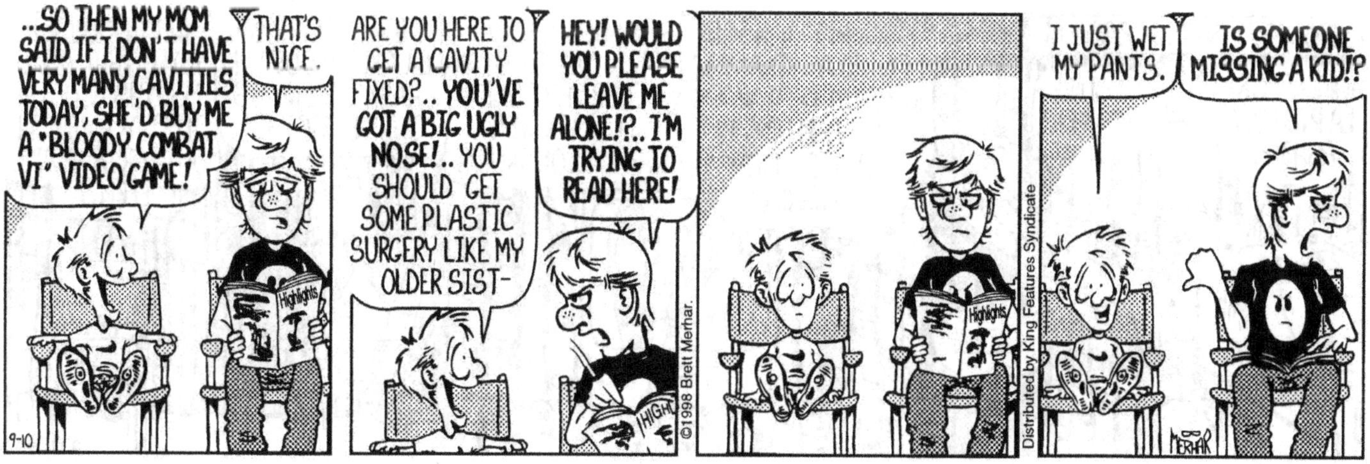
...SO THEN MY MOM SAID IF I DON'T HAVE VERY MANY CAVITIES TODAY, SHE'D BUY ME A "BLOODY COMBAT VI" VIDEO GAME!
THAT'S NICE.
Highlights
9-10
ARE YOU HERE TO GET A CAVITY FIXED?.. YOU'VE GOT A BIG UGLY NOSE!.. YOU SHOULD GET SOME PLASTIC SURGERY LIKE MY OLDER SIST-
HEY! WOULD YOU PLEASE LEAVE ME ALONE!?.. I'M TRYING TO READ HERE!
©1998 Brett Merhar.
Highlights
Distributed by King Features Syndicate
I JUST WET MY PANTS.
IS SOMEONE MISSING A KID!?
MERHAR

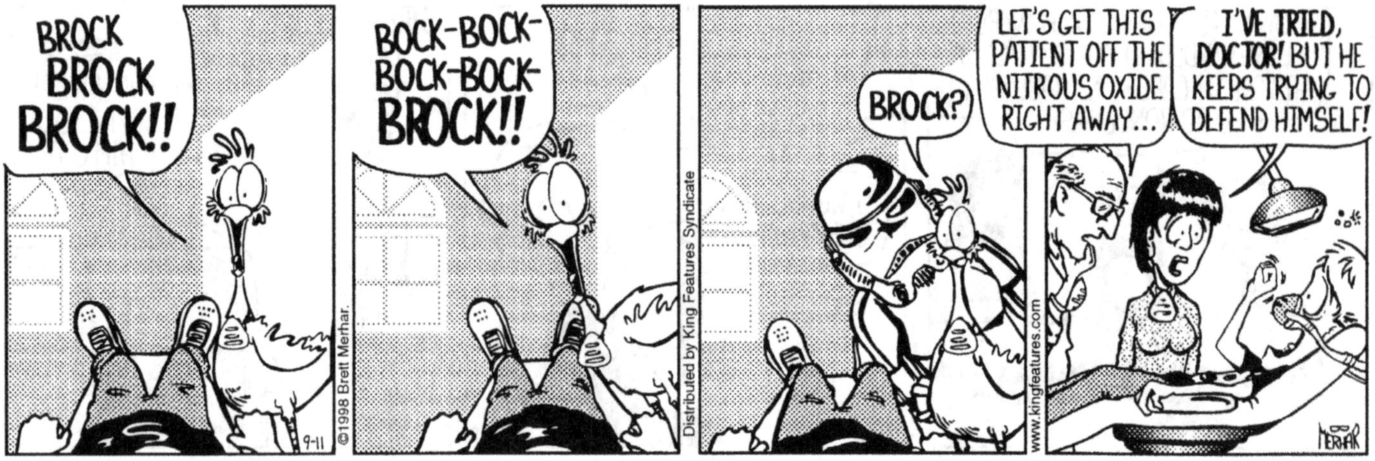
BROCK BROCK BROCK!!
BOCK-BOCK-BOCK-BOCK-BROCK!!
BROCK?
LET'S GET THIS PATIENT OFF THE NITROUS OXIDE RIGHT AWAY...
I'VE TRIED, DOCTOR! BUT HE KEEPS TRYING TO DEFEND HIMSELF!
9-11
©1998 Brett Merhar.
Distributed by King Features Syndicate
www.kingfeatures.com
MERHAR

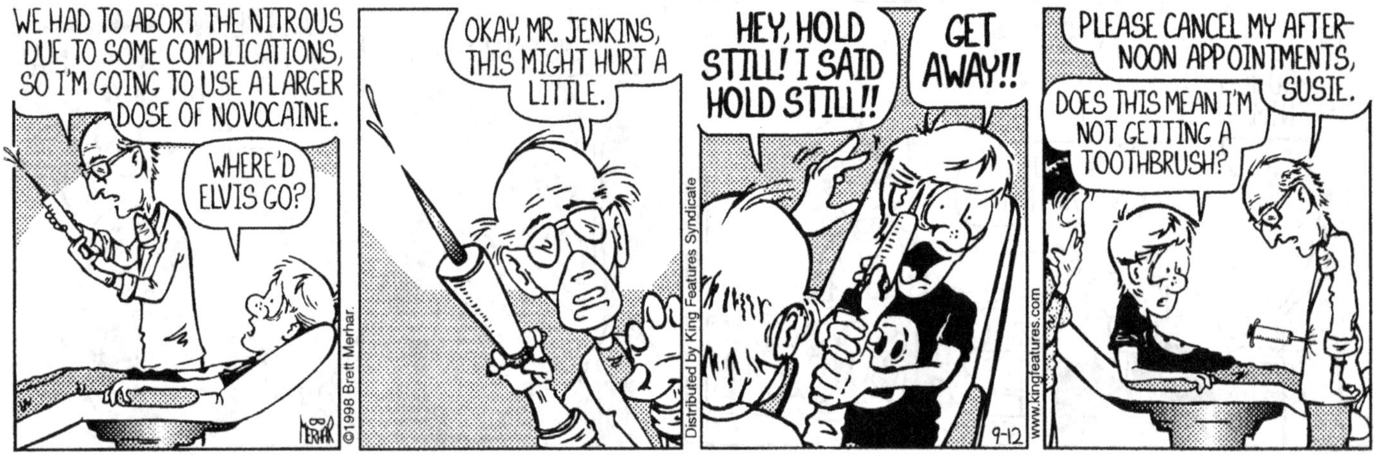
WE HAD TO ABORT THE NITROUS DUE TO SOME COMPLICATIONS, SO I'M GOING TO USE A LARGER DOSE OF NOVOCAINE.
WHERE'D ELVIS GO?
MERHAR
©1998 Brett Merhar.
OKAY, MR. JENKINS, THIS MIGHT HURT A LITTLE.
Distributed by King Features Syndicate
HEY, HOLD STILL! I SAID HOLD STILL!!
GET AWAY!!
9-12
www.kingfeatures.com
PLEASE CANCEL MY AFTER-NOON APPOINTMENTS, SUSIE.
DOES THIS MEAN I'M NOT GETTING A TOOTHBRUSH?

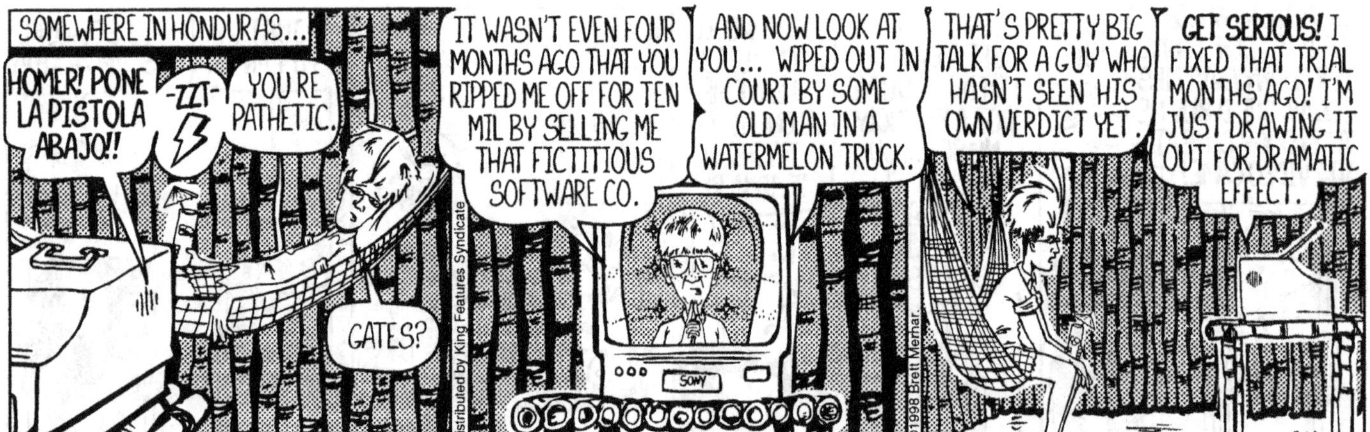
SOMEWHERE IN HONDURAS...
HOMER! PONE LA PISTOLA ABAJO!!
-ZZT-
YOU'RE PATHETIC.
GATES?
Distributed by King Features Syndicate
IT WASN'T EVEN FOUR MONTHS AGO THAT YOU RIPPED ME OFF FOR TEN MIL BY SELLING ME THAT FICTITIOUS SOFTWARE CO.
AND NOW LOOK AT YOU... WIPED OUT IN COURT BY SOME OLD MAN IN A WATERMELON TRUCK.
SONY
©1998 Brett Merhar.
THAT'S PRETTY BIG TALK FOR A GUY WHO HASN'T SEEN HIS OWN VERDICT YET.
GET SERIOUS! I FIXED THAT TRIAL MONTHS AGO! I'M JUST DRAWING IT OUT FOR DRAMATIC EFFECT.
BRETT
9-14

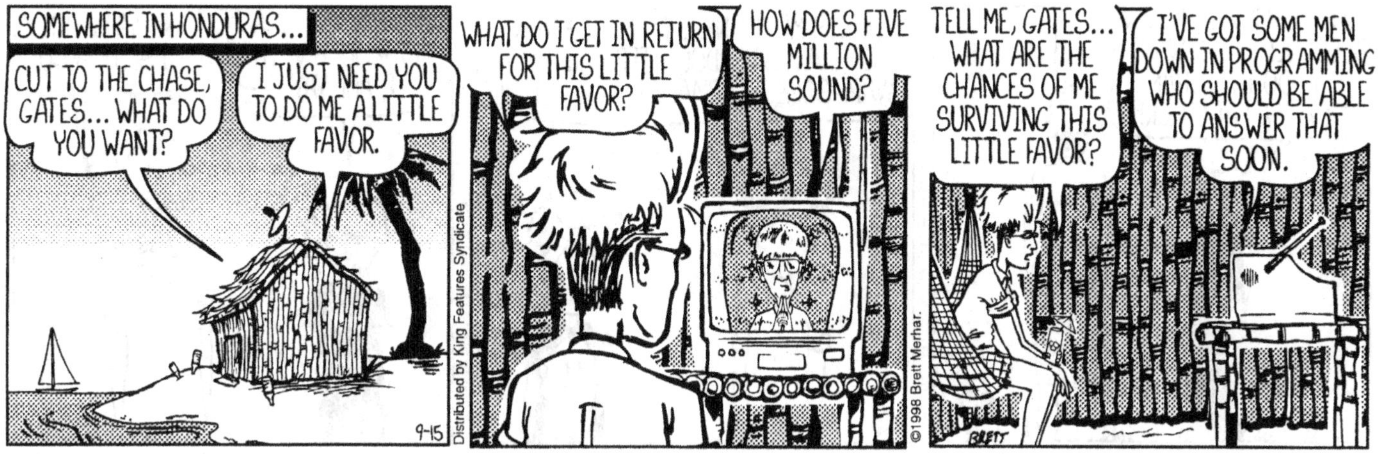
SOMEWHERE IN HONDURAS...
CUT TO THE CHASE, GATES... WHAT DO YOU WANT?
I JUST NEED YOU TO DO ME A LITTLE FAVOR.
9-15
Distributed by King Features Syndicate
WHAT DO I GET IN RETURN FOR THIS LITTLE FAVOR?
HOW DOES FIVE MILLION SOUND?
©1998 Brett Merhar.
TELL ME, GATES... WHAT ARE THE CHANCES OF ME SURVIVING THIS LITTLE FAVOR?
I'VE GOT SOME MEN DOWN IN PROGRAMMING WHO SHOULD BE ABLE TO ANSWER THAT SOON.
BRETT

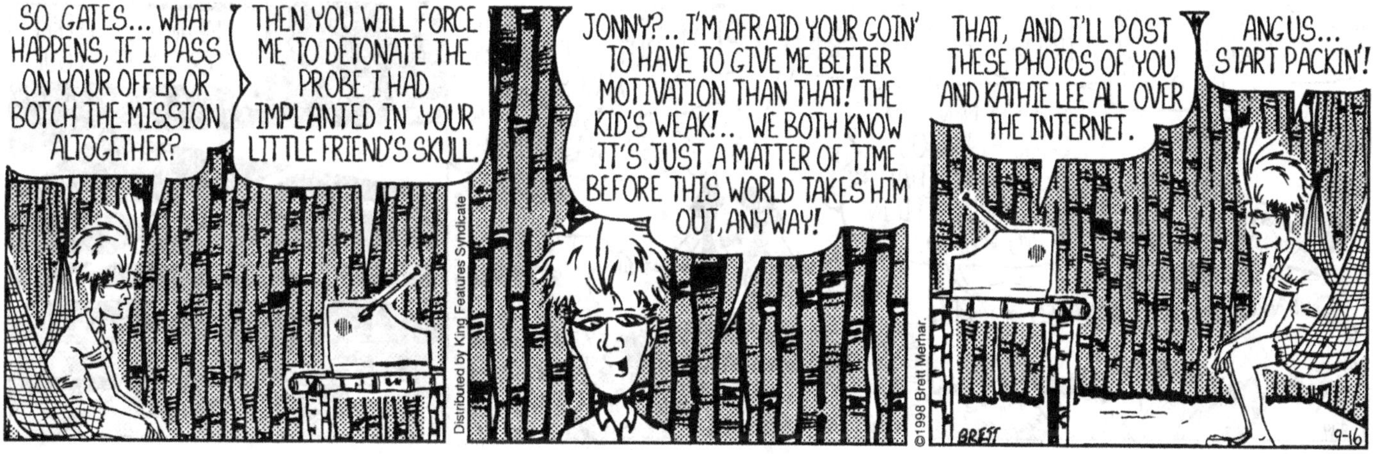
SO GATES... WHAT HAPPENS, IF I PASS ON YOUR OFFER OR BOTCH THE MISSION ALTOGETHER?
THEN YOU WILL FORCE ME TO DETONATE THE PROBE I HAD IMPLANTED IN YOUR LITTLE FRIEND'S SKULL.
Distributed by King Features Syndicate
JONNY?.. I'M AFRAID YOUR GOIN' TO HAVE TO GIVE ME BETTER MOTIVATION THAN THAT! THE KID'S WEAK!.. WE BOTH KNOW IT'S JUST A MATTER OF TIME BEFORE THIS WORLD TAKES HIM OUT, ANYWAY!
©1998 Brett Merhar.
THAT, AND I'LL POST THESE PHOTOS OF YOU AND KATHIE LEE ALL OVER THE INTERNET.
ANGUS... START PACKIN'!
BRETT
9-16

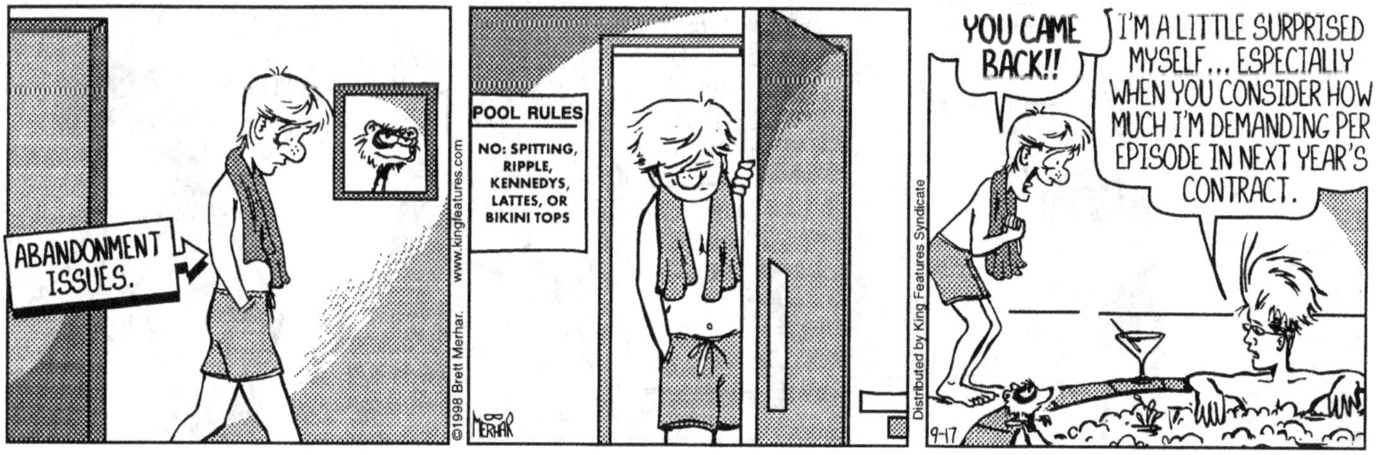
ABANDONMENT ISSUES.
©1998 Brett Merhar. www.kingfeatures.com
POOL RULES
NO: SPITTING, RIPPLE, KENNEDYS, LATTES, OR BIKINI TOPS
MERHAR
Distributed by King Features Syndicate
YOU CAME BACK!!
I'M A LITTLE SURPRISED MYSELF... ESPECIALLY WHEN YOU CONSIDER HOW MUCH I'M DEMANDING PER EPISODE IN NEXT YEAR'S CONTRACT.
9-17

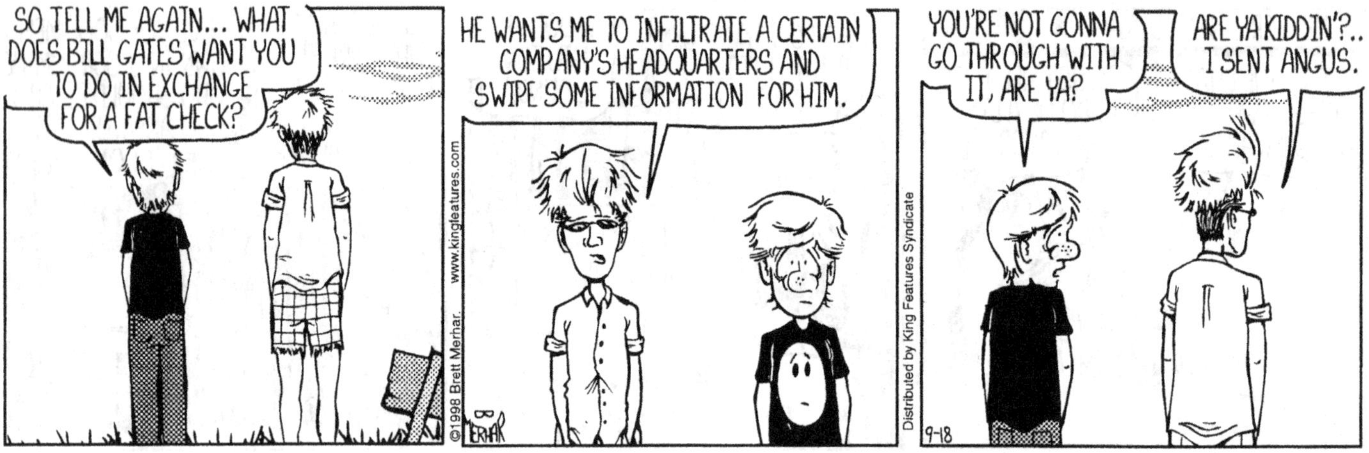
SO TELL ME AGAIN... WHAT DOES BILL GATES WANT YOU TO DO IN EXCHANGE FOR A FAT CHECK?
HE WANTS ME TO INFILTRATE A CERTAIN COMPANY'S HEADQUARTERS AND SWIPE SOME INFORMATION FOR HIM.
YOU'RE NOT GONNA GO THROUGH WITH IT, ARE YA?
ARE YA KIDDIN'?.. I SENT ANGUS.
©1998 Brett Merhar. www.kingfeatures.com
Distributed by King Features Syndicate
MERHAR
9-18

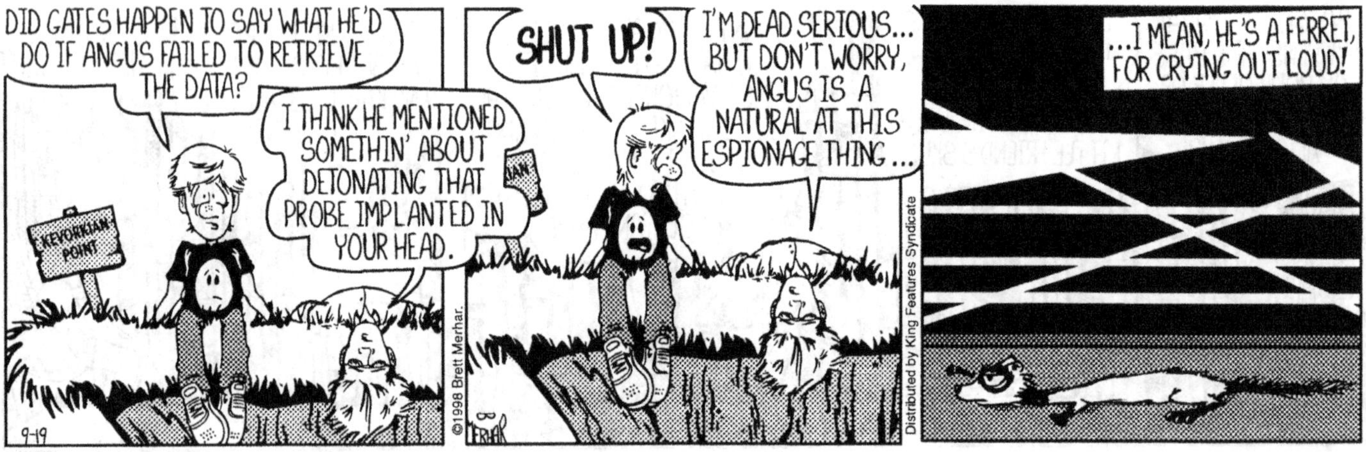
DID GATES HAPPEN TO SAY WHAT HE'D DO IF ANGUS FAILED TO RETRIEVE THE DATA?
I THINK HE MENTIONED SOMETHIN' ABOUT DETONATING THAT PROBE IMPLANTED IN YOUR HEAD.
KEVORKIAN POINT
SHUT UP!
I'M DEAD SERIOUS... BUT DON'T WORRY, ANGUS IS A NATURAL AT THIS ESPIONAGE THING...
...I MEAN, HE'S A FERRET, FOR CRYING OUT LOUD!
©1998 Brett Merhar.
Distributed by King Features Syndicate
MERHAR
9-19

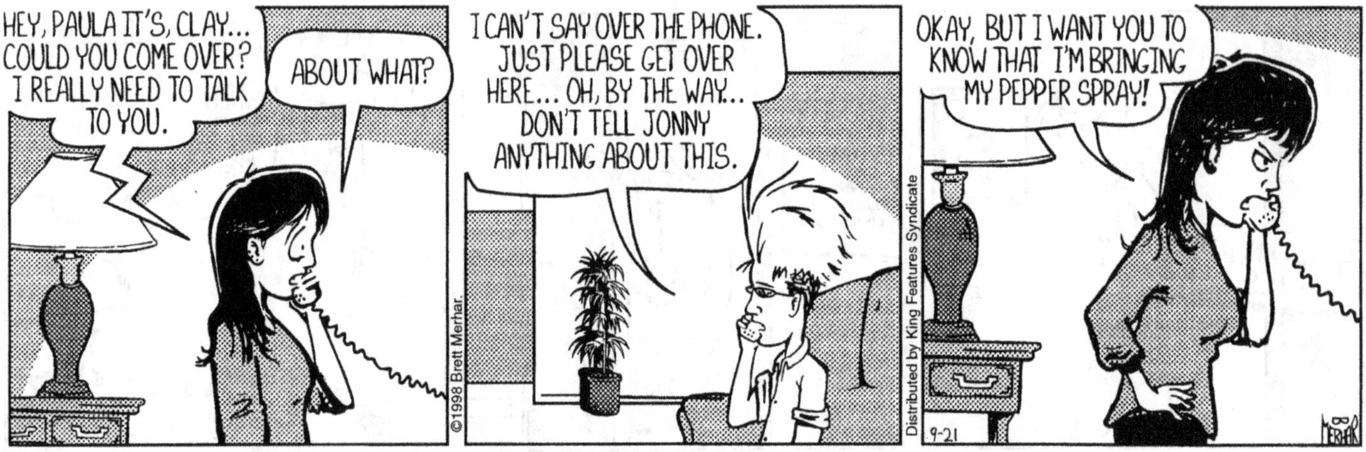
HEY, PAULA IT'S, CLAY... COULD YOU COME OVER? I REALLY NEED TO TALK TO YOU.
ABOUT WHAT?
I CAN'T SAY OVER THE PHONE. JUST PLEASE GET OVER HERE... OH, BY THE WAY... DON'T TELL JONNY ANYTHING ABOUT THIS.
OKAY, BUT I WANT YOU TO KNOW THAT I'M BRINGING MY PEPPER SPRAY!
©1998 Brett Merhar.
Distributed by King Features Syndicate
9-21
MERHAR

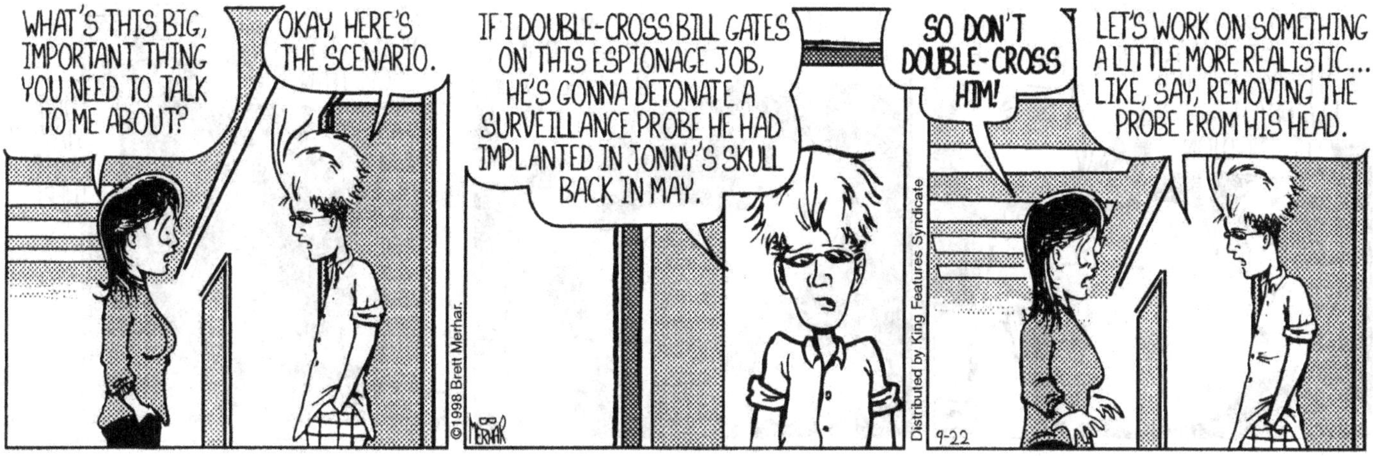
WHAT'S THIS BIG, IMPORTANT THING YOU NEED TO TALK TO ME ABOUT?
OKAY, HERE'S THE SCENARIO.
©1998 Brett Merhar.
IF I DOUBLE-CROSS BILL GATES ON THIS ESPIONAGE JOB, HE'S GONNA DETONATE A SURVEILLANCE PROBE HE HAD IMPLANTED IN JONNY'S SKULL BACK IN MAY.
Distributed by King Features Syndicate
SO DON'T DOUBLE-CROSS HIM!
LET'S WORK ON SOMETHING A LITTLE MORE REALISTIC... LIKE, SAY, REMOVING THE PROBE FROM HIS HEAD.
9-22

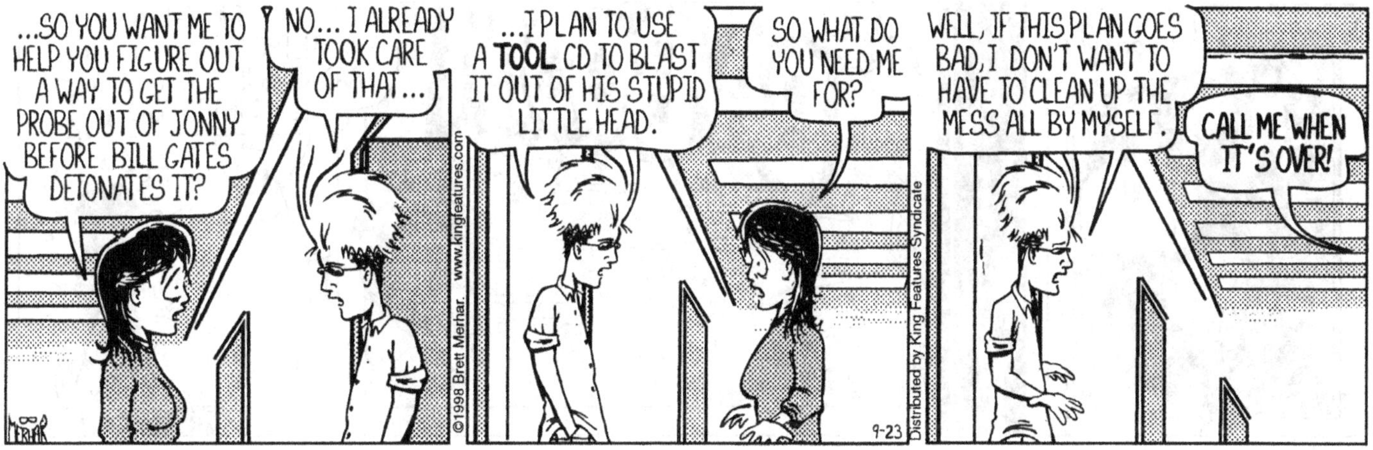
...SO YOU WANT ME TO HELP YOU FIGURE OUT A WAY TO GET THE PROBE OUT OF JONNY BEFORE BILL GATES DETONATES IT?
NO... I ALREADY TOOK CARE OF THAT...
©1998 Brett Merhar. www.kingfeatures.com
...I PLAN TO USE A TOOL CD TO BLAST IT OUT OF HIS STUPID LITTLE HEAD.
SO WHAT DO YOU NEED ME FOR?
9-23
Distributed by King Features Syndicate
WELL, IF THIS PLAN GOES BAD, I DON'T WANT TO HAVE TO CLEAN UP THE MESS ALL BY MYSELF.
CALL ME WHEN IT'S OVER!

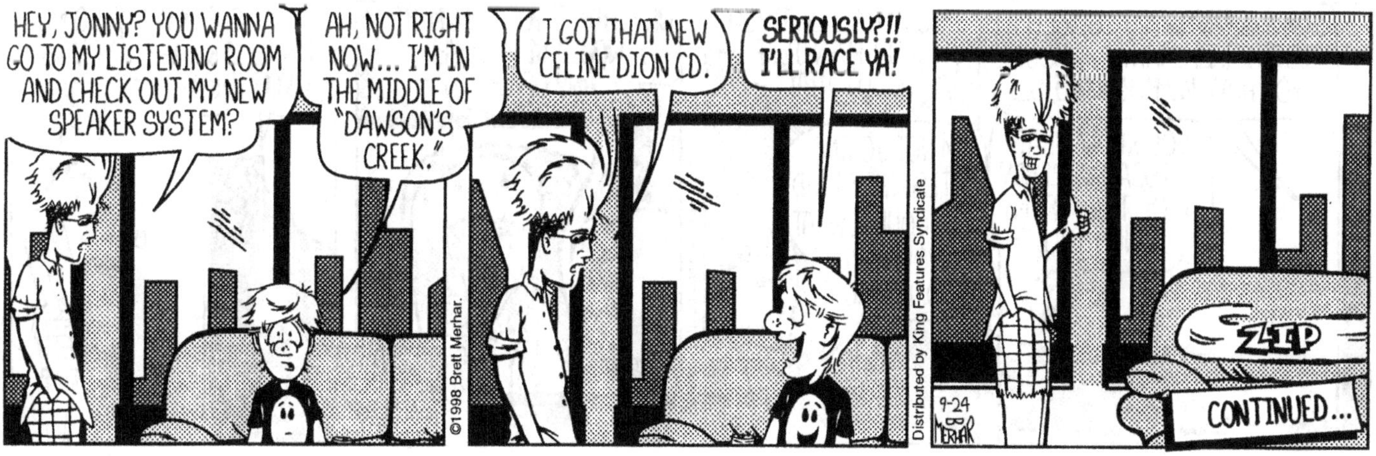
HEY, JONNY? YOU WANNA GO TO MY LISTENING ROOM AND CHECK OUT MY NEW SPEAKER SYSTEM?
AH, NOT RIGHT NOW... I'M IN THE MIDDLE OF "DAWSON'S CREEK."
©1998 Brett Merhar.
I GOT THAT NEW CELINE DION CD.
SERIOUSLY?!! I'LL RACE YA!
Distributed by King Features Syndicate
ZIP
9-24
CONTINUED...

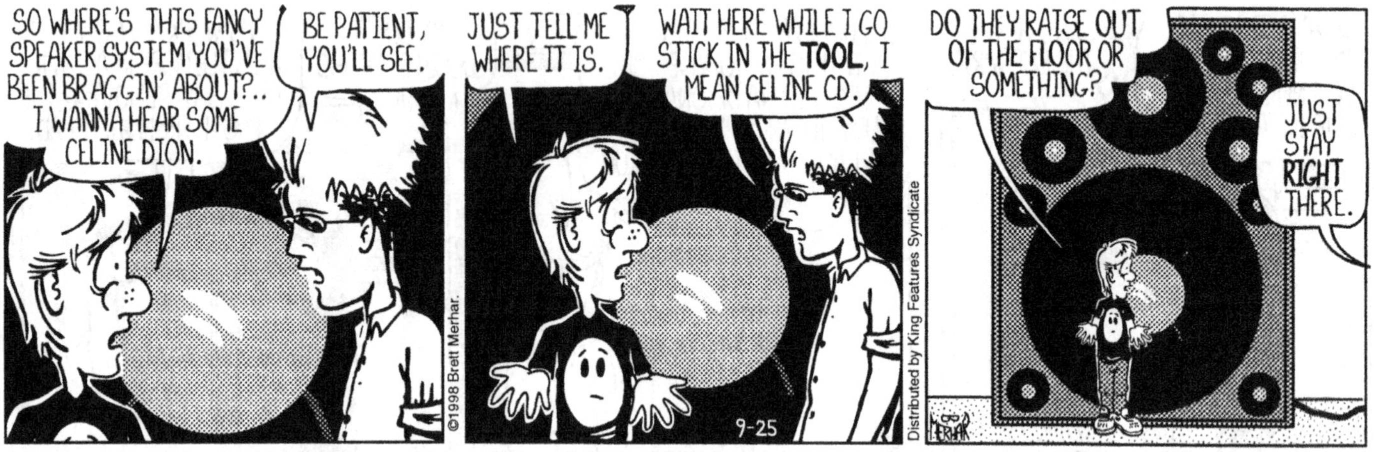
SO WHERE'S THIS FANCY SPEAKER SYSTEM YOU'VE BEEN BRAGGIN' ABOUT?.. I WANNA HEAR SOME CELINE DION.
BE PATIENT, YOU'LL SEE.
©1998 Brett Merhar.
JUST TELL ME WHERE IT IS.
WAIT HERE WHILE I GO STICK IN THE TOOL, I MEAN CELINE CD.
9-25
Distributed by King Features Syndicate
DO THEY RAISE OUT OF THE FLOOR OR SOMETHING?
JUST STAY RIGHT THERE.
MERHAR

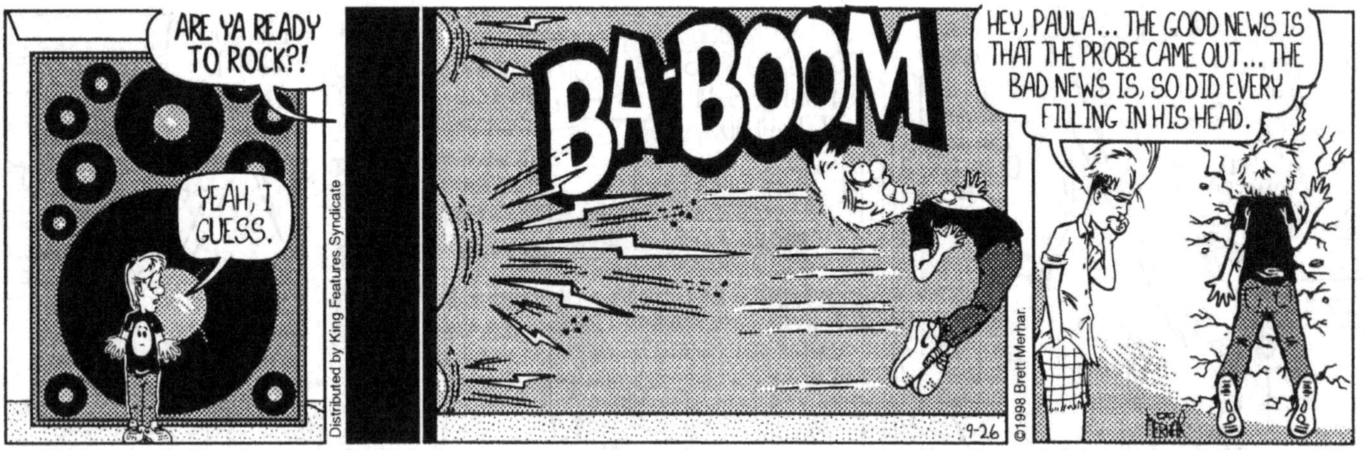
ARE YA READY TO ROCK?!
YEAH, I GUESS.
Distributed by King Features Syndicate
BA-BOOM
9-26
©1998 Brett Merhar.
HEY, PAULA... THE GOOD NEWS IS THAT THE PROBE CAME OUT... THE BAD NEWS IS, SO DID EVERY FILLING IN HIS HEAD.
MERHAR

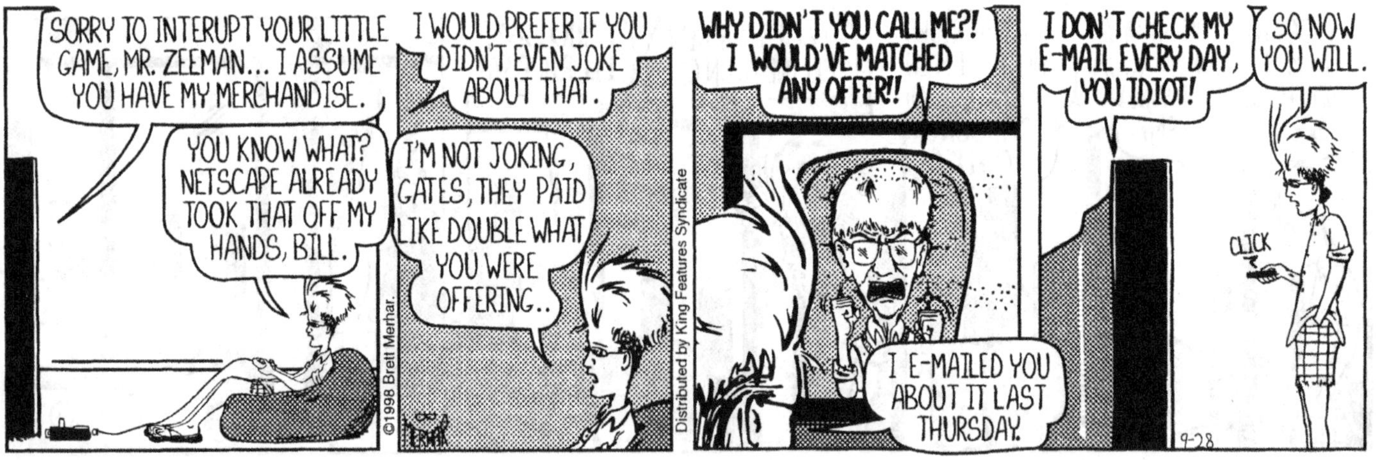
SORRY TO INTERUPT YOUR LITTLE GAME, MR. ZEEMAN... I ASSUME YOU HAVE MY MERCHANDISE.
YOU KNOW WHAT? NETSCAPE ALREADY TOOK THAT OFF MY HANDS, BILL.
©1998 Brett Merhar.
I WOULD PREFER IF YOU DIDN'T EVEN JOKE ABOUT THAT.
I'M NOT JOKING, GATES, THEY PAID LIKE DOUBLE WHAT YOU WERE OFFERING..
MERHAR
Distributed by King Features Syndicate
WHY DIDN'T YOU CALL ME?! I WOULD'VE MATCHED ANY OFFER!!
I E-MAILED YOU ABOUT IT LAST THURSDAY.
I DON'T CHECK MY E-MAIL EVERY DAY, YOU IDIOT!
SO NOW YOU WILL.
CLICK
9-28

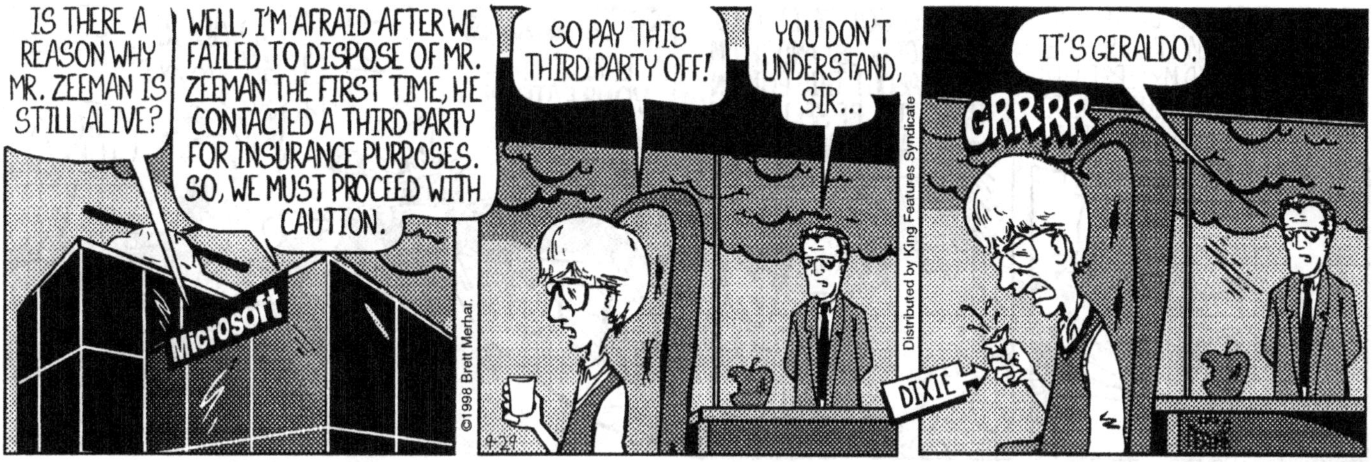
IS THERE A REASON WHY MR. ZEEMAN IS STILL ALIVE?
WELL, I'M AFRAID AFTER WE FAILED TO DISPOSE OF MR. ZEEMAN THE FIRST TIME, HE CONTACTED A THIRD PARTY FOR INSURANCE PURPOSES. SO, WE MUST PROCEED WITH CAUTION.
Microsoft
©1998 Brett Merhar.
4-29
SO PAY THIS THIRD PARTY OFF!
YOU DON'T UNDERSTAND, SIR...
Distributed by King Features Syndicate
GRRRR
IT'S GERALDO.
DIXIE

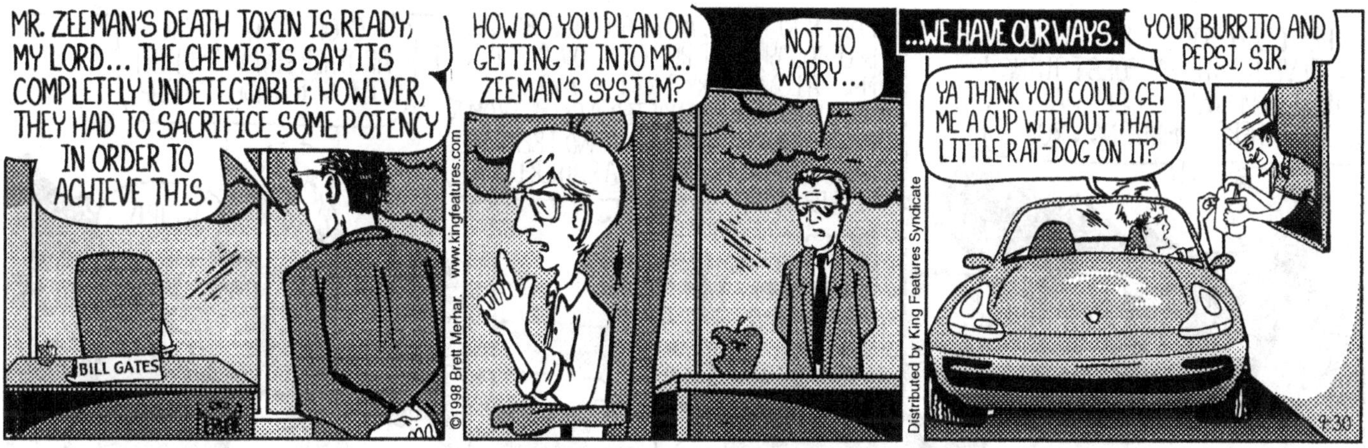
MR. ZEEMAN'S DEATH TOXIN IS READY, MY LORD... THE CHEMISTS SAY ITS COMPLETELY UNDETECTABLE; HOWEVER, THEY HAD TO SACRIFICE SOME POTENCY IN ORDER TO ACHIEVE THIS.
BILL GATES
©1998 Brett Merhar. www.kingfeatures.com
HOW DO YOU PLAN ON GETTING IT INTO MR.. ZEEMAN'S SYSTEM?
NOT TO WORRY...
Distributed by King Features Syndicate
...WE HAVE OUR WAYS.
YOUR BURRITO AND PEPSI, SIR.
YA THINK YOU COULD GET ME A CUP WITHOUT THAT LITTLE RAT-DOG ON IT?
4-30

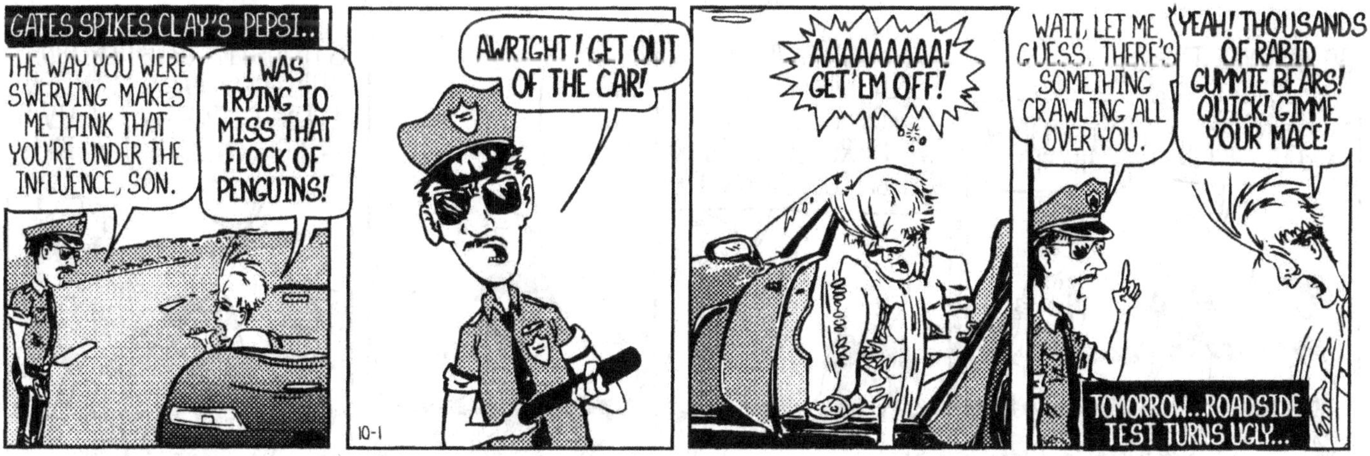
GATES SPIKES CLAY'S PEPSI..
THE WAY YOU WERE SWERVING MAKES ME THINK THAT YOU'RE UNDER THE INFLUENCE, SON.
I WAS TRYING TO MISS THAT FLOCK OF PENGUINS!
AWRIGHT! GET OUT OF THE CAR!
10-1
AAAAAAAAA! GET'EM OFF!
WAIT, LET ME GUESS. THERE'S SOMETHING CRAWLING ALL OVER YOU.
YEAH! THOUSANDS OF RABID GUMMIE BEARS! QUICK! GIMME YOUR MACE!
TOMORROW...ROADSIDE TEST TURNS UGLY...

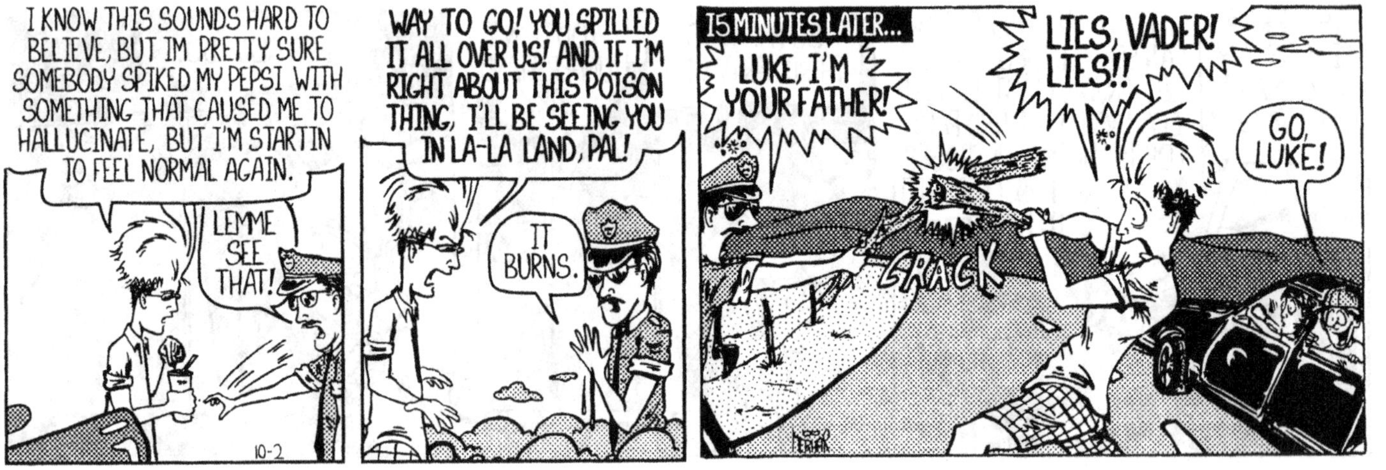
I KNOW THIS SOUNDS HARD TO BELIEVE, BUT IM PRETTY SURE SOMEBODY SPIKED MY PEPSI WITH SOMETHING THAT CAUSED ME TO HALLUCINATE, BUT I'M STARTIN TO FEEL NORMAL AGAIN.
LEMME SEE THAT!
10-2
WAY TO GO! YOU SPILLED IT ALL OVER US! AND IF I'M RIGHT ABOUT THIS POISON THING, I'LL BE SEEING YOU IN LA-LA LAND, PAL!
IT BURNS.
15 MINUTES LATER...
LUKE, I'M YOUR FATHER!
LIES, VADER! LIES!!
GO, LUKE!
CRACK
MERHAR

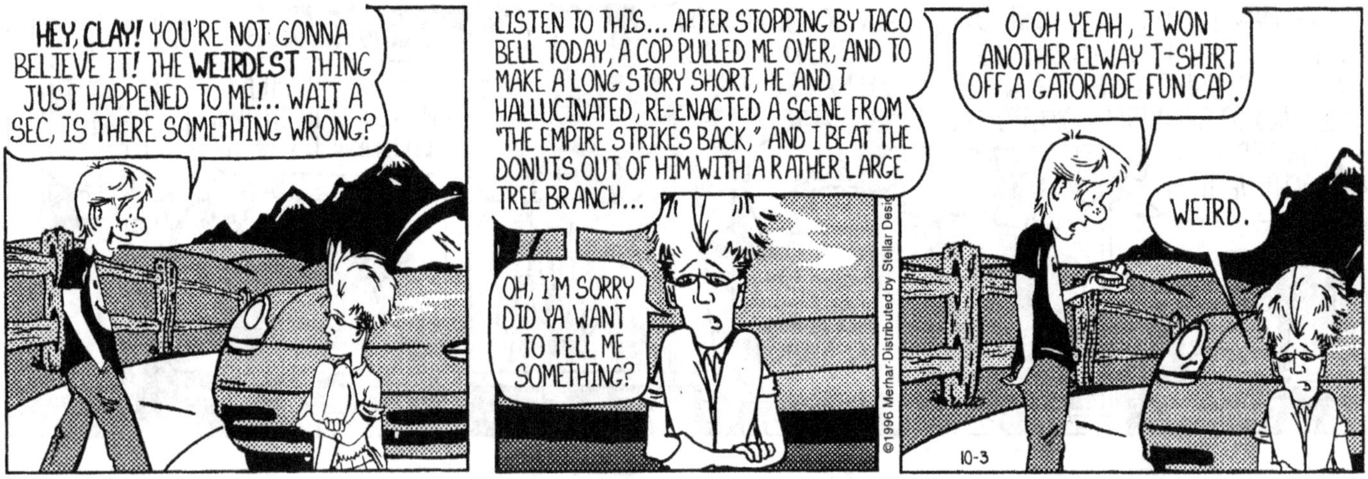
HEY, CLAY! YOU'RE NOT GONNA BELIEVE IT! THE WEIRDEST THING JUST HAPPENED TO ME!.. WAIT A SEC, IS THERE SOMETHING WRONG?
LISTEN TO THIS... AFTER STOPPING BY TACO BELL TODAY, A COP PULLED ME OVER, AND TO MAKE A LONG STORY SHORT, HE AND I HALLUCINATED, RE-ENACTED A SCENE FROM "THE EMPIRE STRIKES BACK," AND I BEAT THE DONUTS OUT OF HIM WITH A RATHER LARGE TREE BRANCH...
OH, I'M SORRY DID YA WANT TO TELL ME SOMETHING?
©1996 Merhar-Distributed by Stellar Desig
O-OH YEAH, I WON ANOTHER ELWAY T-SHIRT OFF A GATORADE FUN CAP.
WEIRD.
10-3

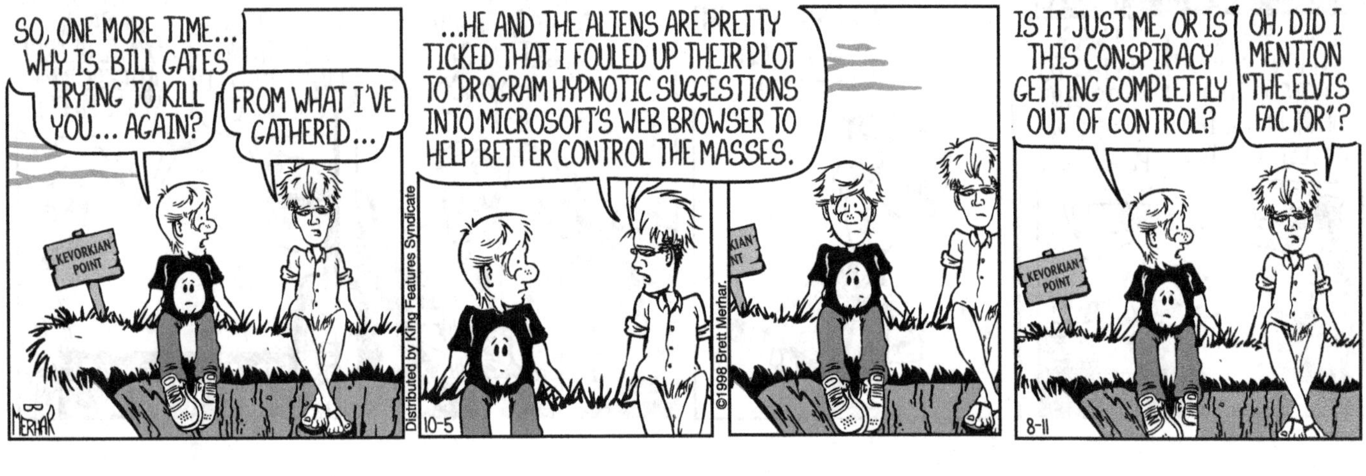
SO, ONE MORE TIME... WHY IS BILL GATES TRYING TO KILL YOU... AGAIN?
FROM WHAT I'VE GATHERED...
KEVORKIAN POINT
MERHAR
Distributed by King Features Syndicate
...HE AND THE ALIENS ARE PRETTY TICKED THAT I FOULED UP THEIR PLOT TO PROGRAM HYPNOTIC SUGGESTIONS INTO MICROSOFT'S WEB BROWSER TO HELP BETTER CONTROL THE MASSES.
10-5
©1998 Brett Merhar.
IS IT JUST ME, OR IS THIS CONSPIRACY GETTING COMPLETELY OUT OF CONTROL?
OH, DID I MENTION "THE ELVIS FACTOR"?
KEVORKIAN POINT
8-11

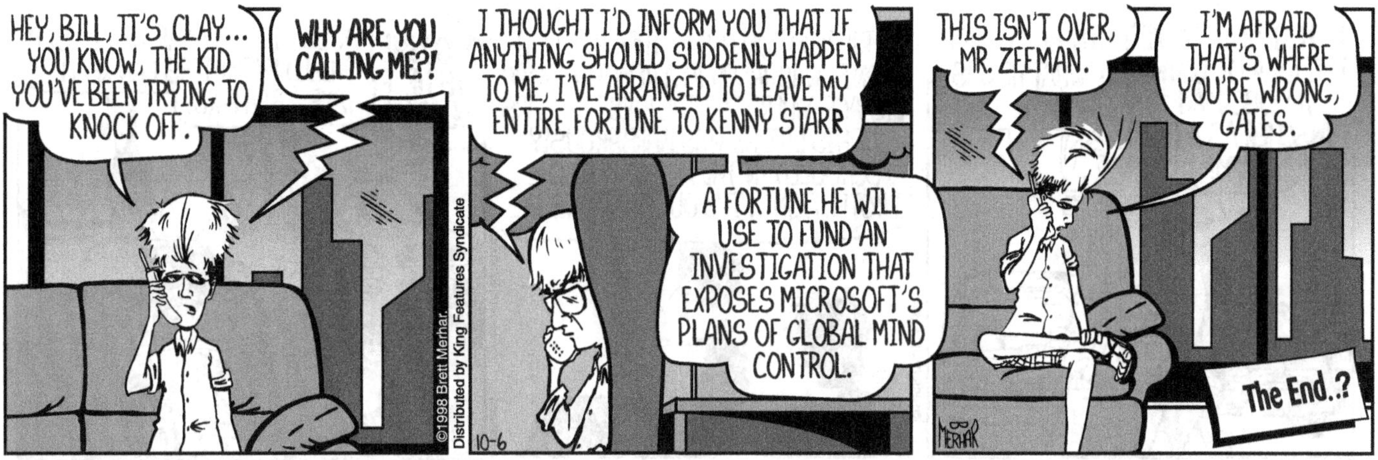
HEY, BILL, IT'S CLAY... YOU KNOW, THE KID YOU'VE BEEN TRYING TO KNOCK OFF.
WHY ARE YOU CALLING ME?!
©1998 Brett Merhar.
Distributed by King Features Syndicate
10-6
I THOUGHT I'D INFORM YOU THAT IF ANYTHING SHOULD SUDDENLY HAPPEN TO ME, I'VE ARRANGED TO LEAVE MY ENTIRE FORTUNE TO KENNY STARR
A FORTUNE HE WILL USE TO FUND AN INVESTIGATION THAT EXPOSES MICROSOFT'S PLANS OF GLOBAL MIND CONTROL.
THIS ISN'T OVER, MR. ZEEMAN.
I'M AFRAID THAT'S WHERE YOU'RE WRONG, GATES.
The End..?
MERHAR

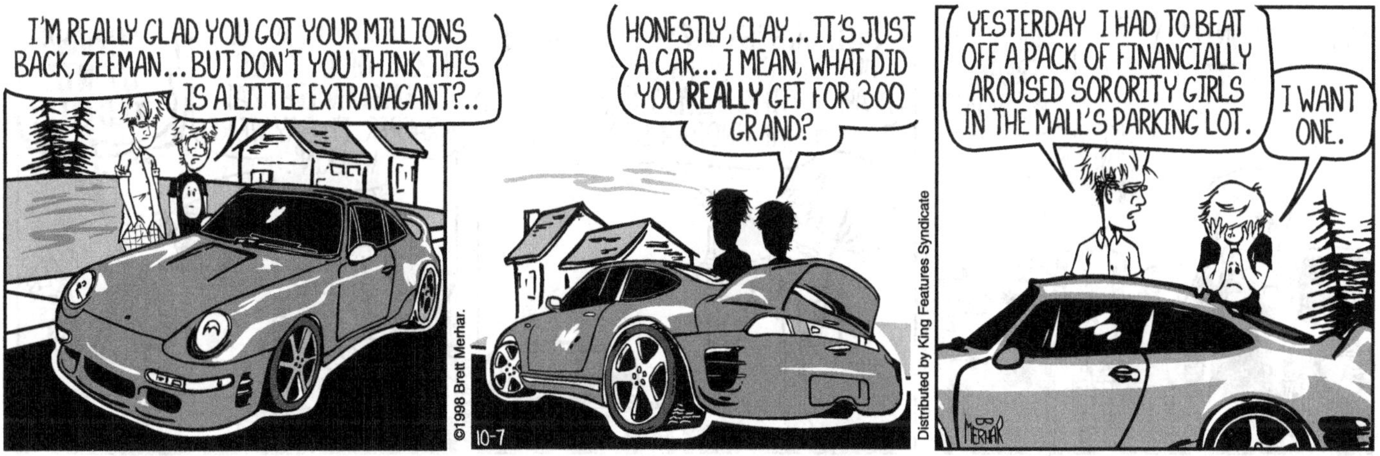
I'M REALLY GLAD YOU GOT YOUR MILLIONS BACK, ZEEMAN... BUT DON'T YOU THINK THIS IS A LITTLE EXTRAVAGANT?..
©1998 Brett Merhar.
10-7
HONESTLY, CLAY... IT'S JUST A CAR... I MEAN, WHAT DID YOU REALLY GET FOR 300 GRAND?
Distributed by King Features Syndicate
YESTERDAY I HAD TO BEAT OFF A PACK OF FINANCIALLY AROUSED SORORITY GIRLS IN THE MALL'S PARKING LOT.
I WANT ONE.
MERHAR

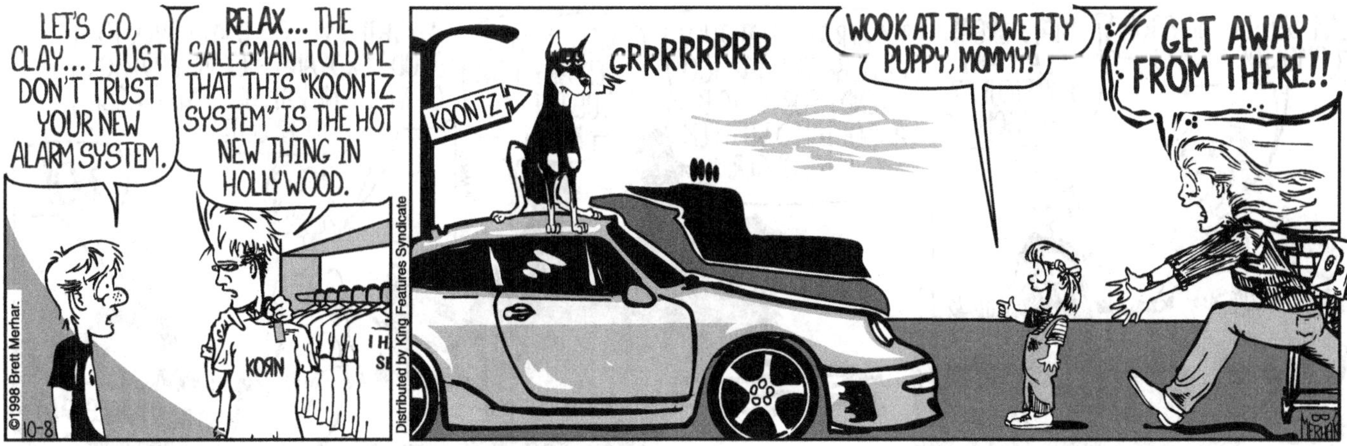
LET'S GO, CLAY... I JUST DON'T TRUST YOUR NEW ALARM SYSTEM.
RELAX... THE SALESMAN TOLD ME THAT THIS "KOONTZ SYSTEM" IS THE HOT NEW THING IN HOLLYWOOD.
KORN
©1998 Brett Merhar.
10-8
Distributed by King Features Syndicate
KOONTZ
GRRRRRRRR
WOOK AT THE PWETTY PUPPY, MOMMY!
GET AWAY FROM THERE!!
MERHAR

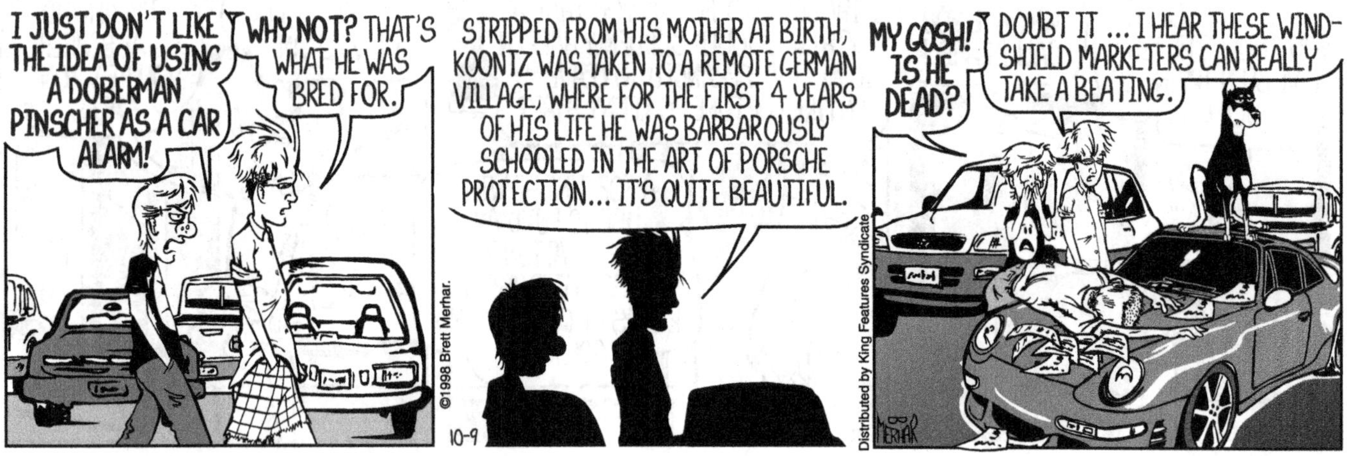
I JUST DON'T LIKE THE IDEA OF USING A DOBERMAN PINSCHER AS A CAR ALARM!
WHY NOT? THAT'S WHAT HE WAS BRED FOR.
©1998 Brett Merhar.
10-9
STRIPPED FROM HIS MOTHER AT BIRTH, KOONTZ WAS TAKEN TO A REMOTE GERMAN VILLAGE, WHERE FOR THE FIRST 4 YEARS OF HIS LIFE HE WAS BARBAROUSLY SCHOOLED IN THE ART OF PORSCHE PROTECTION... IT'S QUITE BEAUTIFUL.
Distributed by King Features Syndicate
MY GOSH! IS HE DEAD?
DOUBT IT ... I HEAR THESE WIND-SHIELD MARKETERS CAN REALLY TAKE A BEATING.
MERHAR

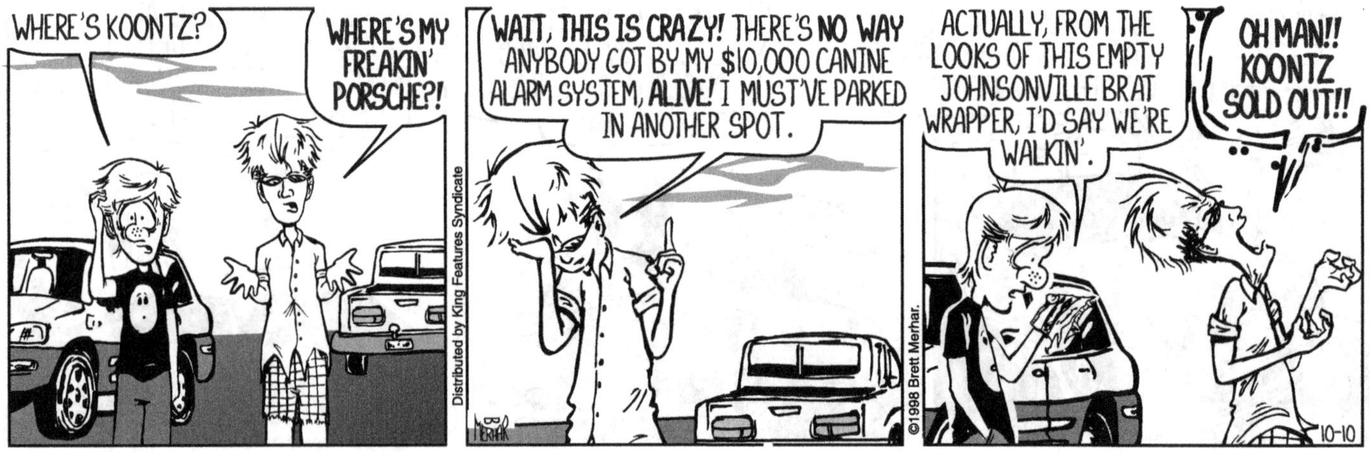
WHERE'S KOONTZ?
WHERE'S MY FREAKIN' PORSCHE?!
Distributed by King Features Syndicate
WAIT, THIS IS CRAZY! THERE'S NO WAY ANYBODY GOT BY MY $10,000 CANINE ALARM SYSTEM, ALIVE! I MUST'VE PARKED IN ANOTHER SPOT.
MERHAR
©1998 Brett Merhar.
ACTUALLY, FROM THE LOOKS OF THIS EMPTY JOHNSONVILLE BRAT WRAPPER, I'D SAY WE'RE WALKIN'.
OH MAN!! KOONTZ SOLD OUT!!
10-10

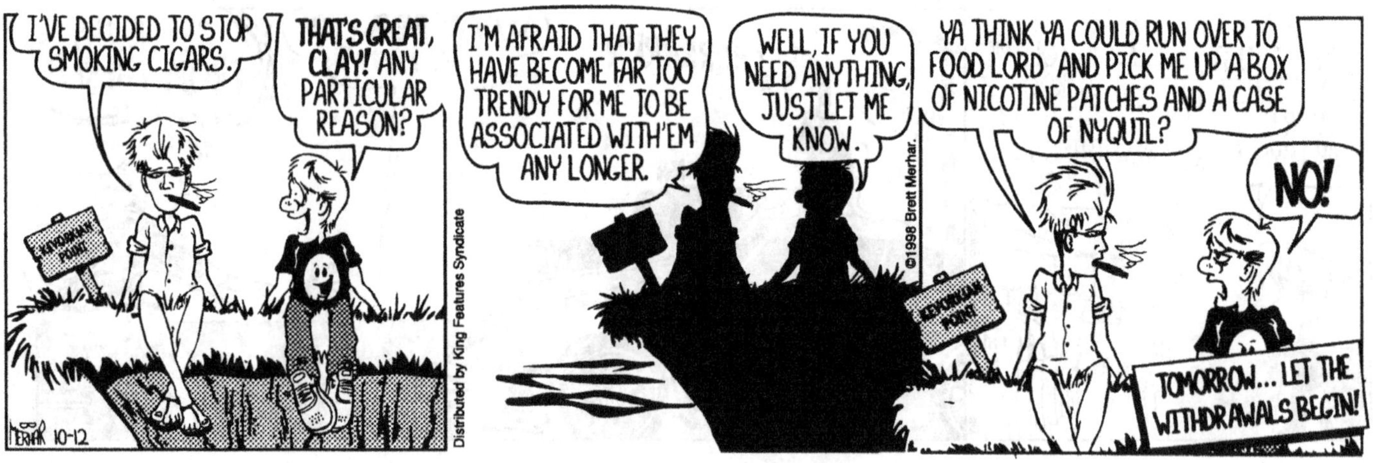
I'VE DECIDED TO STOP SMOKING CIGARS.
THAT'S GREAT, CLAY! ANY PARTICULAR REASON?
MERHAR 10-12
Distributed by King Features Syndicate
I'M AFRAID THAT THEY HAVE BECOME FAR TOO TRENDY FOR ME TO BE ASSOCIATED WITH'EM ANY LONGER.
WELL, IF YOU NEED ANYTHING, JUST LET ME KNOW.
©1998 Brett Merhar.
YA THINK YA COULD RUN OVER TO FOOD LORD AND PICK ME UP A BOX OF NICOTINE PATCHES AND A CASE OF NYQUIL?
NO!
TOMORROW... LET THE WITHDRAWALS BEGIN!

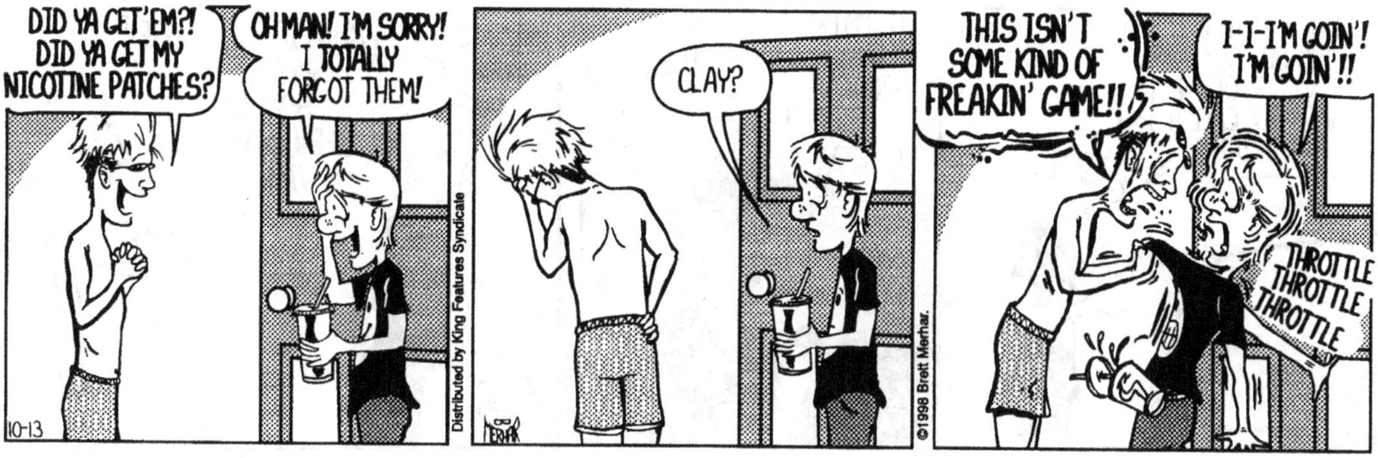
DID YA GET 'EM?! DID YA GET MY NICOTINE PATCHES?
OH MAN! I'M SORRY! I TOTALLY FORGOT THEM!
CLAY?
THIS ISN'T SOME KIND OF FREAKIN' GAME!!
I-I-I'M GOIN'! I'M GOIN'!!
THROTTLE THROTTLE THROTTLE
10-13
Distributed by King Features Syndicate
MERHAR
©1998 Brett Merhar.

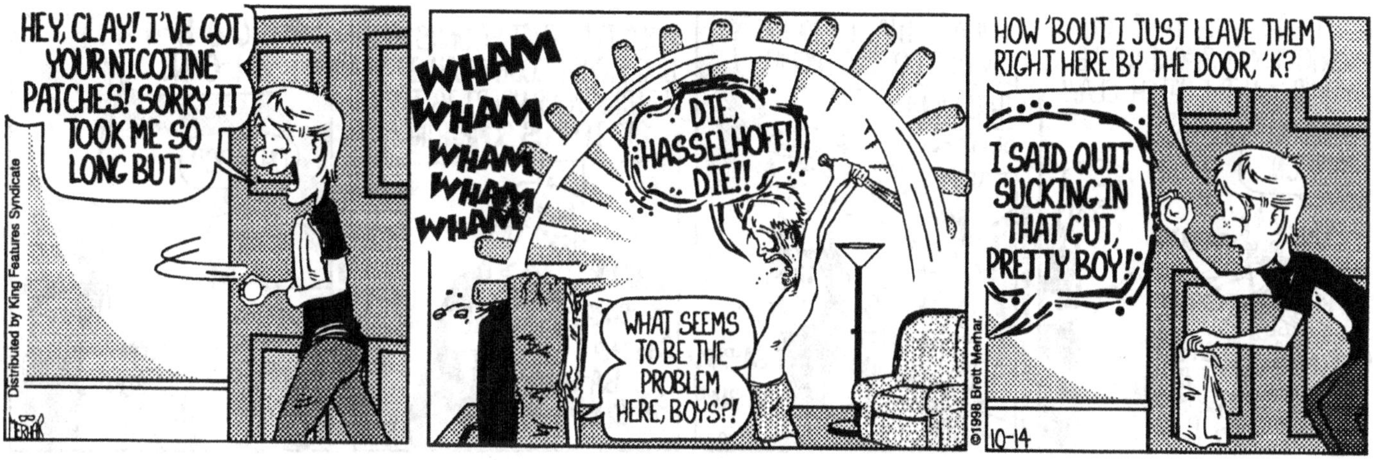
HEY, CLAY! I'VE GOT YOUR NICOTINE PATCHES! SORRY IT TOOK ME SO LONG BUT-
WHAM WHAM WHAM WHAM WHAM
DIE, HASSELHOFF! DIE!!
WHAT SEEMS TO BE THE PROBLEM HERE, BOYS?!
HOW 'BOUT I JUST LEAVE THEM RIGHT HERE BY THE DOOR, 'K?
I SAID QUIT SUCKING IN THAT GUT, PRETTY BOY!
Distributed by King Features Syndicate
MERHAR
©1998 Brett Merhar.
10-14

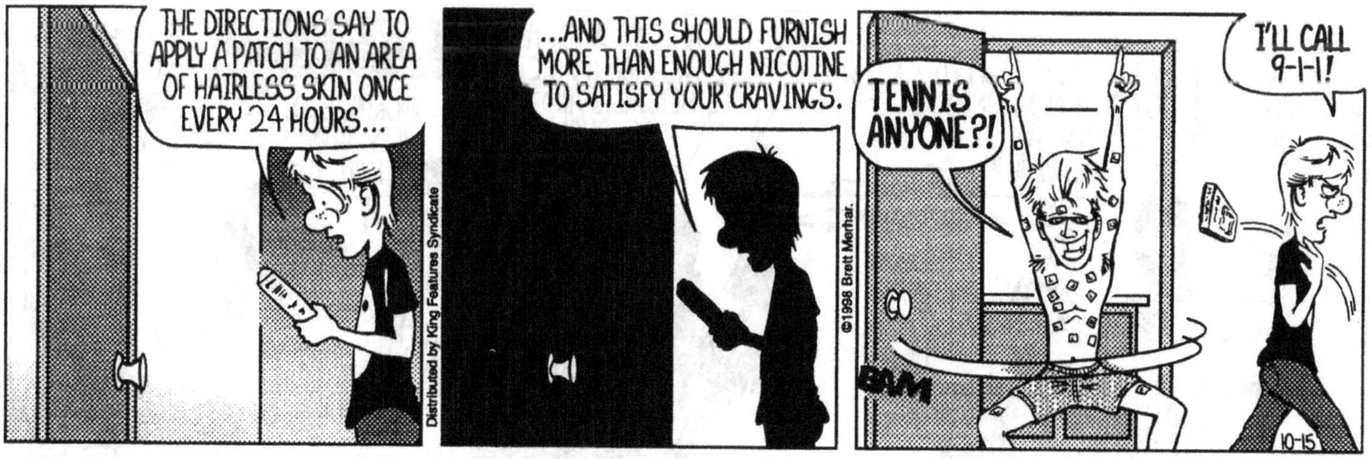
THE DIRECTIONS SAY TO APPLY A PATCH TO AN AREA OF HAIRLESS SKIN ONCE EVERY 24 HOURS...
...AND THIS SHOULD FURNISH MORE THAN ENOUGH NICOTINE TO SATISFY YOUR CRAVINGS.
TENNIS ANYONE?!
I'LL CALL 9-1-1!
BAM
Distributed by King Features Syndicate
©1998 Brett Merhar.
10-15

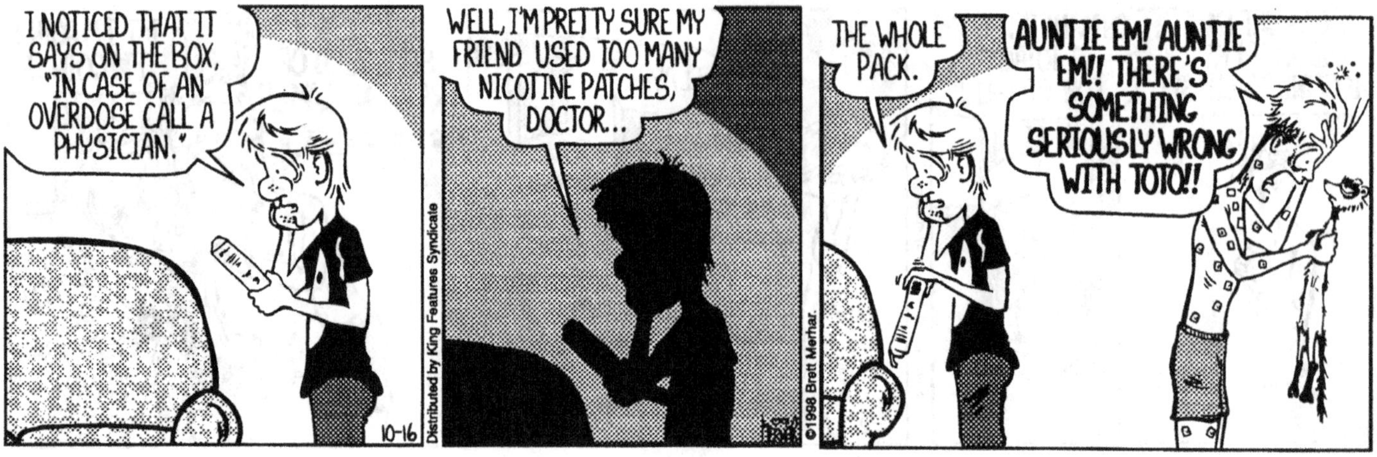
I NOTICED THAT IT SAYS ON THE BOX, "IN CASE OF AN OVERDOSE CALL A PHYSICIAN."
10-16
Distributed by King Features Syndicate
WELL, I'M PRETTY SURE MY FRIEND USED TOO MANY NICOTINE PATCHES, DOCTOR...
©1998 Brett Merhar.
THE WHOLE PACK.
AUNTIE EM! AUNTIE EM!! THERE'S SOMETHING SERIOUSLY WRONG WITH TOTO!!

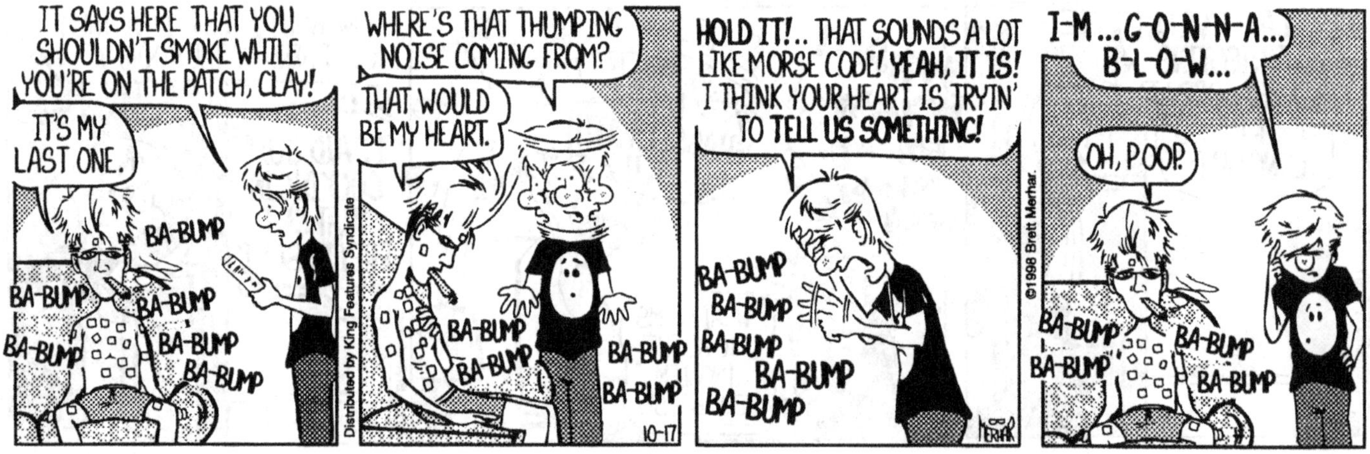
IT SAYS HERE THAT YOU SHOULDN'T SMOKE WHILE YOU'RE ON THE PATCH, CLAY!
IT'S MY LAST ONE.
BA-BUMP
BA-BUMP
BA-BUMP
BA-BUMP
BA-BUMP
BA-BUMP
Distributed by King Features Syndicate
WHERE'S THAT THUMPING NOISE COMING FROM?
THAT WOULD BE MY HEART.
BA-BUMP
BA-BUMP
BA-BUMP
BA-BUMP
10-17
HOLD IT!.. THAT SOUNDS A LOT LIKE MORSE CODE! YEAH, IT IS! I THINK YOUR HEART IS TRYIN' TO TELL US SOMETHING!
BA-BUMP
BA-BUMP
BA-BUMP
BA-BUMP
BA-BUMP
MERHAR
©1998 Brett Merhar.
I-M...G-O-N-N-A... B-L-O-W...
OH, POOP.
BA-BUMP
BA-BUMP
BA-BUMP
BA-BUMP

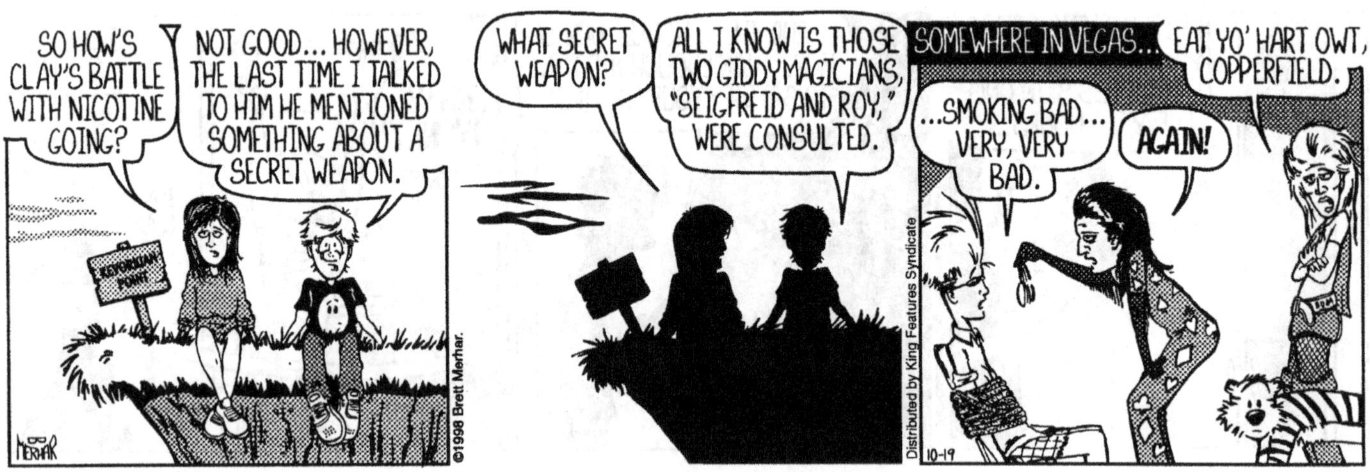
SO HOW'S CLAY'S BATTLE WITH NICOTINE GOING?
NOT GOOD... HOWEVER, THE LAST TIME I TALKED TO HIM HE MENTIONED SOMETHING ABOUT A SECRET WEAPON.
MERHAR
©1998 Brett Merhar.
WHAT SECRET WEAPON?
ALL I KNOW IS THOSE TWO GIDDY MAGICIANS, "SEIGFREID AND ROY," WERE CONSULTED.
Distributed by King Features Syndicate
SOMEWHERE IN VEGAS...
EAT YO' HART OWT, COPPERFIELD.
...SMOKING BAD... VERY, VERY BAD.
AGAIN!
10-19

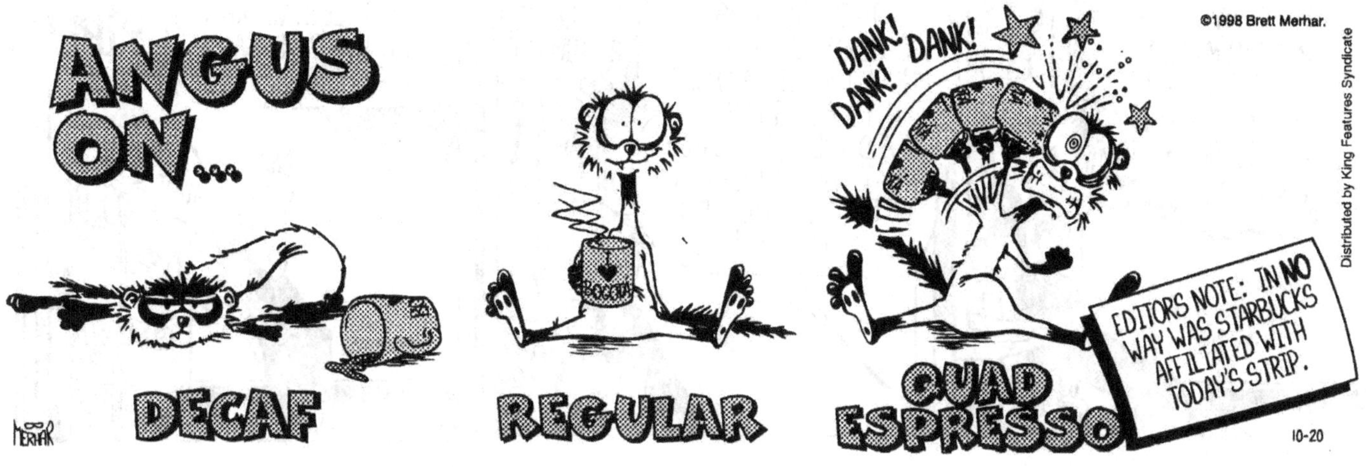

ANGUS ON...
DECAF
REGULAR
BOGOTA
DANK! DANK! DANK!
QUAD ESPRESSO
EDITORS NOTE: IN NO WAY WAS STARBUCKS AFFILIATED WITH TODAY'S STRIP.
©1998 Brett Merhar.
Distributed by King Features Syndicate
MERHAR
10-20

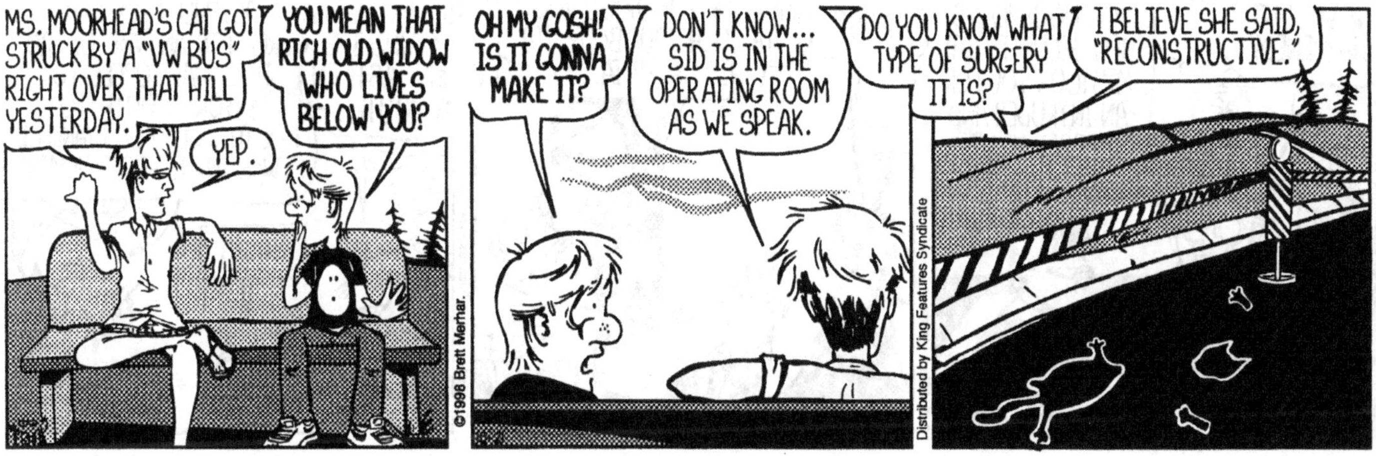

MS. MOORHEAD'S CAT GOT STRUCK BY A "VW BUS" RIGHT OVER THAT HILL YESTERDAY.
YOU MEAN THAT RICH OLD WIDOW WHO LIVES BELOW YOU?
YEP.
OH MY GOSH! IS IT GONNA MAKE IT?
DON'T KNOW... SID IS IN THE OPERATING ROOM AS WE SPEAK.
DO YOU KNOW WHAT TYPE OF SURGERY IT IS?
I BELIEVE SHE SAID, "RECONSTRUCTIVE."
©1998 Brett Merhar.
Distributed by King Features Syndicate

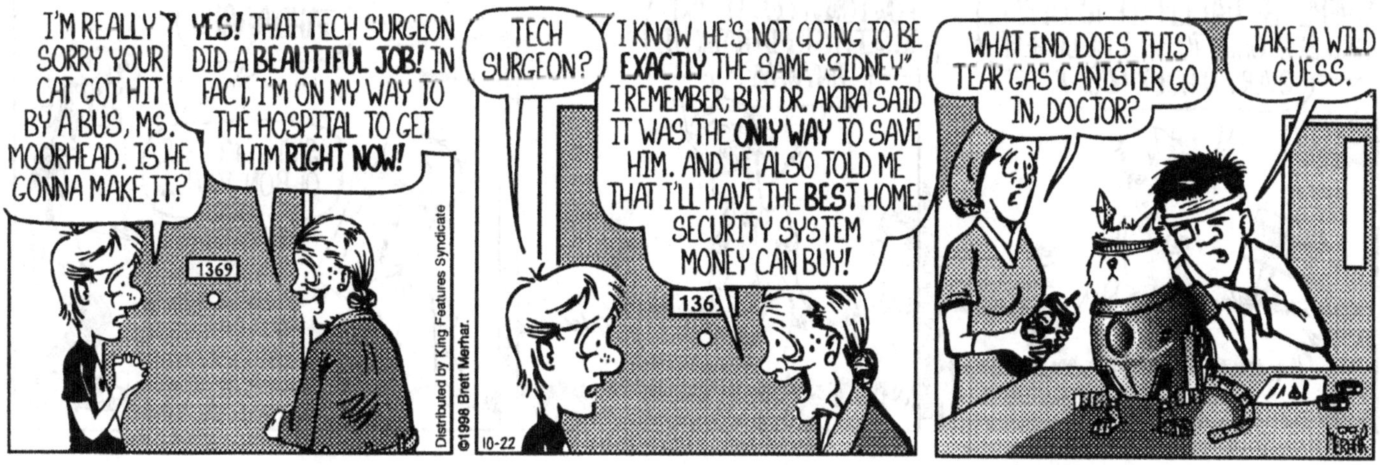

I'M REALLY SORRY YOUR CAT GOT HIT BY A BUS, MS. MOORHEAD. IS HE GONNA MAKE IT?
YES! THAT TECH SURGEON DID A BEAUTIFUL JOB! IN FACT, I'M ON MY WAY TO THE HOSPITAL TO GET HIM RIGHT NOW!
1369
TECH SURGEON?
I KNOW HE'S NOT GOING TO BE EXACTLY THE SAME "SIDNEY" I REMEMBER, BUT DR. AKIRA SAID IT WAS THE ONLY WAY TO SAVE HIM. AND HE ALSO TOLD ME THAT I'LL HAVE THE BEST HOME-SECURITY SYSTEM MONEY CAN BUY!
WHAT END DOES THIS TEAR GAS CANISTER GO IN, DOCTOR?
TAKE A WILD GUESS.
Distributed by King Features Syndicate
©1998 Brett Merhar.
10-22
MERHAR

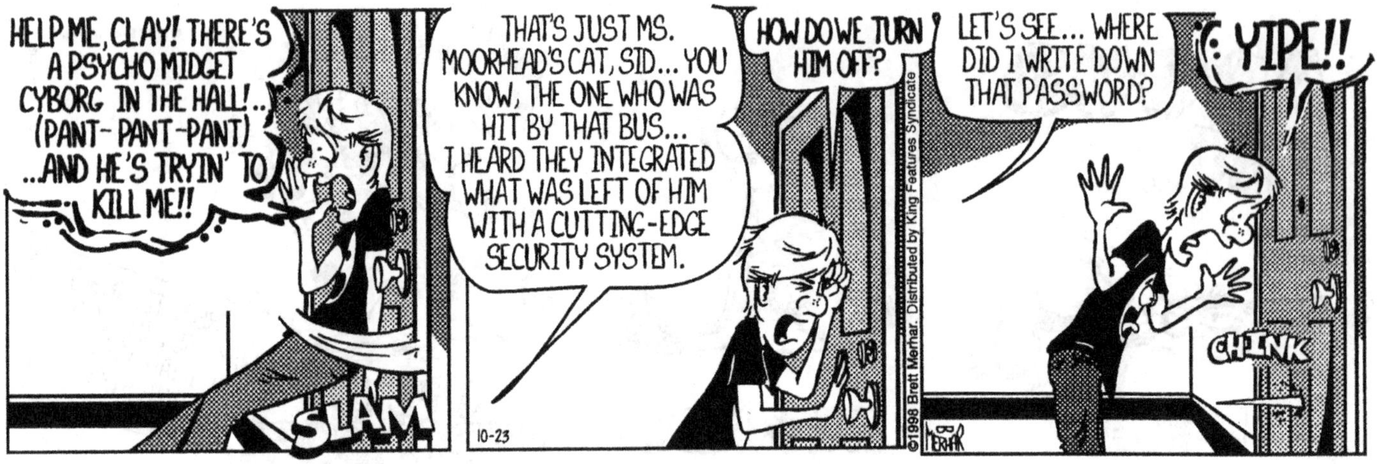
HELP ME, CLAY! THERE'S A PSYCHO MIDGET CYBORG IN THE HALL!.. (PANT-PANT-PANT) ...AND HE'S TRYIN' TO KILL ME!!
SLAM
THAT'S JUST MS. MOORHEAD'S CAT, SID... YOU KNOW, THE ONE WHO WAS HIT BY THAT BUS... I HEARD THEY INTEGRATED WHAT WAS LEFT OF HIM WITH A CUTTING-EDGE SECURITY SYSTEM.
10-23
HOW DO WE TURN HIM OFF?
©1998 Brett Merhar. Distributed by King Features Syndicate
LET'S SEE... WHERE DID I WRITE DOWN THAT PASSWORD?
YIPE!!
CHINK
MERHAR

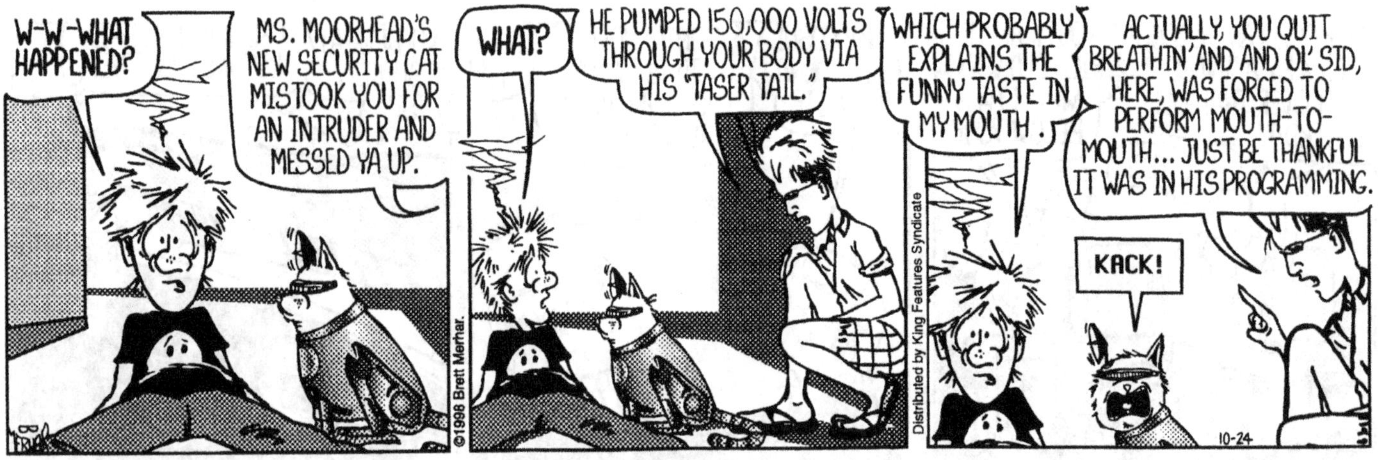
W-W-WHAT HAPPENED?
MS. MOORHEAD'S NEW SECURITY CAT MISTOOK YOU FOR AN INTRUDER AND MESSED YA UP.
MERHAR
©1998 Brett Merhar.
WHAT?
HE PUMPED 150,000 VOLTS THROUGH YOUR BODY VIA HIS "TASER TAIL."
Distributed by King Features Syndicate
WHICH PROBABLY EXPLAINS THE FUNNY TASTE IN MY MOUTH.
ACTUALLY, YOU QUIT BREATHIN' AND AND OL' SID, HERE, WAS FORCED TO PERFORM MOUTH-TO-MOUTH... JUST BE THANKFUL IT WAS IN HIS PROGRAMMING.
KACK!
10-24

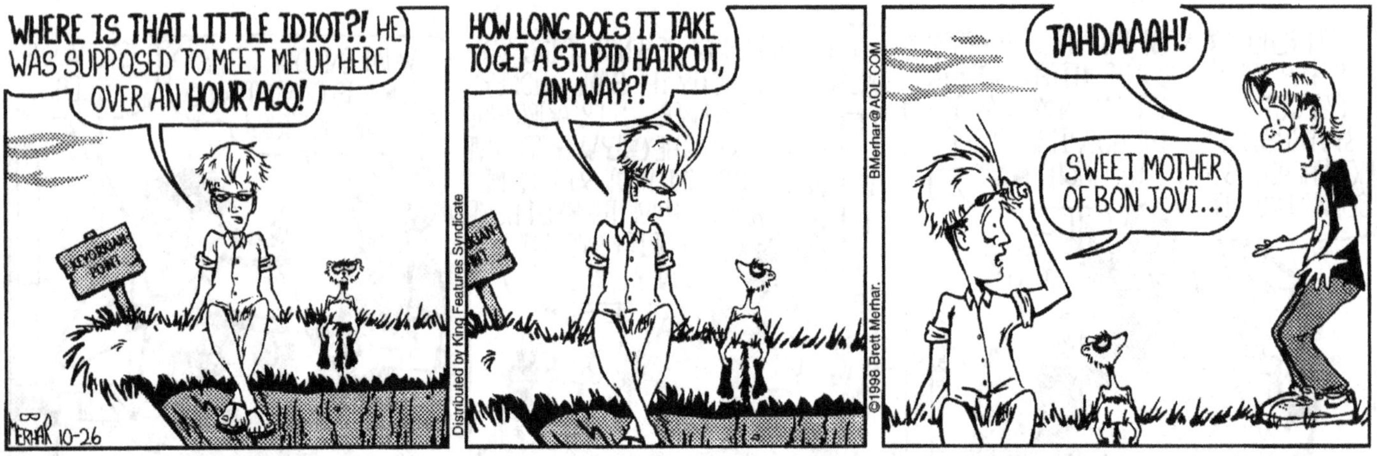
WHERE IS THAT LITTLE IDIOT?! HE WAS SUPPOSED TO MEET ME UP HERE OVER AN HOUR AGO!
KEVORKIAN POINT
MERHAR 10-26
Distributed by King Features Syndicate
HOW LONG DOES IT TAKE TO GET A STUPID HAIRCUT, ANYWAY?!
BMerhar@AOL.COM
©1998 Brett Merhar.
TAHDAAAH!
SWEET MOTHER OF BON JOVI...

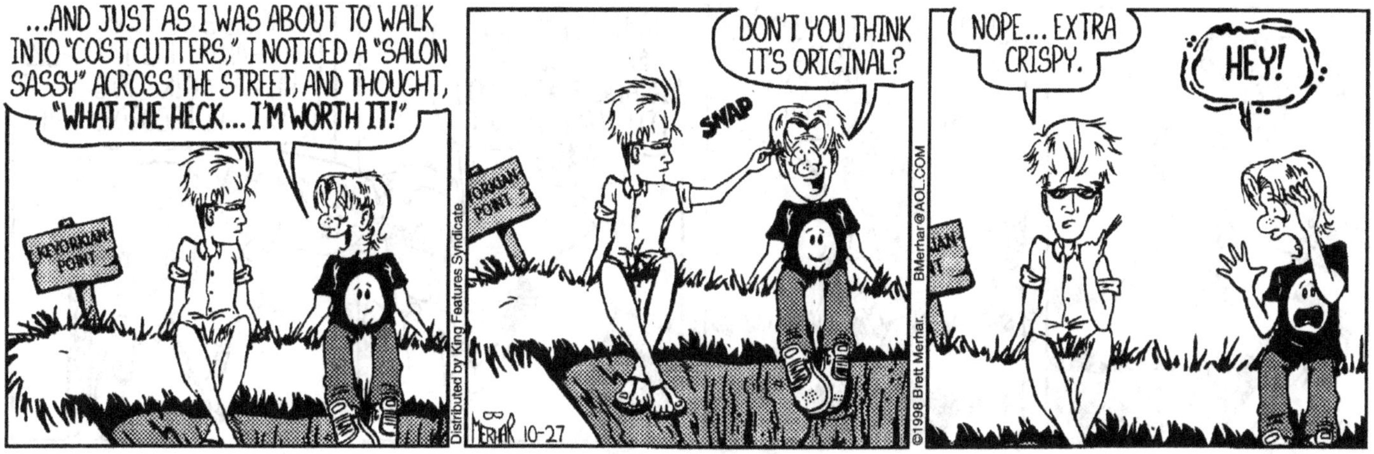
...AND JUST AS I WAS ABOUT TO WALK INTO "COST CUTTERS," I NOTICED A "SALON SASSY" ACROSS THE STREET, AND THOUGHT, "WHAT THE HECK... I'M WORTH IT!"
KEVORKIAN POINT
Distributed by King Features Syndicate
MERHAR 10-27
DON'T YOU THINK IT'S ORIGINAL?
SNAP
©1998 Brett Merhar. BMerhar@AOL.COM
NOPE... EXTRA CRISPY.
HEY!

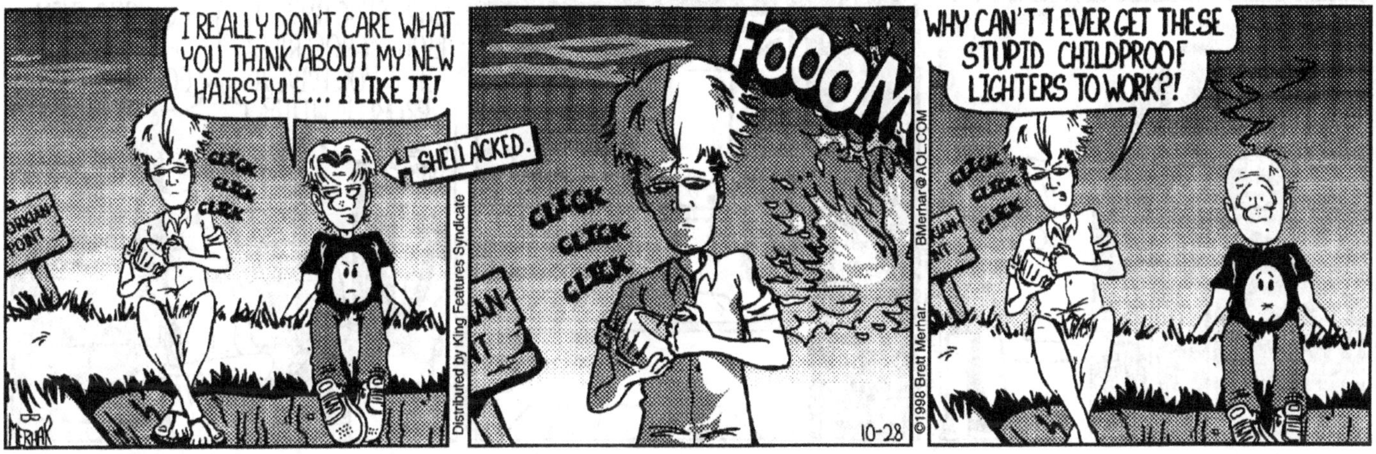
I REALLY DON'T CARE WHAT YOU THINK ABOUT MY NEW HAIRSTYLE... I LIKE IT!
CLICK CLICK CLICK
SHELLACKED.
MERHAR
Distributed by King Features Syndicate
FOOOM
CLICK CLICK CLICK
10-28
©1998 Brett Merhar. BMerhar@AOL.COM
WHY CAN'T I EVER GET THESE STUPID CHILDPROOF LIGHTERS TO WORK?!
CLICK CLICK CLICK

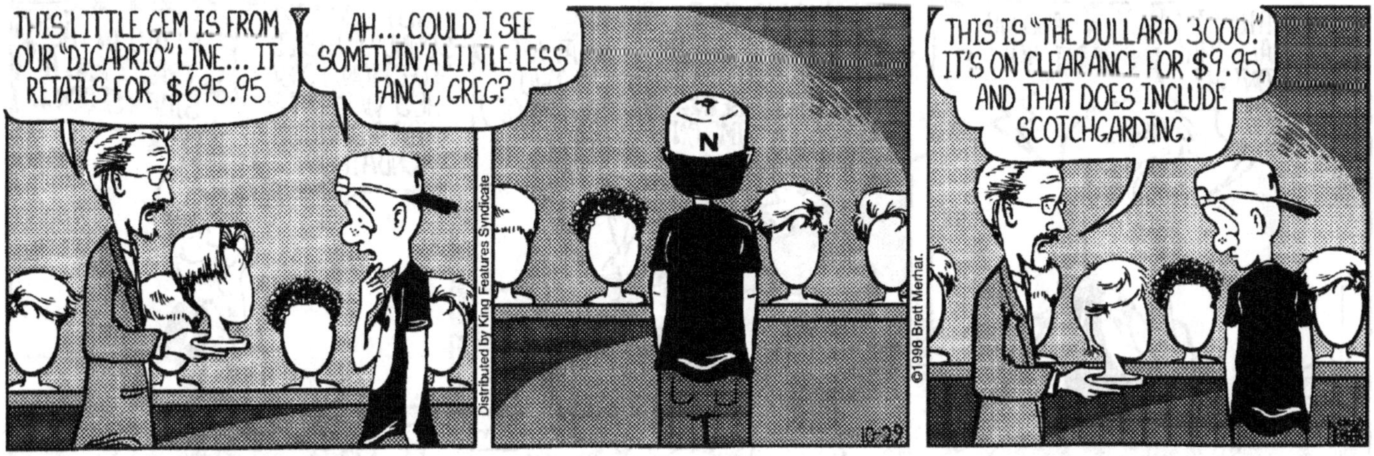
THIS LITTLE GEM IS FROM OUR "DICAPRIO" LINE... IT RETAILS FOR $695.95
AH... COULD I SEE SOMETHIN' A LITTLE LESS FANCY, GREG?
Distributed by King Features Syndicate
N
10-29
©1998 Brett Merhar.
THIS IS "THE DULLARD 3000." IT'S ON CLEARANCE FOR $9.95, AND THAT DOES INCLUDE SCOTCHGARDING.

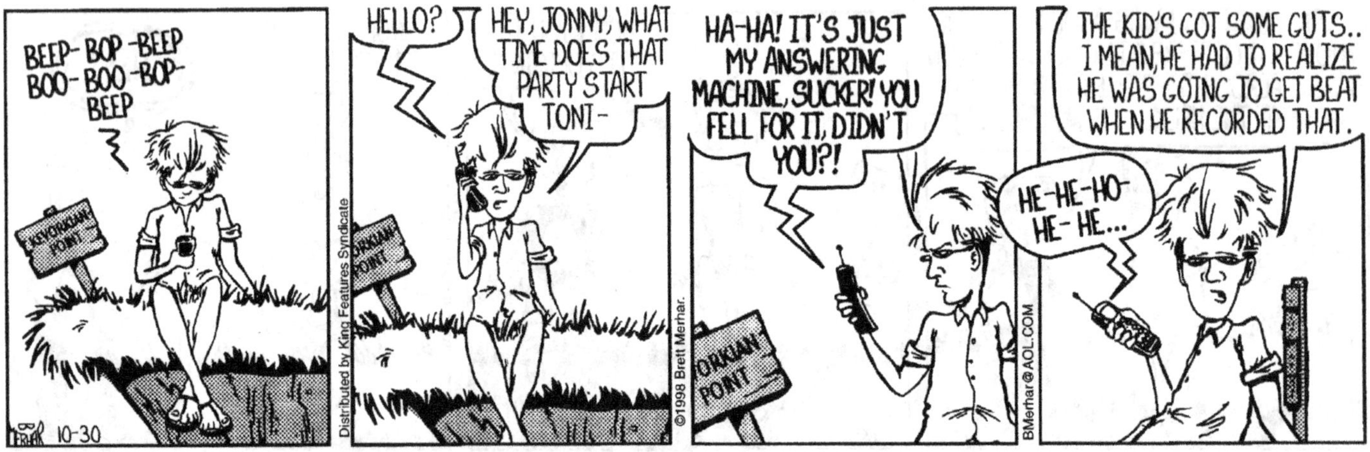
BEEP- BOP -BEEP BOO- BOO -BOP- BEEP
KEVORKIAN POINT
MERHAR 10-30
Distributed by King Features Syndicate
HELLO?
HEY, JONNY, WHAT TIME DOES THAT PARTY START TONI-
©1998 Brett Merhar.
HA-HA! IT'S JUST MY ANSWERING MACHINE, SUCKER! YOU FELL FOR IT, DIDN'T YOU?!
BMerhar@AOL.COM
THE KID'S GOT SOME GUTS.. I MEAN, HE HAD TO REALIZE HE WAS GOING TO GET BEAT WHEN HE RECORDED THAT.
HE-HE-HO- HE- HE...

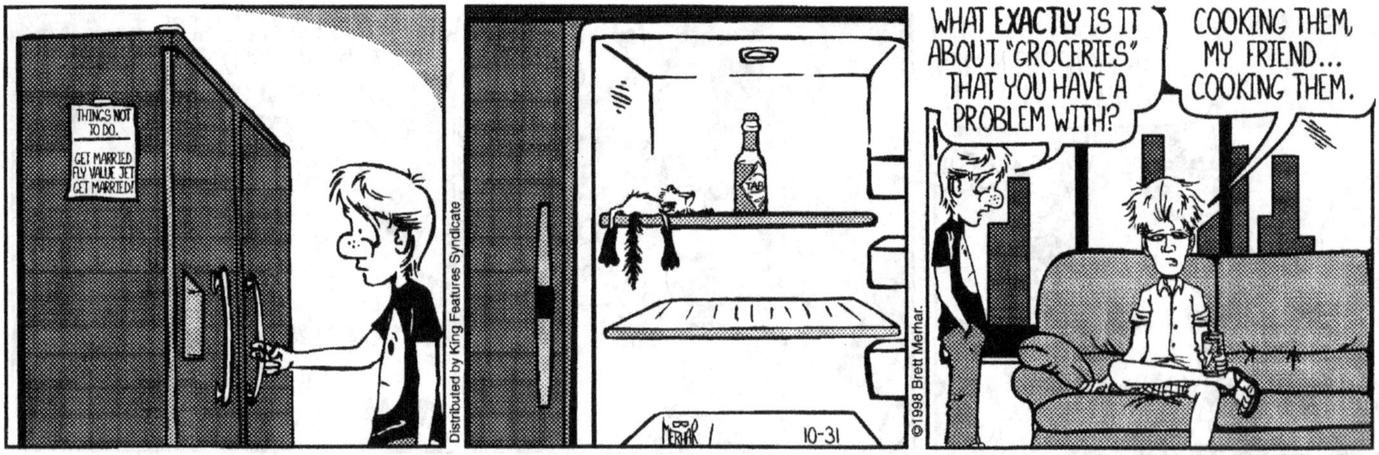
THINGS NOT TO DO.
GET MARRIED
FLY VALUE JET
GET MARRIED!
Distributed by King Features Syndicate
MERHAR 10-31
©1998 Brett Merhar.
WHAT EXACTLY IS IT ABOUT "GROCERIES" THAT YOU HAVE A PROBLEM WITH?
COOKING THEM, MY FRIEND... COOKING THEM.

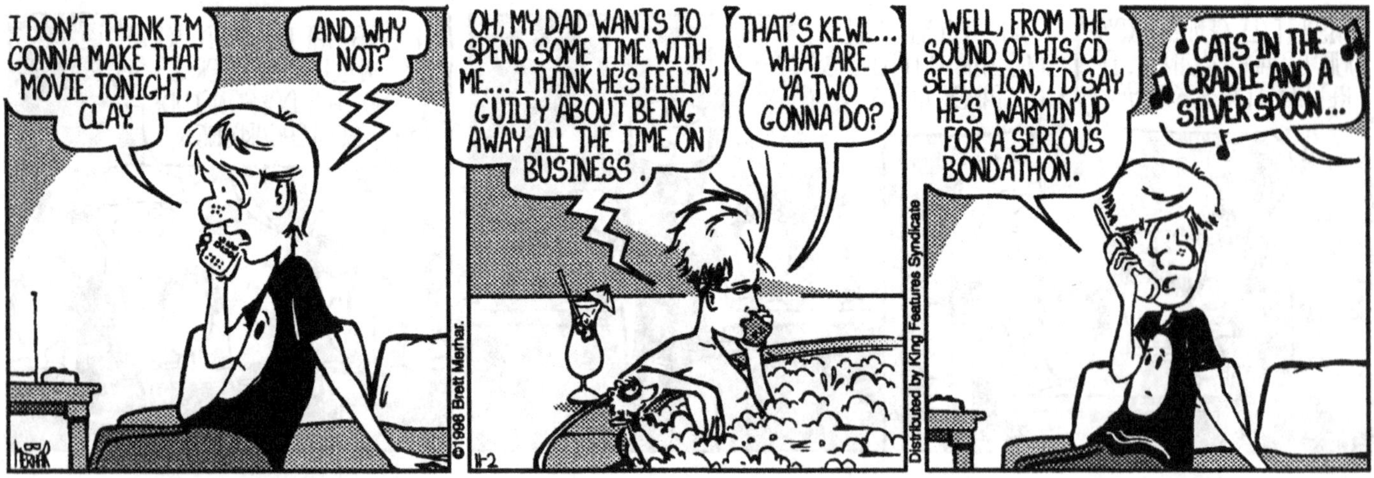
I DON'T THINK I'M GONNA MAKE THAT MOVIE TONIGHT, CLAY.
AND WHY NOT?
MERHAR
OH, MY DAD WANTS TO SPEND SOME TIME WITH ME... I THINK HE'S FEELIN' GUILTY ABOUT BEING AWAY ALL THE TIME ON BUSINESS.
THAT'S KEWL... WHAT ARE YA TWO GONNA DO?
©1998 Brett Merhar.
11-2
Distributed by King Features Syndicate
WELL, FROM THE SOUND OF HIS CD SELECTION, I'D SAY HE'S WARMIN' UP FOR A SERIOUS BONDATHON.
CATS IN THE CRADLE AND A SILVER SPOON...

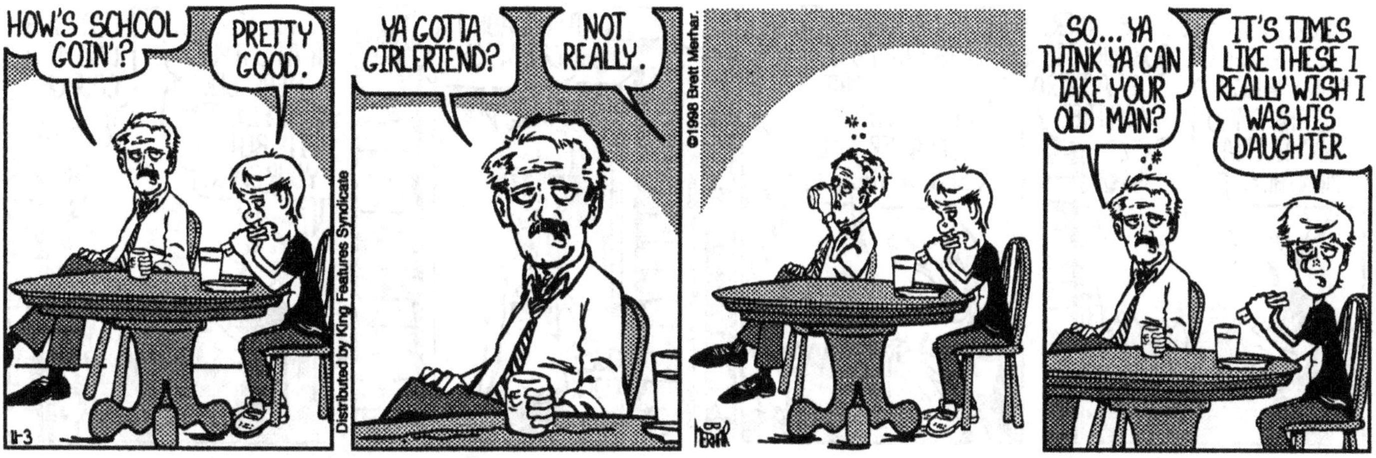
HOW'S SCHOOL GOIN'?
PRETTY GOOD.
YA GOTTA GIRLFRIEND?
NOT REALLY.
SO... YA THINK YA CAN TAKE YOUR OLD MAN?
IT'S TIMES LIKE THESE I REALLY WISH I WAS HIS DAUGHTER.
Distributed by King Features Syndicate
©1998 Brett Merhar.

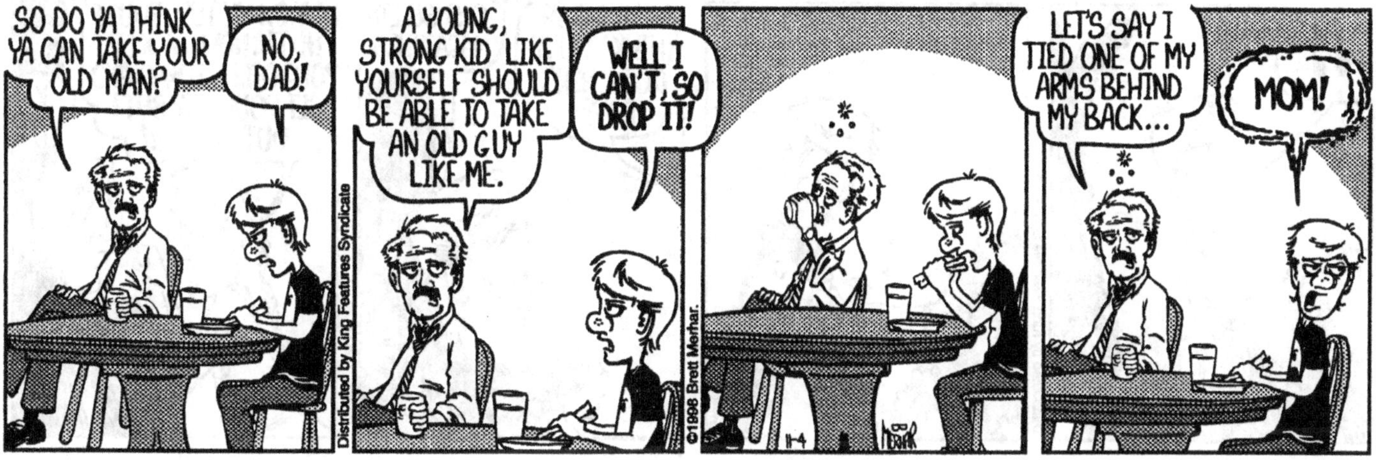
SO DO YA THINK YA CAN TAKE YOUR OLD MAN?
NO, DAD!
A YOUNG, STRONG KID LIKE YOURSELF SHOULD BE ABLE TO TAKE AN OLD GUY LIKE ME.
WELL I CAN'T, SO DROP IT!
LET'S SAY I TIED ONE OF MY ARMS BEHIND MY BACK...
MOM!
Distributed by King Features Syndicate
©1998 Brett Merhar.

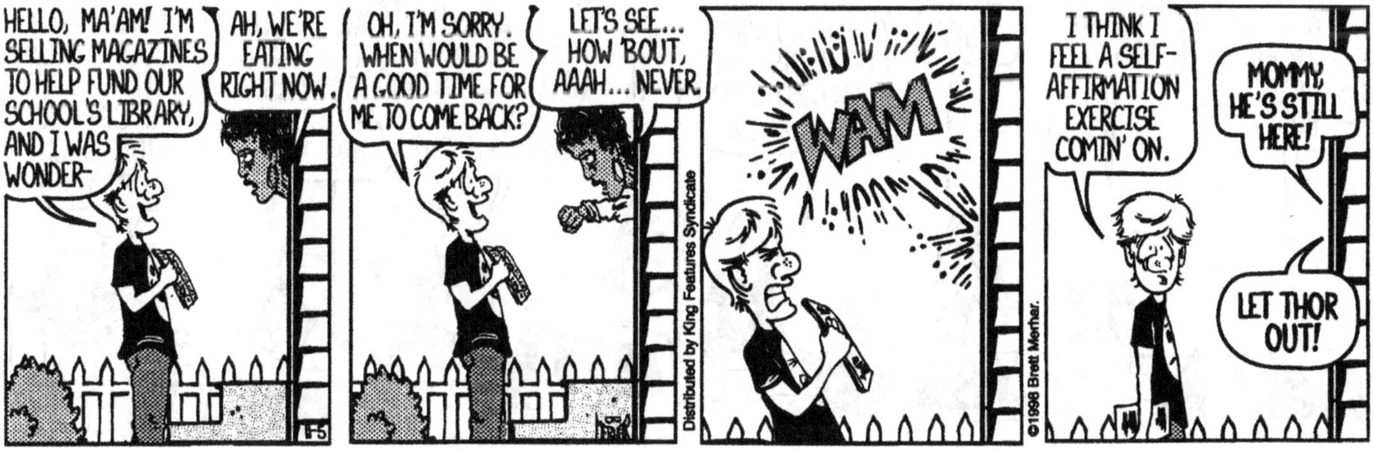
HELLO, MA'AM! I'M SELLING MAGAZINES TO HELP FUND OUR SCHOOL'S LIBRARY, AND I WAS WONDER-
AH, WE'RE EATING RIGHT NOW.
OH, I'M SORRY. WHEN WOULD BE A GOOD TIME FOR ME TO COME BACK?
LET'S SEE... HOW 'BOUT, AAAH... NEVER.
WAM
I THINK I FEEL A SELF-AFFIRMATION EXERCISE COMIN' ON.
MOMMY, HE'S STILL HERE!
LET THOR OUT!
Distributed by King Features Syndicate
©1998 Brett Merhar.

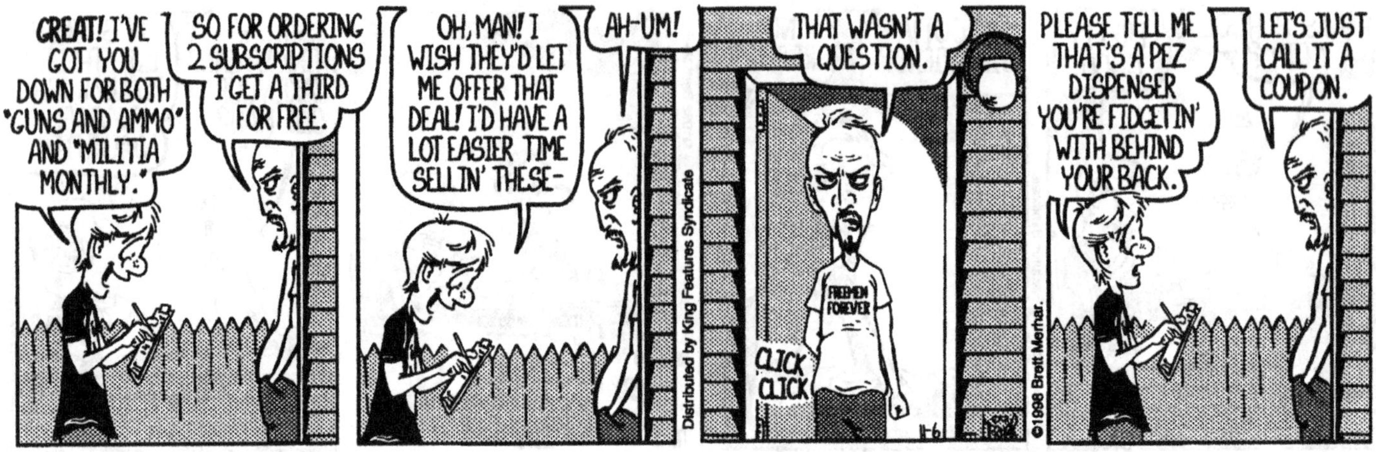
GREAT! I'VE GOT YOU DOWN FOR BOTH "GUNS AND AMMO" AND "MILITIA MONTHLY."
SO FOR ORDERING 2 SUBSCRIPTIONS I GET A THIRD FOR FREE.
OH, MAN! I WISH THEY'D LET ME OFFER THAT DEAL! I'D HAVE A LOT EASIER TIME SELLIN' THESE-
AH-UM!
Distributed by King Features Syndicate
THAT WASN'T A QUESTION.
FREEMEN FOREVER
CLICK CLICK
11-6
©1998 Brett Merhar.
PLEASE TELL ME THAT'S A PEZ DISPENSER YOU'RE FIDGETIN' WITH BEHIND YOUR BACK.
LET'S JUST CALL IT A COUPON.

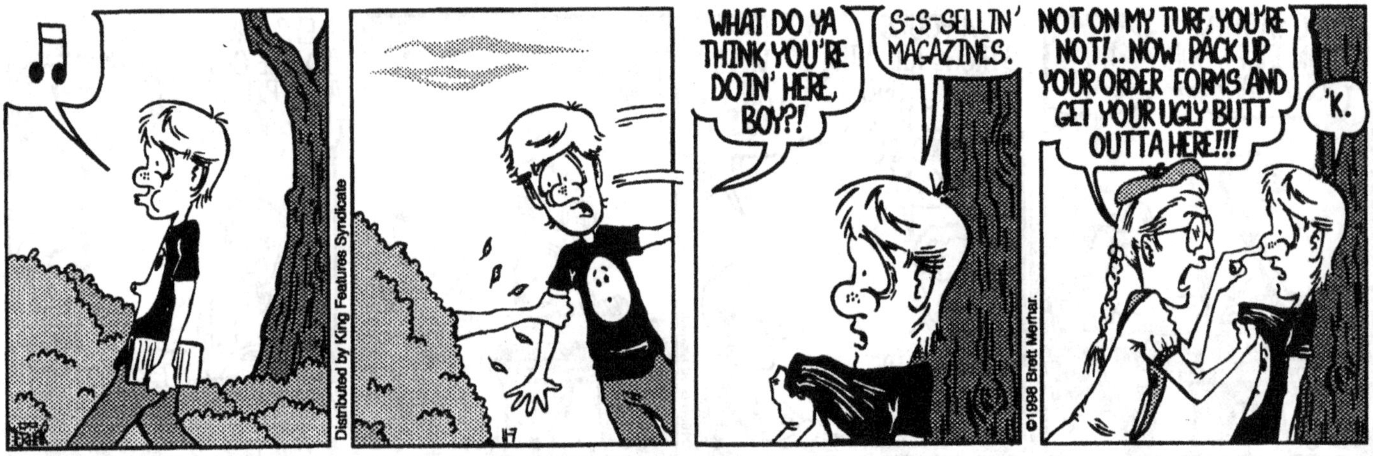
Distributed by King Features Syndicate
11-7
WHAT DO YA THINK YOU'RE DOIN' HERE, BOY?!
S-S-SELLIN' MAGAZINES.
©1998 Brett Merhar.
NOT ON MY TURF, YOU'RE NOT!.. NOW PACK UP YOUR ORDER FORMS AND GET YOUR UGLY BUTT OUTTA HERE!!!
'K.

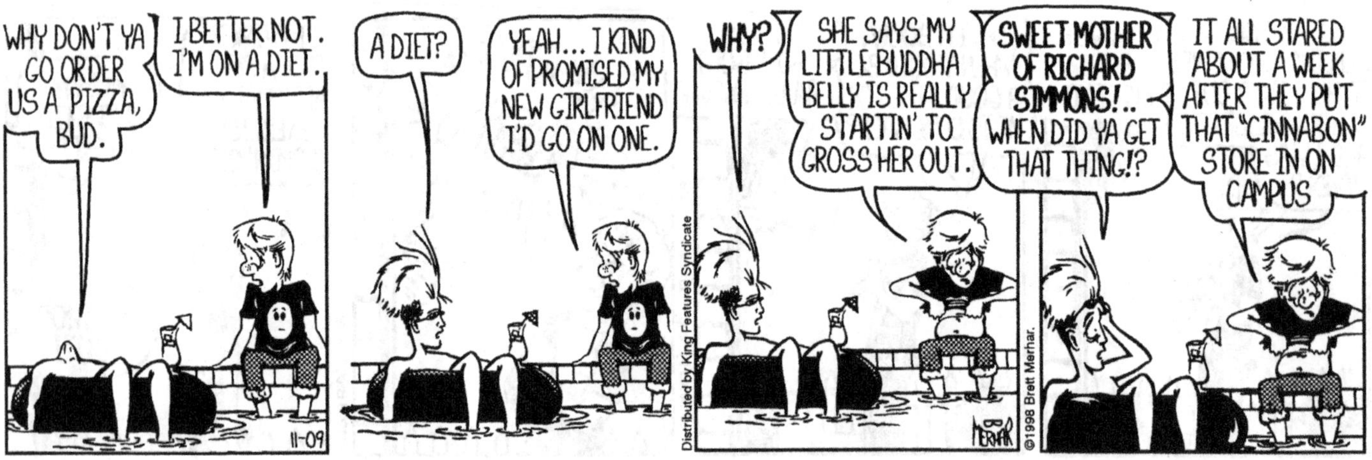
WHY DON'T YA GO ORDER US A PIZZA, BUD.
I BETTER NOT. I'M ON A DIET.
11-09
A DIET?
YEAH... I KIND OF PROMISED MY NEW GIRLFRIEND I'D GO ON ONE.
Distributed by King Features Syndicate
WHY?
SHE SAYS MY LITTLE BUDDHA BELLY IS REALLY STARTIN' TO GROSS HER OUT.
MERHAR
©1998 Brett Merhar.
SWEET MOTHER OF RICHARD SIMMONS!.. WHEN DID YA GET THAT THING!?
IT ALL STARED ABOUT A WEEK AFTER THEY PUT THAT "CINNABON" STORE IN ON CAMPUS

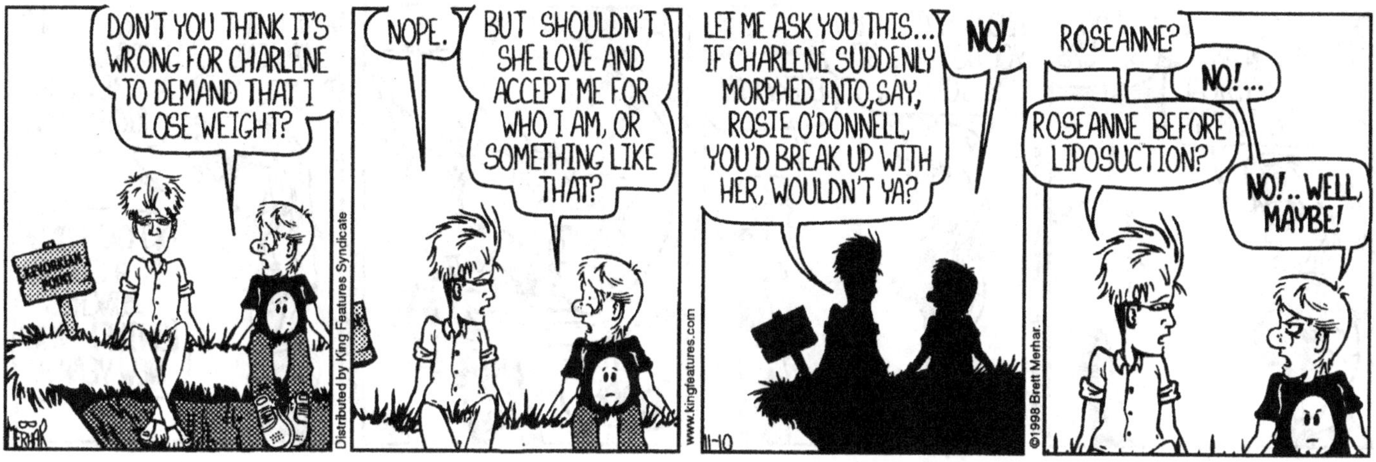
DON'T YOU THINK IT'S WRONG FOR CHARLENE TO DEMAND THAT I LOSE WEIGHT?
MERHAR
Distributed by King Features Syndicate
NOPE.
BUT SHOULDN'T SHE LOVE AND ACCEPT ME FOR WHO I AM, OR SOMETHING LIKE THAT?
www.kingfeatures.com
LET ME ASK YOU THIS... IF CHARLENE SUDDENLY MORPHED INTO, SAY, ROSIE O'DONNELL, YOU'D BREAK UP WITH HER, WOULDN'T YA?
NO!
11-10
©1998 Brett Merhar.
ROSEANNE?
NO!...
ROSEANNE BEFORE LIPOSUCTION?
NO!.. WELL, MAYBE!

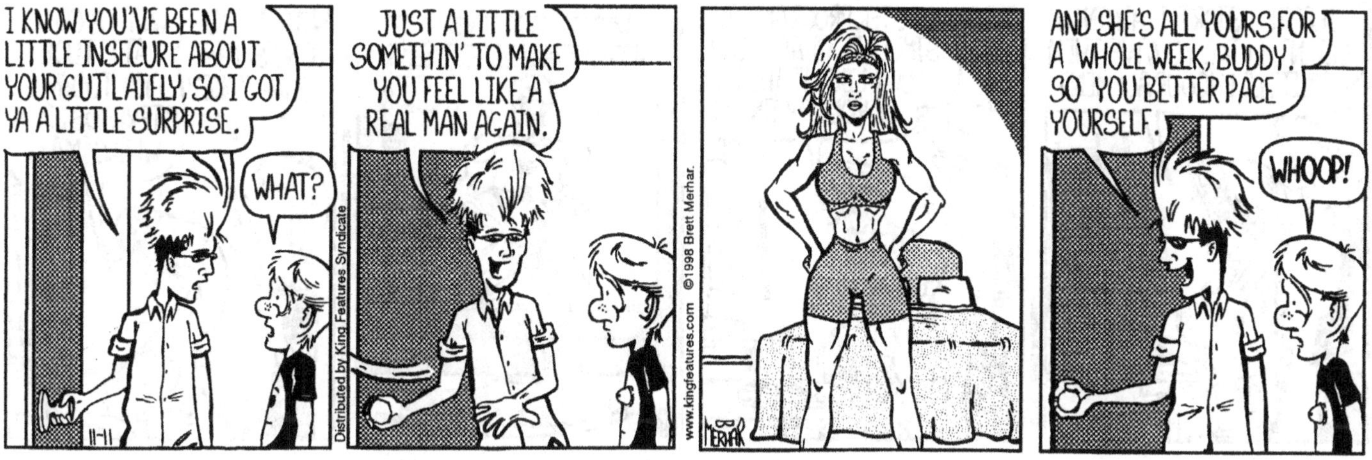
I KNOW YOU'VE BEEN A LITTLE INSECURE ABOUT YOUR GUT LATELY, SO I GOT YA A LITTLE SURPRISE.
WHAT?
11-11
Distributed by King Features Syndicate
JUST A LITTLE SOMETHIN' TO MAKE YOU FEEL LIKE A REAL MAN AGAIN.
www.kingfeatures.com ©1998 Brett Merhar.
MERHAR
AND SHE'S ALL YOURS FOR A WHOLE WEEK, BUDDY. SO YOU BETTER PACE YOURSELF.
WHOOP!

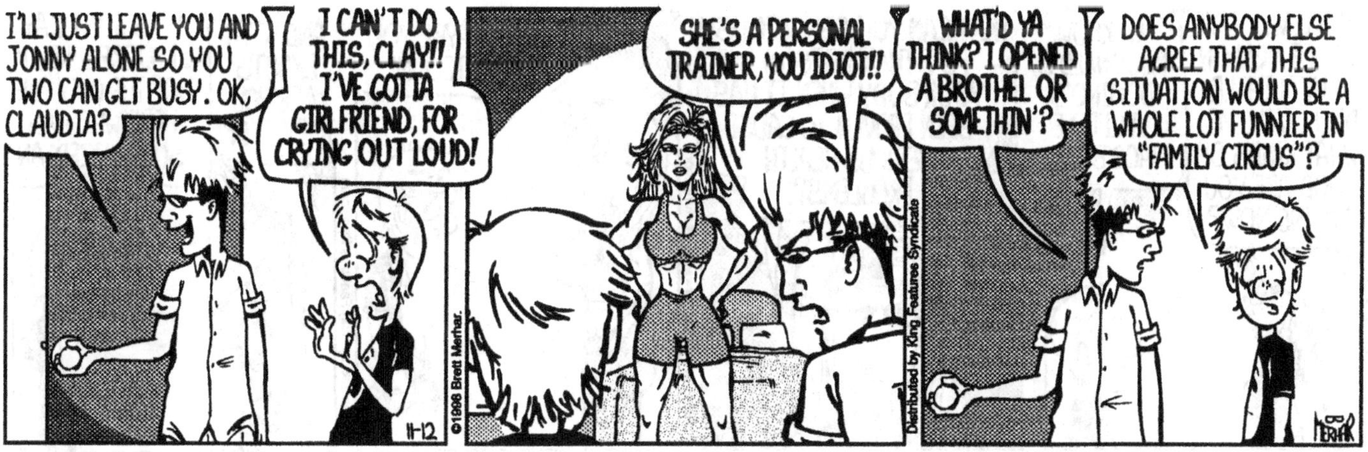
I'LL JUST LEAVE YOU AND JONNY ALONE SO YOU TWO CAN GET BUSY. OK, CLAUDIA?
I CAN'T DO THIS, CLAY!! I'VE GOTTA GIRLFRIEND, FOR CRYING OUT LOUD!
11-12
©1998 Brett Merhar.
SHE'S A PERSONAL TRAINER, YOU IDIOT!!
Distributed by King Features Syndicate
WHAT'D YA THINK? I OPENED A BROTHEL OR SOMETHIN'?
DOES ANYBODY ELSE AGREE THAT THIS SITUATION WOULD BE A WHOLE LOT FUNNIER IN "FAMILY CIRCUS"?
MERHAR

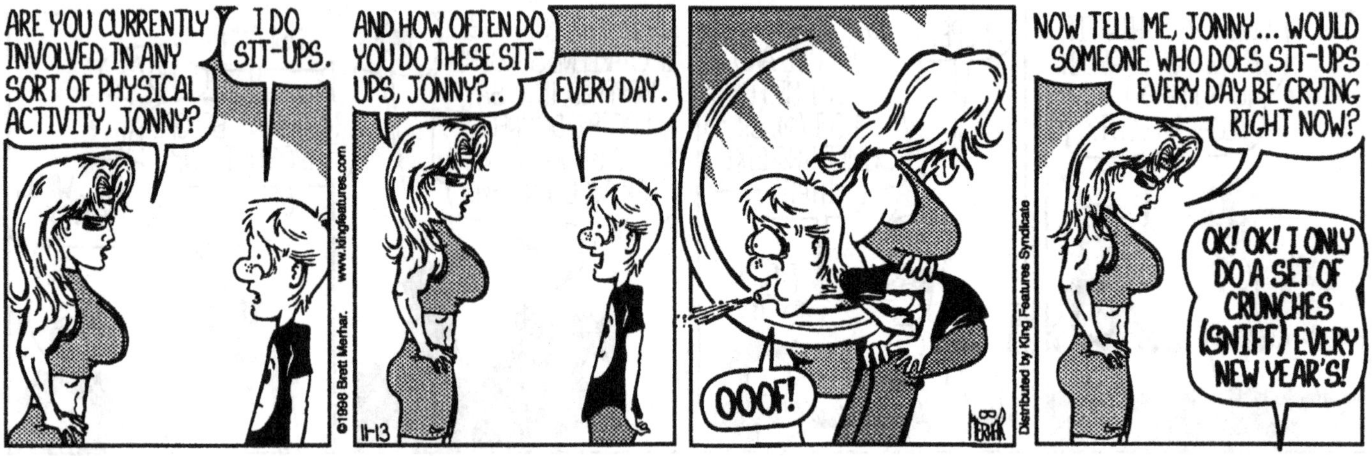
ARE YOU CURRENTLY INVOLVED IN ANY SORT OF PHYSICAL ACTIVITY, JONNY?
I DO SIT-UPS.
©1998 Brett Merhar. www.kingfeatures.com
11-13
AND HOW OFTEN DO YOU DO THESE SIT-UPS, JONNY?..
EVERY DAY.
OOOF!
MERHAR
Distributed by King Features Syndicate
NOW TELL ME, JONNY... WOULD SOMEONE WHO DOES SIT-UPS EVERY DAY BE CRYING RIGHT NOW?
OK! OK! I ONLY DO A SET OF CRUNCHES (SNIFF) EVERY NEW YEAR'S!

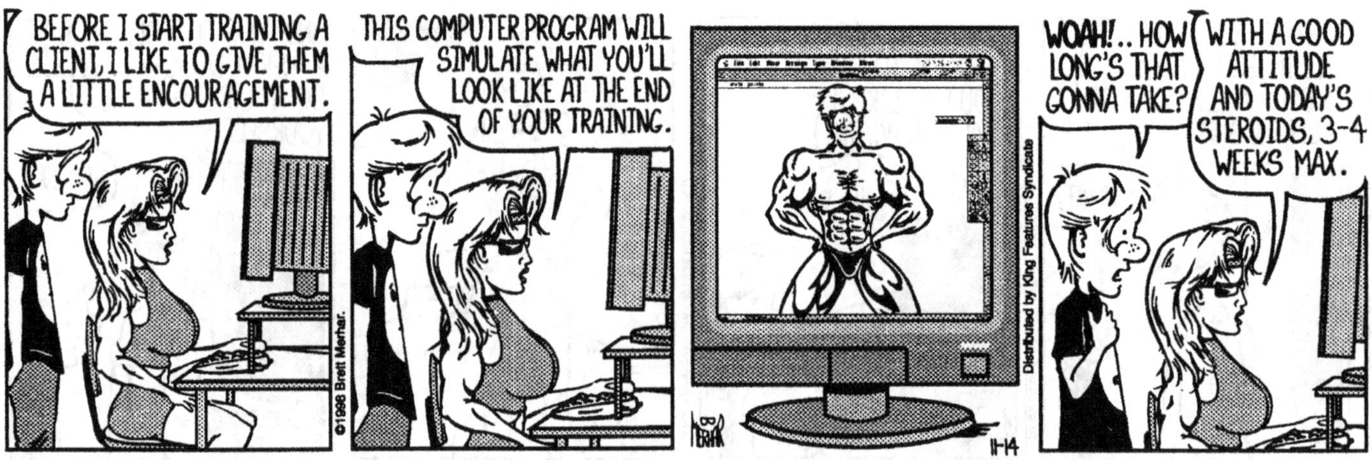
BEFORE I START TRAINING A CLIENT, I LIKE TO GIVE THEM A LITTLE ENCOURAGEMENT.
©1998 Brett Merhar.
THIS COMPUTER PROGRAM WILL SIMULATE WHAT YOU'LL LOOK LIKE AT THE END OF YOUR TRAINING.
MERHAR
11-14
Distributed by King Features Syndicate
WOAH!.. HOW LONG'S THAT GONNA TAKE?
WITH A GOOD ATTITUDE AND TODAY'S STEROIDS, 3-4 WEEKS MAX.

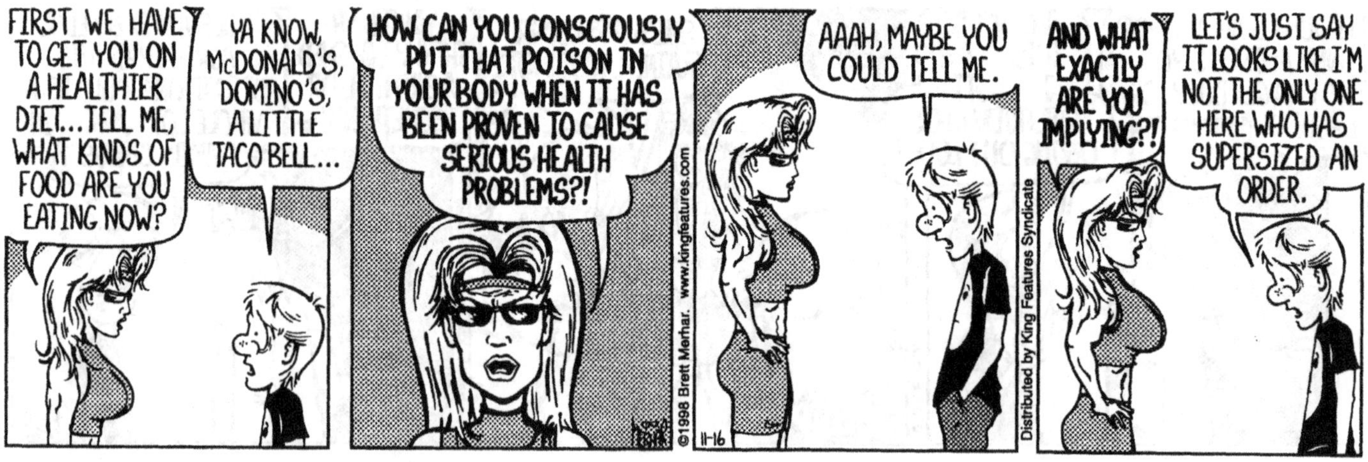
FIRST WE HAVE TO GET YOU ON A HEALTHIER DIET...TELL ME, WHAT KINDS OF FOOD ARE YOU EATING NOW?
YA KNOW, McDONALD'S, DOMINO'S, A LITTLE TACO BELL...
HOW CAN YOU CONSCIOUSLY PUT THAT POISON IN YOUR BODY WHEN IT HAS BEEN PROVEN TO CAUSE SERIOUS HEALTH PROBLEMS?!
MERHAR
©1998 Brett Merhar. www.kingfeatures.com
11-16
AAAH, MAYBE YOU COULD TELL ME.
Distributed by King Features Syndicate
AND WHAT EXACTLY ARE YOU IMPLYING?!
LET'S JUST SAY IT LOOKS LIKE I'M NOT THE ONLY ONE HERE WHO HAS SUPERSIZED AN ORDER.

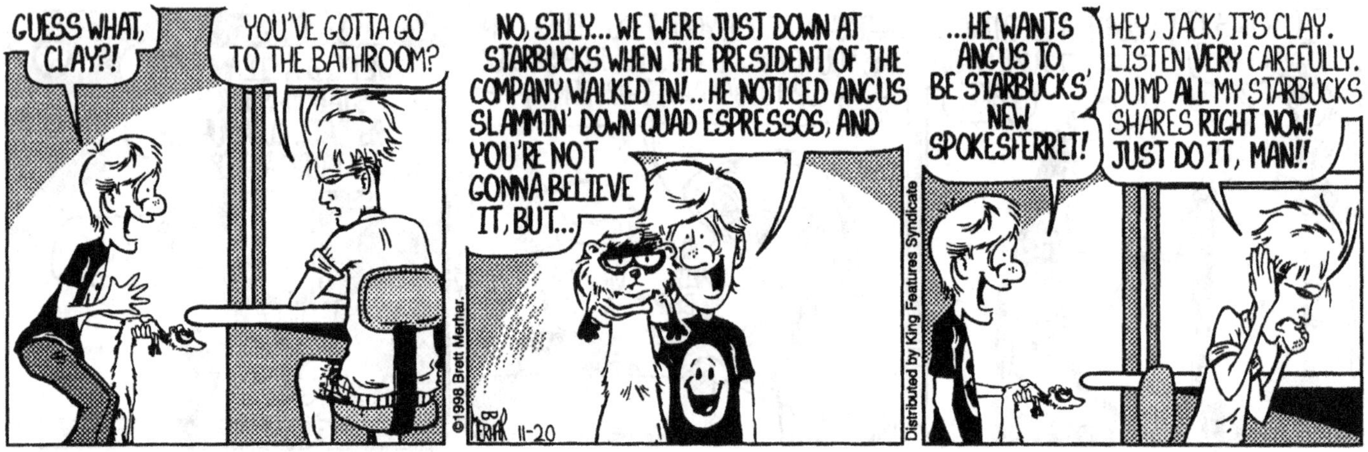
GUESS WHAT, CLAY?!
YOU'VE GOTTA GO TO THE BATHROOM?
NO, SILLY... WE WERE JUST DOWN AT STARBUCKS WHEN THE PRESIDENT OF THE COMPANY WALKED IN!.. HE NOTICED ANGUS SLAMMIN' DOWN QUAD ESPRESSOS, AND YOU'RE NOT GONNA BELIEVE IT, BUT...
©1998 Brett Merhar.
11-20
...HE WANTS ANGUS TO BE STARBUCKS' NEW SPOKESFERRET!
HEY, JACK, IT'S CLAY. LISTEN VERY CAREFULLY. DUMP ALL MY STARBUCKS SHARES RIGHT NOW! JUST DO IT, MAN!!
Distributed by King Features Syndicate

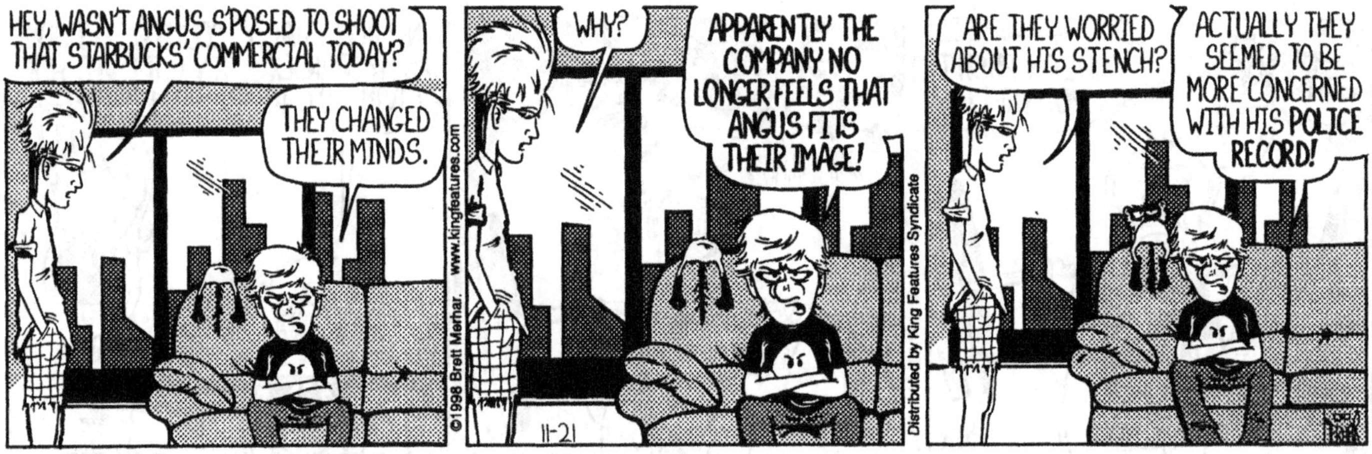
HEY, WASN'T ANGUS S'POSED TO SHOOT THAT STARBUCKS' COMMERCIAL TODAY?
THEY CHANGED THEIR MINDS.
©1998 Brett Merhar. www.kingfeatures.com
WHY?
APPARENTLY THE COMPANY NO LONGER FEELS THAT ANGUS FITS THEIR IMAGE!
11-21
Distributed by King Features Syndicate
ARE THEY WORRIED ABOUT HIS STENCH?
ACTUALLY THEY SEEMED TO BE MORE CONCERNED WITH HIS POLICE RECORD!

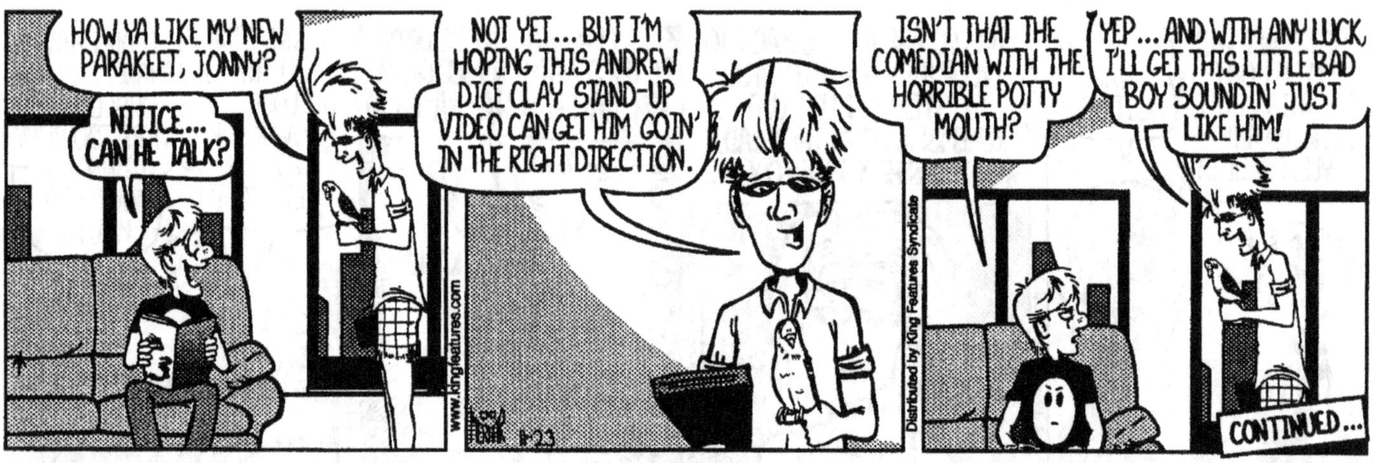
HOW YA LIKE MY NEW PARAKEET, JONNY?
NIIICE... CAN HE TALK?
www.kingfeatures.com
NOT YET... BUT I'M HOPING THIS ANDREW DICE CLAY STAND-UP VIDEO CAN GET HIM GOIN' IN THE RIGHT DIRECTION.
11-23
Distributed by King Features Syndicate
ISN'T THAT THE COMEDIAN WITH THE HORRIBLE POTTY MOUTH?
YEP... AND WITH ANY LUCK, I'LL GET THIS LITTLE BAD BOY SOUNDIN' JUST LIKE HIM!
CONTINUED...

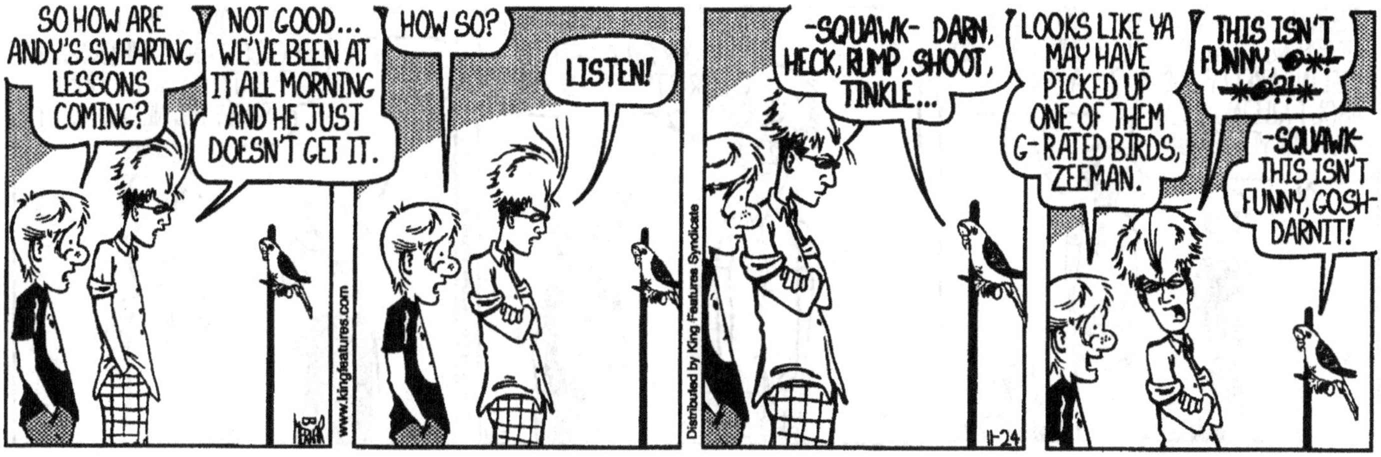
SO HOW ARE ANDY'S SWEARING LESSONS COMING?
NOT GOOD... WE'VE BEEN AT IT ALL MORNING AND HE JUST DOESN'T GET IT.
HOW SO?
LISTEN!
-SQUAWK- DARN, HECK, RUMP, SHOOT, TINKLE...
LOOKS LIKE YA MAY HAVE PICKED UP ONE OF THEM G-RATED BIRDS, ZEEMAN.
THIS ISN'T FUNNY, @*! *@?!*
-SQUAWK- THIS ISN'T FUNNY, GOSH-DARNIT!
www.kingfeatures.com
Distributed by King Features Syndicate
11-24

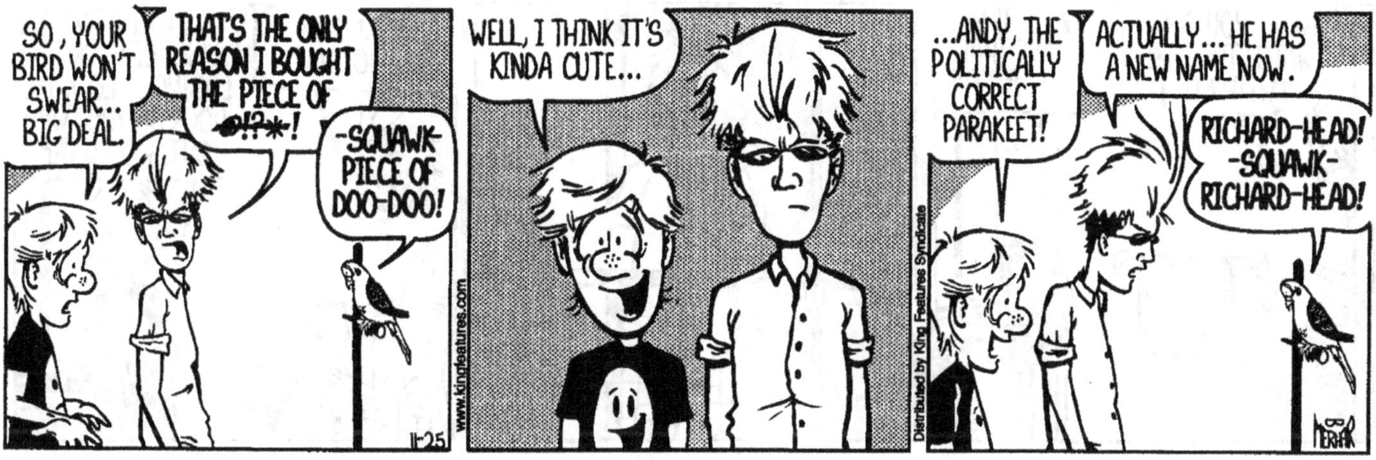
SO, YOUR BIRD WON'T SWEAR... BIG DEAL.
THAT'S THE ONLY REASON I BOUGHT THE PIECE OF @!?*!
-SQUAWK- PIECE OF DOO-DOO!
11-25
WELL, I THINK IT'S KINDA CUTE...
www.kingfeatures.com
...ANDY, THE POLITICALLY CORRECT PARAKEET!
ACTUALLY... HE HAS A NEW NAME NOW.
RICHARD-HEAD! -SQUAWK- RICHARD-HEAD!
Distributed by King Features Syndicate

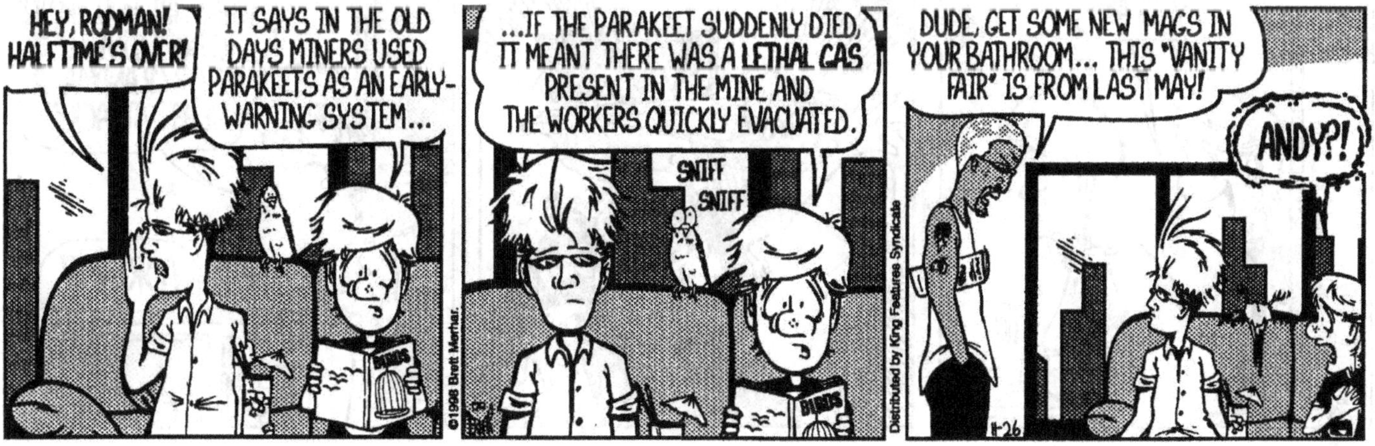
HEY, RODMAN! HALFTIME'S OVER!
IT SAYS IN THE OLD DAYS MINERS USED PARAKEETS AS AN EARLY-WARNING SYSTEM...
BIRDS
©1998 Brett Merhar.
...IF THE PARAKEET SUDDENLY DIED, IT MEANT THERE WAS A LETHAL GAS PRESENT IN THE MINE AND THE WORKERS QUICKLY EVACUATED.
SNIFF
SNIFF
BIRDS
DUDE, GET SOME NEW MAGS IN YOUR BATHROOM... THIS "VANITY FAIR" IS FROM LAST MAY!
ANDY?!
Distributed by King Features Syndicate
11-26

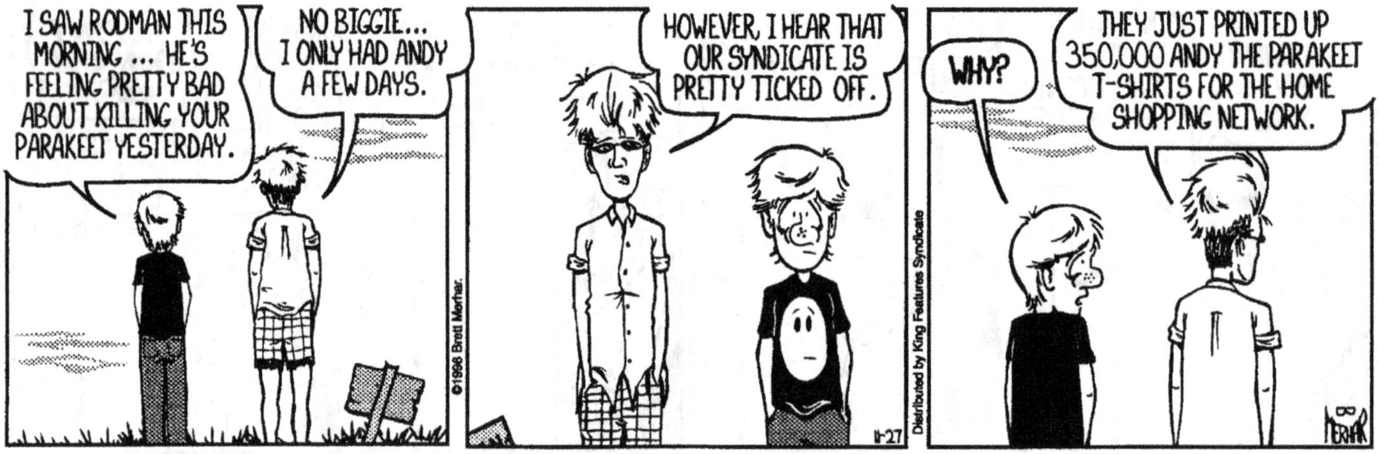
I SAW RODMAN THIS MORNING ... HE'S FEELING PRETTY BAD ABOUT KILLING YOUR PARAKEET YESTERDAY.
NO BIGGIE... I ONLY HAD ANDY A FEW DAYS.
HOWEVER, I HEAR THAT OUR SYNDICATE IS PRETTY TICKED OFF.
WHY?
THEY JUST PRINTED UP 350,000 ANDY THE PARAKEET T-SHIRTS FOR THE HOME SHOPPING NETWORK.
©1998 Brett Merhar.
Distributed by King Features Syndicate
11-27
MERHAR

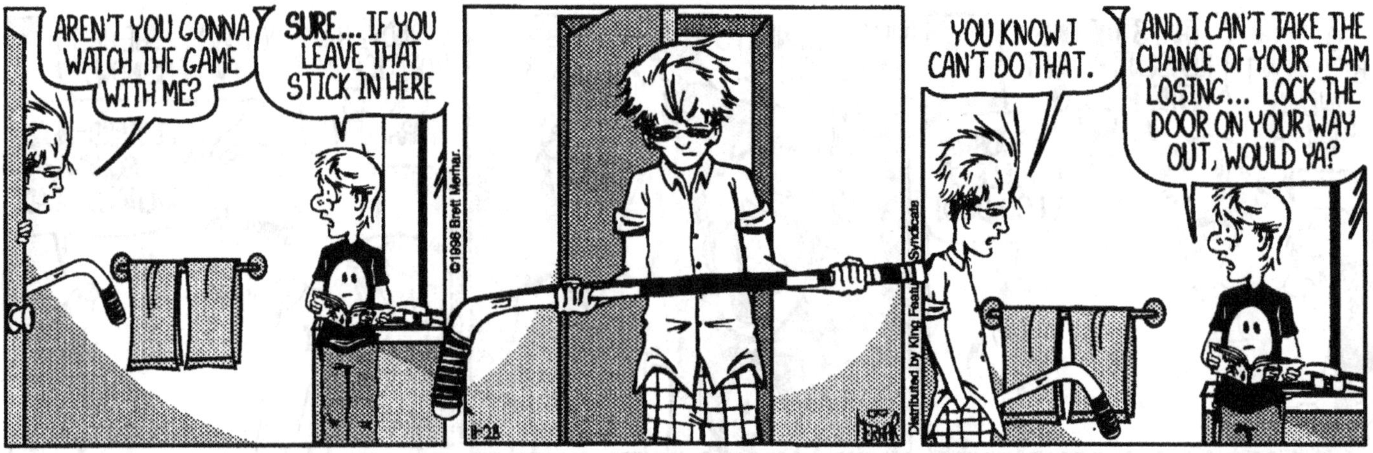
AREN'T YOU GONNA WATCH THE GAME WITH ME?
SURE... IF YOU LEAVE THAT STICK IN HERE
YOU KNOW I CAN'T DO THAT.
AND I CAN'T TAKE THE CHANCE OF YOUR TEAM LOSING... LOCK THE DOOR ON YOUR WAY OUT, WOULD YA?
©1998 Brett Merhar.
Distributed by King Features Syndicate
11-28
MERHAR

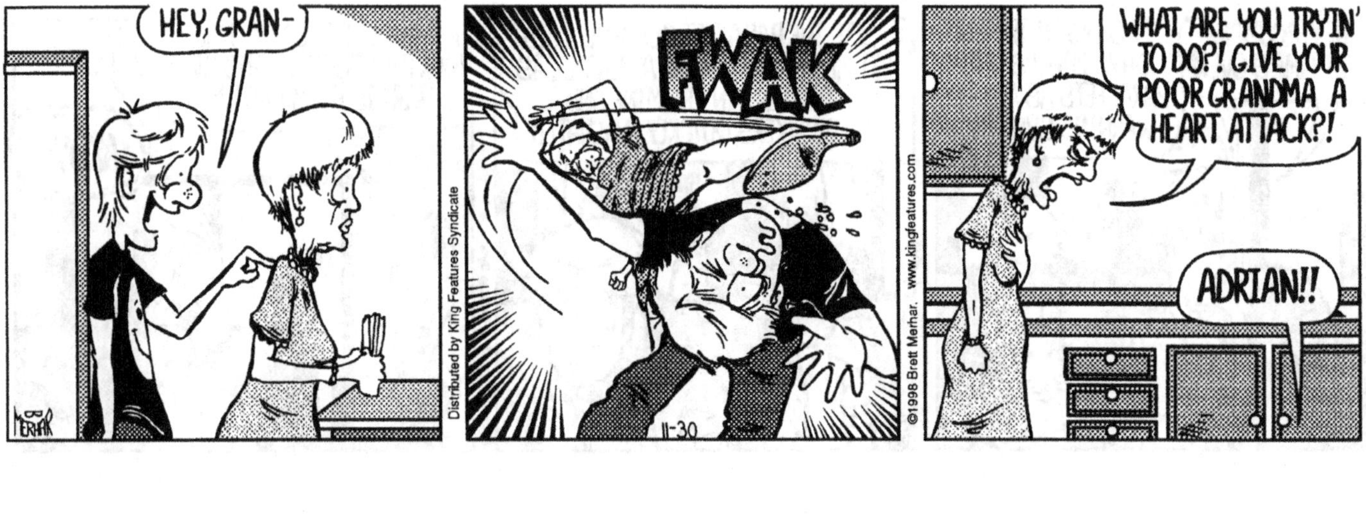
HEY, GRAN-
FWAK
WHAT ARE YOU TRYIN' TO DO?! GIVE YOUR POOR GRANDMA A HEART ATTACK?!
ADRIAN!!
Distributed by King Features Syndicate
©1998 Brett Merhar. www.kingfeatures.com
11-30
MERHAR

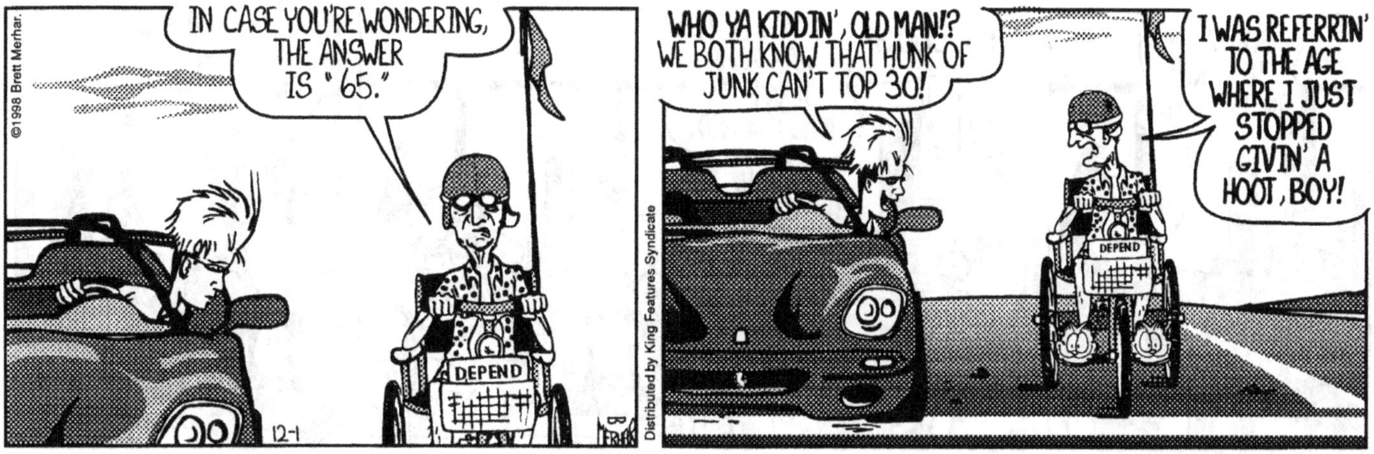
©1998 Brett Merhar.
IN CASE YOU'RE WONDERING, THE ANSWER IS "65."
DEPEND
12-1
Distributed by King Features Syndicate
WHO YA KIDDIN', OLD MAN!? WE BOTH KNOW THAT HUNK OF JUNK CAN'T TOP 30!
I WAS REFERRIN' TO THE AGE WHERE I JUST STOPPED GIVIN' A HOOT, BOY!
DEPEND

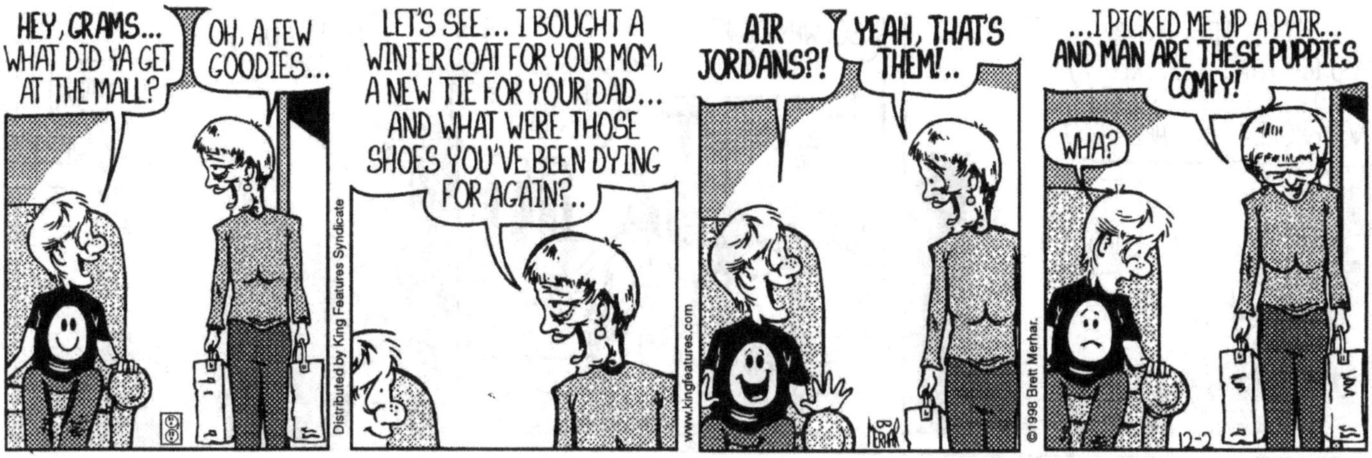
HEY, GRAMS... WHAT DID YA GET AT THE MALL?
OH, A FEW GOODIES...
Distributed by King Features Syndicate
LET'S SEE... I BOUGHT A WINTER COAT FOR YOUR MOM, A NEW TIE FOR YOUR DAD... AND WHAT WERE THOSE SHOES YOU'VE BEEN DYING FOR AGAIN?..
www.kingfeatures.com
AIR JORDANS?!
YEAH, THAT'S THEM!..
©1998 Brett Merhar.
WHA?
...I PICKED ME UP A PAIR... AND MAN ARE THESE PUPPIES COMFY!
12-2

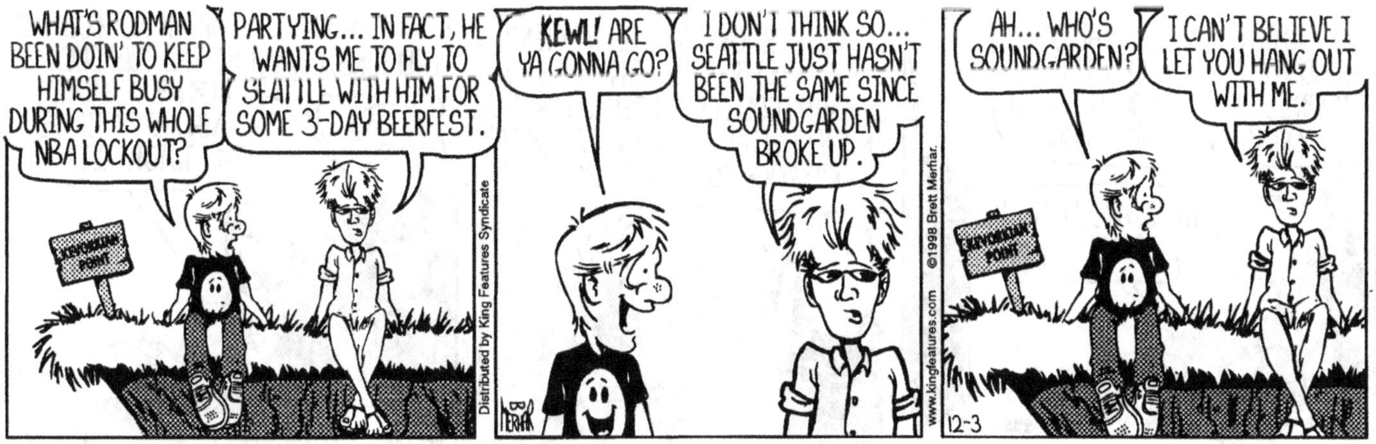
WHAT'S RODMAN BEEN DOIN' TO KEEP HIMSELF BUSY DURING THIS WHOLE NBA LOCKOUT?
PARTYING... IN FACT, HE WANTS ME TO FLY TO SEATTLE WITH HIM FOR SOME 3-DAY BEERFEST.
Distributed by King Features Syndicate
KEWL! ARE YA GONNA GO?
I DON'T THINK SO... SEATTLE JUST HASN'T BEEN THE SAME SINCE SOUNDGARDEN BROKE UP.
©1998 Brett Merhar.
www.kingfeatures.com
AH... WHO'S SOUNDGARDEN?
I CAN'T BELIEVE I LET YOU HANG OUT WITH ME.
12-3

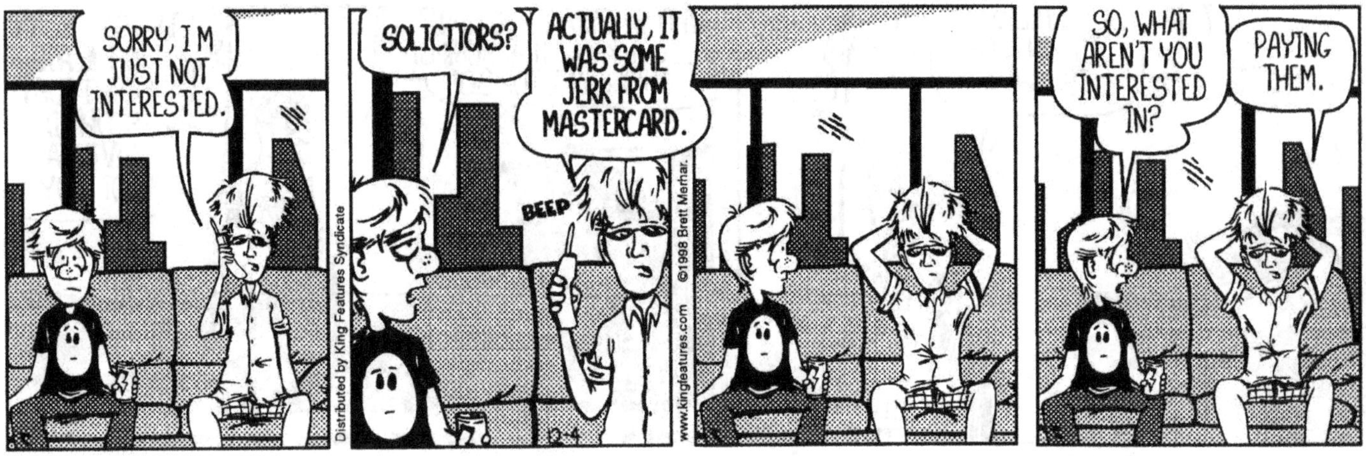
SORRY, I M JUST NOT INTERESTED.
Distributed by King Features Syndicate
SOLICITORS?
ACTUALLY, IT WAS SOME JERK FROM MASTERCARD.
BEEP
12-4
©1998 Brett Merhar.
www.kingfeatures.com
SO, WHAT AREN'T YOU INTERESTED IN?
PAYING THEM.

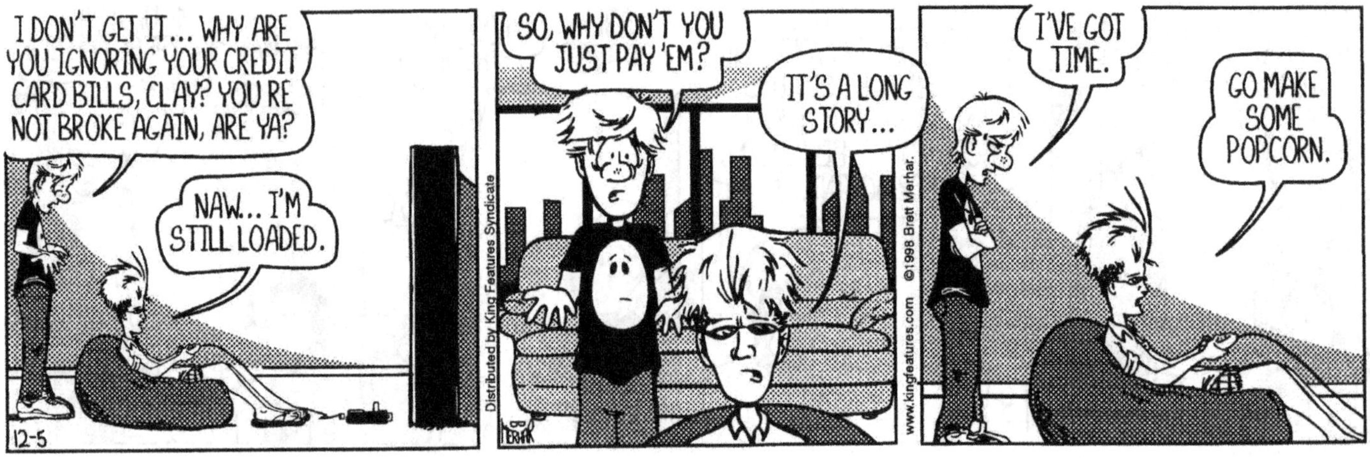
I DON'T GET IT... WHY ARE YOU IGNORING YOUR CREDIT CARD BILLS, CLAY? YOU RE NOT BROKE AGAIN, ARE YA?
NAW... I'M STILL LOADED.
12-5
Distributed by King Features Syndicate
SO, WHY DON'T YOU JUST PAY 'EM?
IT'S A LONG STORY...
©1998 Brett Merhar
www.kingfeatures.com
I'VE GOT TIME.
GO MAKE SOME POPCORN.

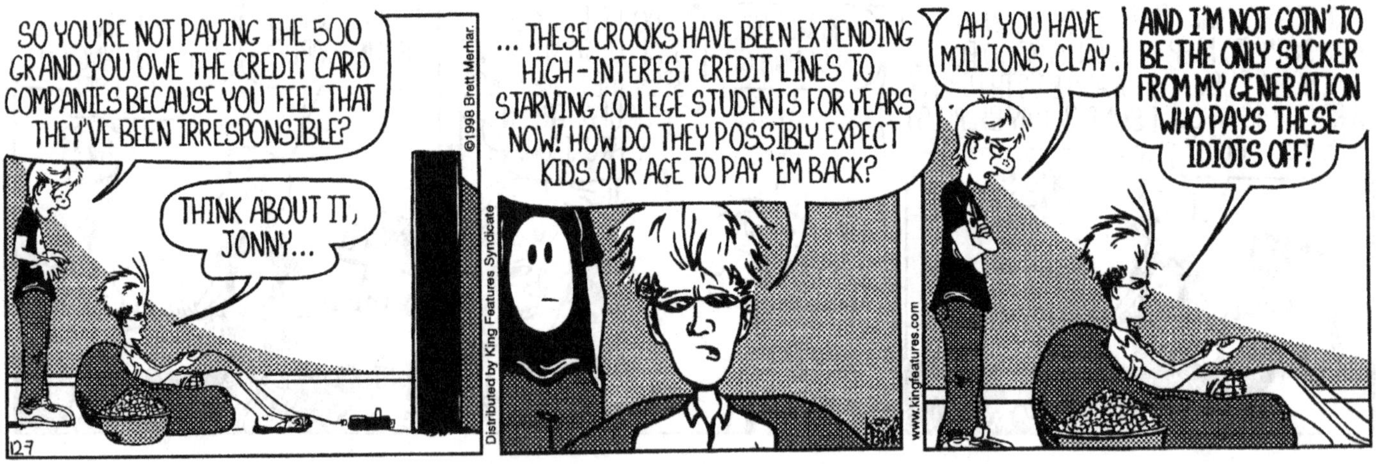
SO YOU'RE NOT PAYING THE 500 GRAND YOU OWE THE CREDIT CARD COMPANIES BECAUSE YOU FEEL THAT THEY'VE BEEN IRRESPONSIBLE?
THINK ABOUT IT, JONNY...
12-7
©1998 Brett Merhar.
Distributed by King Features Syndicate
... THESE CROOKS HAVE BEEN EXTENDING HIGH-INTEREST CREDIT LINES TO STARVING COLLEGE STUDENTS FOR YEARS NOW! HOW DO THEY POSSIBLY EXPECT KIDS OUR AGE TO PAY 'EM BACK?
www.kingfeatures.com
AH, YOU HAVE MILLIONS, CLAY.
AND I'M NOT GOIN' TO BE THE ONLY SUCKER FROM MY GENERATION WHO PAYS THESE IDIOTS OFF!

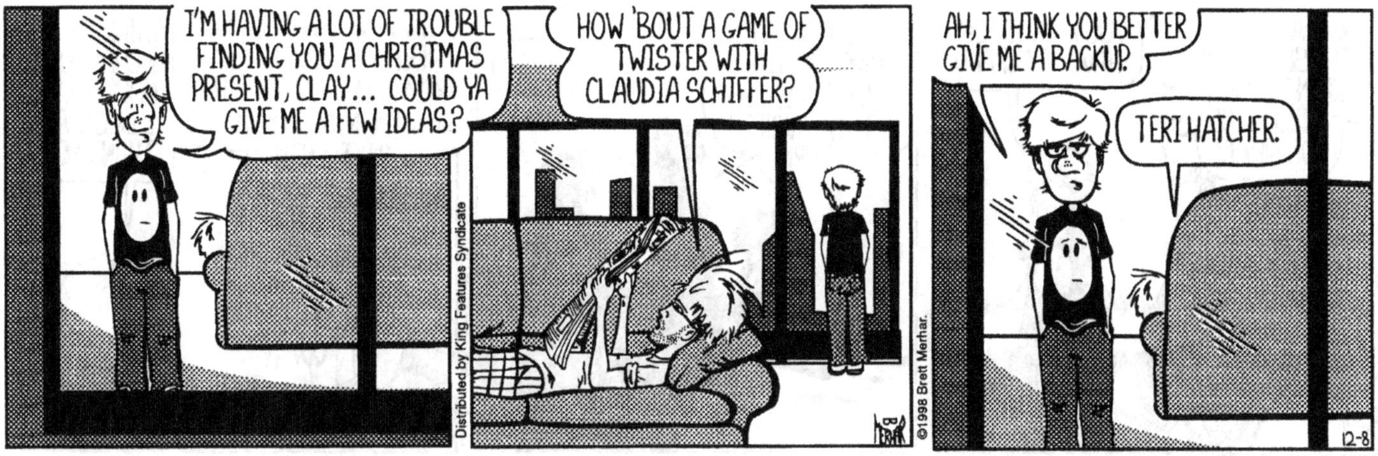
I'M HAVING A LOT OF TROUBLE FINDING YOU A CHRISTMAS PRESENT, CLAY... COULD YA GIVE ME A FEW IDEAS?
HOW 'BOUT A GAME OF TWISTER WITH CLAUDIA SCHIFFER?
AH, I THINK YOU BETTER GIVE ME A BACKUP.
TERI HATCHER.
Distributed by King Features Syndicate
©1998 Brett Merhar.
MERHAR
12-8

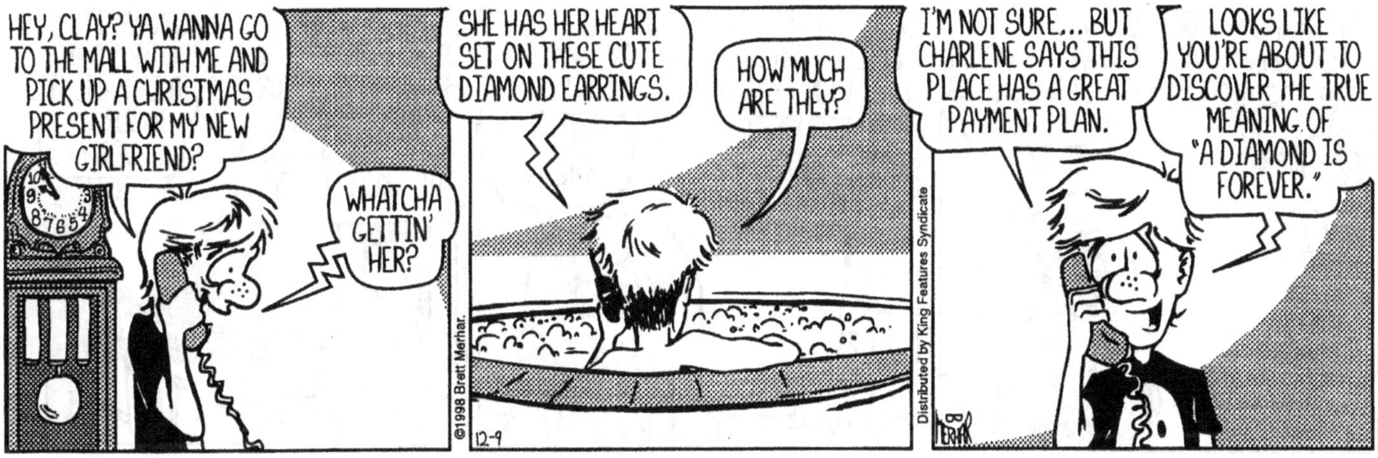
HEY, CLAY? YA WANNA GO TO THE MALL WITH ME AND PICK UP A CHRISTMAS PRESENT FOR MY NEW GIRLFRIEND?
WHATCHA GETTIN' HER?
SHE HAS HER HEART SET ON THESE CUTE DIAMOND EARRINGS.
HOW MUCH ARE THEY?
I'M NOT SURE... BUT CHARLENE SAYS THIS PLACE HAS A GREAT PAYMENT PLAN.
LOOKS LIKE YOU'RE ABOUT TO DISCOVER THE TRUE MEANING OF "A DIAMOND IS FOREVER."
©1998 Brett Merhar.
12-9
Distributed by King Features Syndicate
MERHAR

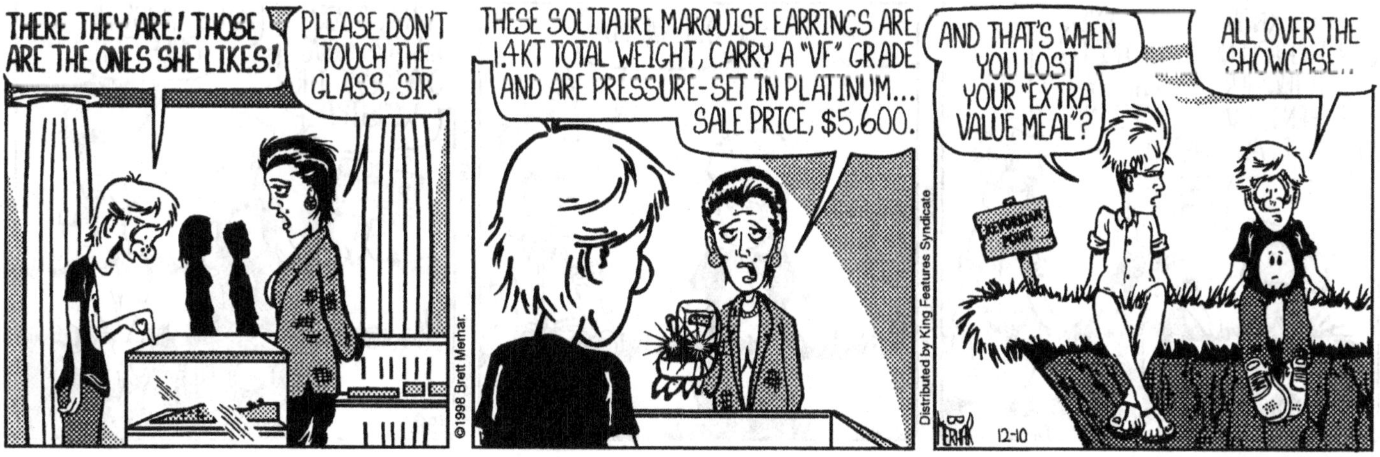
THERE THEY ARE! THOSE ARE THE ONES SHE LIKES!
PLEASE DON'T TOUCH THE GLASS, SIR.
THESE SOLITAIRE MARQUISE EARRINGS ARE 1.4KT TOTAL WEIGHT, CARRY A "VF" GRADE AND ARE PRESSURE-SET IN PLATINUM... SALE PRICE, $5,600.
AND THAT'S WHEN YOU LOST YOUR "EXTRA VALUE MEAL"?
ALL OVER THE SHOWCASE...
©1998 Brett Merhar.
Distributed by King Features Syndicate
MERHAR
12-10

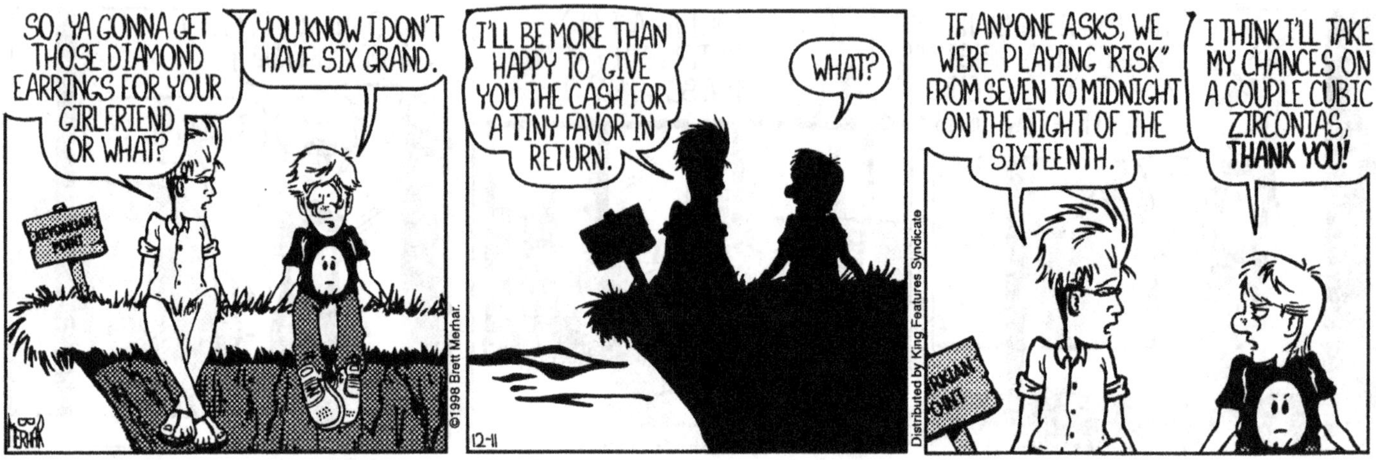
SO, YA GONNA GET THOSE DIAMOND EARRINGS FOR YOUR GIRLFRIEND OR WHAT?
YOU KNOW I DON'T HAVE SIX GRAND.
KEVORKIAN POINT
©1998 Brett Merhar.
I'LL BE MORE THAN HAPPY TO GIVE YOU THE CASH FOR A TINY FAVOR IN RETURN.
WHAT?
12-11
Distributed by King Features Syndicate
IF ANYONE ASKS, WE WERE PLAYING "RISK" FROM SEVEN TO MIDNIGHT ON THE NIGHT OF THE SIXTEENTH.
I THINK I'LL TAKE MY CHANCES ON A COUPLE CUBIC ZIRCONIAS, **THANK YOU!**

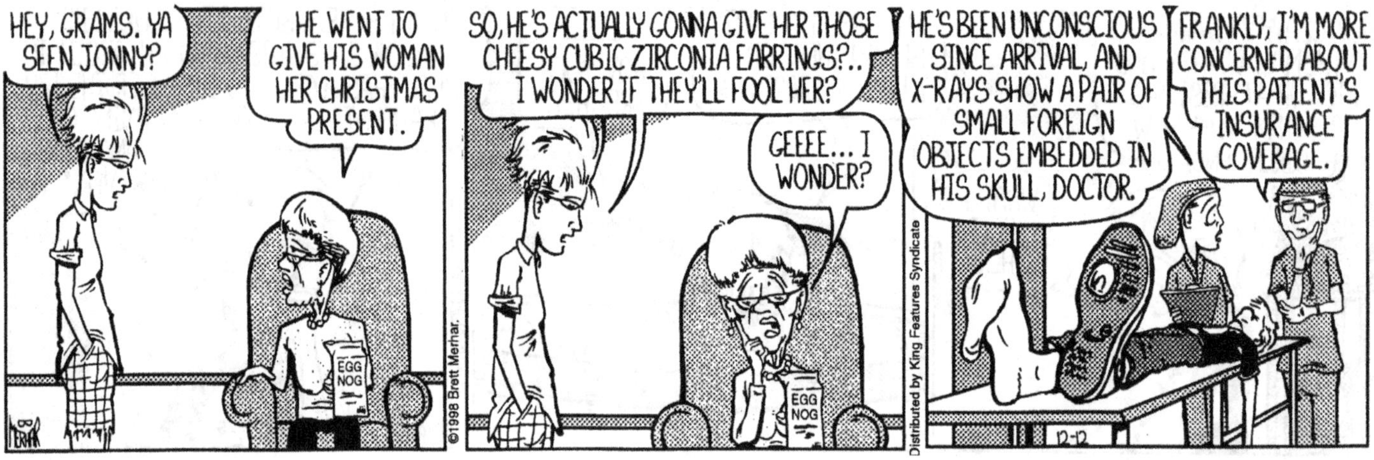
HEY, GRAMS. YA SEEN JONNY?
HE WENT TO GIVE HIS WOMAN HER CHRISTMAS PRESENT.
EGG NOG
©1998 Brett Merhar.
SO, HE'S ACTUALLY GONNA GIVE HER THOSE CHEESY CUBIC ZIRCONIA EARRINGS?.. I WONDER IF THEY'LL FOOL HER?
GEEEE... I WONDER?
EGG NOG
Distributed by King Features Syndicate
HE'S BEEN UNCONSCIOUS SINCE ARRIVAL, AND X-RAYS SHOW A PAIR OF SMALL FOREIGN OBJECTS EMBEDDED IN HIS SKULL, DOCTOR.
FRANKLY, I'M MORE CONCERNED ABOUT THIS PATIENT'S INSURANCE COVERAGE.
12-12

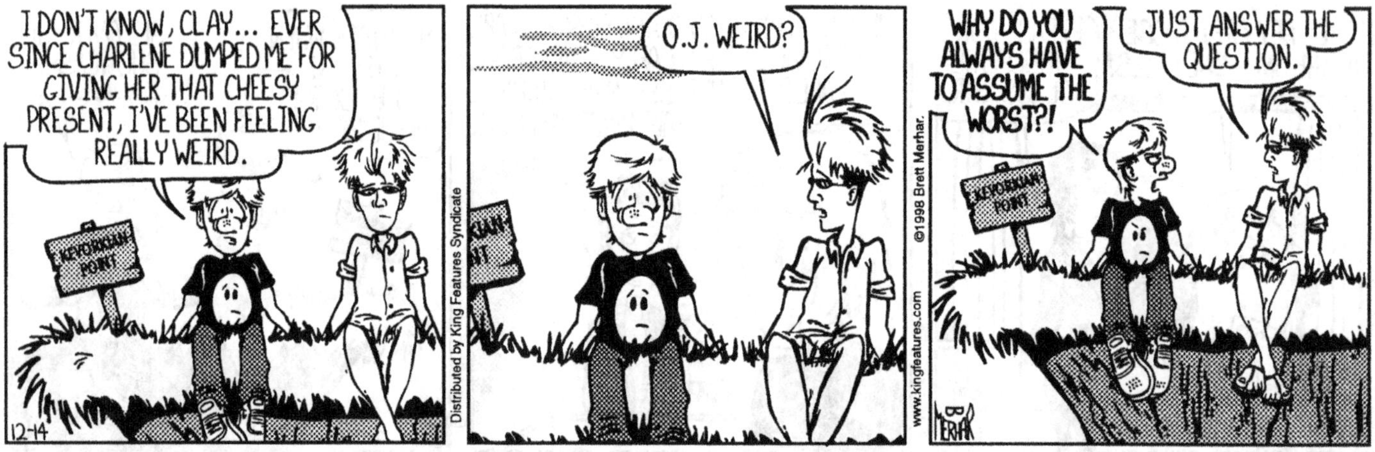
I DON'T KNOW, CLAY... EVER SINCE CHARLENE DUMPED ME FOR GIVING HER THAT CHEESY PRESENT, I'VE BEEN FEELING REALLY WEIRD.
KEVORKIAN POINT
12-14
Distributed by King Features Syndicate
O.J. WEIRD?
©1998 Brett Merhar.
www.kingfeatures.com
WHY DO YOU ALWAYS HAVE TO ASSUME THE WORST?!
JUST ANSWER THE QUESTION.
KEVORKIAN POINT

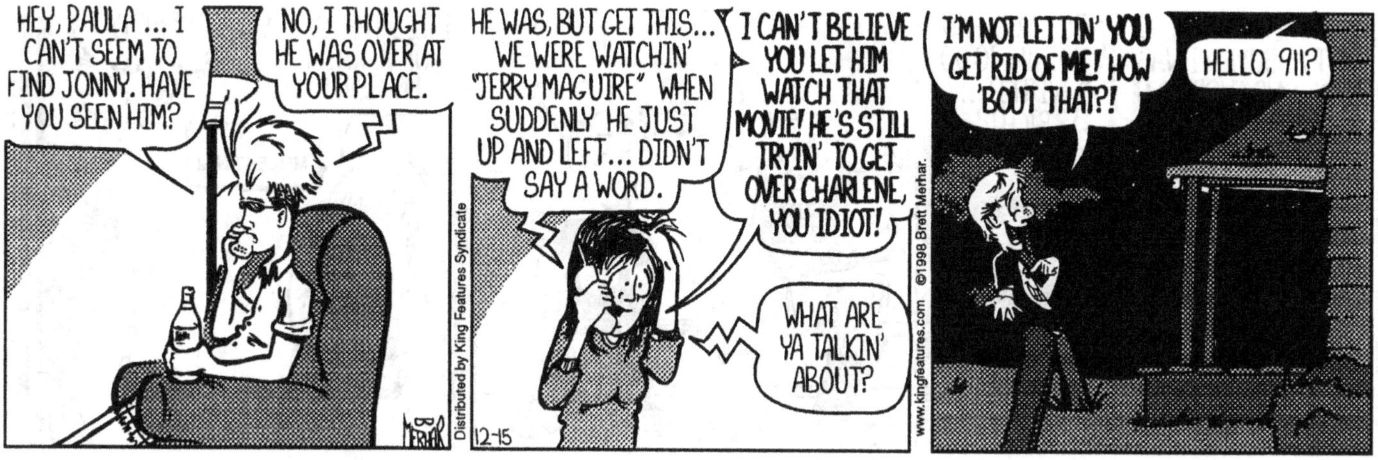
HEY, PAULA ... I CAN'T SEEM TO FIND JONNY. HAVE YOU SEEN HIM?
NO, I THOUGHT HE WAS OVER AT YOUR PLACE.
HE WAS, BUT GET THIS... WE WERE WATCHIN' "JERRY MAGUIRE" WHEN SUDDENLY HE JUST UP AND LEFT... DIDN'T SAY A WORD.
I CAN'T BELIEVE YOU LET HIM WATCH THAT MOVIE! HE'S STILL TRYIN' TO GET OVER CHARLENE, YOU IDIOT!
WHAT ARE YA TALKIN' ABOUT?
I'M NOT LETTIN' YOU GET RID OF ME! HOW 'BOUT THAT?!
HELLO, 911?
MERHAR
12-15
Distributed by King Features Syndicate
www.kingfeatures.com
©1998 Brett Merhar.

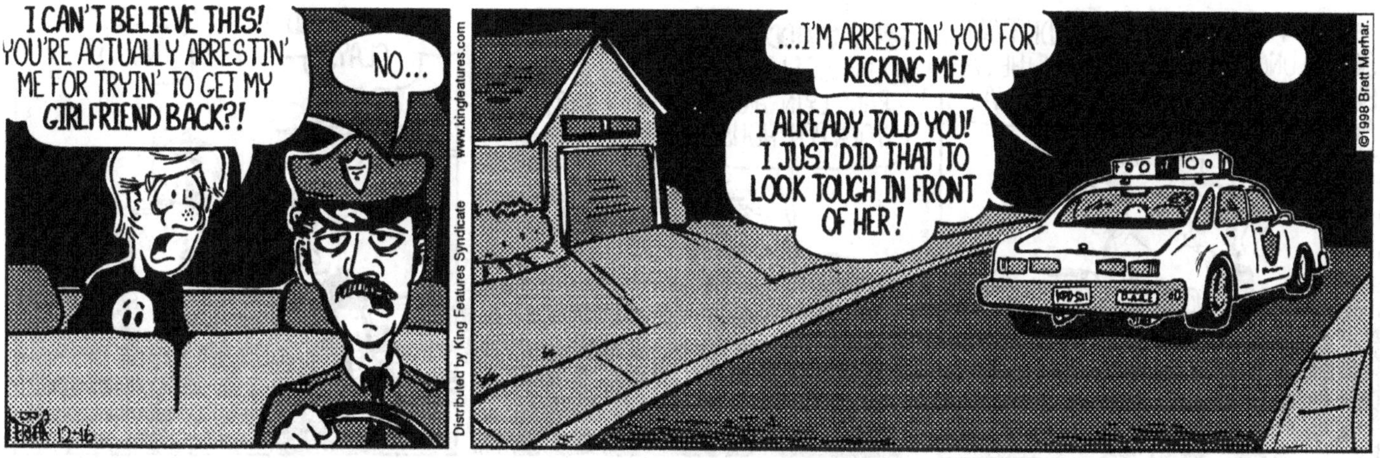
I CAN'T BELIEVE THIS! YOU'RE ACTUALLY ARRESTIN' ME FOR TRYIN' TO GET MY GIRLFRIEND BACK?!
NO...
...I'M ARRESTIN' YOU FOR KICKING ME!
I ALREADY TOLD YOU! I JUST DID THAT TO LOOK TOUGH IN FRONT OF HER!
12-16
www.kingfeatures.com
Distributed by King Features Syndicate
©1998 Brett Merhar.

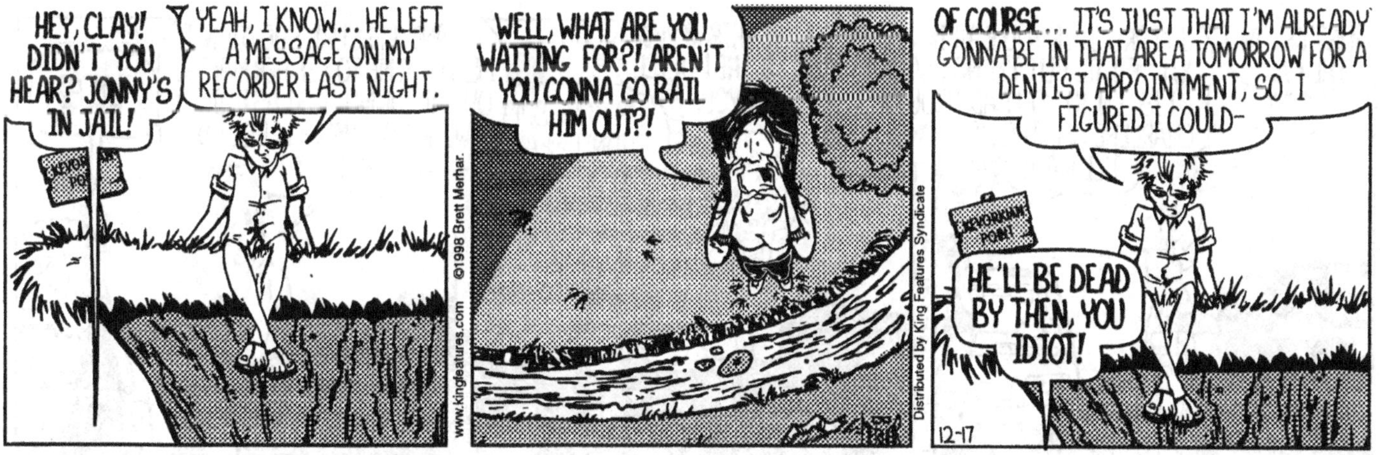
HEY, CLAY! DIDN'T YOU HEAR? JONNY'S IN JAIL!
YEAH, I KNOW... HE LEFT A MESSAGE ON MY RECORDER LAST NIGHT.
WELL, WHAT ARE YOU WAITING FOR?! AREN'T YOU GONNA GO BAIL HIM OUT?!
OF COURSE... IT'S JUST THAT I'M ALREADY GONNA BE IN THAT AREA TOMORROW FOR A DENTIST APPOINTMENT, SO I FIGURED I COULD-
HE'LL BE DEAD BY THEN, YOU IDIOT!
12-17
©1998 Brett Merhar.
www.kingfeatures.com
Distributed by King Features Syndicate

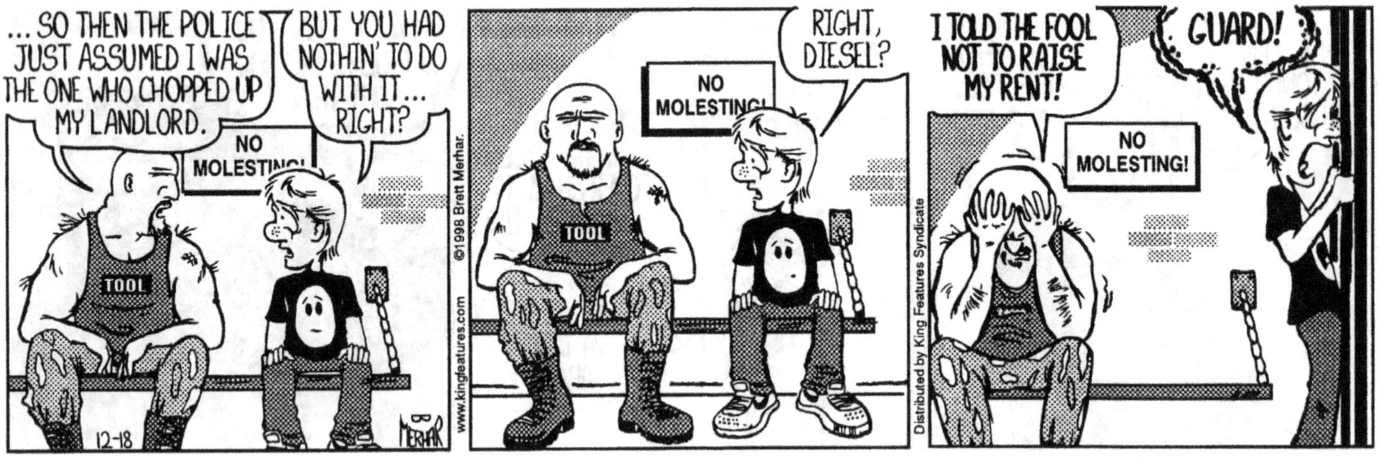
...SO THEN THE POLICE JUST ASSUMED I WAS THE ONE WHO CHOPPED UP MY LANDLORD.
BUT YOU HAD NOTHIN' TO DO WITH IT... RIGHT?
NO MOLESTING!
TOOL
12-18
MERHAR
©1998 Brett Merhar.
www.kingfeatures.com
RIGHT, DIESEL?
NO MOLESTING!
TOOL
Distributed by King Features Syndicate
I TOLD THE FOOL NOT TO RAISE MY RENT!
GUARD!
NO MOLESTING!

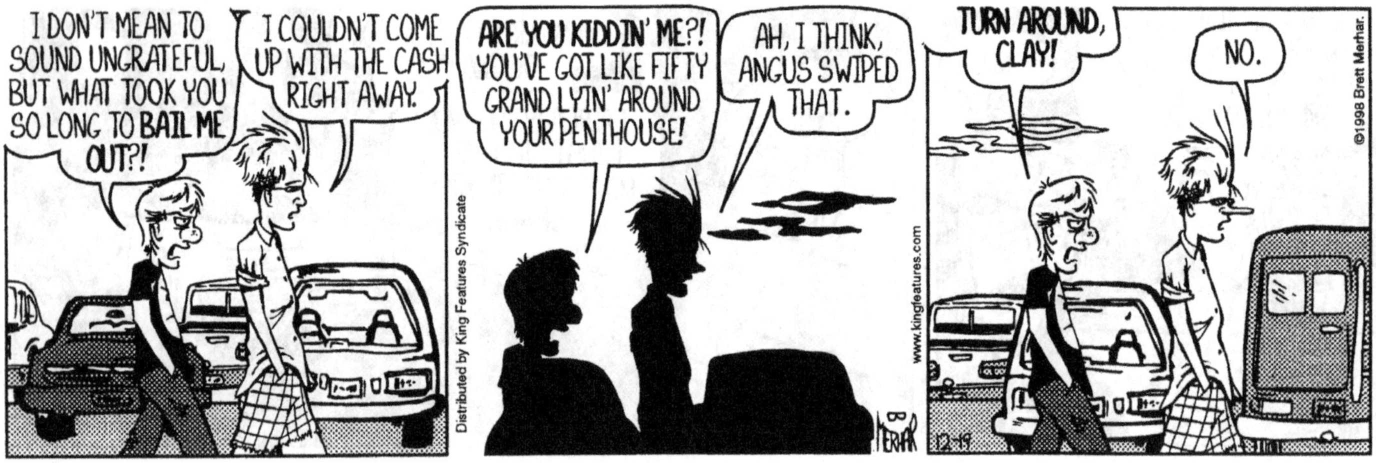
I DON'T MEAN TO SOUND UNGRATEFUL, BUT WHAT TOOK YOU SO LONG TO BAIL ME OUT?!
I COULDN'T COME UP WITH THE CASH RIGHT AWAY.
Distributed by King Features Syndicate
ARE YOU KIDDIN' ME?! YOU'VE GOT LIKE FIFTY GRAND LYIN' AROUND YOUR PENTHOUSE!
AH, I THINK, ANGUS SWIPED THAT.
MERHAR
www.kingfeatures.com
TURN AROUND, CLAY!
NO.
12-19
©1998 Brett Merhar.

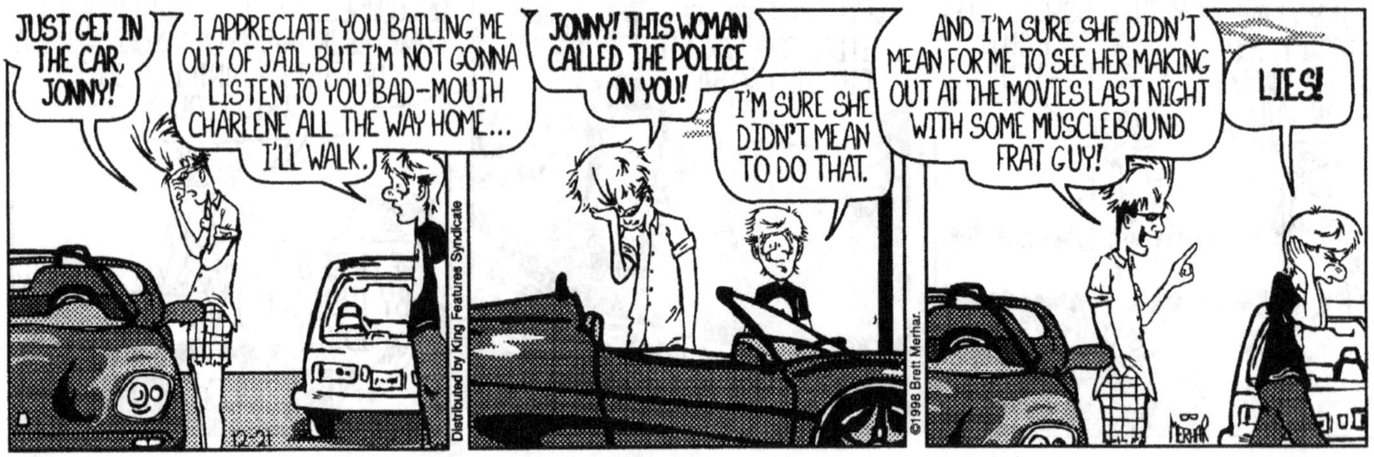
JUST GET IN THE CAR, JONNY!
I APPRECIATE YOU BAILING ME OUT OF JAIL, BUT I'M NOT GONNA LISTEN TO YOU BAD-MOUTH CHARLENE ALL THE WAY HOME... I'LL WALK.
12-21
Distributed by King Features Syndicate
JONNY! THIS WOMAN CALLED THE POLICE ON YOU!
I'M SURE SHE DIDN'T MEAN TO DO THAT.
©1998 Brett Merhar.
AND I'M SURE SHE DIDN'T MEAN FOR ME TO SEE HER MAKING OUT AT THE MOVIES LAST NIGHT WITH SOME MUSCLEBOUND FRAT GUY!
LIES!
MERHAR

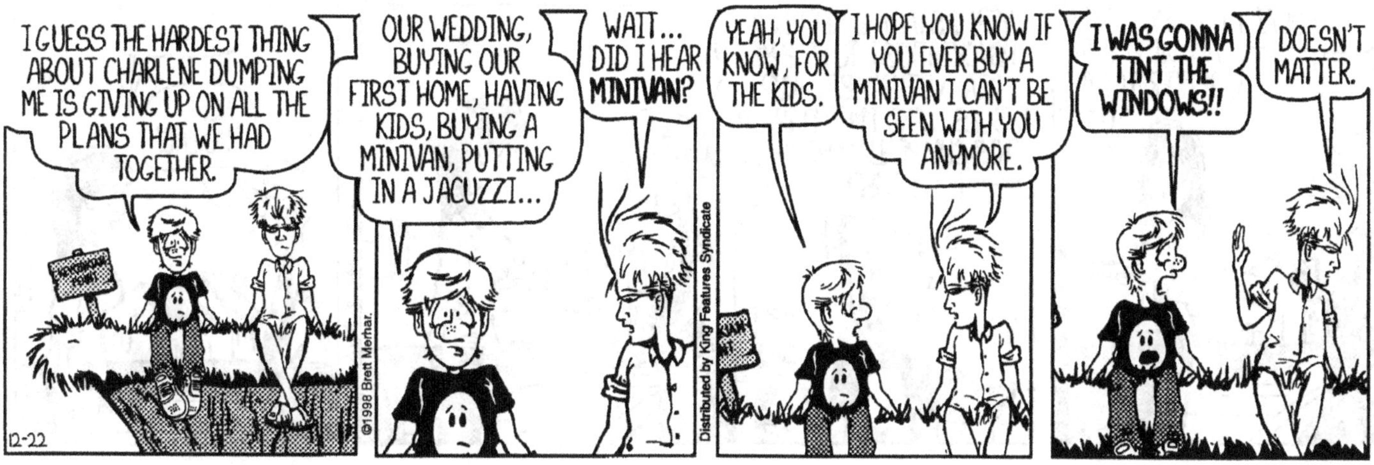
I GUESS THE HARDEST THING ABOUT CHARLENE DUMPING ME IS GIVING UP ON ALL THE PLANS THAT WE HAD TOGETHER.
12-22
OUR WEDDING, BUYING OUR FIRST HOME, HAVING KIDS, BUYING A MINIVAN, PUTTING IN A JACUZZI...
©1998 Brett Merhar.
WAIT... DID I HEAR **MINIVAN?**
YEAH, YOU KNOW, FOR THE KIDS.
Distributed by King Features Syndicate
I HOPE YOU KNOW IF YOU EVER BUY A MINIVAN I CAN'T BE SEEN WITH YOU ANYMORE.
I WAS GONNA TINT THE WINDOWS!!
DOESN'T MATTER.

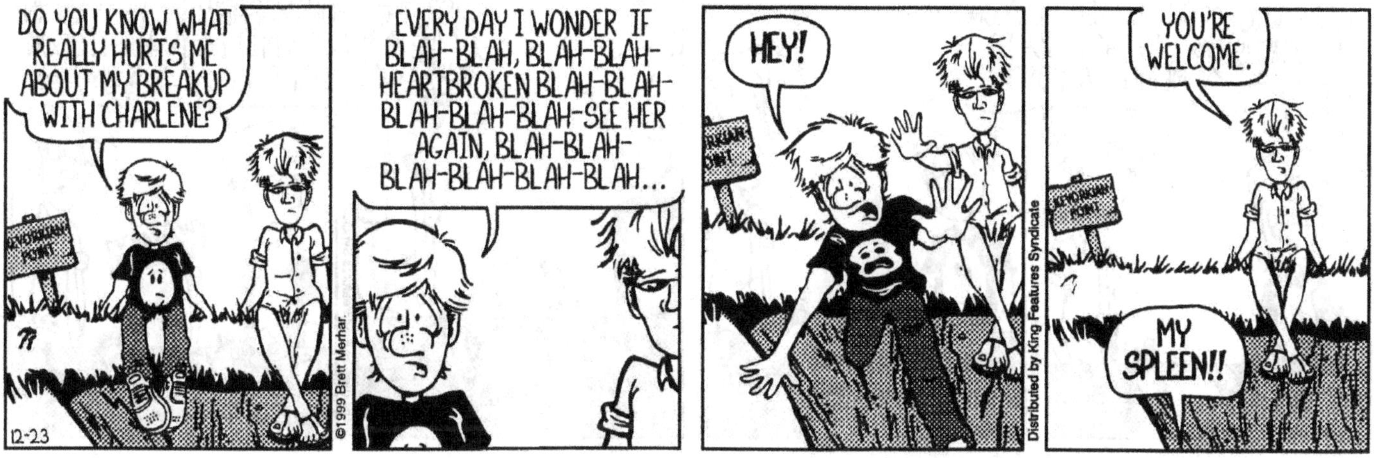
DO YOU KNOW WHAT REALLY HURTS ME ABOUT MY BREAKUP WITH CHARLENE?
12-23
©1999 Brett Merhar.
EVERY DAY I WONDER IF BLAH-BLAH, BLAH-BLAH-HEARTBROKEN BLAH-BLAH-BLAH-BLAH-BLAH-SEE HER AGAIN, BLAH-BLAH-BLAH-BLAH-BLAH-BLAH...
HEY!
Distributed by King Features Syndicate
YOU'RE WELCOME.
MY SPLEEN!!

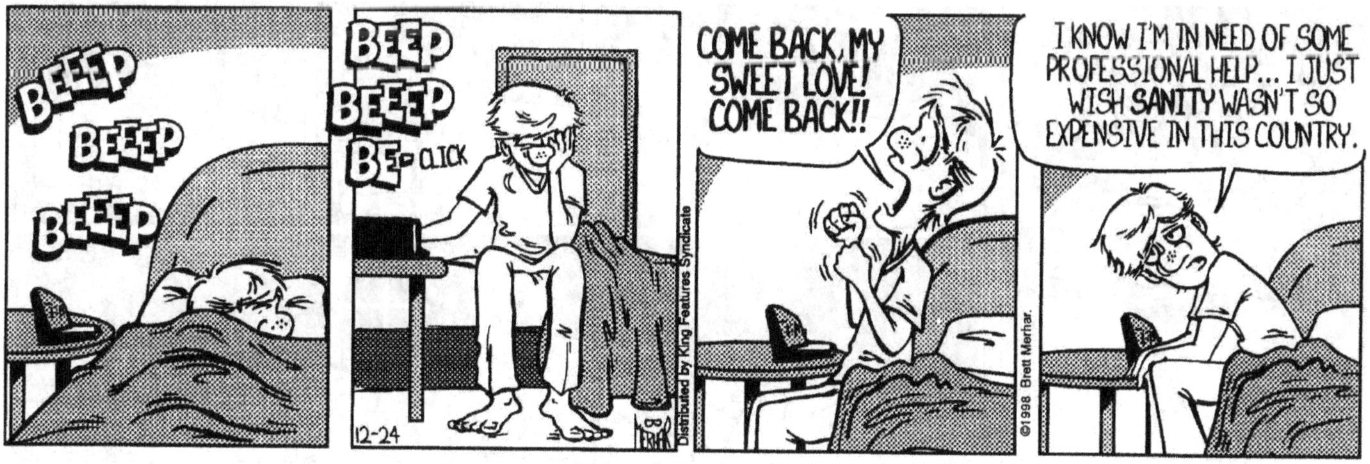
BEEEP
BEEEP
BEEEP
BEEP
BEEEP
BE-CLICK
12-24
MERHAR
Distributed by King Features Syndicate
COME BACK, MY SWEET LOVE! COME BACK!!
©1998 Brett Merhar.
I KNOW I'M IN NEED OF SOME PROFESSIONAL HELP... I JUST WISH **SANITY** WASN'T SO EXPENSIVE IN THIS COUNTRY.

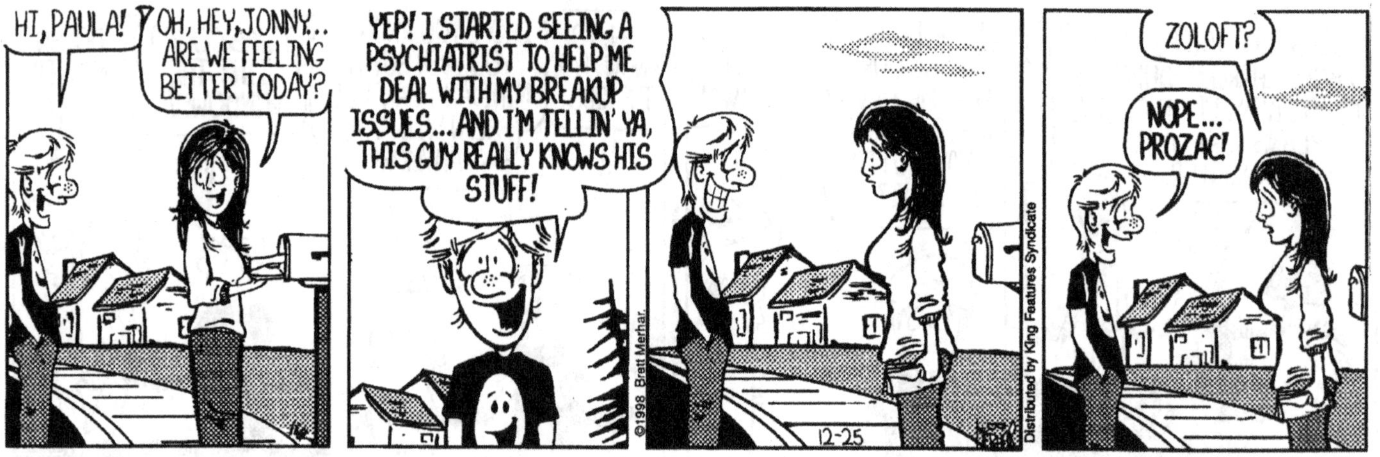
HI, PAULA!
OH, HEY, JONNY... ARE WE FEELING BETTER TODAY?
YEP! I STARTED SEEING A PSYCHIATRIST TO HELP ME DEAL WITH MY BREAKUP ISSUES... AND I'M TELLIN' YA, THIS GUY REALLY KNOWS HIS STUFF!
©1998 Brett Merhar.
12-25
Distributed by King Features Syndicate
ZOLOFT?
NOPE... PROZAC!

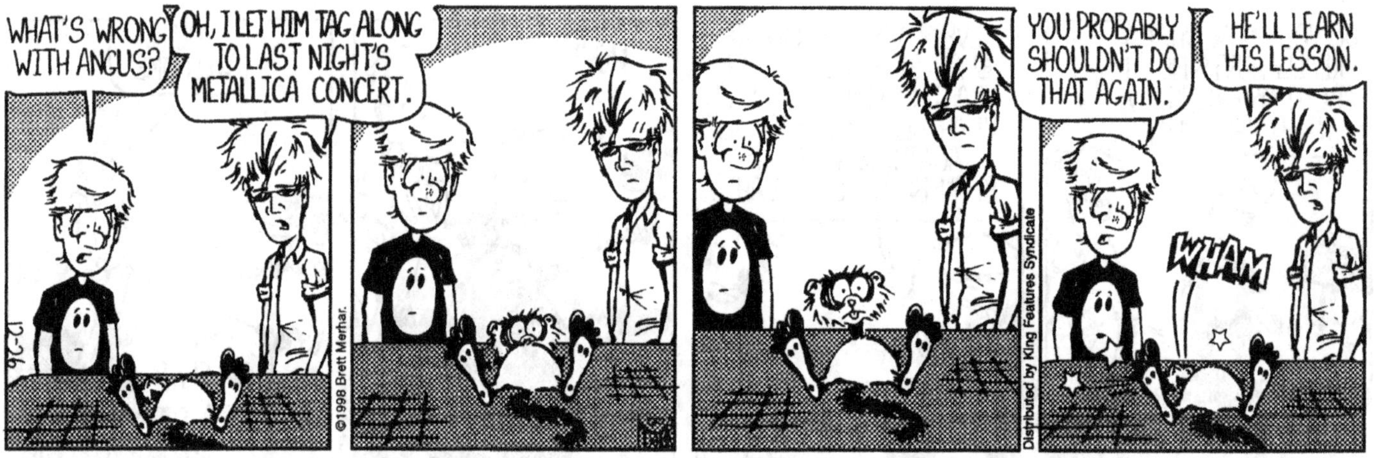
WHAT'S WRONG WITH ANGUS?
OH, I LET HIM TAG ALONG TO LAST NIGHT'S METALLICA CONCERT.
12-26
©1998 Brett Merhar.
Distributed by King Features Syndicate
YOU PROBABLY SHOULDN'T DO THAT AGAIN.
HE'LL LEARN HIS LESSON.
WHAM

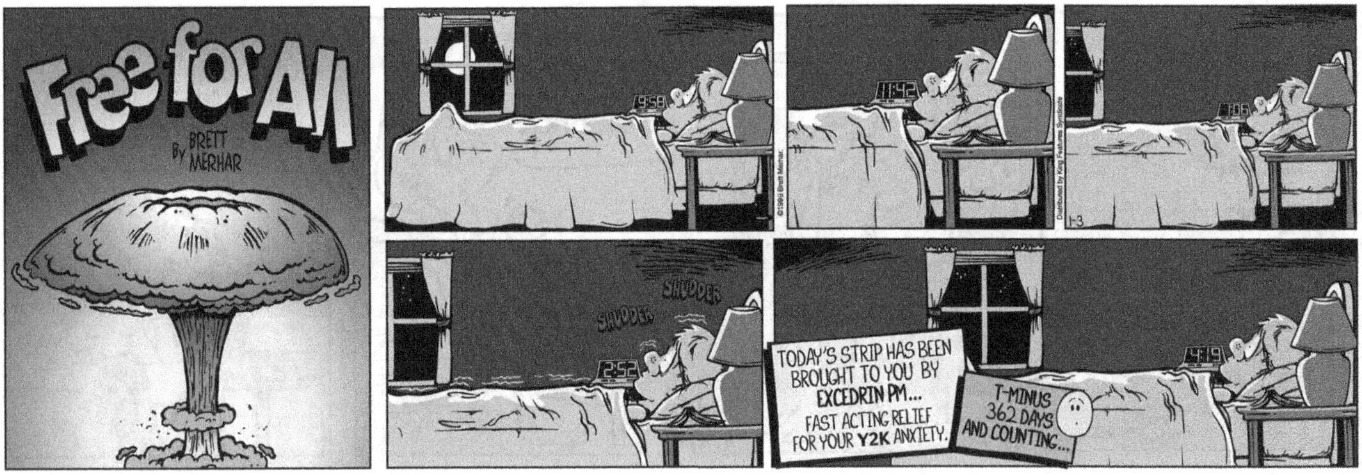
Free for All
BY BRETT MERHAR
9:58
11:42
1:06
1-3
SHUDDER
SHUDDER
2:52
4:19
TODAY'S STRIP HAS BEEN BROUGHT TO YOU BY EXCEDRIN PM... FAST ACTING RELIEF FOR YOUR Y2K ANXIETY.
T-MINUS 362 DAYS AND COUNTING...

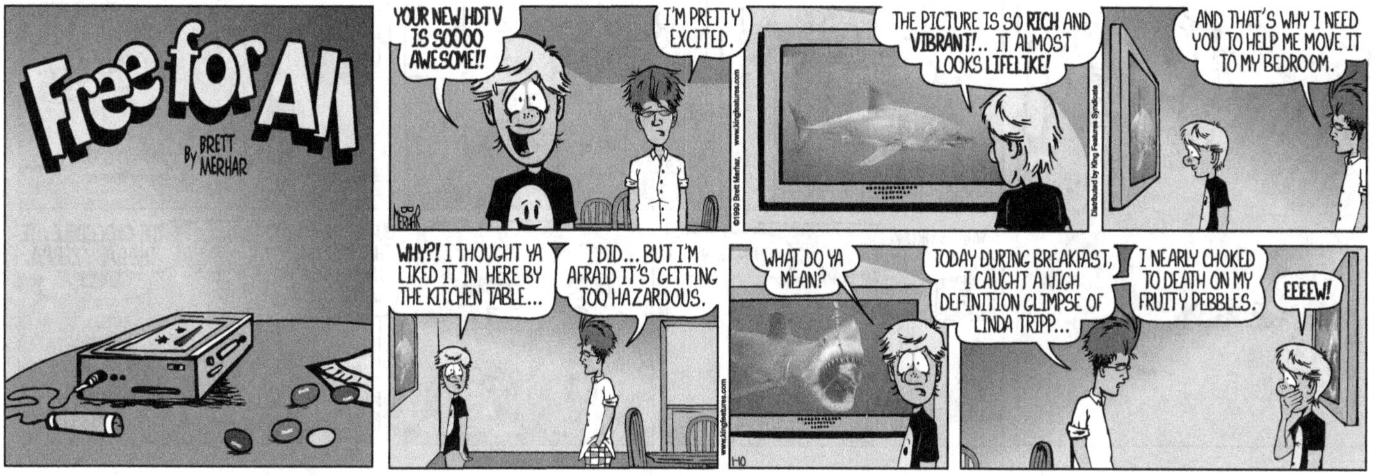
Free for All
By Brett Merhar
YOUR NEW HDTV IS SOOOO AWESOME!!
I'M PRETTY EXCITED.
THE PICTURE IS SO RICH AND VIBRANT!.. IT ALMOST LOOKS LIFELIKE!
AND THAT'S WHY I NEED YOU TO HELP ME MOVE IT TO MY BEDROOM.
WHY?! I THOUGHT YA LIKED IT IN HERE BY THE KITCHEN TABLE...
I DID... BUT I'M AFRAID IT'S GETTING TOO HAZARDOUS.
WHAT DO YA MEAN?
TODAY DURING BREAKFAST, I CAUGHT A HIGH DEFINITION GLIMPSE OF LINDA TRIPP...
I NEARLY CHOKED TO DEATH ON MY FRUITY PEBBLES.
EEEEW!

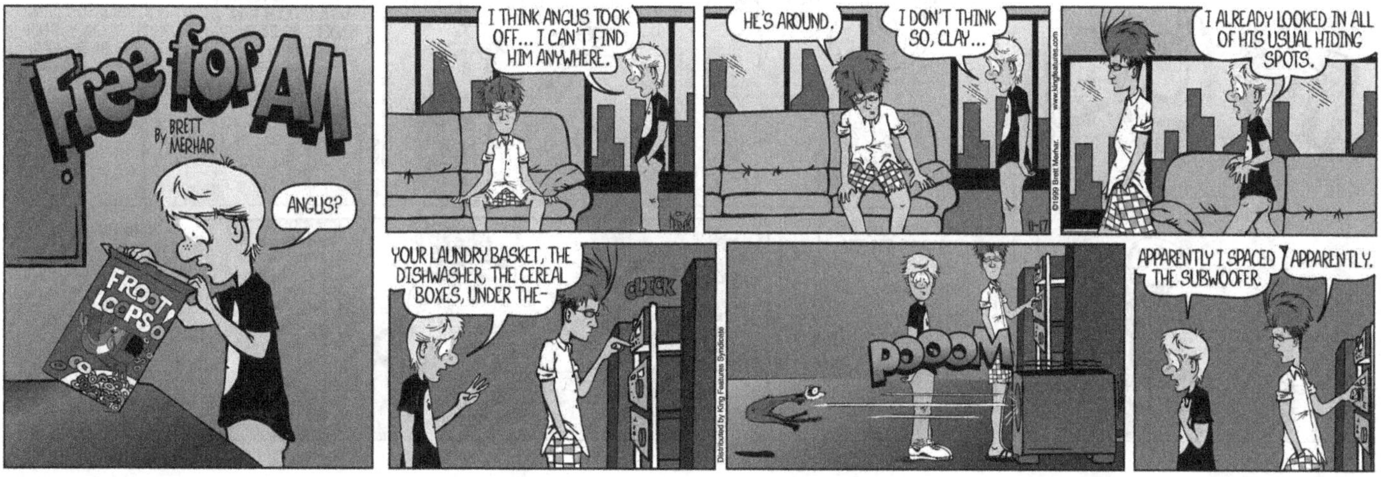
Free for All
By Brett Merhar
ANGUS?
FROOT LOOPS
I THINK ANGUS TOOK OFF... I CAN'T FIND HIM ANYWHERE.
HE'S AROUND.
I DON'T THINK SO, CLAY...
I ALREADY LOOKED IN ALL OF HIS USUAL HIDING SPOTS.
YOUR LAUNDRY BASKET, THE DISHWASHER, THE CEREAL BOXES, UNDER THE-
CLICK
POOOM
APPARENTLY I SPACED THE SUBWOOFER.
APPARENTLY.

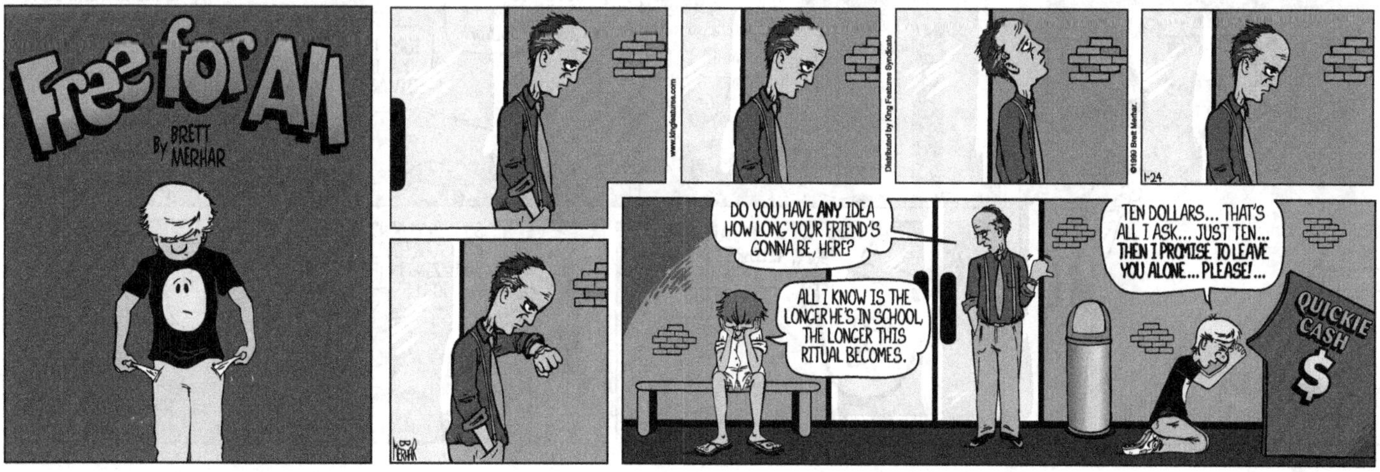
Free for All
By Brett Merhar
DO YOU HAVE ANY IDEA HOW LONG YOUR FRIEND'S GONNA BE, HERE?
ALL I KNOW IS THE LONGER HE'S IN SCHOOL, THE LONGER THIS RITUAL BECOMES.
TEN DOLLARS... THAT'S ALL I ASK... JUST TEN... THEN I PROMISE TO LEAVE YOU ALONE... PLEASE!...
QUICKIE CASH
$

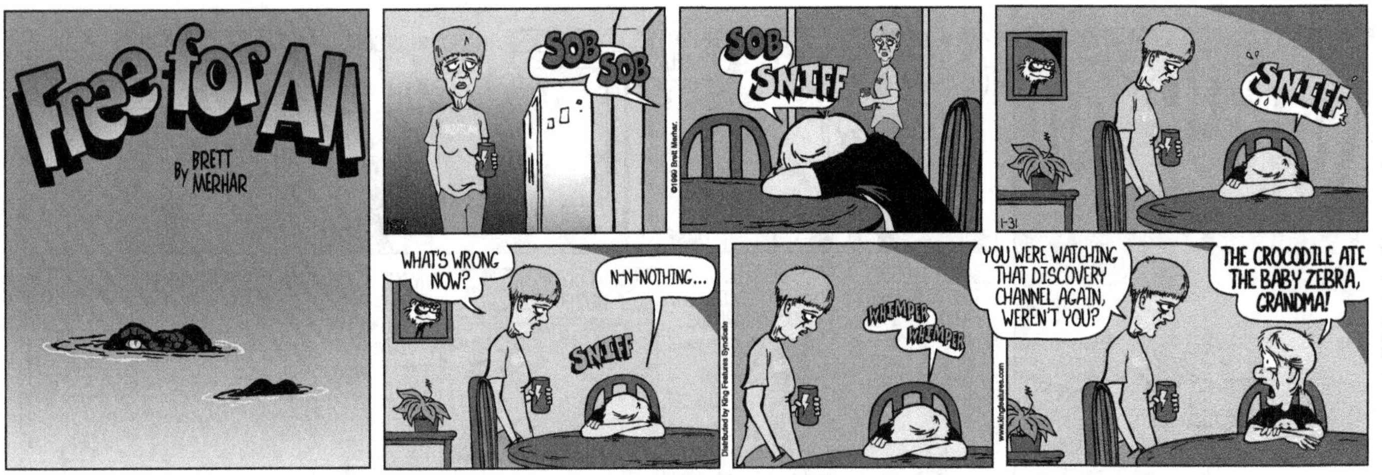
Free for All
By BRETT MERHAR
SOB SOB
SOB
SNIFF
SNIFF
1-31
WHAT'S WRONG NOW?
N-N-NOTHING...
SNIFF
WHIMPER WHIMPER
YOU WERE WATCHING THAT DISCOVERY CHANNEL AGAIN, WEREN'T YOU?
THE CROCODILE ATE THE BABY ZEBRA, GRANDMA!

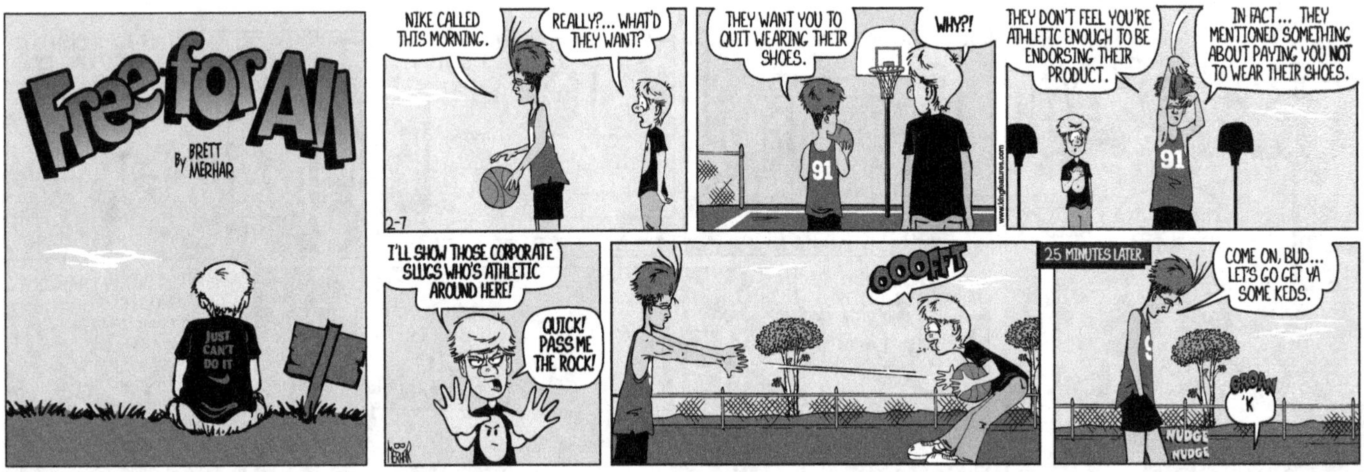
Free for All
By BRETT MERHAR
JUST CAN'T DO IT
NIKE CALLED THIS MORNING.
REALLY?... WHAT'D THEY WANT?
2-7
THEY WANT YOU TO QUIT WEARING THEIR SHOES.
WHY?!
91
THEY DON'T FEEL YOU'RE ATHLETIC ENOUGH TO BE ENDORSING THEIR PRODUCT.
IN FACT... THEY MENTIONED SOMETHING ABOUT PAYING YOU NOT TO WEAR THEIR SHOES.
91
I'LL SHOW THOSE CORPORATE SLUGS WHO'S ATHLETIC AROUND HERE!
QUICK! PASS ME THE ROCK!
OOOFFT
25 MINUTES LATER.
COME ON, BUD... LET'S GO GET YA SOME KEDS.
GROAN
'K
NUDGE
NUDGE

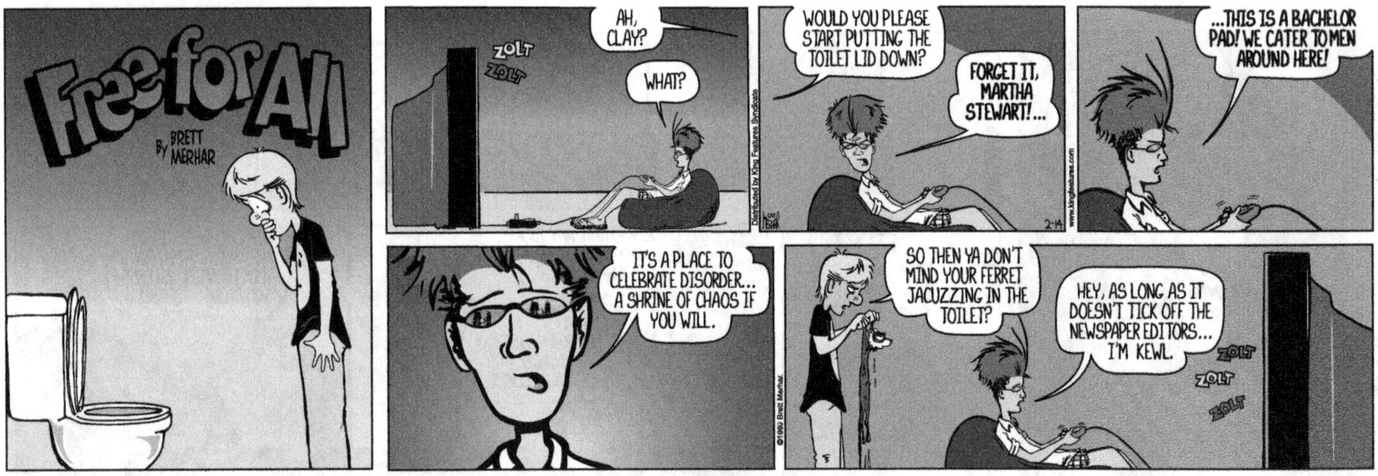
Free for All
By BRETT MERHAR
AH, CLAY?
ZOLT
ZOLT
WHAT?
WOULD YOU PLEASE START PUTTING THE TOILET LID DOWN?
FORGET IT, MARTHA STEWART!...
2-14
...THIS IS A BACHELOR PAD! WE CATER TO MEN AROUND HERE!
IT'S A PLACE TO CELEBRATE DISORDER... A SHRINE OF CHAOS IF YOU WILL.
SO THEN YA DON'T MIND YOUR FERRET JACUZZING IN THE TOILET?
HEY, AS LONG AS IT DOESN'T TICK OFF THE NEWSPAPER EDITORS... I'M KEWL.
ZOLT
ZOLT
ZOLT

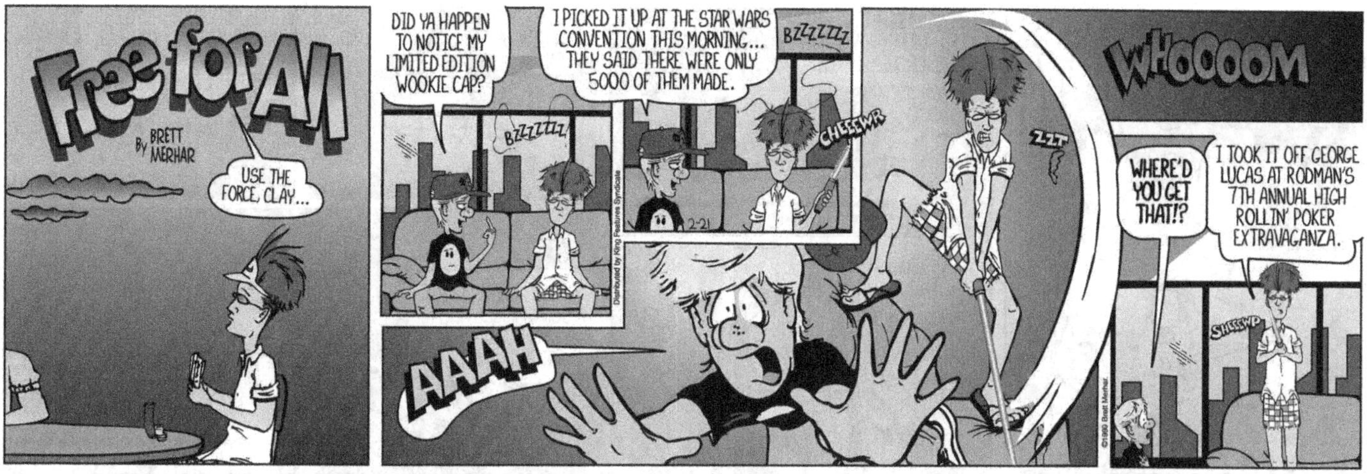
Free for All
By BRETT MERHAR
USE THE FORCE, CLAY...
DID YA HAPPEN TO NOTICE MY LIMITED EDITION WOOKIE CAP?
I PICKED IT UP AT THE STAR WARS CONVENTION THIS MORNING... THEY SAID THERE WERE ONLY 5000 OF THEM MADE.
BZZZZZZ
2-21
Distributed by King Features Syndicate
CHEEEWR
AAAH
WHOOOOM
WHERE'D YOU GET THAT!?
I TOOK IT OFF GEORGE LUCAS AT RODMAN'S 7TH ANNUAL HIGH ROLLIN' POKER EXTRAVAGANZA.

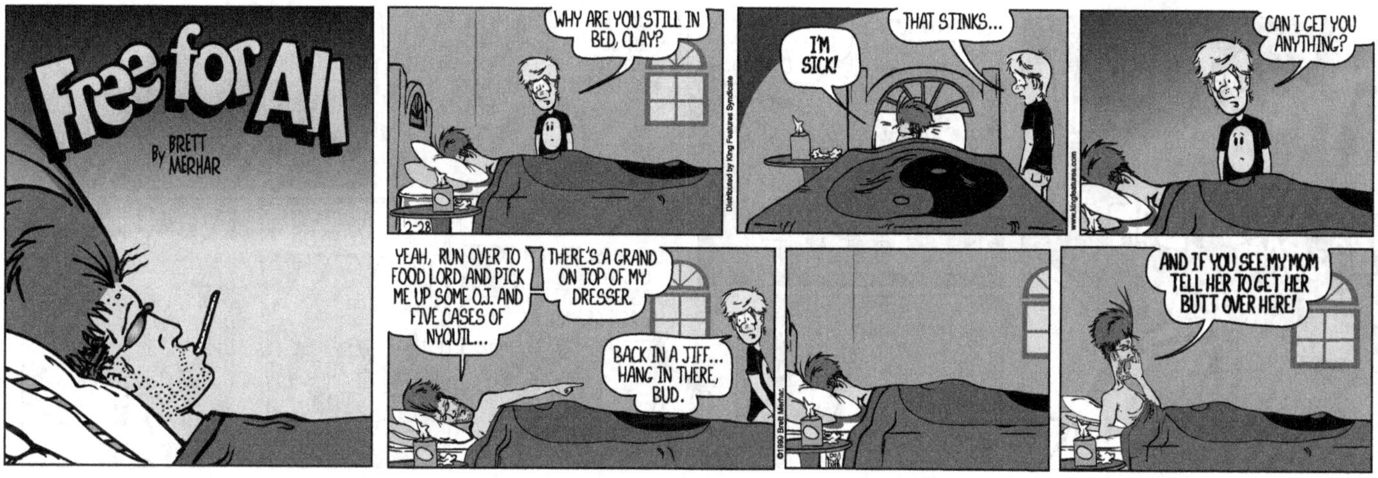
Free for All
By BRETT MERHAR
WHY ARE YOU STILL IN BED, CLAY?
2-28
Distributed by King Features Syndicate
I'M SICK!
THAT STINKS...
www.kingfeatures.com
CAN I GET YOU ANYTHING?
YEAH, RUN OVER TO FOOD LORD AND PICK ME UP SOME O.J. AND FIVE CASES OF NYQUIL...
THERE'S A GRAND ON TOP OF MY DRESSER.
BACK IN A JIFF... HANG IN THERE, BUD.
©1999 Brett Merhar
AND IF YOU SEE MY MOM TELL HER TO GET HER BUTT OVER HERE!

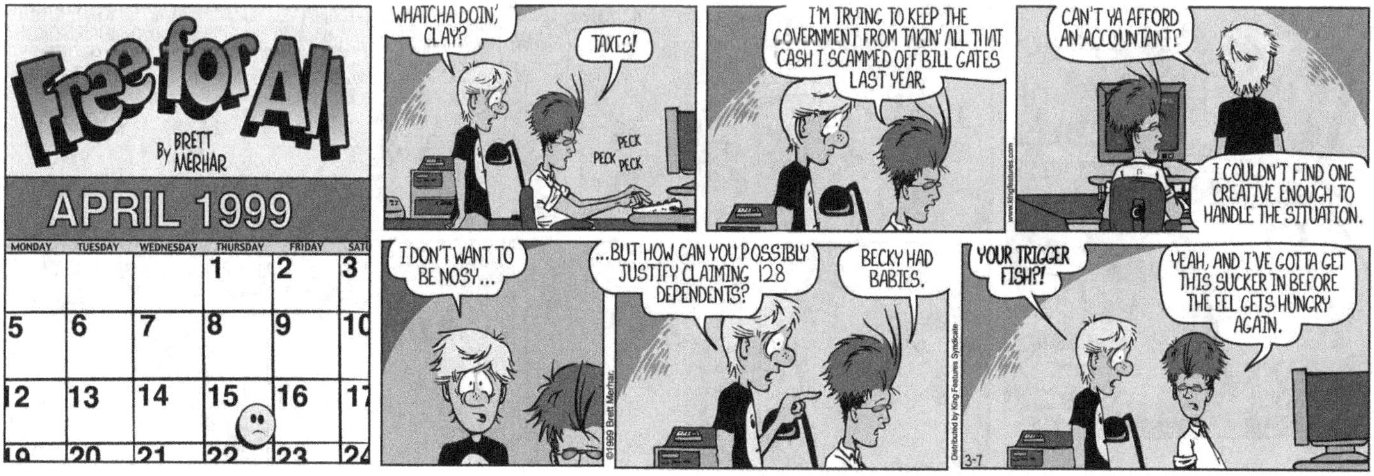
Free for All
By BRETT MERHAR
APRIL 1999
MONDAY TUESDAY WEDNESDAY THURSDAY FRIDAY
1 2 3
5 6 7 8 9 10
12 13 14 15 16 17
WHATCHA DOIN', CLAY?
TAXES!
PECK PECK PECK PECK
I'M TRYING TO KEEP THE GOVERNMENT FROM TAKIN' ALL THAT CASH I SCAMMED OFF BILL GATES LAST YEAR.
www.kingfeatures.com
CAN'T YA AFFORD AN ACCOUNTANT?
I COULDN'T FIND ONE CREATIVE ENOUGH TO HANDLE THE SITUATION.
I DON'T WANT TO BE NOSY...
©1999 Brett Merhar
...BUT HOW CAN YOU POSSIBLY JUSTIFY CLAIMING 128 DEPENDENTS?
BECKY HAD BABIES.
Distributed by King Features Syndicate
3-7
YOUR TRIGGER FISH?!
YEAH, AND I'VE GOTTA GET THIS SUCKER IN BEFORE THE EEL GETS HUNGRY AGAIN.

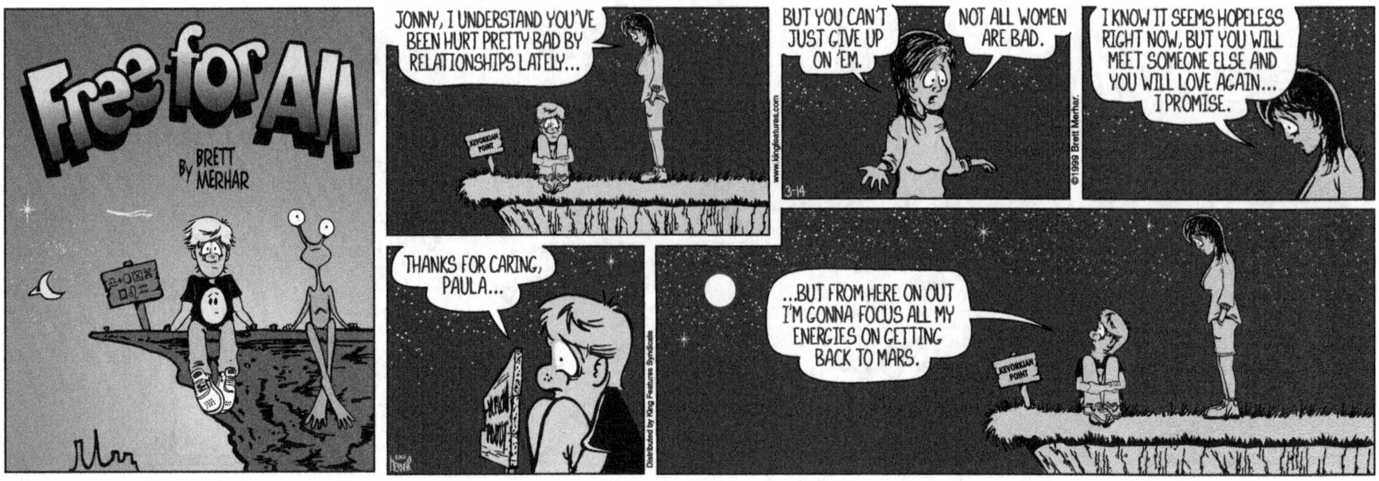

Free for All
By BRETT MERHAR
JONNY, I UNDERSTAND YOU'VE BEEN HURT PRETTY BAD BY RELATIONSHIPS LATELY...
KEVORKIAN POINT
BUT YOU CAN'T JUST GIVE UP ON 'EM.
NOT ALL WOMEN ARE BAD.
I KNOW IT SEEMS HOPELESS RIGHT NOW, BUT YOU WILL MEET SOMEONE ELSE AND YOU WILL LOVE AGAIN... I PROMISE.
THANKS FOR CARING, PAULA...
...BUT FROM HERE ON OUT I'M GONNA FOCUS ALL MY ENERGIES ON GETTING BACK TO MARS.
KEVORKIAN POINT
3-14
www.kingfeatures.com
©1999 Brett Merhar
Distributed by King Features Syndicate

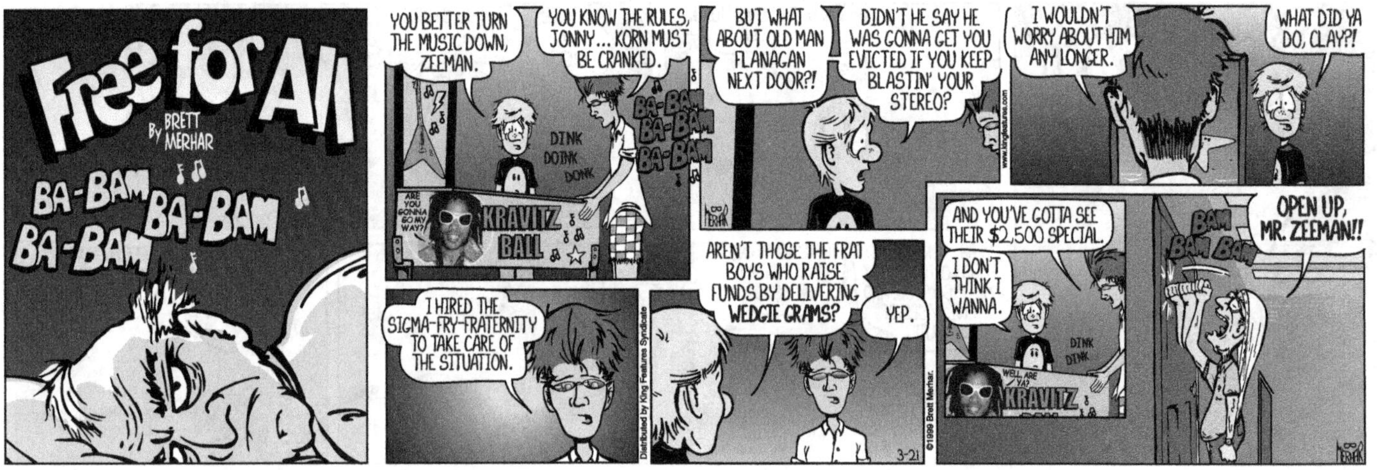

Free for All
By BRETT MERHAR
BA-BAM BA-BAM BA-BAM
YOU BETTER TURN THE MUSIC DOWN, ZEEMAN.
YOU KNOW THE RULES, JONNY... KORN MUST BE CRANKED.
BA-BAM BA-BAM BA-BAM
DINK DOINK DONK
ARE YOU GONNA GO MY WAY?
KRAVITZ BALL
BUT WHAT ABOUT OLD MAN FLANAGAN NEXT DOOR?!
DIDN'T HE SAY HE WAS GONNA GET YOU EVICTED IF YOU KEEP BLASTIN' YOUR STEREO?
I WOULDN'T WORRY ABOUT HIM ANY LONGER.
WHAT DID YA DO, CLAY?!
I HIRED THE SIGMA-FRY-FRATERNITY TO TAKE CARE OF THE SITUATION.
AREN'T THOSE THE FRAT BOYS WHO RAISE FUNDS BY DELIVERING WEDGIE GRAMS?
YEP.
AND YOU'VE GOTTA SEE THEIR $2,500 SPECIAL.
I DON'T THINK I WANNA.
DINK DINK
KRAVITZ
BAM BAM BAM
OPEN UP, MR. ZEEMAN!!
3-21
www.kingfeatures.com
©1999 Brett Merhar
Distributed by King Features Syndicate

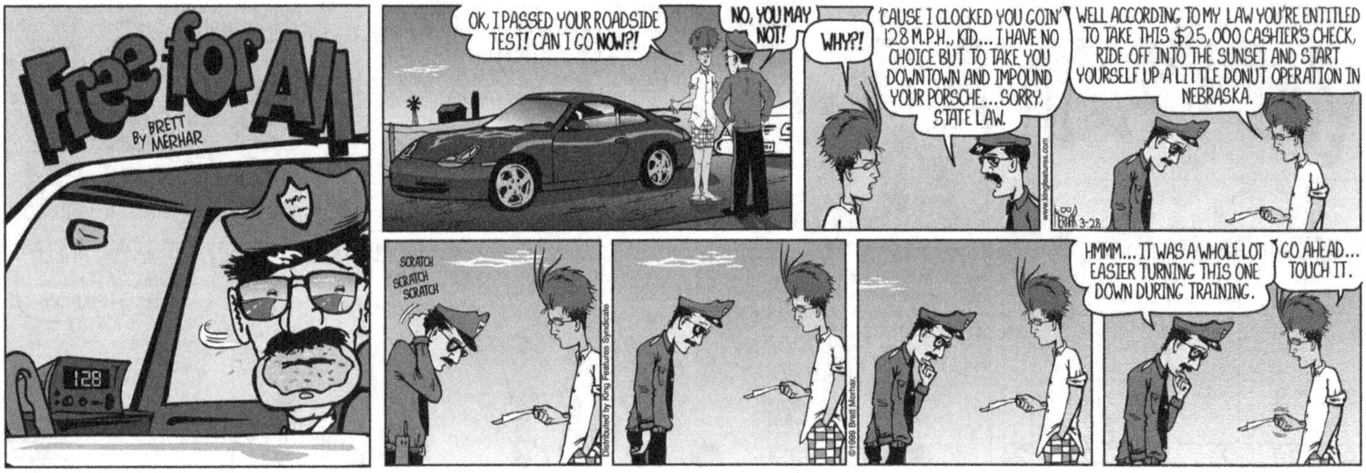

Free for All
By BRETT MERHAR
128
OK, I PASSED YOUR ROADSIDE TEST! CAN I GO NOW?!
NO, YOU MAY NOT!
WHY?!
'CAUSE I CLOCKED YOU GOIN' 128 M.P.H., KID... I HAVE NO CHOICE BUT TO TAKE YOU DOWNTOWN AND IMPOUND YOUR PORSCHE... SORRY, STATE LAW.
WELL ACCORDING TO MY LAW YOU'RE ENTITLED TO TAKE THIS $25,000 CASHIER'S CHECK, RIDE OFF INTO THE SUNSET AND START YOURSELF UP A LITTLE DONUT OPERATION IN NEBRASKA.
SCRATCH SCRATCH SCRATCH
HMMM... IT WAS A WHOLE LOT EASIER TURNING THIS ONE DOWN DURING TRAINING.
GO AHEAD... TOUCH IT.
3-28
www.kingfeatures.com
©1999 Brett Merhar
Distributed by King Features Syndicate

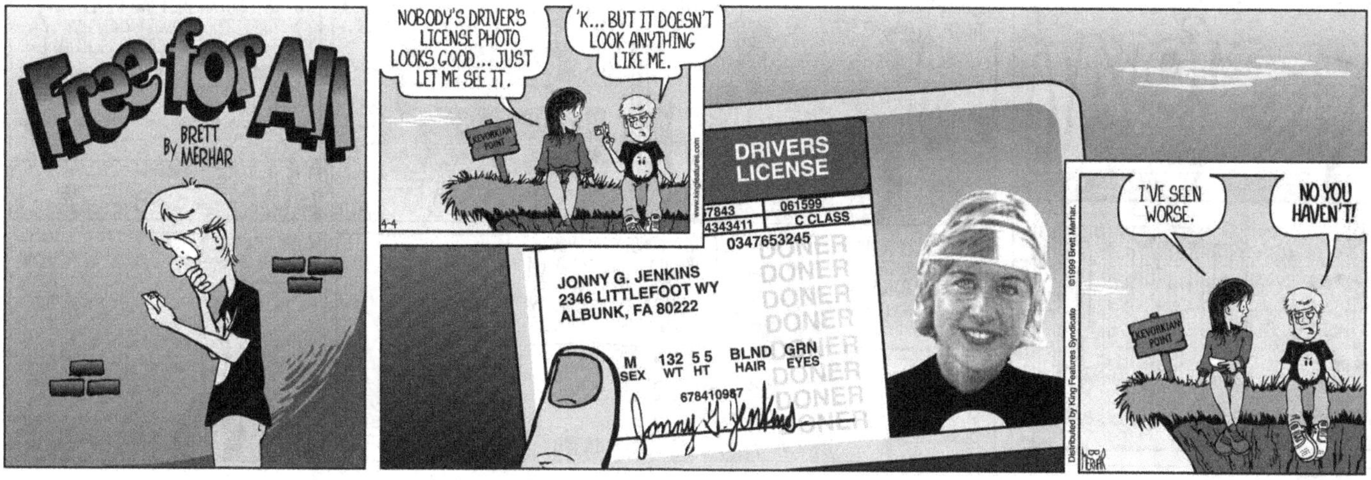
Free for All
BY BRETT MERHAR
NOBODY'S DRIVER'S LICENSE PHOTO LOOKS GOOD... JUST LET ME SEE IT.
'K... BUT IT DOESN'T LOOK ANYTHING LIKE ME.
KEVORKIAN POINT
4-4
DRIVERS LICENSE
JONNY G. JENKINS
2346 LITTLEFOOT WY
ALBUNK, FA 80222
M SEX
132 WT
5 5 HT
BLND HAIR
GRN EYES
DONER
I'VE SEEN WORSE.
NO YOU HAVEN'T!
©1999 Brett Merhar.
Distributed by King Features Syndicate

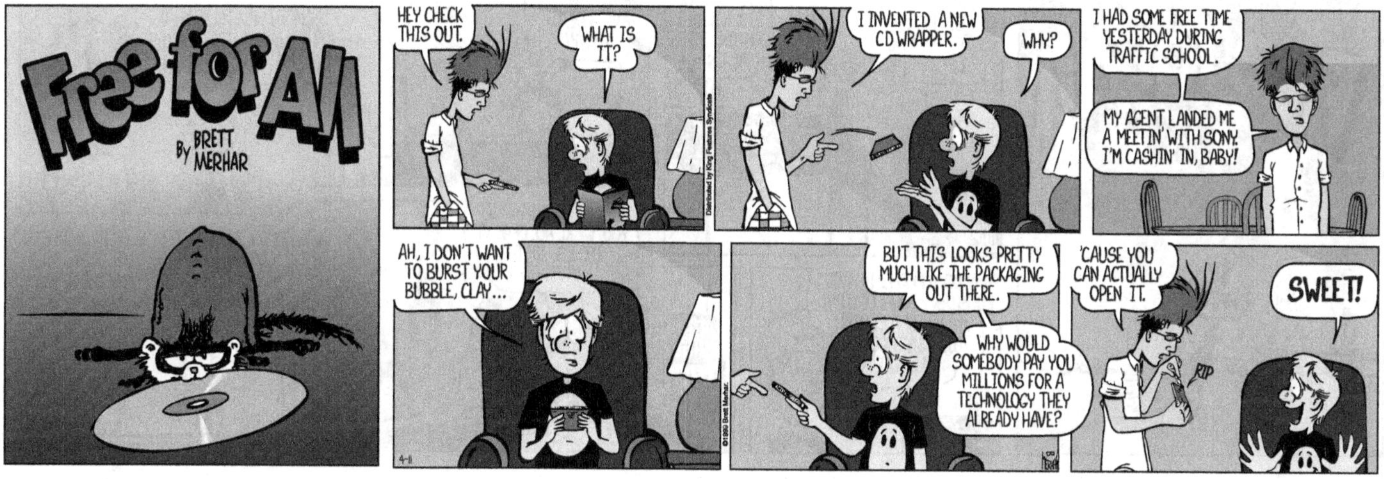
Free for All
BY BRETT MERHAR
HEY CHECK THIS OUT.
WHAT IS IT?
I INVENTED A NEW CD WRAPPER.
WHY?
I HAD SOME FREE TIME YESTERDAY DURING TRAFFIC SCHOOL.
MY AGENT LANDED ME A MEETIN' WITH SONY. I'M CASHIN' IN, BABY!
AH, I DON'T WANT TO BURST YOUR BUBBLE, CLAY...
4-11
BUT THIS LOOKS PRETTY MUCH LIKE THE PACKAGING OUT THERE.
WHY WOULD SOMEBODY PAY YOU MILLIONS FOR A TECHNOLOGY THEY ALREADY HAVE?
'CAUSE YOU CAN ACTUALLY OPEN IT.
RIP
SWEET!

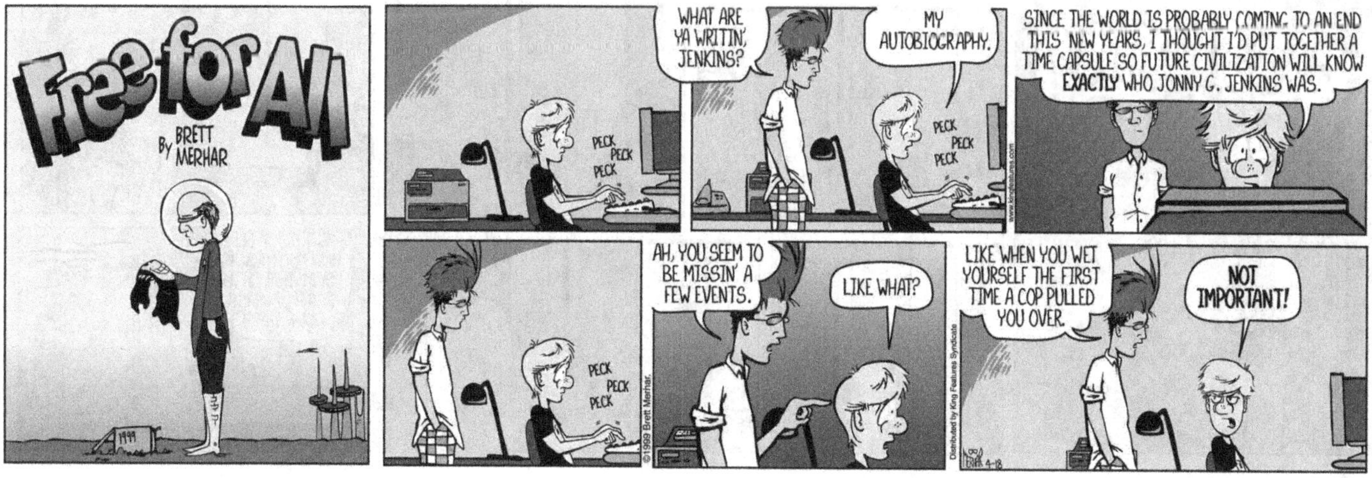
Free for All
BY BRETT MERHAR
1999
PECK PECK PECK
WHAT ARE YA WRITIN', JENKINS?
MY AUTOBIOGRAPHY.
PECK PECK PECK
SINCE THE WORLD IS PROBABLY COMING TO AN END THIS NEW YEARS, I THOUGHT I'D PUT TOGETHER A TIME CAPSULE SO FUTURE CIVILIZATION WILL KNOW EXACTLY WHO JONNY G. JENKINS WAS.
PECK PECK PECK
AH, YOU SEEM TO BE MISSIN' A FEW EVENTS.
LIKE WHAT?
LIKE WHEN YOU WET YOURSELF THE FIRST TIME A COP PULLED YOU OVER.
NOT IMPORTANT!
4-18

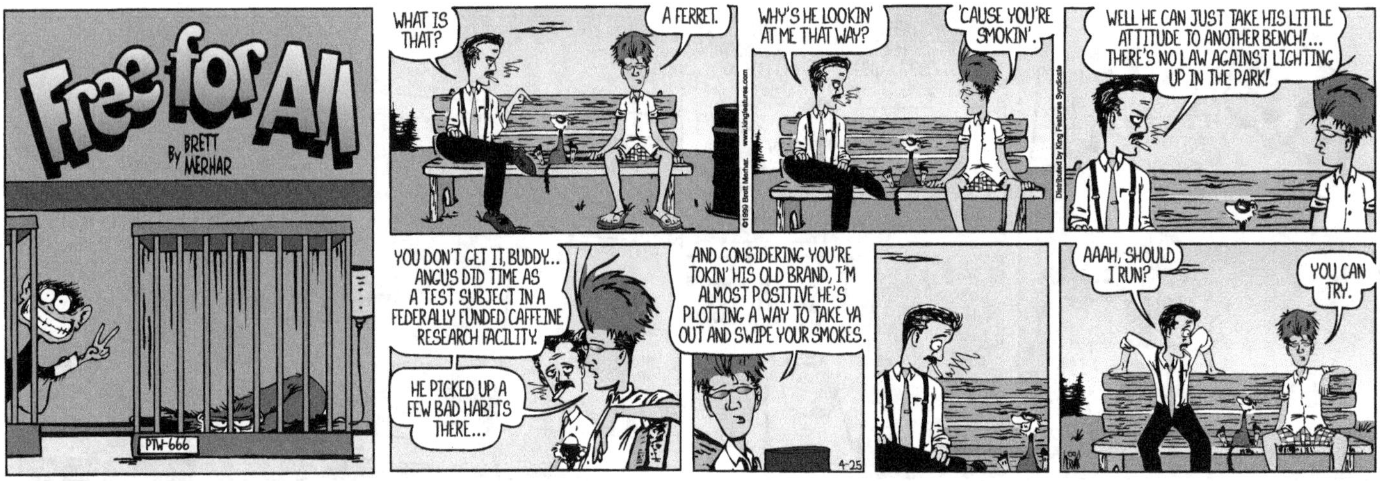
Free for All
By Brett Merhar
PTW-666
WHAT IS THAT?
A FERRET.
WHY'S HE LOOKIN' AT ME THAT WAY?
'CAUSE YOU'RE SMOKIN'.
WELL HE CAN JUST TAKE HIS LITTLE ATTITUDE TO ANOTHER BENCH!... THERE'S NO LAW AGAINST LIGHTING UP IN THE PARK!
YOU DON'T GET IT, BUDDY... ANGUS DID TIME AS A TEST SUBJECT IN A FEDERALLY FUNDED CAFFEINE RESEARCH FACILITY.
HE PICKED UP A FEW BAD HABITS THERE...
AND CONSIDERING YOU'RE TOKIN' HIS OLD BRAND, I'M ALMOST POSITIVE HE'S PLOTTING A WAY TO TAKE YA OUT AND SWIPE YOUR SMOKES.
AAAH, SHOULD I RUN?
YOU CAN TRY.
4-25
©1999 Brett Merhar.
www.kingfeatures.com
Distributed by King Features Syndicate

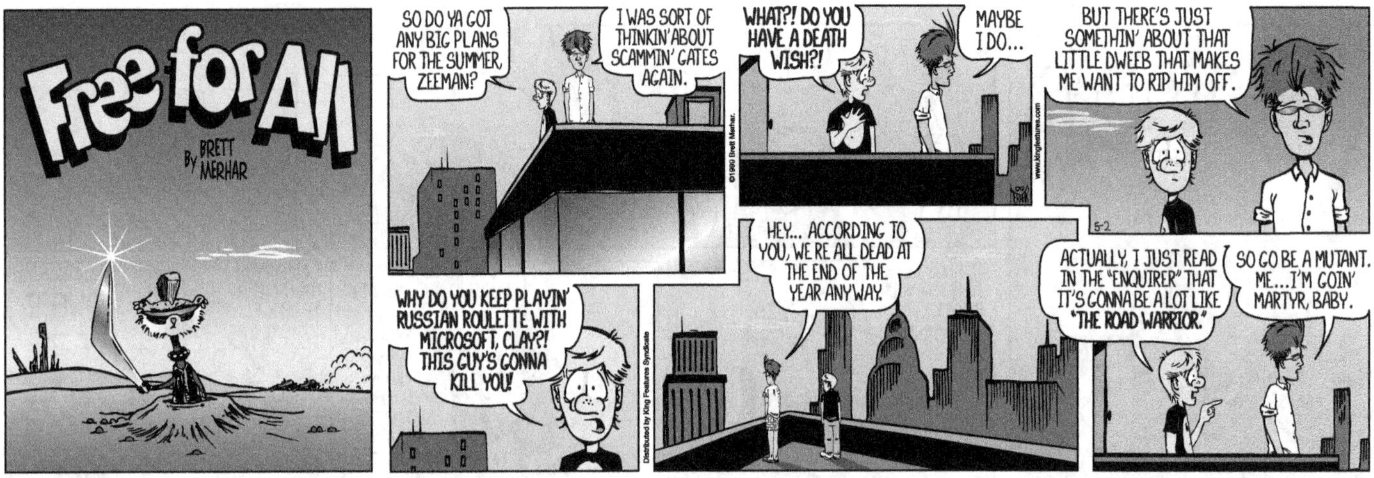
Free for All
By Brett Merhar
SO DO YA GOT ANY BIG PLANS FOR THE SUMMER, ZEEMAN?
I WAS SORT OF THINKIN' ABOUT SCAMMIN' GATES AGAIN.
WHAT?! DO YOU HAVE A DEATH WISH?!
MAYBE I DO...
BUT THERE'S JUST SOMETHIN' ABOUT THAT LITTLE DWEEB THAT MAKES ME WANT TO RIP HIM OFF.
WHY DO YOU KEEP PLAYIN' RUSSIAN ROULETTE WITH MICROSOFT, CLAY?! THIS GUY'S GONNA KILL YOU!
HEY... ACCORDING TO YOU, WE'RE ALL DEAD AT THE END OF THE YEAR ANYWAY.
ACTUALLY, I JUST READ IN THE "ENQUIRER" THAT IT'S GONNA BE A LOT LIKE "THE ROAD WARRIOR."
SO GO BE A MUTANT. ME...I'M GOIN' MARTYR, BABY.
5-2
©1999 Brett Merhar.
www.kingfeatures.com
Distributed by King Features Syndicate

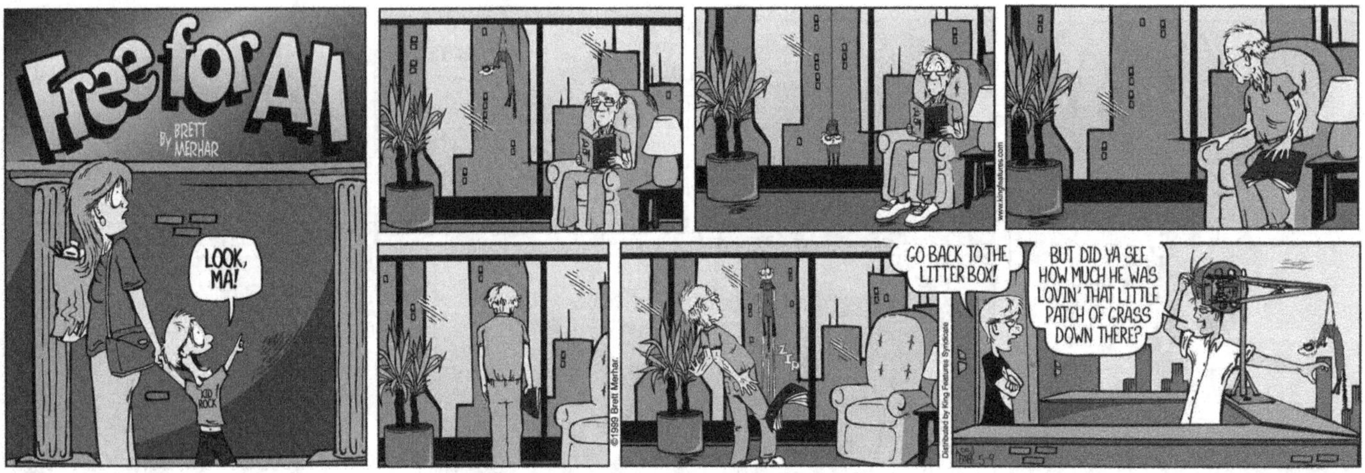
Free for All
By Brett Merhar
LOOK, MA!
KID ROCK
ZIP
GO BACK TO THE LITTER BOX!
BUT DID YA SEE HOW MUCH HE WAS LOVIN' THAT LITTLE PATCH OF GRASS DOWN THERE?
5-9
©1999 Brett Merhar.
www.kingfeatures.com
Distributed by King Features Syndicate

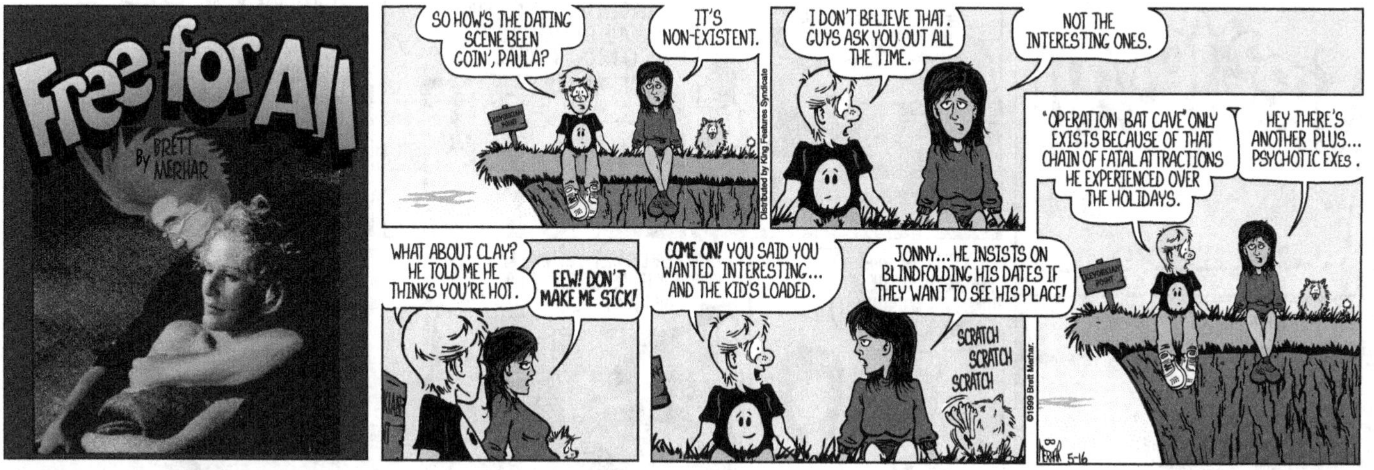
Free for All
By BRETT MERHAR
SO HOW'S THE DATING SCENE BEEN GOIN', PAULA?
IT'S NON-EXISTENT.
I DON'T BELIEVE THAT. GUYS ASK YOU OUT ALL THE TIME.
NOT THE INTERESTING ONES.
Distributed by King Features Syndicate
WHAT ABOUT CLAY? HE TOLD ME HE THINKS YOU'RE HOT.
EEW! DON'T MAKE ME SICK!
COME ON! YOU SAID YOU WANTED INTERESTING... AND THE KID'S LOADED.
JONNY... HE INSISTS ON BLINDFOLDING HIS DATES IF THEY WANT TO SEE HIS PLACE!
SCRATCH
SCRATCH
SCRATCH
©1999 Brett Merhar
"OPERATION BAT CAVE" ONLY EXISTS BECAUSE OF THAT CHAIN OF FATAL ATTRACTIONS HE EXPERIENCED OVER THE HOLIDAYS.
HEY THERE'S ANOTHER PLUS... PSYCHOTIC EXES.
5-16

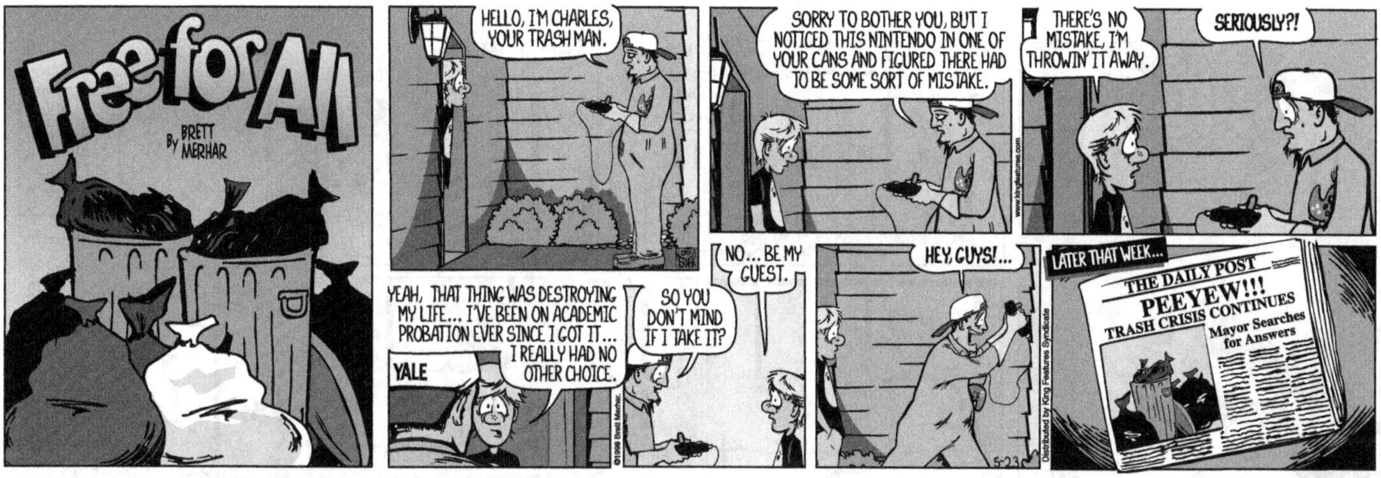
Free for All
By BRETT MERHAR
HELLO, I'M CHARLES, YOUR TRASH MAN.
SORRY TO BOTHER YOU, BUT I NOTICED THIS NINTENDO IN ONE OF YOUR CANS AND FIGURED THERE HAD TO BE SOME SORT OF MISTAKE.
www.kingfeatures.com
THERE'S NO MISTAKE, I'M THROWIN' IT AWAY.
SERIOUSLY?!
YEAH, THAT THING WAS DESTROYING MY LIFE... I'VE BEEN ON ACADEMIC PROBATION EVER SINCE I GOT IT... I REALLY HAD NO OTHER CHOICE.
YALE
©1999 Brett Merhar
SO YOU DON'T MIND IF I TAKE IT?
NO... BE MY GUEST.
HEY, GUYS!...
5-23
Distributed by King Features Syndicate
LATER THAT WEEK...
THE DAILY POST
PEEYEW!!!
TRASH CRISIS CONTINUES
Mayor Searches for Answers

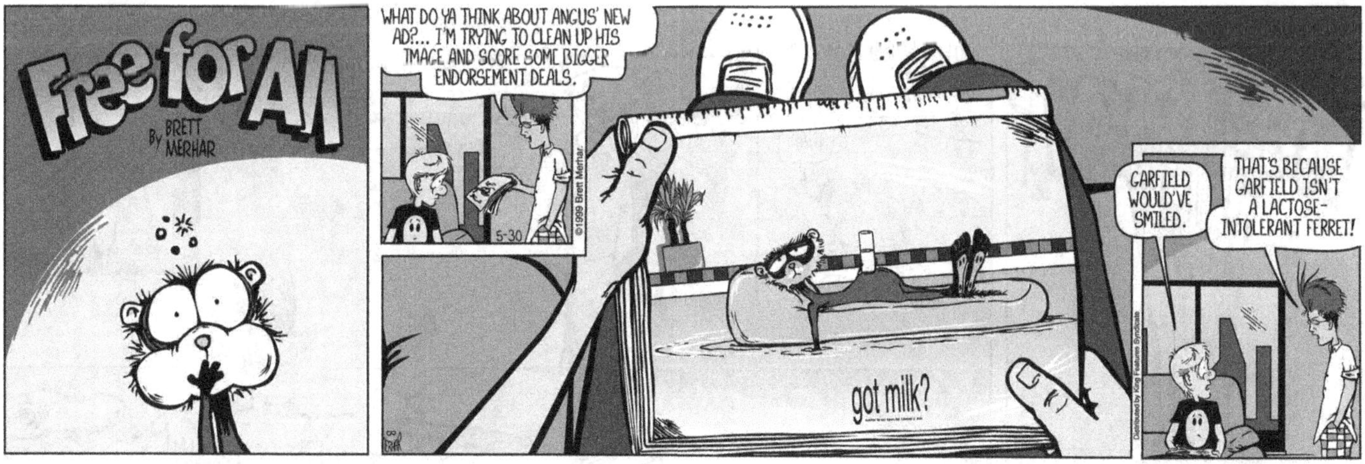
Free for All
By BRETT MERHAR
WHAT DO YA THINK ABOUT ANGUS' NEW AD?... I'M TRYING TO CLEAN UP HIS IMAGE AND SCORE SOME BIGGER ENDORSEMENT DEALS.
©1999 Brett Merhar
5-30
got milk?
GARFIELD WOULD'VE SMILED.
THAT'S BECAUSE GARFIELD ISN'T A LACTOSE-INTOLERANT FERRET!
Distributed by King Features Syndicate

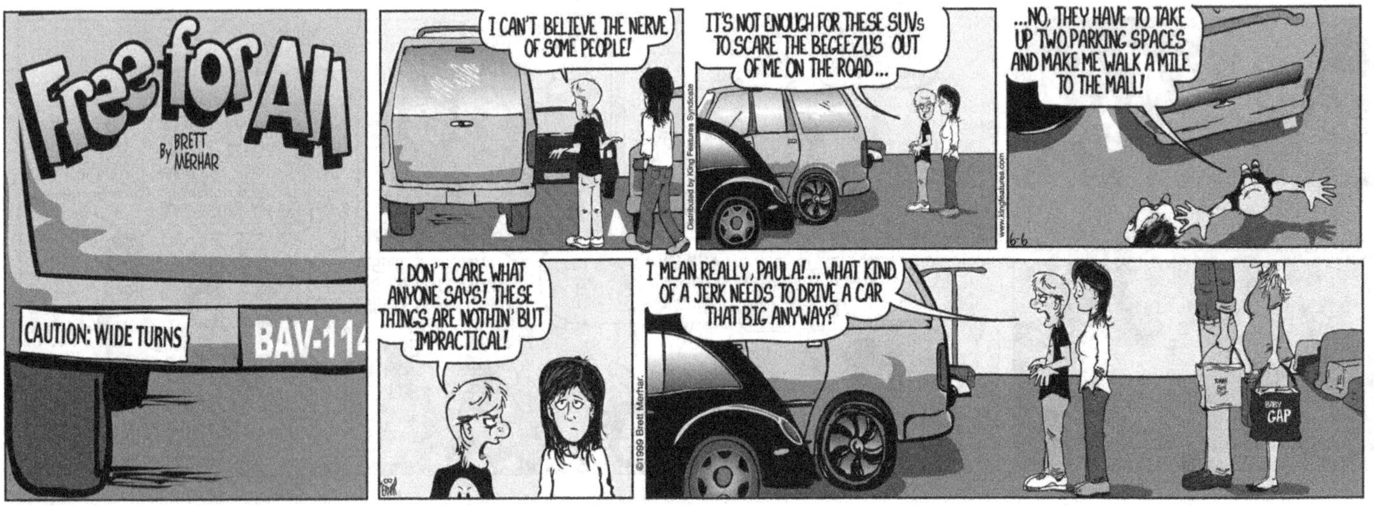
Free for All
By BRETT MERHAR
CAUTION: WIDE TURNS
BAV-114
I CAN'T BELIEVE THE NERVE OF SOME PEOPLE!
IT'S NOT ENOUGH FOR THESE SUVs TO SCARE THE BEGEEZUS OUT OF ME ON THE ROAD...
...NO, THEY HAVE TO TAKE UP TWO PARKING SPACES AND MAKE ME WALK A MILE TO THE MALL!
I DON'T CARE WHAT ANYONE SAYS! THESE THINGS ARE NOTHIN' BUT IMPRACTICAL!
I MEAN REALLY, PAULA!... WHAT KIND OF A JERK NEEDS TO DRIVE A CAR THAT BIG ANYWAY?
BABY GAP
Distributed by King Features Syndicate
www.kingfeatures.com
©1999 Brett Merhar.
6-6

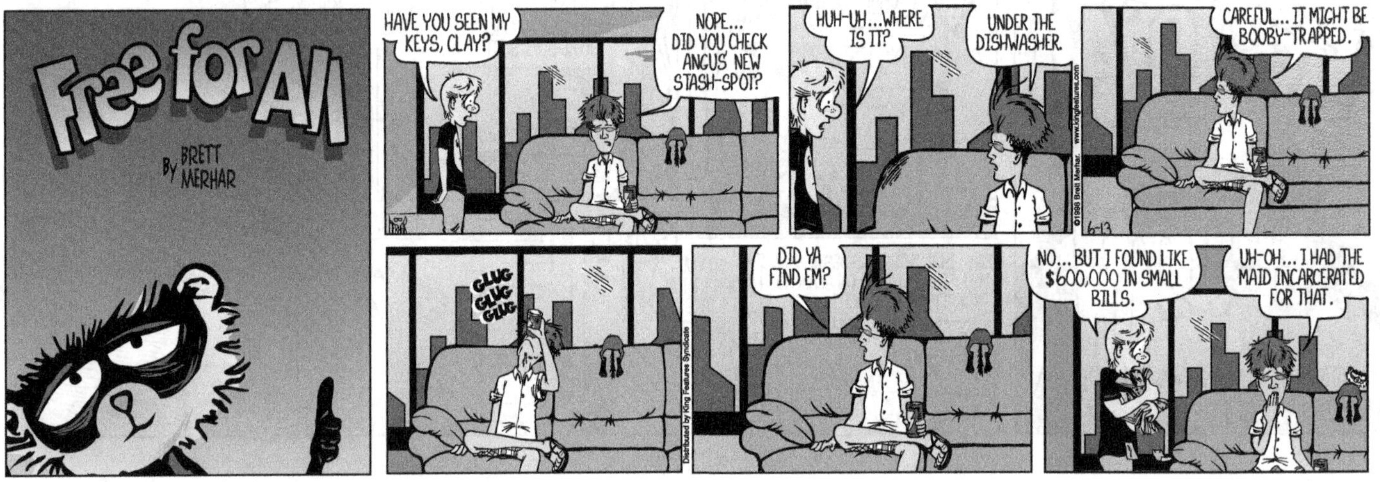
Free for All
By BRETT MERHAR
HAVE YOU SEEN MY KEYS, CLAY?
NOPE... DID YOU CHECK ANGUS' NEW STASH-SPOT?
HUH-UH... WHERE IS IT?
UNDER THE DISHWASHER.
CAREFUL... IT MIGHT BE BOOBY-TRAPPED.
GLUG GLUG GLUG
DID YA FIND EM?
NO... BUT I FOUND LIKE $600,000 IN SMALL BILLS.
UH-OH... I HAD THE MAID INCARCERATED FOR THAT.
Distributed by King Features Syndicate
www.kingfeatures.com
6-13

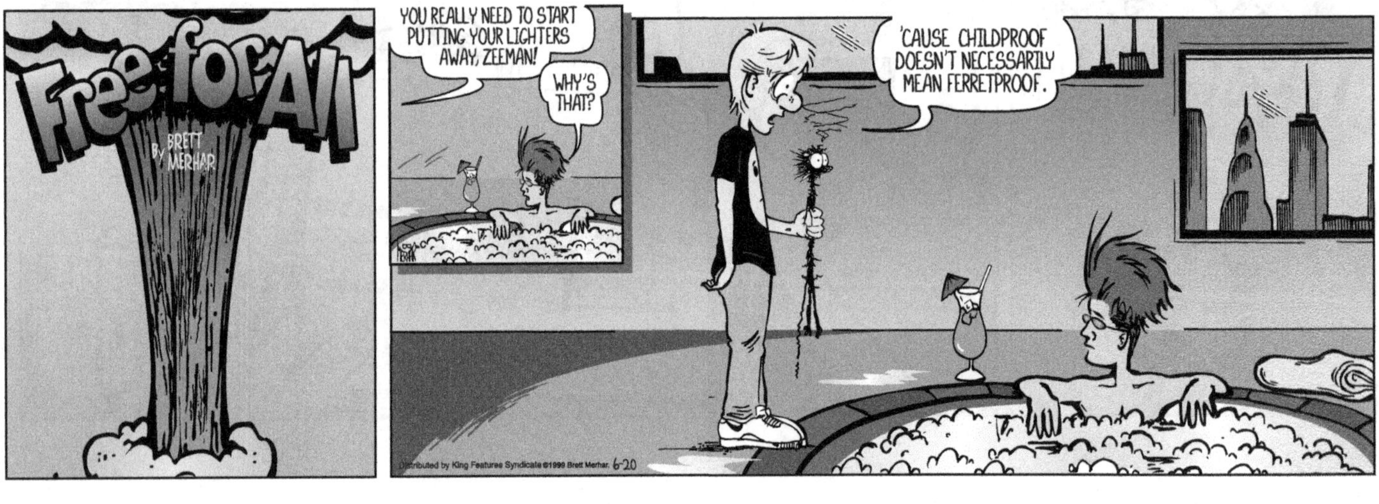
Free for All
By BRETT MERHAR
YOU REALLY NEED TO START PUTTING YOUR LIGHTERS AWAY, ZEEMAN!
WHY'S THAT?
'CAUSE CHILDPROOF DOESN'T NECESSARILY MEAN FERRETPROOF.
Distributed by King Features Syndicate ©1999 Brett Merhar. 6-20

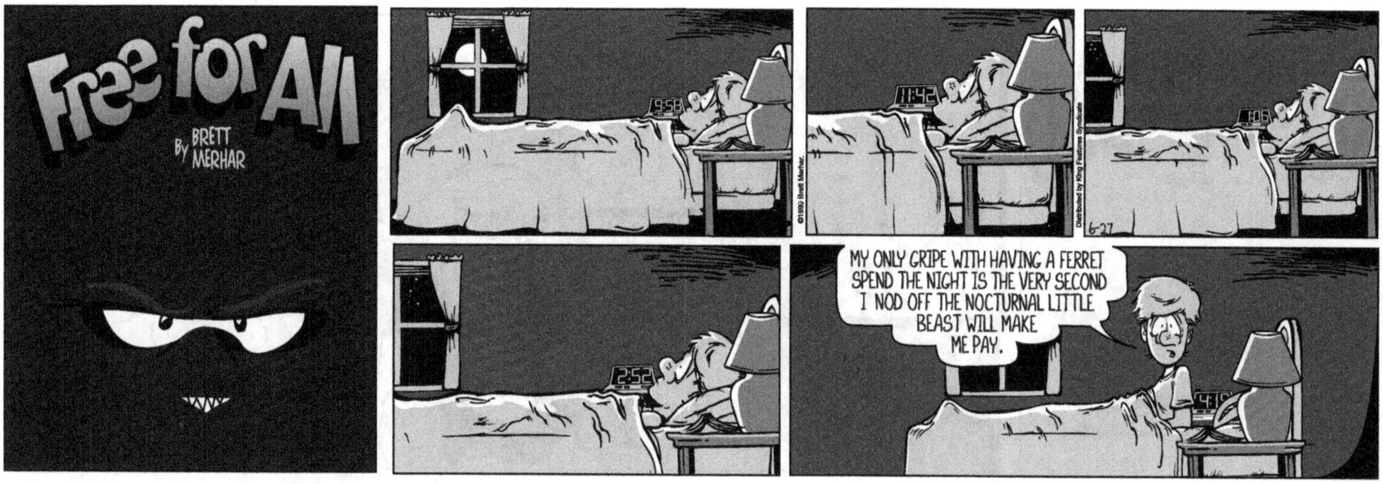
Free for All
By BRETT MERHAR
MY ONLY GRIPE WITH HAVING A FERRET SPEND THE NIGHT IS THE VERY SECOND I NOD OFF THE NOCTURNAL LITTLE BEAST WILL MAKE ME PAY.

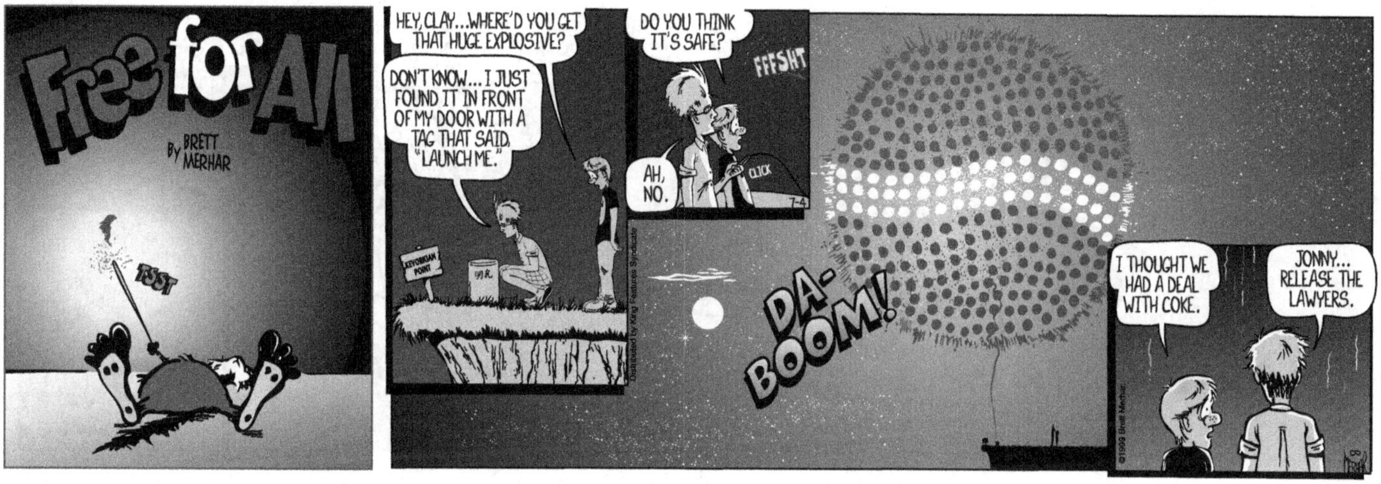
Free for All
By BRETT MERHAR
HEY, CLAY...WHERE'D YOU GET THAT HUGE EXPLOSIVE?
DON'T KNOW... I JUST FOUND IT IN FRONT OF MY DOOR WITH A TAG THAT SAID, "LAUNCH ME."
DO YOU THINK IT'S SAFE?
FFFSHT
AH, NO.
CLICK
DA-BOOM!
I THOUGHT WE HAD A DEAL WITH COKE.
JONNY... RELEASE THE LAWYERS.

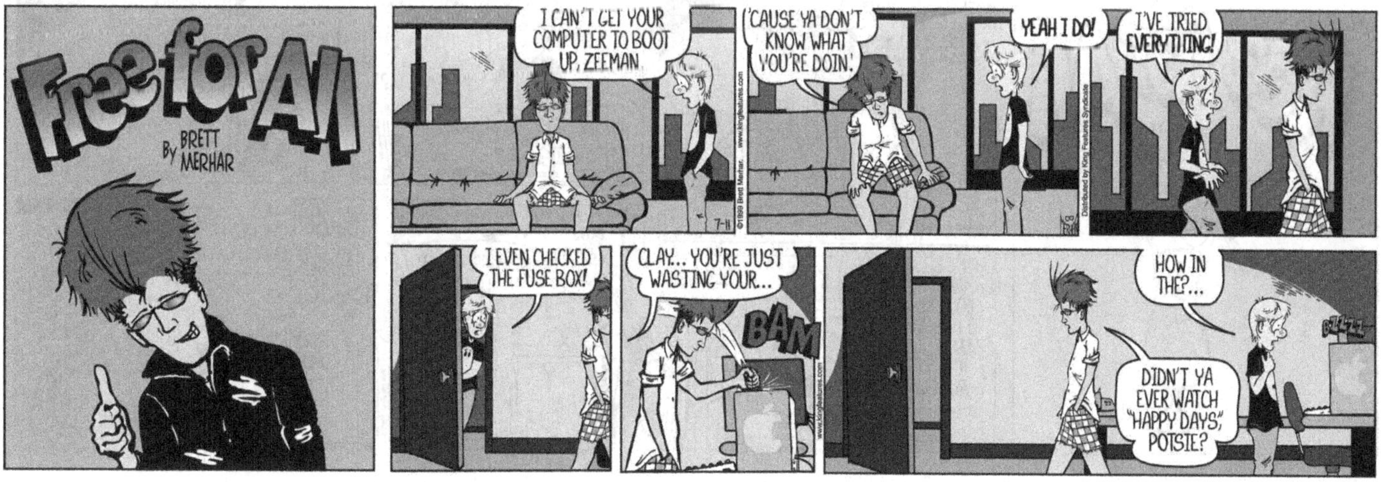
Free for All
By BRETT MERHAR
I CAN'T GET YOUR COMPUTER TO BOOT UP, ZEEMAN.
'CAUSE YA DON'T KNOW WHAT YOU'RE DOIN'.
YEAH I DO!
I'VE TRIED EVERYTHING!
I EVEN CHECKED THE FUSE BOX!
CLAY... YOU'RE JUST WASTING YOUR...
BAM
HOW IN THE?...
DIDN'T YA EVER WATCH "HAPPY DAYS," POTSIE?

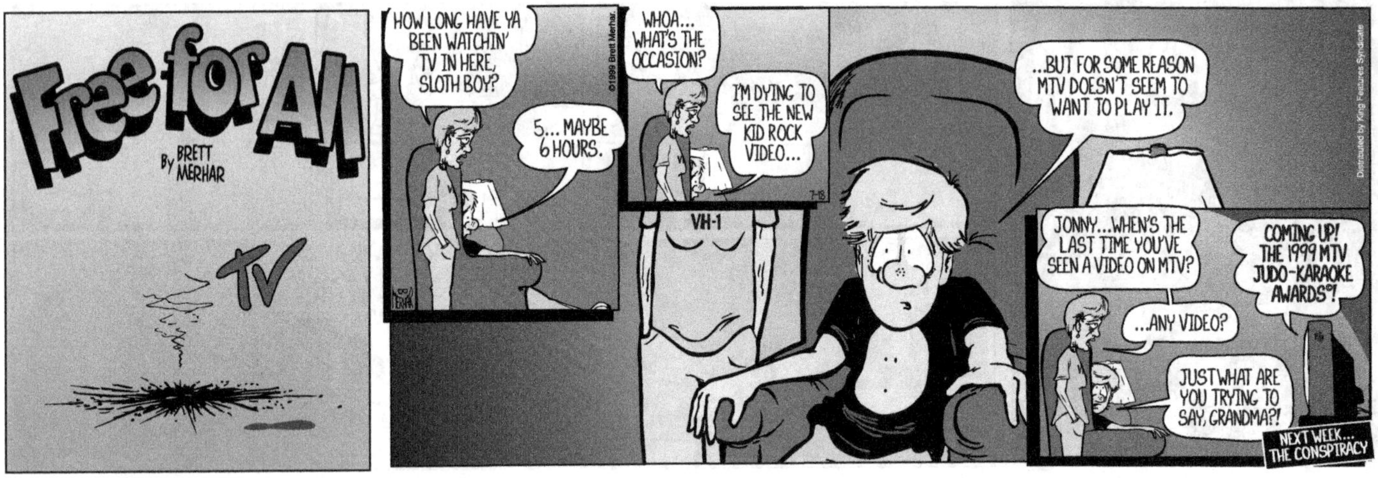
Free for All
By BRETT MERHAR
TV
HOW LONG HAVE YA BEEN WATCHIN' TV IN HERE, SLOTH BOY?
5... MAYBE 6 HOURS.
©1999 Brett Merhar.
WHOA... WHAT'S THE OCCASION?
I'M DYING TO SEE THE NEW KID ROCK VIDEO...
7-18
VH-1
...BUT FOR SOME REASON MTV DOESN'T SEEM TO WANT TO PLAY IT.
JONNY...WHEN'S THE LAST TIME YOU'VE SEEN A VIDEO ON MTV?
...ANY VIDEO?
JUST WHAT ARE YOU TRYING TO SAY, GRANDMA?!
COMING UP! THE 1999 MTV JUDO-KARAOKE AWARDS©!
NEXT WEEK... THE CONSPIRACY
Distributed by King Features Syndicate

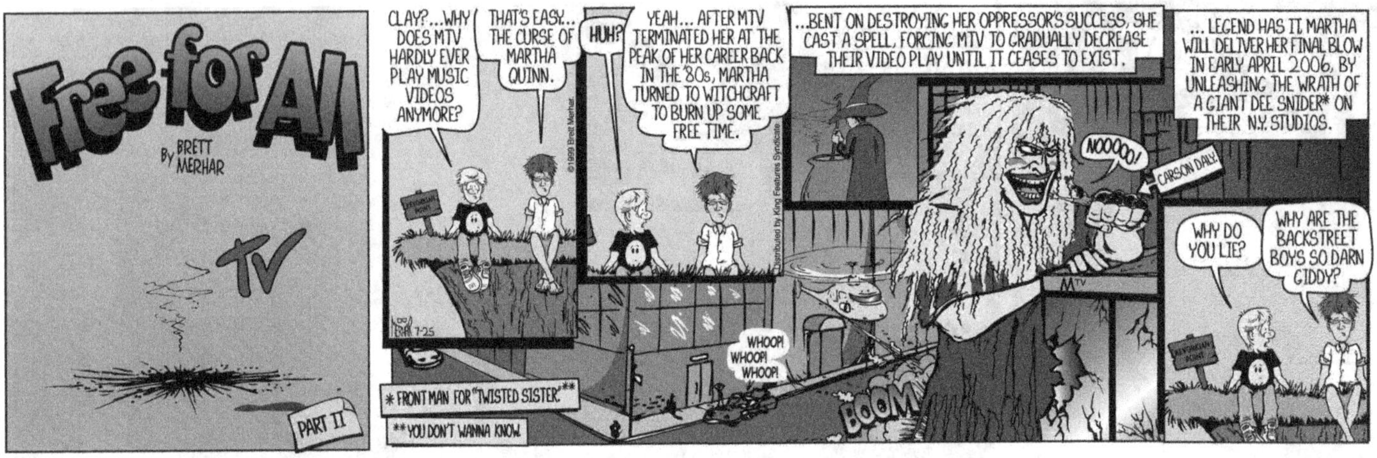
Free for All
By BRETT MERHAR
TV
PART II
CLAY?...WHY DOES MTV HARDLY EVER PLAY MUSIC VIDEOS ANYMORE?
THAT'S EASY... THE CURSE OF MARTHA QUINN.
©1999 Brett Merhar.
7-25
HUH?
YEAH... AFTER MTV TERMINATED HER AT THE PEAK OF HER CAREER BACK IN THE '80s, MARTHA TURNED TO WITCHCRAFT TO BURN UP SOME FREE TIME.
Distributed by King Features Syndicate
...BENT ON DESTROYING HER OPPRESSOR'S SUCCESS, SHE CAST A SPELL, FORCING MTV TO GRADUALLY DECREASE THEIR VIDEO PLAY UNTIL IT CEASES TO EXIST.
NOOOOO!
CARSON DALY
WHOOP! WHOOP! WHOOP!
BOOM
...LEGEND HAS IT, MARTHA WILL DELIVER HER FINAL BLOW IN EARLY APRIL 2006, BY UNLEASHING THE WRATH OF A GIANT DEE SNIDER* ON THEIR N.Y. STUDIOS.
WHY DO YOU LIE?
WHY ARE THE BACKSTREET BOYS SO DARN GIDDY?
* FRONT MAN FOR "TWISTED SISTER."**
** YOU DON'T WANNA KNOW.

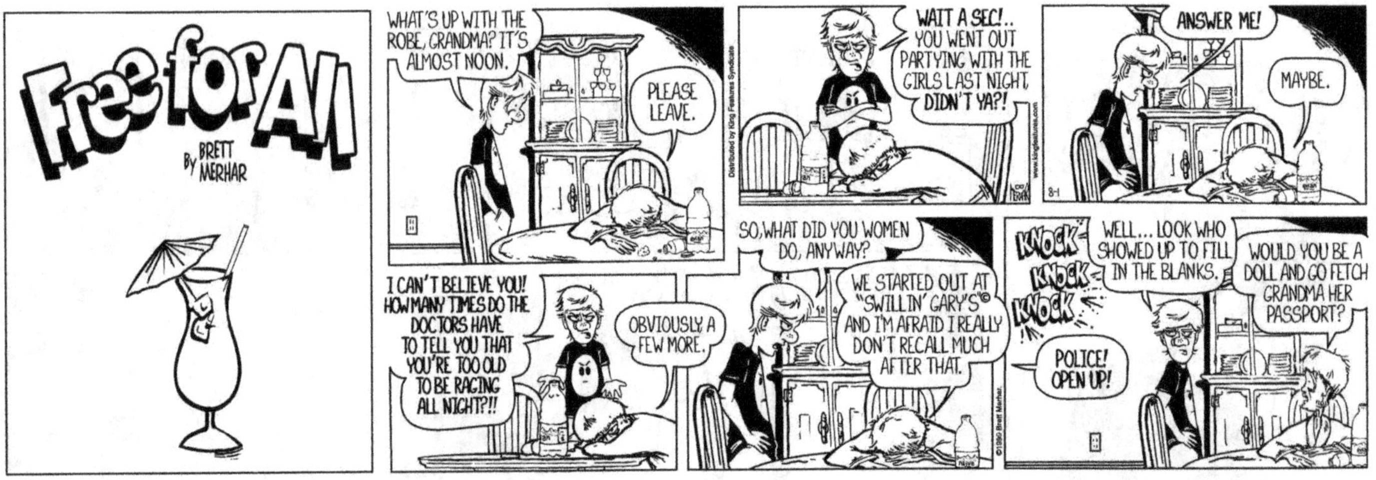
Free for All
By BRETT MERHAR
WHAT'S UP WITH THE ROBE, GRANDMA? IT'S ALMOST NOON.
PLEASE LEAVE.
Distributed by King Features Syndicate
WAIT A SEC!.. YOU WENT OUT PARTYING WITH THE GIRLS LAST NIGHT, DIDN'T YA?!
www.kingfeatures.com
ANSWER ME!
MAYBE.
8-1
I CAN'T BELIEVE YOU! HOW MANY TIMES DO THE DOCTORS HAVE TO TELL YOU THAT YOU'RE TOO OLD TO BE RACING ALL NIGHT?!!
OBVIOUSLY, A FEW MORE.
SO, WHAT DID YOU WOMEN DO, ANYWAY?
WE STARTED OUT AT "SWILL'IN' GARY'S"© AND I'M AFRAID I REALLY DON'T RECALL MUCH AFTER THAT.
©1999 Brett Merhar.
KNOCK KNOCK KNOCK
POLICE! OPEN UP!
WELL... LOOK WHO SHOWED UP TO FILL IN THE BLANKS.
WOULD YOU BE A DOLL AND GO FETCH GRANDMA HER PASSPORT?

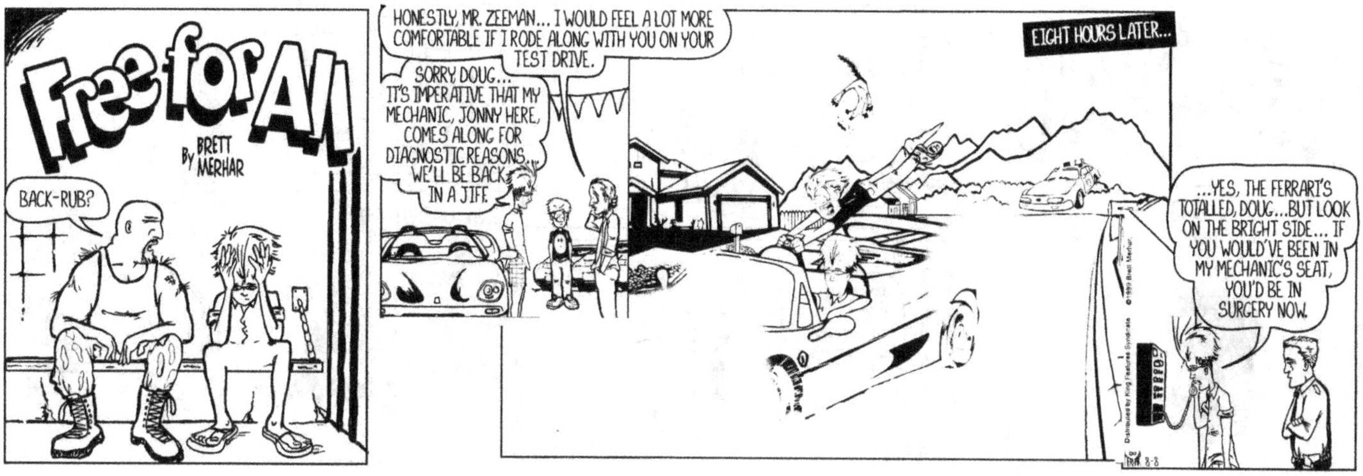
Free for All
By BRETT MERHAR
BACK-RUB?
HONESTLY, MR. ZEEMAN... I WOULD FEEL A LOT MORE COMFORTABLE IF I RODE ALONG WITH YOU ON YOUR TEST DRIVE.
SORRY, DOUG... IT'S IMPERATIVE THAT MY MECHANIC, JONNY HERE, COMES ALONG FOR DIAGNOSTIC REASONS. WE'LL BE BACK IN A JIFF.
EIGHT HOURS LATER...
...YES, THE FERRARI'S TOTALLED, DOUG... BUT LOOK ON THE BRIGHT SIDE... IF YOU WOULD'VE BEEN IN MY MECHANIC'S SEAT, YOU'D BE IN SURGERY NOW.
8-8

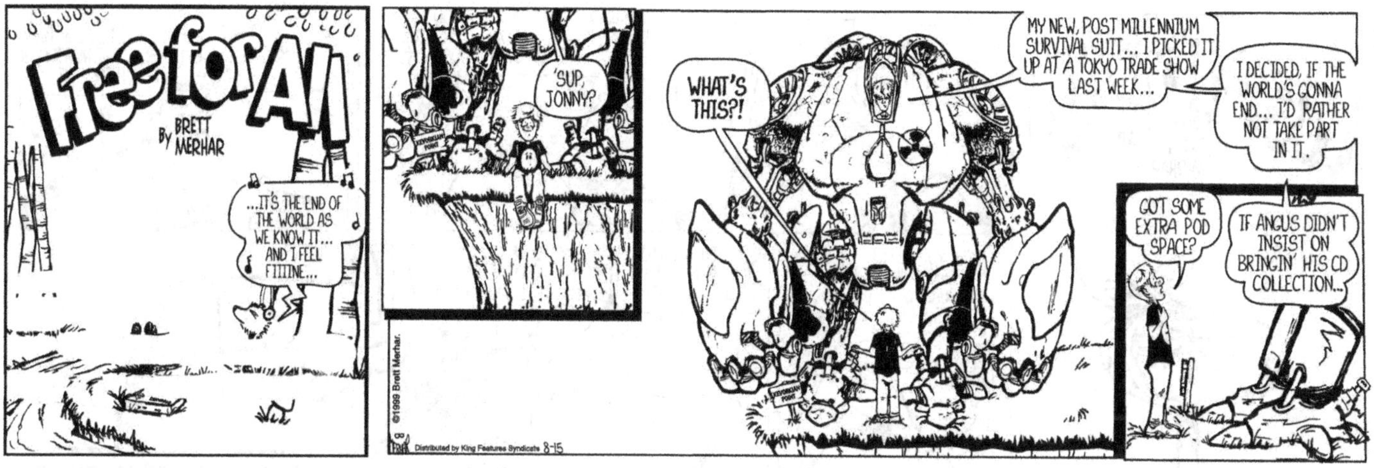
Free for All
By BRETT MERHAR
...IT'S THE END OF THE WORLD AS WE KNOW IT... AND I FEEL FIIIINE...
'SUP, JONNY?
WHAT'S THIS?!
MY NEW, POST MILLENNIUM SURVIVAL SUIT... I PICKED IT UP AT A TOKYO TRADE SHOW LAST WEEK...
I DECIDED, IF THE WORLD'S GONNA END... I'D RATHER NOT TAKE PART IN IT.
GOT SOME EXTRA POD SPACE?
IF ANGUS DIDN'T INSIST ON BRINGIN' HIS CD COLLECTION...
©1999 Brett Merhar.
Distributed by King Features Syndicate 8-15

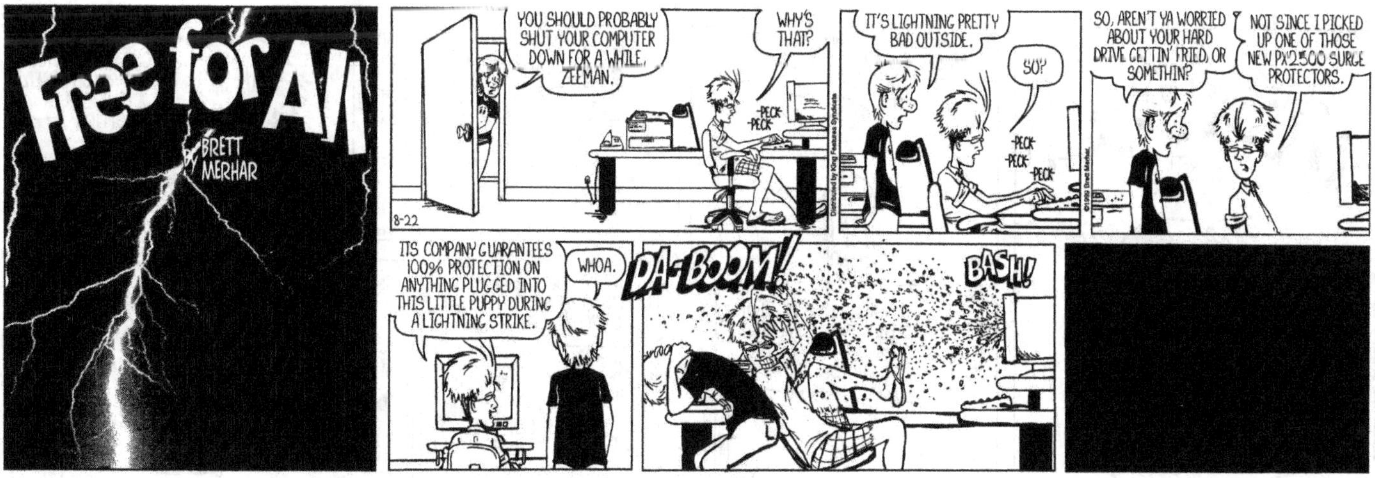
Free for All
BY BRETT MERHAR
YOU SHOULD PROBABLY SHUT YOUR COMPUTER DOWN FOR A WHILE, ZEEMAN.
WHY'S THAT?
-PECK -PECK
8-22
IT'S LIGHTNING PRETTY BAD OUTSIDE.
SO?
-PECK -PECK -PECK
SO, AREN'T YA WORRIED ABOUT YOUR HARD DRIVE GETTIN' FRIED, OR SOMETHIN?
NOT SINCE I PICKED UP ONE OF THOSE NEW PX2500 SURGE PROTECTORS.
ITS COMPANY GUARANTEES 100% PROTECTION ON ANYTHING PLUGGED INTO THIS LITTLE PUPPY DURING A LIGHTNING STRIKE.
WHOA.
DA-BOOM!
BASH!

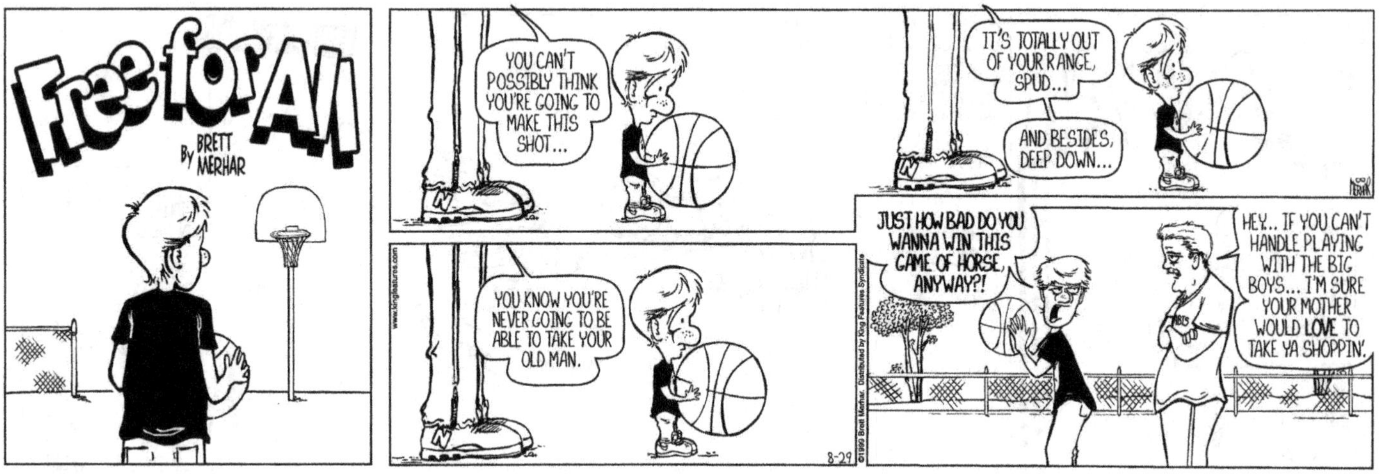
Free for All
By Brett Merhar
YOU CAN'T POSSIBLY THINK YOU'RE GOING TO MAKE THIS SHOT...
YOU KNOW YOU'RE NEVER GOING TO BE ABLE TO TAKE YOUR OLD MAN.
IT'S TOTALLY OUT OF YOUR RANGE, SPUD...
AND BESIDES, DEEP DOWN...
JUST HOW BAD DO YOU WANNA WIN THIS GAME OF HORSE, ANYWAY?!
HEY.. IF YOU CAN'T HANDLE PLAYING WITH THE BIG BOYS... I'M SURE YOUR MOTHER WOULD LOVE TO TAKE YA SHOPPIN'.
8-29

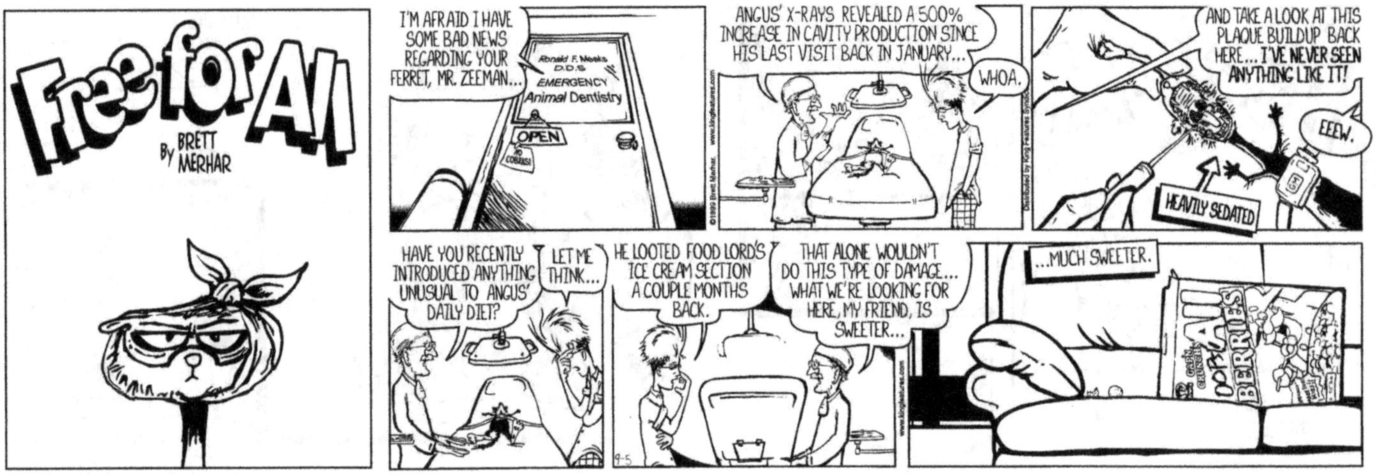
Free for All
By Brett Merhar
I'M AFRAID I HAVE SOME BAD NEWS REGARDING YOUR FERRET, MR. ZEEMAN...
Ronald F. Meeks D.D.S
EMERGENCY
Animal Dentistry
OPEN
ANGUS' X-RAYS REVEALED A 500% INCREASE IN CAVITY PRODUCTION SINCE HIS LAST VISIT BACK IN JANUARY...
WHOA.
AND TAKE A LOOK AT THIS PLAQUE BUILDUP BACK HERE... I'VE NEVER SEEN ANYTHING LIKE IT!
EEEW.
HEAVILY SEDATED
HAVE YOU RECENTLY INTRODUCED ANYTHING UNUSUAL TO ANGUS' DAILY DIET?
LET ME THINK...
HE LOOTED FOOD LORD'S ICE CREAM SECTION A COUPLE MONTHS BACK.
THAT ALONE WOULDN'T DO THIS TYPE OF DAMAGE... WHAT WE'RE LOOKING FOR HERE, MY FRIEND, IS SWEETER...
...MUCH SWEETER.
9-5

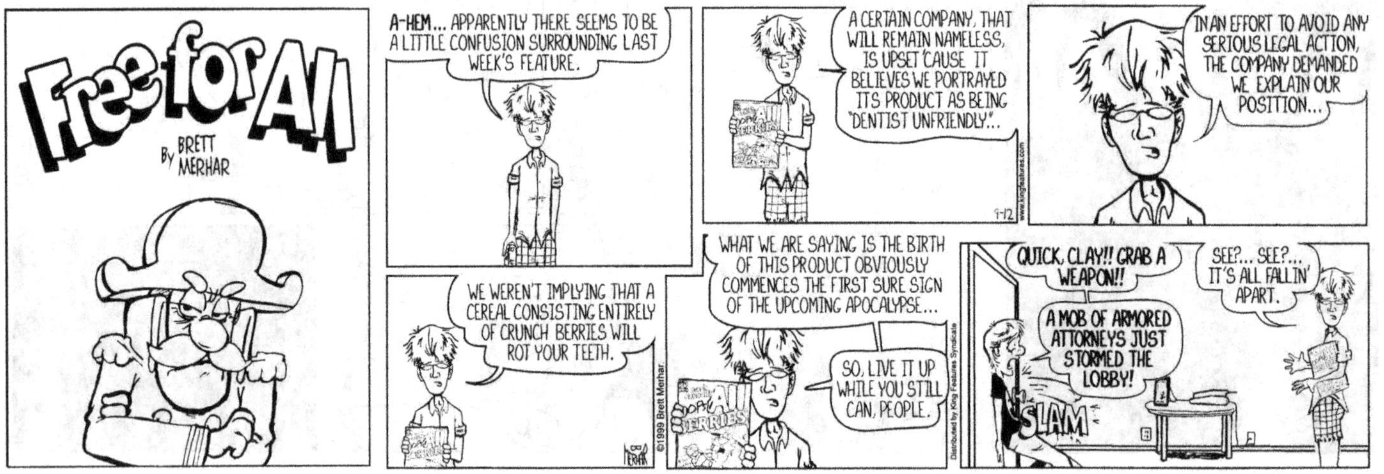
Free for All
By Brett Merhar
A-HEM... APPARENTLY THERE SEEMS TO BE A LITTLE CONFUSION SURROUNDING LAST WEEK'S FEATURE.
A CERTAIN COMPANY, THAT WILL REMAIN NAMELESS, IS UPSET 'CAUSE IT BELIEVES WE PORTRAYED ITS PRODUCT AS BEING "DENTIST UNFRIENDLY"...
IN AN EFFORT TO AVOID ANY SERIOUS LEGAL ACTION, THE COMPANY DEMANDED WE EXPLAIN OUR POSITION...
9-12
WE WEREN'T IMPLYING THAT A CEREAL CONSISTING ENTIRELY OF CRUNCH BERRIES WILL ROT YOUR TEETH.
WHAT WE ARE SAYING IS THE BIRTH OF THIS PRODUCT OBVIOUSLY COMMENCES THE FIRST SURE SIGN OF THE UPCOMING APOCALYPSE...
SO, LIVE IT UP WHILE YOU STILL CAN, PEOPLE.
QUICK, CLAY!! GRAB A WEAPON!!
A MOB OF ARMORED ATTORNEYS JUST STORMED THE LOBBY!
SLAM
SEE?... SEE?... IT'S ALL FALLIN' APART.

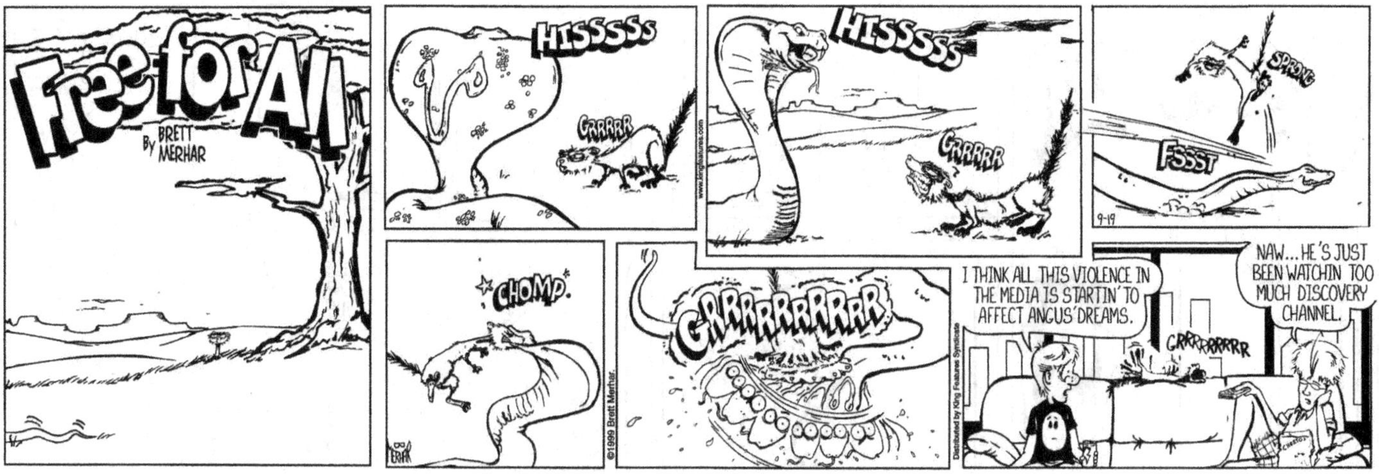
Free for All
BY BRETT MERHAR
HISSSSS
GRRRRR
HISSSSS
GRRRRR
SPRONG
FSSST
9-19
CHOMP
GRRRRRRRRRR
I THINK ALL THIS VIOLENCE IN THE MEDIA IS STARTIN' TO AFFECT ANGUS' DREAMS.
GRRRRRRRR
NAW... HE'S JUST BEEN WATCHIN' TOO MUCH DISCOVERY CHANNEL.
©1999 Brett Merhar.
Distributed by King Features Syndicate

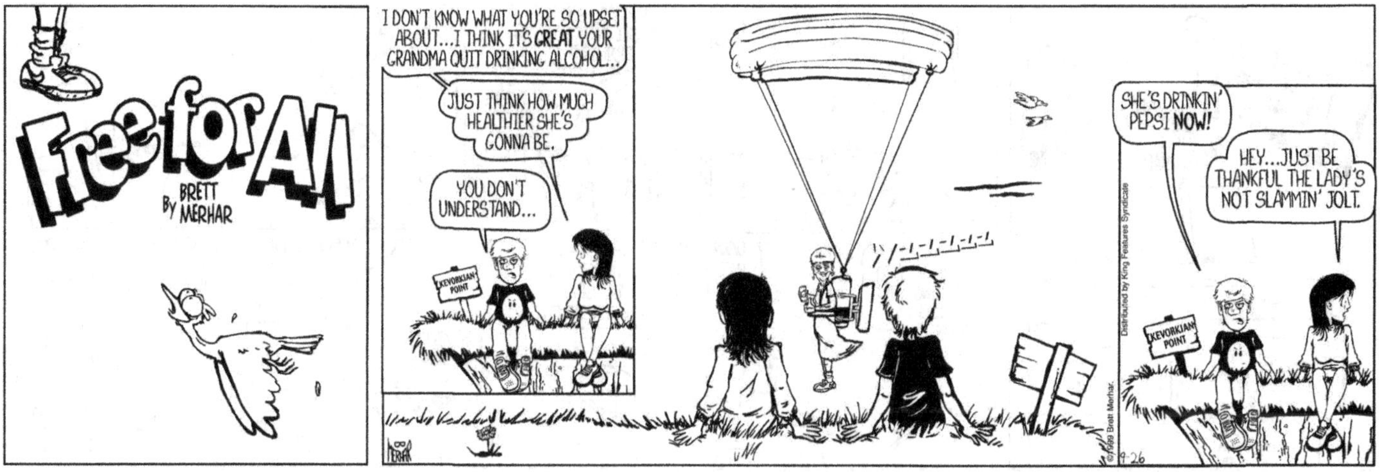
Free for All
BY BRETT MERHAR
I DON'T KNOW WHAT YOU'RE SO UPSET ABOUT... I THINK IT'S GREAT YOUR GRANDMA QUIT DRINKING ALCOHOL...
JUST THINK HOW MUCH HEALTHIER SHE'S GONNA BE.
YOU DON'T UNDERSTAND...
KEVORKIAN POINT
SHE'S DRINKIN' PEPSI NOW!
HEY... JUST BE THANKFUL THE LADY'S NOT SLAMMIN' JOLT.
KEVORKIAN POINT
9-26
Distributed by King Features Syndicate

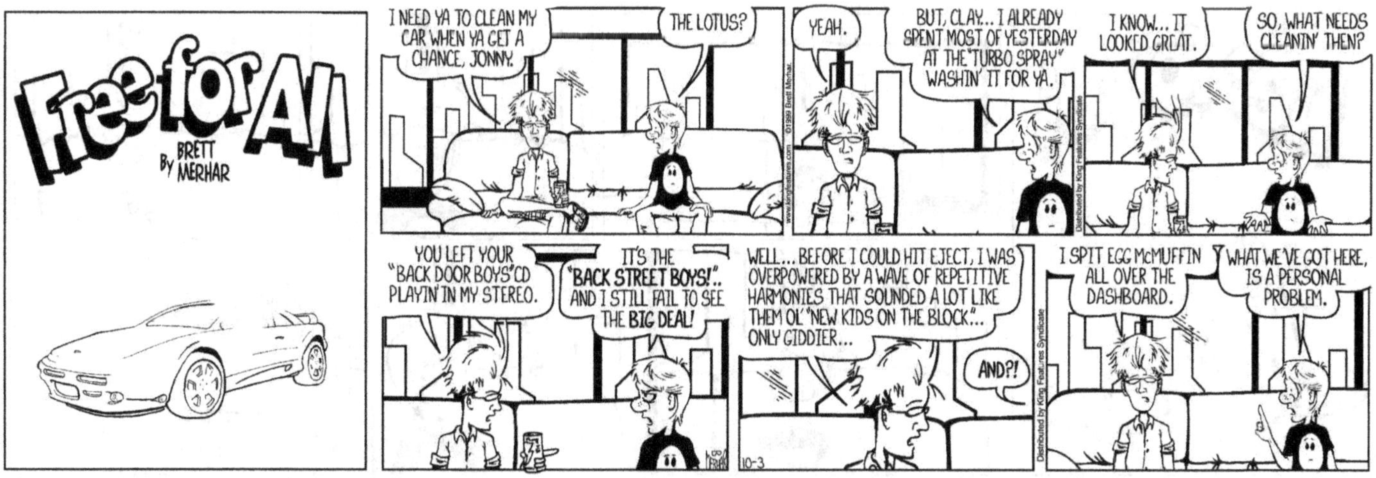
Free for All
BY BRETT MERHAR
I NEED YA TO CLEAN MY CAR WHEN YA GET A CHANCE, JONNY.
THE LOTUS?
YEAH.
BUT, CLAY... I ALREADY SPENT MOST OF YESTERDAY AT THE "TURBO SPRAY" WASHIN' IT FOR YA.
I KNOW... IT LOOKED GREAT.
SO, WHAT NEEDS CLEANIN' THEN?
YOU LEFT YOUR "BACK DOOR BOYS" CD PLAYIN' IN MY STEREO.
IT'S THE "BACK STREET BOYS!".. AND I STILL FAIL TO SEE THE BIG DEAL!
WELL... BEFORE I COULD HIT EJECT, I WAS OVERPOWERED BY A WAVE OF REPETITIVE HARMONIES THAT SOUNDED A LOT LIKE THEM OL' "NEW KIDS ON THE BLOCK"... ONLY GIDDIER...
AND?!
I SPIT EGG McMUFFIN ALL OVER THE DASHBOARD.
WHAT WE'VE GOT HERE, IS A PERSONAL PROBLEM.
10-3
Distributed by King Features Syndicate

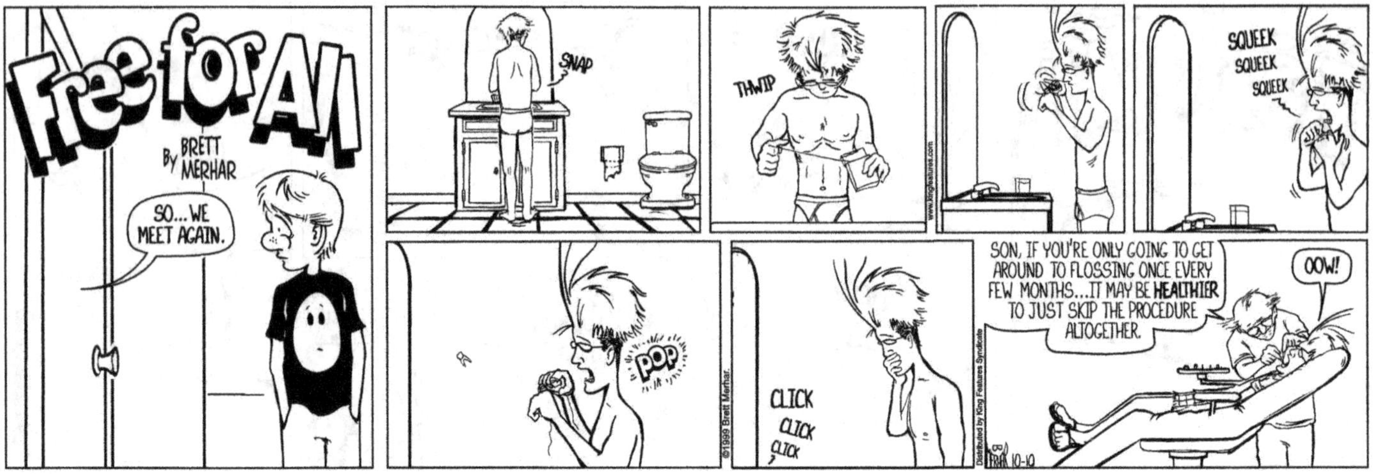
Free for All
BY BRETT MERHAR
SO... WE MEET AGAIN.
SNAP
THWIP
SQUEEK
SQUEEK
SQUEEK
POP
CLICK
CLICK
CLICK
SON, IF YOU'RE ONLY GOING TO GET AROUND TO FLOSSING ONCE EVERY FEW MONTHS... IT MAY BE HEALTHIER TO JUST SKIP THE PROCEDURE ALTOGETHER.
OOW!
10-10
©1999 Brett Merhar
Distributed by King Features Syndicate
www.kingfeatures.com

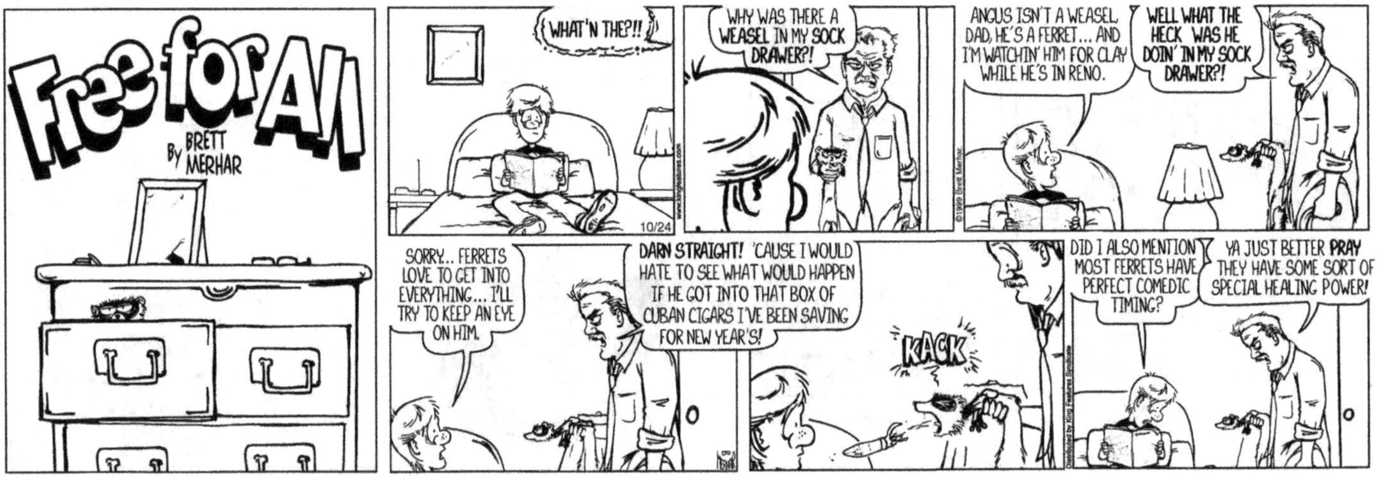
Free for All
BY BRETT MERHAR
WHAT'N THE?!!
10/24
WHY WAS THERE A WEASEL IN MY SOCK DRAWER?!
ANGUS ISN'T A WEASEL DAD, HE'S A FERRET... AND I'M WATCHIN' HIM FOR CLAY WHILE HE'S IN RENO.
WELL WHAT THE HECK WAS HE DOIN' IN MY SOCK DRAWER?!
SORRY... FERRETS LOVE TO GET INTO EVERYTHING... I'LL TRY TO KEEP AN EYE ON HIM.
DARN STRAIGHT! 'CAUSE I WOULD HATE TO SEE WHAT WOULD HAPPEN IF HE GOT INTO THAT BOX OF CUBAN CIGARS I'VE BEEN SAVING FOR NEW YEAR'S!
KACK
DID I ALSO MENTION MOST FERRETS HAVE PERFECT COMEDIC TIMING?
YA JUST BETTER PRAY THEY HAVE SOME SORT OF SPECIAL HEALING POWER!
©1999 Brett Merhar
Distributed by King Features Syndicate
www.kingfeatures.com

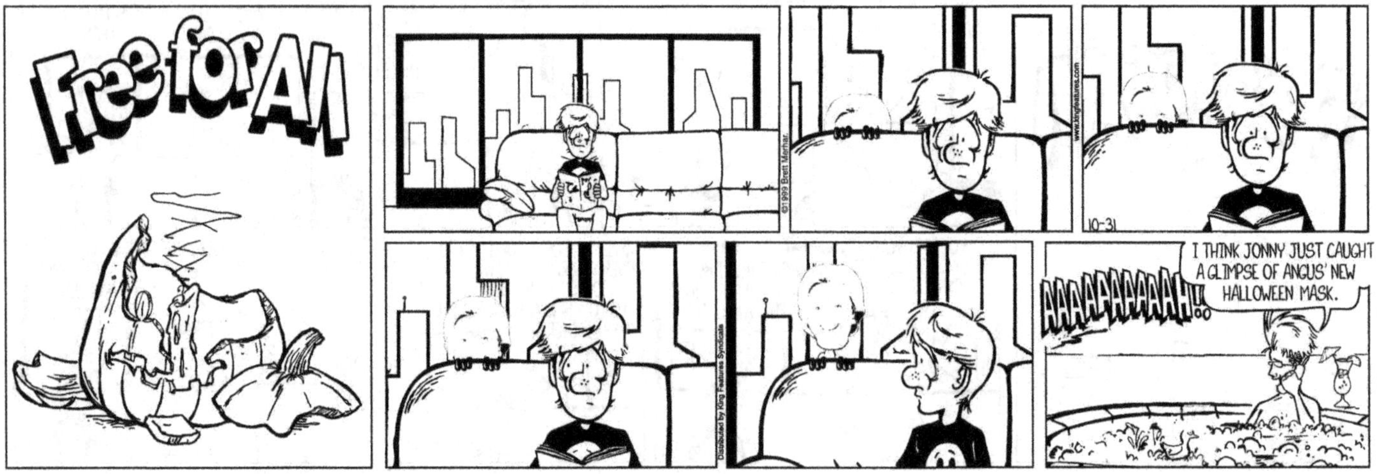
Free for All
10-31
AAAAAAAAAAH!!
I THINK JONNY JUST CAUGHT A GLIMPSE OF ANGUS' NEW HALLOWEEN MASK.
©1999 Brett Merhar
Distributed by King Features Syndicate
www.kingfeatures.com

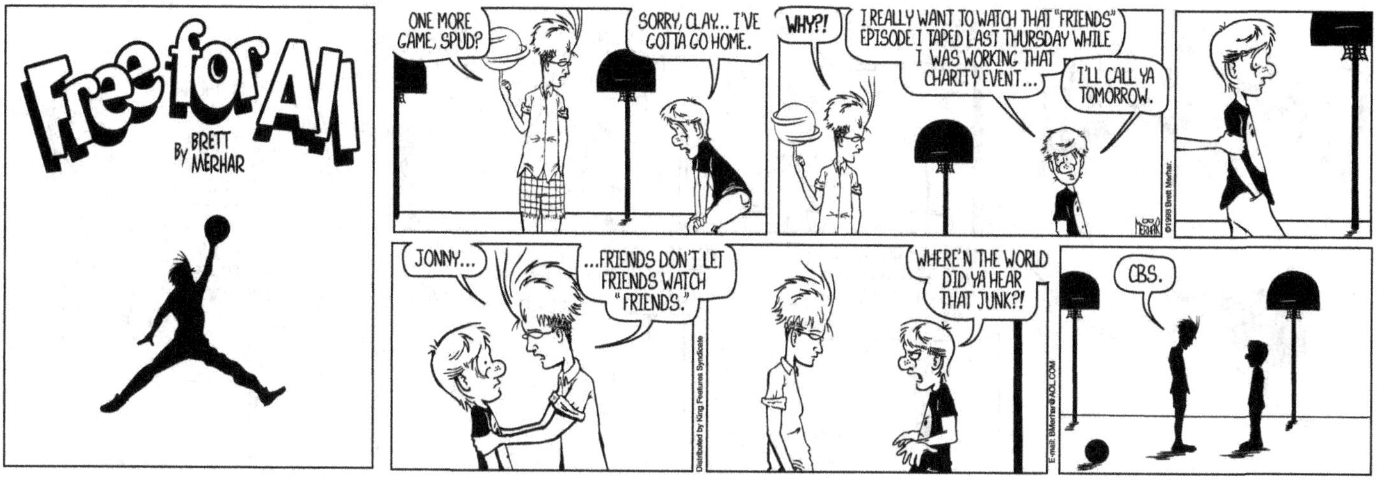
Free for All
By Brett Merhar
ONE MORE GAME, SPUD?
SORRY, CLAY... I'VE GOTTA GO HOME.
WHY?!
I REALLY WANT TO WATCH THAT "FRIENDS" EPISODE I TAPED LAST THURSDAY WHILE I WAS WORKING THAT CHARITY EVENT...
I'LL CALL YA TOMORROW.
JONNY...
...FRIENDS DON'T LET FRIENDS WATCH "FRIENDS."
WHERE'N THE WORLD DID YA HEAR THAT JUNK?!
CBS.

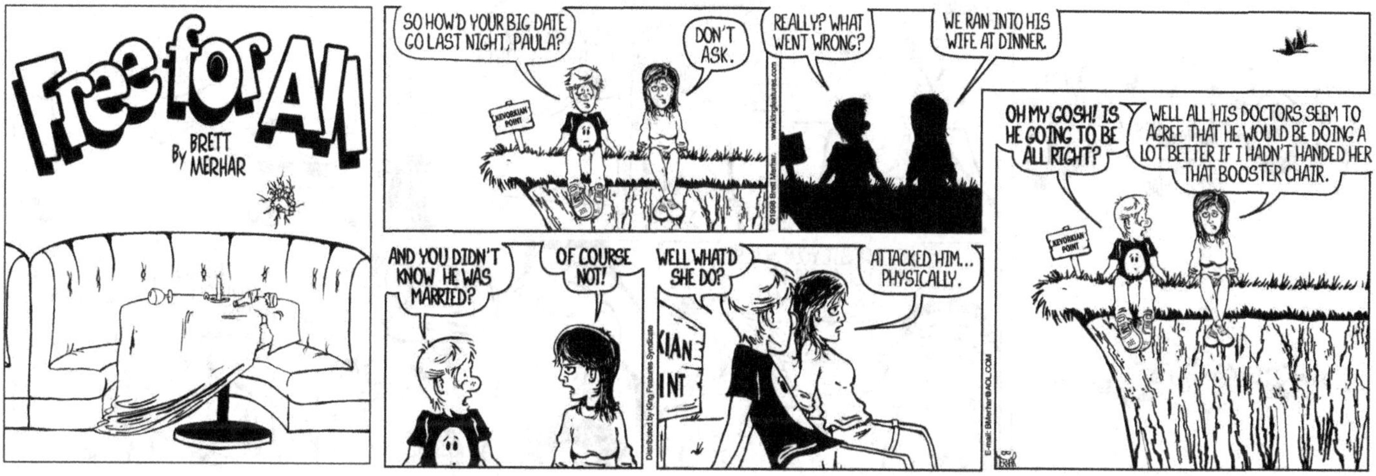
Free for All
By Brett Merhar
SO HOW'D YOUR BIG DATE GO LAST NIGHT, PAULA?
DON'T ASK.
KEVORKIAN POINT
REALLY? WHAT WENT WRONG?
WE RAN INTO HIS WIFE AT DINNER.
AND YOU DIDN'T KNOW HE WAS MARRIED?
OF COURSE NOT!
WELL WHAT'D SHE DO?
ATTACKED HIM... PHYSICALLY.
OH MY GOSH! IS HE GOING TO BE ALL RIGHT?
WELL ALL HIS DOCTORS SEEM TO AGREE THAT HE WOULD BE DOING A LOT BETTER IF I HADN'T HANDED HER THAT BOOSTER CHAIR.
KEVORKIAN POINT

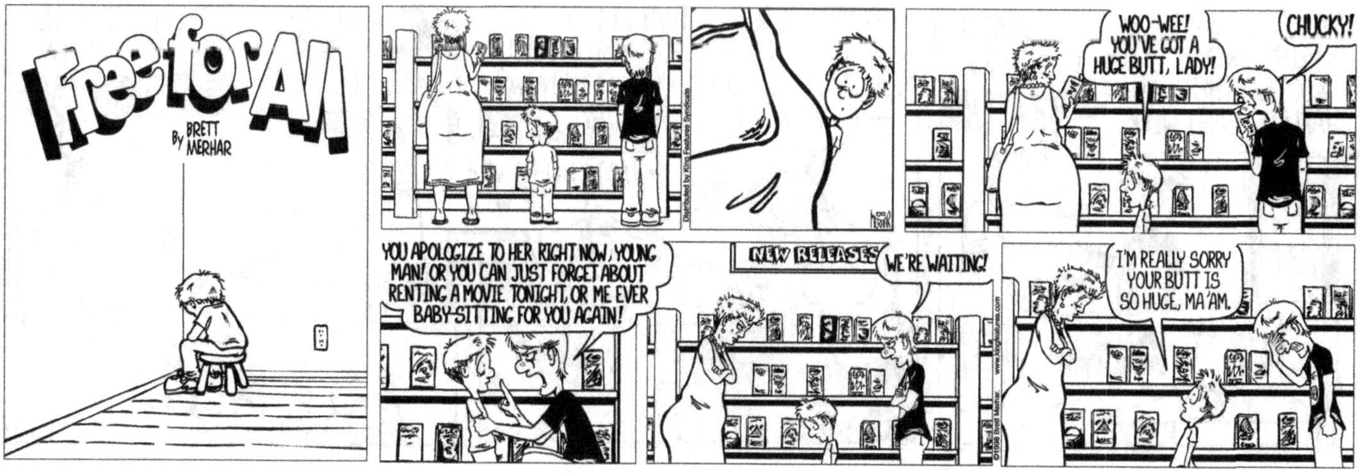
Free for All
By Brett Merhar
WOO-WEE! YOU'VE GOT A HUGE BUTT, LADY!
CHUCKY!
YOU APOLOGIZE TO HER RIGHT NOW, YOUNG MAN! OR YOU CAN JUST FORGET ABOUT RENTING A MOVIE TONIGHT, OR ME EVER BABY-SITTING FOR YOU AGAIN!
NEW RELEASES
WE'RE WAITING!
I'M REALLY SORRY YOUR BUTT IS SO HUGE, MA'AM.

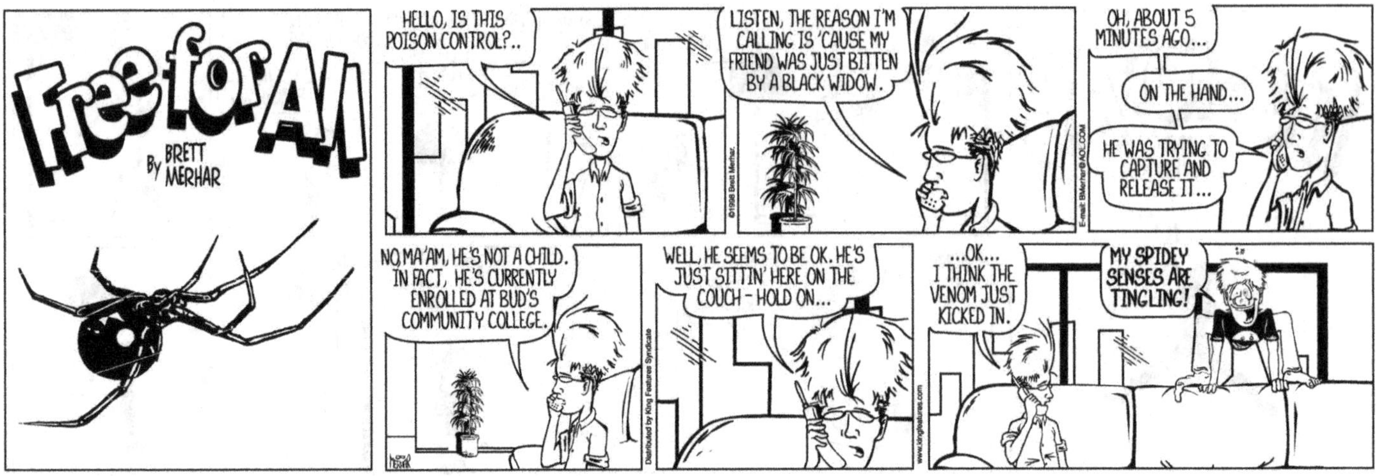
Free for All
By BRETT MERHAR
HELLO, IS THIS POISON CONTROL?..
LISTEN, THE REASON I'M CALLING IS 'CAUSE MY FRIEND WAS JUST BITTEN BY A BLACK WIDOW.
©1998 Brett Merhar.
OH, ABOUT 5 MINUTES AGO...
ON THE HAND...
HE WAS TRYING TO CAPTURE AND RELEASE IT...
E-mail: BMerhar@AOL.COM
NO, MA'AM, HE'S NOT A CHILD. IN FACT, HE'S CURRENTLY ENROLLED AT BUD'S COMMUNITY COLLEGE.
Distributed by King Features Syndicate
WELL, HE SEEMS TO BE OK. HE'S JUST SITTIN' HERE ON THE COUCH - HOLD ON...
www.kingfeatures.com
...OK... I THINK THE VENOM JUST KICKED IN.
MY SPIDEY SENSES ARE TINGLING!

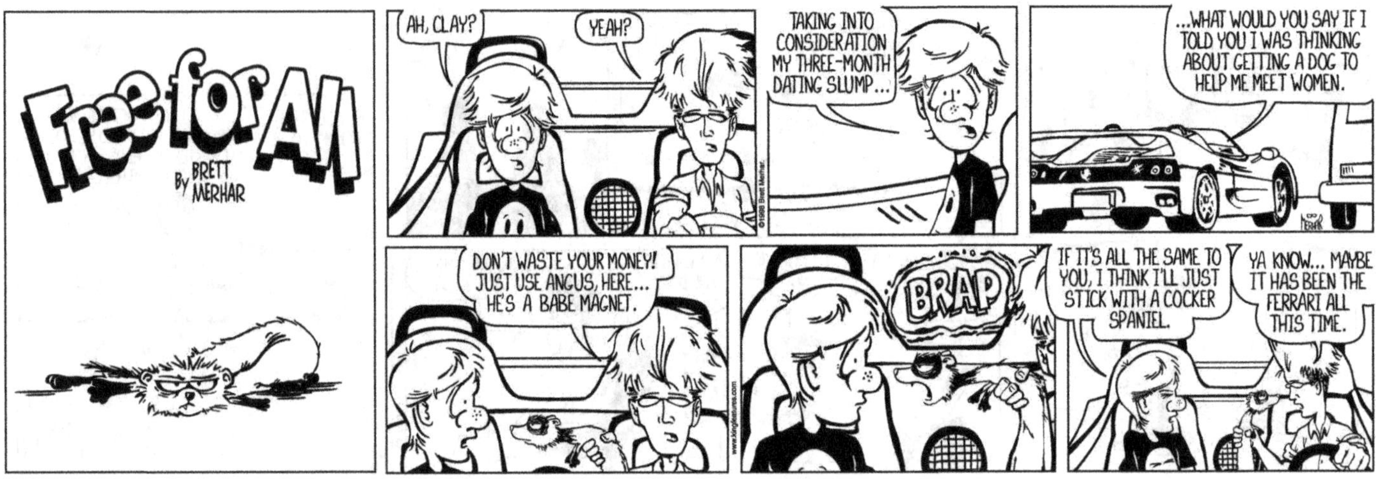
Free for All
By BRETT MERHAR
AH, CLAY?
YEAH?
TAKING INTO CONSIDERATION MY THREE-MONTH DATING SLUMP...
...WHAT WOULD YOU SAY IF I TOLD YOU I WAS THINKING ABOUT GETTING A DOG TO HELP ME MEET WOMEN.
DON'T WASTE YOUR MONEY! JUST USE ANGUS, HERE... HE'S A BABE MAGNET.
www.kingfeatures.com
BRAP
IF IT'S ALL THE SAME TO YOU, I THINK I'LL JUST STICK WITH A COCKER SPANIEL.
YA KNOW... MAYBE IT HAS BEEN THE FERRARI ALL THIS TIME.

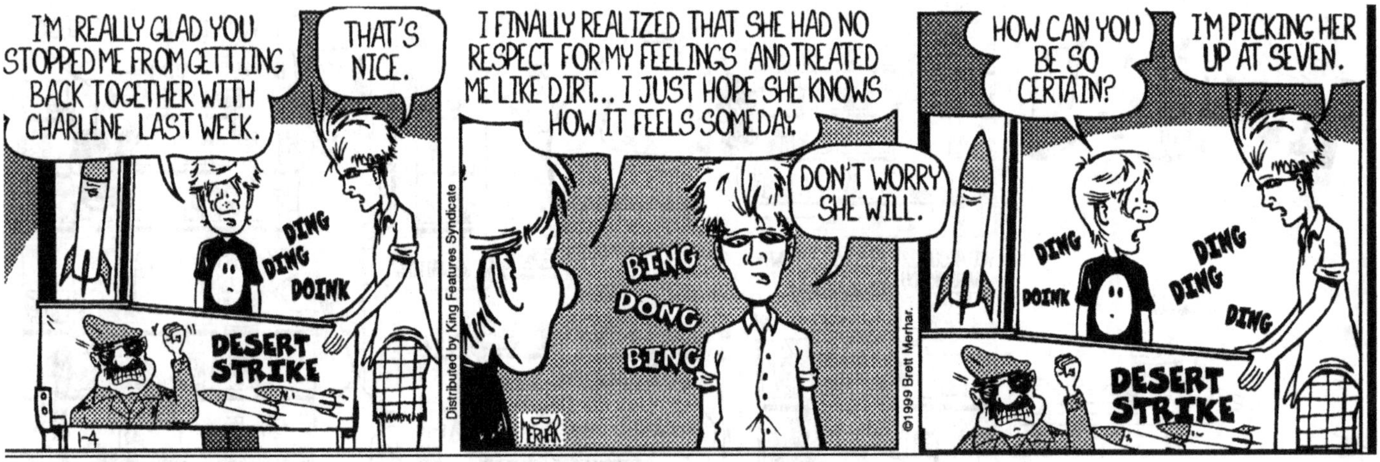
I'M REALLY GLAD YOU STOPPED ME FROM GETTIING BACK TOGETHER WITH CHARLENE LAST WEEK.
THAT'S NICE.
DING
DING
DOINK
DESERT STRIKE
1-4
Distributed by King Features Syndicate
I FINALLY REALIZED THAT SHE HAD NO RESPECT FOR MY FEELINGS AND TREATED ME LIKE DIRT... I JUST HOPE SHE KNOWS HOW IT FEELS SOMEDAY.
DON'T WORRY SHE WILL.
BING
DONG
BING
©1999 Brett Merhar.
HOW CAN YOU BE SO CERTAIN?
I'M PICKING HER UP AT SEVEN.
DING
DOINK
DING
DING
DING
DESERT STRIKE

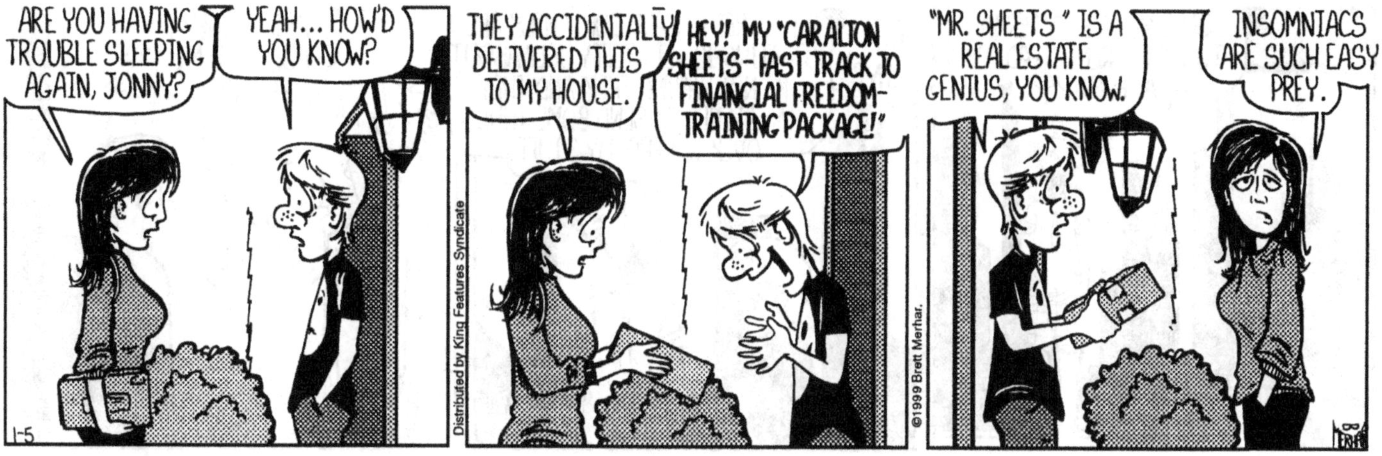
ARE YOU HAVING TROUBLE SLEEPING AGAIN, JONNY?
YEAH... HOW'D YOU KNOW?
1-5
Distributed by King Features Syndicate
THEY ACCIDENTALLY DELIVERED THIS TO MY HOUSE.
HEY! MY "CARALTON SHEETS-FAST TRACK TO FINANCIAL FREEDOM-TRAINING PACKAGE!"
©1999 Brett Merhar.
"MR. SHEETS" IS A REAL ESTATE GENIUS, YOU KNOW.
INSOMNIACS ARE SUCH EASY PREY.

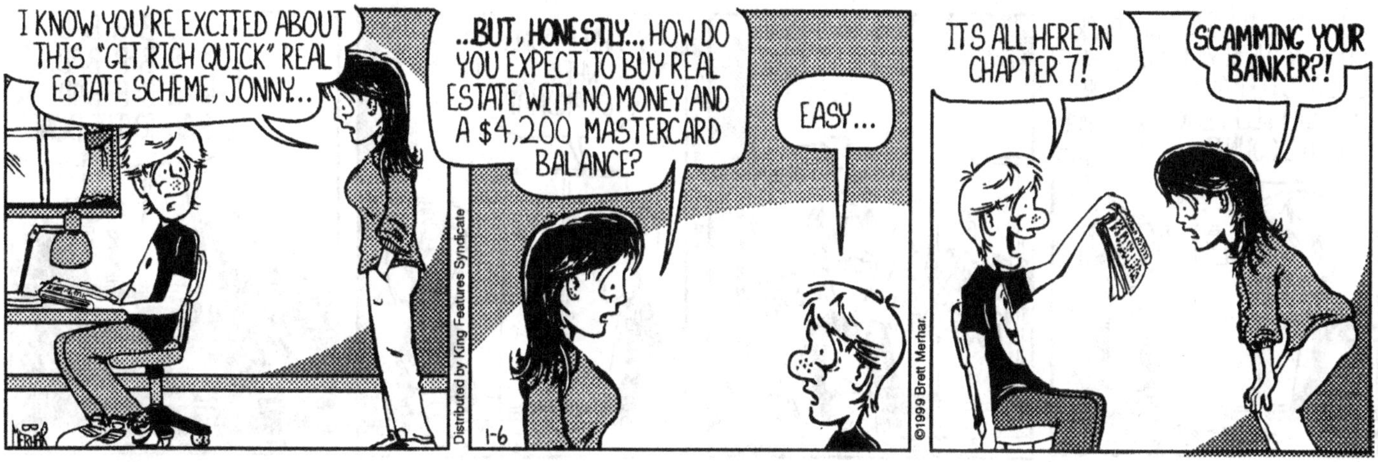
I KNOW YOU'RE EXCITED ABOUT THIS "GET RICH QUICK" REAL ESTATE SCHEME, JONNY...
Distributed by King Features Syndicate
..BUT, HONESTLY... HOW DO YOU EXPECT TO BUY REAL ESTATE WITH NO MONEY AND A $4,200 MASTERCARD BALANCE?
EASY...
1-6
©1999 Brett Merhar.
ITS ALL HERE IN CHAPTER 7!
SCAMMING YOUR BANKER?!

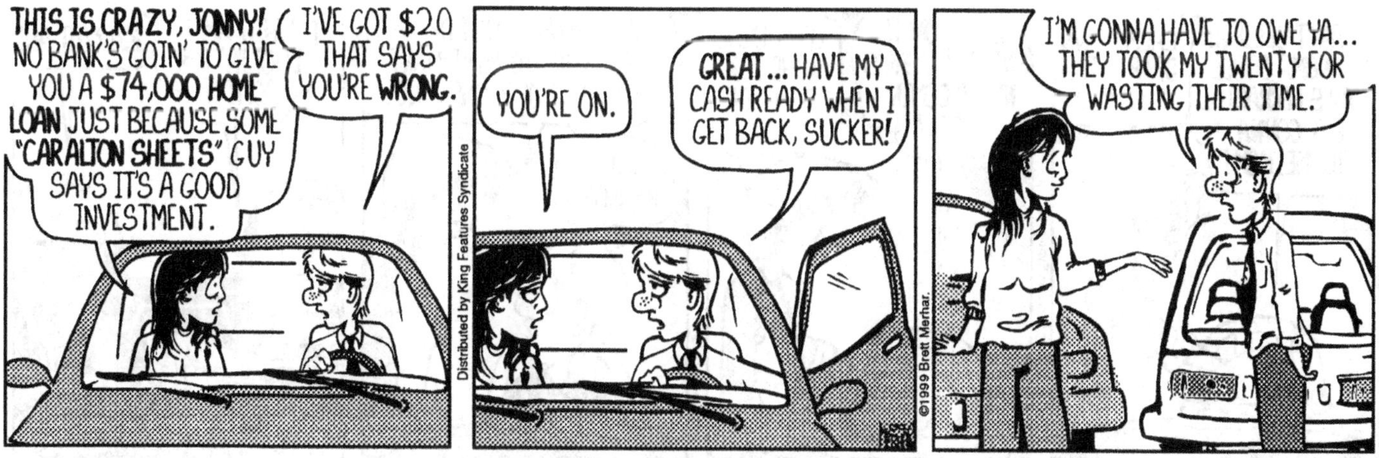
THIS IS CRAZY, JONNY! NO BANK'S GOIN' TO GIVE YOU A $74,000 HOME LOAN JUST BECAUSE SOME "CARALTON SHEETS" GUY SAYS IT'S A GOOD INVESTMENT.
I'VE GOT $20 THAT SAYS YOU'RE WRONG.
Distributed by King Features Syndicate
YOU'RE ON.
GREAT... HAVE MY CASH READY WHEN I GET BACK, SUCKER!
©1999 Brett Merhar.
I'M GONNA HAVE TO OWE YA... THEY TOOK MY TWENTY FOR WASTING THEIR TIME.

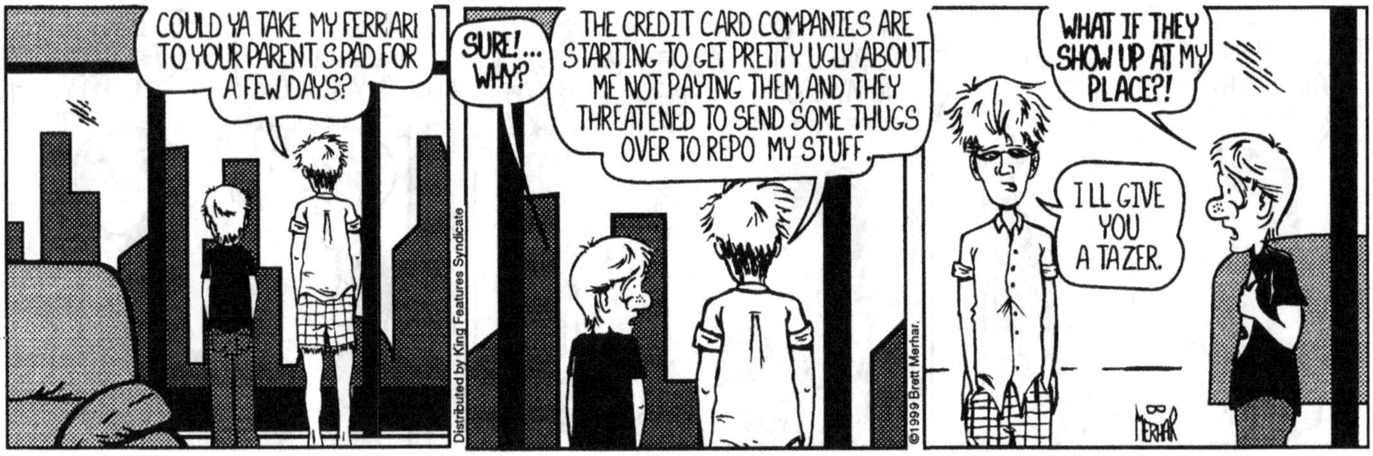
COULD YA TAKE MY FERRARI TO YOUR PARENT S PAD FOR A FEW DAYS?
SURE!... WHY?
THE CREDIT CARD COMPANIES ARE STARTING TO GET PRETTY UGLY ABOUT ME NOT PAYING THEM, AND THEY THREATENED TO SEND SOME THUGS OVER TO REPO MY STUFF.
Distributed by King Features Syndicate
WHAT IF THEY SHOW UP AT MY PLACE?!
I'LL GIVE YOU A TAZER.
©1999 Brett Merhar.
MERHAR

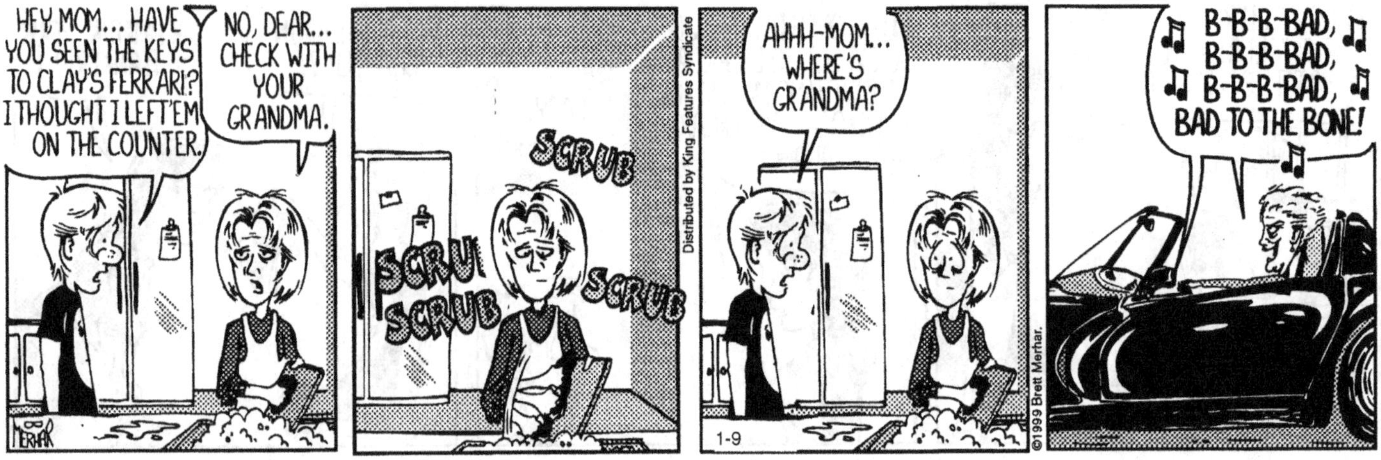
HEY, MOM... HAVE YOU SEEN THE KEYS TO CLAY'S FERRARI? I THOUGHT I LEFT'EM ON THE COUNTER.
NO, DEAR... CHECK WITH YOUR GRANDMA.
MERHAR
SCRUB
SCRUB
SCRUB
SCRUB
Distributed by King Features Syndicate
AHHH-MOM... WHERE'S GRANDMA?
1-9
©1999 Brett Merhar.
B-B-B-BAD, B-B-B-BAD, B-B-B-BAD, BAD TO THE BONE!

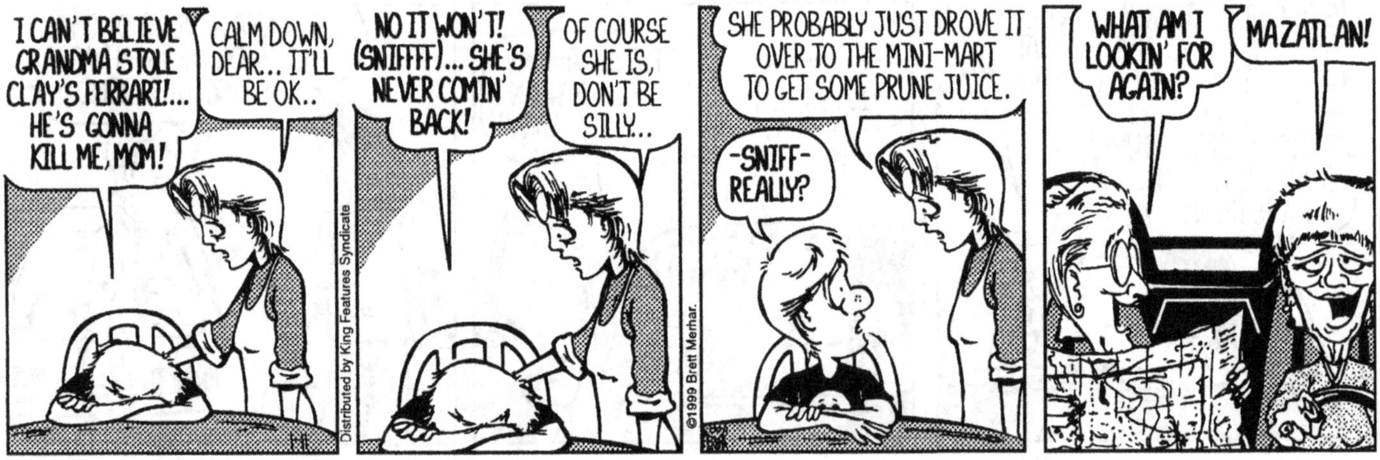
I CAN'T BELIEVE GRANDMA STOLE CLAY'S FERRARI!... HE'S GONNA KILL ME, MOM!
CALM DOWN, DEAR... IT'LL BE OK..
Distributed by King Features Syndicate
NO IT WON'T! (SNIFFFF)... SHE'S NEVER COMIN' BACK!
OF COURSE SHE IS, DON'T BE SILLY...
©1999 Brett Merhar.
SHE PROBABLY JUST DROVE IT OVER TO THE MINI-MART TO GET SOME PRUNE JUICE.
-SNIFF- REALLY?
WHAT AM I LOOKIN' FOR AGAIN?
MAZATLAN!

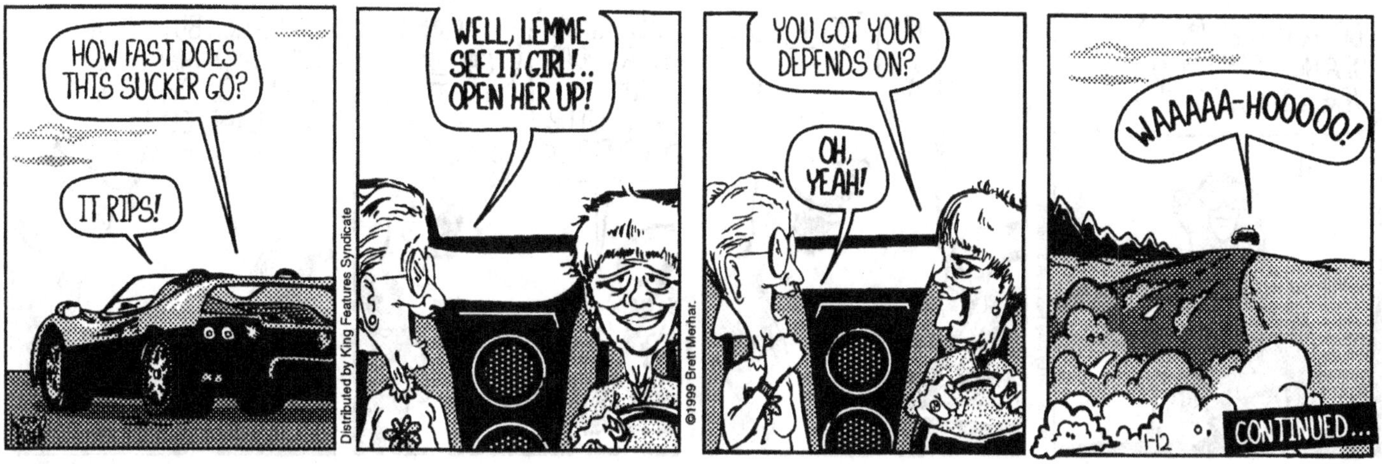
HOW FAST DOES THIS SUCKER GO?
IT RIPS!
Distributed by King Features Syndicate
WELL, LEMME SEE IT, GIRL!.. OPEN HER UP!
©1999 Brett Merhar.
YOU GOT YOUR DEPENDS ON?
OH, YEAH!
WAAAAA-HOOOOO!
1-12
CONTINUED...

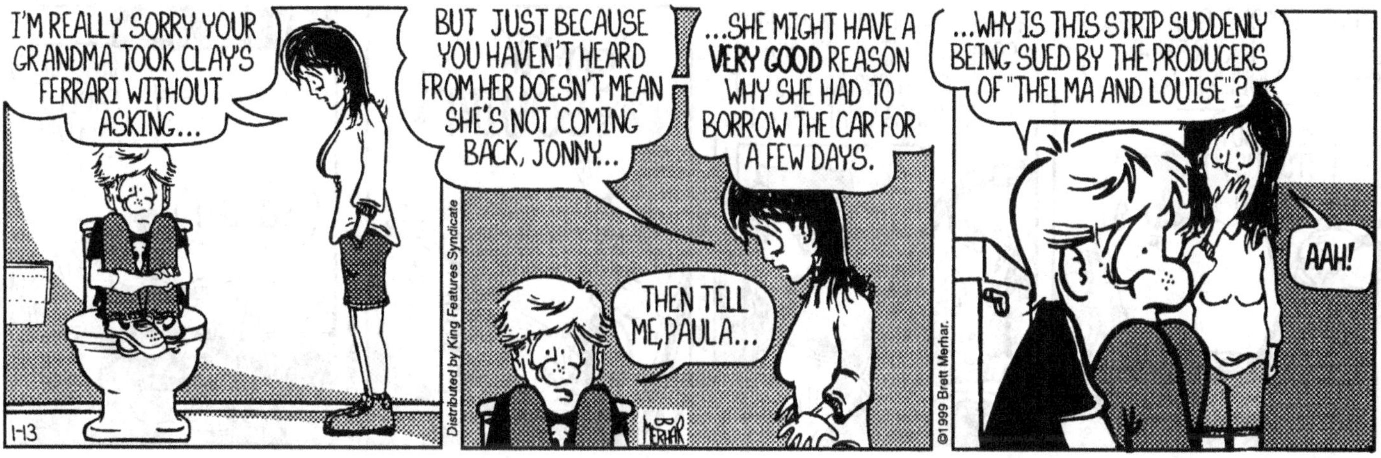
I'M REALLY SORRY YOUR GRANDMA TOOK CLAY'S FERRARI WITHOUT ASKING...
1-13
Distributed by King Features Syndicate
BUT JUST BECAUSE YOU HAVEN'T HEARD FROM HER DOESN'T MEAN SHE'S NOT COMING BACK, JONNY...
THEN TELL ME, PAULA...
...SHE MIGHT HAVE A VERY GOOD REASON WHY SHE HAD TO BORROW THE CAR FOR A FEW DAYS.
©1999 Brett Merhar.
...WHY IS THIS STRIP SUDDENLY BEING SUED BY THE PRODUCERS OF "THELMA AND LOUISE"?
AAH!

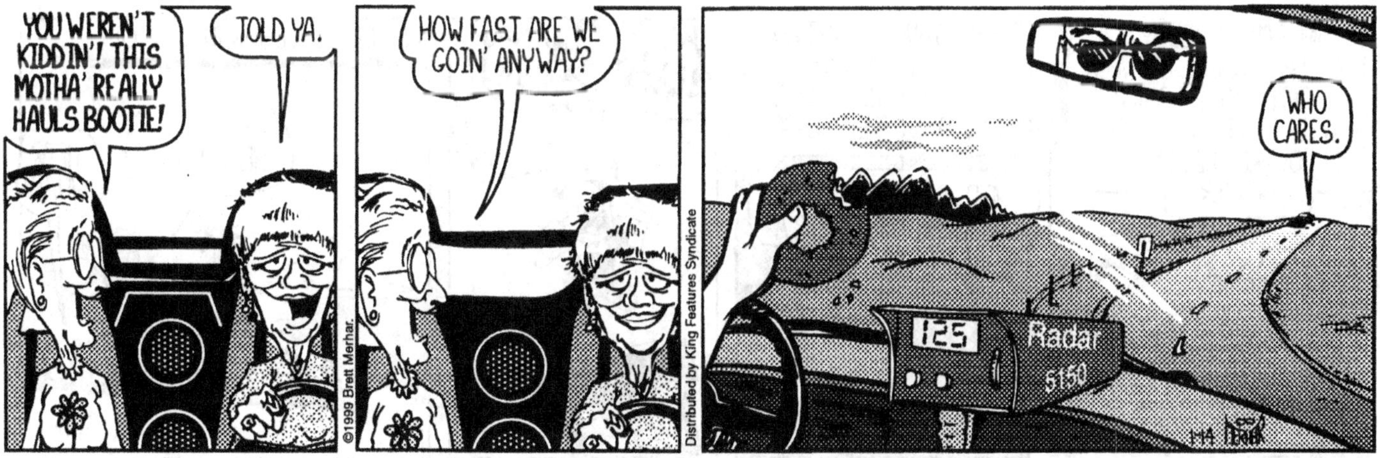
YOU WEREN'T KIDDIN'! THIS MOTHA' REALLY HAULS BOOTIE!
TOLD YA.
©1999 Brett Merhar.
HOW FAST ARE WE GOIN' ANYWAY?
Distributed by King Features Syndicate
125
Radar
5150
WHO CARES.
1-14

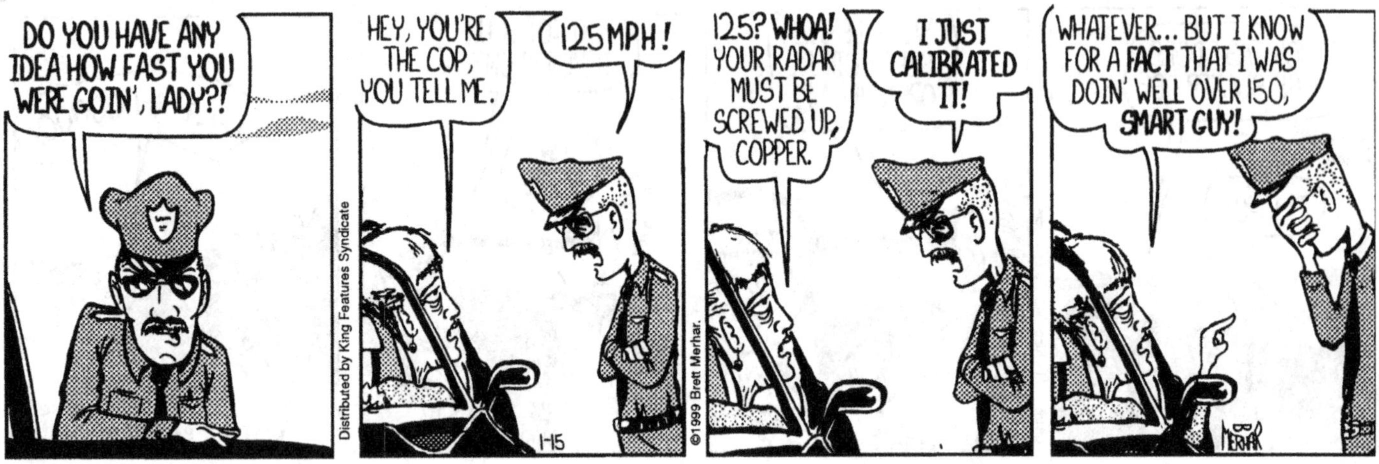
DO YOU HAVE ANY IDEA HOW FAST YOU WERE GOIN', LADY?!
HEY, YOU'RE THE COP, YOU TELL ME.
125 MPH!
125? WHOA! YOUR RADAR MUST BE SCREWED UP, COPPER.
I JUST CALIBRATED IT!
WHATEVER... BUT I KNOW FOR A FACT THAT I WAS DOIN' WELL OVER 150, SMART GUY!
Distributed by King Features Syndicate
1-15
©1999 Brett Merhar.
MERHAR

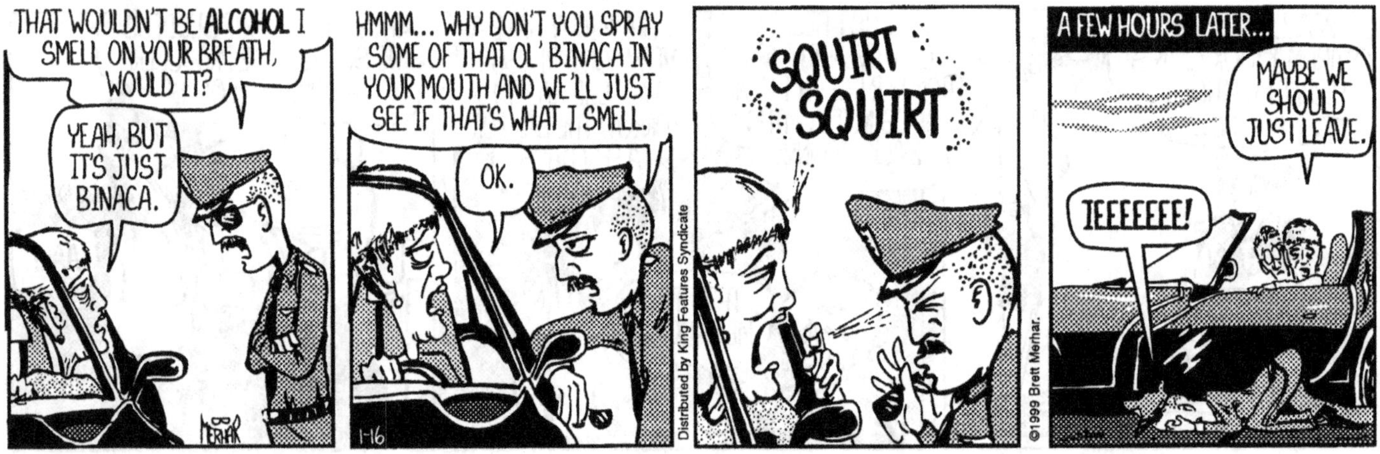
THAT WOULDN'T BE ALCOHOL I SMELL ON YOUR BREATH, WOULD IT?
YEAH, BUT IT'S JUST BINACA.
HMMM... WHY DON'T YOU SPRAY SOME OF THAT OL' BINACA IN YOUR MOUTH AND WE'LL JUST SEE IF THAT'S WHAT I SMELL.
OK.
SQUIRT SQUIRT
A FEW HOURS LATER...
MAYBE WE SHOULD JUST LEAVE.
IEEEEEEE!
MERHAR
1-16
Distributed by King Features Syndicate
©1999 Brett Merhar.

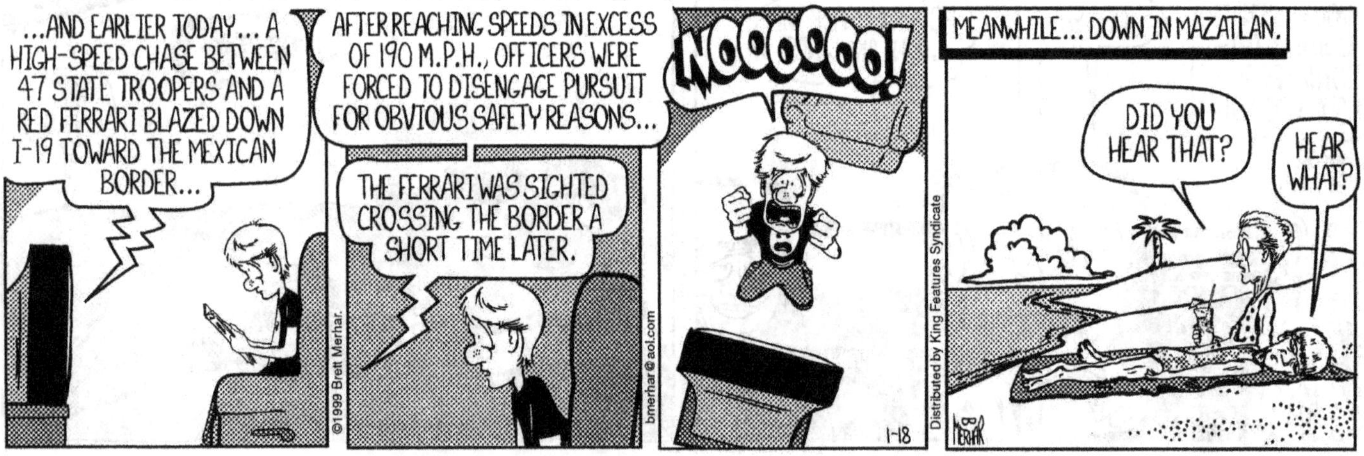
...AND EARLIER TODAY... A HIGH-SPEED CHASE BETWEEN 47 STATE TROOPERS AND A RED FERRARI BLAZED DOWN I-19 TOWARD THE MEXICAN BORDER...
AFTER REACHING SPEEDS IN EXCESS OF 190 M.P.H., OFFICERS WERE FORCED TO DISENGAGE PURSUIT FOR OBVIOUS SAFETY REASONS...
THE FERRARI WAS SIGHTED CROSSING THE BORDER A SHORT TIME LATER.
©1999 Brett Merhar.
NOOOOOOO!
bmerhar@aol.com
1-18
Distributed by King Features Syndicate
MEANWHILE... DOWN IN MAZATLAN.
DID YOU HEAR THAT?
HEAR WHAT?
MERHAR

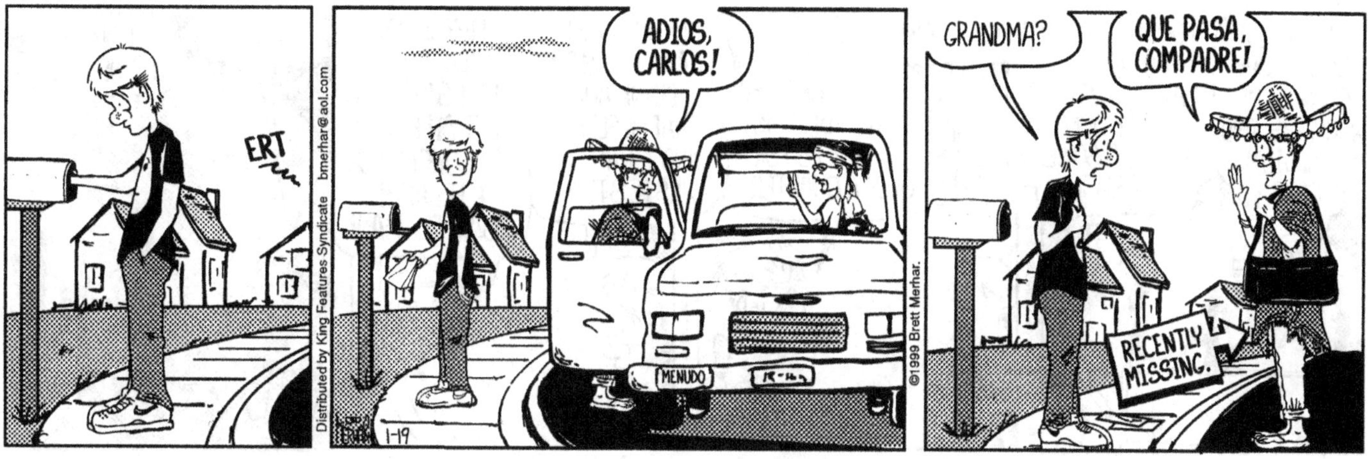
ERT
ADIOS, CARLOS!
MENUDO
GRANDMA?
QUE PASA, COMPADRE!
RECENTLY MISSING.
Distributed by King Features Syndicate bmerhar@aol.com
©1999 Brett Merhar.
1-19

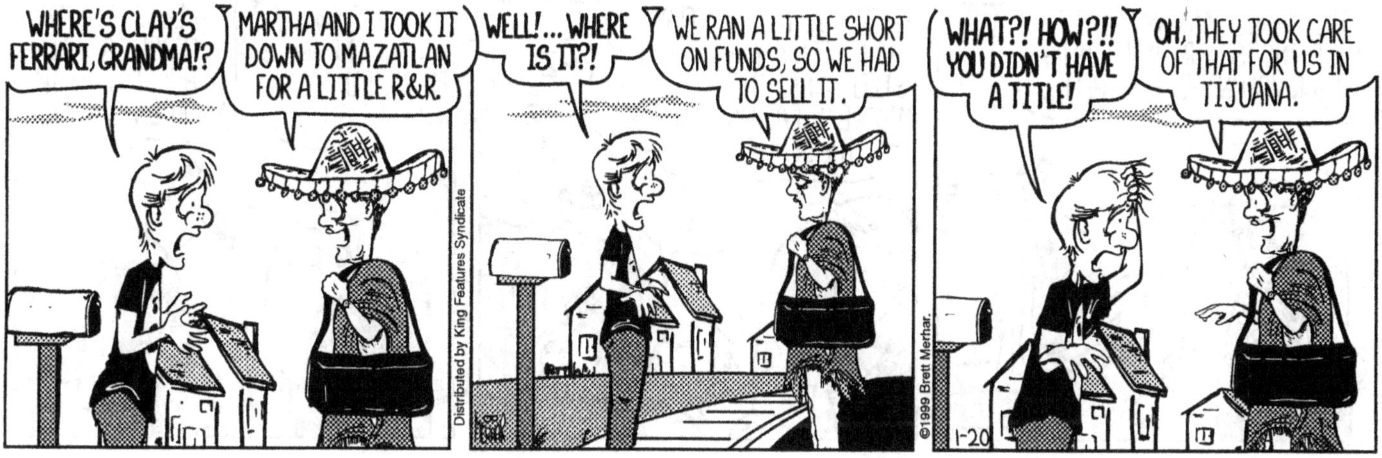
WHERE'S CLAY'S FERRARI, GRANDMA!?
MARTHA AND I TOOK IT DOWN TO MAZATLAN FOR A LITTLE R&R.
WELL!... WHERE IS IT?!
WE RAN A LITTLE SHORT ON FUNDS, SO WE HAD TO SELL IT.
WHAT?! HOW?!! YOU DIDN'T HAVE A TITLE!
OH, THEY TOOK CARE OF THAT FOR US IN TIJUANA.
Distributed by King Features Syndicate
©1999 Brett Merhar.
1-20

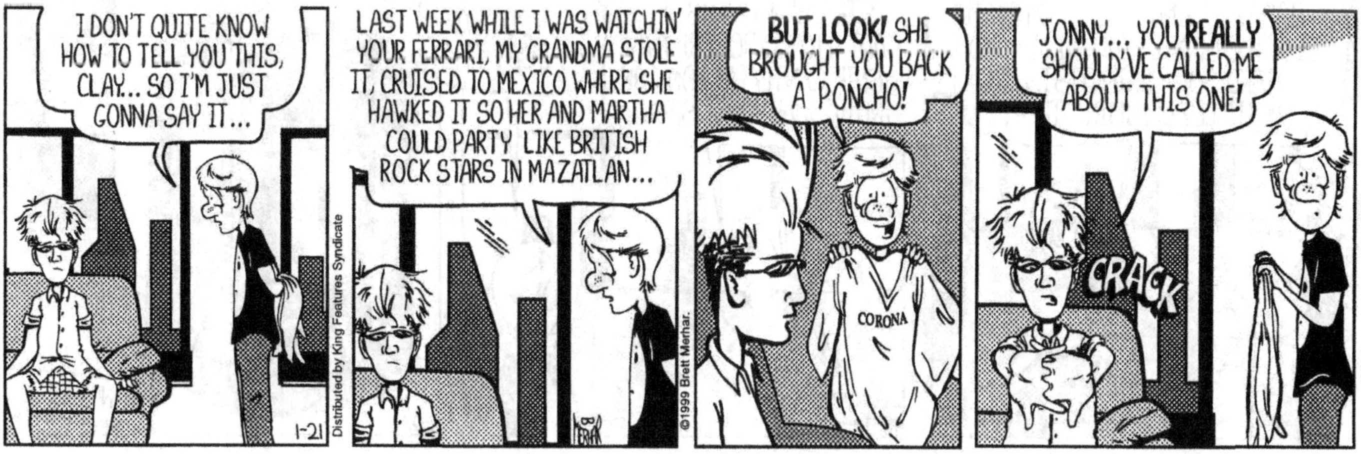
I DON'T QUITE KNOW HOW TO TELL YOU THIS, CLAY... SO I'M JUST GONNA SAY IT...
LAST WEEK WHILE I WAS WATCHIN' YOUR FERRARI, MY GRANDMA STOLE IT, CRUISED TO MEXICO WHERE SHE HAWKED IT SO HER AND MARTHA COULD PARTY LIKE BRITISH ROCK STARS IN MAZATLAN...
BUT, LOOK! SHE BROUGHT YOU BACK A PONCHO!
CORONA
JONNY... YOU REALLY SHOULD'VE CALLED ME ABOUT THIS ONE!
CRACK
Distributed by King Features Syndicate
©1999 Brett Merhar.
1-21

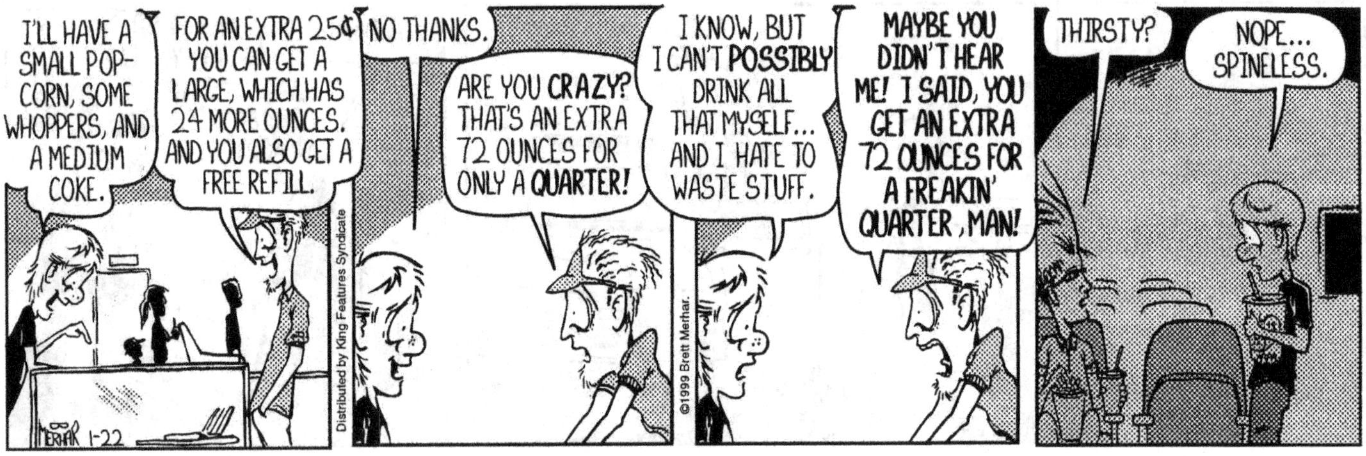
I'LL HAVE A SMALL POPCORN, SOME WHOPPERS, AND A MEDIUM COKE.
FOR AN EXTRA 25¢ YOU CAN GET A LARGE, WHICH HAS 24 MORE OUNCES. AND YOU ALSO GET A FREE REFILL.
MERHAR 1-22
Distributed by King Features Syndicate
NO THANKS.
ARE YOU **CRAZY?** THAT'S AN EXTRA 72 OUNCES FOR ONLY A **QUARTER!**
©1999 Brett Merhar.
I KNOW, BUT I CAN'T **POSSIBLY** DRINK ALL THAT MYSELF... AND I HATE TO WASTE STUFF.
MAYBE YOU DIDN'T HEAR ME! I SAID, YOU GET AN EXTRA 72 OUNCES FOR A FREAKIN' QUARTER, MAN!
THIRSTY?
NOPE... SPINELESS.

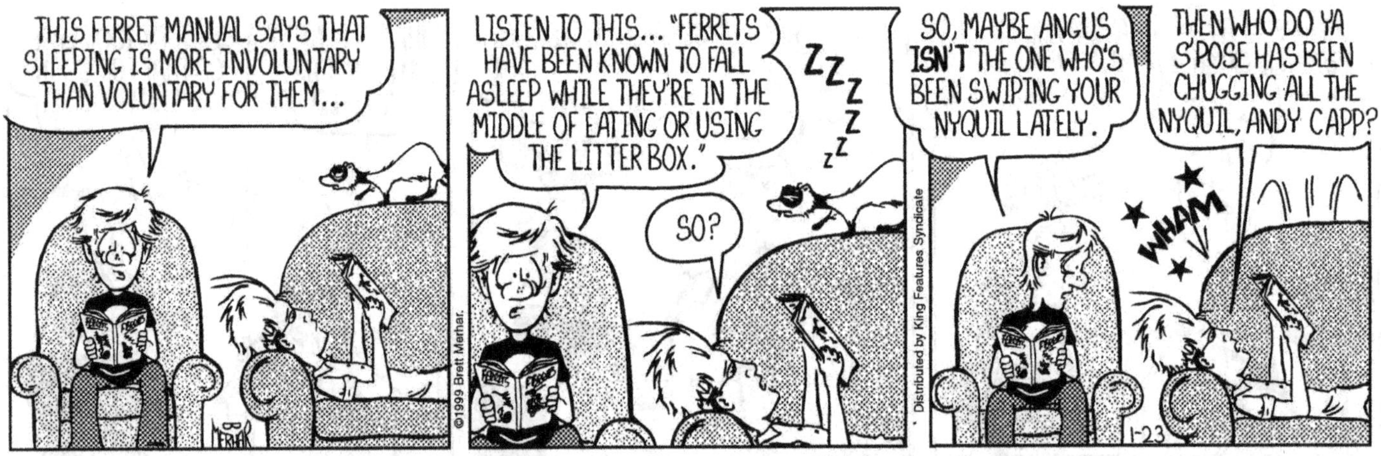
THIS FERRET MANUAL SAYS THAT SLEEPING IS MORE INVOLUNTARY THAN VOLUNTARY FOR THEM...
MERHAR
©1999 Brett Merhar.
LISTEN TO THIS... "FERRETS HAVE BEEN KNOWN TO FALL ASLEEP WHILE THEY'RE IN THE MIDDLE OF EATING OR USING THE LITTER BOX."
ZZZZZ
SO?
Distributed by King Features Syndicate
SO, MAYBE ANGUS **ISN'T** THE ONE WHO'S BEEN SWIPING YOUR NYQUIL LATELY.
WHAM
THEN WHO DO YA S'POSE HAS BEEN CHUGGING ALL THE NYQUIL, ANDY CAPP?
1-23

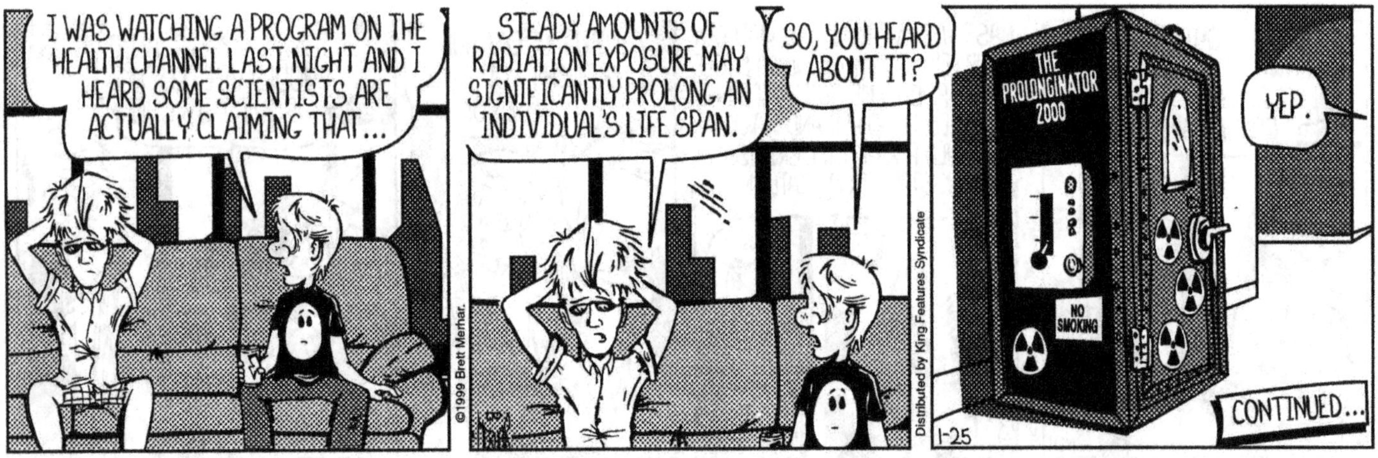
I WAS WATCHING A PROGRAM ON THE HEALTH CHANNEL LAST NIGHT AND I HEARD SOME SCIENTISTS ARE ACTUALLY CLAIMING THAT...
©1999 Brett Merhar.
STEADY AMOUNTS OF RADIATION EXPOSURE MAY SIGNIFICANTLY PROLONG AN INDIVIDUAL'S LIFE SPAN.
SO, YOU HEARD ABOUT IT?
Distributed by King Features Syndicate
THE PROLONGINATOR 2000
NO SMOKING
YEP.
CONTINUED...
1-25

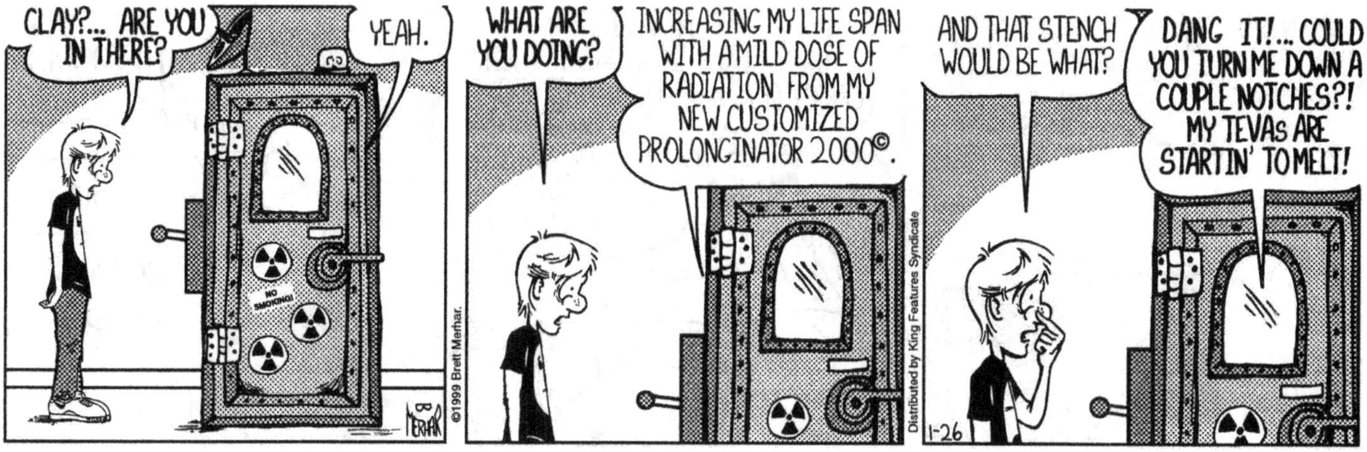
CLAY?... ARE YOU IN THERE?
YEAH.
NO SMOKING!
WHAT ARE YOU DOING?
INCREASING MY LIFE SPAN WITH A MILD DOSE OF RADIATION FROM MY NEW CUSTOMIZED PROLONGINATOR 2000©.
AND THAT STENCH WOULD BE WHAT?
DANG IT!... COULD YOU TURN ME DOWN A COUPLE NOTCHES?! MY TEVAs ARE STARTIN' TO MELT!
©1999 Brett Merhar.
Distributed by King Features Syndicate
1-26

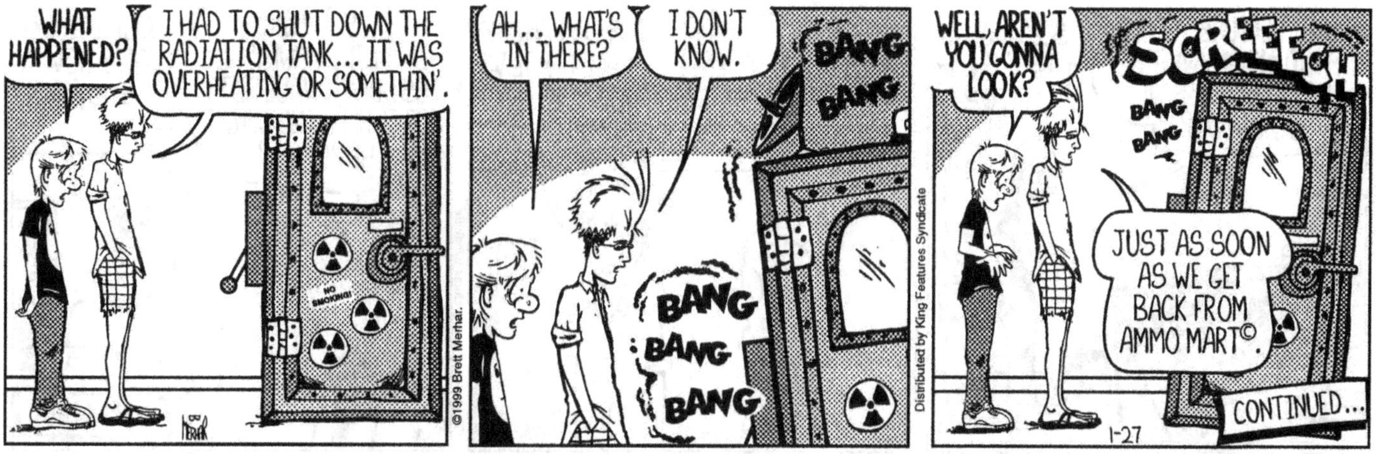
WHAT HAPPENED?
I HAD TO SHUT DOWN THE RADIATION TANK... IT WAS OVERHEATING OR SOMETHIN'.
NO SMOKING!
AH... WHAT'S IN THERE?
I DON'T KNOW.
BANG
BANG
BANG
BANG
BANG
WELL, AREN'T YOU GONNA LOOK?
SCREEECH
BANG
BANG
JUST AS SOON AS WE GET BACK FROM AMMO MART©.
CONTINUED...
©1999 Brett Merhar.
Distributed by King Features Syndicate
1-27

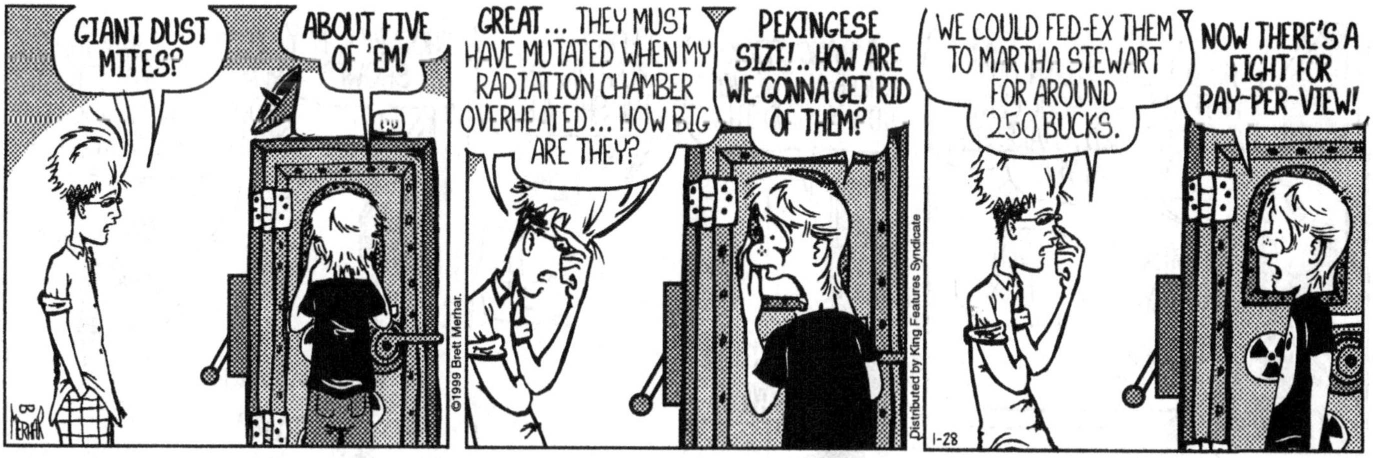
GIANT DUST MITES?
ABOUT FIVE OF 'EM!
GREAT... THEY MUST HAVE MUTATED WHEN MY RADIATION CHAMBER OVERHEATED... HOW BIG ARE THEY?
PEKINGESE SIZE!.. HOW ARE WE GONNA GET RID OF THEM?
WE COULD FED-EX THEM TO MARTHA STEWART FOR AROUND 250 BUCKS.
NOW THERE'S A FIGHT FOR PAY-PER-VIEW!
©1999 Brett Merhar.
Distributed by King Features Syndicate
1-28

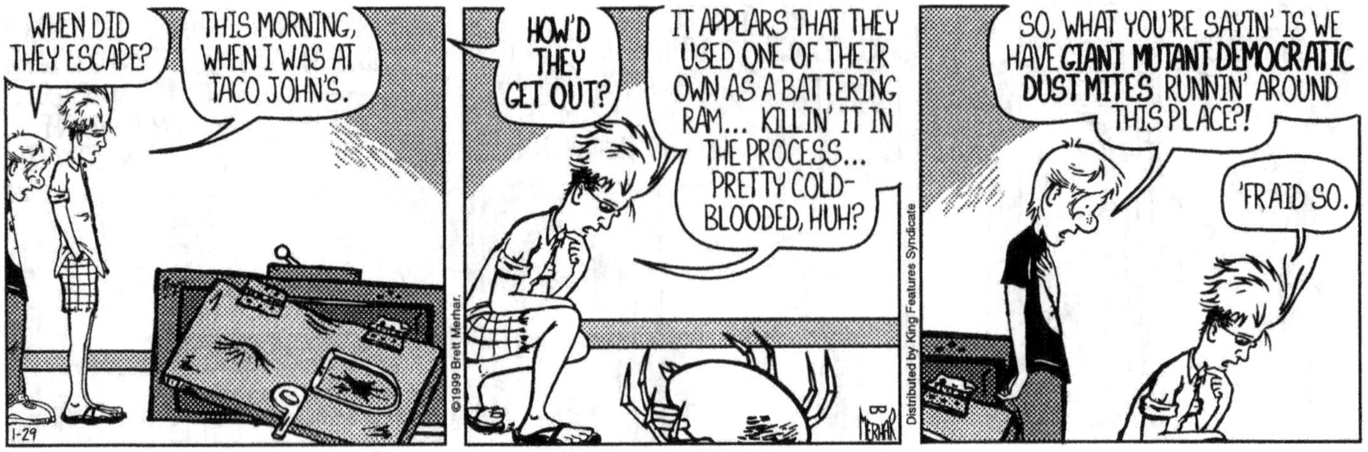
WHEN DID THEY ESCAPE?
THIS MORNING, WHEN I WAS AT TACO JOHN'S.
1-29
©1999 Brett Merhar.
HOW'D THEY GET OUT?
IT APPEARS THAT THEY USED ONE OF THEIR OWN AS A BATTERING RAM... KILLIN' IT IN THE PROCESS... PRETTY COLD-BLOODED, HUH?
MERHAR
Distributed by King Features Syndicate
SO, WHAT YOU'RE SAYIN' IS WE HAVE GIANT MUTANT DEMOCRATIC DUST MITES RUNNIN' AROUND THIS PLACE?!
'FRAID SO.

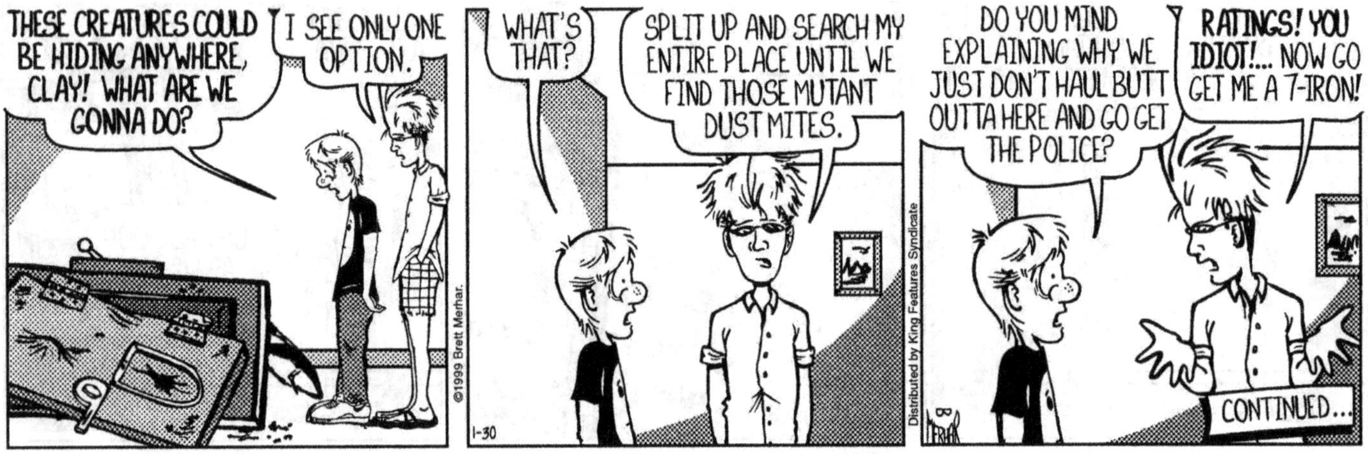
THESE CREATURES COULD BE HIDING ANYWHERE, CLAY! WHAT ARE WE GONNA DO?
I SEE ONLY ONE OPTION.
©1999 Brett Merhar.
WHAT'S THAT?
SPLIT UP AND SEARCH MY ENTIRE PLACE UNTIL WE FIND THOSE MUTANT DUST MITES.
1-30
Distributed by King Features Syndicate
DO YOU MIND EXPLAINING WHY WE JUST DON'T HAUL BUTT OUTTA HERE AND GO GET THE POLICE?
RATINGS! YOU IDIOT!... NOW GO GET ME A 7-IRON!
MERHAR
CONTINUED...

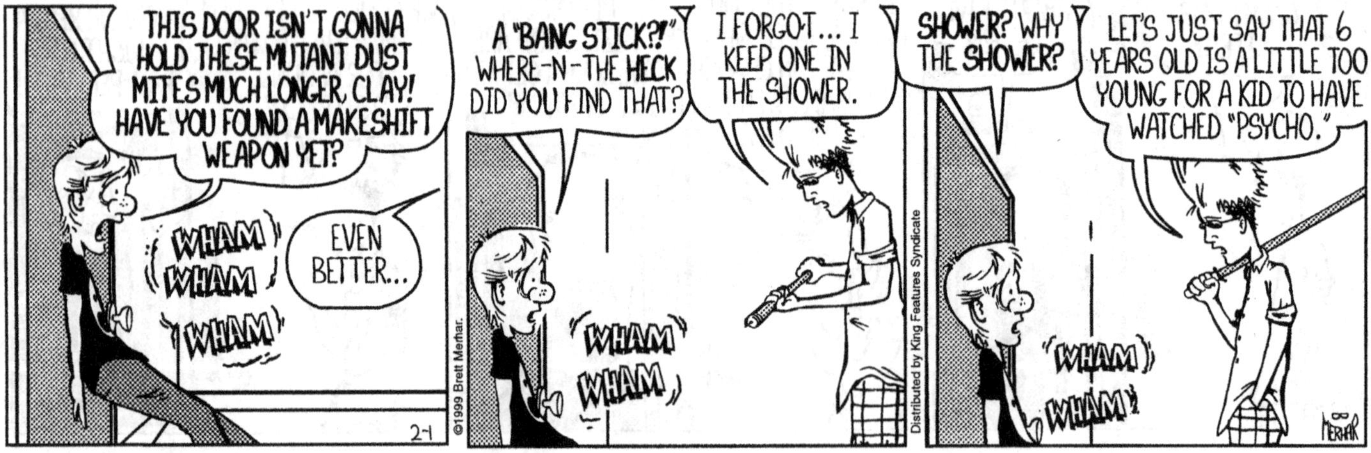
THIS DOOR ISN'T GONNA HOLD THESE MUTANT DUST MITES MUCH LONGER, CLAY! HAVE YOU FOUND A MAKESHIFT WEAPON YET?
WHAM
WHAM
WHAM
EVEN BETTER...
2-1
©1999 Brett Merhar.
A "BANG STICK?!" WHERE-N-THE HECK DID YOU FIND THAT?
I FORGOT... I KEEP ONE IN THE SHOWER.
WHAM
WHAM
Distributed by King Features Syndicate
SHOWER? WHY THE SHOWER?
LET'S JUST SAY THAT 6 YEARS OLD IS A LITTLE TOO YOUNG FOR A KID TO HAVE WATCHED "PSYCHO."
WHAM
WHAM
MERHAR

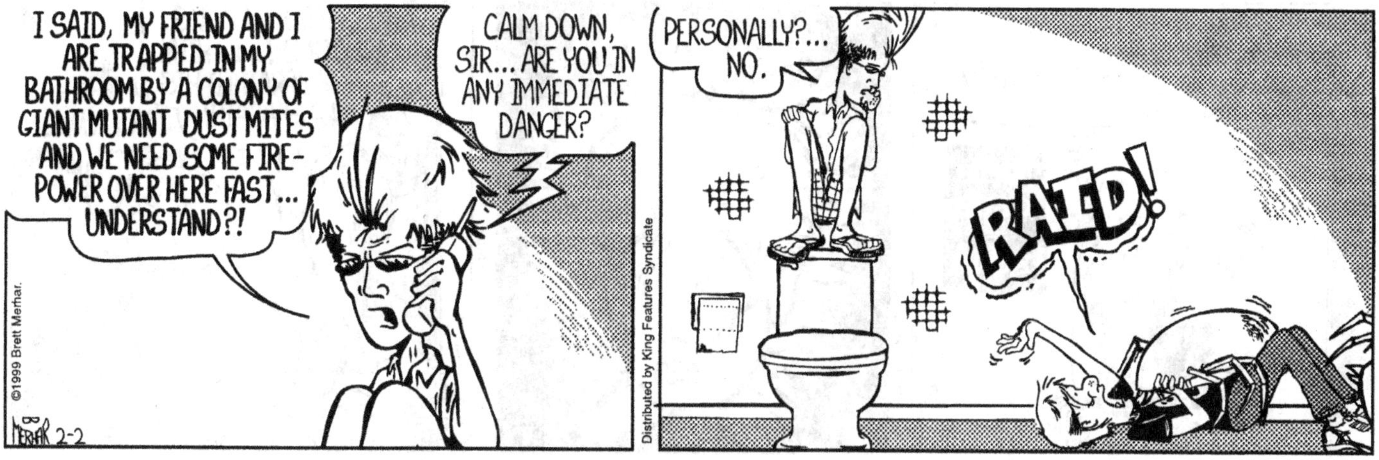
I SAID, MY FRIEND AND I ARE TRAPPED IN MY BATHROOM BY A COLONY OF GIANT MUTANT DUST MITES AND WE NEED SOME FIRE-POWER OVER HERE FAST... UNDERSTAND?!
CALM DOWN, SIR... ARE YOU IN ANY IMMEDIATE DANGER?
©1999 Brett Merhar.
MERHAR 2-2
PERSONALLY?... NO.
RAID!
Distributed by King Features Syndicate

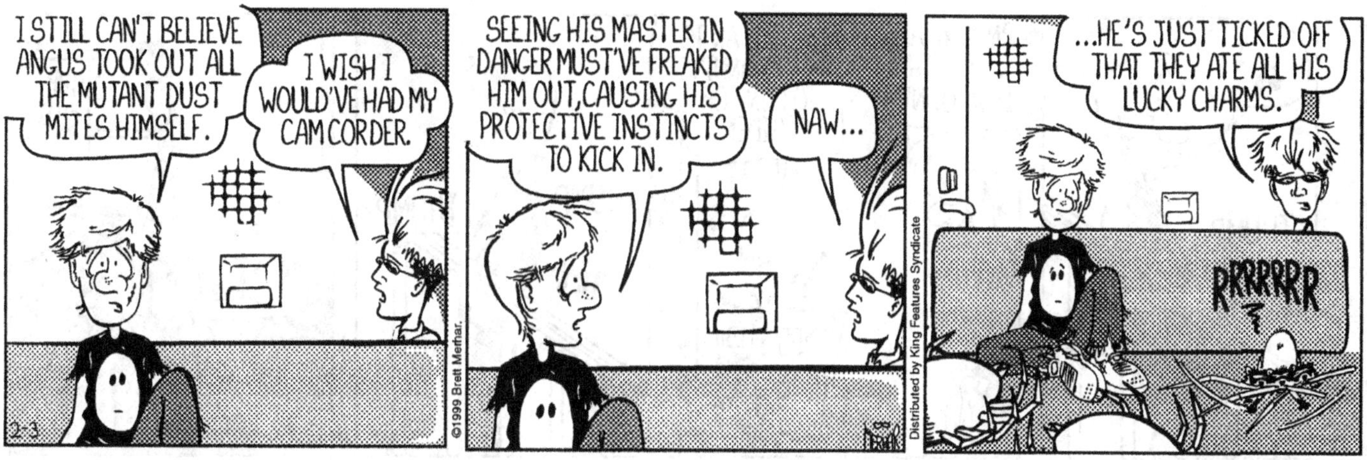
I STILL CAN'T BELIEVE ANGUS TOOK OUT ALL THE MUTANT DUST MITES HIMSELF.
I WISH I WOULD'VE HAD MY CAMCORDER.
2-3
SEEING HIS MASTER IN DANGER MUST'VE FREAKED HIM OUT, CAUSING HIS PROTECTIVE INSTINCTS TO KICK IN.
NAW...
©1999 Brett Merhar.
...HE'S JUST TICKED OFF THAT THEY ATE ALL HIS LUCKY CHARMS.
RRRRRRR
Distributed by King Features Syndicate

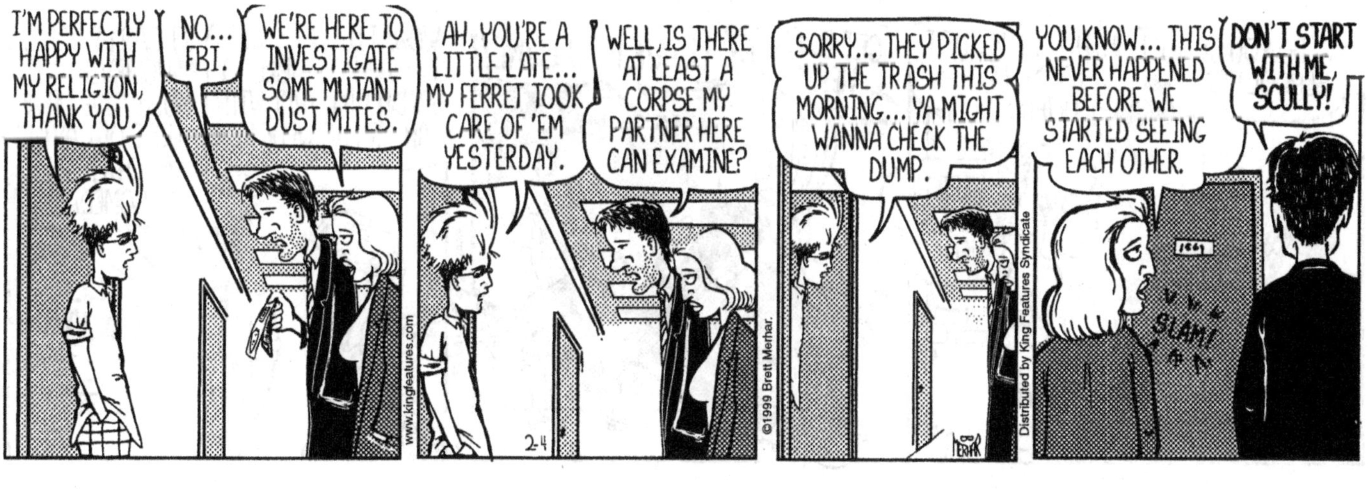
I'M PERFECTLY HAPPY WITH MY RELIGION, THANK YOU.
NO... FBI.
WE'RE HERE TO INVESTIGATE SOME MUTANT DUST MITES.
www.kingfeatures.com
AH, YOU'RE A LITTLE LATE... MY FERRET TOOK CARE OF 'EM YESTERDAY.
WELL, IS THERE AT LEAST A CORPSE MY PARTNER HERE CAN EXAMINE?
2-4
©1999 Brett Merhar.
SORRY... THEY PICKED UP THE TRASH THIS MORNING... YA MIGHT WANNA CHECK THE DUMP.
MERHAR
Distributed by King Features Syndicate
YOU KNOW... THIS NEVER HAPPENED BEFORE WE STARTED SEEING EACH OTHER.
DON'T START WITH ME, SCULLY!
SLAM!

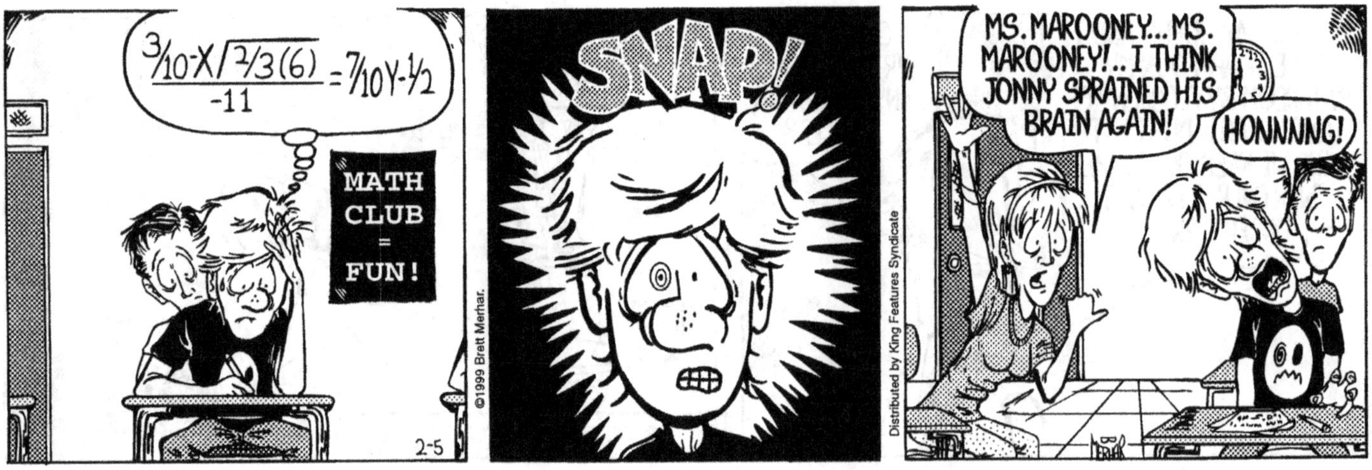
3/10-X/√2/3(6) / -11 = 7/10Y-1/2
MATH CLUB = FUN!
©1999 Brett Merhar.
2-5
SNAP!
MS. MAROONEY... MS. MAROONEY!.. I THINK JONNY SPRAINED HIS BRAIN AGAIN!
HONNNNG!
Distributed by King Features Syndicate

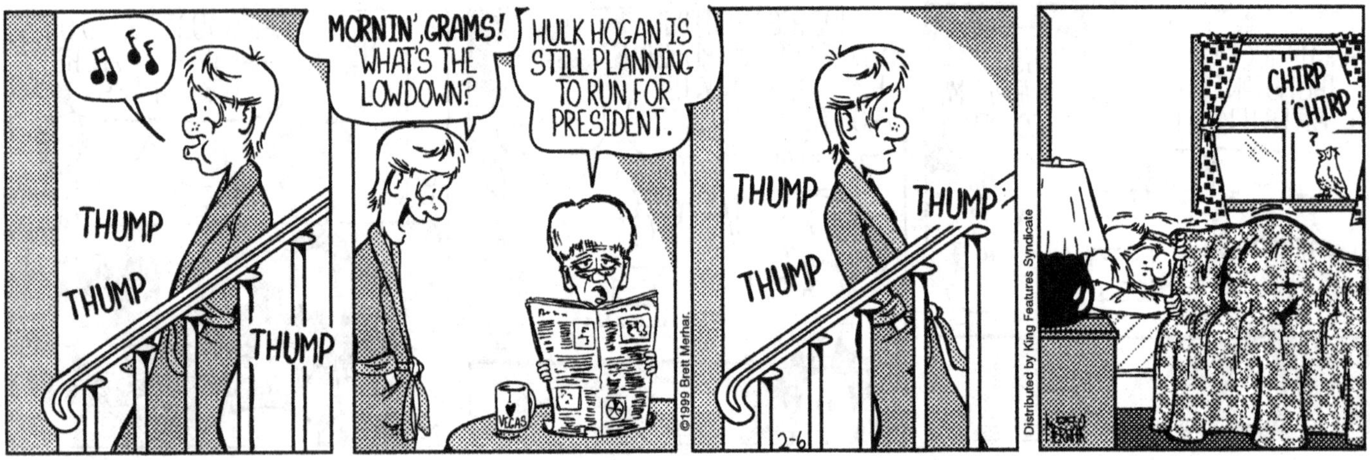
THUMP
THUMP
THUMP
MORNIN', GRAMS! WHAT'S THE LOWDOWN?
HULK HOGAN IS STILL PLANNING TO RUN FOR PRESIDENT.
©1999 Brett Merhar.
THUMP
THUMP
THUMP
2-6
CHIRP
CHIRP
Distributed by King Features Syndicate

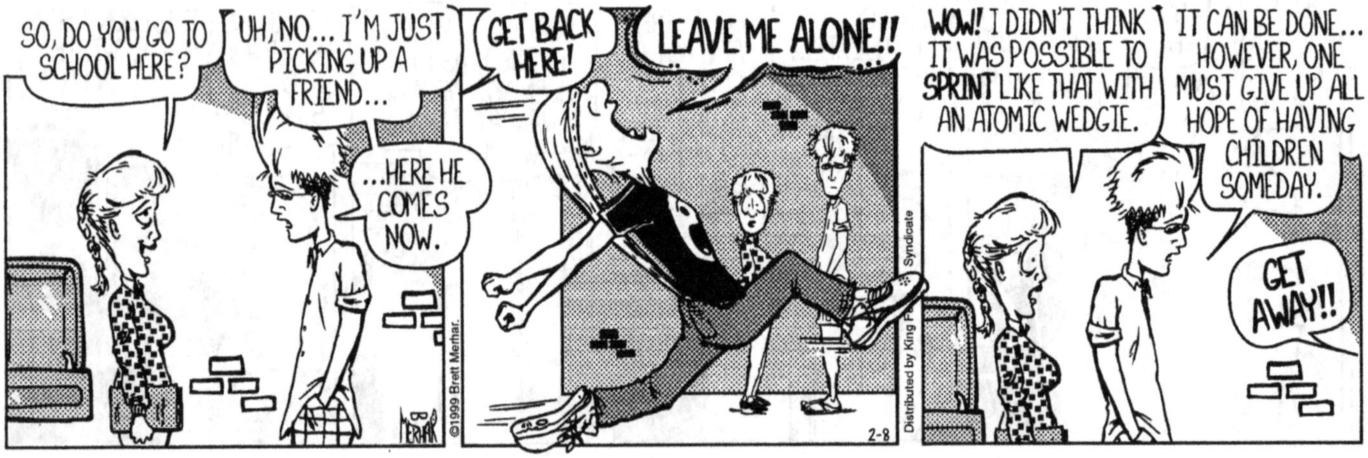
SO, DO YOU GO TO SCHOOL HERE?
UH, NO... I'M JUST PICKING UP A FRIEND...
...HERE HE COMES NOW.
©1999 Brett Merhar.
GET BACK HERE!
LEAVE ME ALONE!!
2-8
WOW! I DIDN'T THINK IT WAS POSSIBLE TO SPRINT LIKE THAT WITH AN ATOMIC WEDGIE.
IT CAN BE DONE... HOWEVER, ONE MUST GIVE UP ALL HOPE OF HAVING CHILDREN SOMEDAY.
GET AWAY!!

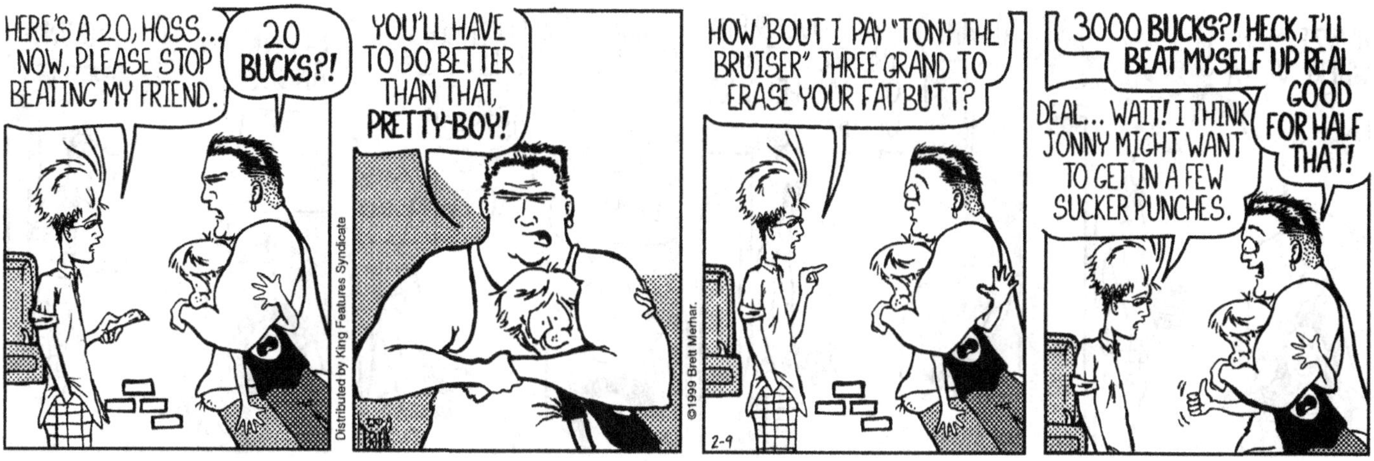
HERE'S A 20, HOSS... NOW, PLEASE STOP BEATING MY FRIEND.
20 BUCKS?!
YOU'LL HAVE TO DO BETTER THAN THAT, PRETTY-BOY!
Distributed by King Features Syndicate
HOW 'BOUT I PAY "TONY THE BRUISER" THREE GRAND TO ERASE YOUR FAT BUTT?
©1999 Brett Merhar.
2-9
3000 BUCKS?! HECK, I'LL BEAT MYSELF UP REAL GOOD FOR HALF THAT!
DEAL... WAIT! I THINK JONNY MIGHT WANT TO GET IN A FEW SUCKER PUNCHES.

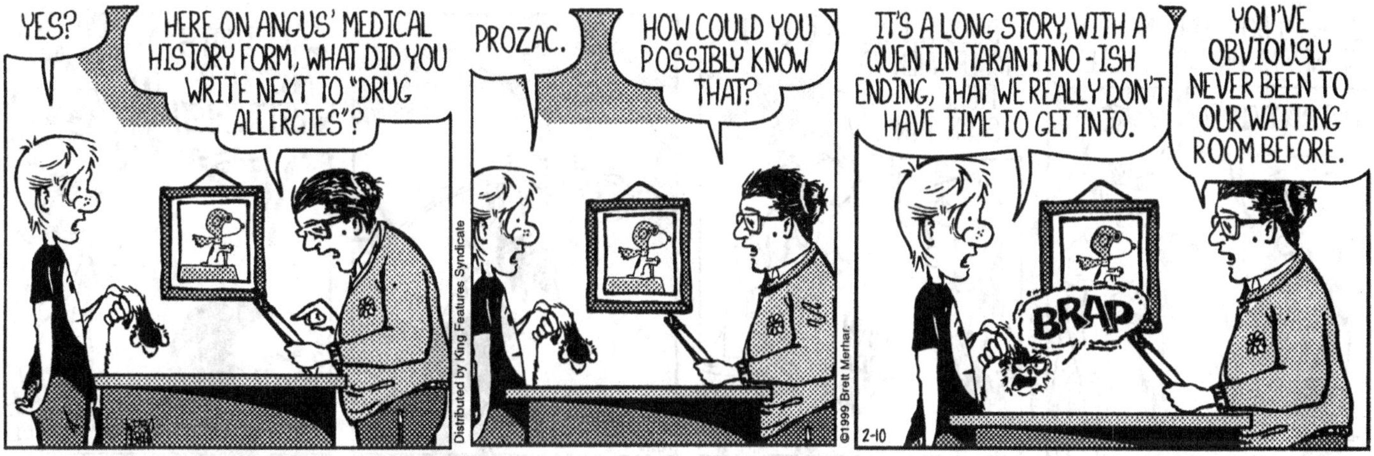
YES?
HERE ON ANGUS' MEDICAL HISTORY FORM, WHAT DID YOU WRITE NEXT TO "DRUG ALLERGIES"?
PROZAC.
HOW COULD YOU POSSIBLY KNOW THAT?
Distributed by King Features Syndicate
©1999 Brett Merhar.
2-10
IT'S A LONG STORY, WITH A QUENTIN TARANTINO - ISH ENDING, THAT WE REALLY DON'T HAVE TIME TO GET INTO.
YOU'VE OBVIOUSLY NEVER BEEN TO OUR WAITING ROOM BEFORE.
BRAP

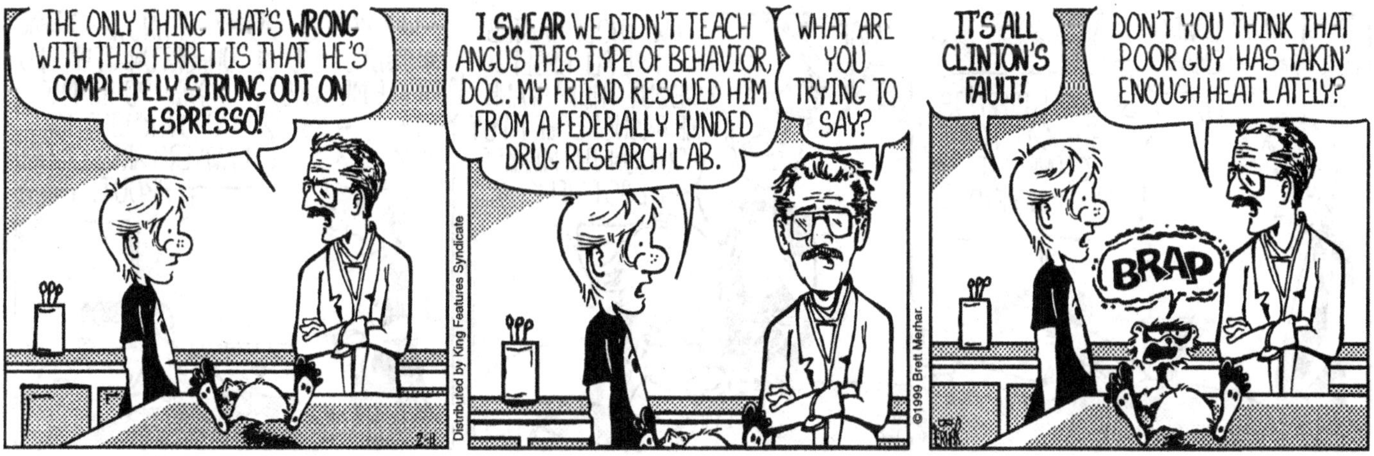
THE ONLY THING THAT'S WRONG WITH THIS FERRET IS THAT HE'S COMPLETELY STRUNG OUT ON ESPRESSO!
I SWEAR WE DIDN'T TEACH ANGUS THIS TYPE OF BEHAVIOR, DOC. MY FRIEND RESCUED HIM FROM A FEDERALLY FUNDED DRUG RESEARCH LAB.
WHAT ARE YOU TRYING TO SAY?
Distributed by King Features Syndicate
©1999 Brett Merhar.
IT'S ALL CLINTON'S FAULT!
DON'T YOU THINK THAT POOR GUY HAS TAKIN' ENOUGH HEAT LATELY?
BRAP

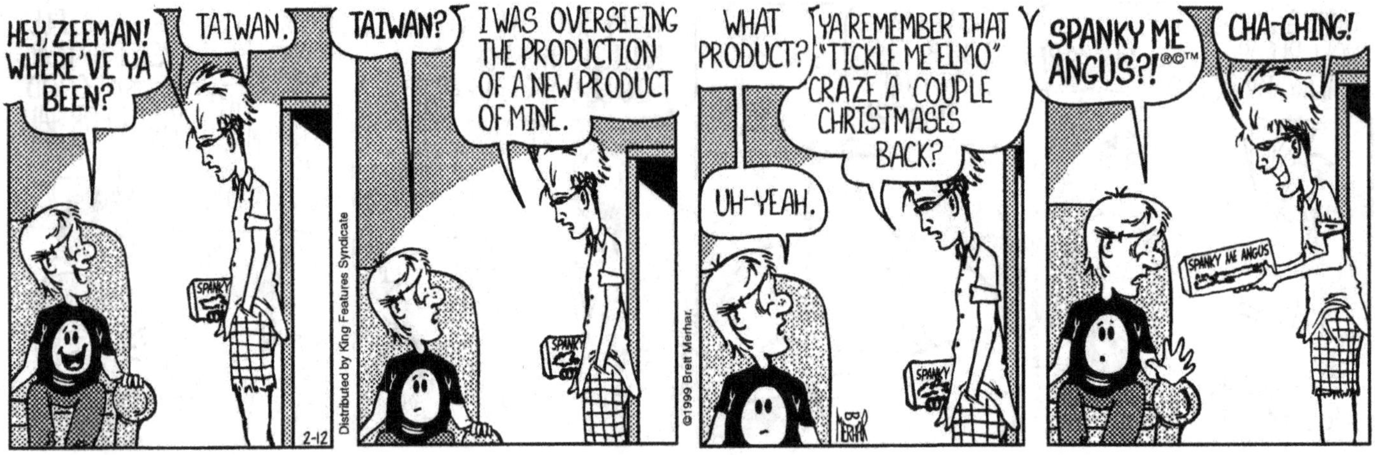
HEY, ZEEMAN! WHERE'VE YA BEEN?
TAIWAN.
2-12
Distributed by King Features Syndicate
TAIWAN?
I WAS OVERSEEING THE PRODUCTION OF A NEW PRODUCT OF MINE.
©1999 Brett Merhar.
WHAT PRODUCT?
UH-YEAH.
YA REMEMBER THAT "TICKLE ME ELMO" CRAZE A COUPLE CHRISTMASES BACK?
MERHAR
SPANKY ME ANGUS?!®©™
CHA-CHING!
SPANKY ME ANGUS

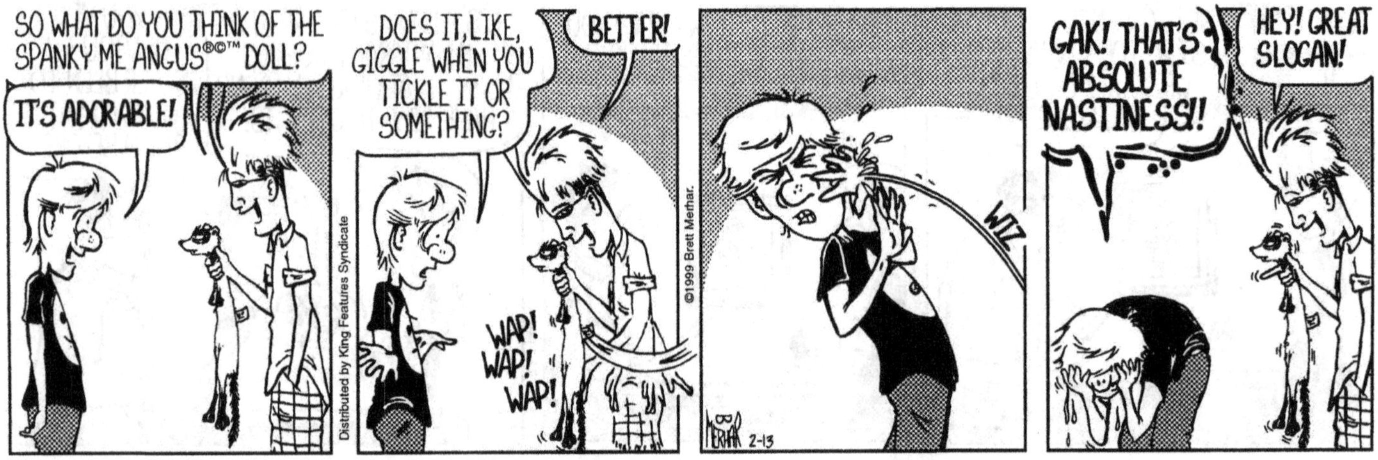
SO WHAT DO YOU THINK OF THE SPANKY ME ANGUS®©™ DOLL?
IT'S ADORABLE!
Distributed by King Features Syndicate
DOES IT, LIKE, GIGGLE WHEN YOU TICKLE IT OR SOMETHING?
BETTER!
WAP! WAP! WAP!
©1999 Brett Merhar.
WIZ
MERHAR 2-13
GAK! THAT'S ABSOLUTE NASTINESS!!
HEY! GREAT SLOGAN!

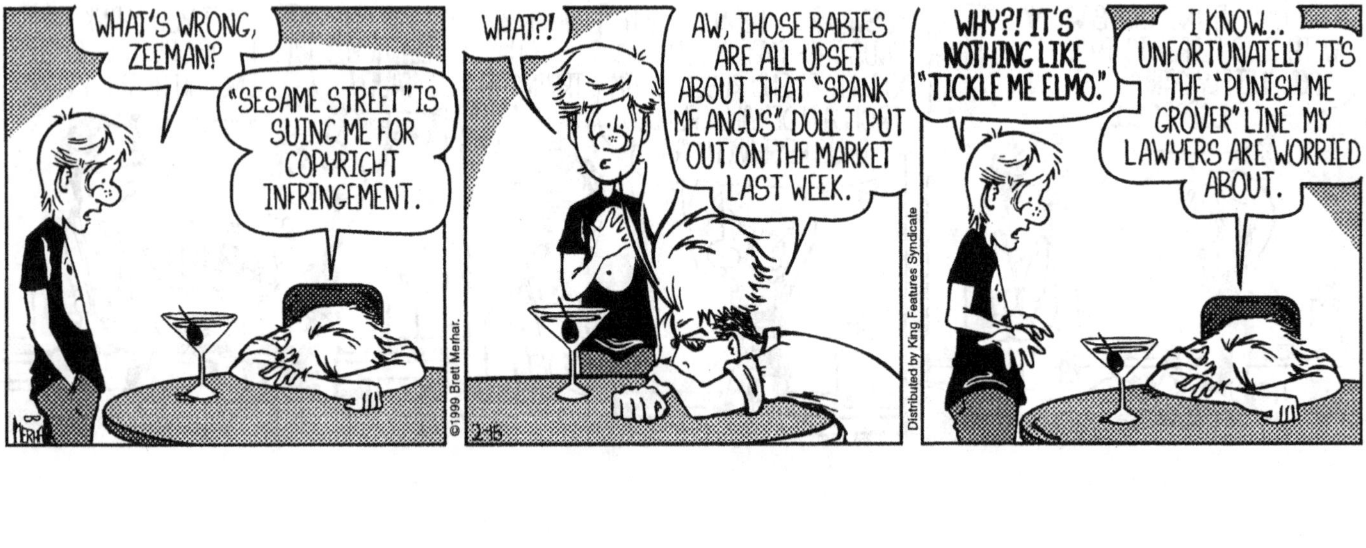
WHAT'S WRONG, ZEEMAN?
"SESAME STREET" IS SUING ME FOR COPYRIGHT INFRINGEMENT.
MERHAR
©1999 Brett Merhar.
2-15
WHAT?!
AW, THOSE BABIES ARE ALL UPSET ABOUT THAT "SPANK ME ANGUS" DOLL I PUT OUT ON THE MARKET LAST WEEK.
Distributed by King Features Syndicate
WHY?! IT'S NOTHING LIKE "TICKLE ME ELMO."
I KNOW... UNFORTUNATELY IT'S THE "PUNISH ME GROVER" LINE MY LAWYERS ARE WORRIED ABOUT.

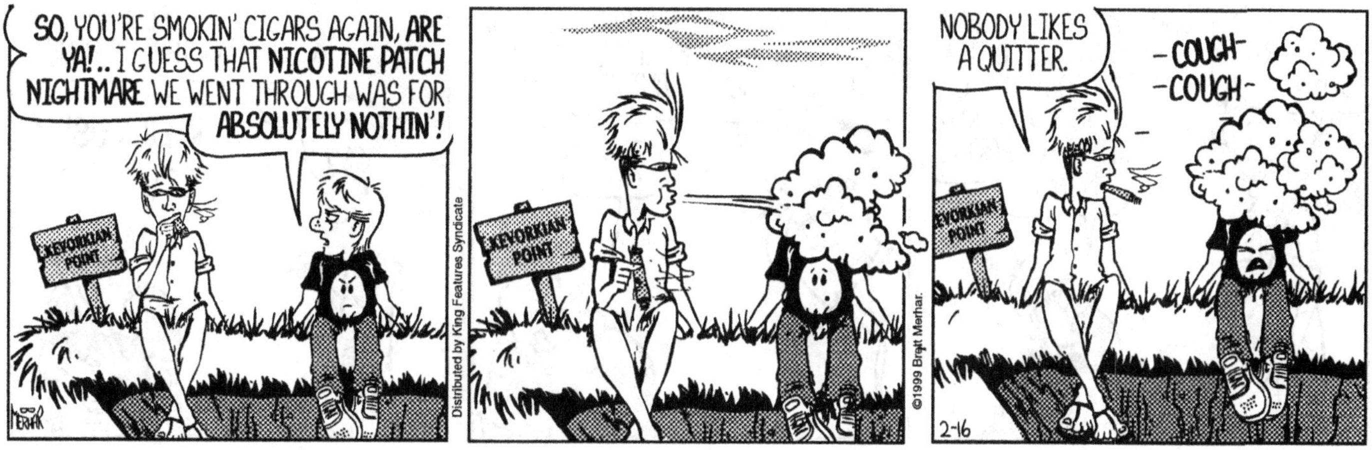
SO, YOU'RE SMOKIN' CIGARS AGAIN, ARE YA!.. I GUESS THAT NICOTINE PATCH NIGHTMARE WE WENT THROUGH WAS FOR ABSOLUTELY NOTHIN'!
KEVORKIAN POINT
MERHAR
Distributed by King Features Syndicate
©1999 Brett Merhar.
NOBODY LIKES A QUITTER.
-COUGH-
-COUGH-
2-16

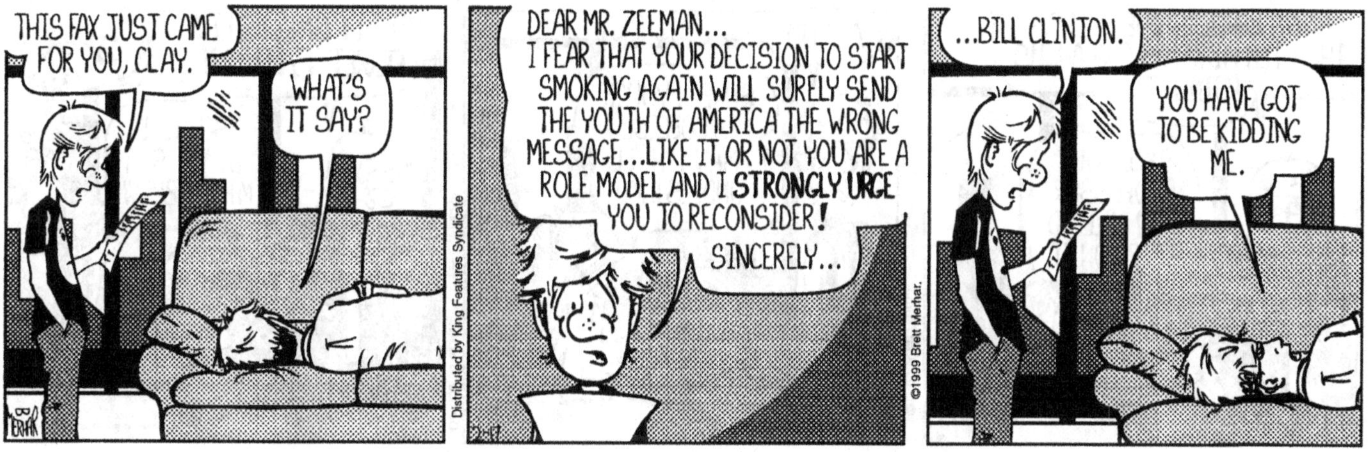
THIS FAX JUST CAME FOR YOU, CLAY.
WHAT'S IT SAY?
MERHAR
Distributed by King Features Syndicate
DEAR MR. ZEEMAN...
I FEAR THAT YOUR DECISION TO START SMOKING AGAIN WILL SURELY SEND THE YOUTH OF AMERICA THE WRONG MESSAGE...LIKE IT OR NOT YOU ARE A ROLE MODEL AND I STRONGLY URGE YOU TO RECONSIDER!
SINCERELY...
©1999 Brett Merhar.
...BILL CLINTON.
YOU HAVE GOT TO BE KIDDING ME.

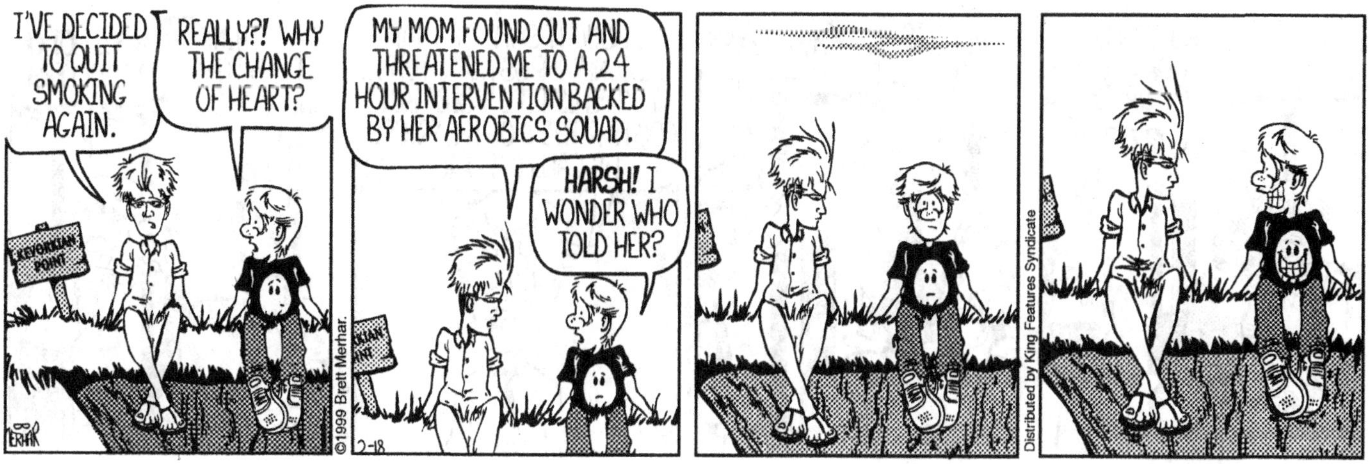
I'VE DECIDED TO QUIT SMOKING AGAIN.
REALLY?! WHY THE CHANGE OF HEART?
KEVORKIAN POINT
MERHAR
©1999 Brett Merhar.
MY MOM FOUND OUT AND THREATENED ME TO A 24 HOUR INTERVENTION BACKED BY HER AEROBICS SQUAD.
HARSH! I WONDER WHO TOLD HER?
2-18
Distributed by King Features Syndicate

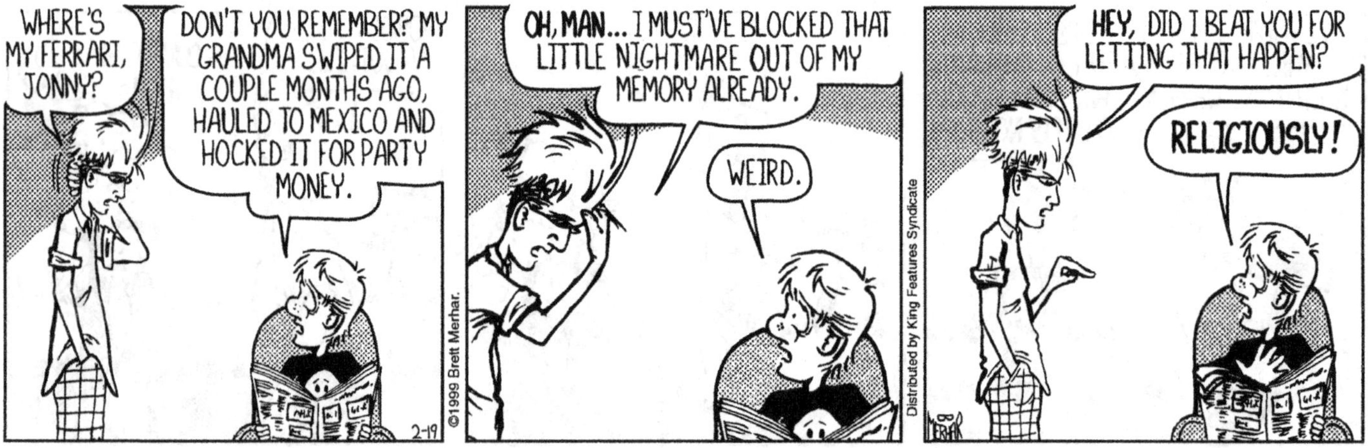
WHERE'S MY FERRARI, JONNY?
DON'T YOU REMEMBER? MY GRANDMA SWIPED IT A COUPLE MONTHS AGO, HAULED TO MEXICO AND HOCKED IT FOR PARTY MONEY.
2-19
©1999 Brett Merhar.
OH, MAN... I MUST'VE BLOCKED THAT LITTLE NIGHTMARE OUT OF MY MEMORY ALREADY.
WEIRD.
Distributed by King Features Syndicate
HEY, DID I BEAT YOU FOR LETTING THAT HAPPEN?
RELIGIOUSLY!
MERHAR

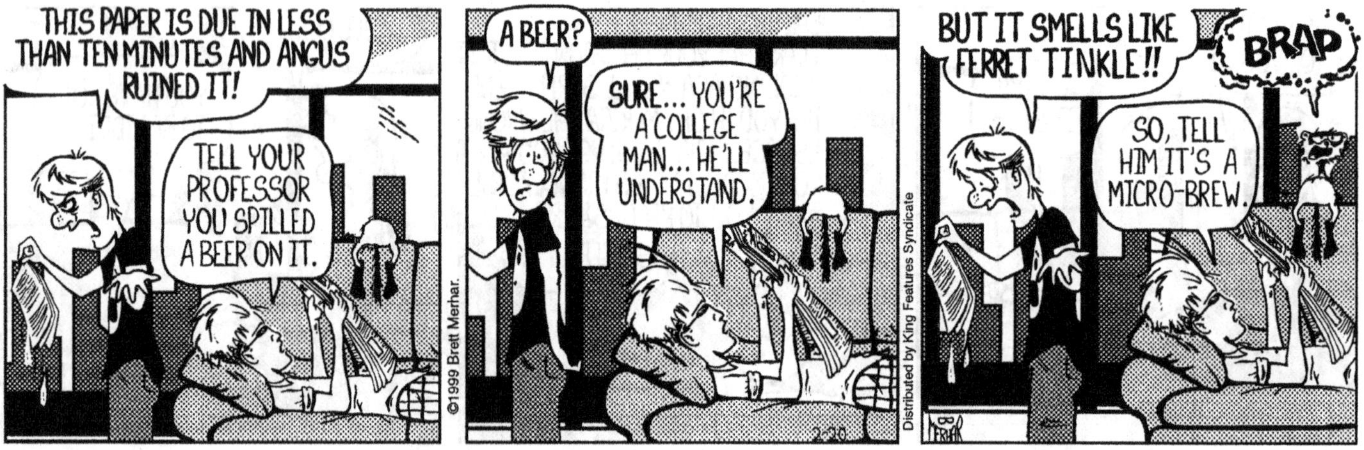
THIS PAPER IS DUE IN LESS THAN TEN MINUTES AND ANGUS RUINED IT!
TELL YOUR PROFESSOR YOU SPILLED A BEER ON IT.
©1999 Brett Merhar.
A BEER?
SURE... YOU'RE A COLLEGE MAN... HE'LL UNDERSTAND.
2-20
Distributed by King Features Syndicate
BUT IT SMELLS LIKE FERRET TINKLE!!
BRAP
SO, TELL HIM IT'S A MICRO-BREW.
MERHAR

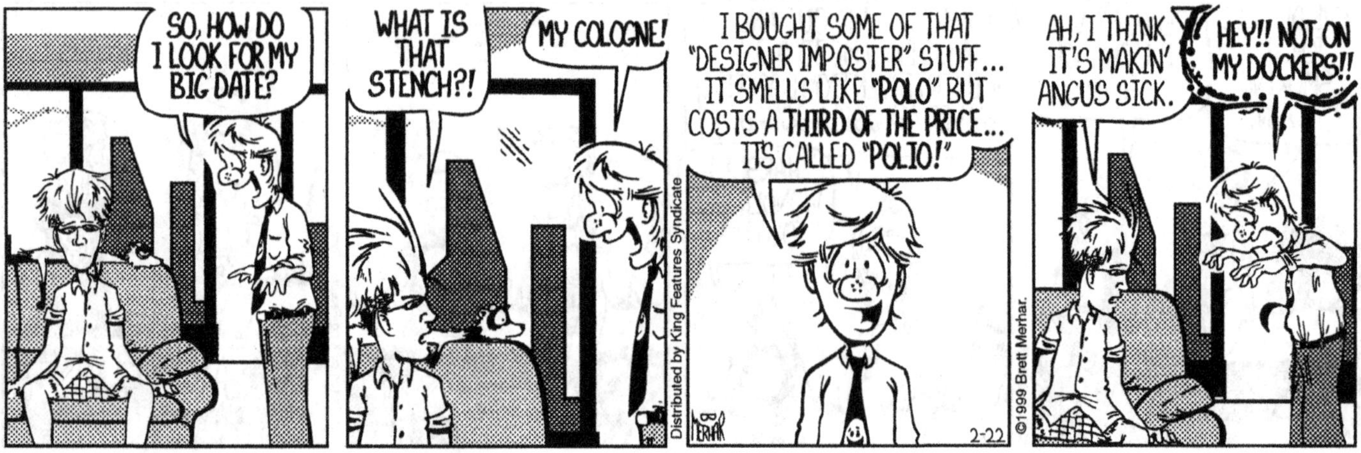
SO, HOW DO I LOOK FOR MY BIG DATE?
WHAT IS THAT STENCH?!
MY COLOGNE!
Distributed by King Features Syndicate
I BOUGHT SOME OF THAT "DESIGNER IMPOSTER" STUFF... IT SMELLS LIKE "POLO" BUT COSTS A THIRD OF THE PRICE... ITS CALLED "POLIO!"
MERHAR
2-22
©1999 Brett Merhar.
AH, I THINK IT'S MAKIN' ANGUS SICK.
HEY!! NOT ON MY DOCKERS!!

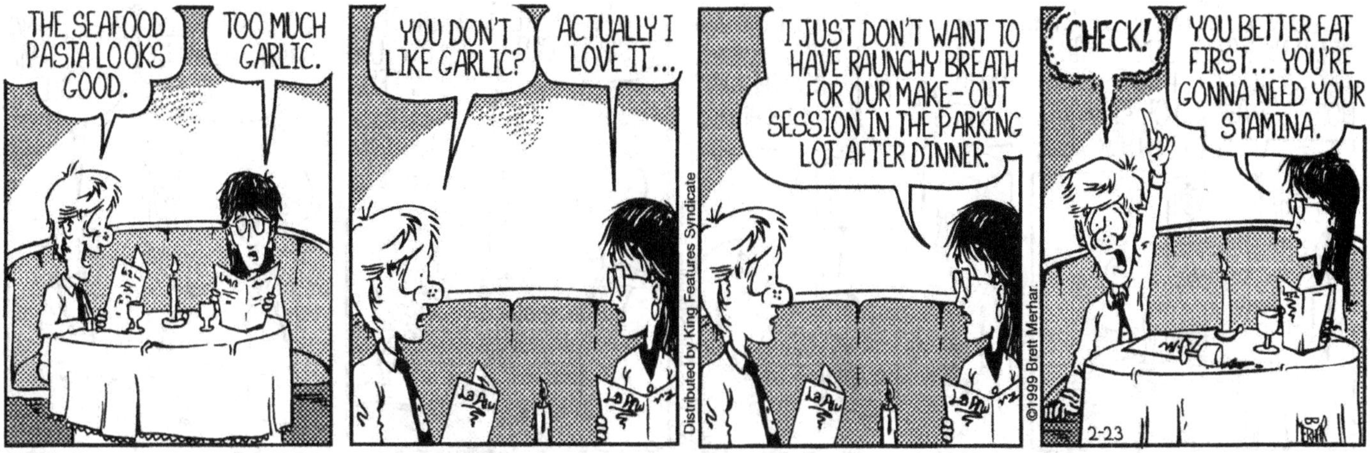
THE SEAFOOD PASTA LOOKS GOOD.
TOO MUCH GARLIC.
YOU DON'T LIKE GARLIC?
ACTUALLY I LOVE IT...
I JUST DON'T WANT TO HAVE RAUNCHY BREATH FOR OUR MAKE-OUT SESSION IN THE PARKING LOT AFTER DINNER.
CHECK!
YOU BETTER EAT FIRST... YOU'RE GONNA NEED YOUR STAMINA.
Distributed by King Features Syndicate
©1999 Brett Merhar.
2-23

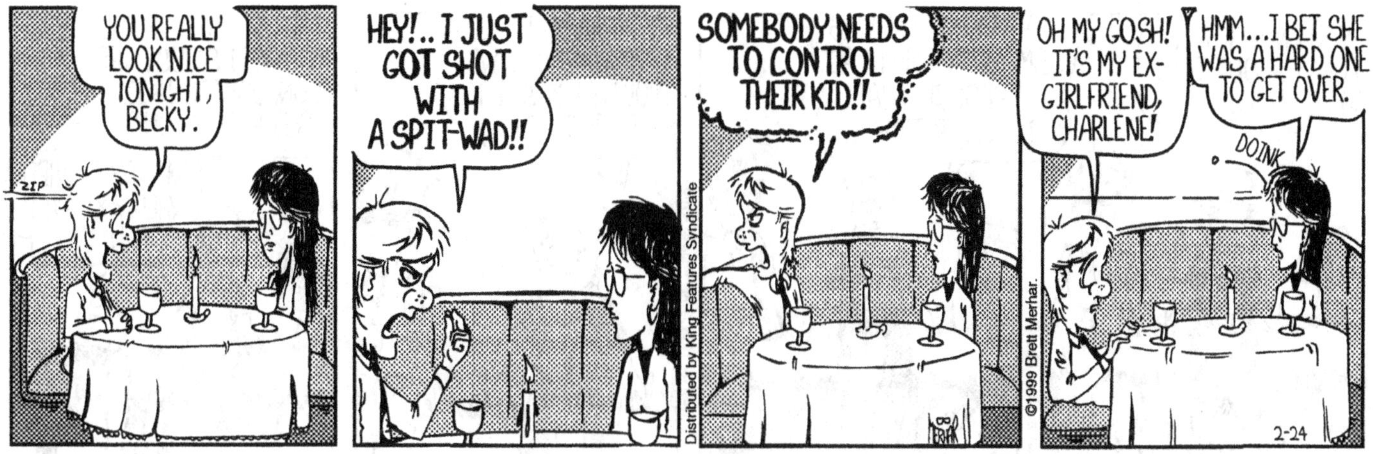
ZIP
YOU REALLY LOOK NICE TONIGHT, BECKY.
HEY!.. I JUST GOT SHOT WITH A SPIT-WAD!!
SOMEBODY NEEDS TO CONTROL THEIR KID!!
OH MY GOSH! IT'S MY EX-GIRLFRIEND, CHARLENE!
HMM...I BET SHE WAS A HARD ONE TO GET OVER.
DOINK
Distributed by King Features Syndicate
©1999 Brett Merhar.
2-24

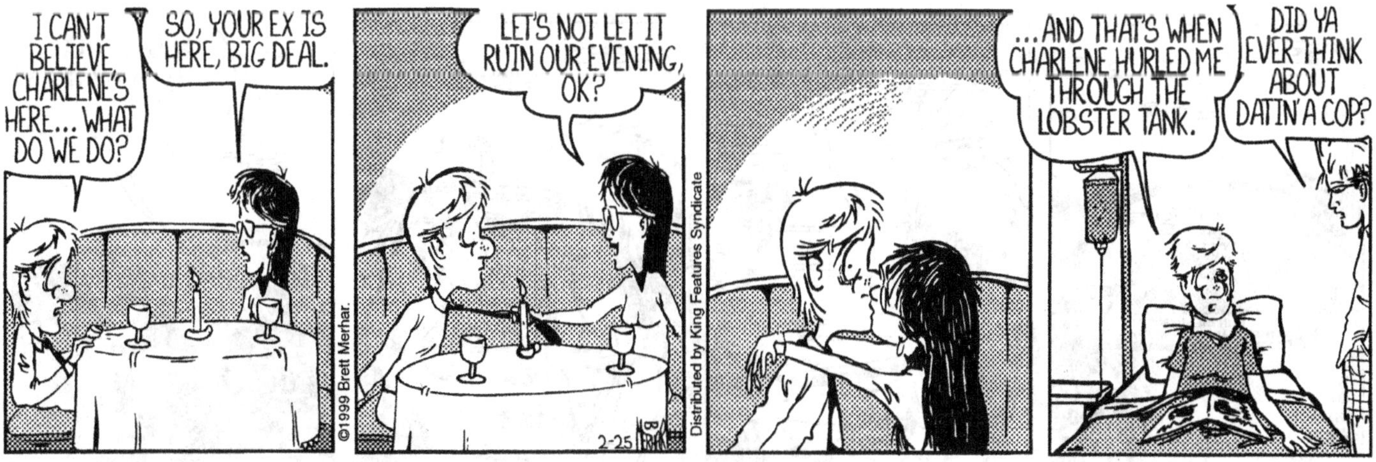
I CAN'T BELIEVE CHARLENE'S HERE... WHAT DO WE DO?
SO, YOUR EX IS HERE, BIG DEAL.
LET'S NOT LET IT RUIN OUR EVENING, OK?
...AND THAT'S WHEN CHARLENE HURLED ME THROUGH THE LOBSTER TANK.
DID YA EVER THINK ABOUT DATIN' A COP?
©1999 Brett Merhar.
Distributed by King Features Syndicate
2-25

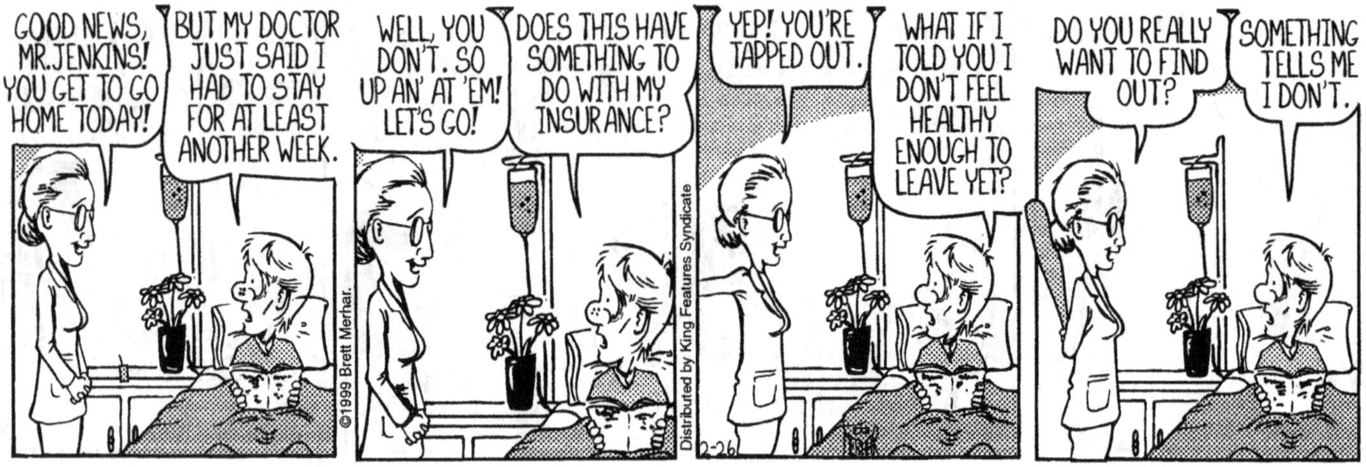
GOOD NEWS, MR. JENKINS! YOU GET TO GO HOME TODAY!
BUT MY DOCTOR JUST SAID I HAD TO STAY FOR AT LEAST ANOTHER WEEK.
WELL, YOU DON'T. SO UP AN' AT 'EM! LET'S GO!
DOES THIS HAVE SOMETHING TO DO WITH MY INSURANCE?
YEP! YOU'RE TAPPED OUT.
WHAT IF I TOLD YOU I DON'T FEEL HEALTHY ENOUGH TO LEAVE YET?
DO YOU REALLY WANT TO FIND OUT?
SOMETHING TELLS ME I DON'T.
©1999 Brett Merhar.
Distributed by King Features Syndicate
2-26

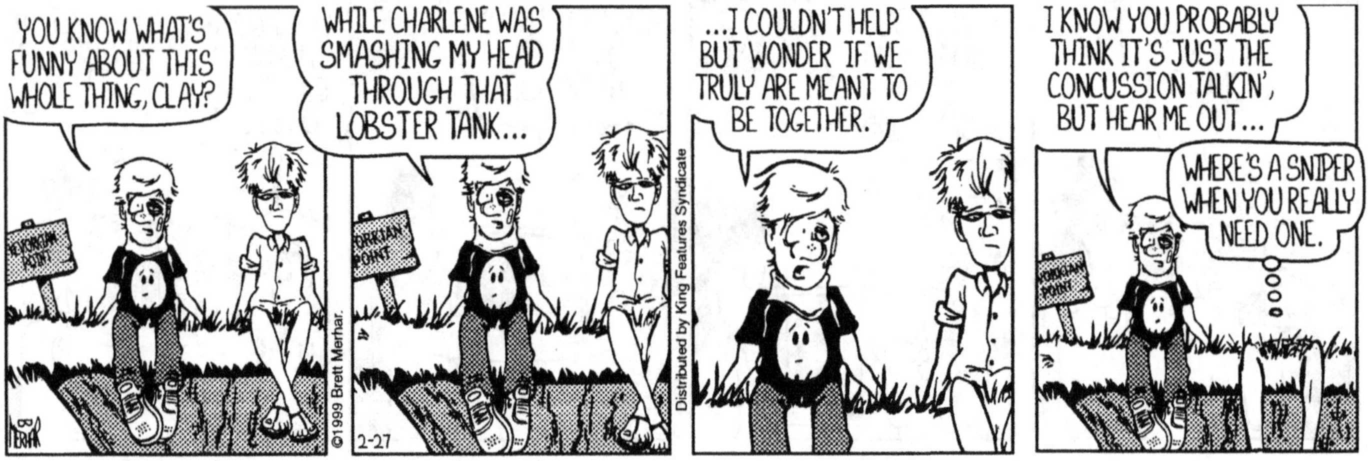
YOU KNOW WHAT'S FUNNY ABOUT THIS WHOLE THING, CLAY?
WHILE CHARLENE WAS SMASHING MY HEAD THROUGH THAT LOBSTER TANK...
...I COULDN'T HELP BUT WONDER IF WE TRULY ARE MEANT TO BE TOGETHER.
I KNOW YOU PROBABLY THINK IT'S JUST THE CONCUSSION TALKIN', BUT HEAR ME OUT...
WHERE'S A SNIPER WHEN YOU REALLY NEED ONE.
©1999 Brett Merhar.
Distributed by King Features Syndicate
2-27

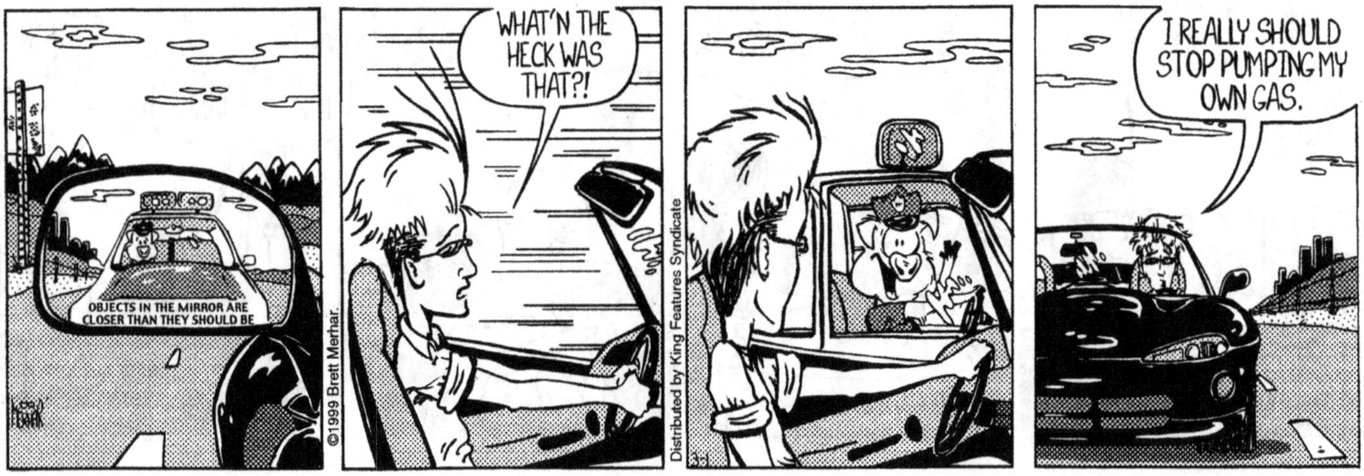
OBJECTS IN THE MIRROR ARE CLOSER THAN THEY SHOULD BE
WHAT'N THE HECK WAS THAT?!
I REALLY SHOULD STOP PUMPING MY OWN GAS.
©1999 Brett Merhar.
Distributed by King Features Syndicate

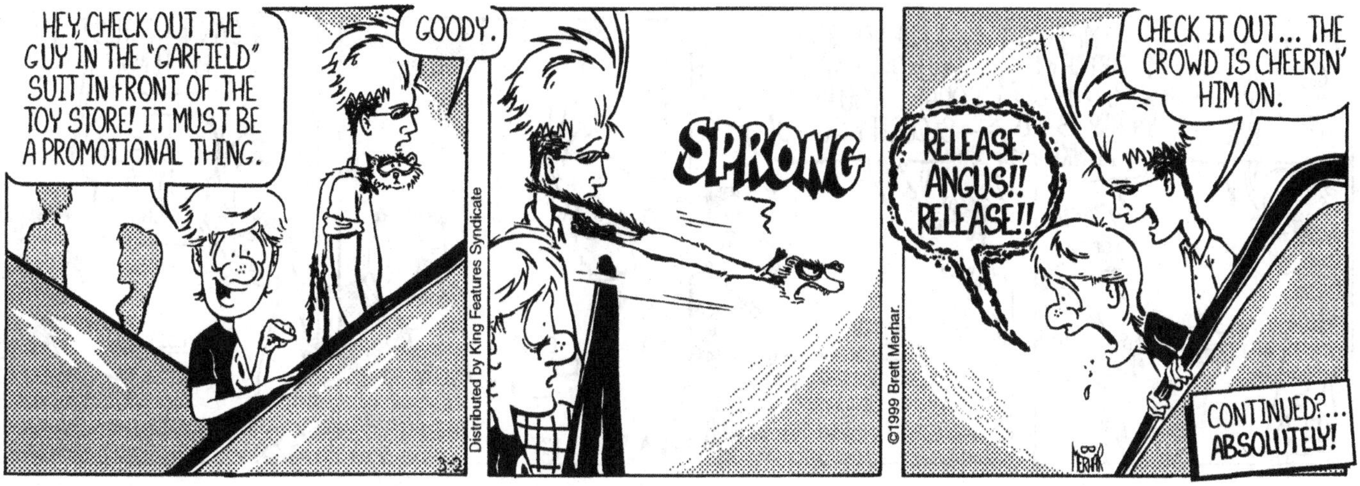
HEY, CHECK OUT THE GUY IN THE "GARFIELD" SUIT IN FRONT OF THE TOY STORE! IT MUST BE A PROMOTIONAL THING.
GOODY.
SPRONG
RELEASE, ANGUS!! RELEASE!!
CHECK IT OUT... THE CROWD IS CHEERIN' HIM ON.
CONTINUED?... ABSOLUTELY!
3-2
Distributed by King Features Syndicate
©1999 Brett Merhar.
MERHAR

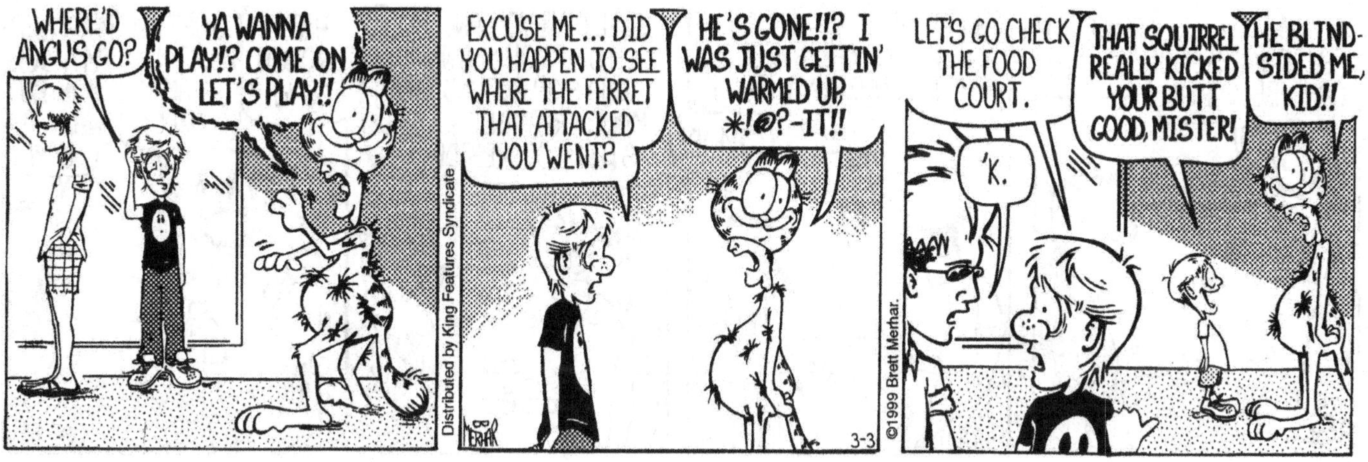
WHERE'D ANGUS GO?
YA WANNA PLAY!? COME ON LET'S PLAY!!
EXCUSE ME... DID YOU HAPPEN TO SEE WHERE THE FERRET THAT ATTACKED YOU WENT?
HE'S GONE!!? I WAS JUST GETTIN' WARMED UP, *!@?-IT!!
LET'S GO CHECK THE FOOD COURT.
'K.
THAT SQUIRREL REALLY KICKED YOUR BUTT GOOD, MISTER!
HE BLIND-SIDED ME, KID!!
3-3
Distributed by King Features Syndicate
©1999 Brett Merhar.
MERHAR

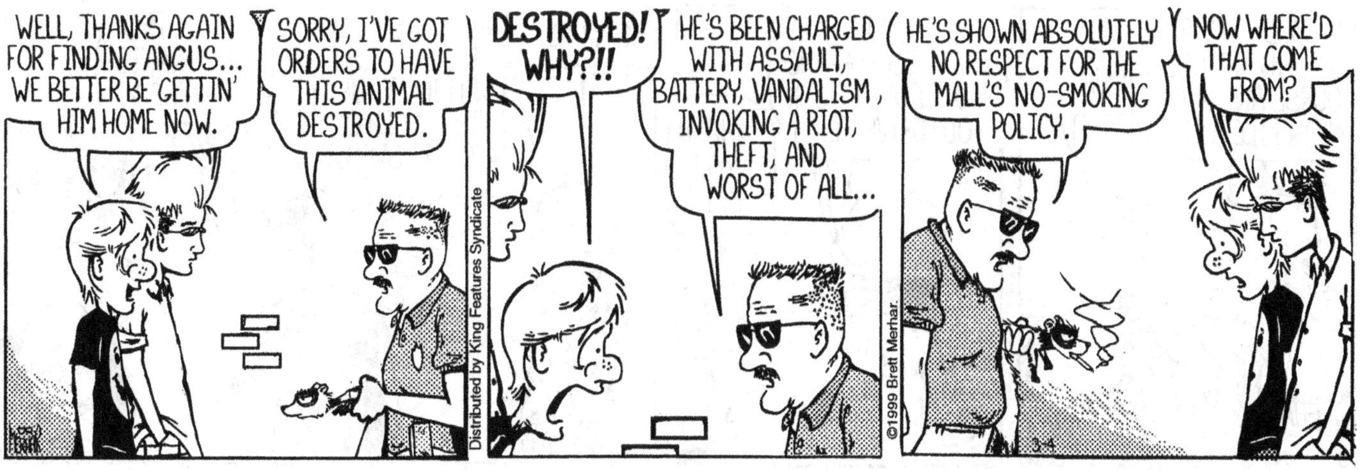
WELL, THANKS AGAIN FOR FINDING ANGUS... WE BETTER BE GETTIN' HIM HOME NOW.
SORRY, I'VE GOT ORDERS TO HAVE THIS ANIMAL DESTROYED.
DESTROYED! WHY?!!
HE'S BEEN CHARGED WITH ASSAULT, BATTERY, VANDALISM, INVOKING A RIOT, THEFT, AND WORST OF ALL...
HE'S SHOWN ABSOLUTELY NO RESPECT FOR THE MALL'S NO-SMOKING POLICY.
NOW WHERE'D THAT COME FROM?
3-4
Distributed by King Features Syndicate
©1999 Brett Merhar.
MERHAR

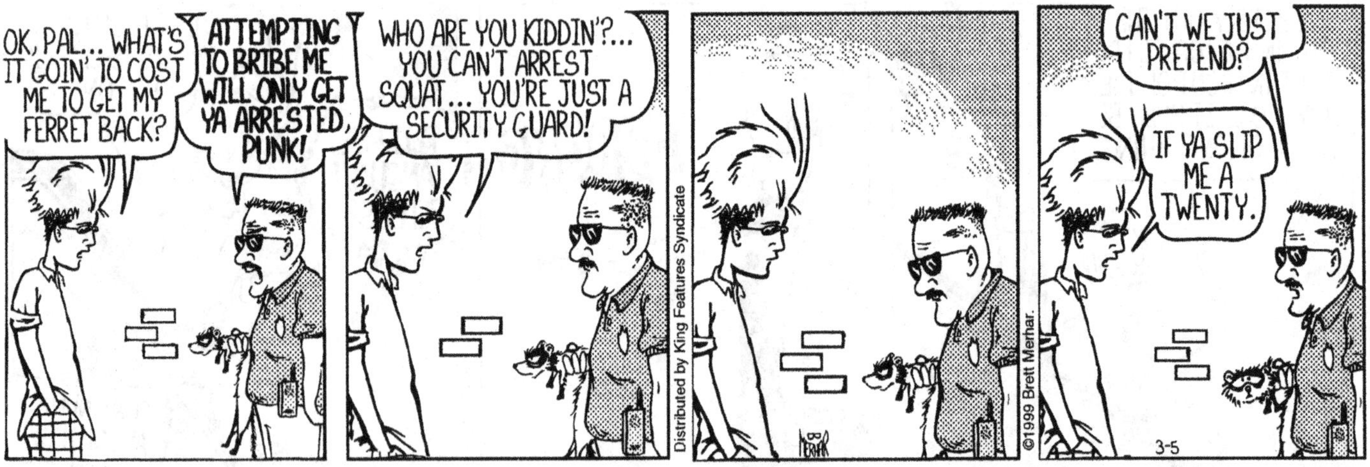
OK, PAL... WHAT'S IT GOIN' TO COST ME TO GET MY FERRET BACK?
ATTEMPTING TO BRIBE ME WILL ONLY GET YA ARRESTED, PUNK!
WHO ARE YOU KIDDIN'?... YOU CAN'T ARREST SQUAT... YOU'RE JUST A SECURITY GUARD!
Distributed by King Features Syndicate
CAN'T WE JUST PRETEND?
IF YA SLIP ME A TWENTY.
©1999 Brett Merhar.
3-5

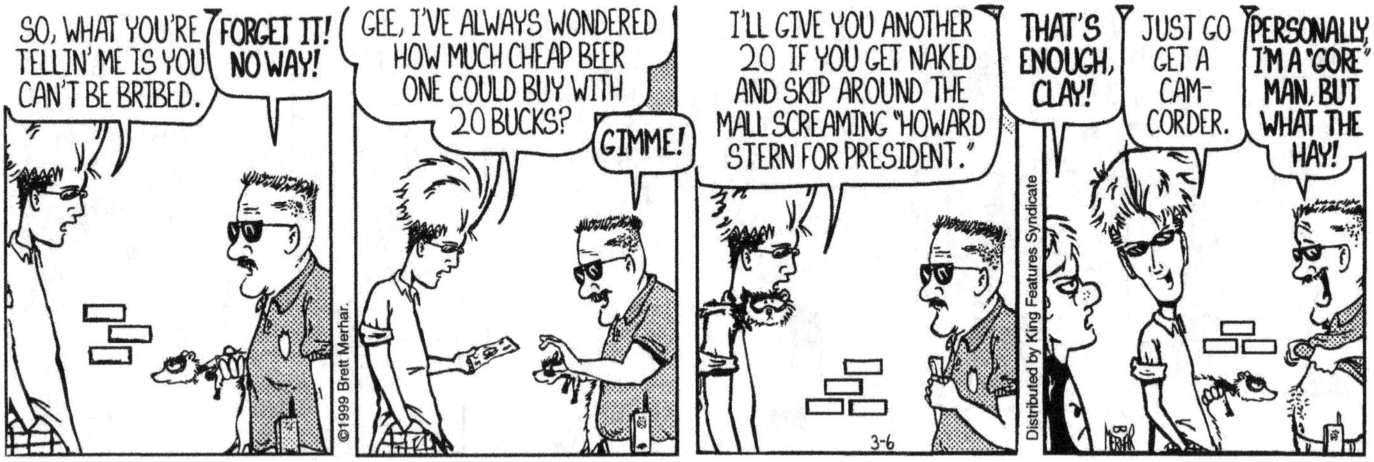
SO, WHAT YOU'RE TELLIN' ME IS YOU CAN'T BE BRIBED.
FORGET IT! NO WAY!
©1999 Brett Merhar.
GEE, I'VE ALWAYS WONDERED HOW MUCH CHEAP BEER ONE COULD BUY WITH 20 BUCKS?
GIMME!
I'LL GIVE YOU ANOTHER 20 IF YOU GET NAKED AND SKIP AROUND THE MALL SCREAMING "HOWARD STERN FOR PRESIDENT."
3-6
Distributed by King Features Syndicate
THAT'S ENOUGH, CLAY!
JUST GO GET A CAM-CORDER.
PERSONALLY, I'M A "GORE" MAN, BUT WHAT THE HAY!

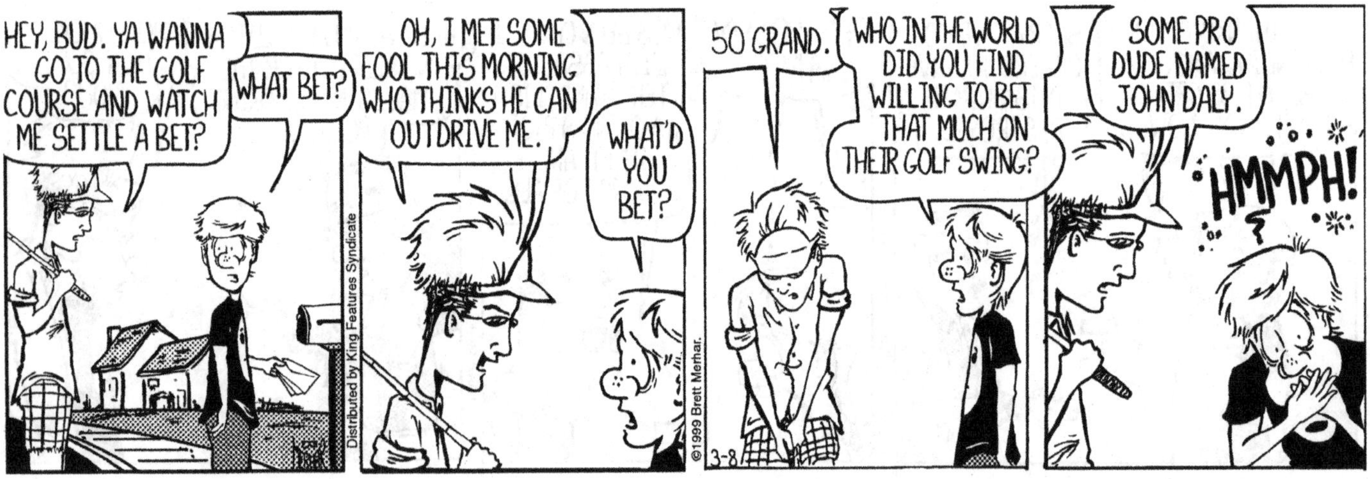
HEY, BUD. YA WANNA GO TO THE GOLF COURSE AND WATCH ME SETTLE A BET?
WHAT BET?
Distributed by King Features Syndicate
OH, I MET SOME FOOL THIS MORNING WHO THINKS HE CAN OUTDRIVE ME.
WHAT'D YOU BET?
©1999 Brett Merhar.
50 GRAND.
WHO IN THE WORLD DID YOU FIND WILLING TO BET THAT MUCH ON THEIR GOLF SWING?
3-8
SOME PRO DUDE NAMED JOHN DALY.
HMMPH!

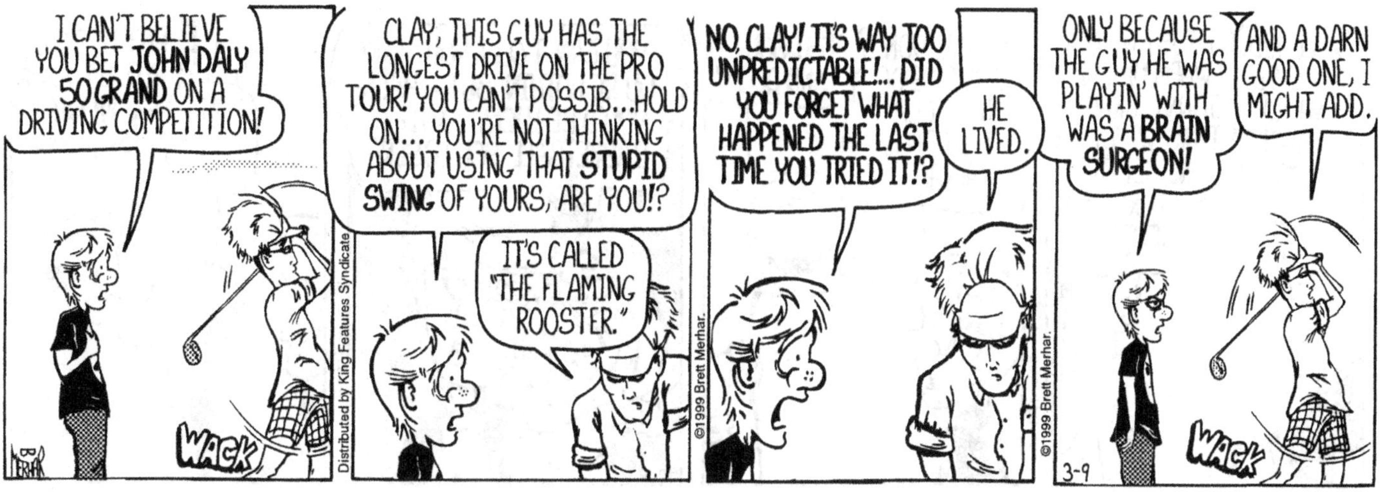
I CAN'T BELIEVE YOU BET JOHN DALY 50 GRAND ON A DRIVING COMPETITION!
WACK
MERHAR
Distributed by King Features Syndicate
CLAY, THIS GUY HAS THE LONGEST DRIVE ON THE PRO TOUR! YOU CAN'T POSSIB...HOLD ON... YOU'RE NOT THINKING ABOUT USING THAT STUPID SWING OF YOURS, ARE YOU!?
IT'S CALLED "THE FLAMING ROOSTER."
©1999 Brett Merhar.
NO, CLAY! IT'S WAY TOO UNPREDICTABLE!... DID YOU FORGET WHAT HAPPENED THE LAST TIME YOU TRIED IT!?
HE LIVED.
©1999 Brett Merhar.
ONLY BECAUSE THE GUY HE WAS PLAYIN' WITH WAS A BRAIN SURGEON!
AND A DARN GOOD ONE, I MIGHT ADD.
WACK
3-9

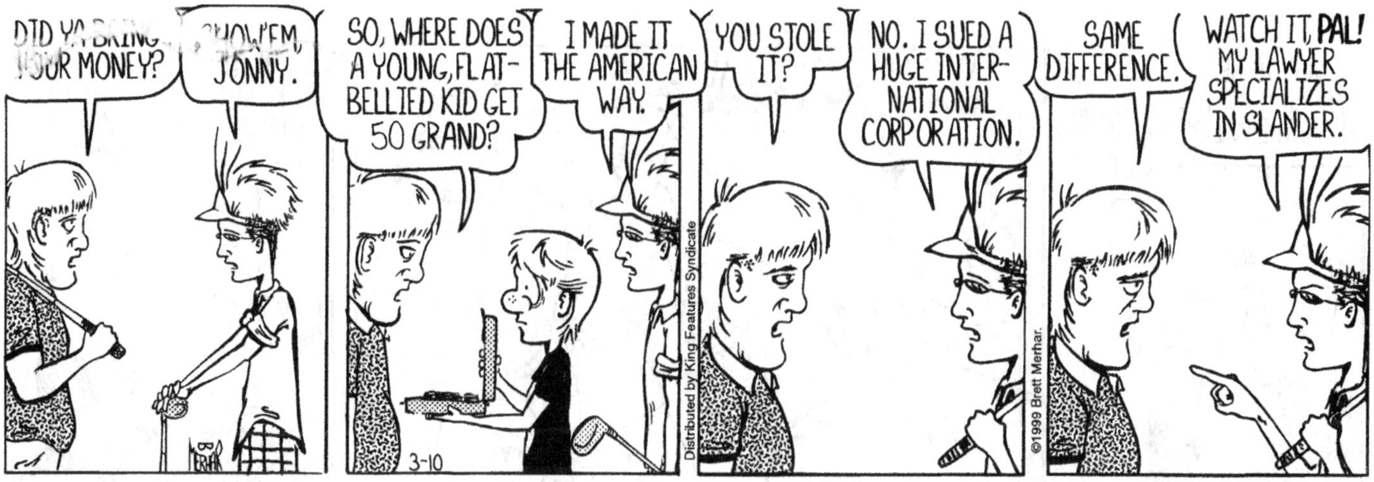
DID YA BRING... YOUR MONEY?
SHOW 'EM, JONNY.
MERHAR
SO, WHERE DOES A YOUNG, FLAT-BELLIED KID GET 50 GRAND?
I MADE IT THE AMERICAN WAY.
3-10
Distributed by King Features Syndicate
YOU STOLE IT?
NO. I SUED A HUGE INTERNATIONAL CORPORATION.
©1999 Brett Merhar.
SAME DIFFERENCE.
WATCH IT, PAL! MY LAWYER SPECIALIZES IN SLANDER.

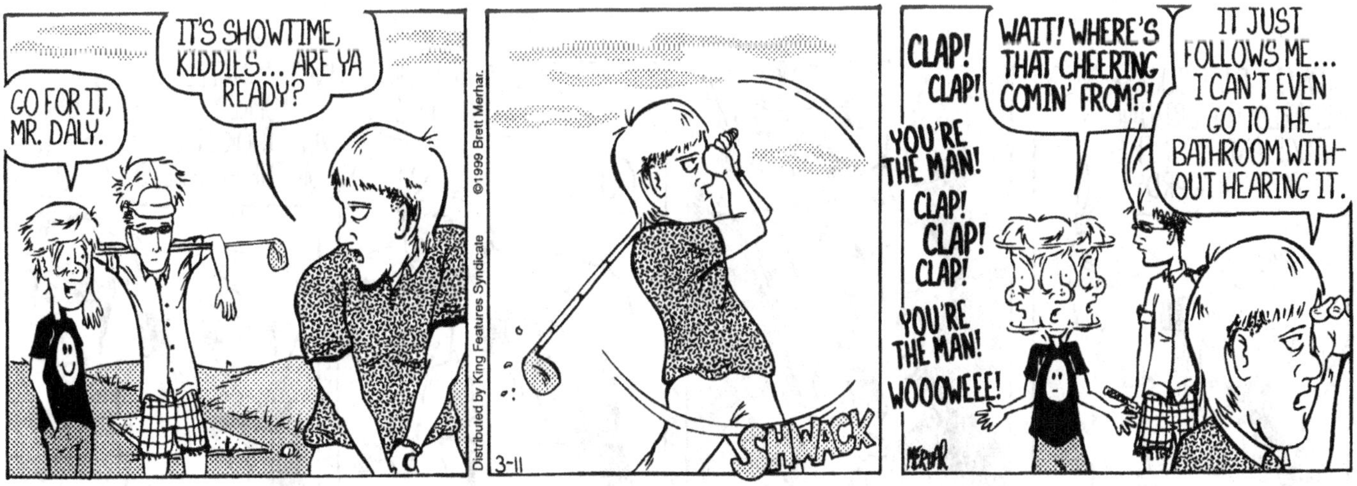
GO FOR IT, MR. DALY.
IT'S SHOWTIME, KIDDIES... ARE YA READY?
©1999 Brett Merhar.
Distributed by King Features Syndicate
SHWACK
3-11
CLAP! CLAP!
YOU'RE THE MAN!
CLAP! CLAP! CLAP!
YOU'RE THE MAN!
WOOOWEEE!
WAIT! WHERE'S THAT CHEERING COMIN' FROM?!
IT JUST FOLLOWS ME... I CAN'T EVEN GO TO THE BATHROOM WITH-OUT HEARING IT.
MERHAR

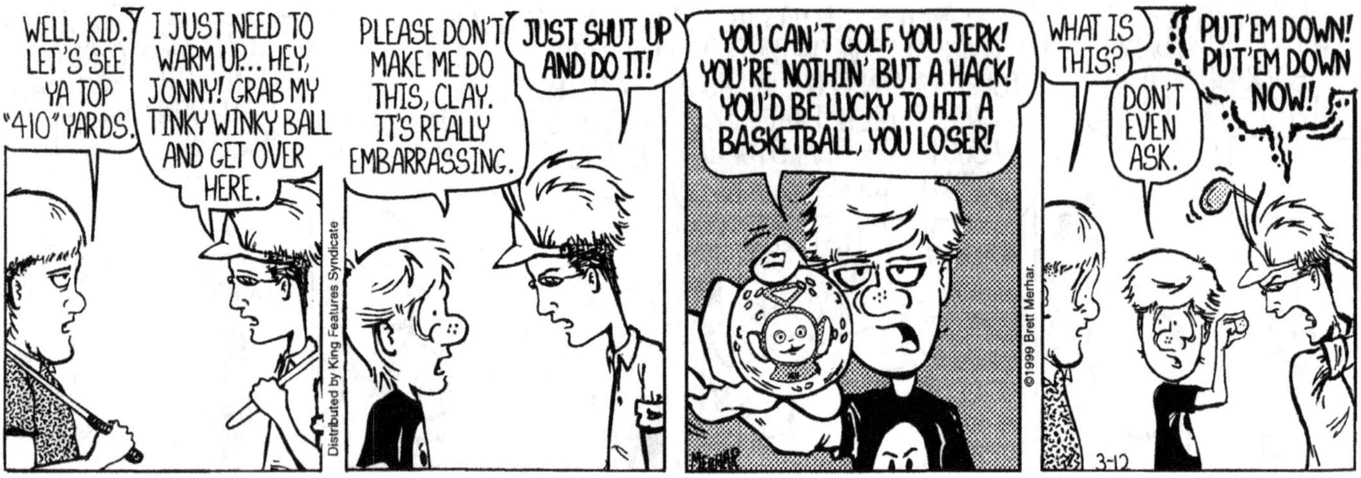
WELL, KID. LET'S SEE YA TOP "410" YARDS.
I JUST NEED TO WARM UP.. HEY, JONNY! GRAB MY TINKY WINKY BALL AND GET OVER HERE.
Distributed by King Features Syndicate
PLEASE DON'T MAKE ME DO THIS, CLAY. IT'S REALLY EMBARRASSING.
JUST SHUT UP AND DO IT!
YOU CAN'T GOLF, YOU JERK! YOU'RE NOTHIN' BUT A HACK! YOU'D BE LUCKY TO HIT A BASKETBALL, YOU LOSER!
©1999 Brett Merhar.
WHAT IS THIS?
DON'T EVEN ASK.
PUT'EM DOWN! PUT'EM DOWN NOW!
3-12

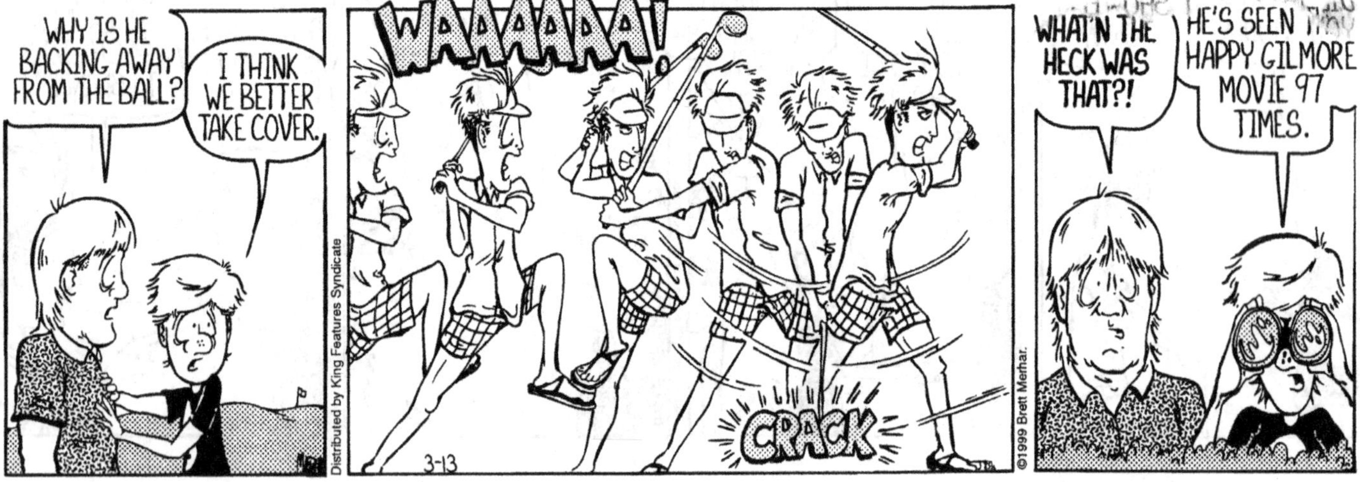
WHY IS HE BACKING AWAY FROM THE BALL?
I THINK WE BETTER TAKE COVER.
Distributed by King Features Syndicate
WAAAAAA!
CRACK
3-13
©1999 Brett Merhar.
WHAT'N THE HECK WAS THAT?!
HE'S SEEN THAT HAPPY GILMORE MOVIE 97 TIMES.

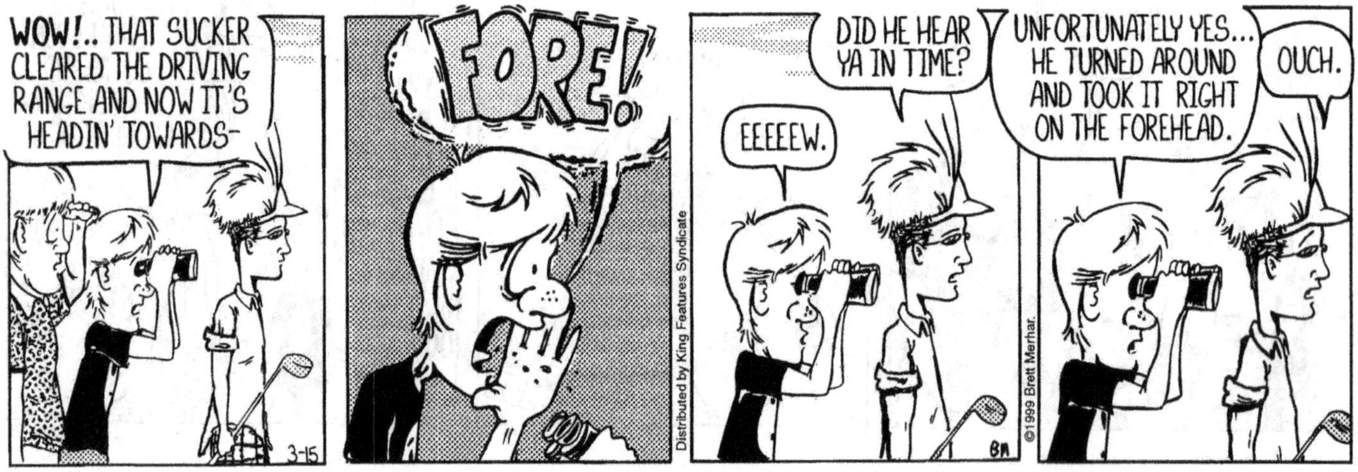
WOW!.. THAT SUCKER CLEARED THE DRIVING RANGE AND NOW IT'S HEADIN' TOWARDS-
3-15
FORE!
Distributed by King Features Syndicate
DID HE HEAR YA IN TIME?
EEEEEW.
©1999 Brett Merhar.
UNFORTUNATELY YES... HE TURNED AROUND AND TOOK IT RIGHT ON THE FOREHEAD.
OUCH.

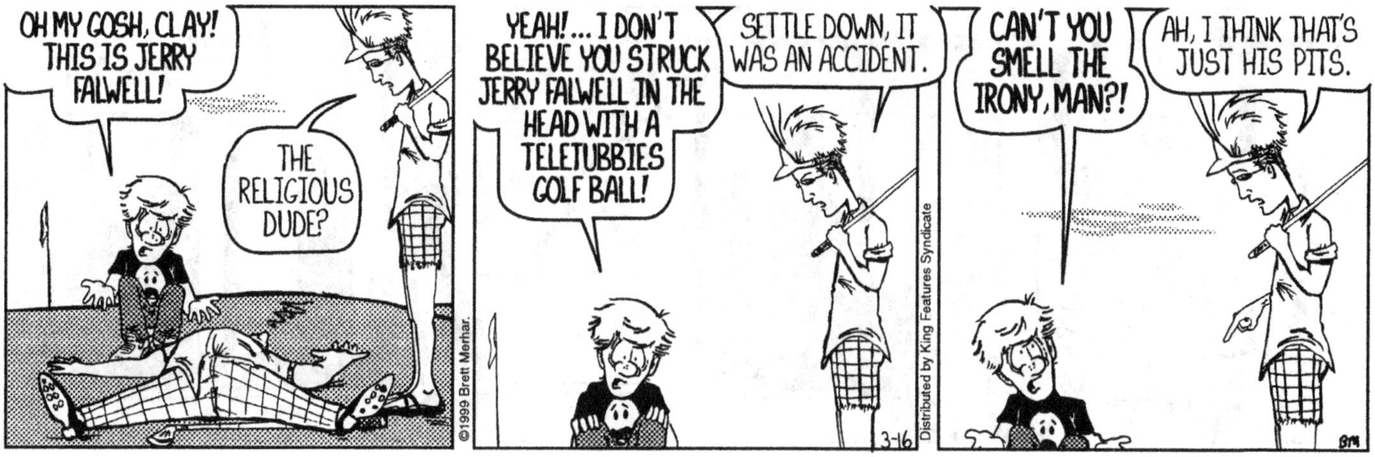
OH MY GOSH, CLAY! THIS IS JERRY FALWELL!
THE RELIGIOUS DUDE?
YEAH!... I DON'T BELIEVE YOU STRUCK JERRY FALWELL IN THE HEAD WITH A TELETUBBIES GOLF BALL!
SETTLE DOWN, IT WAS AN ACCIDENT.
CAN'T YOU SMELL THE IRONY, MAN?!
AH, I THINK THAT'S JUST HIS PITS.
©1999 Brett Merhar.
3-16
Distributed by King Features Syndicate
BM

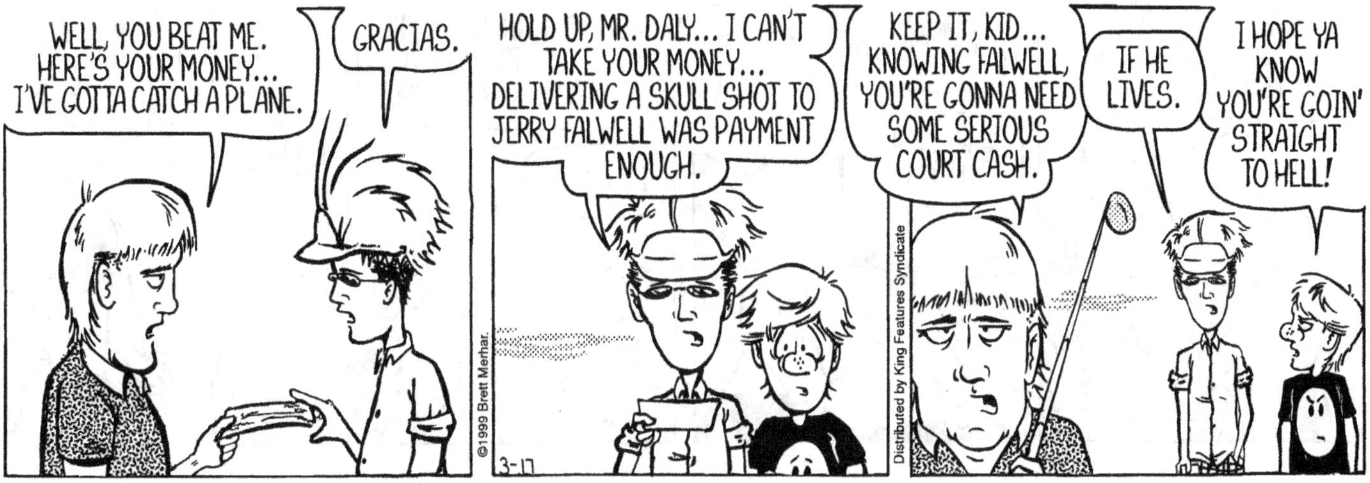
WELL, YOU BEAT ME. HERE'S YOUR MONEY... I'VE GOTTA CATCH A PLANE.
GRACIAS.
HOLD UP, MR. DALY... I CAN'T TAKE YOUR MONEY... DELIVERING A SKULL SHOT TO JERRY FALWELL WAS PAYMENT ENOUGH.
KEEP IT, KID... KNOWING FALWELL, YOU'RE GONNA NEED SOME SERIOUS COURT CASH.
IF HE LIVES.
I HOPE YA KNOW YOU'RE GOIN' STRAIGHT TO HELL!
©1999 Brett Merhar.
3-17
Distributed by King Features Syndicate

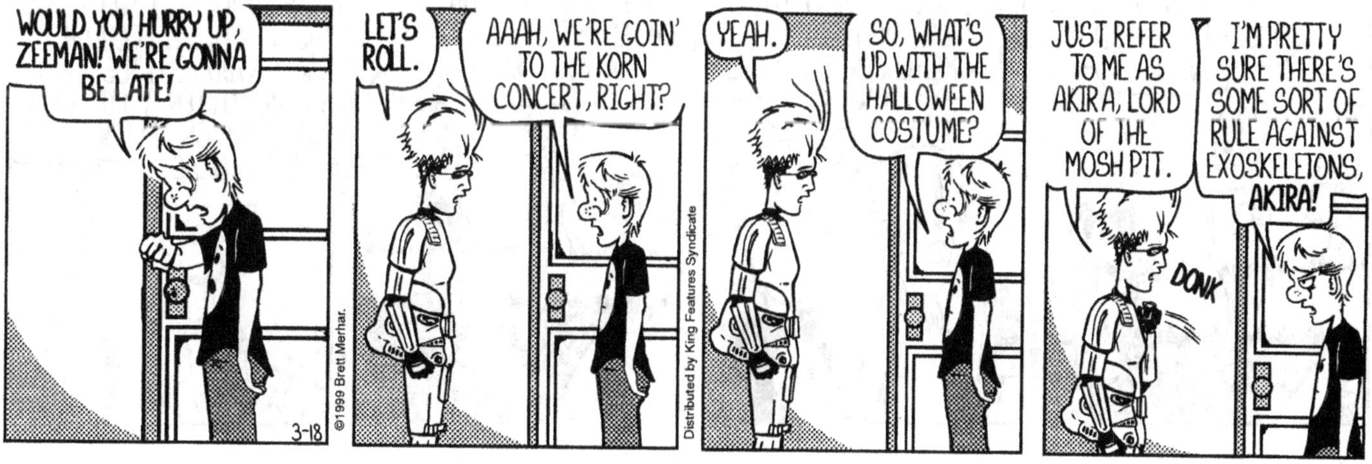
WOULD YOU HURRY UP, ZEEMAN! WE'RE GONNA BE LATE!
LET'S ROLL.
AAAH, WE'RE GOIN' TO THE KORN CONCERT, RIGHT?
YEAH.
SO, WHAT'S UP WITH THE HALLOWEEN COSTUME?
JUST REFER TO ME AS AKIRA, LORD OF THE MOSH PIT.
I'M PRETTY SURE THERE'S SOME SORT OF RULE AGAINST EXOSKELETONS, AKIRA!
DONK
3-18
©1999 Brett Merhar.
Distributed by King Features Syndicate

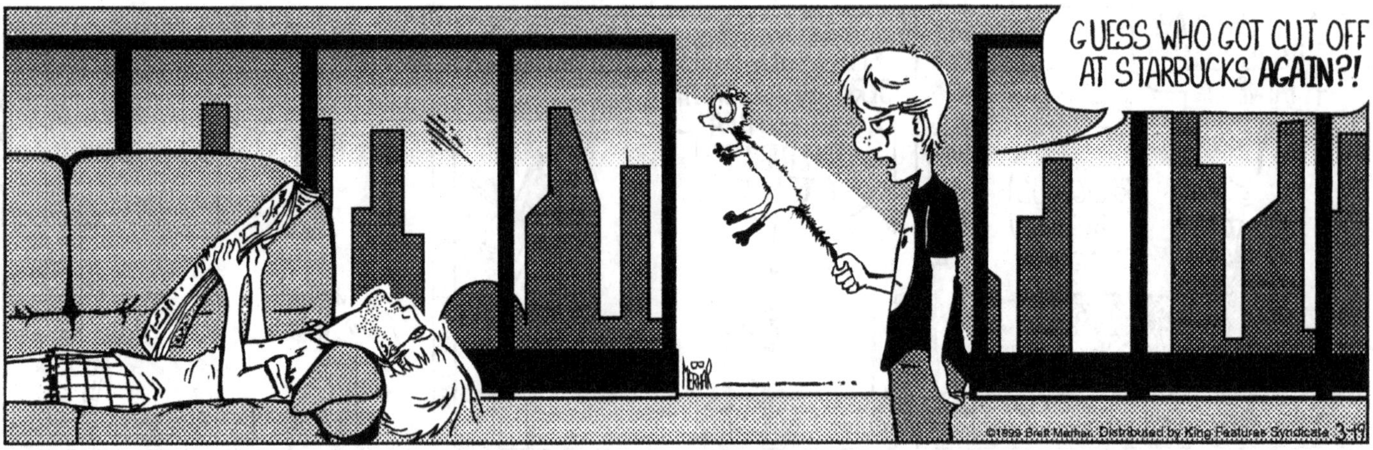
GUESS WHO GOT CUT OFF AT STARBUCKS AGAIN?!
©1999 Brett Merhar. Distributed by King Features Syndicate 3-19

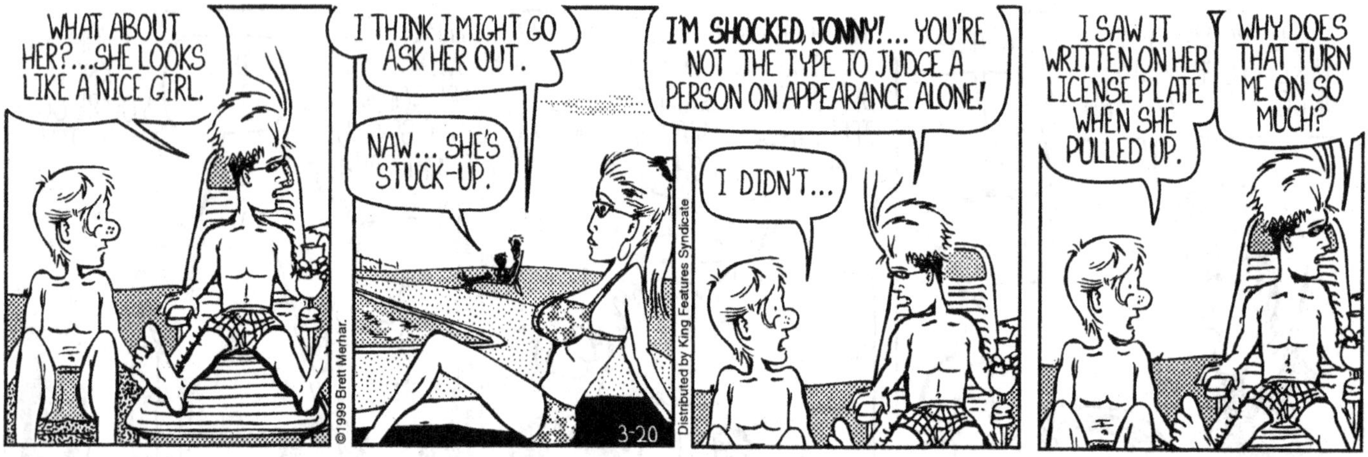
WHAT ABOUT HER?...SHE LOOKS LIKE A NICE GIRL.
NAW... SHE'S STUCK-UP.
I THINK I MIGHT GO ASK HER OUT.
©1999 Brett Merhar.
3-20
Distributed by King Features Syndicate
I'M SHOCKED, JONNY!... YOU'RE NOT THE TYPE TO JUDGE A PERSON ON APPEARANCE ALONE!
I DIDN'T...
I SAW IT WRITTEN ON HER LICENSE PLATE WHEN SHE PULLED UP.
WHY DOES THAT TURN ME ON SO MUCH?

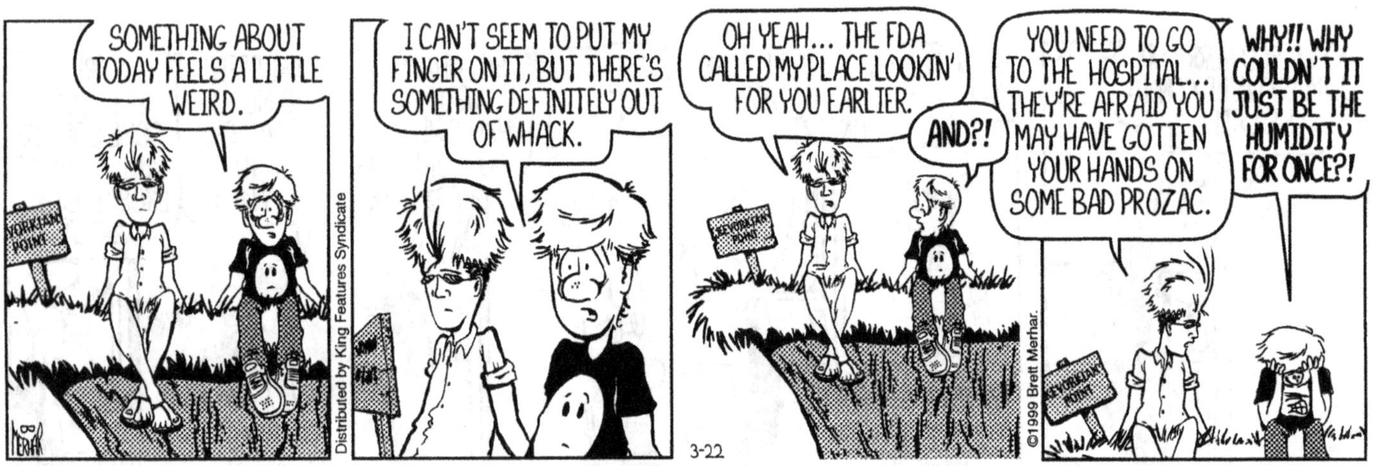
SOMETHING ABOUT TODAY FEELS A LITTLE WEIRD.
Distributed by King Features Syndicate
I CAN'T SEEM TO PUT MY FINGER ON IT, BUT THERE'S SOMETHING DEFINITELY OUT OF WHACK.
OH YEAH... THE FDA CALLED MY PLACE LOOKIN' FOR YOU EARLIER.
AND?!
3-22
©1999 Brett Merhar.
YOU NEED TO GO TO THE HOSPITAL... THEY'RE AFRAID YOU MAY HAVE GOTTEN YOUR HANDS ON SOME BAD PROZAC.
WHY!! WHY COULDN'T IT JUST BE THE HUMIDITY FOR ONCE?!

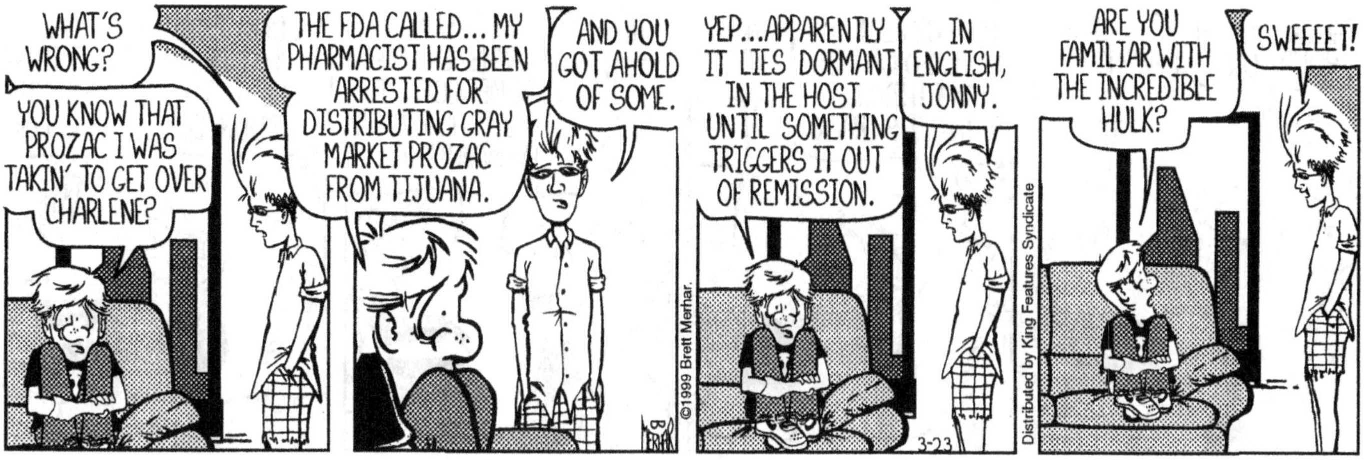
WHAT'S WRONG?
YOU KNOW THAT PROZAC I WAS TAKIN' TO GET OVER CHARLENE?
THE FDA CALLED... MY PHARMACIST HAS BEEN ARRESTED FOR DISTRIBUTING GRAY MARKET PROZAC FROM TIJUANA.
AND YOU GOT AHOLD OF SOME.
©1999 Brett Merhar.
YEP...APPARENTLY IT LIES DORMANT IN THE HOST UNTIL SOMETHING TRIGGERS IT OUT OF REMISSION.
IN ENGLISH, JONNY.
3-23
ARE YOU FAMILIAR WITH THE INCREDIBLE HULK?
SWEEEET!
Distributed by King Features Syndicate

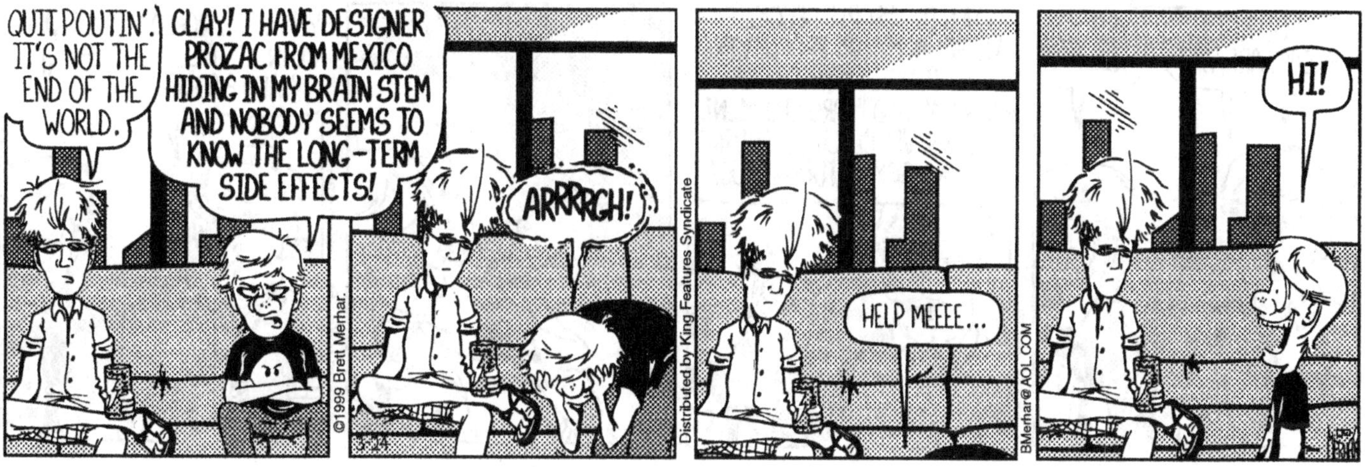
QUIT POUTIN'. IT'S NOT THE END OF THE WORLD.
CLAY! I HAVE DESIGNER PROZAC FROM MEXICO HIDING IN MY BRAIN STEM AND NOBODY SEEMS TO KNOW THE LONG-TERM SIDE EFFECTS!
©1999 Brett Merhar.
3-24
ARRRRGH!
Distributed by King Features Syndicate
HELP MEEEE...
BMerhar@AOL.COM
HI!

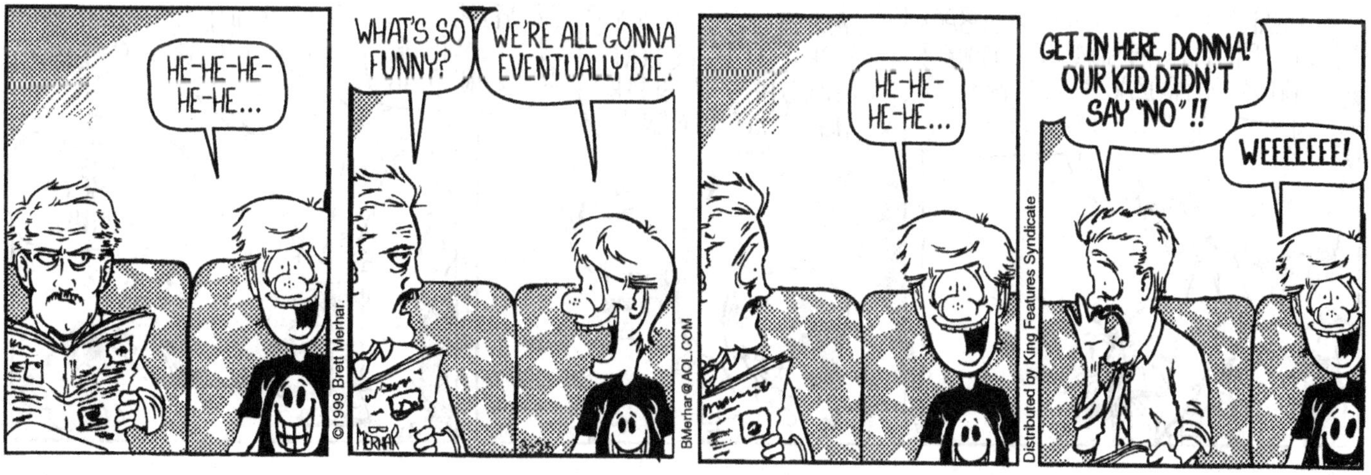
HE-HE-HE-HE-HE...
©1999 Brett Merhar.
WHAT'S SO FUNNY?
WE'RE ALL GONNA EVENTUALLY DIE.
3-25
BMerhar@AOL.COM
HE-HE-HE-HE...
Distributed by King Features Syndicate
GET IN HERE, DONNA! OUR KID DIDN'T SAY "NO"!!
WEEEEEEE!

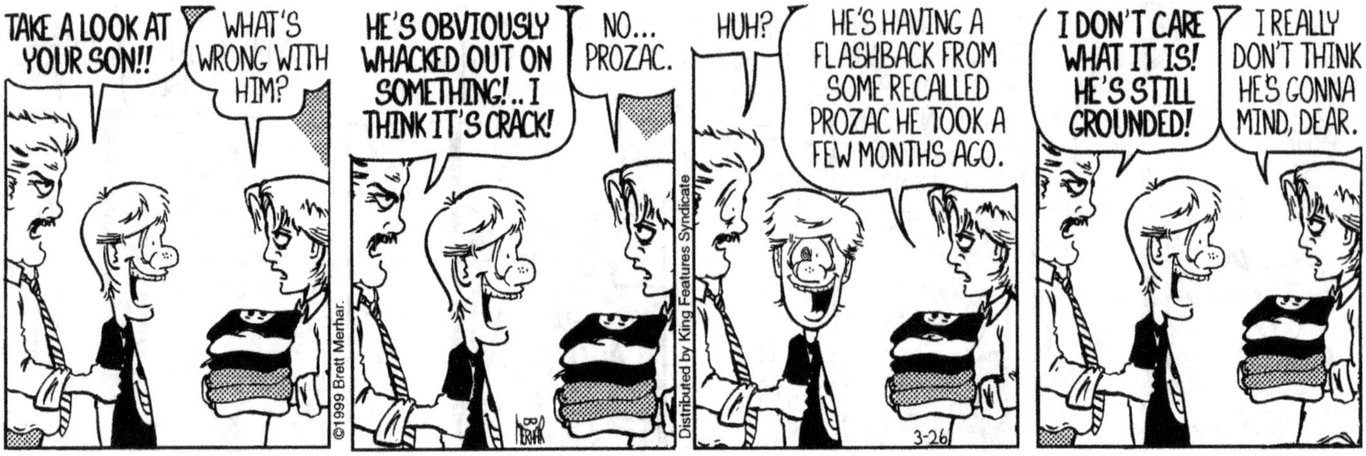
TAKE A LOOK AT YOUR SON!!
WHAT'S WRONG WITH HIM?
©1999 Brett Merhar.
HE'S OBVIOUSLY WHACKED OUT ON SOMETHING!.. I THINK IT'S CRACK!
NO... PROZAC.
Distributed by King Features Syndicate
HUH?
HE'S HAVING A FLASHBACK FROM SOME RECALLED PROZAC HE TOOK A FEW MONTHS AGO.
3-26
I DON'T CARE WHAT IT IS! HE'S STILL GROUNDED!
I REALLY DON'T THINK HE'S GONNA MIND, DEAR.

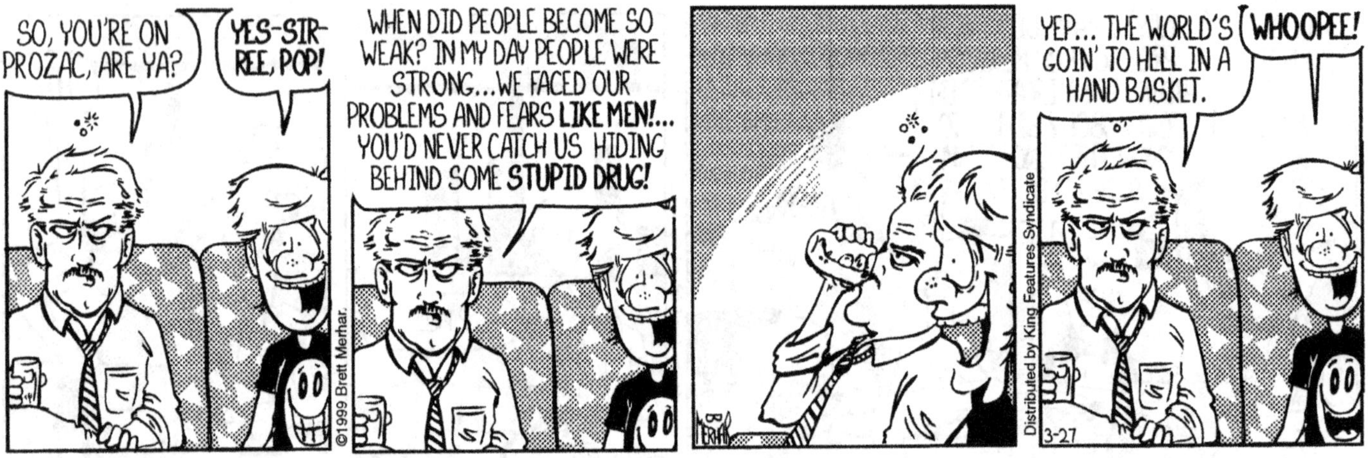
SO, YOU'RE ON PROZAC, ARE YA?
YES-SIR-REE, POP!
©1999 Brett Merhar.
WHEN DID PEOPLE BECOME SO WEAK? IN MY DAY PEOPLE WERE STRONG...WE FACED OUR PROBLEMS AND FEARS LIKE MEN!... YOU'D NEVER CATCH US HIDING BEHIND SOME STUPID DRUG!
YEP... THE WORLD'S GOIN' TO HELL IN A HAND BASKET.
WHOOPEE!
Distributed by King Features Syndicate
3-27

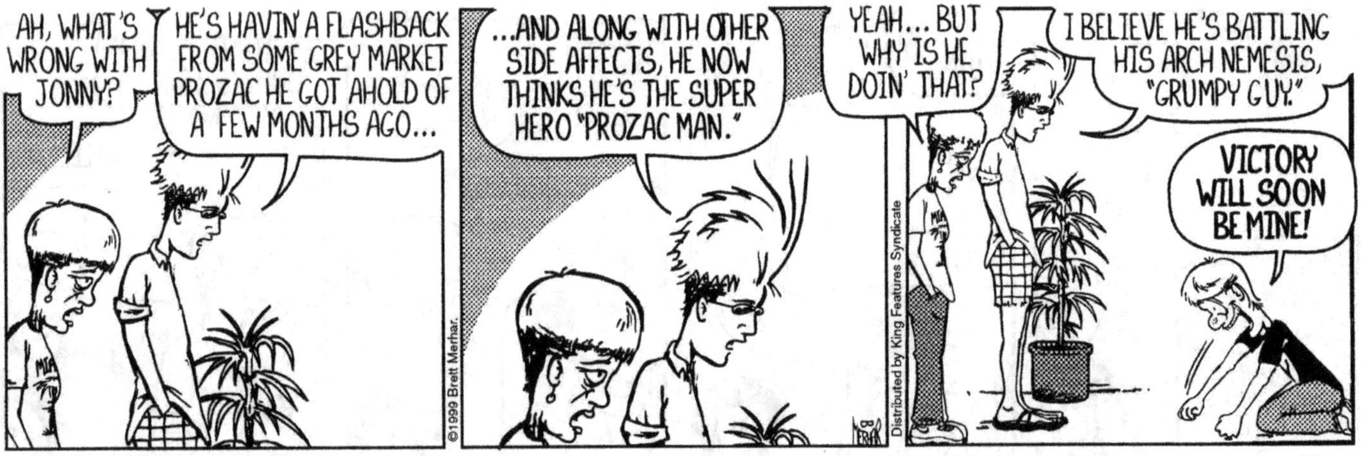
AH, WHAT'S WRONG WITH JONNY?
HE'S HAVIN' A FLASHBACK FROM SOME GREY MARKET PROZAC HE GOT AHOLD OF A FEW MONTHS AGO...
©1999 Brett Merhar.
...AND ALONG WITH OTHER SIDE AFFECTS, HE NOW THINKS HE'S THE SUPER HERO "PROZAC MAN."
Distributed by King Features Syndicate
YEAH... BUT WHY IS HE DOIN' THAT?
I BELIEVE HE'S BATTLING HIS ARCH NEMESIS, "GRUMPY GUY."
VICTORY WILL SOON BE MINE!

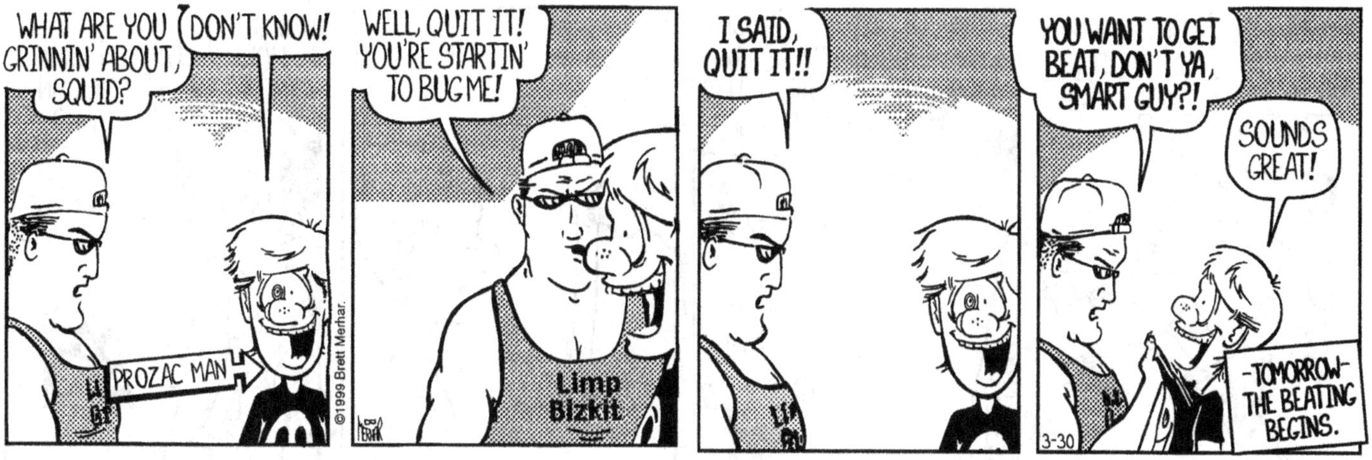
WHAT ARE YOU GRINNIN' ABOUT, SQUID?
DON'T KNOW!
PROZAC MAN
©1999 Brett Merhar.
WELL, QUIT IT! YOU'RE STARTIN' TO BUG ME!
Limp Bizkit
MERHAR
I SAID, QUIT IT!!
YOU WANT TO GET BEAT, DON'T YA, SMART GUY?!
SOUNDS GREAT!
-TOMORROW- THE BEATING BEGINS.
3-30

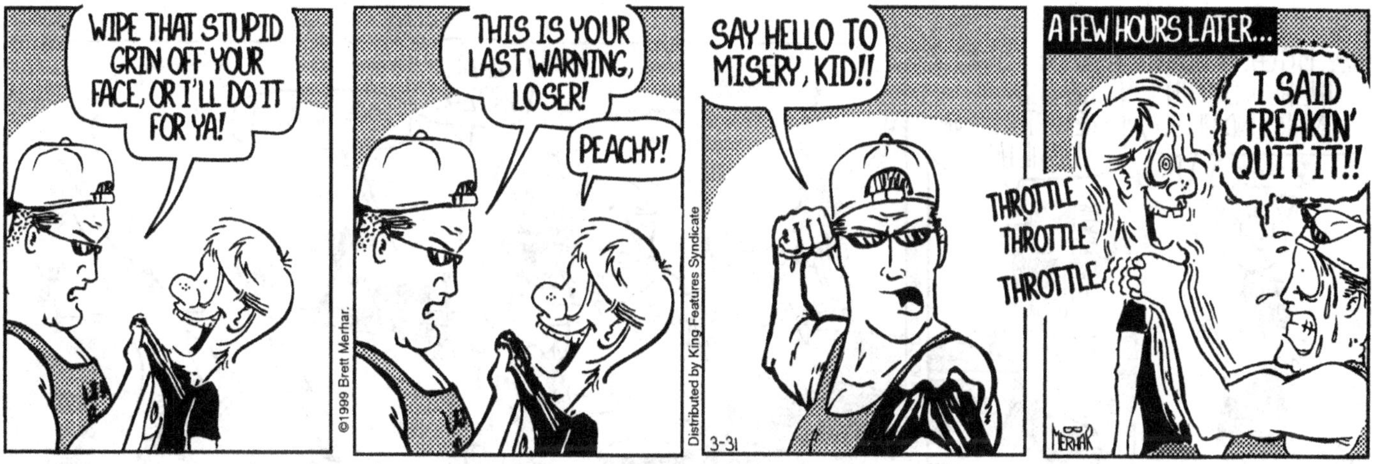
WIPE THAT STUPID GRIN OFF YOUR FACE, OR I'LL DO IT FOR YA!
©1999 Brett Merhar.
THIS IS YOUR LAST WARNING, LOSER!
PEACHY!
Distributed by King Features Syndicate
SAY HELLO TO MISERY, KID!!
3-31
A FEW HOURS LATER...
I SAID FREAKIN' QUIT IT!!
THROTTLE
THROTTLE
THROTTLE
MERHAR

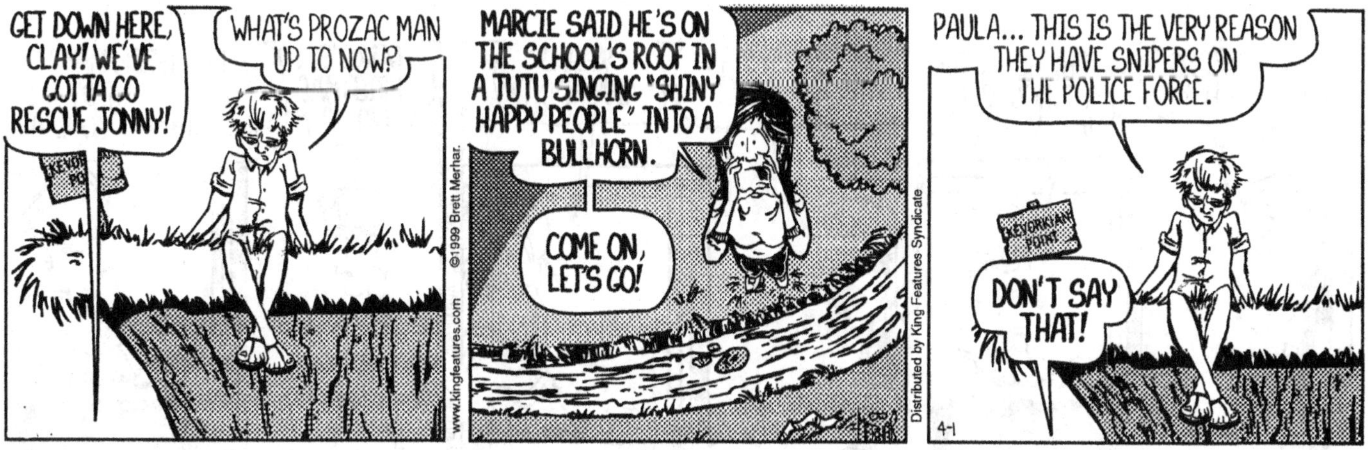
GET DOWN HERE, CLAY! WE'VE GOTTA GO RESCUE JONNY!
WHAT'S PROZAC MAN UP TO NOW?
www.kingfeatures.com
©1999 Brett Merhar.
MARCIE SAID HE'S ON THE SCHOOL'S ROOF IN A TUTU SINGING "SHINY HAPPY PEOPLE" INTO A BULLHORN.
COME ON, LET'S GO!
Distributed by King Features Syndicate
PAULA... THIS IS THE VERY REASON THEY HAVE SNIPERS ON THE POLICE FORCE.
KEVORKIAN POINT
DON'T SAY THAT!
4-1

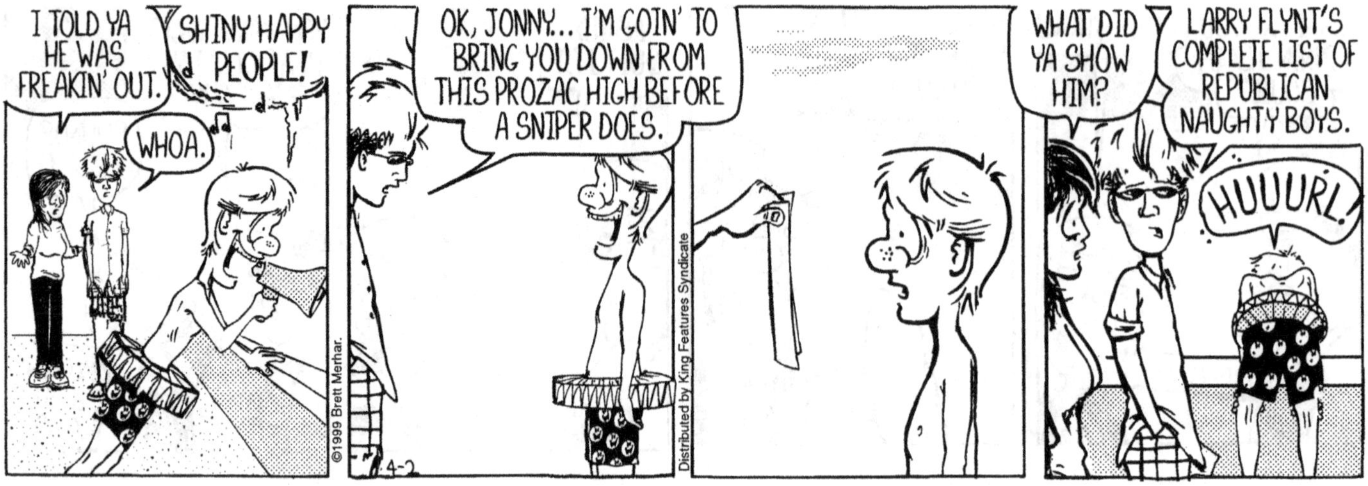
I TOLD YA HE WAS FREAKIN' OUT.
SHINY HAPPY PEOPLE!
WHOA.
©1999 Brett Merhar.
4-2
OK, JONNY... I'M GOIN' TO BRING YOU DOWN FROM THIS PROZAC HIGH BEFORE A SNIPER DOES.
Distributed by King Features Syndicate
WHAT DID YA SHOW HIM?
LARRY FLYNT'S COMPLETE LIST OF REPUBLICAN NAUGHTY BOYS.
HUUURL!

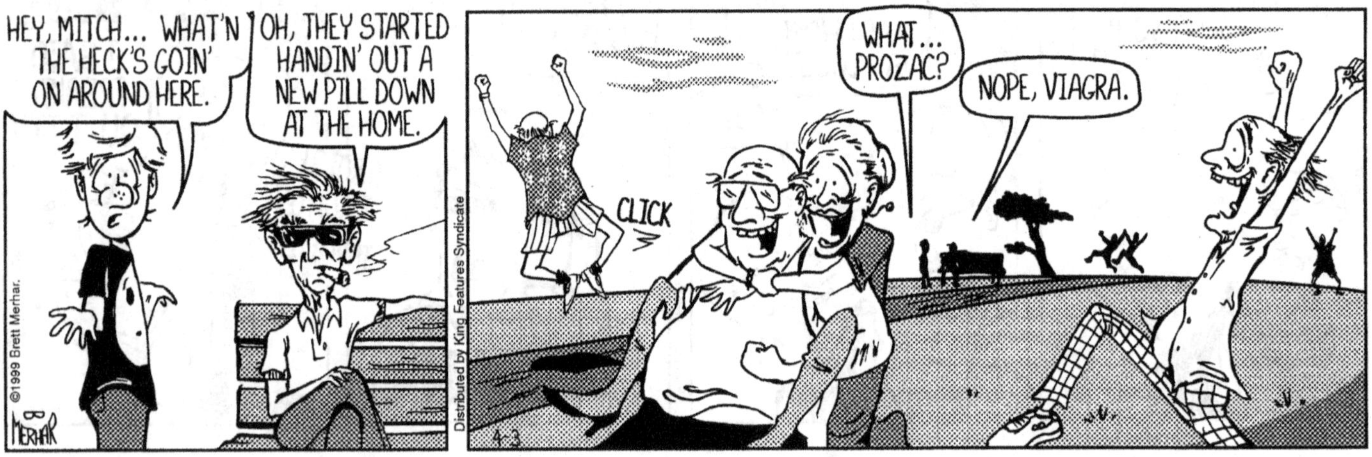
HEY, MITCH... WHAT'N THE HECK'S GOIN' ON AROUND HERE.
OH, THEY STARTED HANDIN' OUT A NEW PILL DOWN AT THE HOME.
©1999 Brett Merhar.
MERHAR
Distributed by King Features Syndicate
4-3
CLICK
WHAT... PROZAC?
NOPE, VIAGRA.

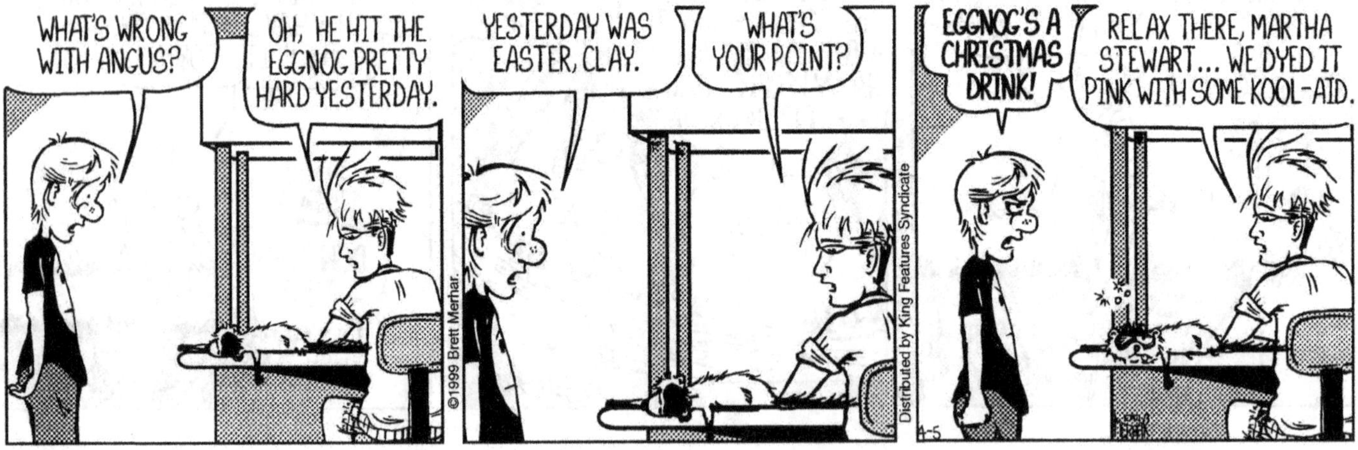
WHAT'S WRONG WITH ANGUS?
OH, HE HIT THE EGGNOG PRETTY HARD YESTERDAY.
YESTERDAY WAS EASTER, CLAY.
WHAT'S YOUR POINT?
©1999 Brett Merhar.
Distributed by King Features Syndicate
4-5
EGGNOG'S A CHRISTMAS DRINK!
RELAX THERE, MARTHA STEWART... WE DYED IT PINK WITH SOME KOOL-AID.

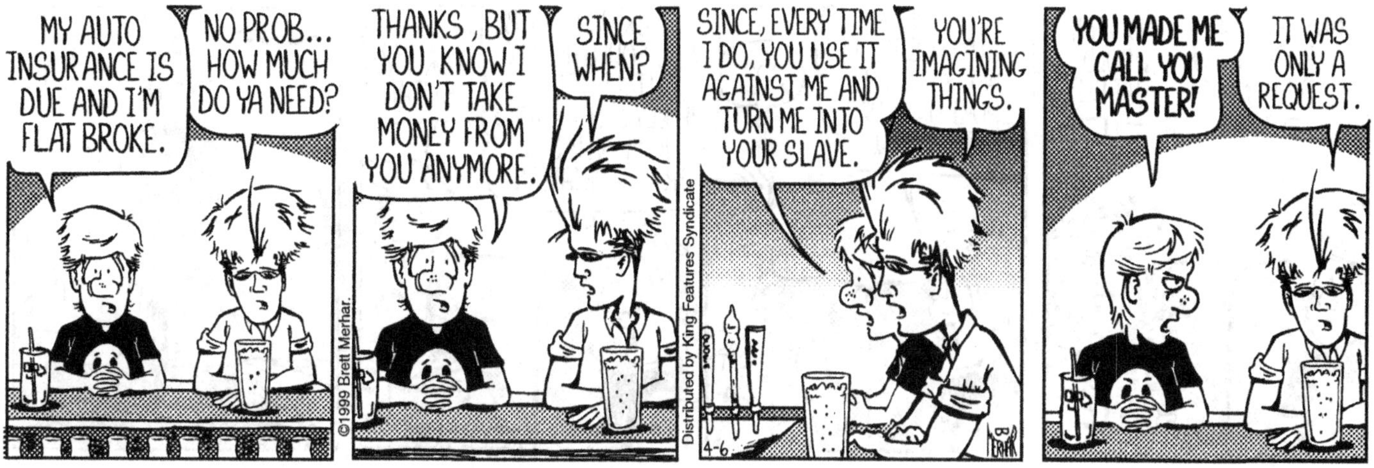
MY AUTO INSURANCE IS DUE AND I'M FLAT BROKE.
NO PROB... HOW MUCH DO YA NEED?
©1999 Brett Merhar.
THANKS, BUT YOU KNOW I DON'T TAKE MONEY FROM YOU ANYMORE.
SINCE WHEN?
Distributed by King Features Syndicate
SINCE, EVERY TIME I DO, YOU USE IT AGAINST ME AND TURN ME INTO YOUR SLAVE.
YOU'RE IMAGINING THINGS.
YOU MADE ME CALL YOU MASTER!
IT WAS ONLY A REQUEST.

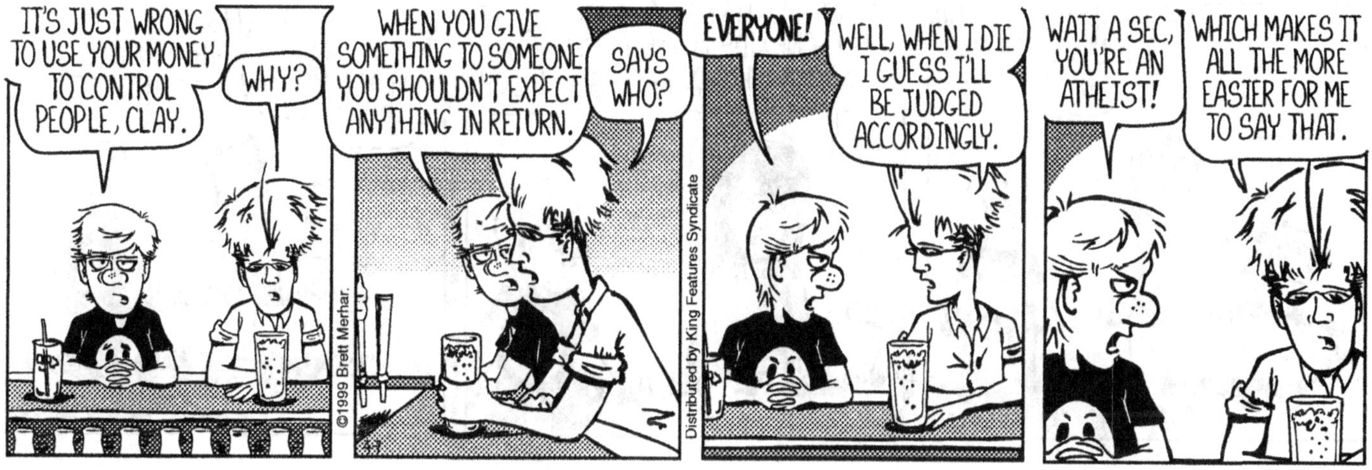
IT'S JUST WRONG TO USE YOUR MONEY TO CONTROL PEOPLE, CLAY.
WHY?
©1999 Brett Merhar.
WHEN YOU GIVE SOMETHING TO SOMEONE YOU SHOULDN'T EXPECT ANYTHING IN RETURN.
SAYS WHO?
Distributed by King Features Syndicate
EVERYONE!
WELL, WHEN I DIE I GUESS I'LL BE JUDGED ACCORDINGLY.
WAIT A SEC, YOU'RE AN ATHEIST!
WHICH MAKES IT ALL THE MORE EASIER FOR ME TO SAY THAT.

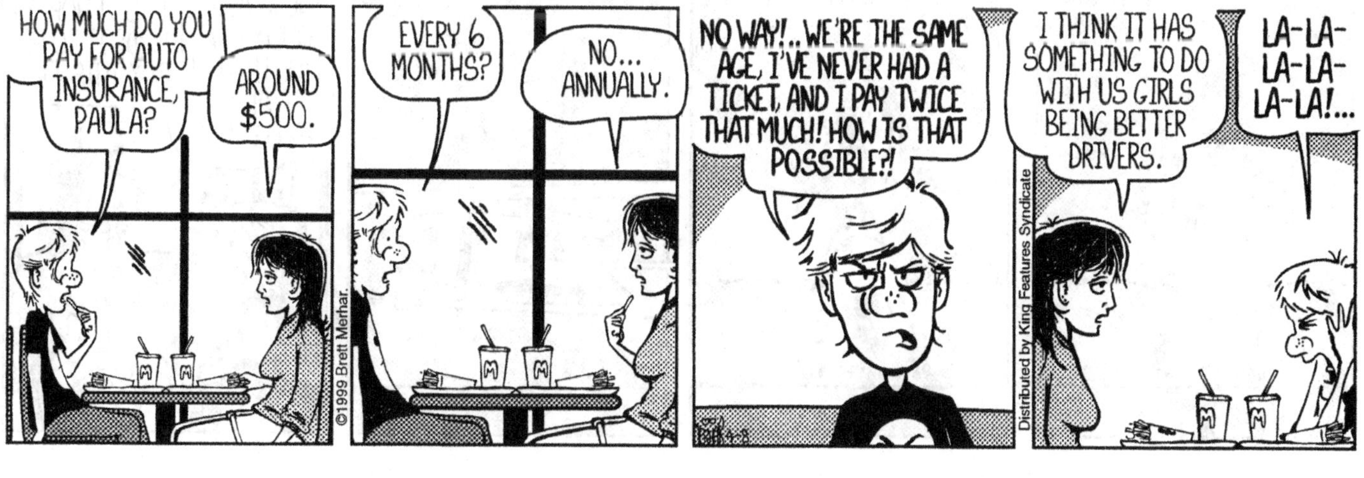
HOW MUCH DO YOU PAY FOR AUTO INSURANCE, PAULA?
AROUND $500.
©1999 Brett Merhar.
EVERY 6 MONTHS?
NO... ANNUALLY.
NO WAY!.. WE'RE THE SAME AGE, I'VE NEVER HAD A TICKET, AND I PAY TWICE THAT MUCH! HOW IS THAT POSSIBLE?!
Distributed by King Features Syndicate
I THINK IT HAS SOMETHING TO DO WITH US GIRLS BEING BETTER DRIVERS.
LA-LA-LA-LA-LA-LA!...

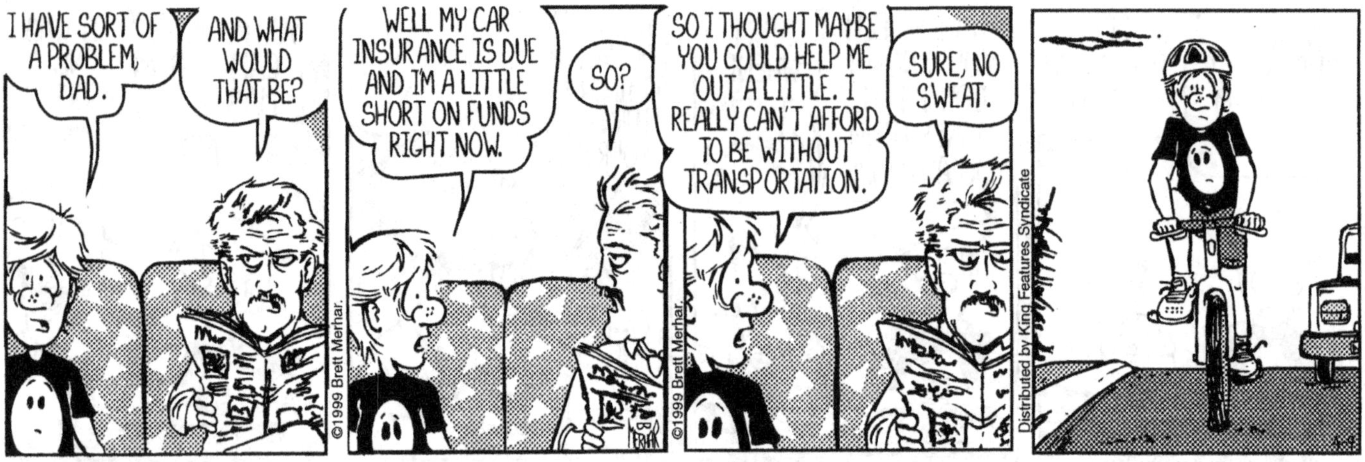
I HAVE SORT OF A PROBLEM, DAD.
AND WHAT WOULD THAT BE?
©1999 Brett Merhar.
WELL MY CAR INSURANCE IS DUE AND I'M A LITTLE SHORT ON FUNDS RIGHT NOW.
SO?
©1999 Brett Merhar
SO I THOUGHT MAYBE YOU COULD HELP ME OUT A LITTLE. I REALLY CAN'T AFFORD TO BE WITHOUT TRANSPORTATION.
SURE, NO SWEAT.
Distributed by King Features Syndicate
4-9

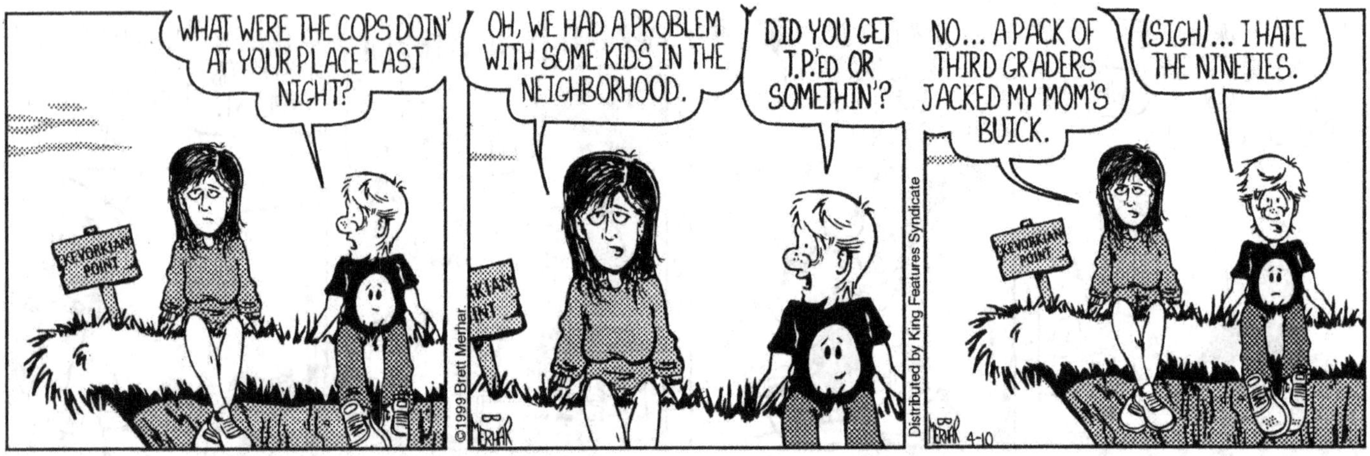
WHAT WERE THE COPS DOIN' AT YOUR PLACE LAST NIGHT?
KEVORKIAN POINT
©1999 Brett Merhar
OH, WE HAD A PROBLEM WITH SOME KIDS IN THE NEIGHBORHOOD.
DID YOU GET T.P.'ED OR SOMETHIN'?
Distributed by King Features Syndicate
4-10
NO... A PACK OF THIRD GRADERS JACKED MY MOM'S BUICK.
(SIGH)... I HATE THE NINETIES.
KEVORKIAN POINT

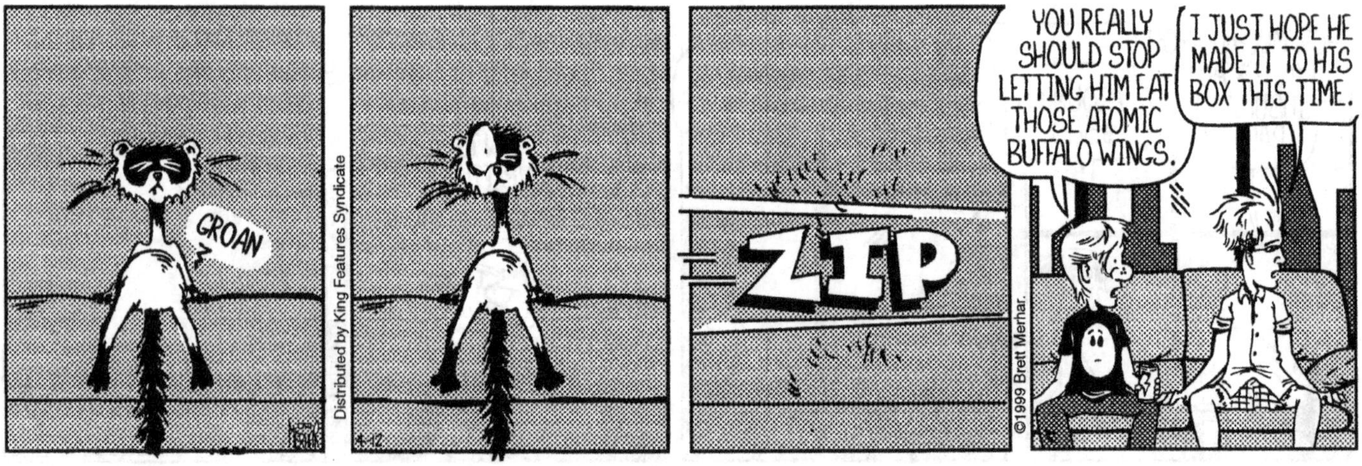
GROAN
Distributed by King Features Syndicate
4-12
ZIP
YOU REALLY SHOULD STOP LETTING HIM EAT THOSE ATOMIC BUFFALO WINGS.
I JUST HOPE HE MADE IT TO HIS BOX THIS TIME.
©1999 Brett Merhar.

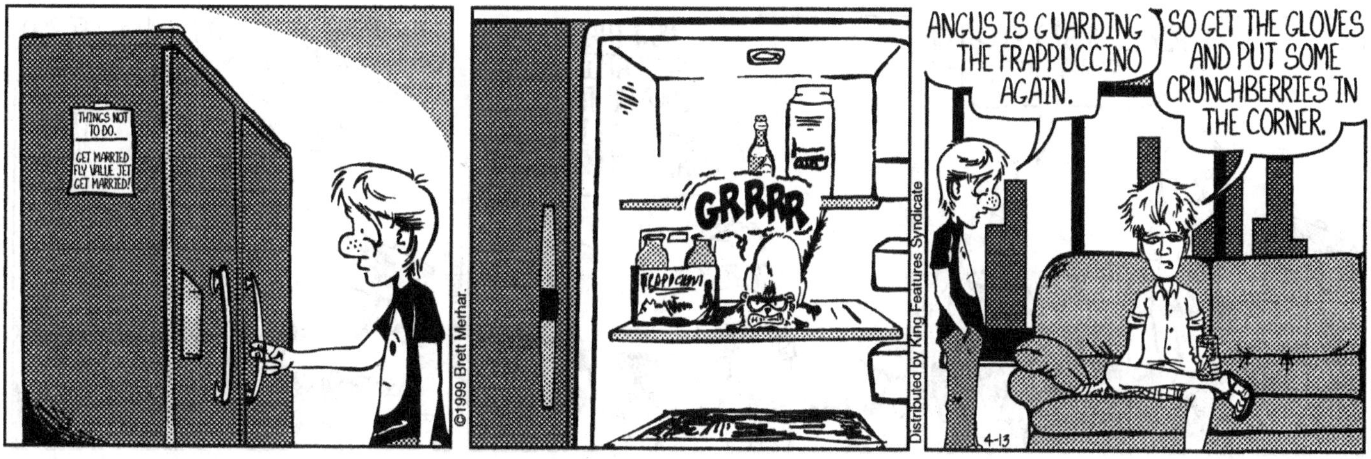
THINGS NOT TO DO.
GET MARRIED
FLY VALUE JET
GET MARRIED!
©1999 Brett Merhar.
GRRRR
Distributed by King Features Syndicate
ANGUS IS GUARDING THE FRAPPUCCINO AGAIN.
SO GET THE GLOVES AND PUT SOME CRUNCHBERRIES IN THE CORNER.
4-13

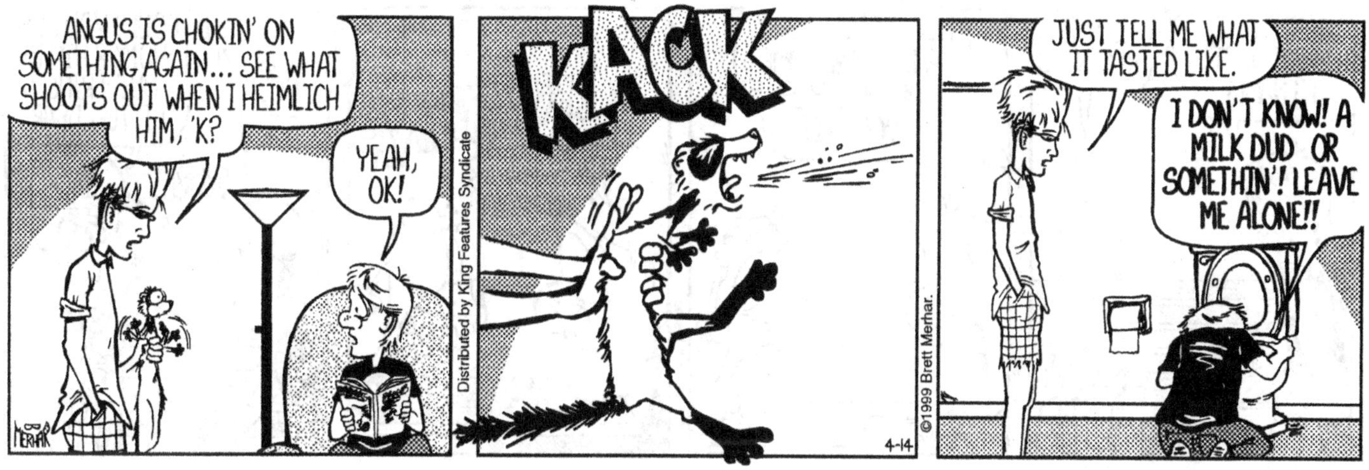
ANGUS IS CHOKIN' ON SOMETHING AGAIN... SEE WHAT SHOOTS OUT WHEN I HEIMLICH HIM, 'K?
YEAH, OK!
MERHAR
Distributed by King Features Syndicate
KACK
4-14
©1999 Brett Merhar.
JUST TELL ME WHAT IT TASTED LIKE.
I DON'T KNOW! A MILK DUD OR SOMETHIN'! LEAVE ME ALONE!!

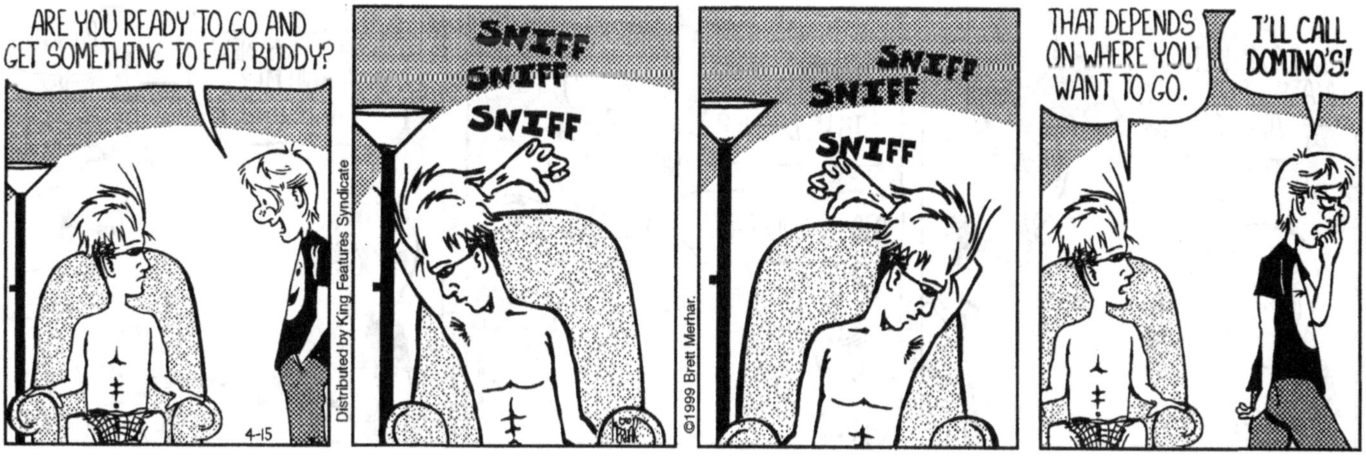
ARE YOU READY TO GO AND GET SOMETHING TO EAT, BUDDY?
4-15
Distributed by King Features Syndicate
SNIFF
SNIFF
SNIFF
©1999 Brett Merhar.
SNIFF
SNIFF
SNIFF
THAT DEPENDS ON WHERE YOU WANT TO GO.
I'LL CALL DOMINO'S!

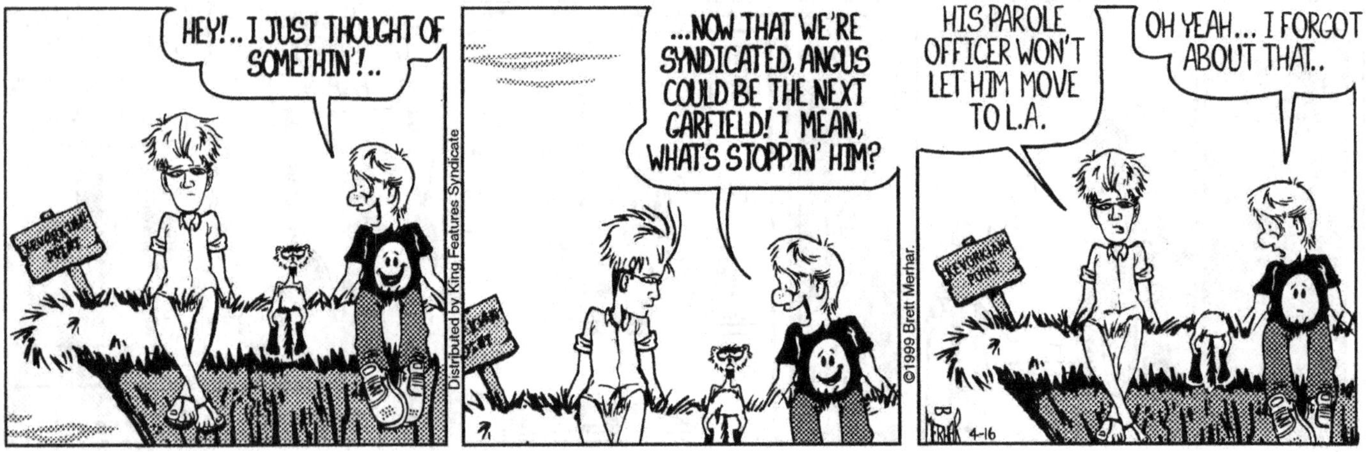
HEY!.. I JUST THOUGHT OF SOMETHIN'!..
Distributed by King Features Syndicate
...NOW THAT WE'RE SYNDICATED, ANGUS COULD BE THE NEXT GARFIELD! I MEAN, WHAT'S STOPPIN' HIM?
©1999 Brett Merhar.
HIS PAROLE OFFICER WON'T LET HIM MOVE TO L.A.
OH YEAH... I FORGOT ABOUT THAT..
4-16

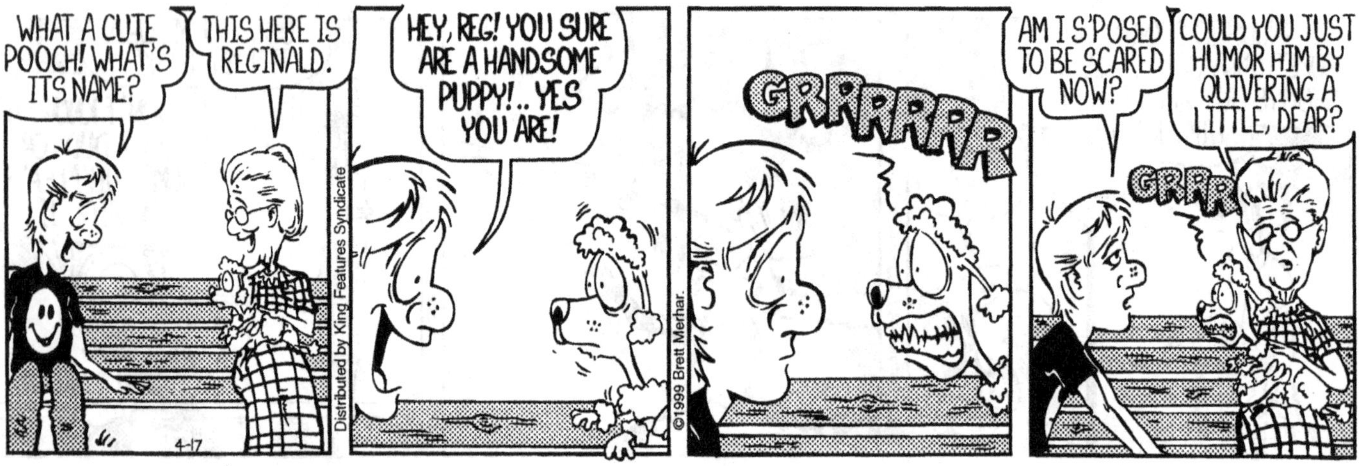
WHAT A CUTE POOCH! WHAT'S ITS NAME?
THIS HERE IS REGINALD.
4-17
Distributed by King Features Syndicate
HEY, REG! YOU SURE ARE A HANDSOME PUPPY!.. YES YOU ARE!
©1999 Brett Merhar.
GRRRRRRR
AM I S'POSED TO BE SCARED NOW?
COULD YOU JUST HUMOR HIM BY QUIVERING A LITTLE, DEAR?
GRRR

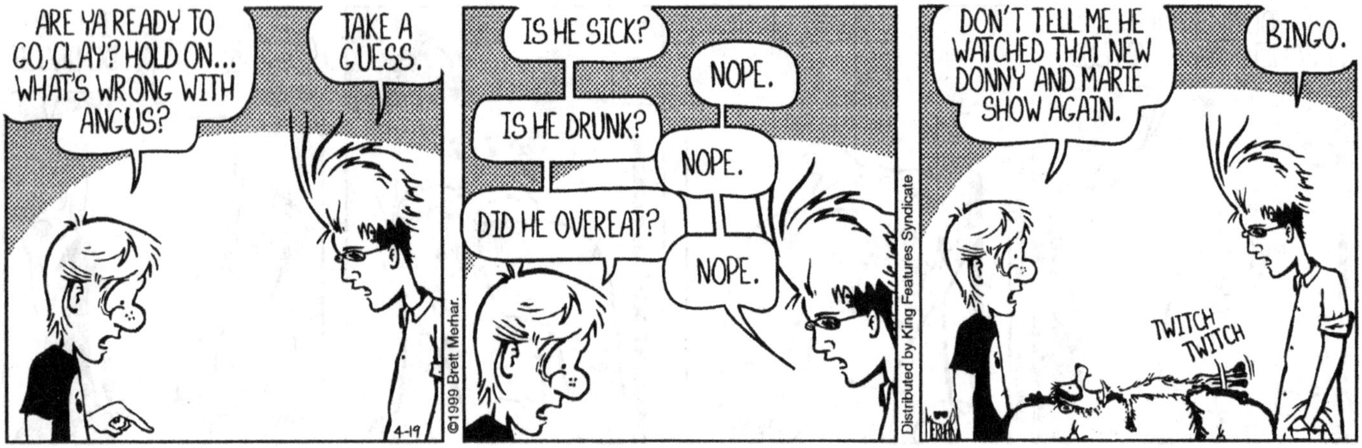
ARE YA READY TO GO, CLAY? HOLD ON... WHAT'S WRONG WITH ANGUS?
TAKE A GUESS.
4-19
©1999 Brett Merhar.
IS HE SICK?
NOPE.
IS HE DRUNK?
NOPE.
DID HE OVEREAT?
NOPE.
Distributed by King Features Syndicate
DON'T TELL ME HE WATCHED THAT NEW DONNY AND MARIE SHOW AGAIN.
BINGO.
TWITCH TWITCH

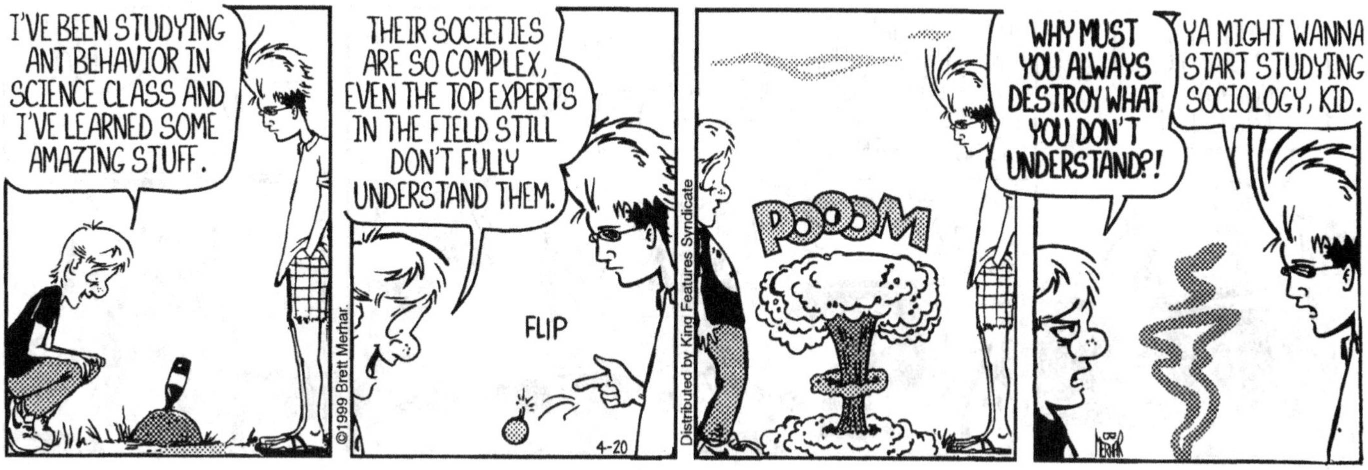
I'VE BEEN STUDYING ANT BEHAVIOR IN SCIENCE CLASS AND I'VE LEARNED SOME AMAZING STUFF.
©1999 Brett Merhar.
THEIR SOCIETIES ARE SO COMPLEX, EVEN THE TOP EXPERTS IN THE FIELD STILL DON'T FULLY UNDERSTAND THEM.
FLIP
4-20
Distributed by King Features Syndicate
POOOM
WHY MUST YOU ALWAYS DESTROY WHAT YOU DON'T UNDERSTAND?!
YA MIGHT WANNA START STUDYING SOCIOLOGY, KID.
MERHAR

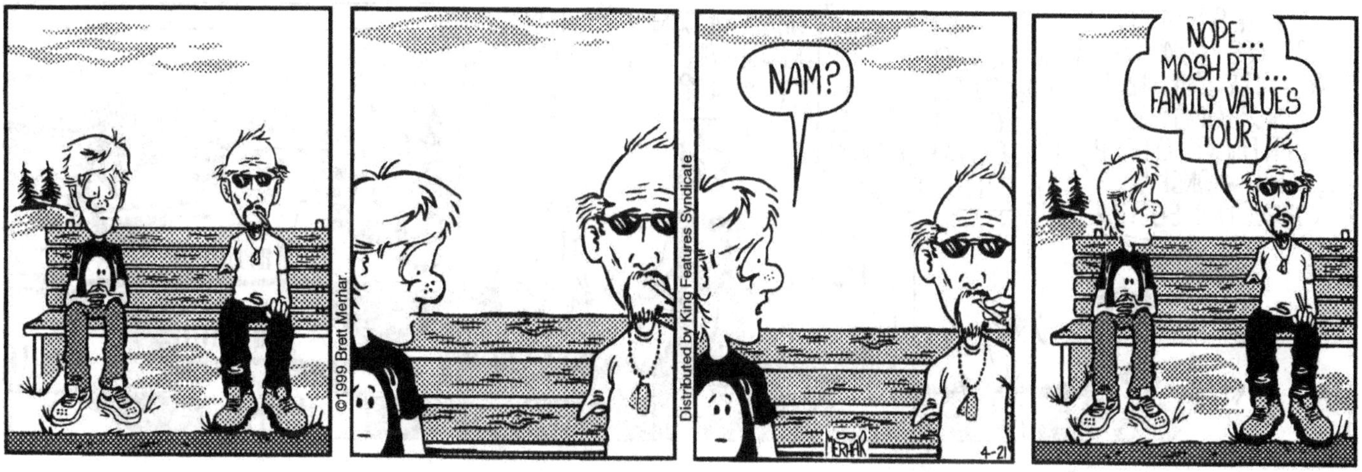
©1999 Brett Merhar.
Distributed by King Features Syndicate
NAM?
MERHAR
4-21
NOPE... MOSH PIT... FAMILY VALUES TOUR

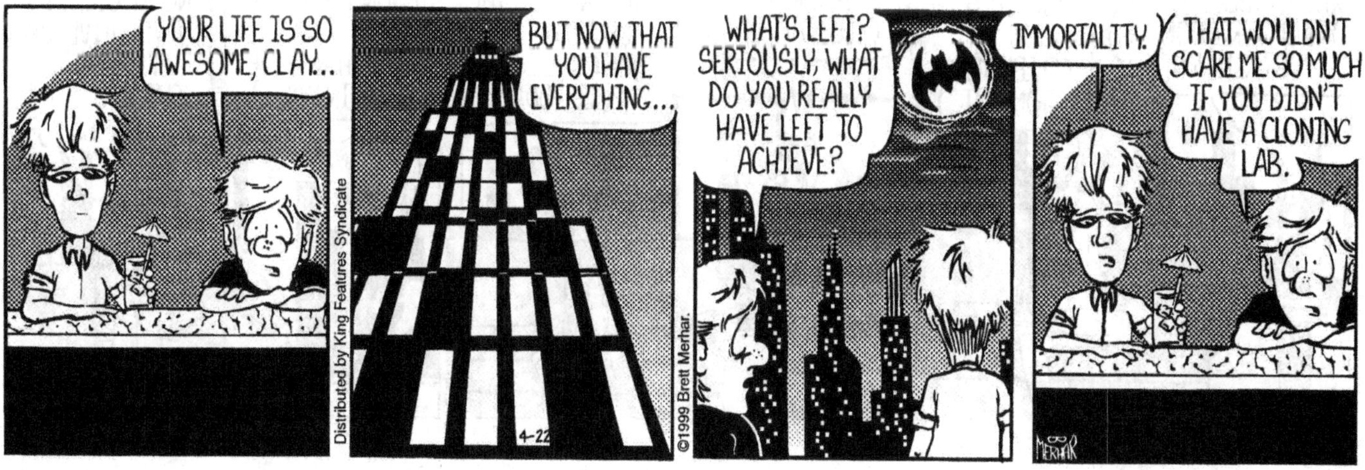
YOUR LIFE IS SO AWESOME, CLAY...
Distributed by King Features Syndicate
BUT NOW THAT YOU HAVE EVERYTHING...
4-22
©1999 Brett Merhar.
WHAT'S LEFT? SERIOUSLY, WHAT DO YOU REALLY HAVE LEFT TO ACHIEVE?
IMMORTALITY.
THAT WOULDN'T SCARE ME SO MUCH IF YOU DIDN'T HAVE A CLONING LAB.
MERHAR

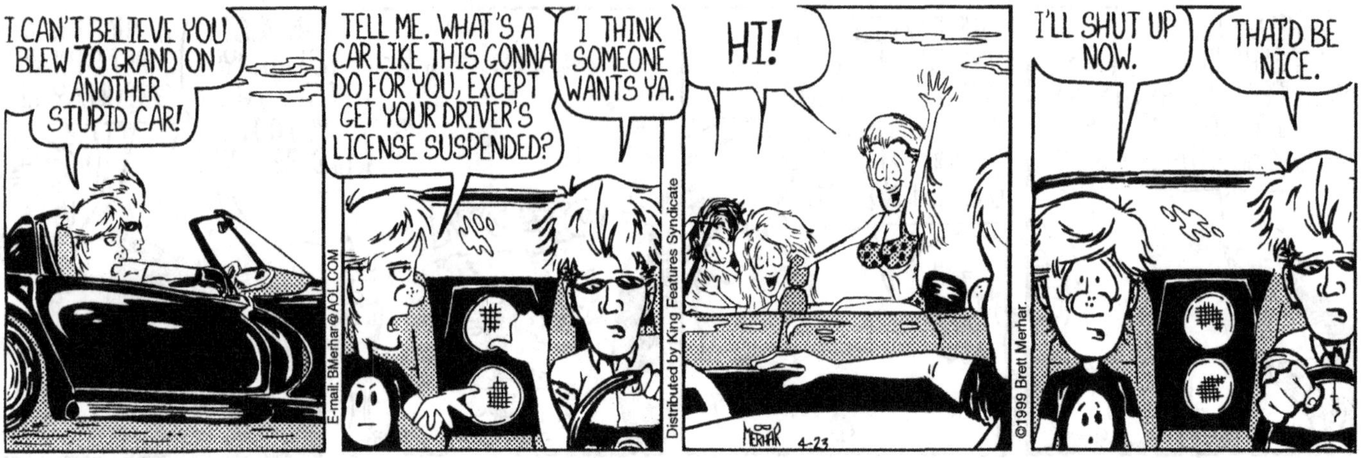
I CAN'T BELIEVE YOU BLEW 70 GRAND ON ANOTHER STUPID CAR!
E-mail: BMerhar@AOL.COM
TELL ME. WHAT'S A CAR LIKE THIS GONNA DO FOR YOU, EXCEPT GET YOUR DRIVER'S LICENSE SUSPENDED?
I THINK SOMEONE WANTS YA.
Distributed by King Features Syndicate
HI!
MERHAR
4-23
©1999 Brett Merhar.
I'LL SHUT UP NOW.
THAT'D BE NICE.

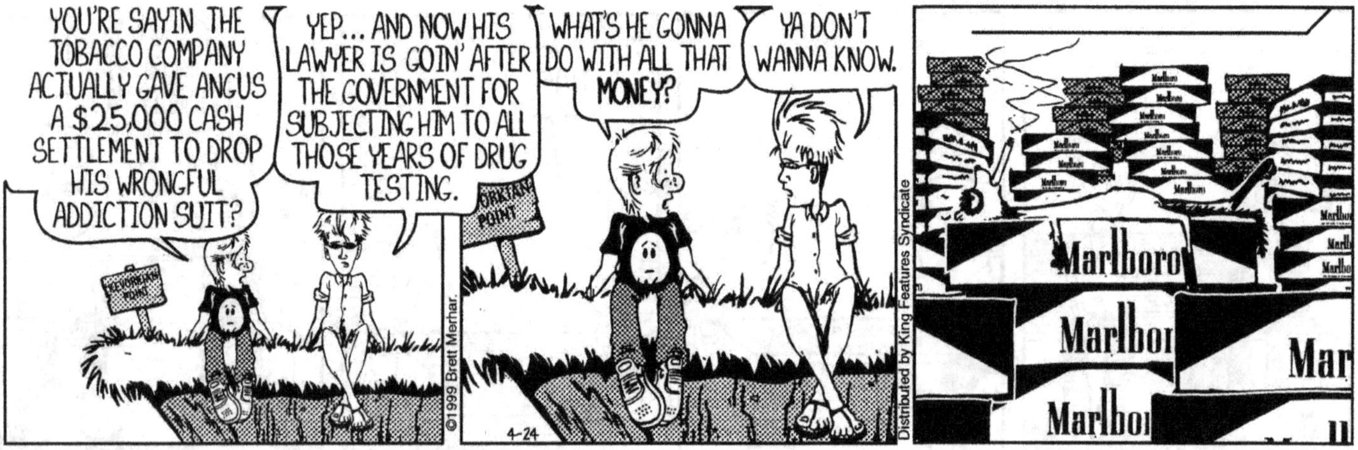
YOU'RE SAYIN THE TOBACCO COMPANY ACTUALLY GAVE ANGUS A $25,000 CASH SETTLEMENT TO DROP HIS WRONGFUL ADDICTION SUIT?
YEP... AND NOW HIS LAWYER IS GOIN' AFTER THE GOVERNMENT FOR SUBJECTING HIM TO ALL THOSE YEARS OF DRUG TESTING.
©1999 Brett Merhar.
WHAT'S HE GONNA DO WITH ALL THAT MONEY?
YA DON'T WANNA KNOW.
4-24
Distributed by King Features Syndicate
Marlboro
Marlboro
Marlboro

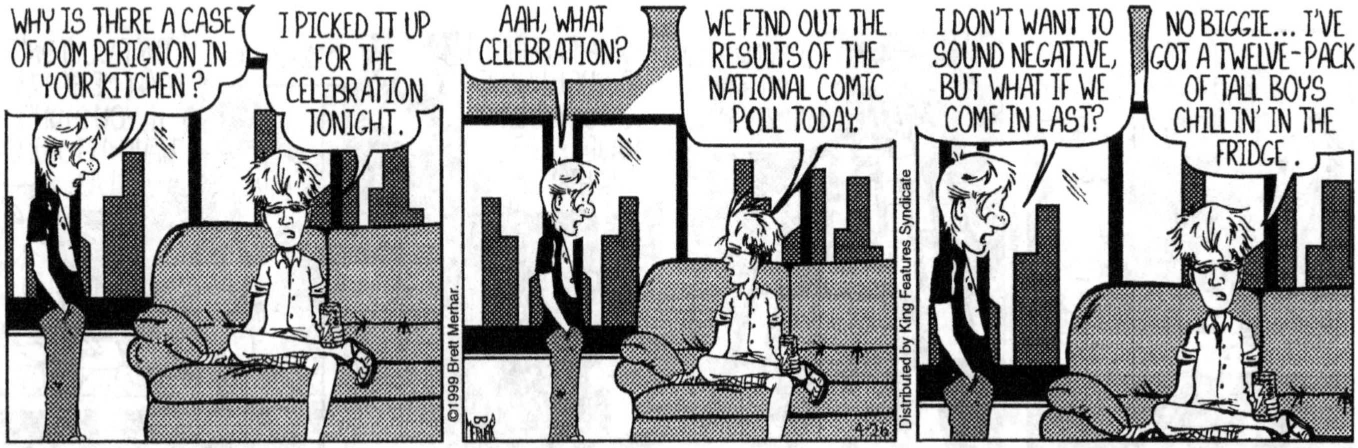
WHY IS THERE A CASE OF DOM PERIGNON IN YOUR KITCHEN?
I PICKED IT UP FOR THE CELEBRATION TONIGHT.
©1999 Brett Merhar.
AAH, WHAT CELEBRATION?
WE FIND OUT THE RESULTS OF THE NATIONAL COMIC POLL TODAY.
4-26
Distributed by King Features Syndicate
I DON'T WANT TO SOUND NEGATIVE, BUT WHAT IF WE COME IN LAST?
NO BIGGIE... I'VE GOT A TWELVE-PACK OF TALL BOYS CHILLIN' IN THE FRIDGE.

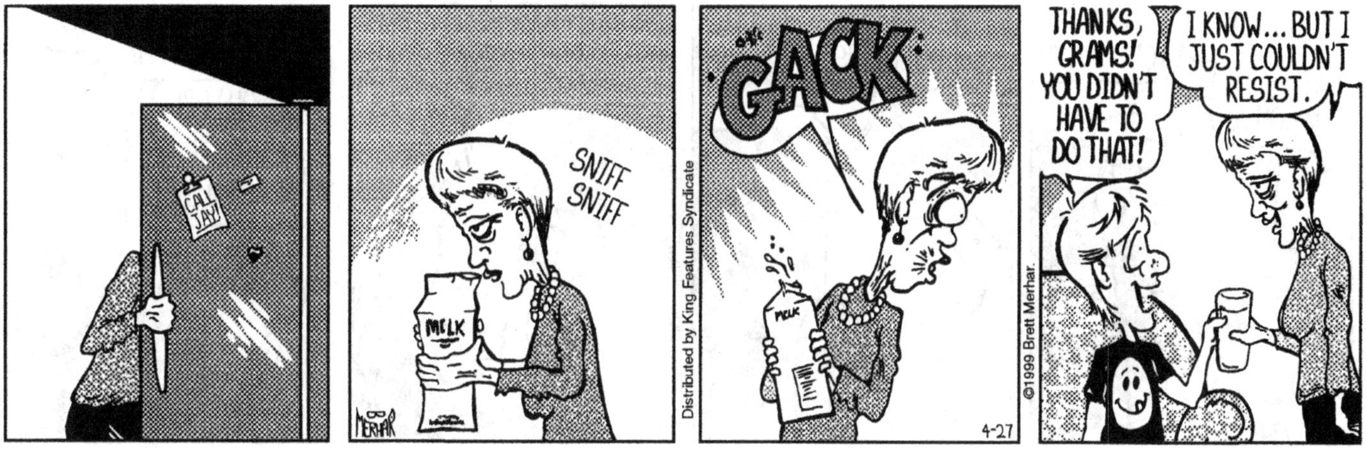
CALL JAY!
MILK
SNIFF SNIFF
MERHAR
Distributed by King Features Syndicate
GACK
MILK
4-27
©1999 Brett Merhar.
THANKS, GRAMS! YOU DIDN'T HAVE TO DO THAT!
I KNOW... BUT I JUST COULDN'T RESIST.

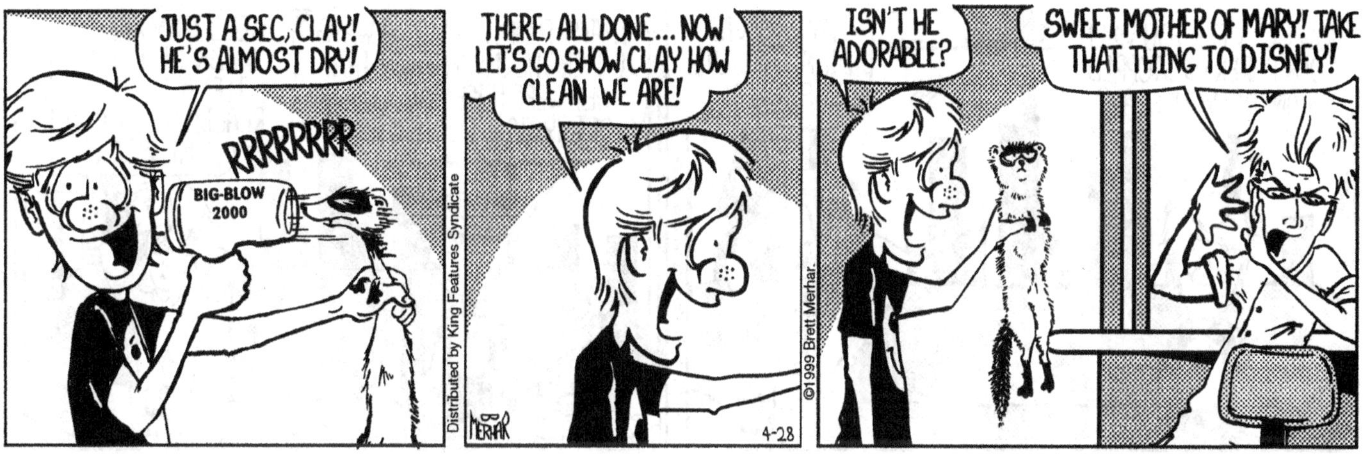
JUST A SEC, CLAY! HE'S ALMOST DRY!
RRRRRRRR
BIG-BLOW 2000
Distributed by King Features Syndicate
THERE, ALL DONE... NOW LET'S GO SHOW CLAY HOW CLEAN WE ARE!
MERHAR
4-28
©1999 Brett Merhar.
ISN'T HE ADORABLE?
SWEET MOTHER OF MARY! TAKE THAT THING TO DISNEY!

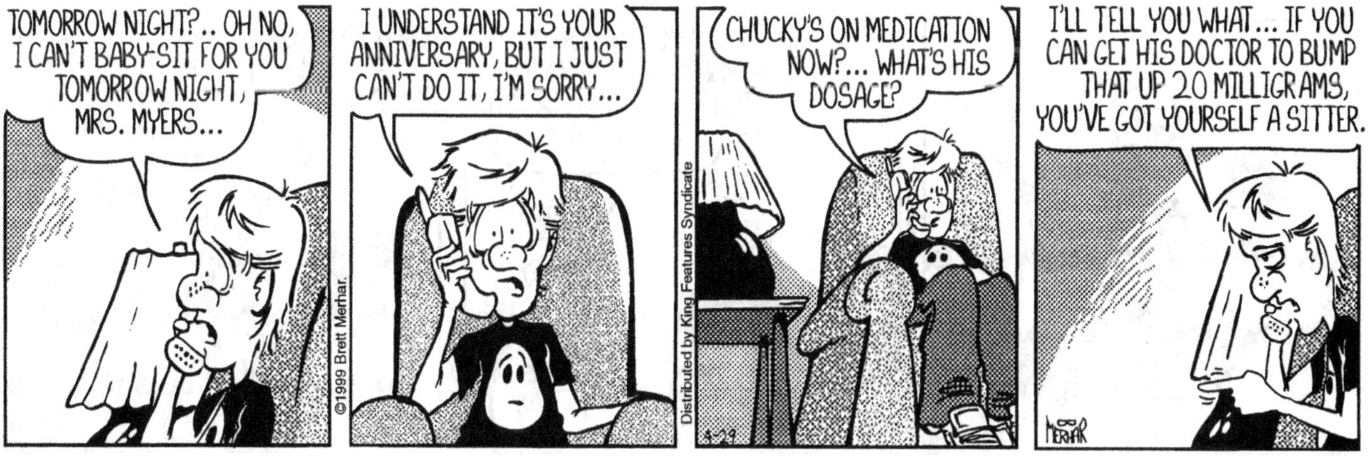
TOMORROW NIGHT?.. OH NO, I CAN'T BABY-SIT FOR YOU TOMORROW NIGHT, MRS. MYERS...
©1999 Brett Merhar.
I UNDERSTAND IT'S YOUR ANNIVERSARY, BUT I JUST CAN'T DO IT, I'M SORRY...
Distributed by King Features Syndicate
CHUCKY'S ON MEDICATION NOW?... WHAT'S HIS DOSAGE?
4-29
I'LL TELL YOU WHAT... IF YOU CAN GET HIS DOCTOR TO BUMP THAT UP 20 MILLIGRAMS, YOU'VE GOT YOURSELF A SITTER.
MERHAR

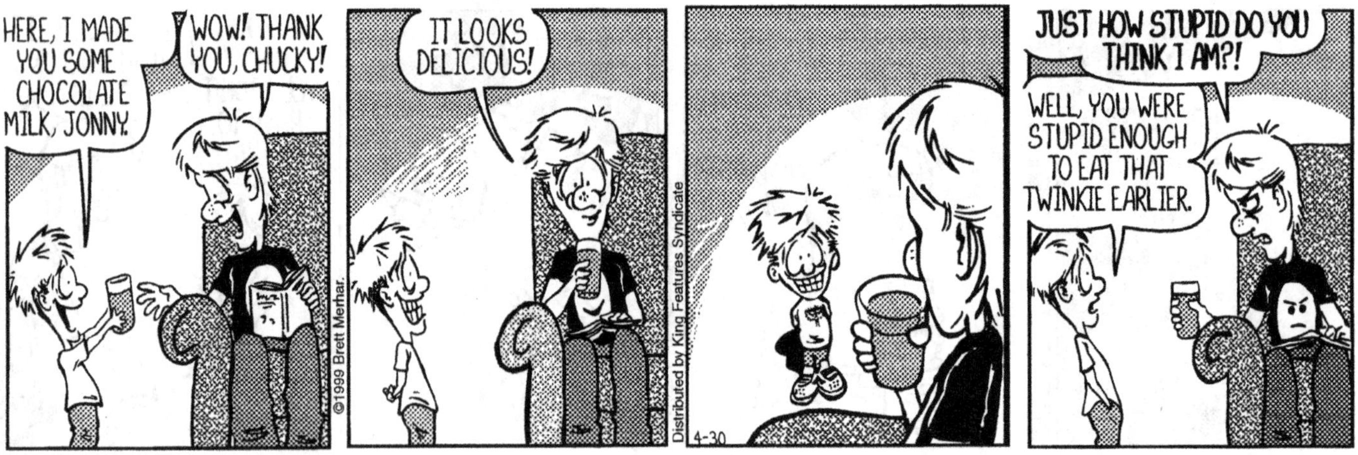
HERE, I MADE YOU SOME CHOCOLATE MILK, JONNY.
WOW! THANK YOU, CHUCKY!
©1999 Brett Merhar.
IT LOOKS DELICIOUS!
Distributed by King Features Syndicate
4-30
JUST HOW STUPID DO YOU THINK I AM?!
WELL, YOU WERE STUPID ENOUGH TO EAT THAT TWINKIE EARLIER.

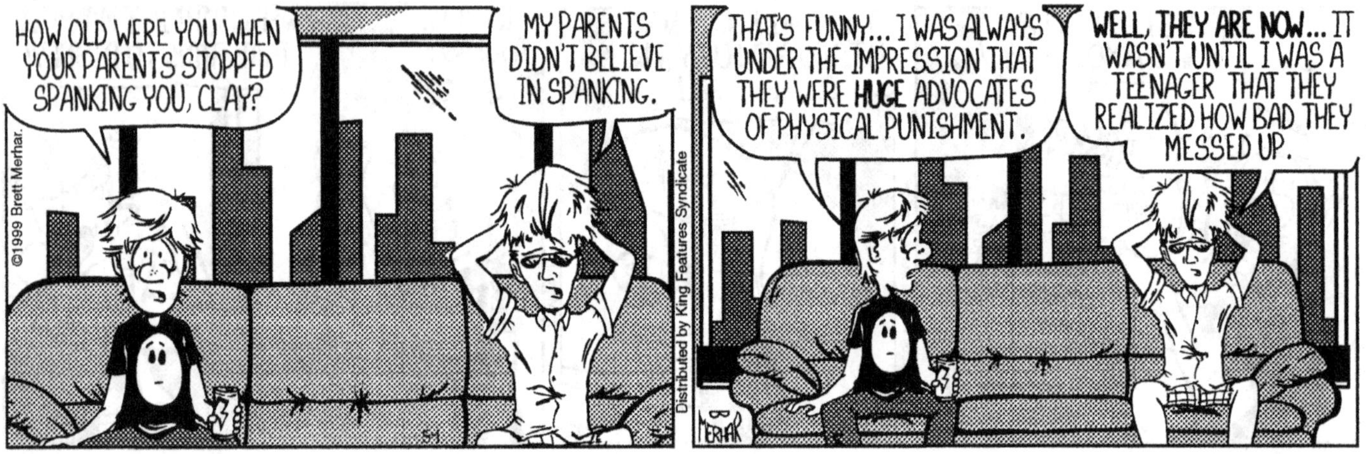
HOW OLD WERE YOU WHEN YOUR PARENTS STOPPED SPANKING YOU, CLAY?
©1999 Brett Merhar.
MY PARENTS DIDN'T BELIEVE IN SPANKING.
Distributed by King Features Syndicate
THAT'S FUNNY... I WAS ALWAYS UNDER THE IMPRESSION THAT THEY WERE HUGE ADVOCATES OF PHYSICAL PUNISHMENT.
WELL, THEY ARE NOW... IT WASN'T UNTIL I WAS A TEENAGER THAT THEY REALIZED HOW BAD THEY MESSED UP.
MERHAR

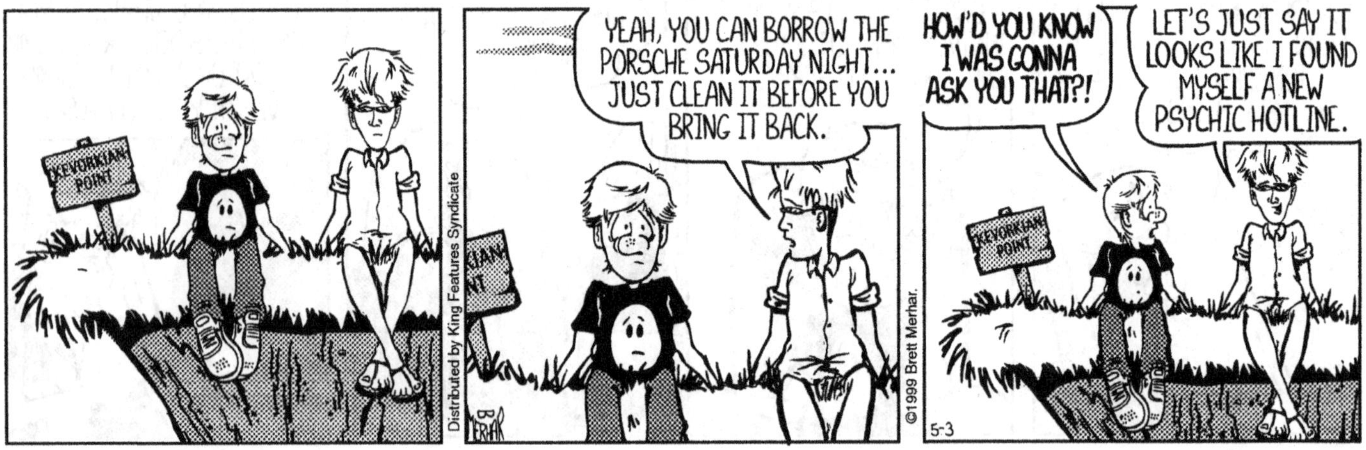
KEVORKIAN POINT
Distributed by King Features Syndicate
YEAH, YOU CAN BORROW THE PORSCHE SATURDAY NIGHT... JUST CLEAN IT BEFORE YOU BRING IT BACK.
MERHAR
©1999 Brett Merhar.
5-3
HOW'D YOU KNOW I WAS GONNA ASK YOU THAT?!
LET'S JUST SAY IT LOOKS LIKE I FOUND MYSELF A NEW PSYCHIC HOTLINE.
KEVORKIAN POINT

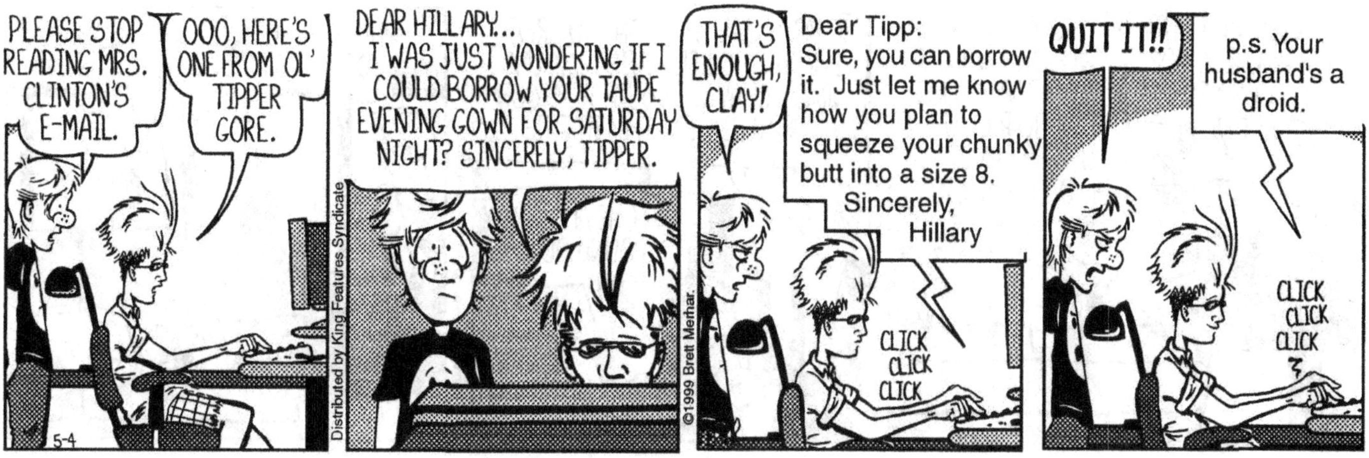
PLEASE STOP READING MRS. CLINTON'S E-MAIL.
OOO, HERE'S ONE FROM OL' TIPPER GORE.
5-4
DEAR HILLARY... I WAS JUST WONDERING IF I COULD BORROW YOUR TAUPE EVENING GOWN FOR SATURDAY NIGHT? SINCERELY, TIPPER.
Distributed by King Features Syndicate
THAT'S ENOUGH, CLAY!
Dear Tipp: Sure, you can borrow it. Just let me know how you plan to squeeze your chunky butt into a size 8. Sincerely, Hillary
CLICK CLICK CLICK
©1999 Brett Merhar.
QUIT IT!!
p.s. Your husband's a droid.
CLICK CLICK CLICK

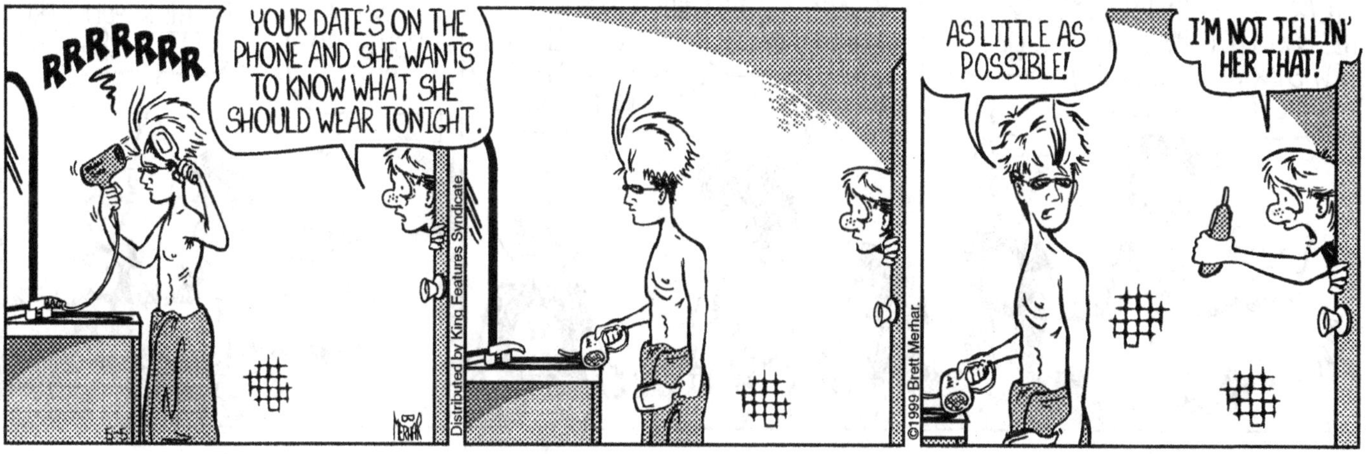
RRRRRRRR
YOUR DATE'S ON THE PHONE AND SHE WANTS TO KNOW WHAT SHE SHOULD WEAR TONIGHT.
5-5
Distributed by King Features Syndicate
AS LITTLE AS POSSIBLE!
I'M NOT TELLIN' HER THAT!
©1999 Brett Merhar.

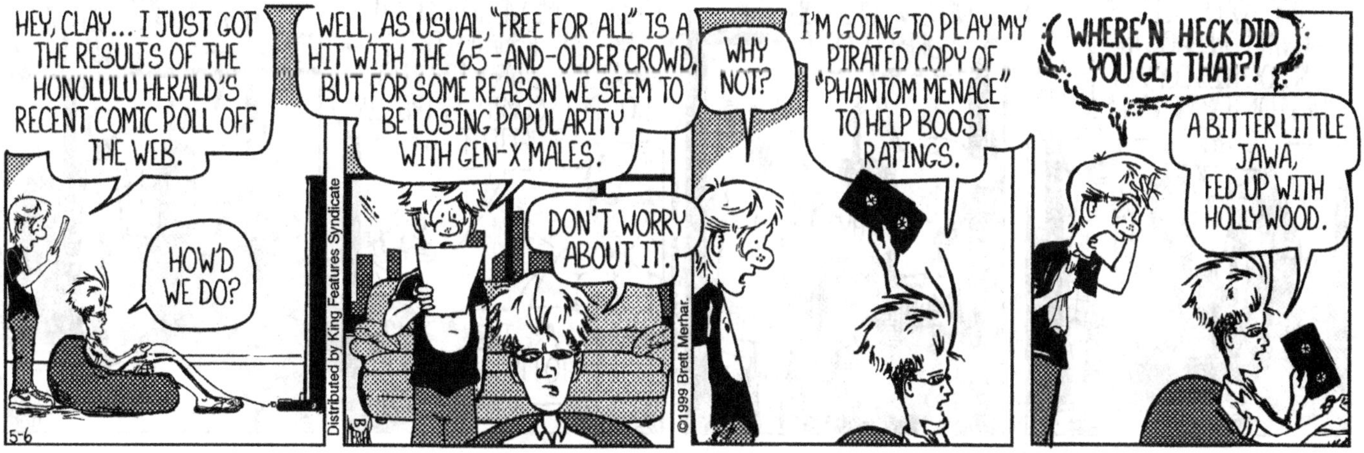
HEY, CLAY... I JUST GOT THE RESULTS OF THE HONOLULU HERALD'S RECENT COMIC POLL OFF THE WEB.
HOW'D WE DO?
5-6
WELL, AS USUAL, "FREE FOR ALL" IS A HIT WITH THE 65-AND-OLDER CROWD, BUT FOR SOME REASON WE SEEM TO BE LOSING POPULARITY WITH GEN-X MALES.
DON'T WORRY ABOUT IT.
Distributed by King Features Syndicate
WHY NOT?
I'M GOING TO PLAY MY PIRATED COPY OF "PHANTOM MENACE" TO HELP BOOST RATINGS.
©1999 Brett Merhar.
WHERE'N HECK DID YOU GET THAT?!
A BITTER LITTLE JAWA, FED UP WITH HOLLYWOOD.

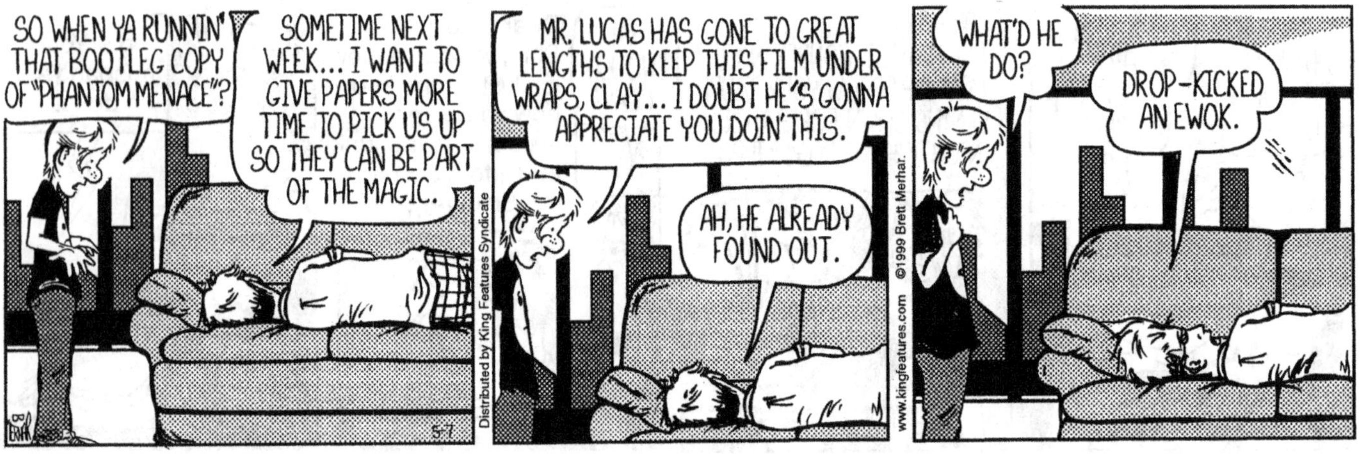
SO WHEN YA RUNNIN' THAT BOOTLEG COPY OF "PHANTOM MENACE"?
SOMETIME NEXT WEEK... I WANT TO GIVE PAPERS MORE TIME TO PICK US UP SO THEY CAN BE PART OF THE MAGIC.
5-7
Distributed by King Features Syndicate
MR. LUCAS HAS GONE TO GREAT LENGTHS TO KEEP THIS FILM UNDER WRAPS, CLAY... I DOUBT HE'S GONNA APPRECIATE YOU DOIN' THIS.
AH, HE ALREADY FOUND OUT.
www.kingfeatures.com ©1999 Brett Merhar.
WHAT'D HE DO?
DROP-KICKED AN EWOK.

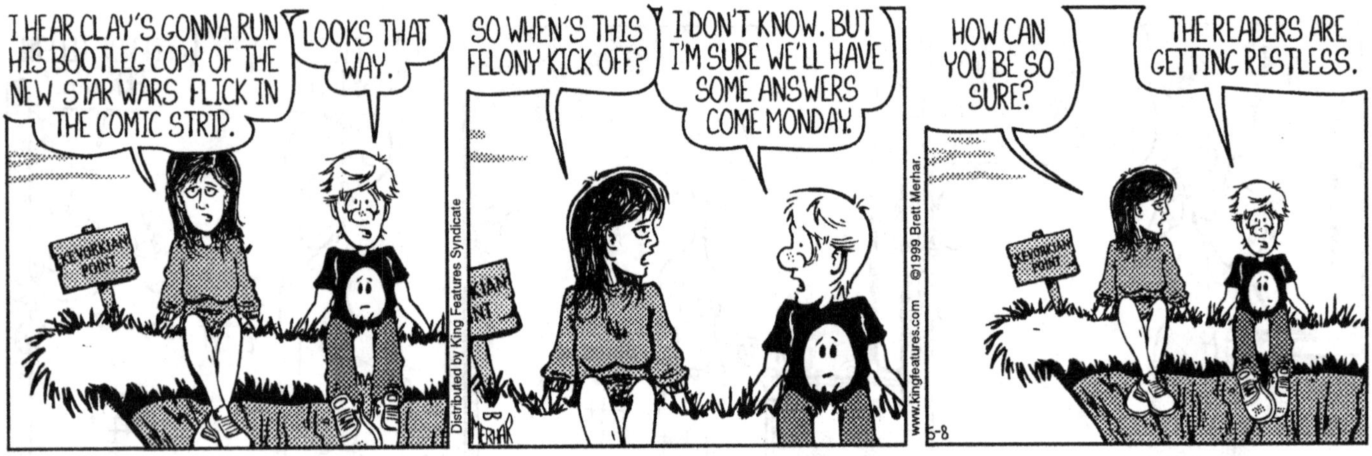
I HEAR CLAY'S GONNA RUN HIS BOOTLEG COPY OF THE NEW STAR WARS FLICK IN THE COMIC STRIP.
LOOKS THAT WAY.
KEVORKIAN POINT
Distributed by King Features Syndicate
SO WHEN'S THIS FELONY KICK OFF?
I DON'T KNOW. BUT I'M SURE WE'LL HAVE SOME ANSWERS COME MONDAY.
www.kingfeatures.com ©1999 Brett Merhar.
5-8
HOW CAN YOU BE SO SURE?
THE READERS ARE GETTING RESTLESS.

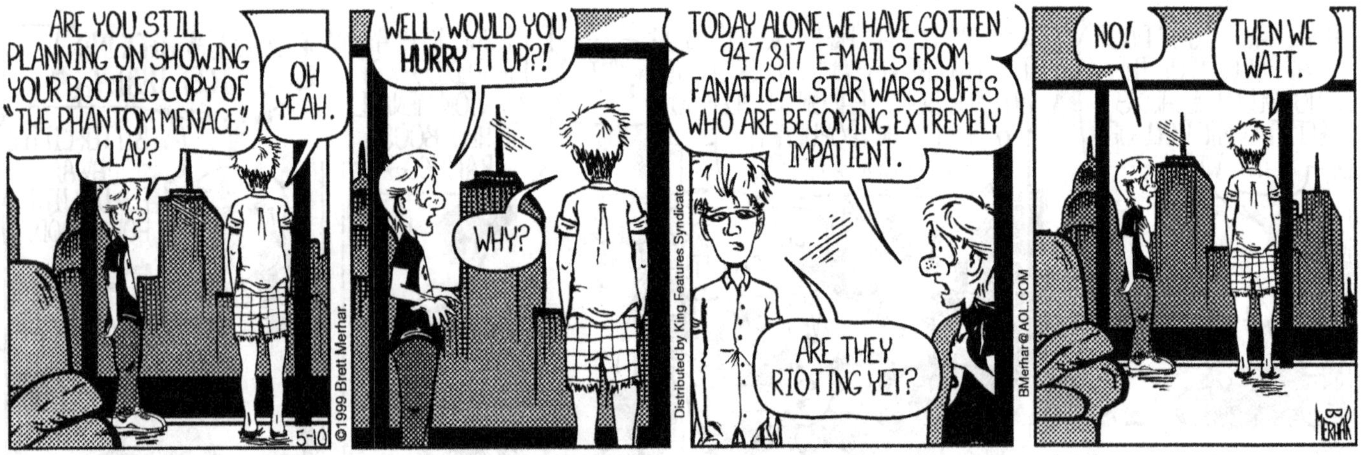
ARE YOU STILL PLANNING ON SHOWING YOUR BOOTLEG COPY OF "THE PHANTOM MENACE," CLAY?
OH YEAH.
©1999 Brett Merhar.
5-10
WELL, WOULD YOU HURRY IT UP?!
WHY?
Distributed by King Features Syndicate
TODAY ALONE WE HAVE GOTTEN 947,817 E-MAILS FROM FANATICAL STAR WARS BUFFS WHO ARE BECOMING EXTREMELY IMPATIENT.
ARE THEY RIOTING YET?
BMerhar@AOL.COM
NO!
THEN WE WAIT.

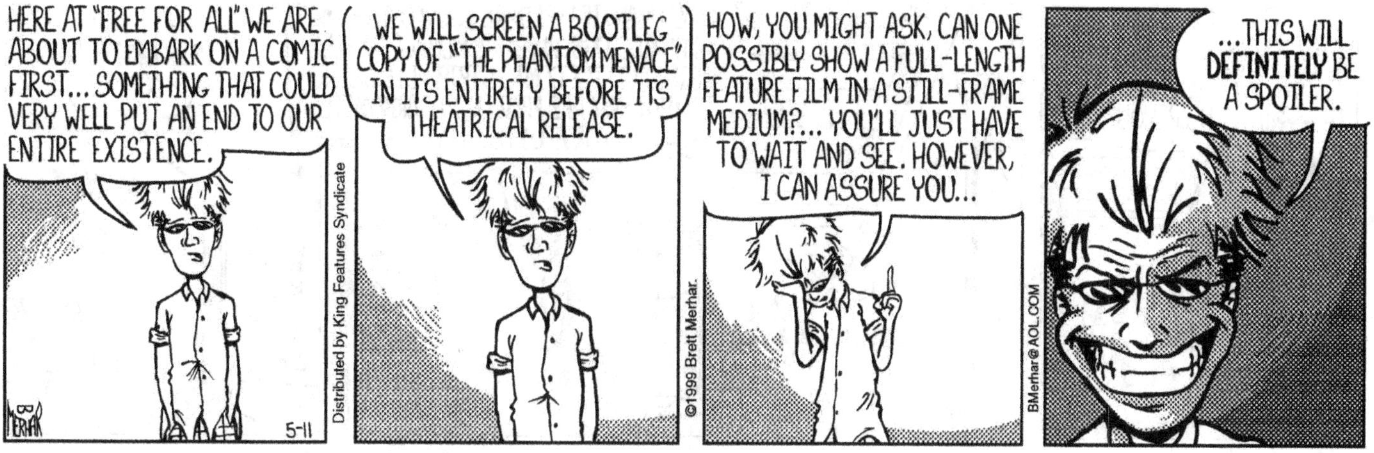
HERE AT "FREE FOR ALL" WE ARE ABOUT TO EMBARK ON A COMIC FIRST... SOMETHING THAT COULD VERY WELL PUT AN END TO OUR ENTIRE EXISTENCE.
B MERHAR
5-11
Distributed by King Features Syndicate
WE WILL SCREEN A BOOTLEG COPY OF "THE PHANTOM MENACE" IN ITS ENTIRETY BEFORE ITS THEATRICAL RELEASE.
©1999 Brett Merhar.
HOW, YOU MIGHT ASK, CAN ONE POSSIBLY SHOW A FULL-LENGTH FEATURE FILM IN A STILL-FRAME MEDIUM?... YOU'LL JUST HAVE TO WAIT AND SEE. HOWEVER, I CAN ASSURE YOU...
BMerhar@AOL.COM
...THIS WILL DEFINITELY BE A SPOILER.

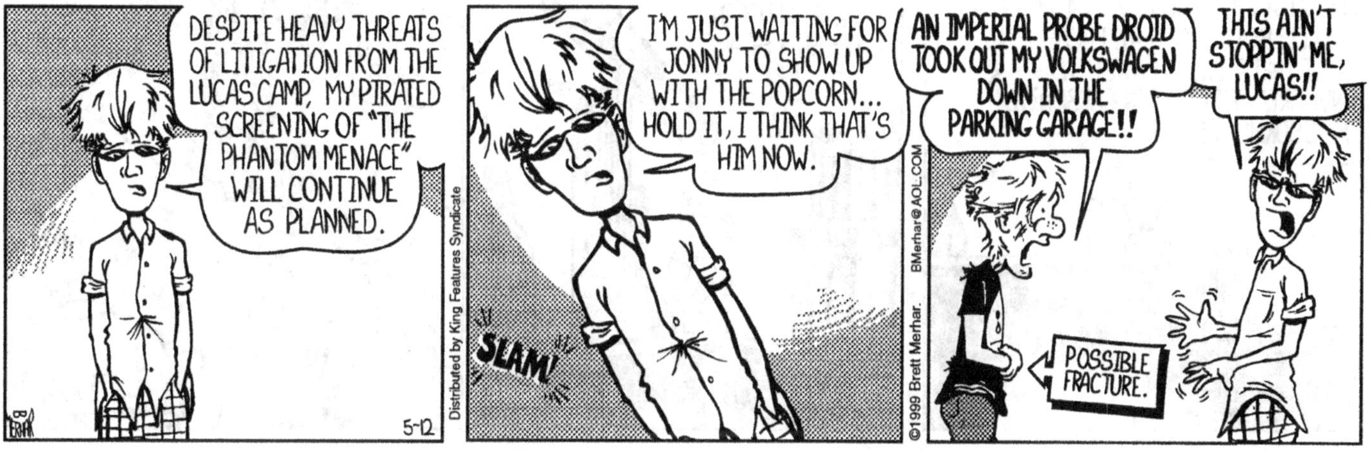
DESPITE HEAVY THREATS OF LITIGATION FROM THE LUCAS CAMP, MY PIRATED SCREENING OF "THE PHANTOM MENACE" WILL CONTINUE AS PLANNED.
B MERHAR
5-12
Distributed by King Features Syndicate
I'M JUST WAITING FOR JONNY TO SHOW UP WITH THE POPCORN... HOLD IT, I THINK THAT'S HIM NOW.
SLAM!
©1999 Brett Merhar.
BMerhar@AOL.COM
AN IMPERIAL PROBE DROID TOOK OUT MY VOLKSWAGEN DOWN IN THE PARKING GARAGE!!
POSSIBLE FRACTURE.
THIS AIN'T STOPPIN' ME, LUCAS!!

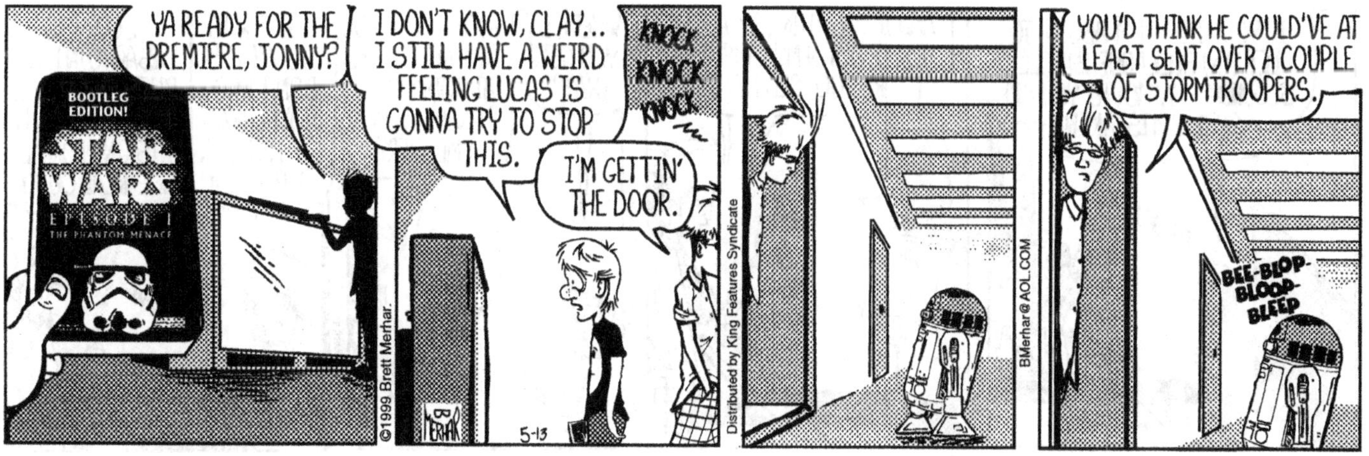
YA READY FOR THE PREMIERE, JONNY?
BOOTLEG EDITION!
STAR WARS
EPISODE I
THE PHANTOM MENACE
©1999 Brett Merhar.
I DON'T KNOW, CLAY... I STILL HAVE A WEIRD FEELING LUCAS IS GONNA TRY TO STOP THIS.
KNOCK KNOCK KNOCK
I'M GETTIN' THE DOOR.
B MERHAR
5-13
Distributed by King Features Syndicate
BMerhar@AOL.COM
YOU'D THINK HE COULD'VE AT LEAST SENT OVER A COUPLE OF STORMTROOPERS.
BEE-BLOP-BLOOP-BLEEP

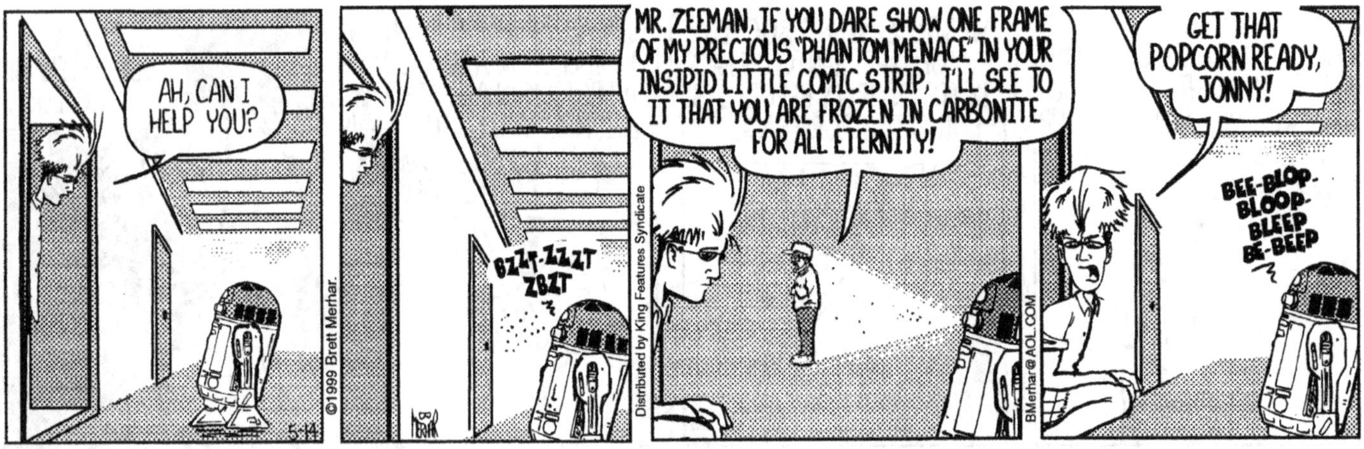
AH, CAN I HELP YOU?
©1999 Brett Merhar.
5-14
BZZT-ZZZT ZBZT
MR. ZEEMAN, IF YOU DARE SHOW ONE FRAME OF MY PRECIOUS "PHANTOM MENACE" IN YOUR INSIPID LITTLE COMIC STRIP, I'LL SEE TO IT THAT YOU ARE FROZEN IN CARBONITE FOR ALL ETERNITY!
Distributed by King Features Syndicate
BMerhar@AOL.COM
GET THAT POPCORN READY, JONNY!
BEE-BLOP-BLOOP-BLEEP BE-BEEP

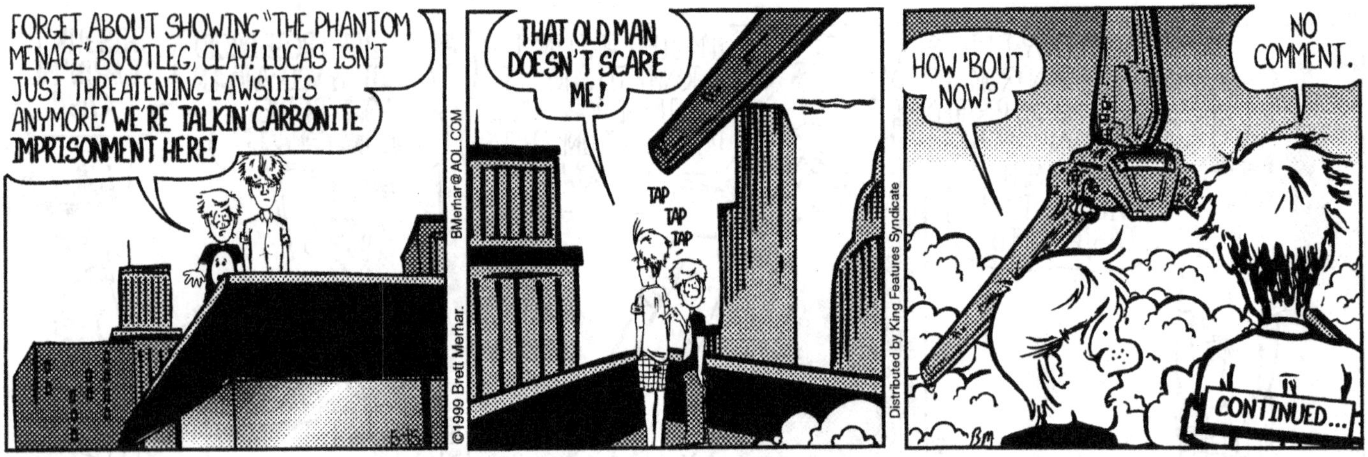
FORGET ABOUT SHOWING "THE PHANTOM MENACE" BOOTLEG, CLAY! LUCAS ISN'T JUST THREATENING LAWSUITS ANYMORE! WE'RE TALKIN' CARBONITE IMPRISONMENT HERE!
BMerhar@AOL.COM
©1999 Brett Merhar.
THAT OLD MAN DOESN'T SCARE ME!
TAP TAP TAP
Distributed by King Features Syndicate
HOW 'BOUT NOW?
NO COMMENT.
CONTINUED...

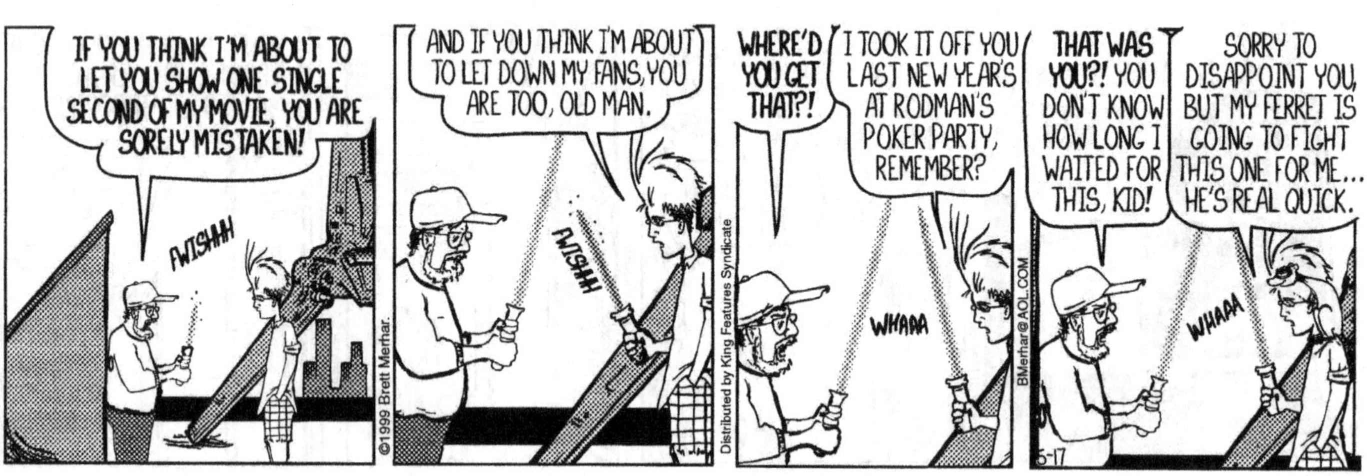
IF YOU THINK I'M ABOUT TO LET YOU SHOW ONE SINGLE SECOND OF MY MOVIE, YOU ARE SORELY MISTAKEN!
FWISHHH
©1999 Brett Merhar.
AND IF YOU THINK I'M ABOUT TO LET DOWN MY FANS, YOU ARE TOO, OLD MAN.
FWISHHH
Distributed by King Features Syndicate
WHERE'D YOU GET THAT?!
I TOOK IT OFF YOU LAST NEW YEAR'S AT RODMAN'S POKER PARTY, REMEMBER?
WHAAA
BMerhar@AOL.COM
THAT WAS YOU?! YOU DON'T KNOW HOW LONG I WAITED FOR THIS, KID!
SORRY TO DISAPPOINT YOU, BUT MY FERRET IS GOING TO FIGHT THIS ONE FOR ME... HE'S REAL QUICK.
WHAAA
5-17

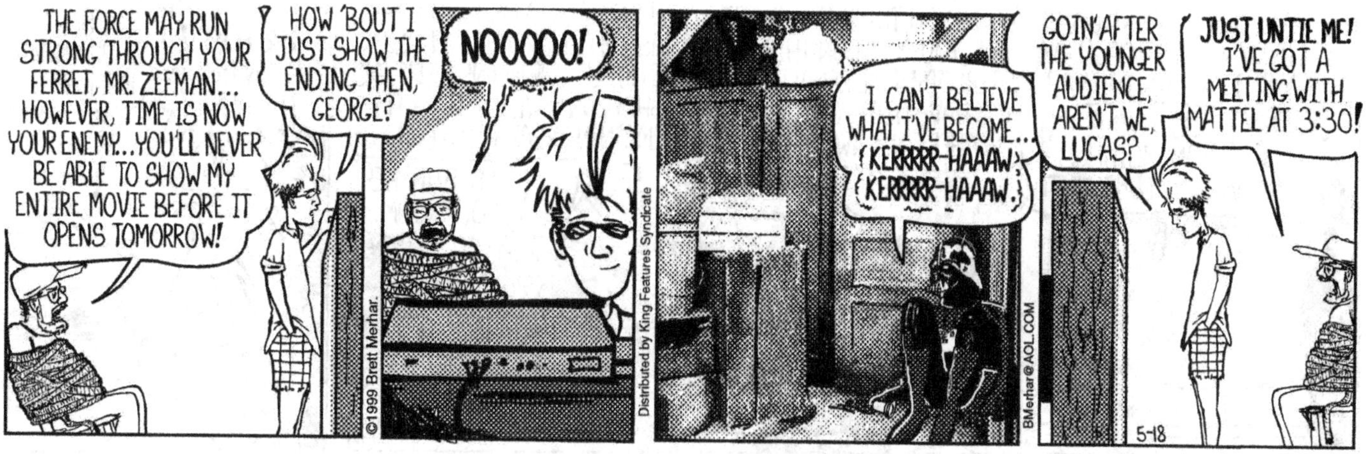
THE FORCE MAY RUN STRONG THROUGH YOUR FERRET, MR. ZEEMAN... HOWEVER, TIME IS NOW YOUR ENEMY...YOU'LL NEVER BE ABLE TO SHOW MY ENTIRE MOVIE BEFORE IT OPENS TOMORROW!
HOW 'BOUT I JUST SHOW THE ENDING THEN, GEORGE?
NOOOOO!
©1999 Brett Merhar.
Distributed by King Features Syndicate
I CAN'T BELIEVE WHAT I'VE BECOME... KERRRRR-HAAAW, KERRRRR-HAAAW,
BMerhar@AOL.COM
GOIN' AFTER THE YOUNGER AUDIENCE, AREN'T WE, LUCAS?
JUST UNTIE ME! I'VE GOT A MEETING WITH MATTEL AT 3:30!
5-18

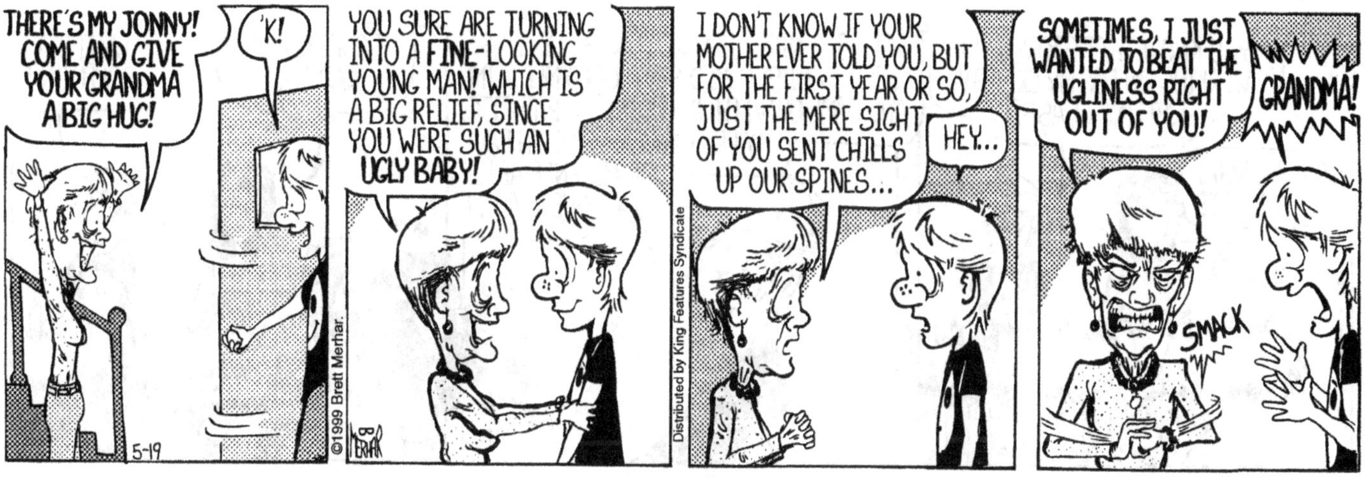
THERE'S MY JONNY! COME AND GIVE YOUR GRANDMA A BIG HUG!
'K!
5-19
YOU SURE ARE TURNING INTO A FINE-LOOKING YOUNG MAN! WHICH IS A BIG RELIEF, SINCE YOU WERE SUCH AN UGLY BABY!
©1999 Brett Merhar.
I DON'T KNOW IF YOUR MOTHER EVER TOLD YOU, BUT FOR THE FIRST YEAR OR SO, JUST THE MERE SIGHT OF YOU SENT CHILLS UP OUR SPINES...
HEY...
Distributed by King Features Syndicate
SOMETIMES, I JUST WANTED TO BEAT THE UGLINESS RIGHT OUT OF YOU!
GRANDMA!
SMACK

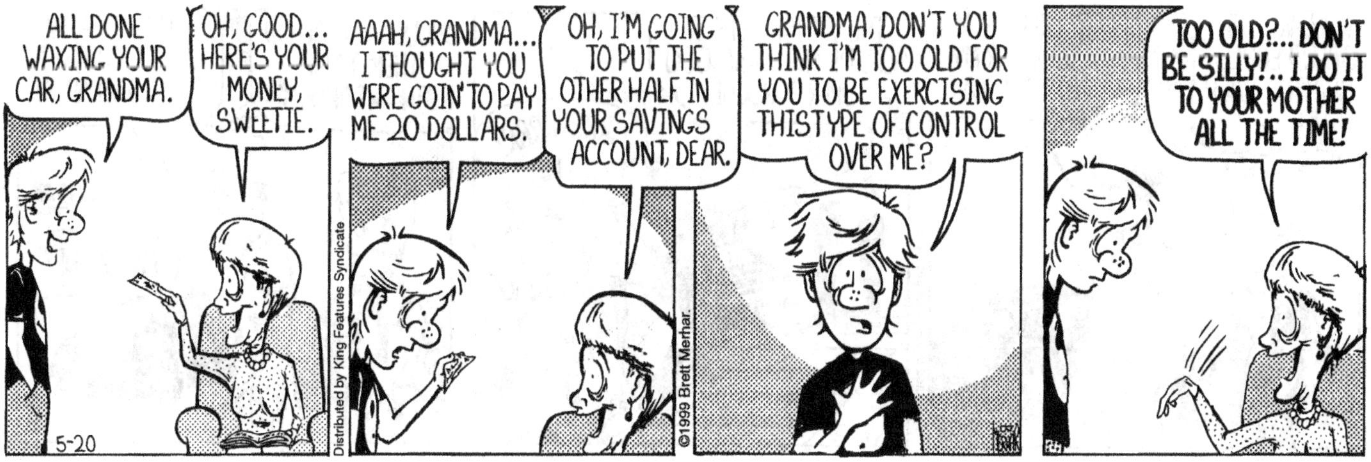
ALL DONE WAXING YOUR CAR, GRANDMA.
OH, GOOD... HERE'S YOUR MONEY, SWEETIE.
5-20
Distributed by King Features Syndicate
AAAH, GRANDMA... I THOUGHT YOU WERE GOIN' TO PAY ME 20 DOLLARS.
OH, I'M GOING TO PUT THE OTHER HALF IN YOUR SAVINGS ACCOUNT, DEAR.
©1999 Brett Merhar.
GRANDMA, DON'T YOU THINK I'M TOO OLD FOR YOU TO BE EXERCISING THISTYPE OF CONTROL OVER ME?
TOO OLD?... DON'T BE SILLY!... I DO IT TO YOUR MOTHER ALL THE TIME!

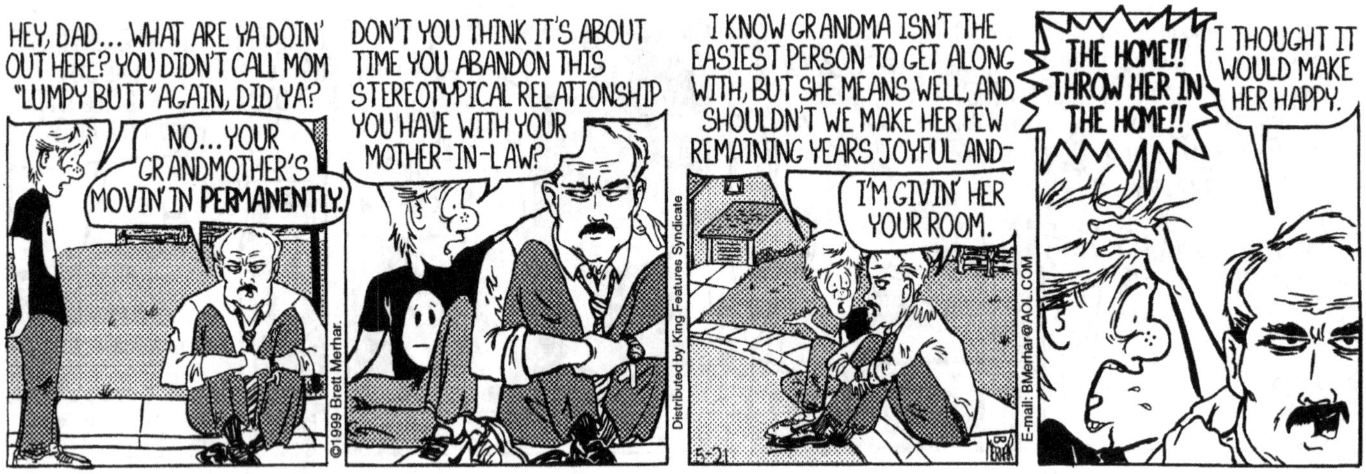
HEY, DAD... WHAT ARE YA DOIN' OUT HERE? YOU DIDN'T CALL MOM "LUMPY BUTT" AGAIN, DID YA?
NO... YOUR GRANDMOTHER'S MOVIN' IN **PERMANENTLY.**
©1999 Brett Merhar.
DON'T YOU THINK IT'S ABOUT TIME YOU ABANDON THIS STEREOTYPICAL RELATIONSHIP YOU HAVE WITH YOUR MOTHER-IN-LAW?
Distributed by King Features Syndicate
I KNOW GRANDMA ISN'T THE EASIEST PERSON TO GET ALONG WITH, BUT SHE MEANS WELL, AND SHOULDN'T WE MAKE HER FEW REMAINING YEARS JOYFUL AND-
I'M GIVIN' HER YOUR ROOM.
5-21
MERHAR
E-mail: BMerhar@AOL.COM
THE HOME!! THROW HER IN THE HOME!!
I THOUGHT IT WOULD MAKE HER HAPPY.

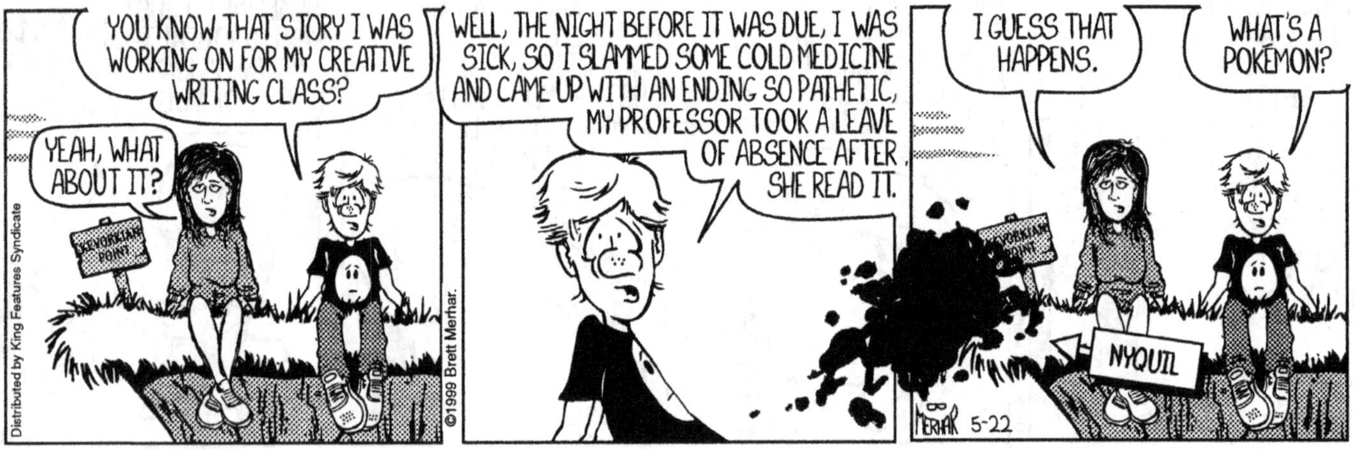
YOU KNOW THAT STORY I WAS WORKING ON FOR MY CREATIVE WRITING CLASS?
YEAH, WHAT ABOUT IT?
KEVORKIAN POINT
Distributed by King Features Syndicate
WELL, THE NIGHT BEFORE IT WAS DUE, I WAS SICK, SO I SLAMMED SOME COLD MEDICINE AND CAME UP WITH AN ENDING SO PATHETIC, MY PROFESSOR TOOK A LEAVE OF ABSENCE AFTER SHE READ IT.
©1999 Brett Merhar.
I GUESS THAT HAPPENS.
WHAT'S A POKÉMON?
NYQUIL
MERHAR 5-22

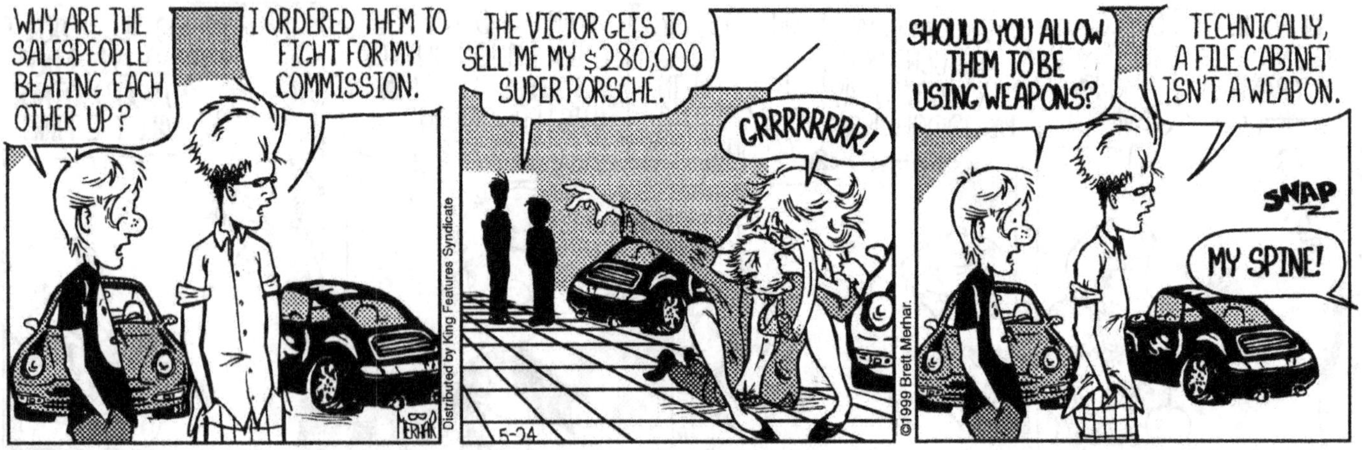
WHY ARE THE SALESPEOPLE BEATING EACH OTHER UP?
I ORDERED THEM TO FIGHT FOR MY COMMISSION.
MERHAR
THE VICTOR GETS TO SELL ME MY $280,000 SUPER PORSCHE.
GRRRRRRRR!
Distributed by King Features Syndicate
5-24
©1999 Brett Merhar.
SHOULD YOU ALLOW THEM TO BE USING WEAPONS?
TECHNICALLY, A FILE CABINET ISN'T A WEAPON.
SNAP
MY SPINE!

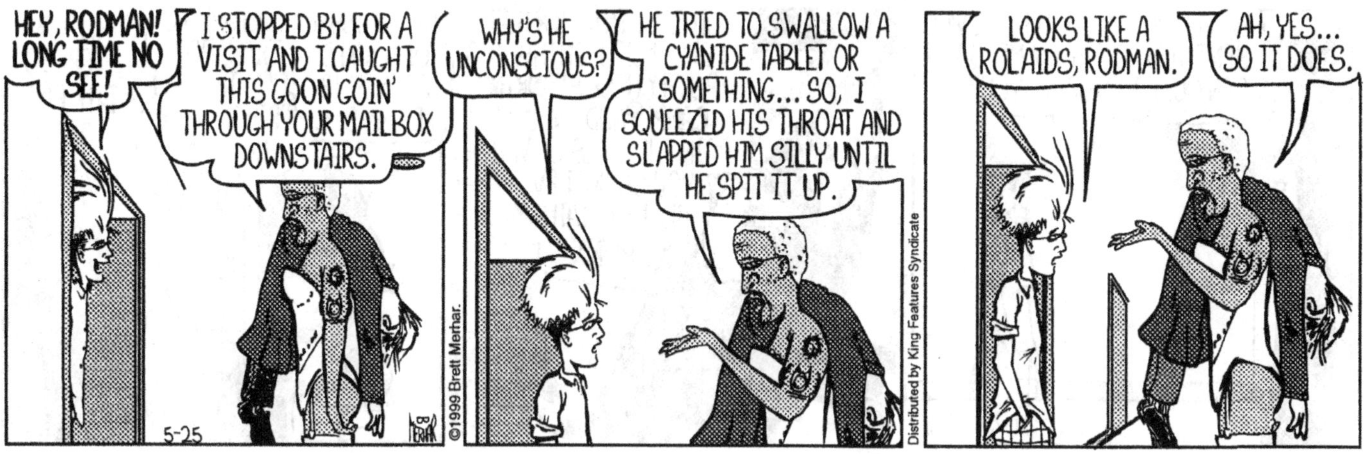
HEY, RODMAN! LONG TIME NO SEE!
I STOPPED BY FOR A VISIT AND I CAUGHT THIS GOON GOIN' THROUGH YOUR MAILBOX DOWNSTAIRS.
WHY'S HE UNCONSCIOUS?
HE TRIED TO SWALLOW A CYANIDE TABLET OR SOMETHING... SO, I SQUEEZED HIS THROAT AND SLAPPED HIM SILLY UNTIL HE SPIT IT UP.
LOOKS LIKE A ROLAIDS, RODMAN.
AH, YES... SO IT DOES.
5-25
©1999 Brett Merhar.
Distributed by King Features Syndicate

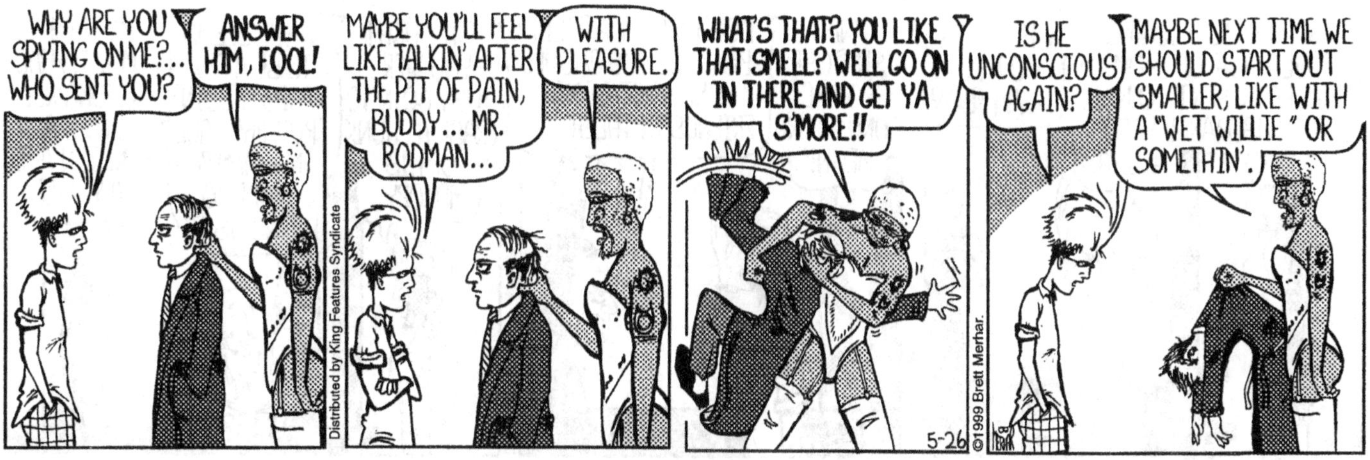
WHY ARE YOU SPYING ON ME?... WHO SENT YOU?
ANSWER HIM, FOOL!
MAYBE YOU'LL FEEL LIKE TALKIN' AFTER THE PIT OF PAIN, BUDDY... MR. RODMAN...
WITH PLEASURE.
WHAT'S THAT? YOU LIKE THAT SMELL? WELL GO ON IN THERE AND GET YA S'MORE!!
IS HE UNCONSCIOUS AGAIN?
MAYBE NEXT TIME WE SHOULD START OUT SMALLER, LIKE WITH A "WET WILLIE" OR SOMETHIN'.
Distributed by King Features Syndicate
5-26
©1999 Brett Merhar.

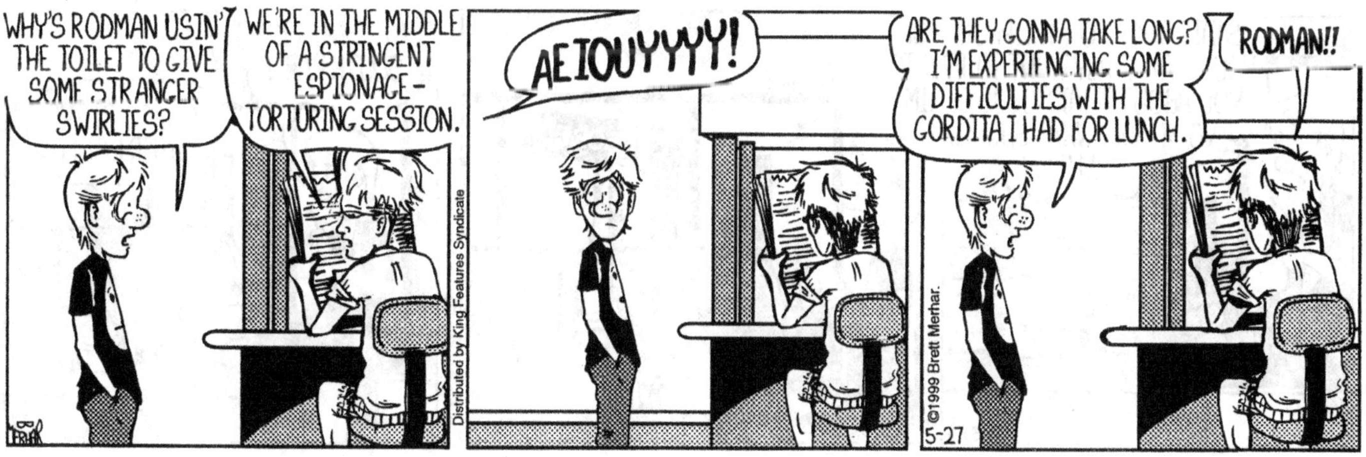
WHY'S RODMAN USIN' THE TOILET TO GIVE SOME STRANGER SWIRLIES?
WE'RE IN THE MIDDLE OF A STRINGENT ESPIONAGE-TORTURING SESSION.
Distributed by King Features Syndicate
AEIOUYYYY!
ARE THEY GONNA TAKE LONG? I'M EXPERIENCING SOME DIFFICULTIES WITH THE GORDITA I HAD FOR LUNCH.
RODMAN!!
©1999 Brett Merhar.
5-27

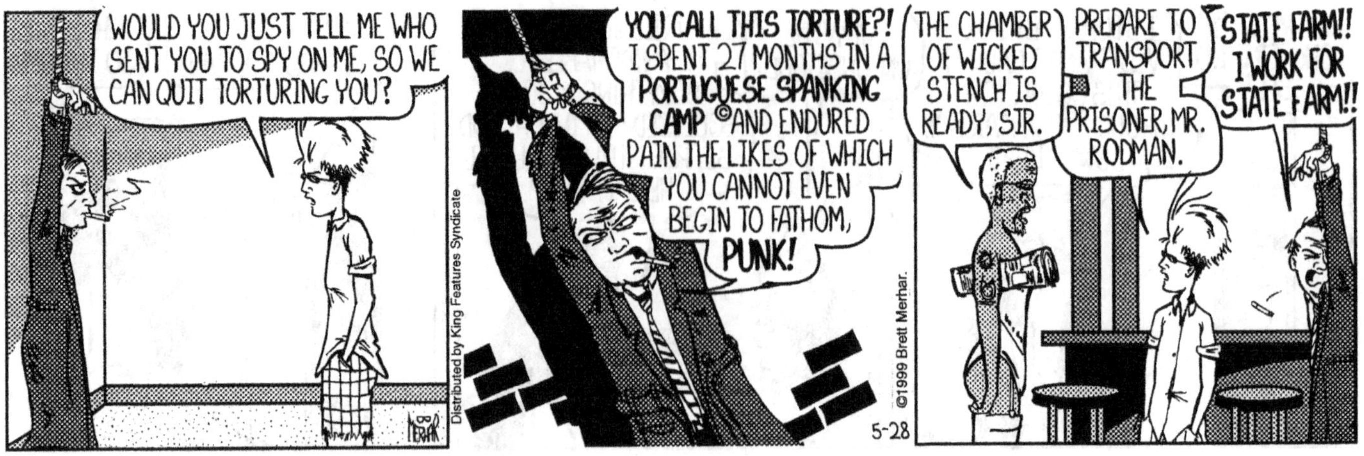
WOULD YOU JUST TELL ME WHO SENT YOU TO SPY ON ME, SO WE CAN QUIT TORTURING YOU?
YOU CALL THIS TORTURE?! I SPENT 27 MONTHS IN A PORTUGUESE SPANKING CAMP © AND ENDURED PAIN THE LIKES OF WHICH YOU CANNOT EVEN BEGIN TO FATHOM, PUNK!
Distributed by King Features Syndicate
5-28
©1999 Brett Merhar.
THE CHAMBER OF WICKED STENCH IS READY, SIR.
PREPARE TO TRANSPORT THE PRISONER, MR. RODMAN.
STATE FARM!! I WORK FOR STATE FARM!!

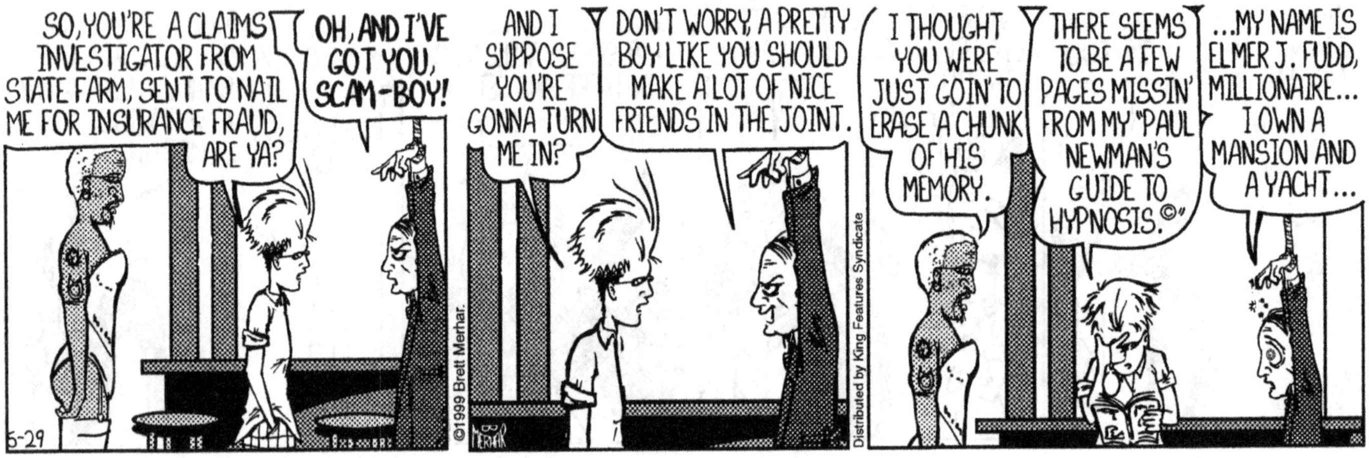
SO, YOU'RE A CLAIMS INVESTIGATOR FROM STATE FARM, SENT TO NAIL ME FOR INSURANCE FRAUD, ARE YA?
OH, AND I'VE GOT YOU, SCAM-BOY!
5-29
©1999 Brett Merhar.
AND I SUPPOSE YOU'RE GONNA TURN ME IN?
DON'T WORRY, A PRETTY BOY LIKE YOU SHOULD MAKE A LOT OF NICE FRIENDS IN THE JOINT.
Distributed by King Features Syndicate
I THOUGHT YOU WERE JUST GOIN' TO ERASE A CHUNK OF HIS MEMORY.
THERE SEEMS TO BE A FEW PAGES MISSIN' FROM MY "PAUL NEWMAN'S GUIDE TO HYPNOSIS.©"
...MY NAME IS ELMER J. FUDD, MILLIONAIRE... I OWN A MANSION AND A YACHT...

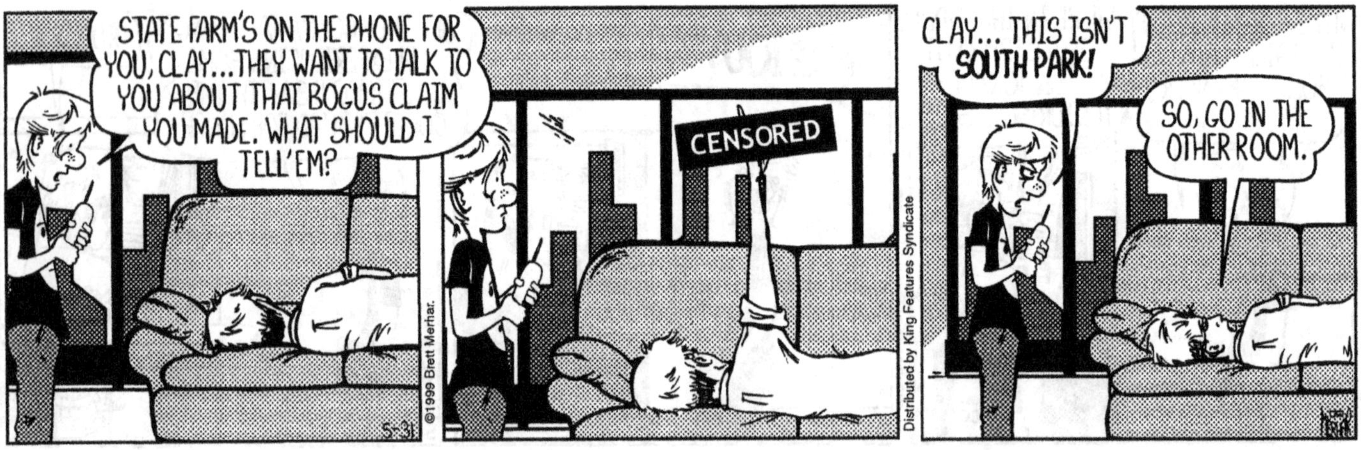
STATE FARM'S ON THE PHONE FOR YOU, CLAY...THEY WANT TO TALK TO YOU ABOUT THAT BOGUS CLAIM YOU MADE. WHAT SHOULD I TELL 'EM?
©1999 Brett Merhar.
5-31
CENSORED
CLAY... THIS ISN'T SOUTH PARK!
SO, GO IN THE OTHER ROOM.
Distributed by King Features Syndicate

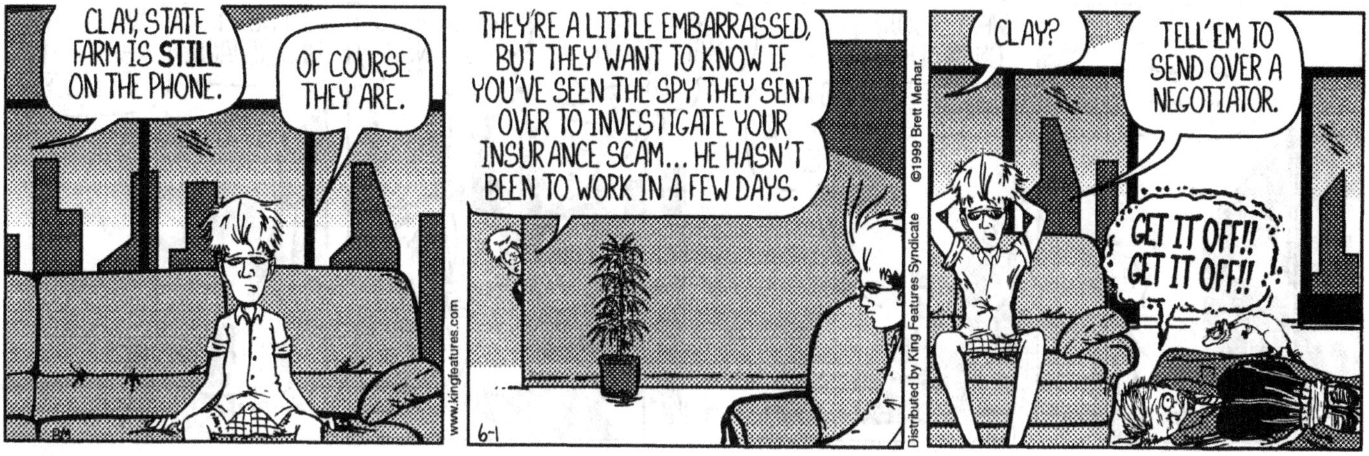
CLAY, STATE FARM IS **STILL** ON THE PHONE.
OF COURSE THEY ARE.
www.kingfeatures.com
THEY'RE A LITTLE EMBARRASSED, BUT THEY WANT TO KNOW IF YOU'VE SEEN THE SPY THEY SENT OVER TO INVESTIGATE YOUR INSURANCE SCAM... HE HASN'T BEEN TO WORK IN A FEW DAYS.
6-1
©1999 Brett Merhar.
Distributed by King Features Syndicate
CLAY?
TELL'EM TO SEND OVER A NEGOTIATOR.
GET IT OFF!! GET IT OFF!!

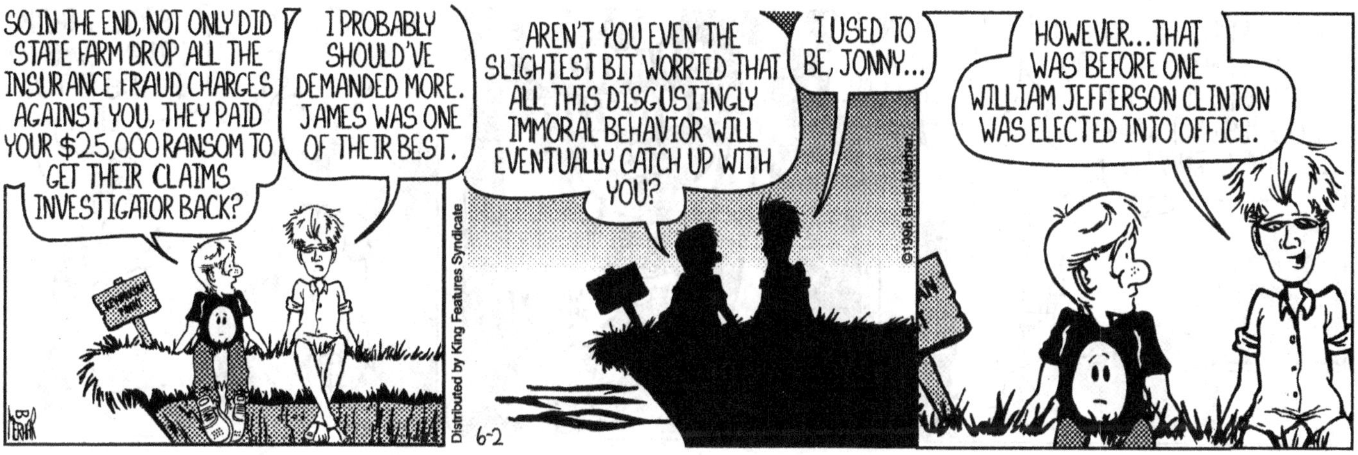
SO IN THE END, NOT ONLY DID STATE FARM DROP ALL THE INSURANCE FRAUD CHARGES AGAINST YOU, THEY PAID YOUR $25,000 RANSOM TO GET THEIR CLAIMS INVESTIGATOR BACK?
I PROBABLY SHOULD'VE DEMANDED MORE. JAMES WAS ONE OF THEIR BEST.
MERHAR
Distributed by King Features Syndicate
AREN'T YOU EVEN THE SLIGHTEST BIT WORRIED THAT ALL THIS DISGUSTINGLY IMMORAL BEHAVIOR WILL EVENTUALLY CATCH UP WITH YOU?
I USED TO BE, JONNY...
6-2
©1998 Brett Merhar.
HOWEVER...THAT WAS BEFORE ONE WILLIAM JEFFERSON CLINTON WAS ELECTED INTO OFFICE.

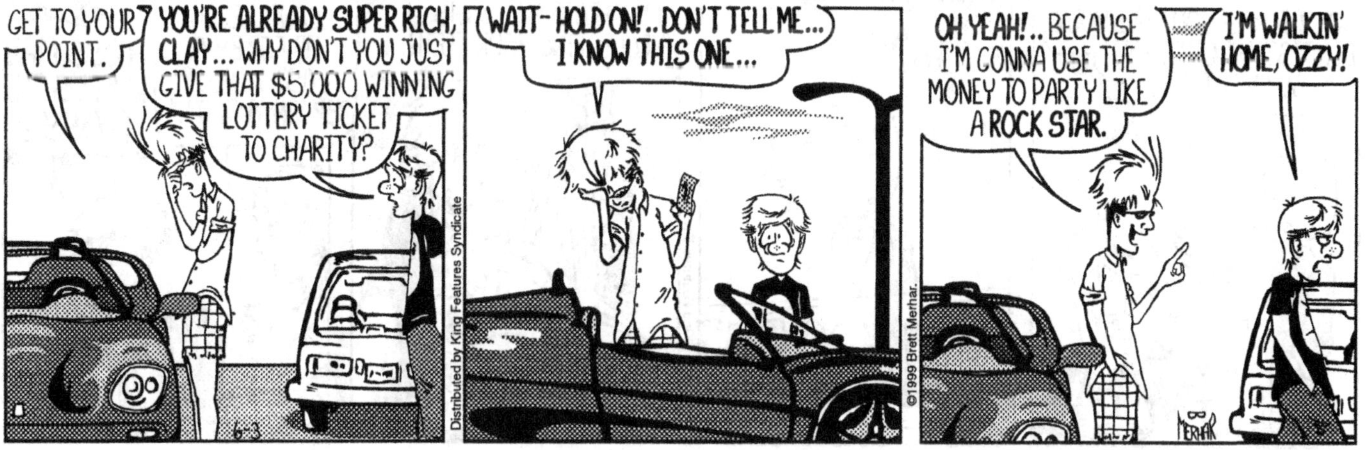
GET TO YOUR POINT.
YOU'RE ALREADY SUPER RICH, CLAY... WHY DON'T YOU JUST GIVE THAT $5,000 WINNING LOTTERY TICKET TO CHARITY?
6-3
Distributed by King Features Syndicate
WAIT- HOLD ON!.. DON'T TELL ME... I KNOW THIS ONE...
©1999 Brett Merhar.
OH YEAH!.. BECAUSE I'M GONNA USE THE MONEY TO PARTY LIKE A **ROCK STAR.**
I'M WALKIN' HOME, OZZY!
MERHAR

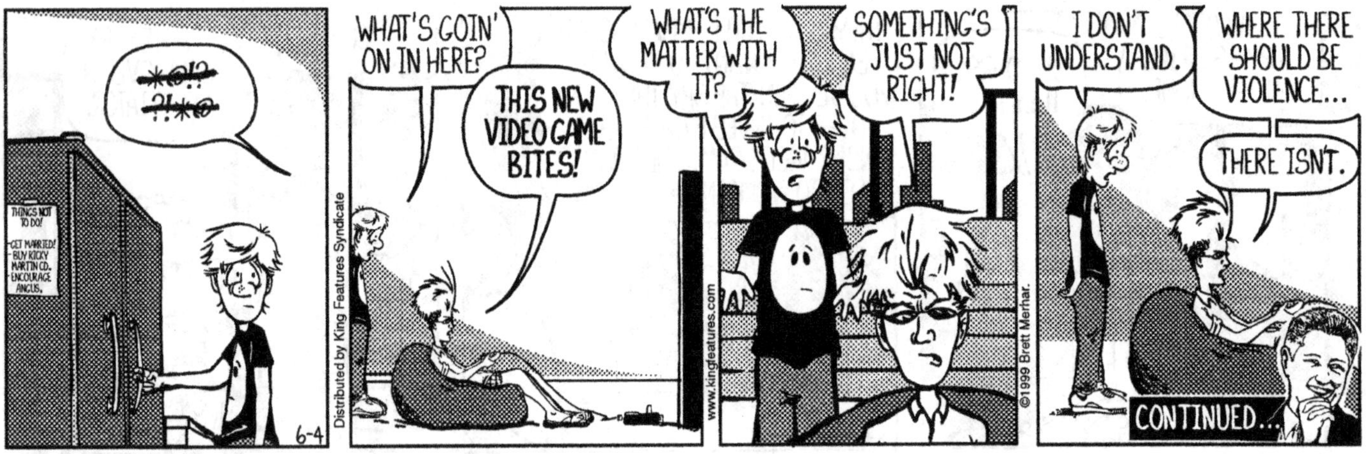
THINGS NOT TO DO! -GET MARRIED! -BUY RICKY MARTIN CD. -ENCOURAGE ANGUS.
6-4
WHAT'S GOIN' ON IN HERE?
THIS NEW VIDEO GAME BITES!
Distributed by King Features Syndicate
WHAT'S THE MATTER WITH IT?
SOMETHING'S JUST NOT RIGHT!
www.kingfeatures.com
I DON'T UNDERSTAND.
WHERE THERE SHOULD BE VIOLENCE...
THERE ISN'T.
©1999 Brett Merhar.
CONTINUED...

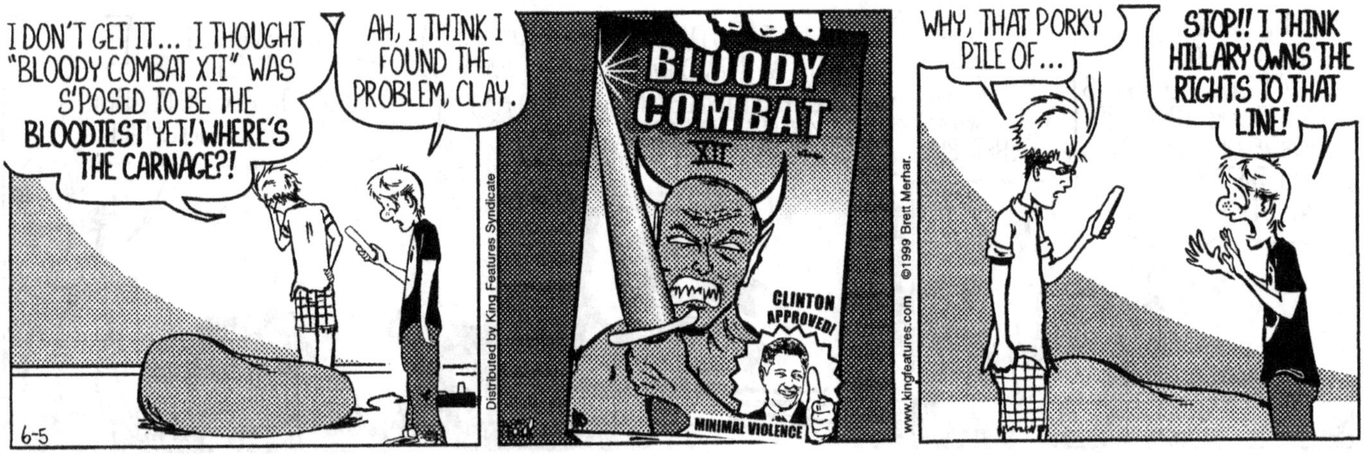
I DON'T GET IT... I THOUGHT "BLOODY COMBAT XII" WAS S'POSED TO BE THE BLOODIEST YET! WHERE'S THE CARNAGE?!
AH, I THINK I FOUND THE PROBLEM, CLAY.
6-5
Distributed by King Features Syndicate
BLOODY COMBAT XII
CLINTON APPROVED!
MINIMAL VIOLENCE
©1999 Brett Merhar.
www.kingfeatures.com
WHY, THAT PORKY PILE OF...
STOP!! I THINK HILLARY OWNS THE RIGHTS TO THAT LINE!

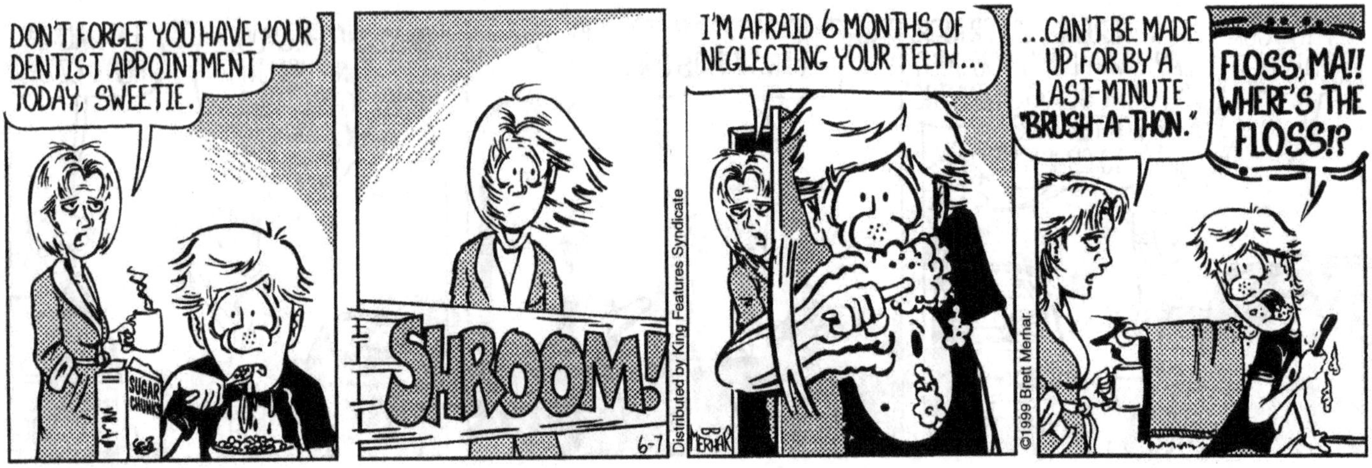
DON'T FORGET YOU HAVE YOUR DENTIST APPOINTMENT TODAY, SWEETIE.
SUGAR CHUNKS
SHROOM!
6-7
Distributed by King Features Syndicate
I'M AFRAID 6 MONTHS OF NEGLECTING YOUR TEETH...
MERHAR
©1999 Brett Merhar.
...CAN'T BE MADE UP FOR BY A LAST-MINUTE "BRUSH-A-THON."
FLOSS, MA!! WHERE'S THE FLOSS!?

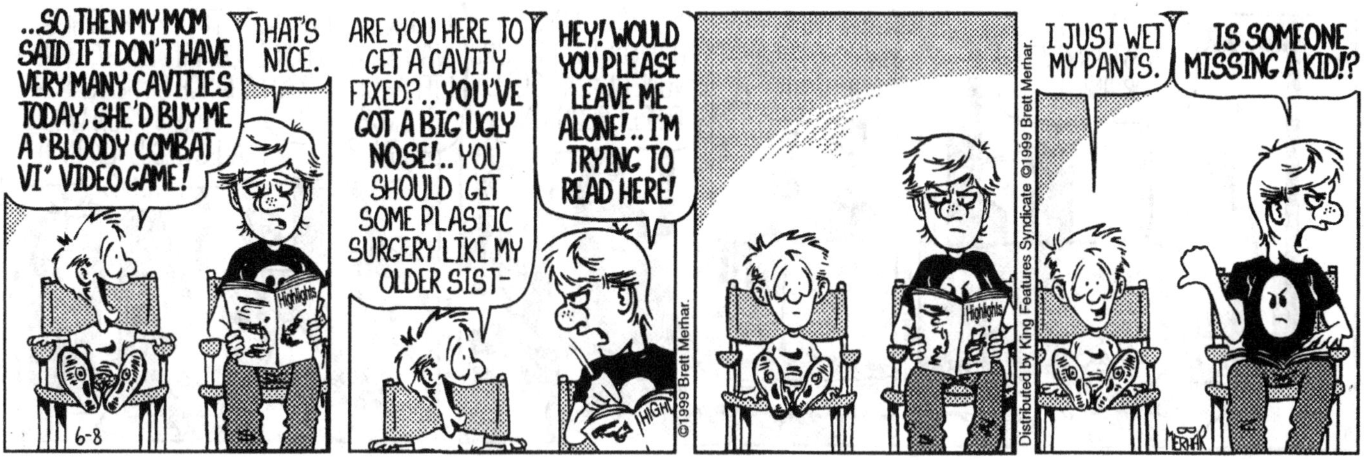
...SO THEN MY MOM SAID IF I DON'T HAVE VERY MANY CAVITIES TODAY, SHE'D BUY ME A "BLOODY COMBAT VI" VIDEO GAME!
THAT'S NICE.
ARE YOU HERE TO GET A CAVITY FIXED?.. YOU'VE GOT A BIG UGLY NOSE!.. YOU SHOULD GET SOME PLASTIC SURGERY LIKE MY OLDER SIST-
HEY! WOULD YOU PLEASE LEAVE ME ALONE!.. I'M TRYING TO READ HERE!
I JUST WET MY PANTS.
IS SOMEONE MISSING A KID!?
6-8
©1999 Brett Merhar.
Distributed by King Features Syndicate ©1999 Brett Merhar.
MERHAR

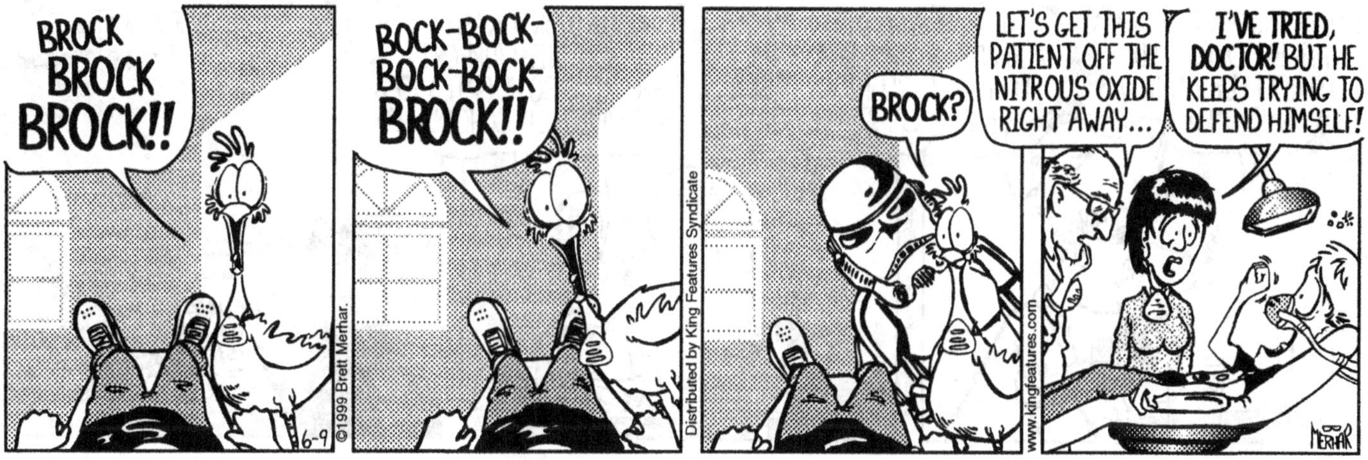
BROCK BROCK BROCK!!
BOCK-BOCK-BOCK-BOCK-BROCK!!
BROCK?
LET'S GET THIS PATIENT OFF THE NITROUS OXIDE RIGHT AWAY...
I'VE TRIED, DOCTOR! BUT HE KEEPS TRYING TO DEFEND HIMSELF!
6-9
©1999 Brett Merhar.
Distributed by King Features Syndicate
www.kingfeatures.com
MERHAR

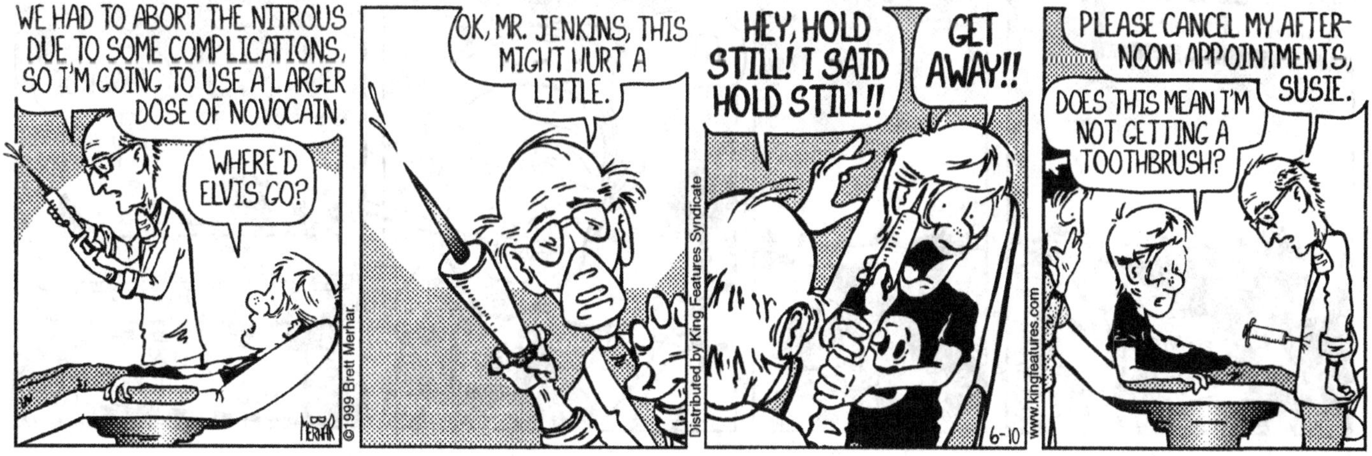
WE HAD TO ABORT THE NITROUS DUE TO SOME COMPLICATIONS, SO I'M GOING TO USE A LARGER DOSE OF NOVOCAIN.
WHERE'D ELVIS GO?
OK, MR. JENKINS, THIS MIGHT HURT A LITTLE.
HEY, HOLD STILL! I SAID HOLD STILL!!
GET AWAY!!
PLEASE CANCEL MY AFTERNOON APPOINTMENTS, SUSIE.
DOES THIS MEAN I'M NOT GETTING A TOOTHBRUSH?
6-10
©1999 Brett Merhar.
Distributed by King Features Syndicate
www.kingfeatures.com
MERHAR

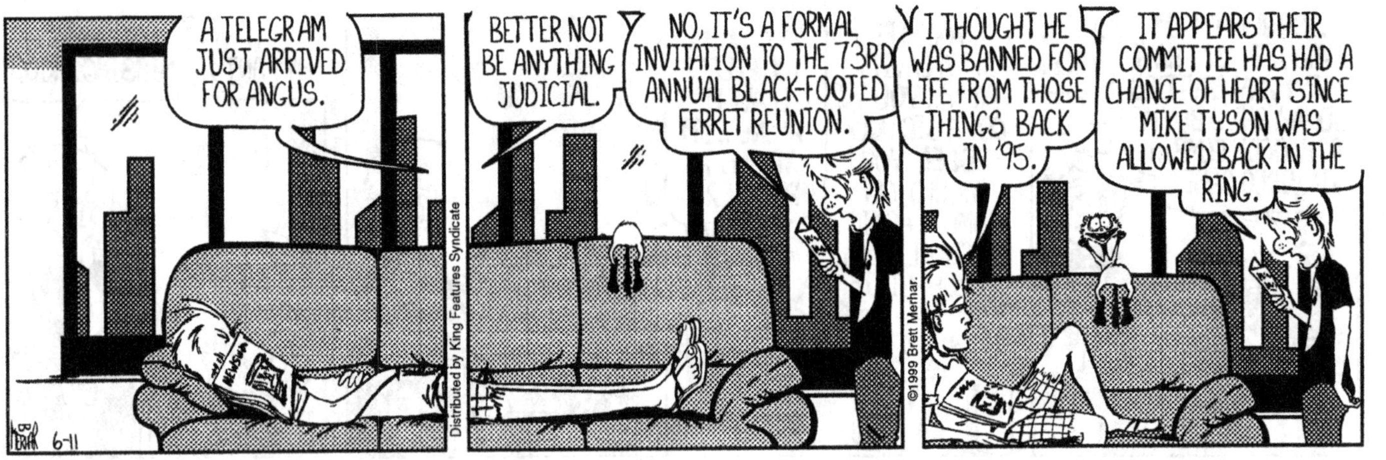
A TELEGRAM JUST ARRIVED FOR ANGUS.
BETTER NOT BE ANYTHING JUDICIAL.
NO, IT'S A FORMAL INVITATION TO THE 73RD ANNUAL BLACK-FOOTED FERRET REUNION.
I THOUGHT HE WAS BANNED FOR LIFE FROM THOSE THINGS BACK IN '95.
IT APPEARS THEIR COMMITTEE HAS HAD A CHANGE OF HEART SINCE MIKE TYSON WAS ALLOWED BACK IN THE RING.
6-11
Distributed by King Features Syndicate
©1999 Brett Merhar.

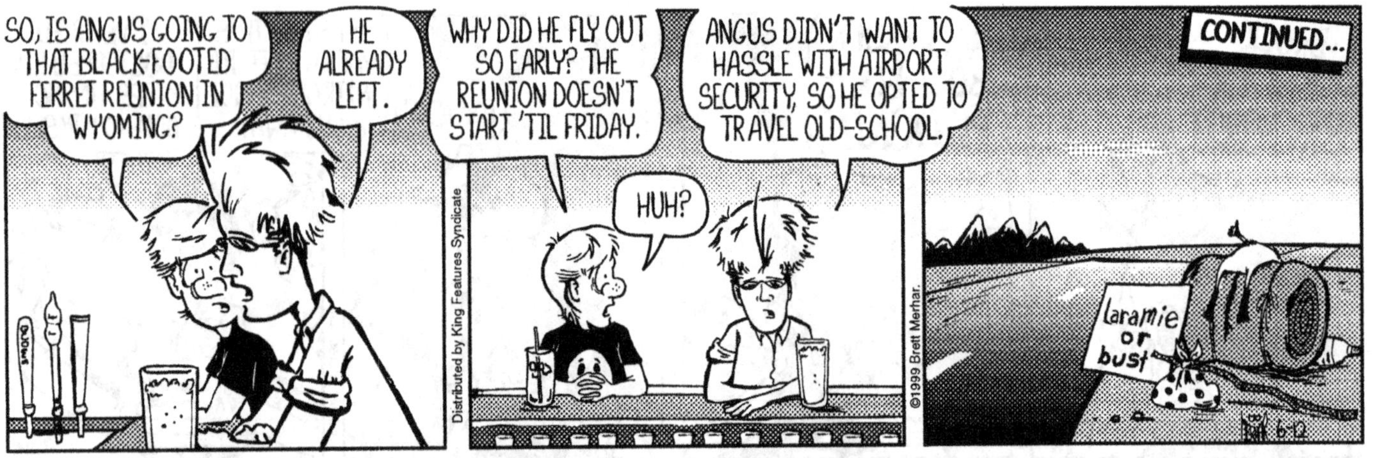
SO, IS ANGUS GOING TO THAT BLACK-FOOTED FERRET REUNION IN WYOMING?
HE ALREADY LEFT.
WHY DID HE FLY OUT SO EARLY? THE REUNION DOESN'T START 'TIL FRIDAY.
HUH?
ANGUS DIDN'T WANT TO HASSLE WITH AIRPORT SECURITY, SO HE OPTED TO TRAVEL OLD-SCHOOL.
CONTINUED...
laramie or bust
6-12
Distributed by King Features Syndicate
©1999 Brett Merhar.

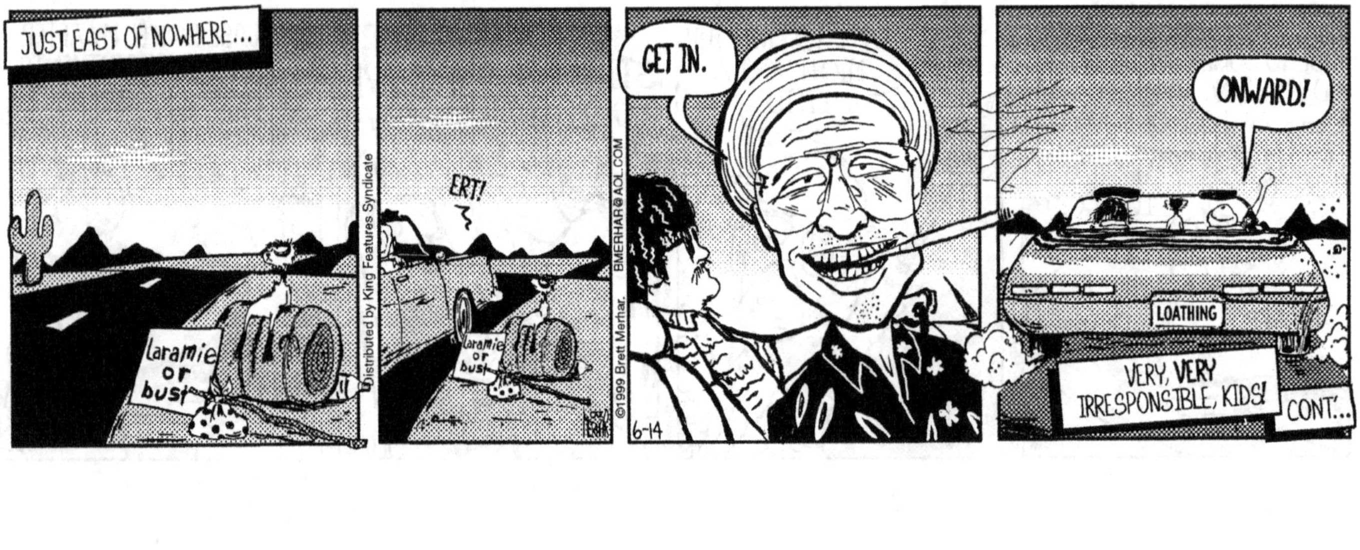
JUST EAST OF NOWHERE...
laramie or bust
ERT!
GET IN.
ONWARD!
LOATHING
VERY, VERY IRRESPONSIBLE, KIDS!
CONT'...
6-14
Distributed by King Features Syndicate
©1999 Brett Merhar.
BMERHAR@AOL.COM

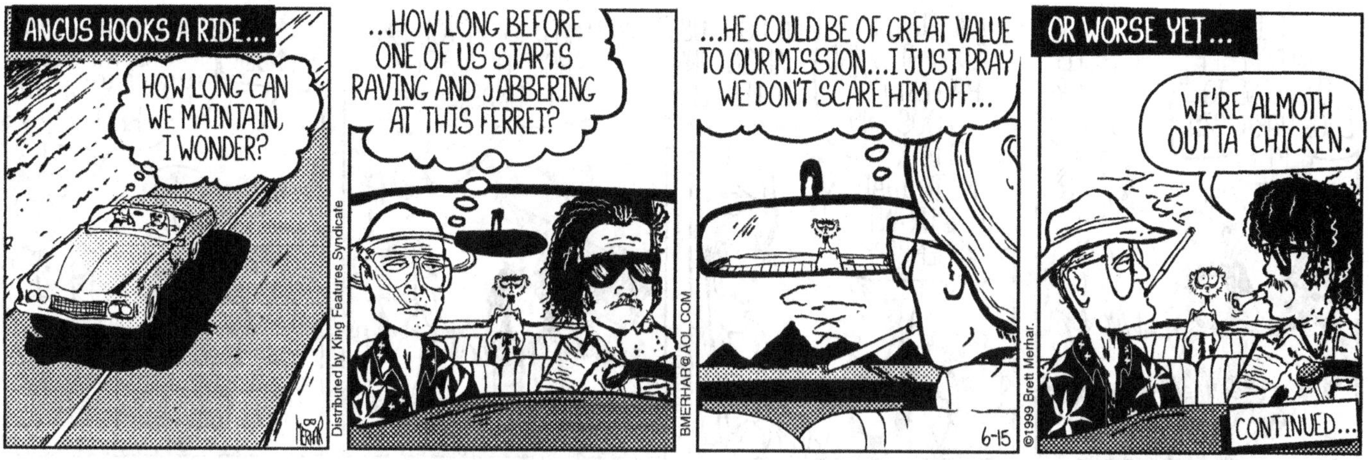
ANGUS HOOKS A RIDE...
HOW LONG CAN WE MAINTAIN, I WONDER?
...HOW LONG BEFORE ONE OF US STARTS RAVING AND JABBERING AT THIS FERRET?
Distributed by King Features Syndicate
...HE COULD BE OF GREAT VALUE TO OUR MISSION...I JUST PRAY WE DON'T SCARE HIM OFF...
BMERHAR@AOL.COM
6-15
OR WORSE YET...
WE'RE ALMOTH OUTTA CHICKEN.
©1999 Brett Merhar.
CONTINUED...

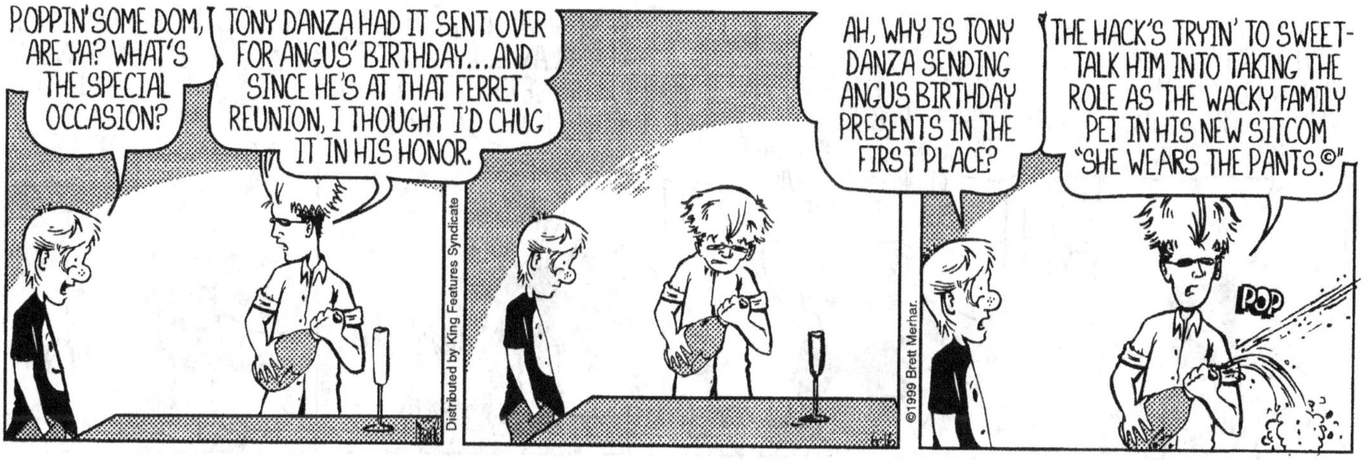
POPPIN' SOME DOM, ARE YA? WHAT'S THE SPECIAL OCCASION?
TONY DANZA HAD IT SENT OVER FOR ANGUS' BIRTHDAY...AND SINCE HE'S AT THAT FERRET REUNION, I THOUGHT I'D CHUG IT IN HIS HONOR.
Distributed by King Features Syndicate
AH, WHY IS TONY DANZA SENDING ANGUS BIRTHDAY PRESENTS IN THE FIRST PLACE?
©1999 Brett Merhar.
THE HACK'S TRYIN' TO SWEET-TALK HIM INTO TAKING THE ROLE AS THE WACKY FAMILY PET IN HIS NEW SITCOM "SHE WEARS THE PANTS.©"
POP

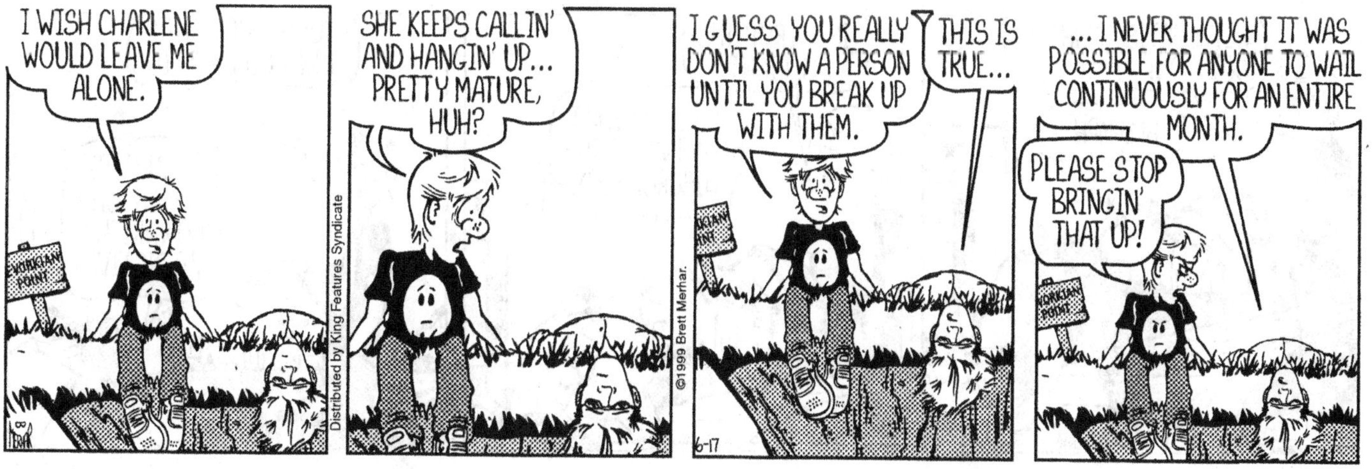
I WISH CHARLENE WOULD LEAVE ME ALONE.
Distributed by King Features Syndicate
SHE KEEPS CALLIN' AND HANGIN' UP... PRETTY MATURE, HUH?
©1999 Brett Merhar.
I GUESS YOU REALLY DON'T KNOW A PERSON UNTIL YOU BREAK UP WITH THEM.
THIS IS TRUE...
6-17
... I NEVER THOUGHT IT WAS POSSIBLE FOR ANYONE TO WAIL CONTINUOUSLY FOR AN ENTIRE MONTH.
PLEASE STOP BRINGIN' THAT UP!

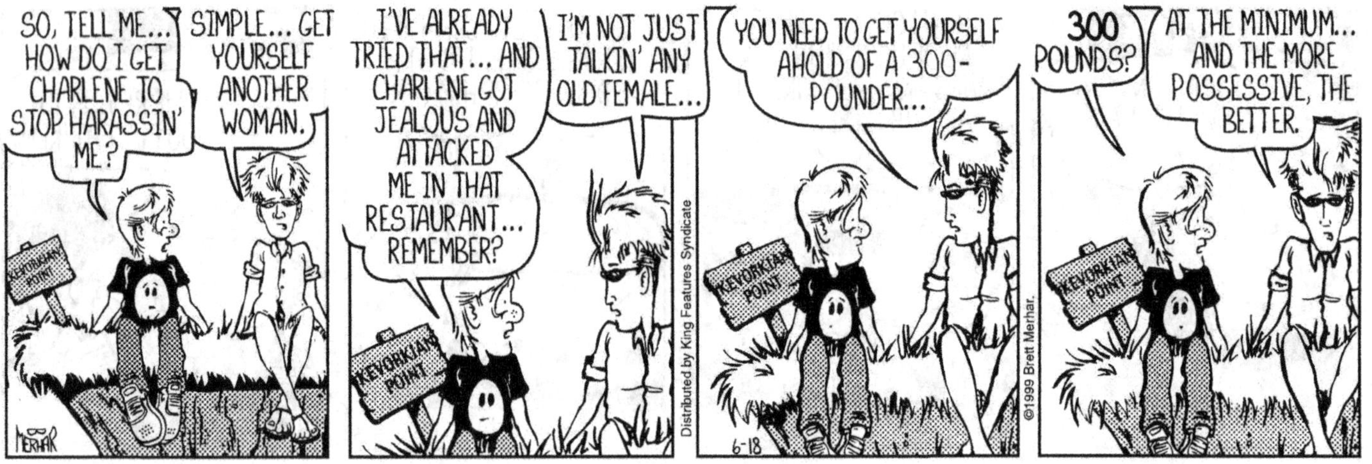
SO, TELL ME... HOW DO I GET CHARLENE TO STOP HARASSIN' ME?
SIMPLE... GET YOURSELF ANOTHER WOMAN.
KEVORKIAN POINT
MERHAR
I'VE ALREADY TRIED THAT... AND CHARLENE GOT JEALOUS AND ATTACKED ME IN THAT RESTAURANT... REMEMBER?
I'M NOT JUST TALKIN' ANY OLD FEMALE...
KEVORKIAN POINT
Distributed by King Features Syndicate
YOU NEED TO GET YOURSELF AHOLD OF A 300-POUNDER...
KEVORKIAN POINT
6-18
©1999 Brett Merhar.
300 POUNDS?
AT THE MINIMUM... AND THE MORE POSSESSIVE, THE BETTER.
KEVORKIAN POINT

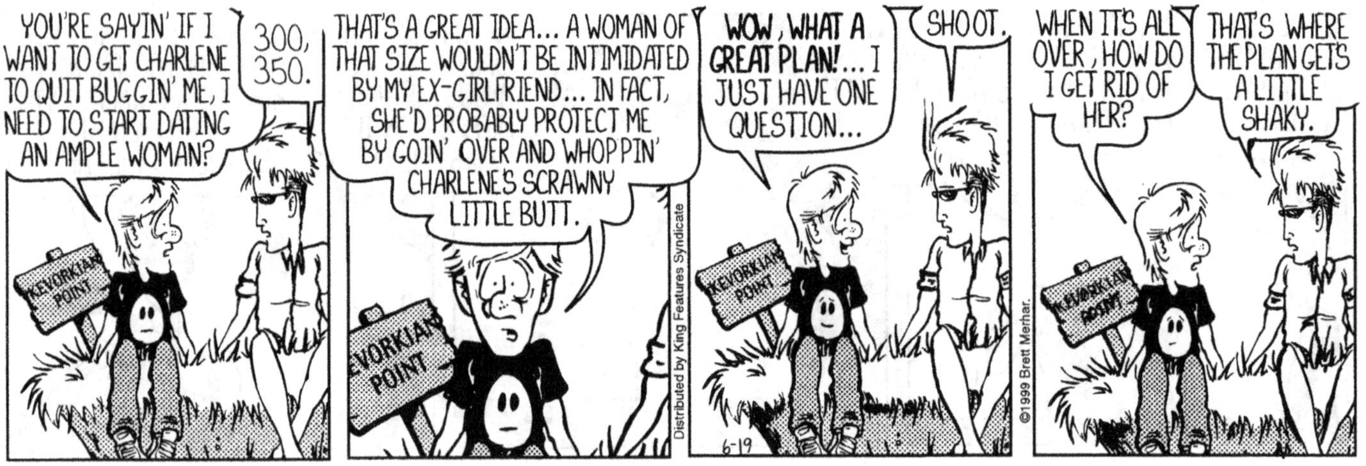
YOU'RE SAYIN' IF I WANT TO GET CHARLENE TO QUIT BUGGIN' ME, I NEED TO START DATING AN AMPLE WOMAN?
300, 350.
KEVORKIAN POINT
THAT'S A GREAT IDEA... A WOMAN OF THAT SIZE WOULDN'T BE INTIMIDATED BY MY EX-GIRLFRIEND... IN FACT, SHE'D PROBABLY PROTECT ME BY GOIN' OVER AND WHOPPIN' CHARLENE'S SCRAWNY LITTLE BUTT.
KEVORKIAN POINT
Distributed by King Features Syndicate
WOW, WHAT A GREAT PLAN!... I JUST HAVE ONE QUESTION...
SHOOT.
KEVORKIAN POINT
6-19
©1999 Brett Merhar.
WHEN IT'S ALL OVER, HOW DO I GET RID OF HER?
THAT'S WHERE THE PLAN GETS A LITTLE SHAKY.

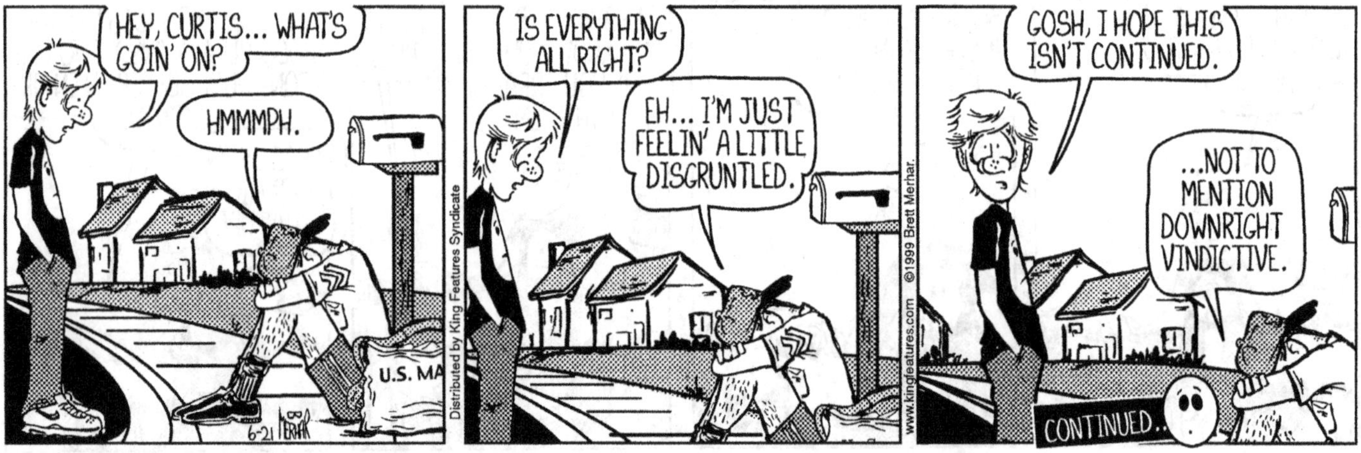
HEY, CURTIS... WHAT'S GOIN' ON?
HMMMPH.
U.S. MA
6-21 MERHAR
Distributed by King Features Syndicate
IS EVERYTHING ALL RIGHT?
EH... I'M JUST FEELIN' A LITTLE DISGRUNTLED.
©1999 Brett Merhar.
www.kingfeatures.com
GOSH, I HOPE THIS ISN'T CONTINUED.
...NOT TO MENTION DOWNRIGHT VINDICTIVE.
CONTINUED...

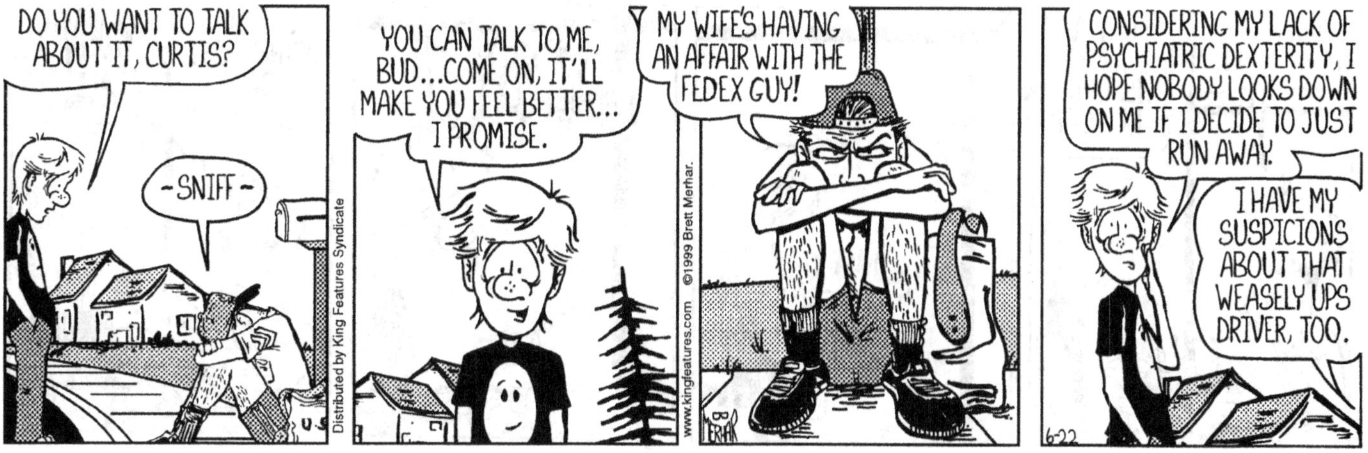
DO YOU WANT TO TALK ABOUT IT, CURTIS?
-SNIFF-
Distributed by King Features Syndicate
YOU CAN TALK TO ME, BUD...COME ON, IT'LL MAKE YOU FEEL BETTER... I PROMISE.
www.kingfeatures.com ©1999 Brett Merhar.
MY WIFE'S HAVING AN AFFAIR WITH THE FEDEX GUY!
CONSIDERING MY LACK OF PSYCHIATRIC DEXTERITY, I HOPE NOBODY LOOKS DOWN ON ME IF I DECIDE TO JUST RUN AWAY.
I HAVE MY SUSPICIONS ABOUT THAT WEASELY UPS DRIVER, TOO.
6-22

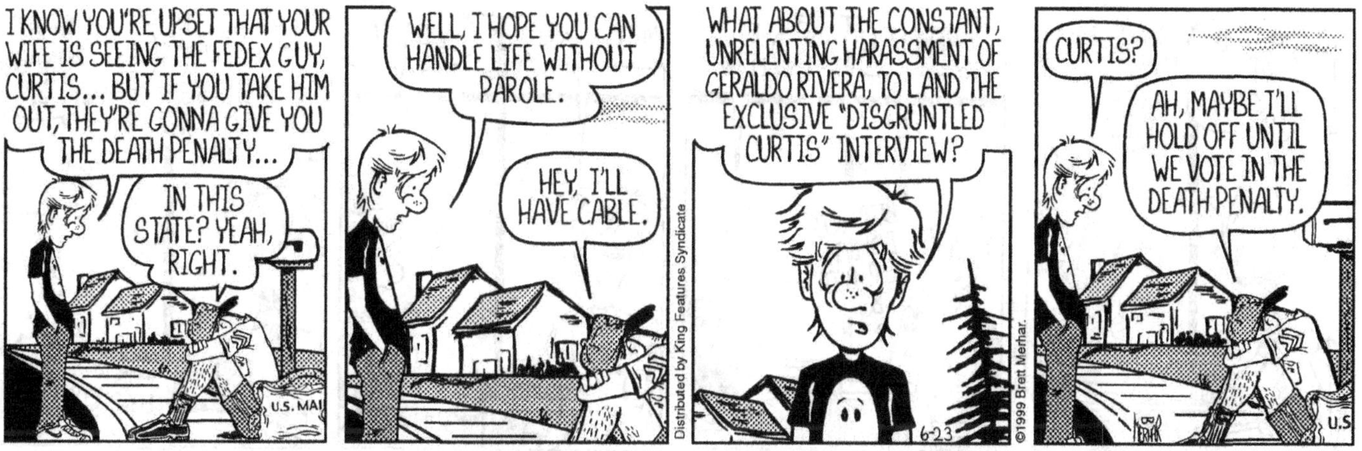
I KNOW YOU'RE UPSET THAT YOUR WIFE IS SEEING THE FEDEX GUY, CURTIS... BUT IF YOU TAKE HIM OUT, THEY'RE GONNA GIVE YOU THE DEATH PENALTY...
IN THIS STATE? YEAH, RIGHT.
WELL, I HOPE YOU CAN HANDLE LIFE WITHOUT PAROLE.
HEY, I'LL HAVE CABLE.
Distributed by King Features Syndicate
WHAT ABOUT THE CONSTANT, UNRELENTING HARASSMENT OF GERALDO RIVERA, TO LAND THE EXCLUSIVE "DISGRUNTLED CURTIS" INTERVIEW?
6-23
©1999 Brett Merhar.
CURTIS?
AH, MAYBE I'LL HOLD OFF UNTIL WE VOTE IN THE DEATH PENALTY.

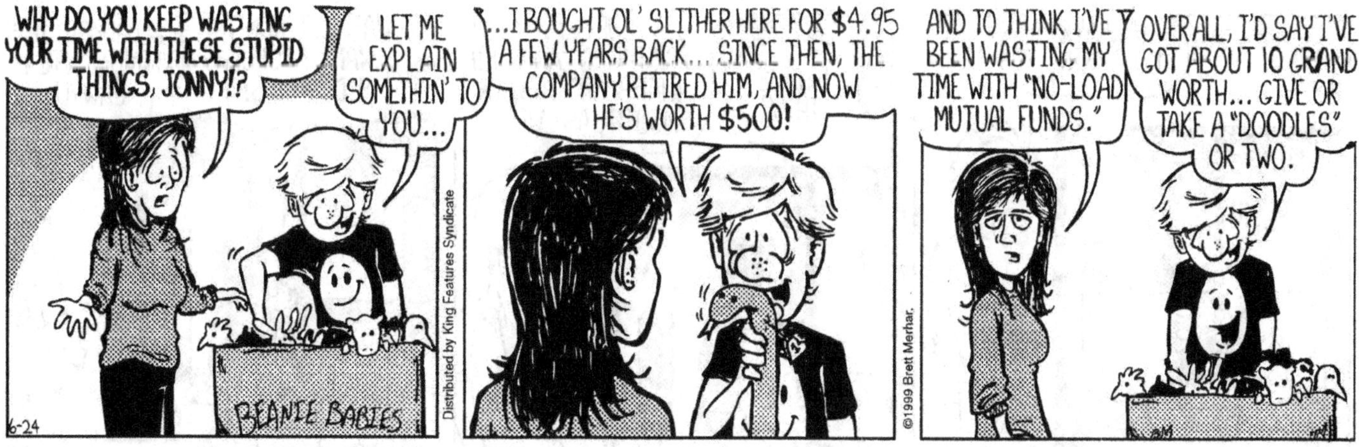
WHY DO YOU KEEP WASTING YOUR TIME WITH THESE STUPID THINGS, JONNY!?
LET ME EXPLAIN SOMETHIN' TO YOU...
BEANIE BABIES
6-24
Distributed by King Features Syndicate
...I BOUGHT OL' SLITHER HERE FOR $4.95 A FEW YEARS BACK... SINCE THEN, THE COMPANY RETIRED HIM, AND NOW HE'S WORTH $500!
©1999 Brett Merhar.
AND TO THINK I'VE BEEN WASTING MY TIME WITH "NO-LOAD MUTUAL FUNDS."
OVERALL, I'D SAY I'VE GOT ABOUT 10 GRAND WORTH... GIVE OR TAKE A "DOODLES" OR TWO.

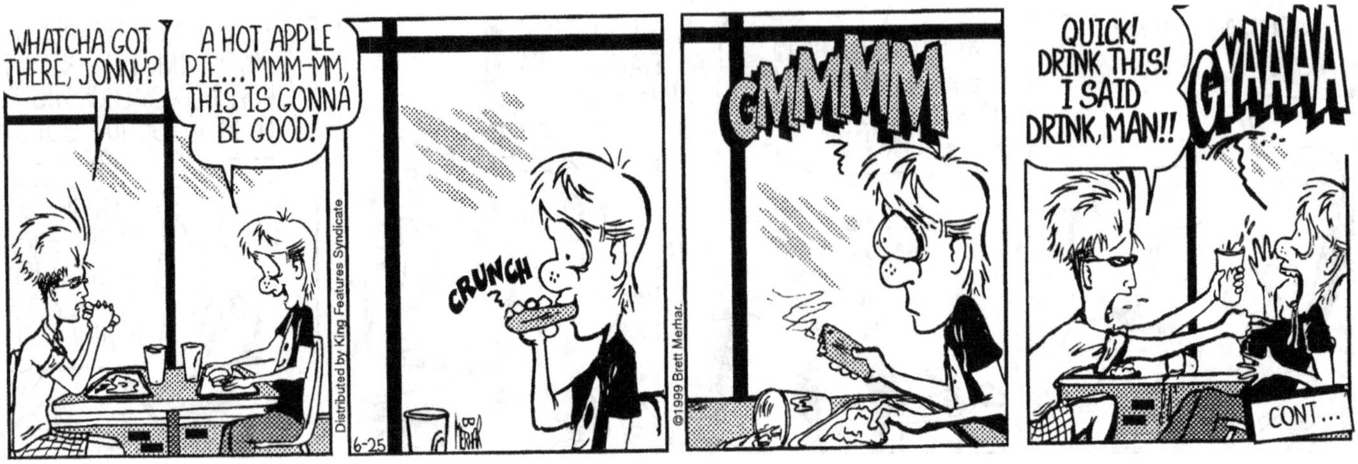
WHATCHA GOT THERE, JONNY?
A HOT APPLE PIE... MMM-MM, THIS IS GONNA BE GOOD!
Distributed by King Features Syndicate
6-25
CRUNCH
©1999 Brett Merhar.
CMMMMM
QUICK! DRINK THIS! I SAID DRINK, MAN!!
GYAAAA
CONT...

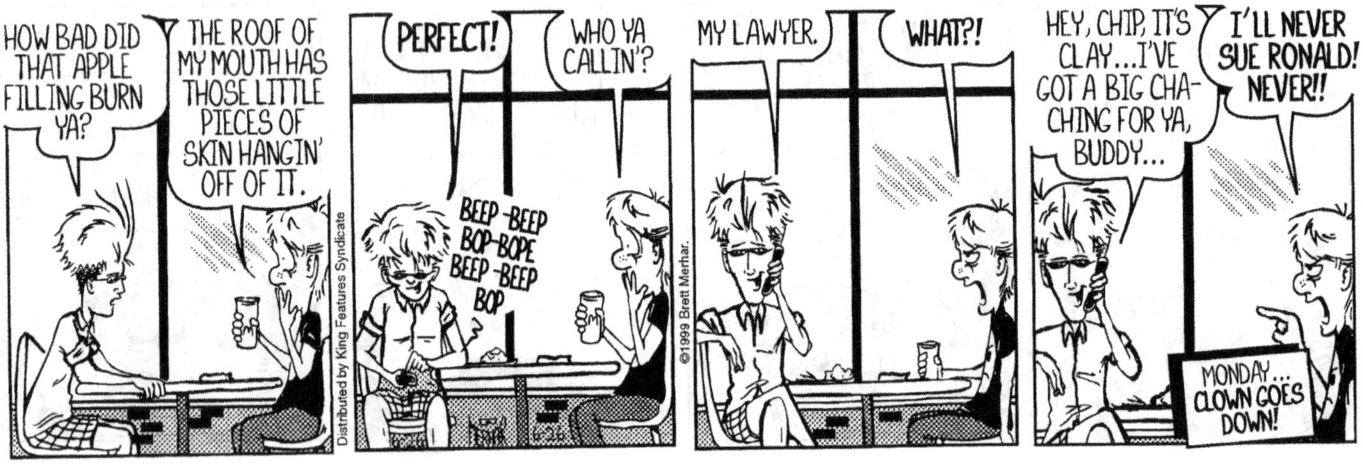
HOW BAD DID THAT APPLE FILLING BURN YA?
THE ROOF OF MY MOUTH HAS THOSE LITTLE PIECES OF SKIN HANGIN' OFF OF IT.
Distributed by King Features Syndicate
PERFECT!
WHO YA CALLIN'?
BEEP-BEEP BOP-BOPE BEEP-BEEP BOP
©1999 Brett Merhar.
MY LAWYER.
WHAT?!
HEY, CHIP, IT'S CLAY...I'VE GOT A BIG CHA-CHING FOR YA, BUDDY...
I'LL NEVER SUE RONALD! NEVER!!
MONDAY... CLOWN GOES DOWN!

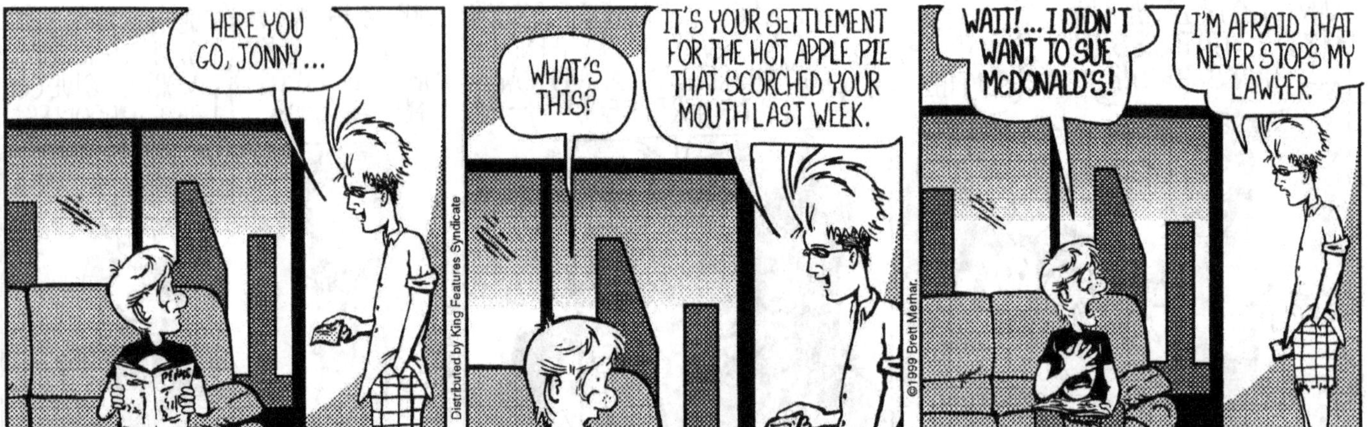
HERE YOU GO, JONNY...
Distributed by King Features Syndicate
WHAT'S THIS?
IT'S YOUR SETTLEMENT FOR THE HOT APPLE PIE THAT SCORCHED YOUR MOUTH LAST WEEK.
©1999 Brett Merhar.
WAIT!...I DIDN'T WANT TO SUE McDONALD'S!
I'M AFRAID THAT NEVER STOPS MY LAWYER.

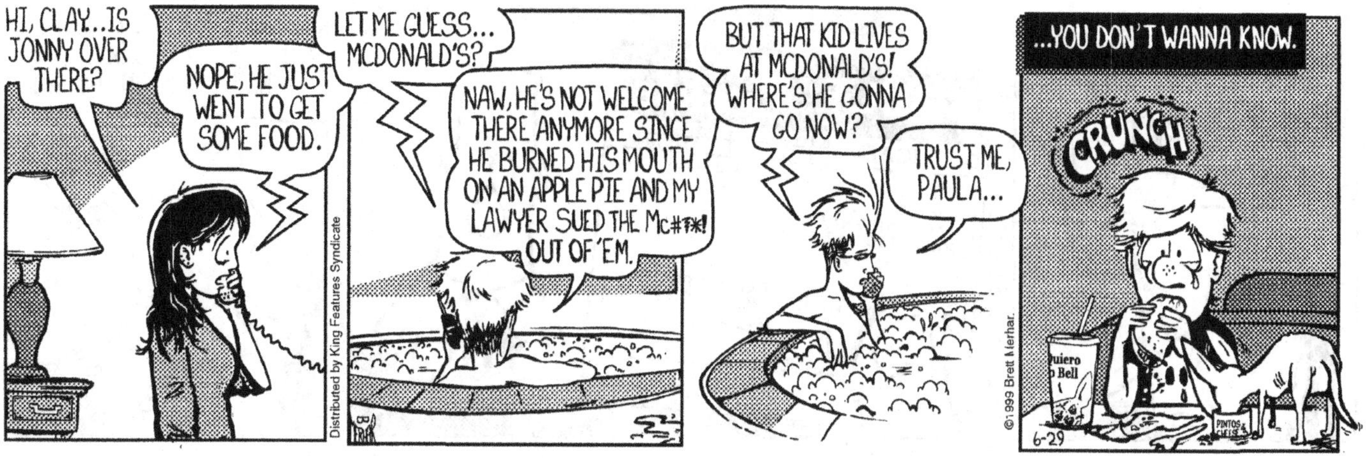
HI, CLAY..IS JONNY OVER THERE?
NOPE, HE JUST WENT TO GET SOME FOOD.
Distributed by King Features Syndicate
LET ME GUESS... MCDONALD'S?
NAW, HE'S NOT WELCOME THERE ANYMORE SINCE HE BURNED HIS MOUTH ON AN APPLE PIE AND MY LAWYER SUED THE Mc#*! OUT OF 'EM.
BUT THAT KID LIVES AT MCDONALD'S! WHERE'S HE GONNA GO NOW?
TRUST ME, PAULA...
...YOU DON'T WANNA KNOW.
CRUNCH
©1999 Brett Merhar.
6-29

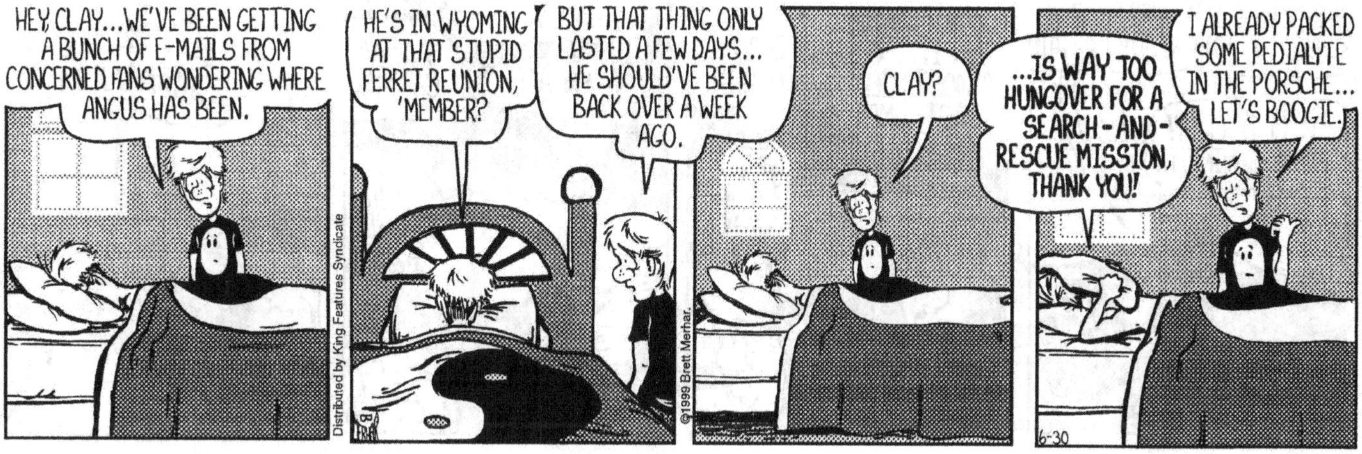
HEY, CLAY...WE'VE BEEN GETTING A BUNCH OF E-MAILS FROM CONCERNED FANS WONDERING WHERE ANGUS HAS BEEN.
Distributed by King Features Syndicate
HE'S IN WYOMING AT THAT STUPID FERRET REUNION, 'MEMBER?
BUT THAT THING ONLY LASTED A FEW DAYS... HE SHOULD'VE BEEN BACK OVER A WEEK AGO.
©1999 Brett Merhar.
CLAY?
...IS WAY TOO HUNGOVER FOR A SEARCH-AND-RESCUE MISSION, THANK YOU!
I ALREADY PACKED SOME PEDIALYTE IN THE PORSCHE... LET'S BOOGIE.
6-30

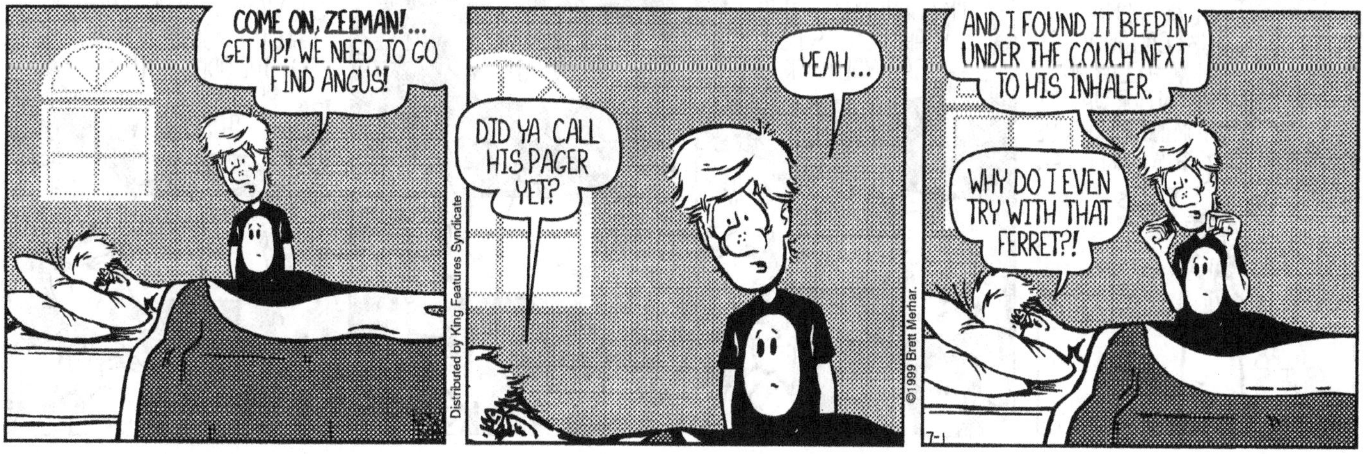
COME ON, ZEEMAN!... GET UP! WE NEED TO GO FIND ANGUS!
Distributed by King Features Syndicate
DID YA CALL HIS PAGER YET?
YEAH...
©1999 Brett Merhar.
AND I FOUND IT BEEPIN' UNDER THE COUCH NEXT TO HIS INHALER.
WHY DO I EVEN TRY WITH THAT FERRET?!
7-1

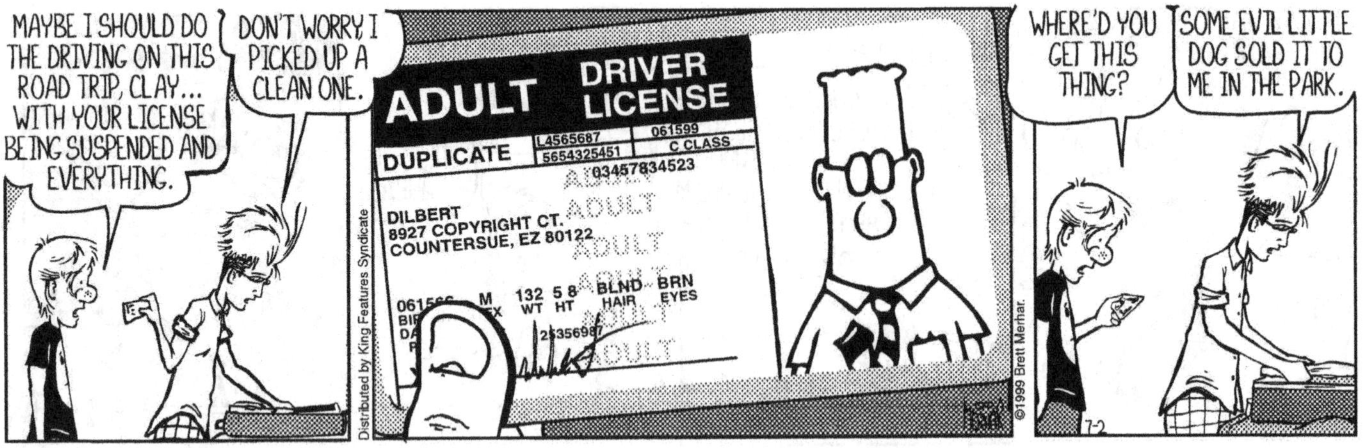
MAYBE I SHOULD DO THE DRIVING ON THIS ROAD TRIP, CLAY... WITH YOUR LICENSE BEING SUSPENDED AND EVERYTHING.
DON'T WORRY, I PICKED UP A CLEAN ONE.
Distributed by King Features Syndicate
ADULT DRIVER LICENSE
DUPLICATE
L4565687
5654325451
061599
C CLASS
03457834523
DILBERT
8927 COPYRIGHT CT.
COUNTERSUE, EZ 80122
M
132 WT
5 8 HT
BLND HAIR
BRN EYES
ADULT
©1999 Brett Merhar.
WHERE'D YOU GET THIS THING?
SOME EVIL LITTLE DOG SOLD IT TO ME IN THE PARK.
7-2

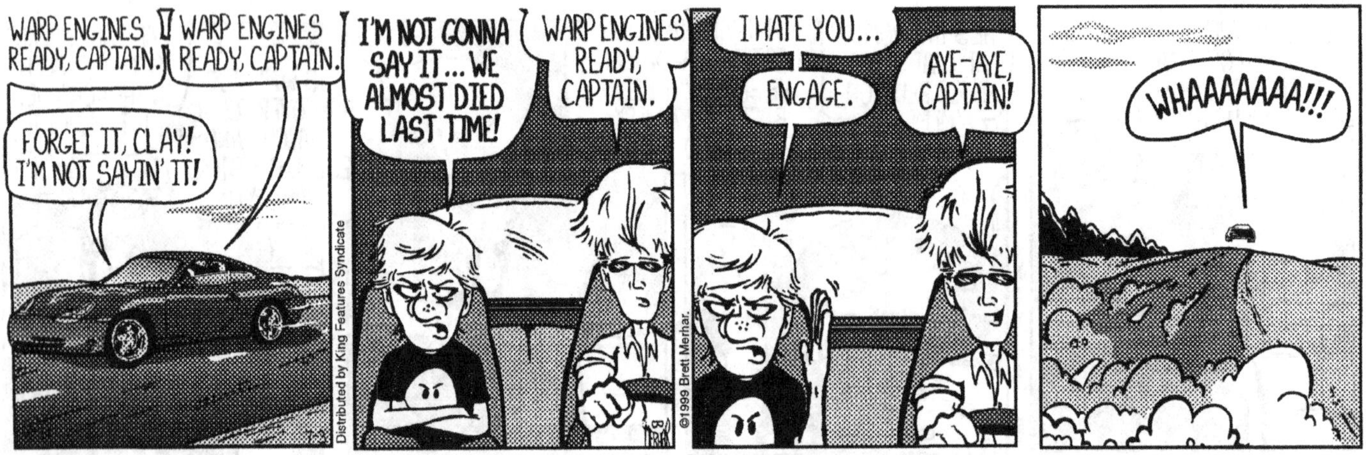
WARP ENGINES READY, CAPTAIN.
WARP ENGINES READY, CAPTAIN.
FORGET IT, CLAY! I'M NOT SAYIN' IT!
7-3
Distributed by King Features Syndicate
I'M NOT GONNA SAY IT... WE ALMOST DIED LAST TIME!
WARP ENGINES READY, CAPTAIN.
©1999 Brett Merhar.
I HATE YOU...
ENGAGE.
AYE-AYE, CAPTAIN!
WHAAAAAAA!!!

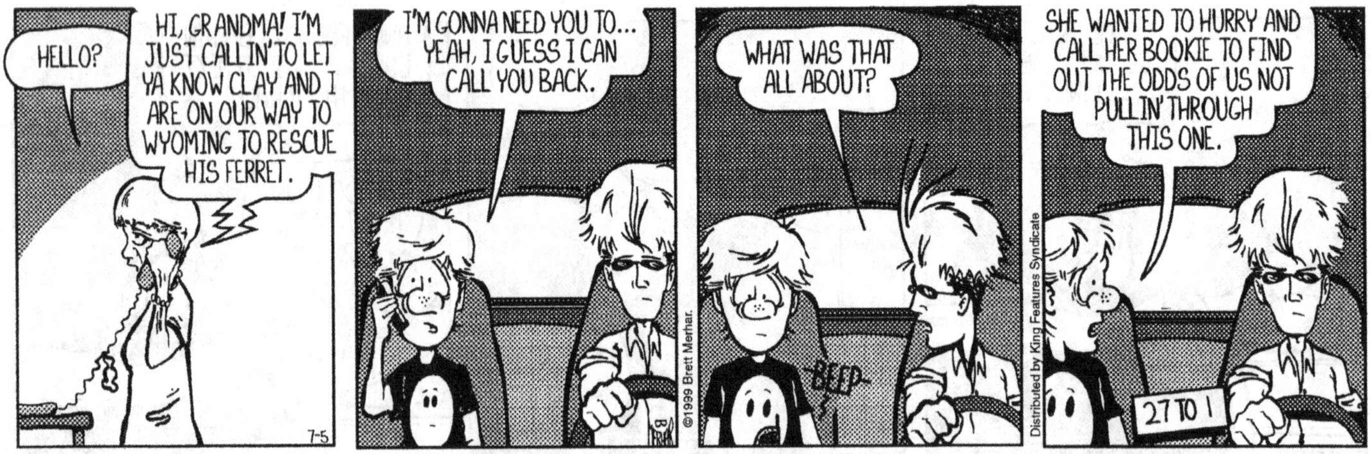
HELLO?
HI, GRANDMA! I'M JUST CALLIN' TO LET YA KNOW CLAY AND I ARE ON OUR WAY TO WYOMING TO RESCUE HIS FERRET.
7-5
I'M GONNA NEED YOU TO... YEAH, I GUESS I CAN CALL YOU BACK.
©1999 Brett Merhar.
WHAT WAS THAT ALL ABOUT?
BEEP
Distributed by King Features Syndicate
SHE WANTED TO HURRY AND CALL HER BOOKIE TO FIND OUT THE ODDS OF US NOT PULLIN' THROUGH THIS ONE.
27 TO 1

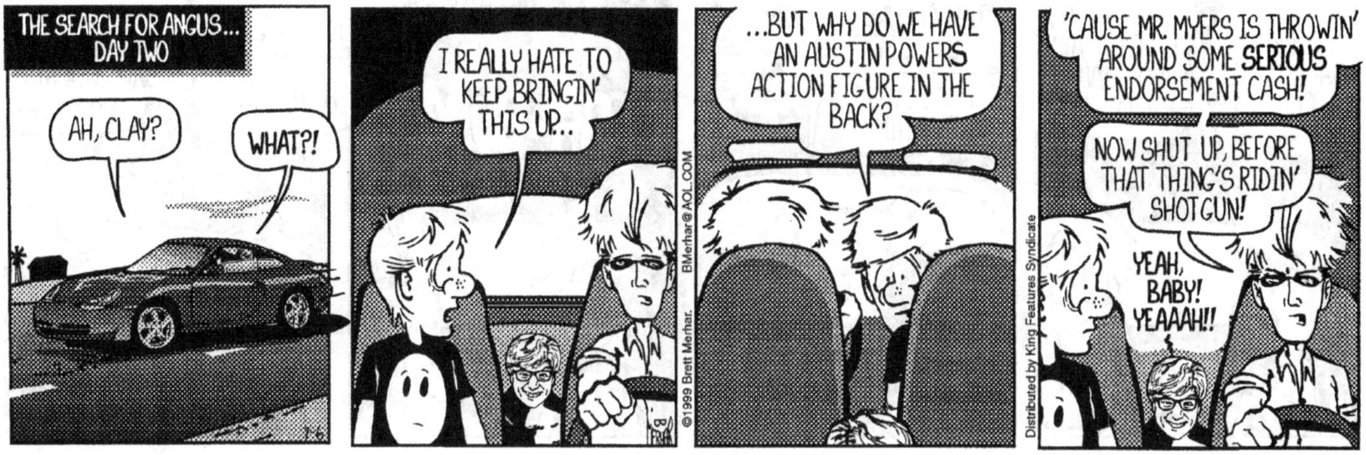
THE SEARCH FOR ANGUS... DAY TWO
AH, CLAY?
WHAT?!
I REALLY HATE TO KEEP BRINGIN' THIS UP..
BMerhar@AOL.COM
©1999 Brett Merhar
...BUT WHY DO WE HAVE AN AUSTIN POWERS ACTION FIGURE IN THE BACK?
Distributed by King Features Syndicate
'CAUSE MR. MYERS IS THROWIN' AROUND SOME SERIOUS ENDORSEMENT CASH!
NOW SHUT UP, BEFORE THAT THING'S RIDIN' SHOTGUN!
YEAH, BABY! YEAAAH!!

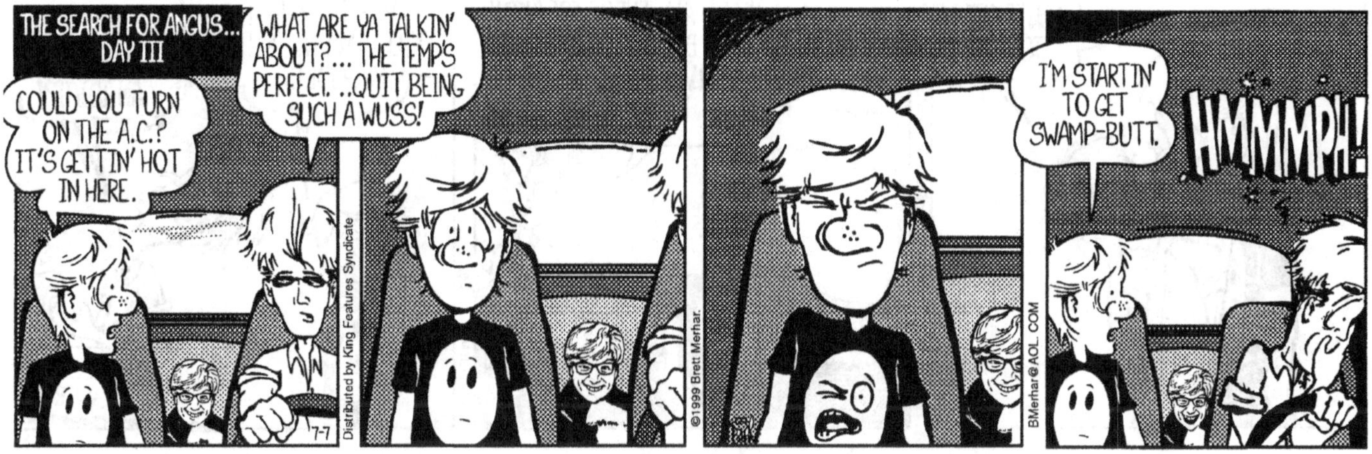
THE SEARCH FOR ANGUS... DAY III
COULD YOU TURN ON THE A.C.? IT'S GETTIN' HOT IN HERE.
WHAT ARE YA TALKIN' ABOUT?... THE TEMP'S PERFECT. ..QUIT BEING SUCH A WUSS!
7-7
Distributed by King Features Syndicate
©1999 Brett Merhar.
BMerhar@AOL.COM
I'M STARTIN' TO GET SWAMP-BUTT.
HMMMPH!

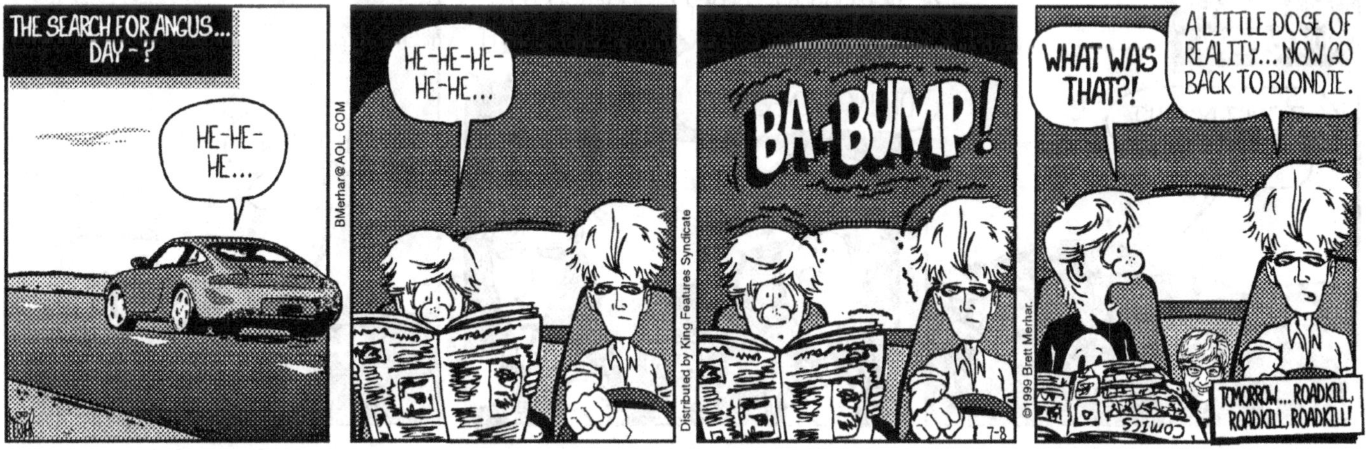
THE SEARCH FOR ANGUS... DAY -?
HE-HE-HE...
BMerhar@AOL.COM
HE-HE-HE-HE-HE...
Distributed by King Features Syndicate
BA-BUMP!
7-8
©1999 Brett Merhar.
WHAT WAS THAT?!
A LITTLE DOSE OF REALITY... NOW GO BACK TO BLONDIE.
COMICS
TOMORROW... ROADKILL, ROADKILL, ROADKILL!

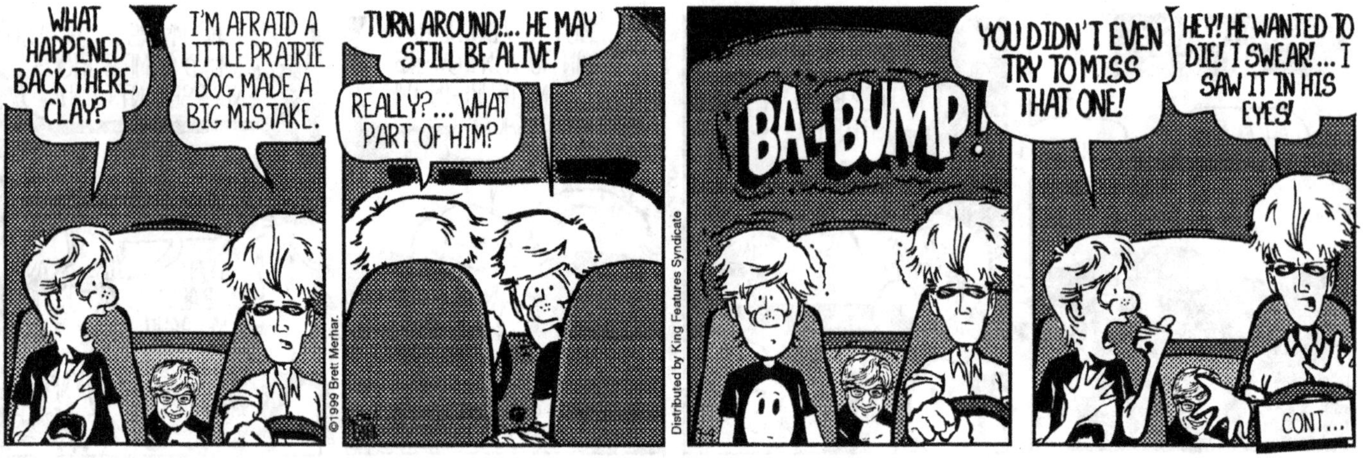
WHAT HAPPENED BACK THERE, CLAY?
I'M AFRAID A LITTLE PRAIRIE DOG MADE A BIG MISTAKE.
TURN AROUND!... HE MAY STILL BE ALIVE!
REALLY?... WHAT PART OF HIM?
BA-BUMP!
YOU DIDN'T EVEN TRY TO MISS THAT ONE!
HEY! HE WANTED TO DIE! I SWEAR!... I SAW IT IN HIS EYES!
CONT...
©1999 Brett Merhar.
Distributed by King Features Syndicate

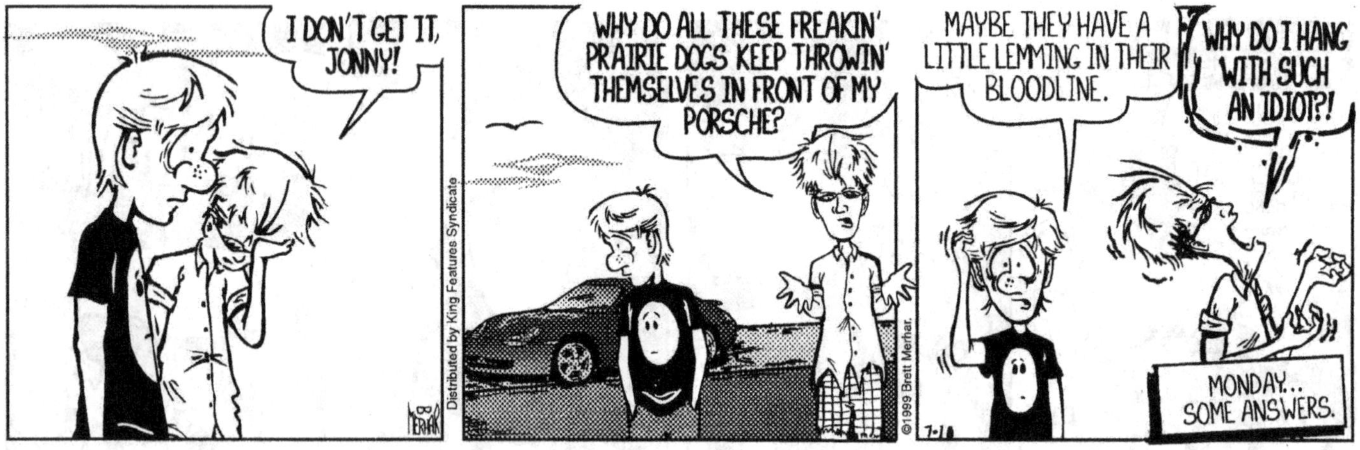
I DON'T GET IT, JONNY!
WHY DO ALL THESE FREAKIN' PRAIRIE DOGS KEEP THROWIN' THEMSELVES IN FRONT OF MY PORSCHE?
MAYBE THEY HAVE A LITTLE LEMMING IN THEIR BLOODLINE.
WHY DO I HANG WITH SUCH AN IDIOT?!
MONDAY... SOME ANSWERS.
Distributed by King Features Syndicate
©1999 Brett Merhar.

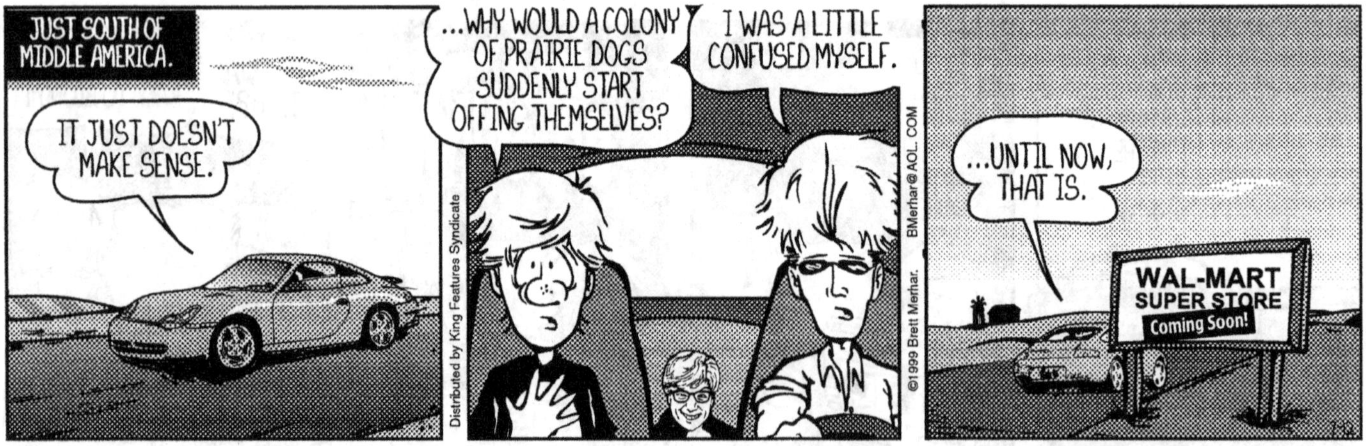
JUST SOUTH OF MIDDLE AMERICA.
IT JUST DOESN'T MAKE SENSE.
...WHY WOULD A COLONY OF PRAIRIE DOGS SUDDENLY START OFFING THEMSELVES?
I WAS A LITTLE CONFUSED MYSELF.
...UNTIL NOW, THAT IS.
WAL-MART SUPER STORE
Coming Soon!
Distributed by King Features Syndicate
©1999 Brett Merhar. BMerhar@AOL.COM

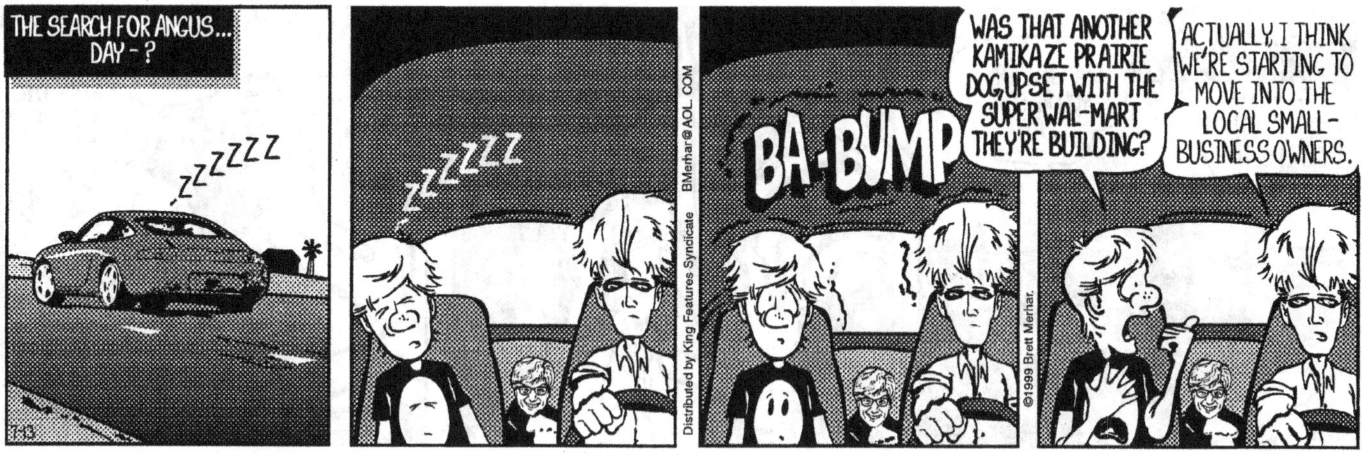
THE SEARCH FOR ANGUS... DAY - ?
ZZZZZZ
ZZZZZZZ
Distributed by King Features Syndicate
BMerhar@AOL.COM
BA-BUMP
©1999 Brett Merhar.
WAS THAT ANOTHER KAMIKAZE PRAIRIE DOG, UPSET WITH THE SUPER WAL-MART THEY'RE BUILDING?
ACTUALLY, I THINK WE'RE STARTING TO MOVE INTO THE LOCAL SMALL-BUSINESS OWNERS.

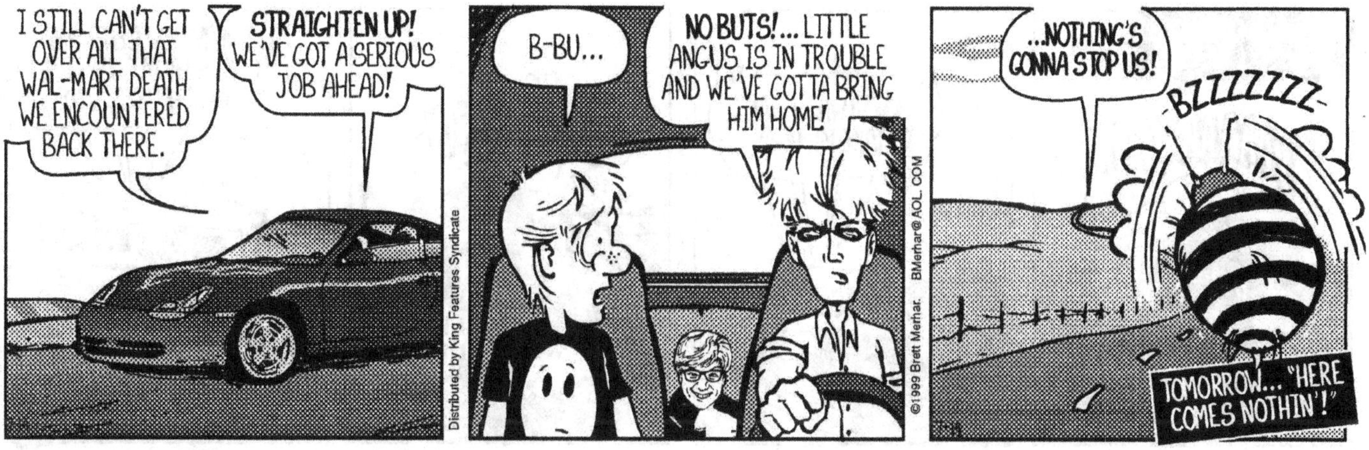
I STILL CAN'T GET OVER ALL THAT WAL-MART DEATH WE ENCOUNTERED BACK THERE.
STRAIGHTEN UP! WE'VE GOT A SERIOUS JOB AHEAD!
Distributed by King Features Syndicate
B-BU...
NO BUTS!... LITTLE ANGUS IS IN TROUBLE AND WE'VE GOTTA BRING HIM HOME!
©1999 Brett Merhar.
BMerhar@AOL.COM
...NOTHING'S GONNA STOP US!
-BZZZZZZZ-
TOMORROW... "HERE COMES NOTHIN'!"

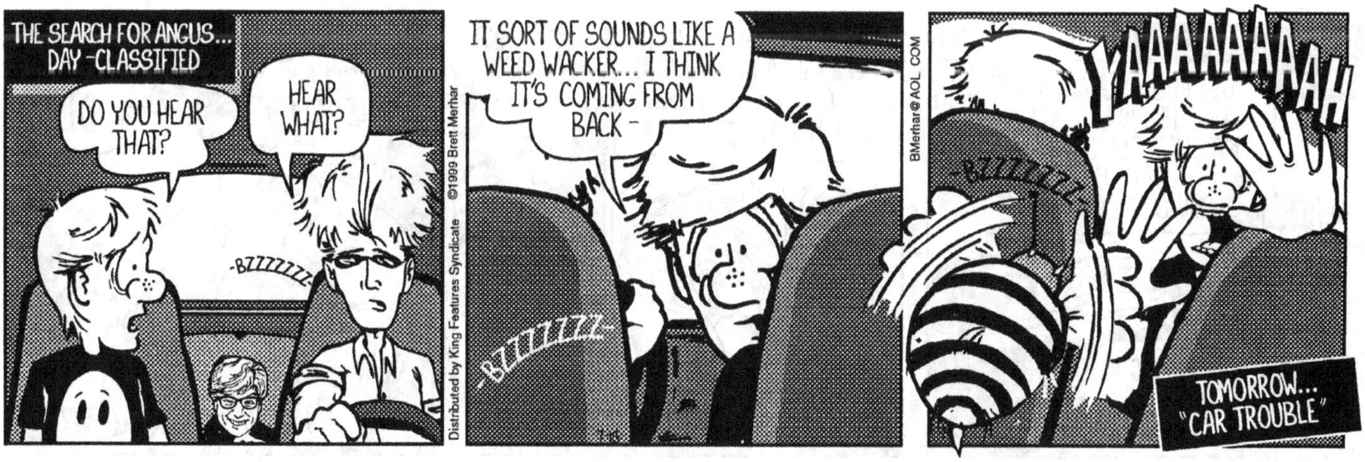
THE SEARCH FOR ANGUS... DAY -CLASSIFIED
DO YOU HEAR THAT?
HEAR WHAT?
-BZZZZZZZ
Distributed by King Features Syndicate
©1999 Brett Merhar
IT SORT OF SOUNDS LIKE A WEED WACKER... I THINK IT'S COMING FROM BACK -
-BZZZZZZZ-
BMerhar@AOL.COM
YAAAAAAAAH
-BZZZZZZZ
TOMORROW... "CAR TROUBLE"

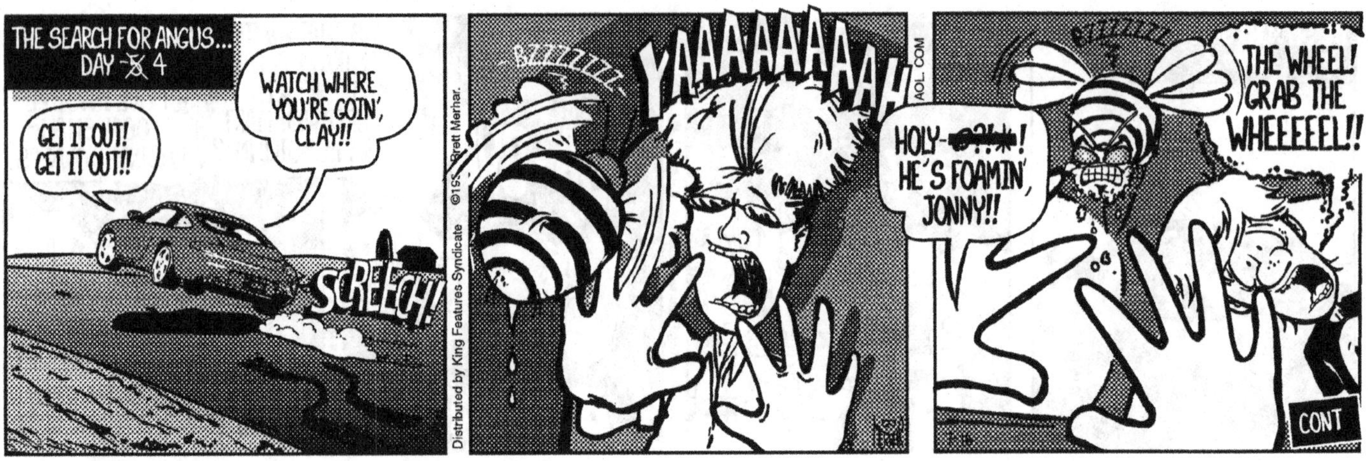
THE SEARCH FOR ANGUS... DAY -5 4
GET IT OUT! GET IT OUT!!
WATCH WHERE YOU'RE GOIN', CLAY!!
SCREECH!
Distributed by King Features Syndicate
Brett Merhar.
-BZZZZZZZ-
YAAAAAAAAAH
AOL. COM
HOLY-@?!*! HE'S FOAMIN', JONNY!!
BZZZZZZZ
THE WHEEL! GRAB THE WHEEEEEL!!
CONT

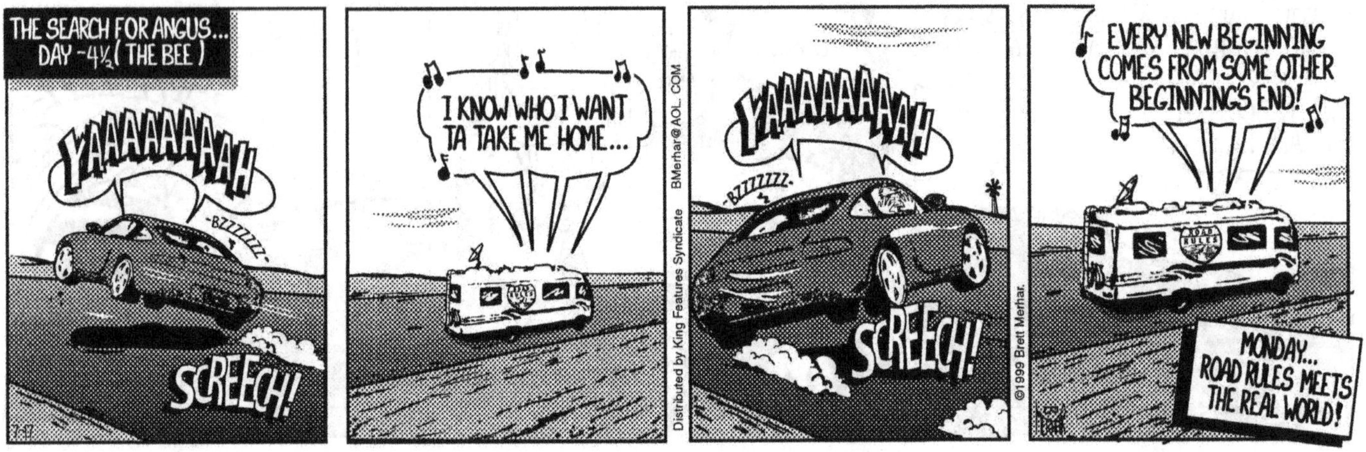
THE SEARCH FOR ANGUS... DAY -4½ (THE BEE)
YAAAAAAAAAH
-BZZZZZZZ-
SCREECH!
I KNOW WHO I WANT TA TAKE ME HOME...
Distributed by King Features Syndicate
BMerhar@AOL.COM
YAAAAAAAAAH
-BZZZZZZZ-
SCREECH!
©1999 Brett Merhar.
EVERY NEW BEGINNING COMES FROM SOME OTHER BEGINNING'S END!
MONDAY... ROAD RULES MEETS THE REAL WORLD!

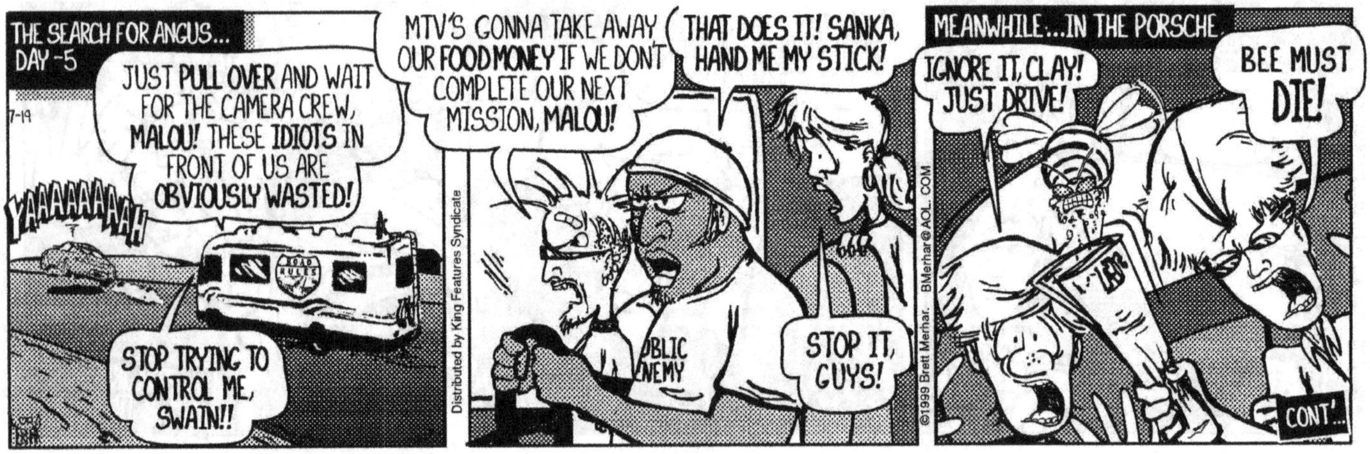
THE SEARCH FOR ANGUS... DAY -5
JUST PULL OVER AND WAIT FOR THE CAMERA CREW, MALOU! THESE IDIOTS IN FRONT OF US ARE OBVIOUSLY WASTED!
YAAAAAAAAAH
STOP TRYING TO CONTROL ME, SWAIN!!
MTV'S GONNA TAKE AWAY OUR FOOD MONEY IF WE DON'T COMPLETE OUR NEXT MISSION, MALOU!
THAT DOES IT! SANKA, HAND ME MY STICK!
Distributed by King Features Syndicate
BLIC NEMY
STOP IT, GUYS!
©1999 Brett Merhar.
BMerhar@AOL.COM
MEANWHILE...IN THE PORSCHE
IGNORE IT, CLAY! JUST DRIVE!
BEE MUST DIE!
CONT'...

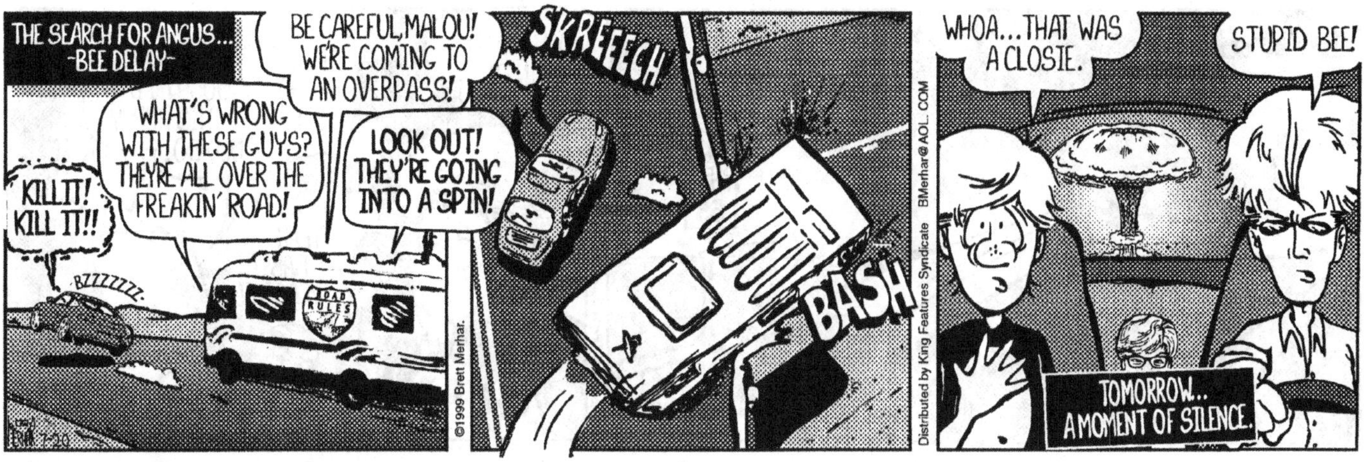
THE SEARCH FOR ANGUS...
-BEE DELAY-
KILL IT! KILL IT!!
BZZZZZZZ
WHAT'S WRONG WITH THESE GUYS? THEY'RE ALL OVER THE FREAKIN' ROAD!
BE CAREFUL, MALOU! WE'RE COMING TO AN OVERPASS!
LOOK OUT! THEY'RE GOING INTO A SPIN!
ROAD RULES
©1999 Brett Merhar.
SKREEEECH
BASH
Distributed by King Features Syndicate
BMerhar@AOL.COM
WHOA... THAT WAS A CLOSIE.
STUPID BEE!
TOMORROW... A MOMENT OF SILENCE.

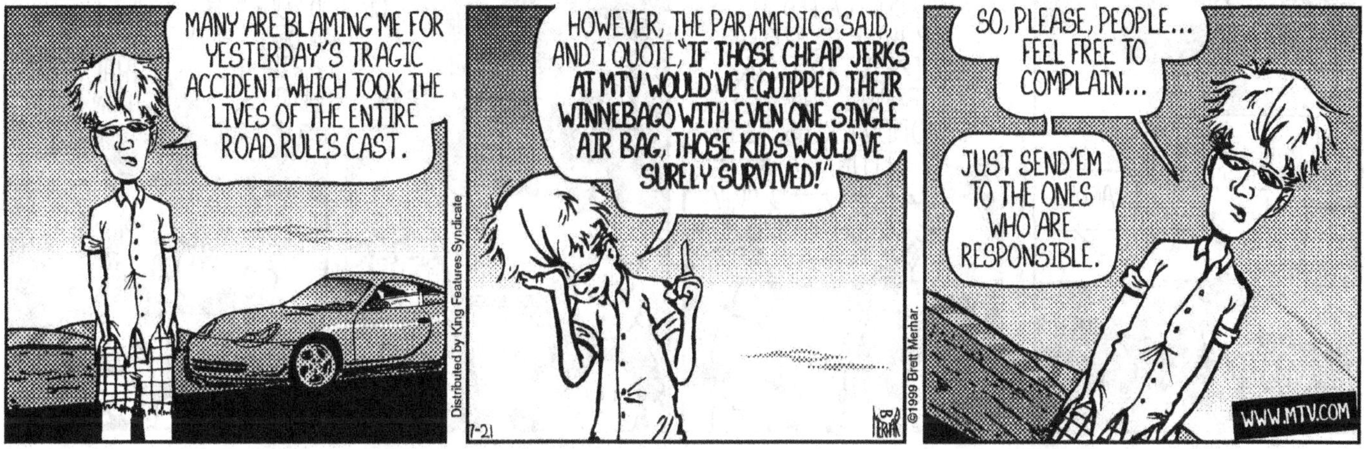
MANY ARE BLAMING ME FOR YESTERDAY'S TRAGIC ACCIDENT WHICH TOOK THE LIVES OF THE ENTIRE ROAD RULES CAST.
Distributed by King Features Syndicate
HOWEVER, THE PARAMEDICS SAID, AND I QUOTE, "IF THOSE CHEAP JERKS AT MTV WOULD'VE EQUIPPED THEIR WINNEBAGO WITH EVEN ONE SINGLE AIR BAG, THOSE KIDS WOULD'VE SURELY SURVIVED!"
7-21
©1999 Brett Merhar.
SO, PLEASE, PEOPLE... FEEL FREE TO COMPLAIN...
JUST SEND 'EM TO THE ONES WHO ARE RESPONSIBLE.
WWW.MTV.COM

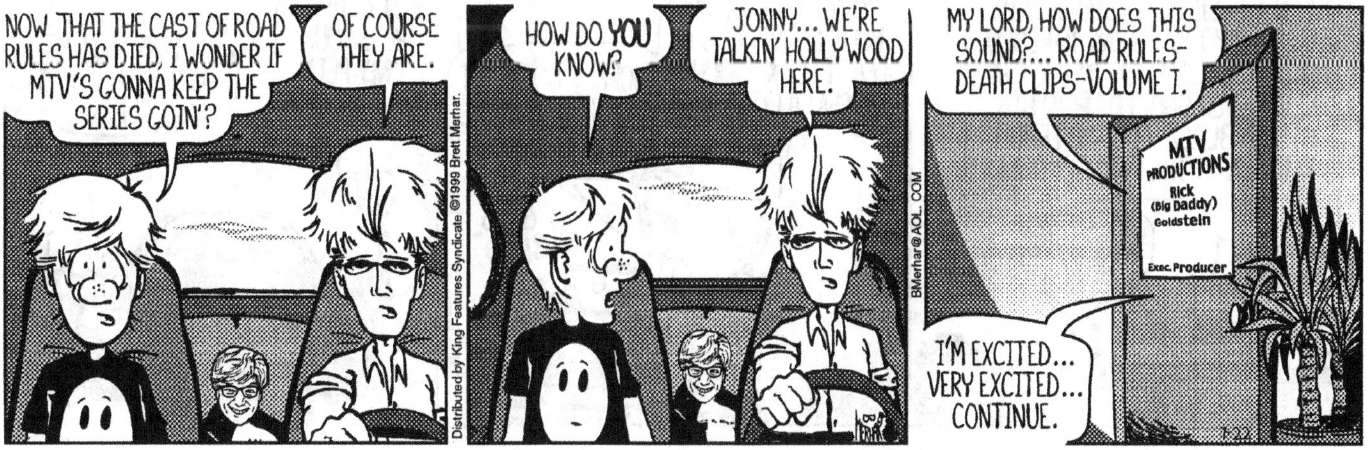
NOW THAT THE CAST OF ROAD RULES HAS DIED, I WONDER IF MTV'S GONNA KEEP THE SERIES GOIN'?
OF COURSE THEY ARE.
Distributed by King Features Syndicate ©1999 Brett Merhar.
HOW DO YOU KNOW?
JONNY... WE'RE TALKIN' HOLLYWOOD HERE.
BMerhar@AOL.COM
MY LORD, HOW DOES THIS SOUND?... ROAD RULES-DEATH CLIPS-VOLUME I.
MTV PRODUCTIONS
Rick (Big Daddy) Goldstein
Exec. Producer
I'M EXCITED... VERY EXCITED... CONTINUE.

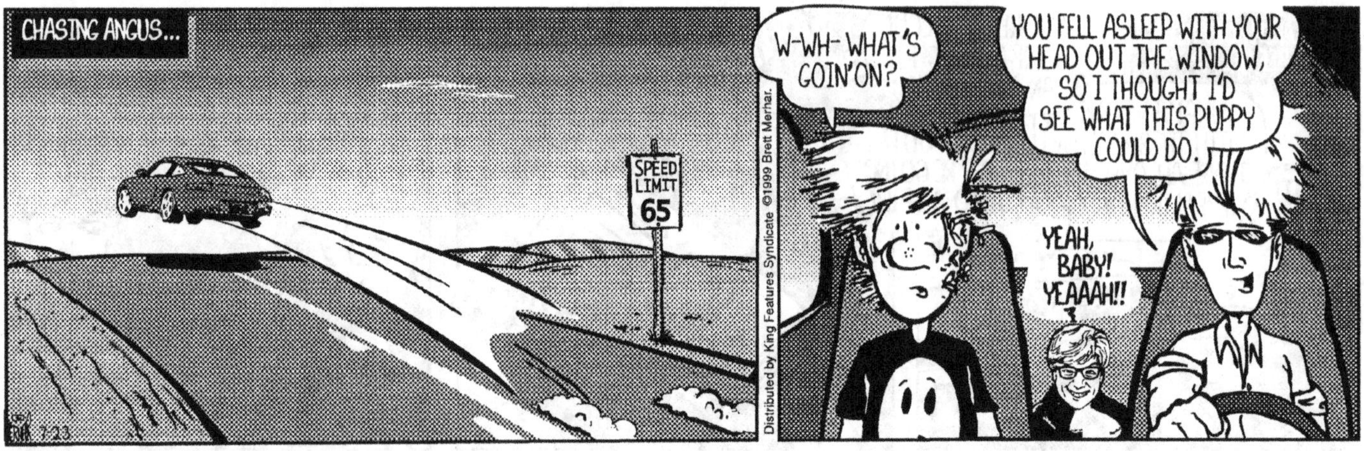
CHASING ANGUS...
SPEED LIMIT 65
7-23
Distributed by King Features Syndicate ©1999 Brett Merhar.
W-WH- WHAT'S GOIN'ON?
YOU FELL ASLEEP WITH YOUR HEAD OUT THE WINDOW, SO I THOUGHT I'D SEE WHAT THIS PUPPY COULD DO.
YEAH, BABY! YEAAAH!!

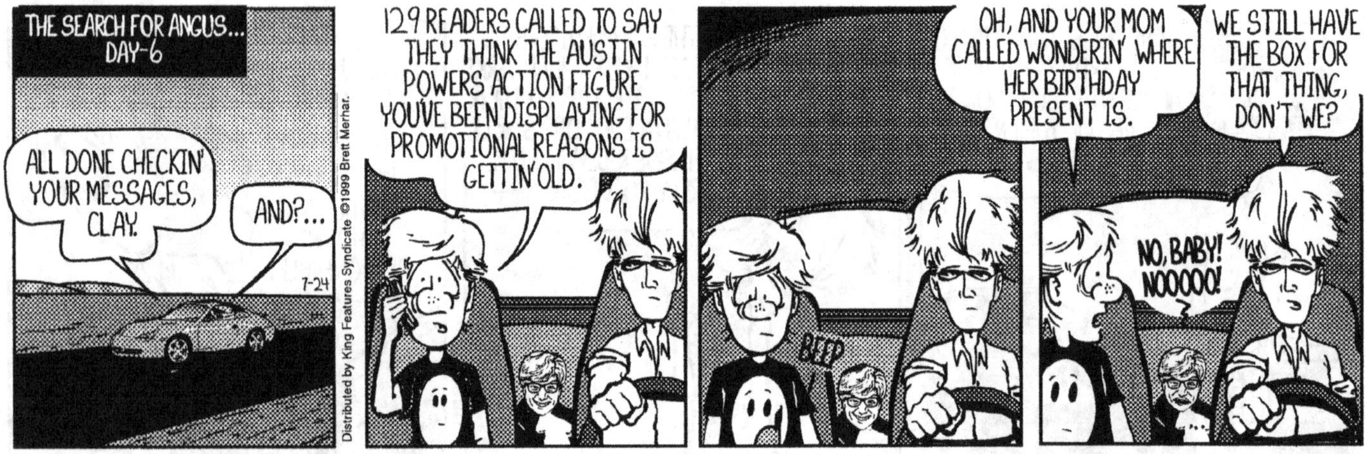
THE SEARCH FOR ANGUS... DAY-6
ALL DONE CHECKIN' YOUR MESSAGES, CLAY.
AND?...
7-24
Distributed by King Features Syndicate ©1999 Brett Merhar.
129 READERS CALLED TO SAY THEY THINK THE AUSTIN POWERS ACTION FIGURE YOU'VE BEEN DISPLAYING FOR PROMOTIONAL REASONS IS GETTIN'OLD.
BEEP
OH, AND YOUR MOM CALLED WONDERIN' WHERE HER BIRTHDAY PRESENT IS.
WE STILL HAVE THE BOX FOR THAT THING, DON'T WE?
NO, BABY! NOOOOO!
...

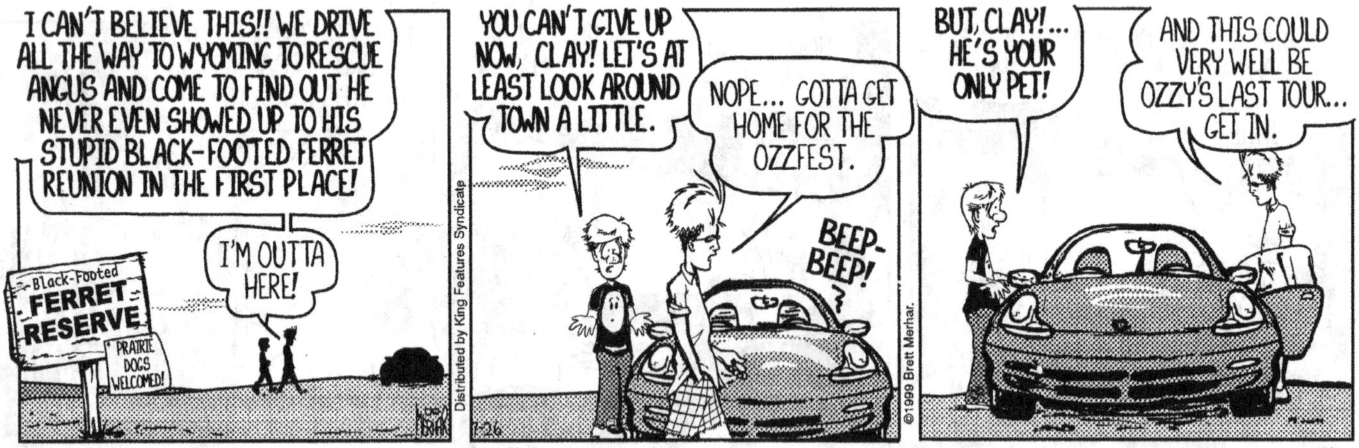
I CAN'T BELIEVE THIS!! WE DRIVE ALL THE WAY TO WYOMING TO RESCUE ANGUS AND COME TO FIND OUT HE NEVER EVEN SHOWED UP TO HIS STUPID BLACK-FOOTED FERRET REUNION IN THE FIRST PLACE!
I'M OUTTA HERE!
Black-Footed FERRET RESERVE
PRAIRIE DOGS WELCOMED!
Distributed by King Features Syndicate
7-26
YOU CAN'T GIVE UP NOW, CLAY! LET'S AT LEAST LOOK AROUND TOWN A LITTLE.
NOPE... GOTTA GET HOME FOR THE OZZFEST.
BEEP-BEEP!
©1999 Brett Merhar.
BUT, CLAY!... HE'S YOUR ONLY PET!
AND THIS COULD VERY WELL BE OZZY'S LAST TOUR... GET IN.

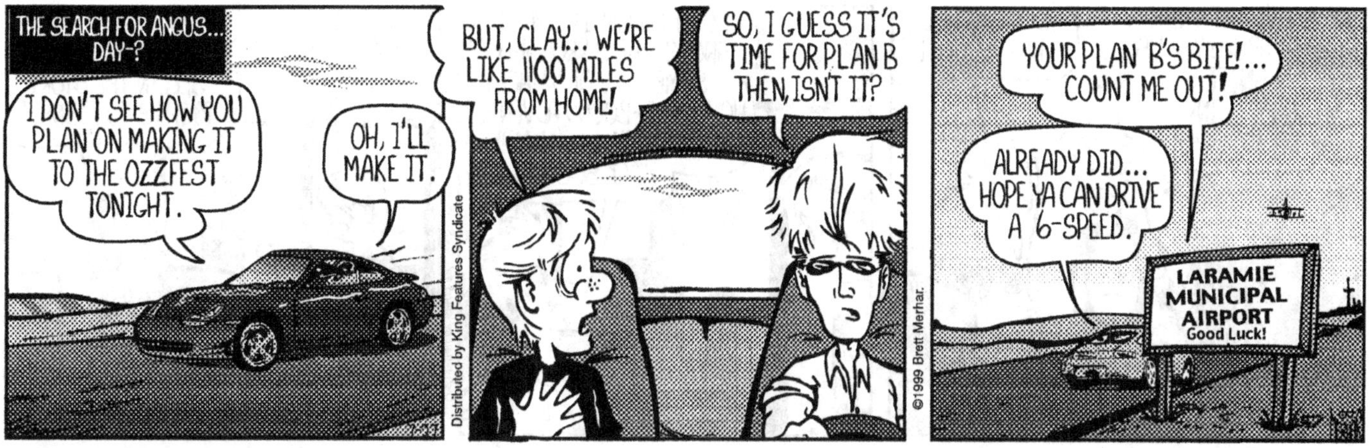
THE SEARCH FOR ANGUS... DAY-?
I DON'T SEE HOW YOU PLAN ON MAKING IT TO THE OZZFEST TONIGHT.
OH, I'LL MAKE IT.
Distributed by King Features Syndicate
BUT, CLAY... WE'RE LIKE 1100 MILES FROM HOME!
SO, I GUESS IT'S TIME FOR PLAN B THEN, ISN'T IT?
©1999 Brett Merhar.
YOUR PLAN B'S BITE!... COUNT ME OUT!
ALREADY DID... HOPE YA CAN DRIVE A 6-SPEED.
LARAMIE MUNICIPAL AIRPORT
Good Luck!

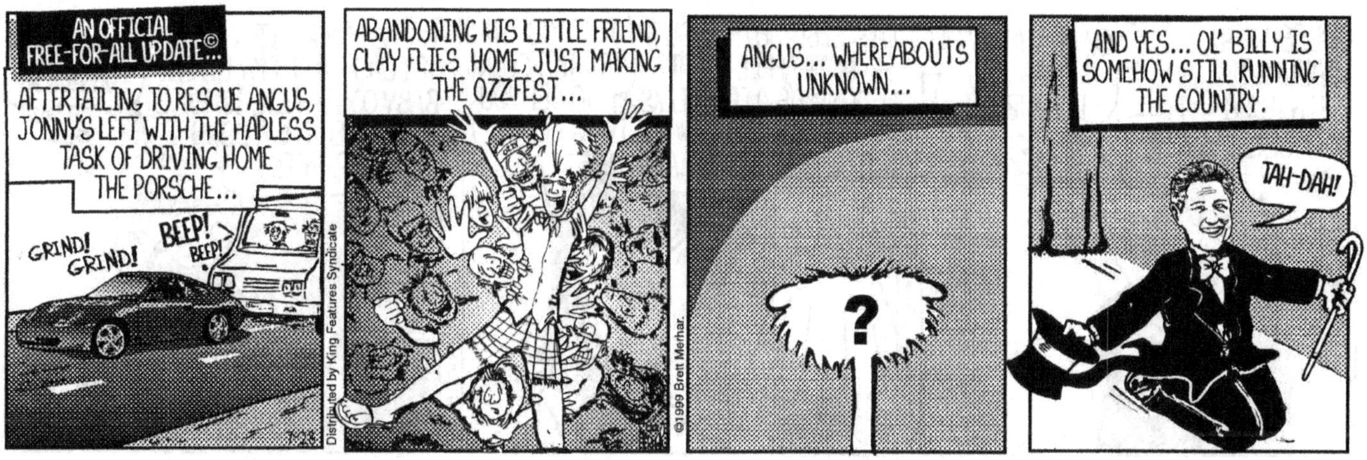
AN OFFICIAL FREE-FOR-ALL UPDATE©...
AFTER FAILING TO RESCUE ANGUS, JONNY'S LEFT WITH THE HAPLESS TASK OF DRIVING HOME THE PORSCHE...
GRIND! GRIND!
BEEP! BEEP!
Distributed by King Features Syndicate
ABANDONING HIS LITTLE FRIEND, CLAY FLIES HOME, JUST MAKING THE OZZFEST...
©1999 Brett Merhar.
ANGUS... WHEREABOUTS UNKNOWN...
?
AND YES... OL' BILLY IS SOMEHOW STILL RUNNING THE COUNTRY.
TAH-DAH!

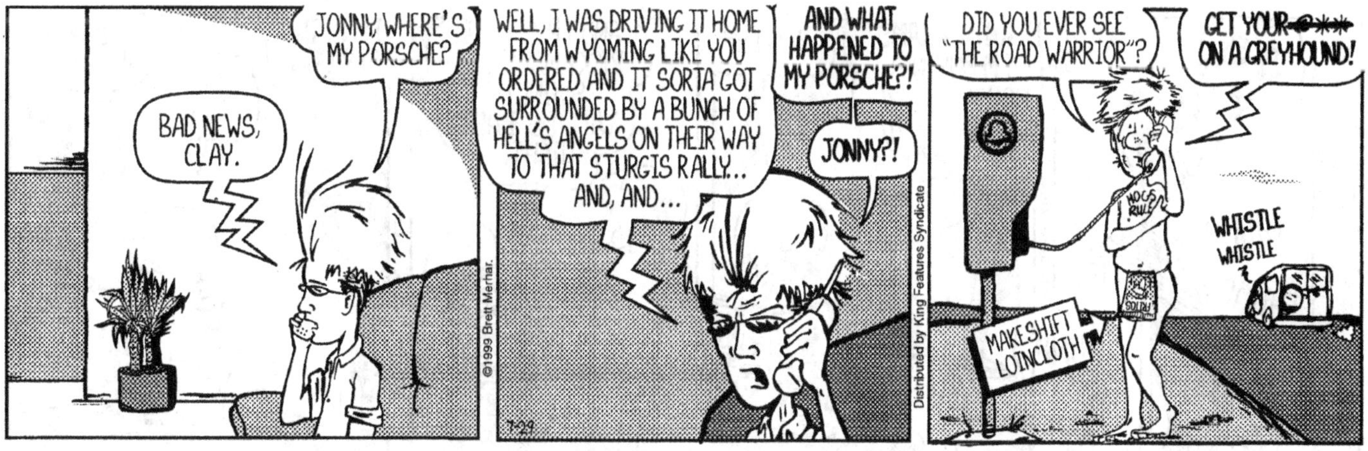
JONNY, WHERE'S MY PORSCHE?
BAD NEWS, CLAY.
©1999 Brett Merhar.
WELL, I WAS DRIVING IT HOME FROM WYOMING LIKE YOU ORDERED AND IT SORTA GOT SURROUNDED BY A BUNCH OF HELL'S ANGELS ON THEIR WAY TO THAT STURGIS RALLY... AND, AND...
AND WHAT HAPPENED TO MY PORSCHE?!
JONNY?!
Distributed by King Features Syndicate
DID YOU EVER SEE "THE ROAD WARRIOR"?
GET YOUR @*** ON A GREYHOUND!
WHISTLE WHISTLE
MAKESHIFT LOINCLOTH

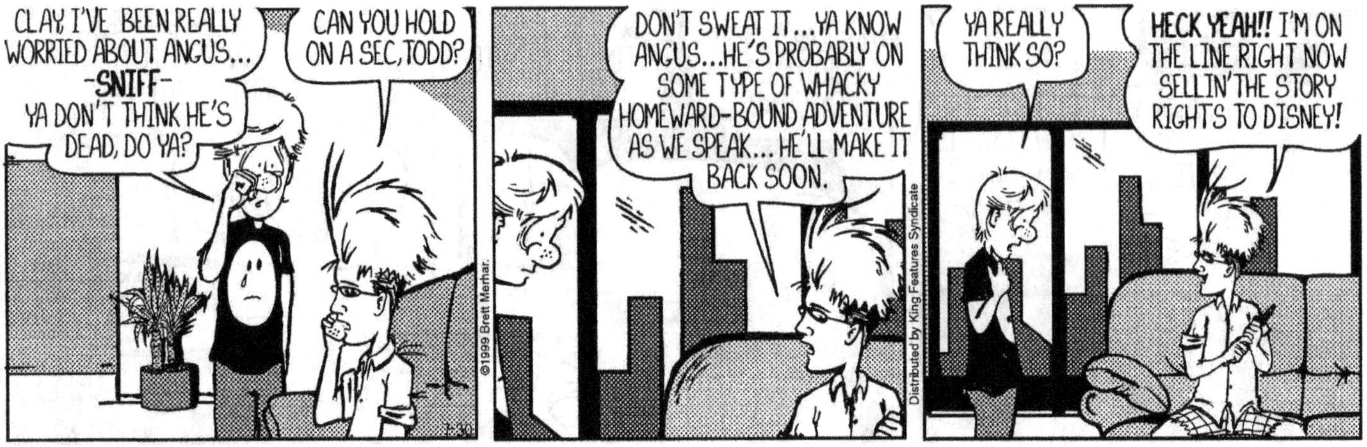
CLAY, I'VE BEEN REALLY WORRIED ABOUT ANGUS... -SNIFF- YA DON'T THINK HE'S DEAD, DO YA?
CAN YOU HOLD ON A SEC, TODD?
©1999 Brett Merhar.
DON'T SWEAT IT...YA KNOW ANGUS...HE'S PROBABLY ON SOME TYPE OF WHACKY HOMEWARD-BOUND ADVENTURE AS WE SPEAK... HE'LL MAKE IT BACK SOON.
Distributed by King Features Syndicate
YA REALLY THINK SO?
HECK YEAH!! I'M ON THE LINE RIGHT NOW SELLIN' THE STORY RIGHTS TO DISNEY!

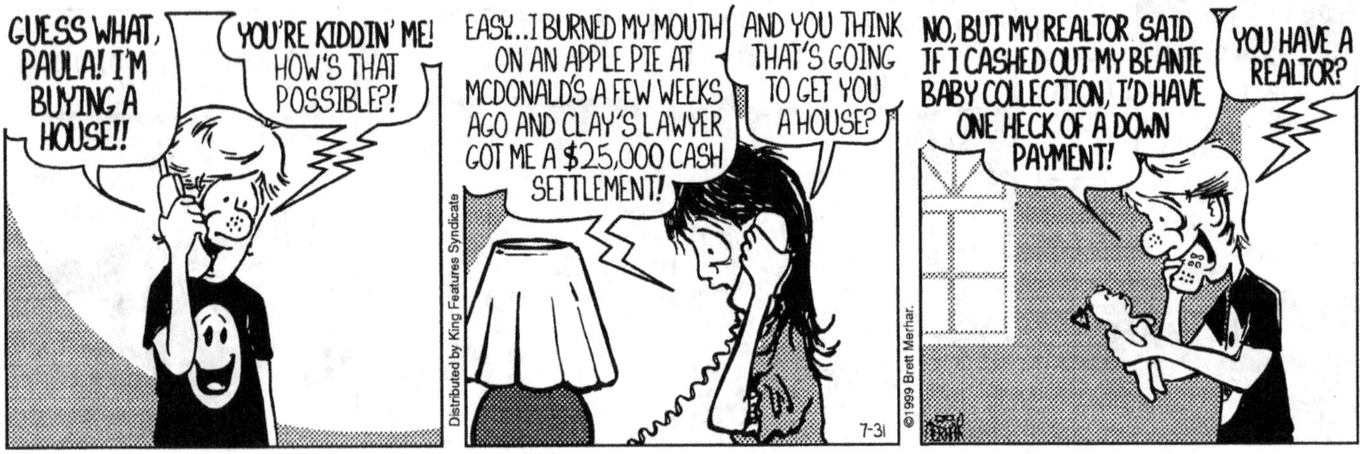
GUESS WHAT, PAULA! I'M BUYING A HOUSE!!
YOU'RE KIDDIN' ME! HOW'S THAT POSSIBLE?!
Distributed by King Features Syndicate
EASY...I BURNED MY MOUTH ON AN APPLE PIE AT MCDONALD'S A FEW WEEKS AGO AND CLAY'S LAWYER GOT ME A $25,000 CASH SETTLEMENT!
AND YOU THINK THAT'S GOING TO GET YOU A HOUSE?
7-31
©1999 Brett Merhar.
NO, BUT MY REALTOR SAID IF I CASHED OUT MY BEANIE BABY COLLECTION, I'D HAVE ONE HECK OF A DOWN PAYMENT!
YOU HAVE A REALTOR?

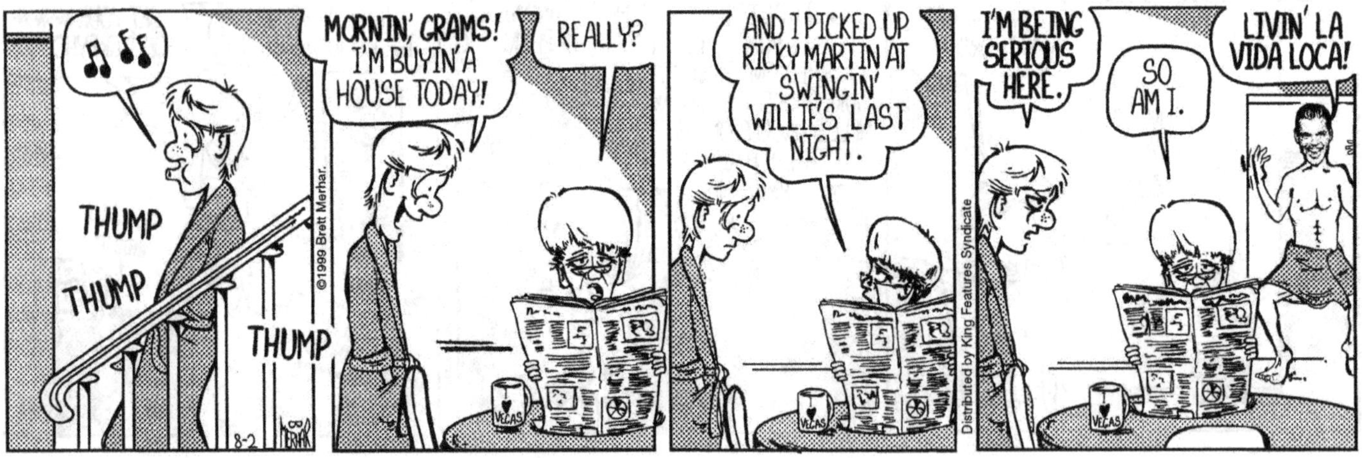
THUMP
THUMP
THUMP
8-2
©1999 Brett Merhar.
MORNIN', GRAMS! I'M BUYIN' A HOUSE TODAY!
REALLY?
AND I PICKED UP RICKY MARTIN AT SWINGIN' WILLIE'S LAST NIGHT.
Distributed by King Features Syndicate
I'M BEING SERIOUS HERE.
SO AM I.
LIVIN' LA VIDA LOCA!

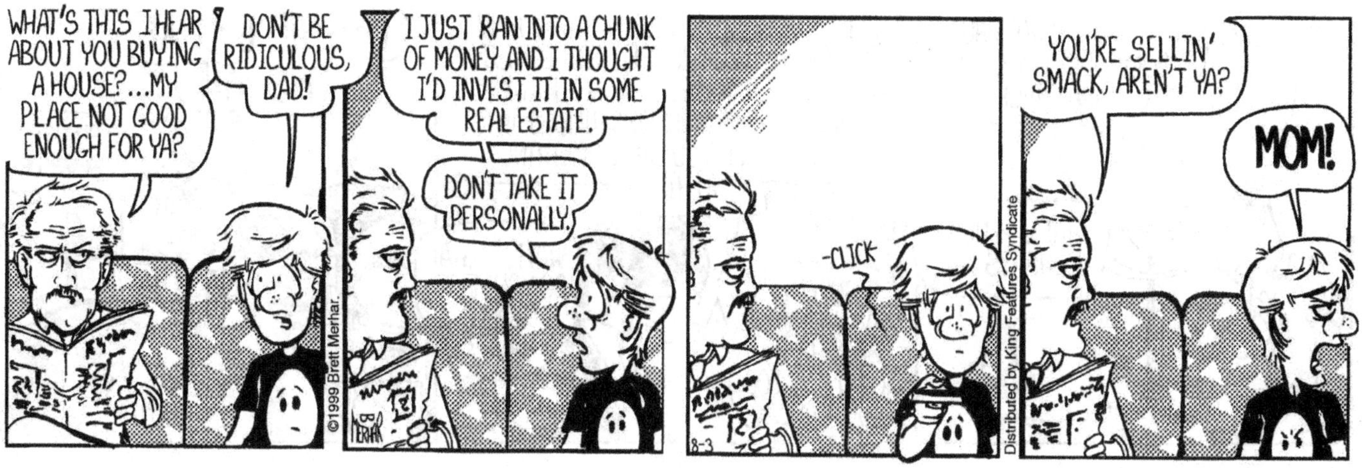
WHAT'S THIS I HEAR ABOUT YOU BUYING A HOUSE?...MY PLACE NOT GOOD ENOUGH FOR YA?
DON'T BE RIDICULOUS, DAD!
©1999 Brett Merhar.
I JUST RAN INTO A CHUNK OF MONEY AND I THOUGHT I'D INVEST IT IN SOME REAL ESTATE.
DON'T TAKE IT PERSONALLY.
-CLICK
8-3
Distributed by King Features Syndicate
YOU'RE SELLIN' SMACK, AREN'T YA?
MOM!

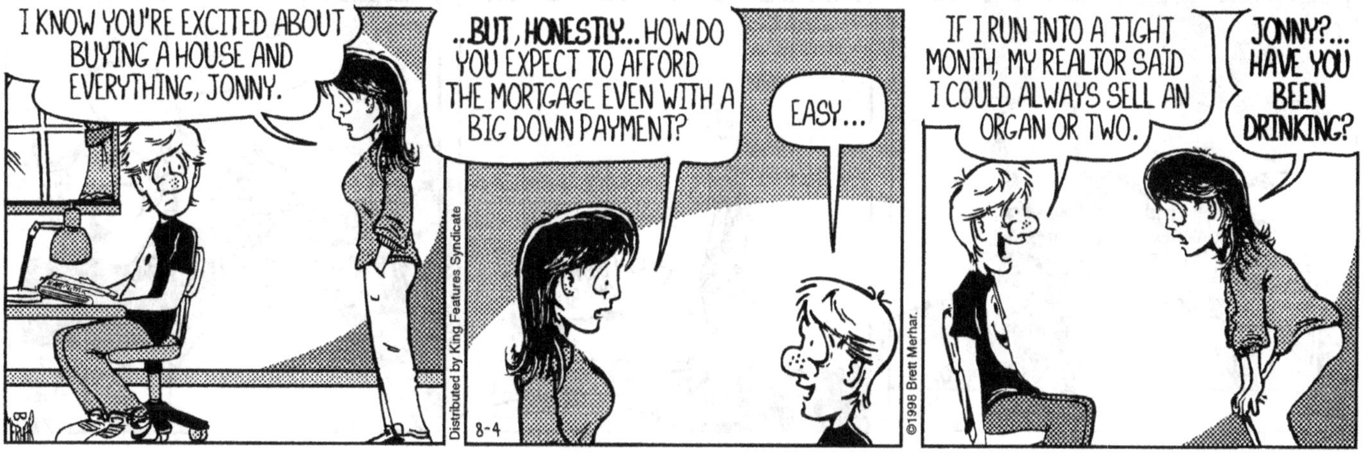
I KNOW YOU'RE EXCITED ABOUT BUYING A HOUSE AND EVERYTHING, JONNY.
Distributed by King Features Syndicate
...BUT, HONESTLY... HOW DO YOU EXPECT TO AFFORD THE MORTGAGE EVEN WITH A BIG DOWN PAYMENT?
EASY...
8-4
©1998 Brett Merhar.
IF I RUN INTO A TIGHT MONTH, MY REALTOR SAID I COULD ALWAYS SELL AN ORGAN OR TWO.
JONNY?... HAVE YOU BEEN DRINKING?

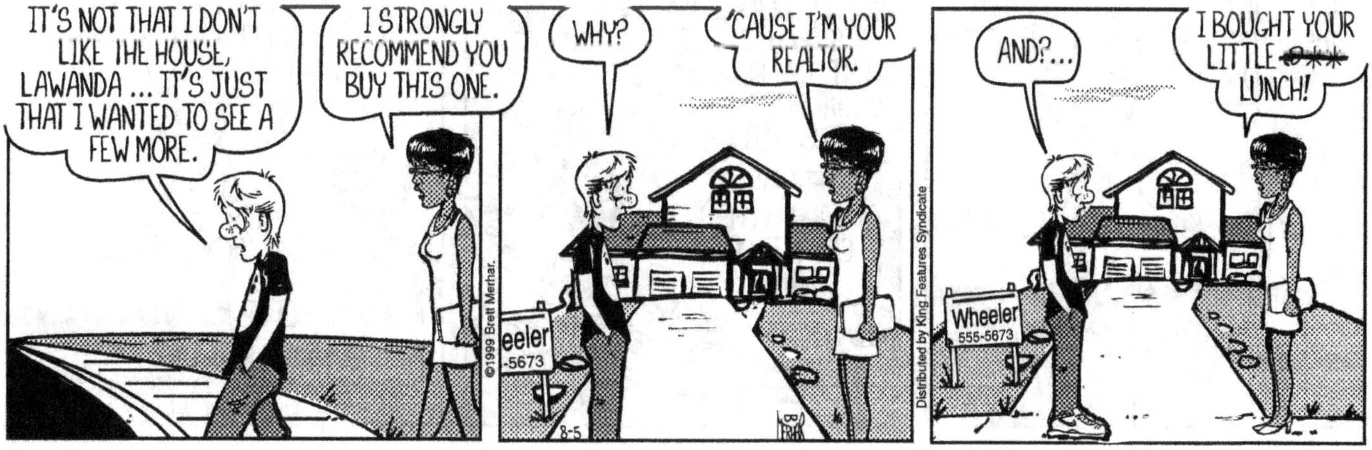
IT'S NOT THAT I DON'T LIKE THE HOUSE, LAWANDA ... IT'S JUST THAT I WANTED TO SEE A FEW MORE.
I STRONGLY RECOMMEND YOU BUY THIS ONE.
©1999 Brett Merhar.
WHY?
'CAUSE I'M YOUR REALTOR.
eeler
-5673
8-5
Distributed by King Features Syndicate
AND?...
I BOUGHT YOUR LITTLE LUNCH!
Wheeler
555-5673

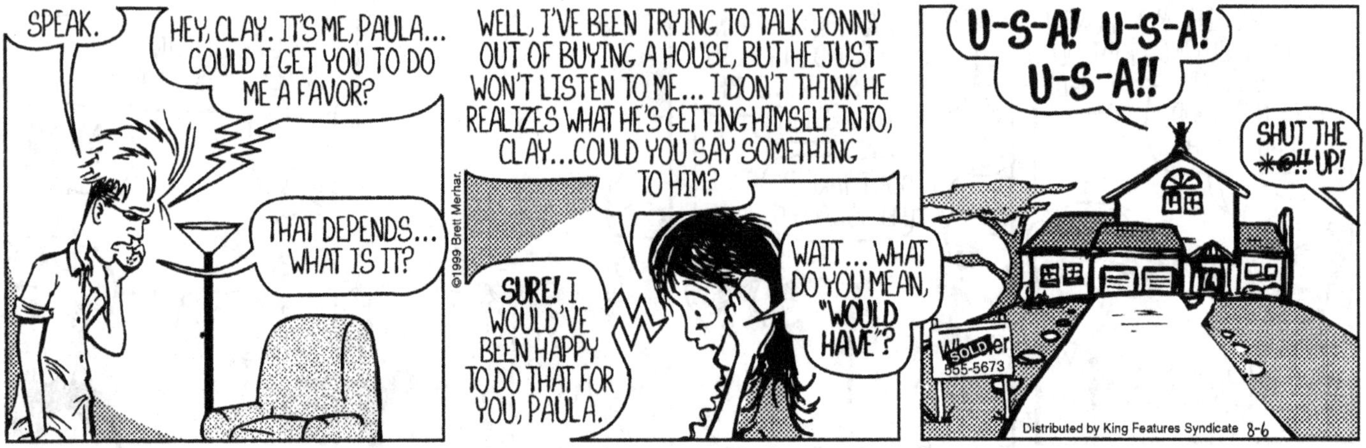
SPEAK.
HEY, CLAY. IT'S ME, PAULA... COULD I GET YOU TO DO ME A FAVOR?
THAT DEPENDS... WHAT IS IT?
©1999 Brett Merhar.
WELL, I'VE BEEN TRYING TO TALK JONNY OUT OF BUYING A HOUSE, BUT HE JUST WON'T LISTEN TO ME... I DON'T THINK HE REALIZES WHAT HE'S GETTING HIMSELF INTO, CLAY...COULD YOU SAY SOMETHING TO HIM?
SURE! I WOULD'VE BEEN HAPPY TO DO THAT FOR YOU, PAULA.
WAIT... WHAT DO YOU MEAN, "WOULD HAVE"?
U-S-A! U-S-A! U-S-A!!
SHUT THE *@!! UP!
SOLD
555-5673
Distributed by King Features Syndicate 8-6

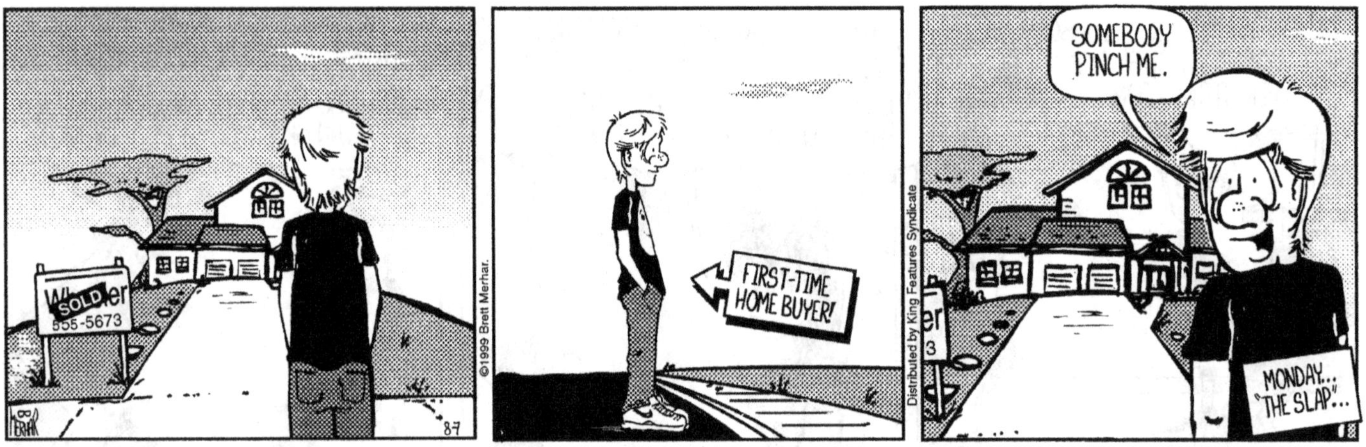
SOLD
555-5673
8-7
©1999 Brett Merhar.
FIRST-TIME HOME BUYER!
Distributed by King Features Syndicate
SOMEBODY PINCH ME.
MONDAY... "THE SLAP"...

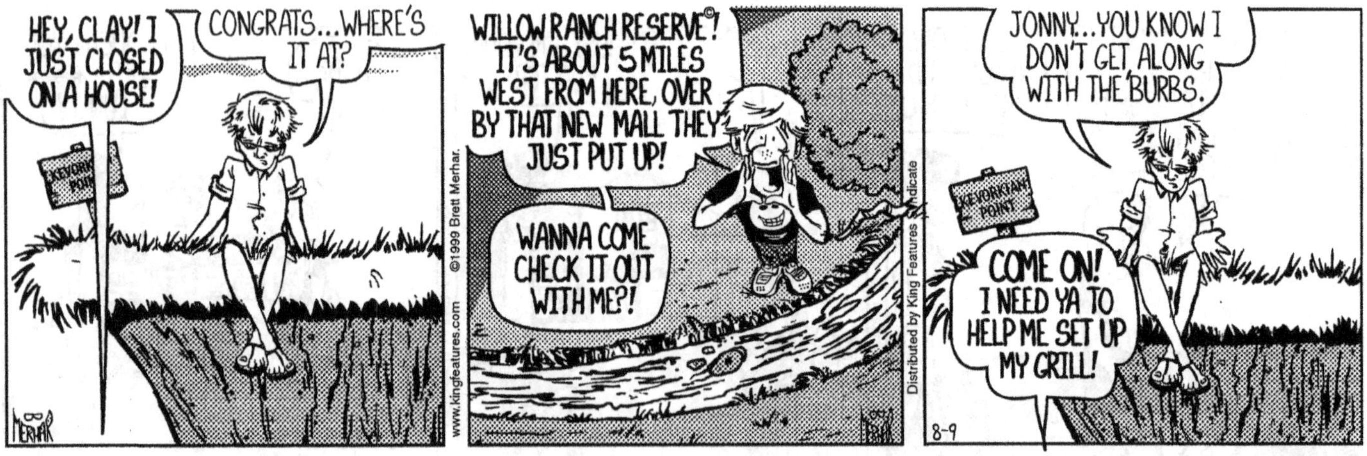
HEY, CLAY! I JUST CLOSED ON A HOUSE!
CONGRATS...WHERE'S IT AT?
www.kingfeatures.com ©1999 Brett Merhar.
WILLOW RANCH RESERVE! IT'S ABOUT 5 MILES WEST FROM HERE, OVER BY THAT NEW MALL THEY JUST PUT UP!
WANNA COME CHECK IT OUT WITH ME?!
Distributed by King Features Syndicate
JONNY...YOU KNOW I DON'T GET ALONG WITH THE 'BURBS.
KEVORKIAN POINT
COME ON! I NEED YA TO HELP ME SET UP MY GRILL!
8-9

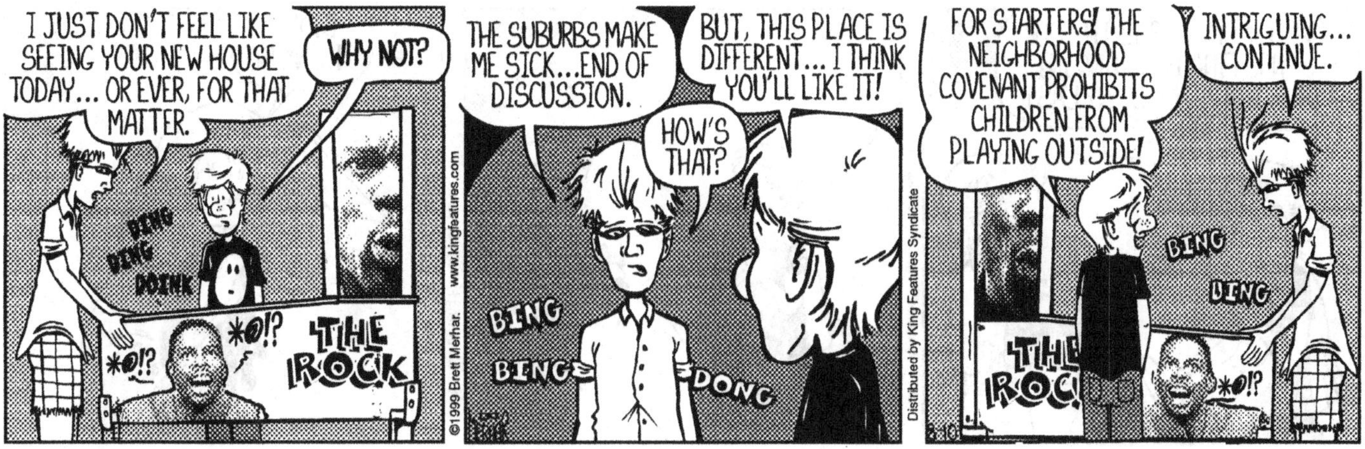
I JUST DON'T FEEL LIKE SEEING YOUR NEW HOUSE TODAY... OR EVER, FOR THAT MATTER.
WHY NOT?
BING BING DOINK
*@!?
*@!?
THE ROCK
©1999 Brett Merhar. www.kingfeatures.com
THE SUBURBS MAKE ME SICK...END OF DISCUSSION.
BUT, THIS PLACE IS DIFFERENT... I THINK YOU'LL LIKE IT!
HOW'S THAT?
BING BING DONG
Distributed by King Features Syndicate
FOR STARTERS! THE NEIGHBORHOOD COVENANT PROHIBITS CHILDREN FROM PLAYING OUTSIDE!
INTRIGUING... CONTINUE.
BING BING
*@!?

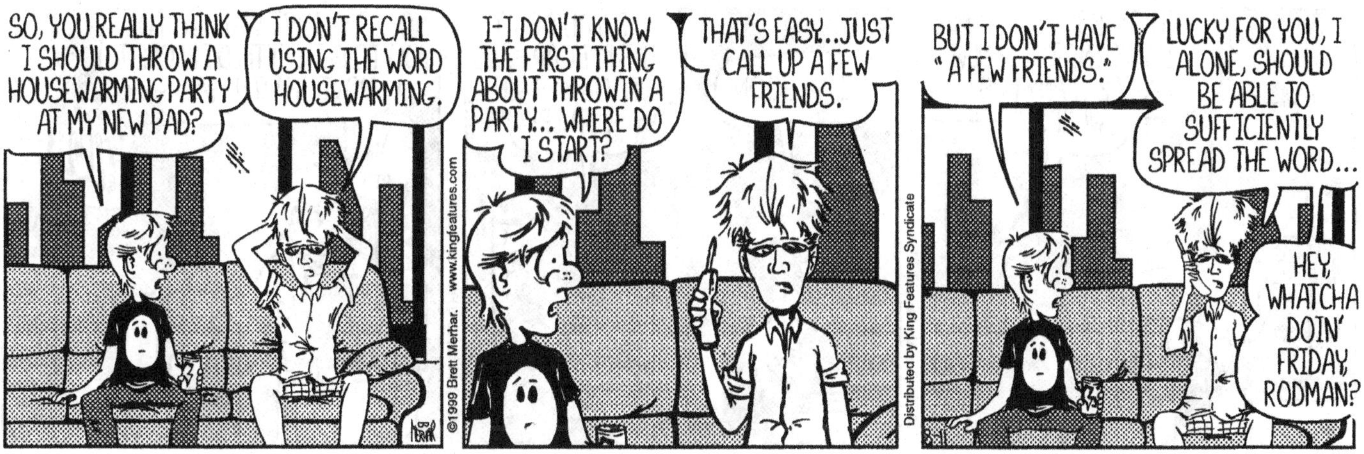
SO, YOU REALLY THINK I SHOULD THROW A HOUSEWARMING PARTY AT MY NEW PAD?
I DON'T RECALL USING THE WORD HOUSEWARMING.
©1999 Brett Merhar. www.kingfeatures.com
I-I DON'T KNOW THE FIRST THING ABOUT THROWIN' A PARTY... WHERE DO I START?
THAT'S EASY...JUST CALL UP A FEW FRIENDS.
Distributed by King Features Syndicate
BUT I DON'T HAVE "A FEW FRIENDS."
LUCKY FOR YOU, I ALONE, SHOULD BE ABLE TO SUFFICIENTLY SPREAD THE WORD...
HEY, WHATCHA DOIN' FRIDAY, RODMAN?

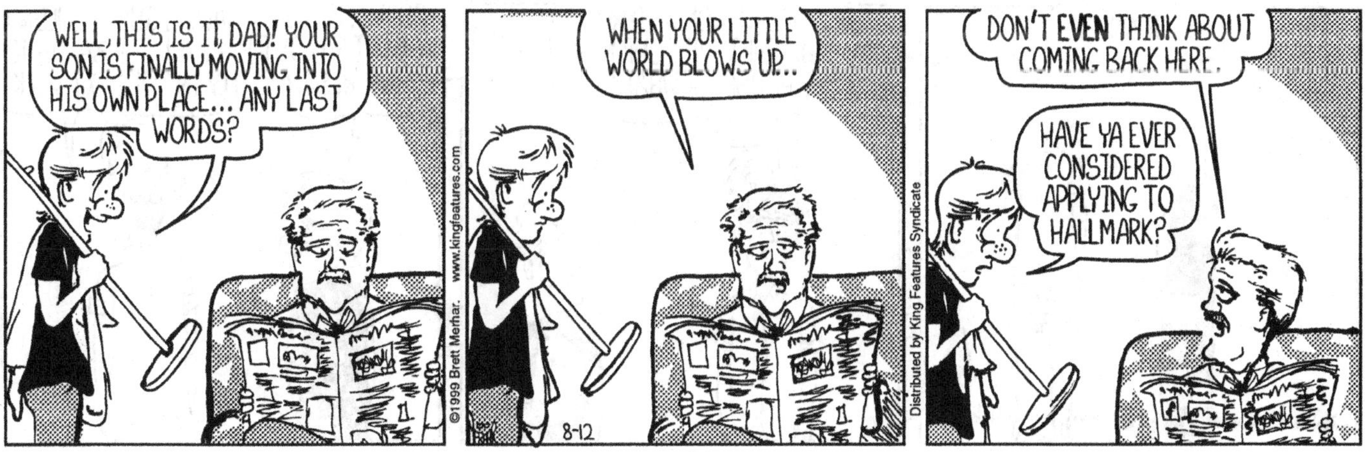
WELL, THIS IS IT, DAD! YOUR SON IS FINALLY MOVING INTO HIS OWN PLACE... ANY LAST WORDS?
©1999 Brett Merhar. www.kingfeatures.com
WHEN YOUR LITTLE WORLD BLOWS UP...
8-12
Distributed by King Features Syndicate
DON'T EVEN THINK ABOUT COMING BACK HERE.
HAVE YA EVER CONSIDERED APPLYING TO HALLMARK?

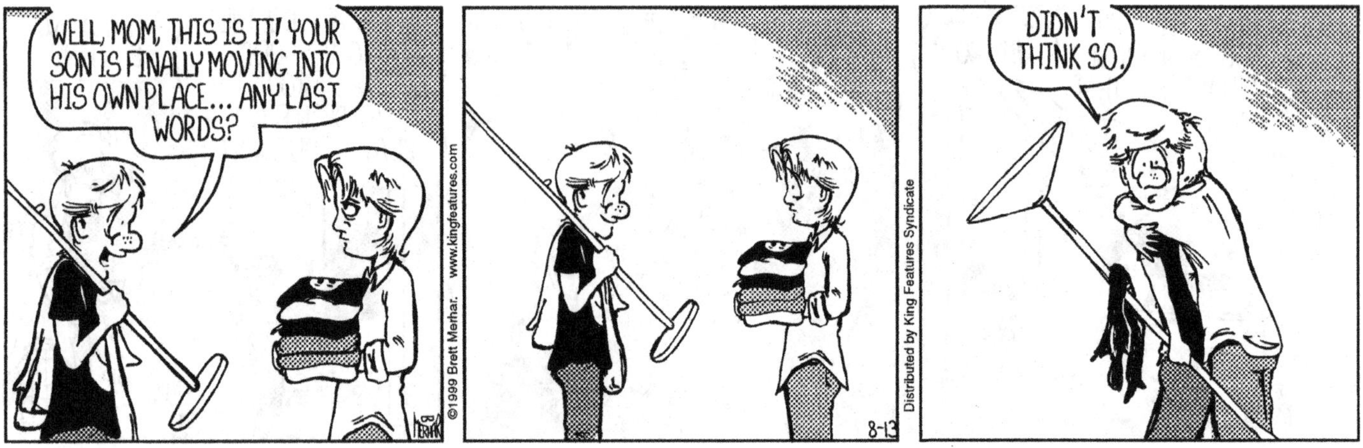
WELL, MOM, THIS IS IT! YOUR SON IS FINALLY MOVING INTO HIS OWN PLACE... ANY LAST WORDS?
©1999 Brett Merhar. www.kingfeatures.com
Distributed by King Features Syndicate
8-13
DIDN'T THINK SO.

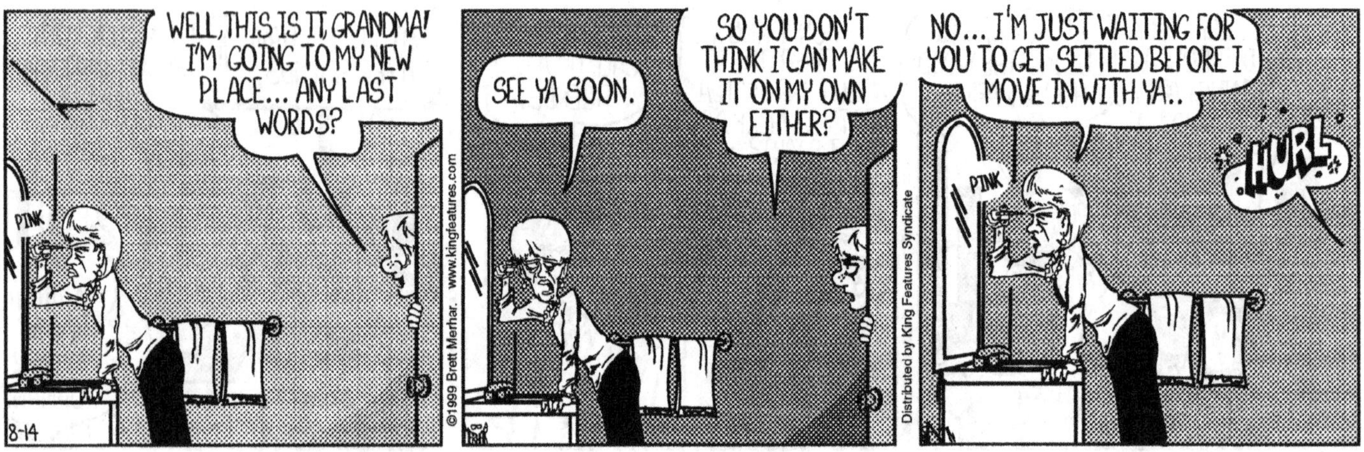
WELL, THIS IS IT, GRANDMA! I'M GOING TO MY NEW PLACE... ANY LAST WORDS?
PINK
8-14
©1999 Brett Merhar. www.kingfeatures.com
SEE YA SOON.
SO YOU DON'T THINK I CAN MAKE IT ON MY OWN EITHER?
Distributed by King Features Syndicate
NO... I'M JUST WAITING FOR YOU TO GET SETTLED BEFORE I MOVE IN WITH YA..
PINK
HURL

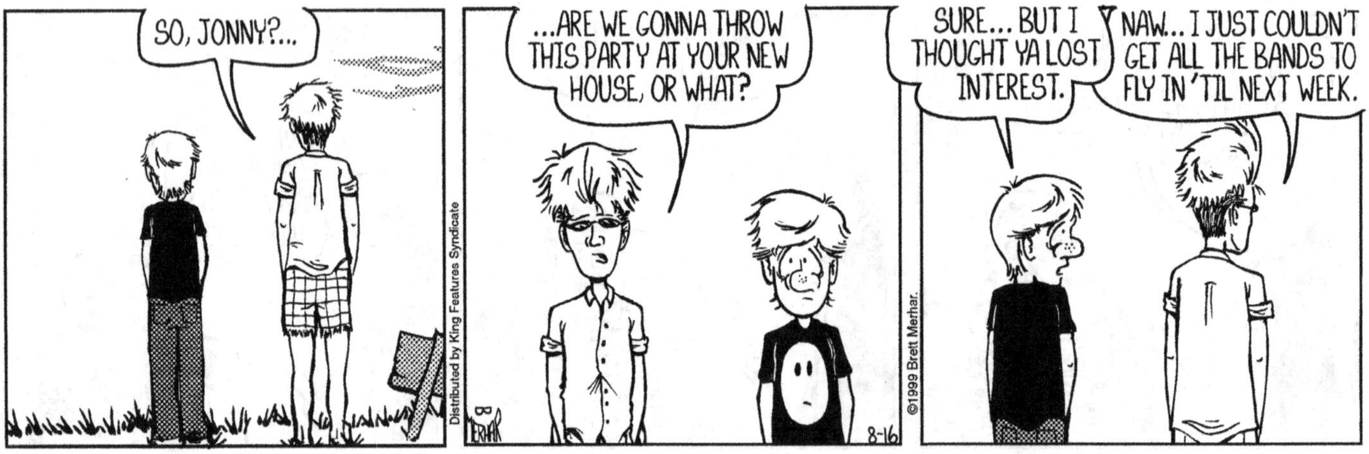
SO, JONNY?...
Distributed by King Features Syndicate
...ARE WE GONNA THROW THIS PARTY AT YOUR NEW HOUSE, OR WHAT?
8-16
©1999 Brett Merhar.
SURE... BUT I THOUGHT YA LOST INTEREST.
NAW... I JUST COULDN'T GET ALL THE BANDS TO FLY IN 'TIL NEXT WEEK.

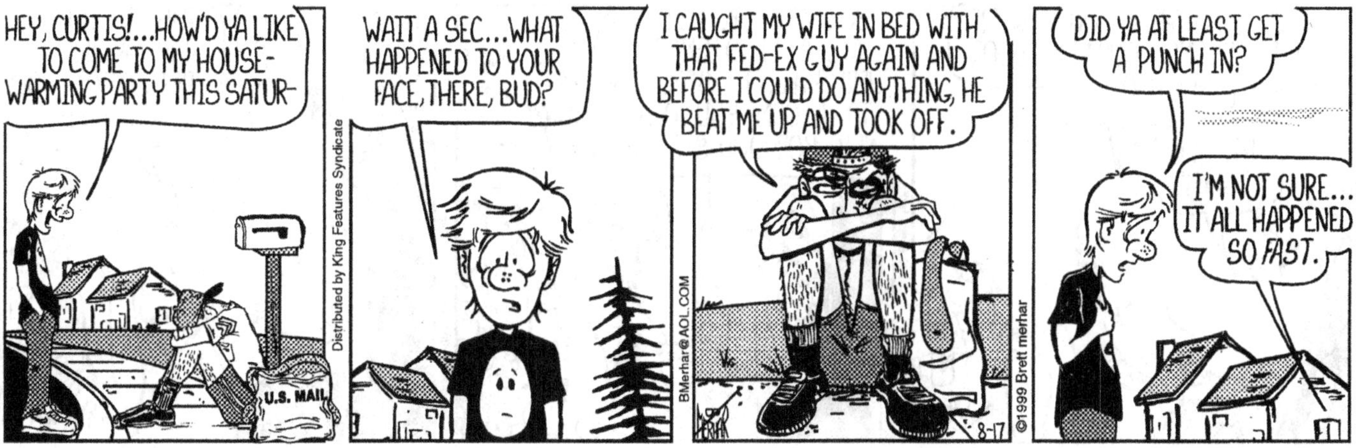
HEY, CURTIS!...HOW'D YA LIKE TO COME TO MY HOUSE-WARMING PARTY THIS SATUR-
U.S. MAIL
Distributed by King Features Syndicate
WAIT A SEC...WHAT HAPPENED TO YOUR FACE, THERE, BUD?
BMerhar@AOL.COM
I CAUGHT MY WIFE IN BED WITH THAT FED-EX GUY AGAIN AND BEFORE I COULD DO ANYTHING, HE BEAT ME UP AND TOOK OFF.
8-17
©1999 Brett merhar
DID YA AT LEAST GET A PUNCH IN?
I'M NOT SURE... IT ALL HAPPENED SO FAST.

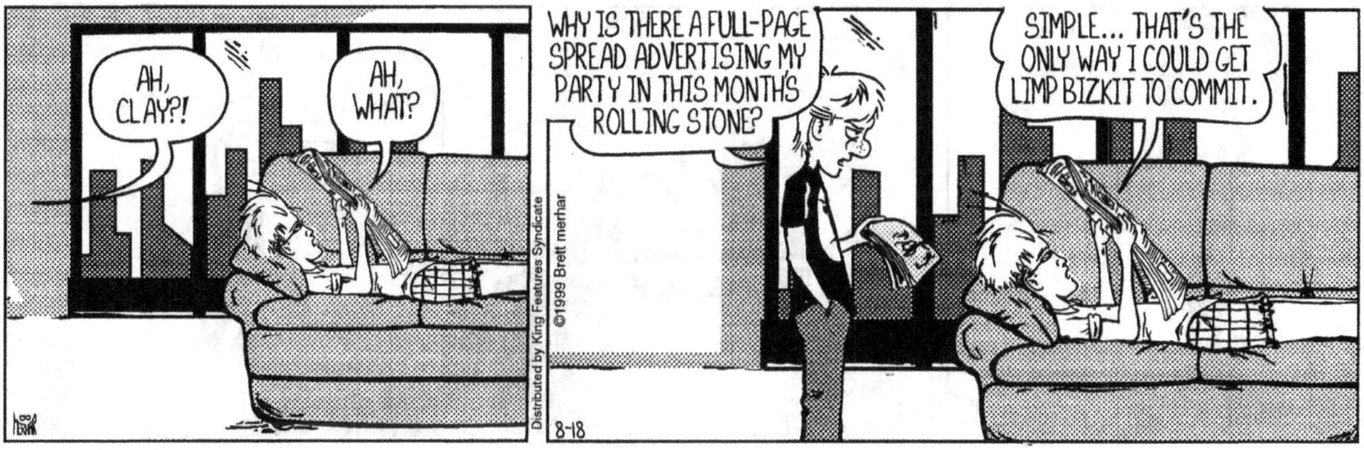
AH, CLAY?!
AH, WHAT?
Distributed by King Features Syndicate
©1999 Brett merhar
8-18
WHY IS THERE A FULL-PAGE SPREAD ADVERTISING MY PARTY IN THIS MONTH'S ROLLING STONE?
SIMPLE... THAT'S THE ONLY WAY I COULD GET LIMP BIZKIT TO COMMIT.

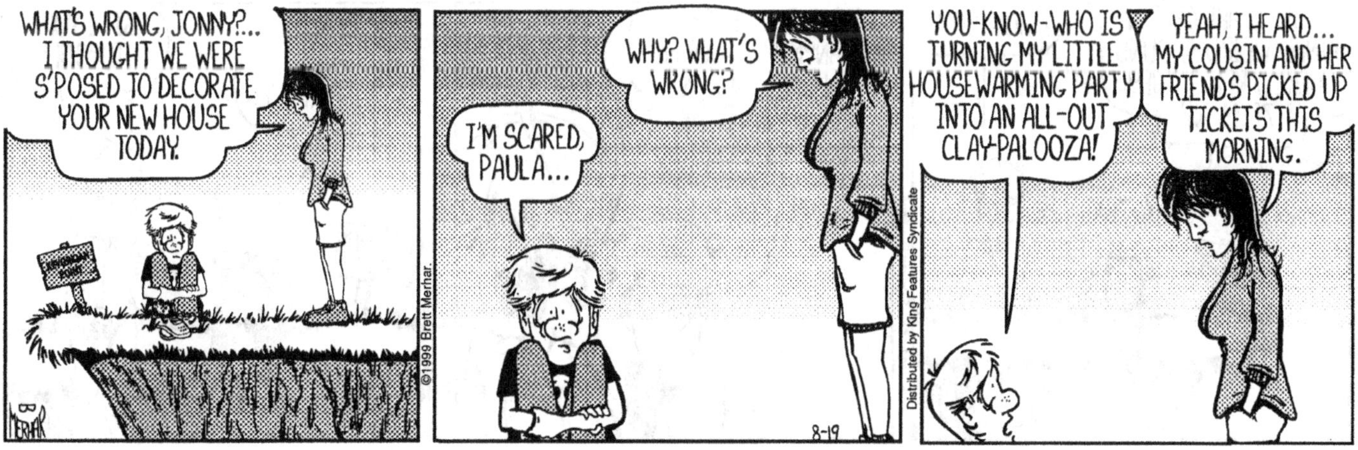
WHAT'S WRONG, JONNY?... I THOUGHT WE WERE S'POSED TO DECORATE YOUR NEW HOUSE TODAY.
©1999 Brett Merhar.
WHY? WHAT'S WRONG?
I'M SCARED, PAULA...
8-19
Distributed by King Features Syndicate
YOU-KNOW-WHO IS TURNING MY LITTLE HOUSEWARMING PARTY INTO AN ALL-OUT CLAY-PALOOZA!
YEAH, I HEARD... MY COUSIN AND HER FRIENDS PICKED UP TICKETS THIS MORNING.

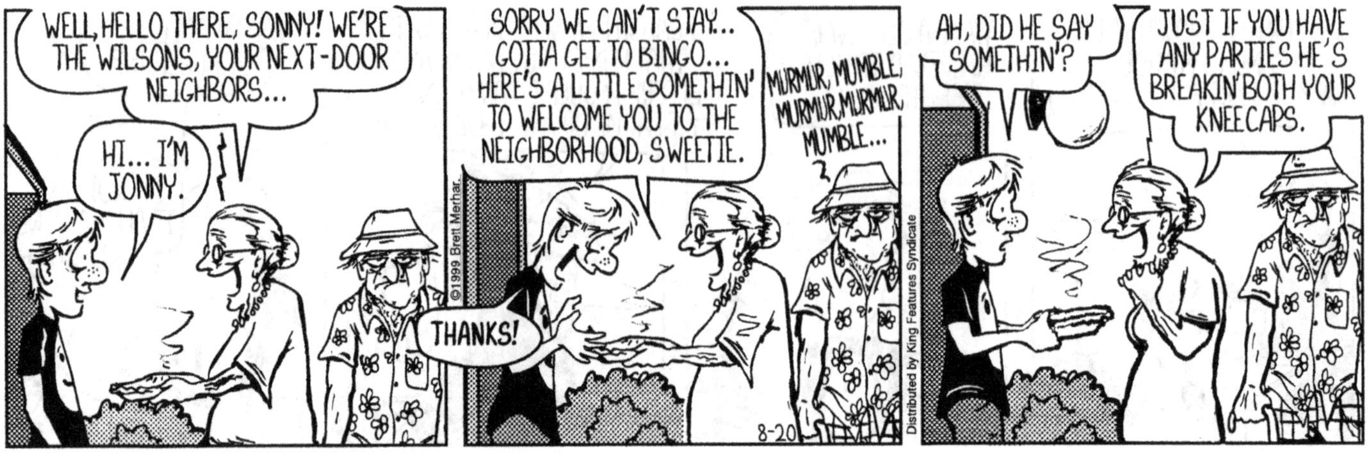
WELL, HELLO THERE, SONNY! WE'RE THE WILSONS, YOUR NEXT-DOOR NEIGHBORS...
HI... I'M JONNY.
SORRY WE CAN'T STAY... GOTTA GET TO BINGO... HERE'S A LITTLE SOMETHIN' TO WELCOME YOU TO THE NEIGHBORHOOD, SWEETIE.
MURMUR, MUMBLE, MURMUR, MURMUR, MUMBLE...
THANKS!
©1999 Brett Merhar.
8-20
AH, DID HE SAY SOMETHIN'?
JUST IF YOU HAVE ANY PARTIES HE'S BREAKIN' BOTH YOUR KNEECAPS.
Distributed by King Features Syndicate

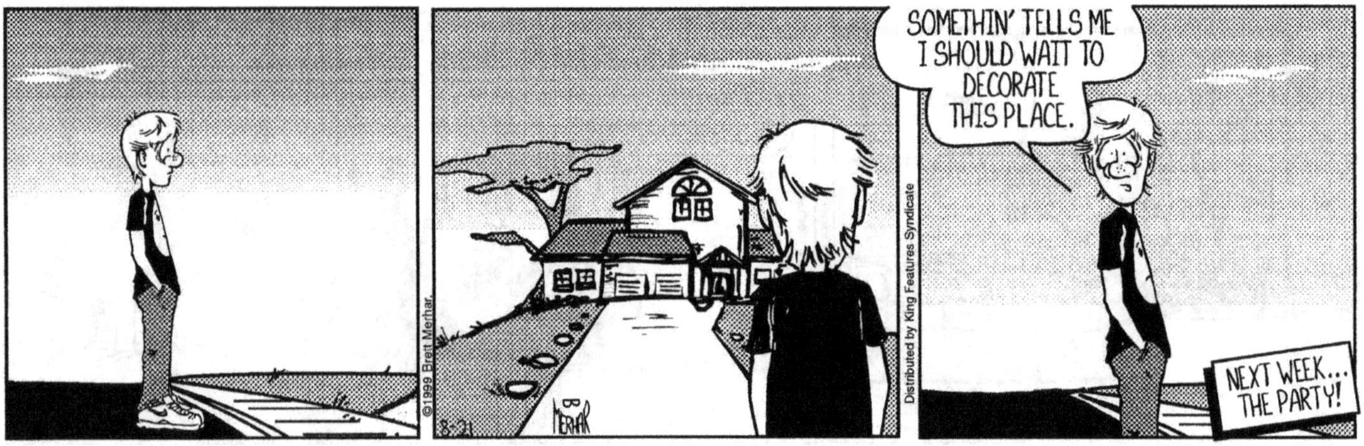
©1999 Brett Merhar.
8-21
B MERHAR
SOMETHIN' TELLS ME I SHOULD WAIT TO DECORATE THIS PLACE.
NEXT WEEK... THE PARTY!
Distributed by King Features Syndicate

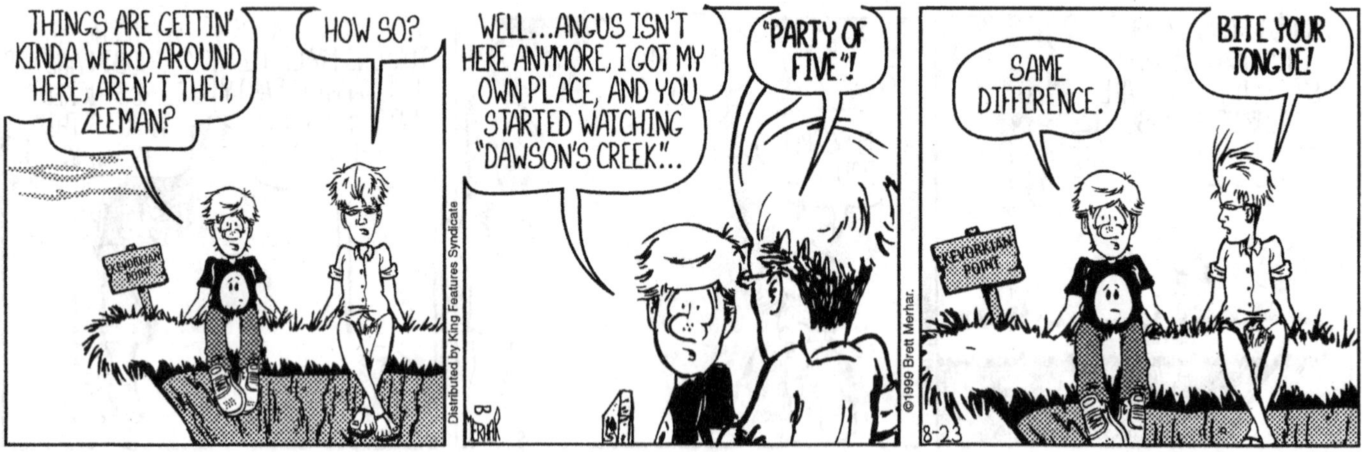
THINGS ARE GETTIN' KINDA WEIRD AROUND HERE, AREN'T THEY, ZEEMAN?
HOW SO?
KEVORKIAN POINT
Distributed by King Features Syndicate
WELL...ANGUS ISN'T HERE ANYMORE, I GOT MY OWN PLACE, AND YOU STARTED WATCHING "DAWSON'S CREEK"...
"PARTY OF FIVE"!
B MERHAR
©1999 Brett Merhar.
8-23
SAME DIFFERENCE.
BITE YOUR TONGUE!
KEVORKIAN POINT

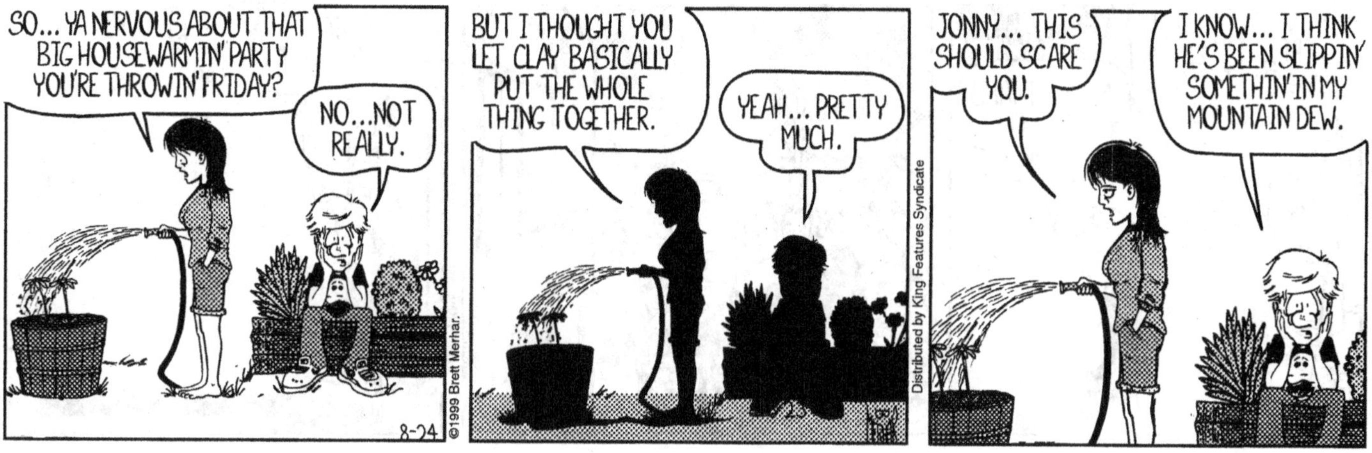
SO... YA NERVOUS ABOUT THAT BIG HOUSEWARMIN' PARTY YOU'RE THROWIN' FRIDAY?
NO...NOT REALLY.
8-24
©1999 Brett Merhar.
BUT I THOUGHT YOU LET CLAY BASICALLY PUT THE WHOLE THING TOGETHER.
YEAH... PRETTY MUCH.
Distributed by King Features Syndicate
JONNY... THIS SHOULD SCARE YOU.
I KNOW... I THINK HE'S BEEN SLIPPIN' SOMETHIN' IN MY MOUNTAIN DEW.

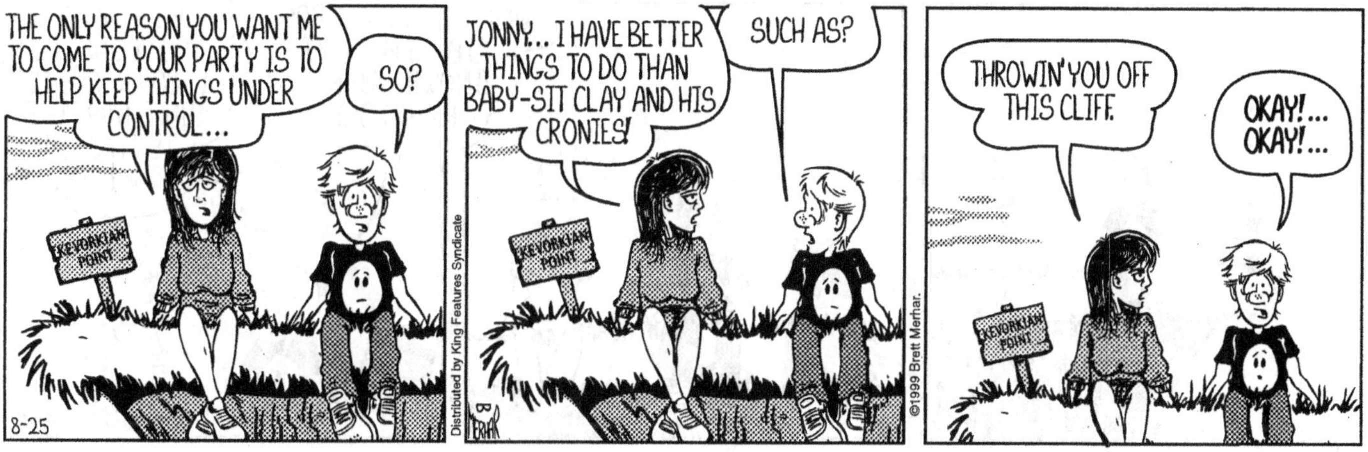
THE ONLY REASON YOU WANT ME TO COME TO YOUR PARTY IS TO HELP KEEP THINGS UNDER CONTROL...
SO?
KEVORKIAN POINT
8-25
Distributed by King Features Syndicate
JONNY... I HAVE BETTER THINGS TO DO THAN BABY-SIT CLAY AND HIS CRONIES!
SUCH AS?
KEVORKIAN POINT
©1999 Brett Merhar.
THROWIN' YOU OFF THIS CLIFF.
OKAY!... OKAY!...
KEVORKIAN POINT

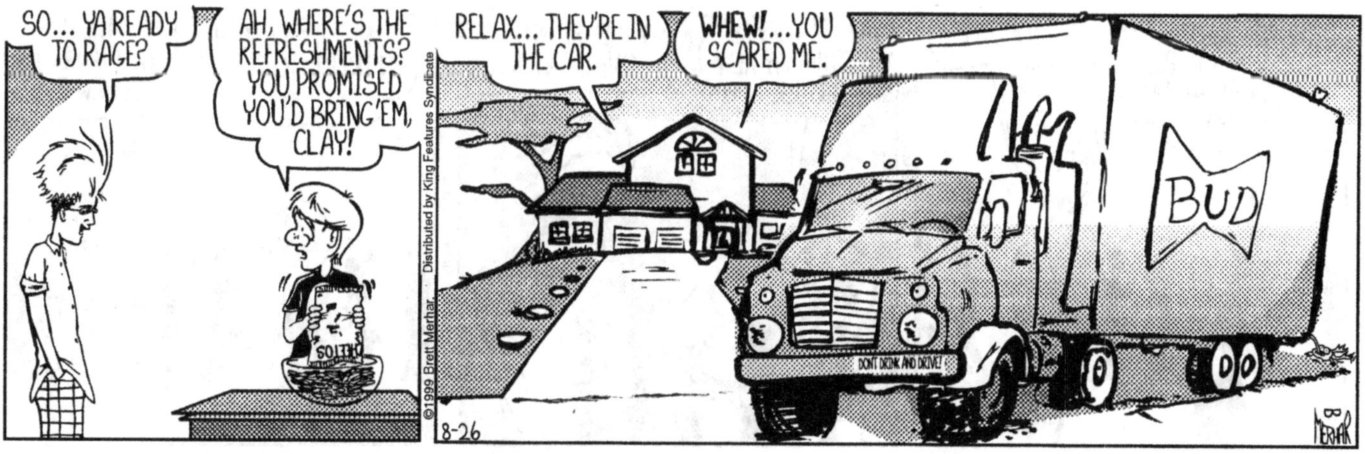
SO... YA READY TO RAGE?
AH, WHERE'S THE REFRESHMENTS? YOU PROMISED YOU'D BRING 'EM, CLAY!
©1999 Brett Merhar. Distributed by King Features Syndicate
RELAX... THEY'RE IN THE CAR.
WHEW!...YOU SCARED ME.
BUD
DON'T DRINK AND DRIVE!
8-26

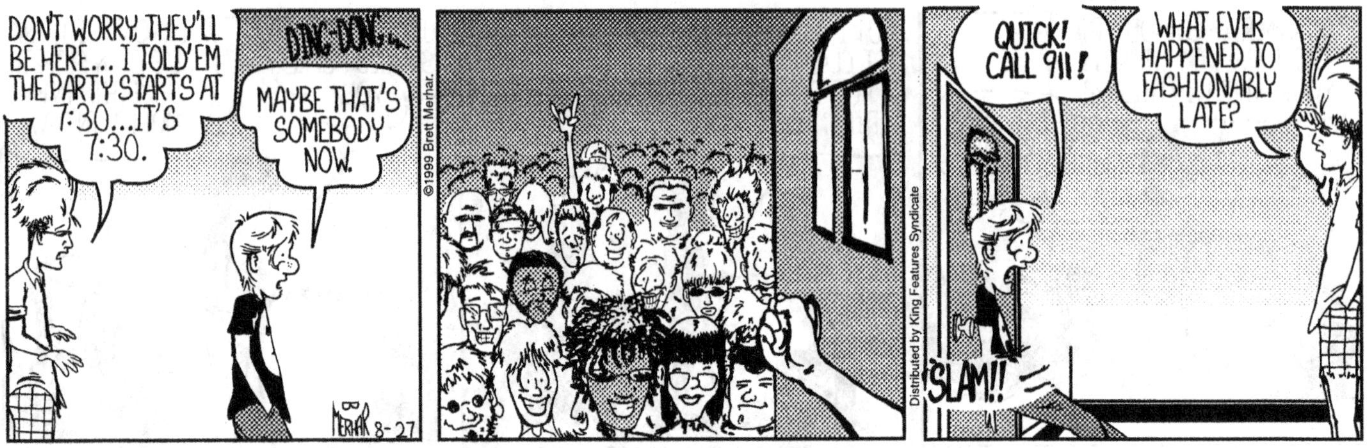
DON'T WORRY, THEY'LL BE HERE... I TOLD 'EM THE PARTY STARTS AT 7:30...IT'S 7:30.
DING-DONG...
MAYBE THAT'S SOMEBODY NOW.
MERHAR 8-27
©1999 Brett Merhar.
Distributed by King Features Syndicate
QUICK! CALL 911!
SLAM!!
WHAT EVER HAPPENED TO FASHIONABLY LATE?

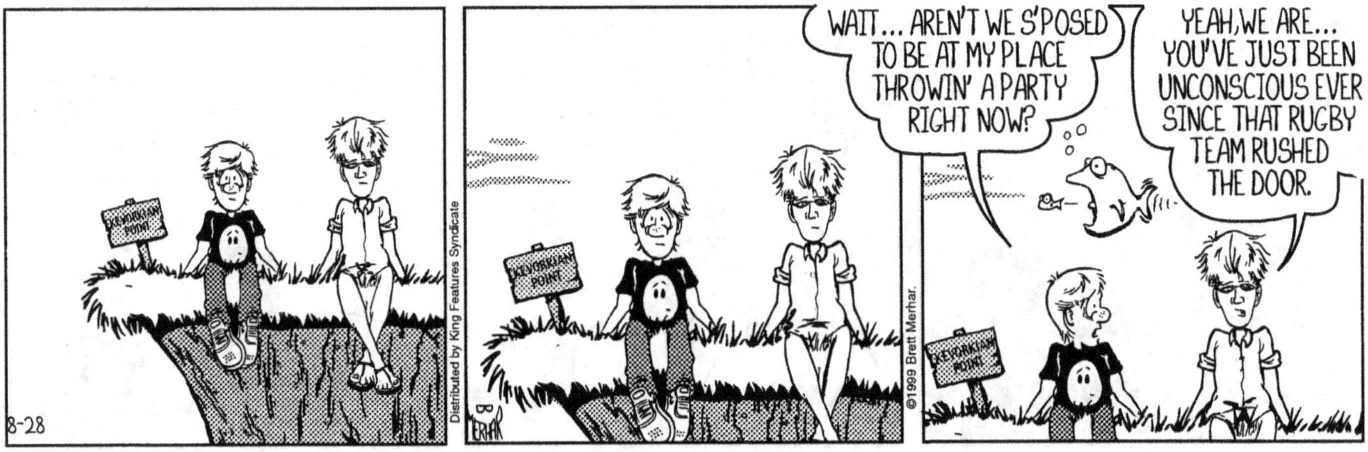
KEVORKIAN POINT
8-28
Distributed by King Features Syndicate
MERHAR
WAIT... AREN'T WE S'POSED TO BE AT MY PLACE THROWIN' A PARTY RIGHT NOW?
YEAH, WE ARE... YOU'VE JUST BEEN UNCONSCIOUS EVER SINCE THAT RUGBY TEAM RUSHED THE DOOR.
©1999 Brett Merhar.

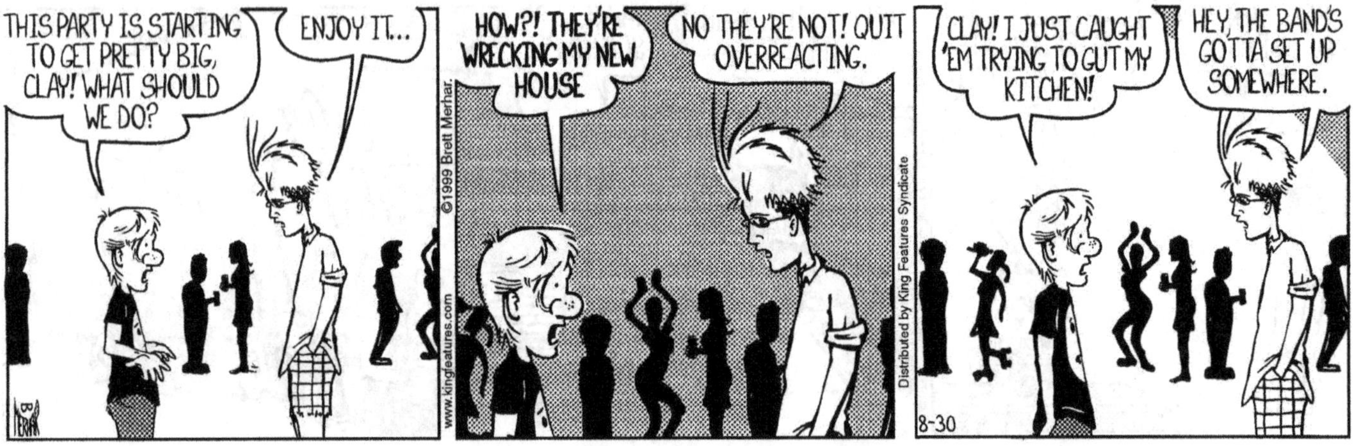
THIS PARTY IS STARTING TO GET PRETTY BIG, CLAY! WHAT SHOULD WE DO?
ENJOY IT...
MERHAR
©1999 Brett Merhar.
www.kingfeatures.com
HOW?! THEY'RE WRECKING MY NEW HOUSE
NO THEY'RE NOT! QUIT OVERREACTING.
Distributed by King Features Syndicate
CLAY! I JUST CAUGHT 'EM TRYING TO GUT MY KITCHEN!
HEY, THE BAND'S GOTTA SET UP SOMEWHERE.
8-30

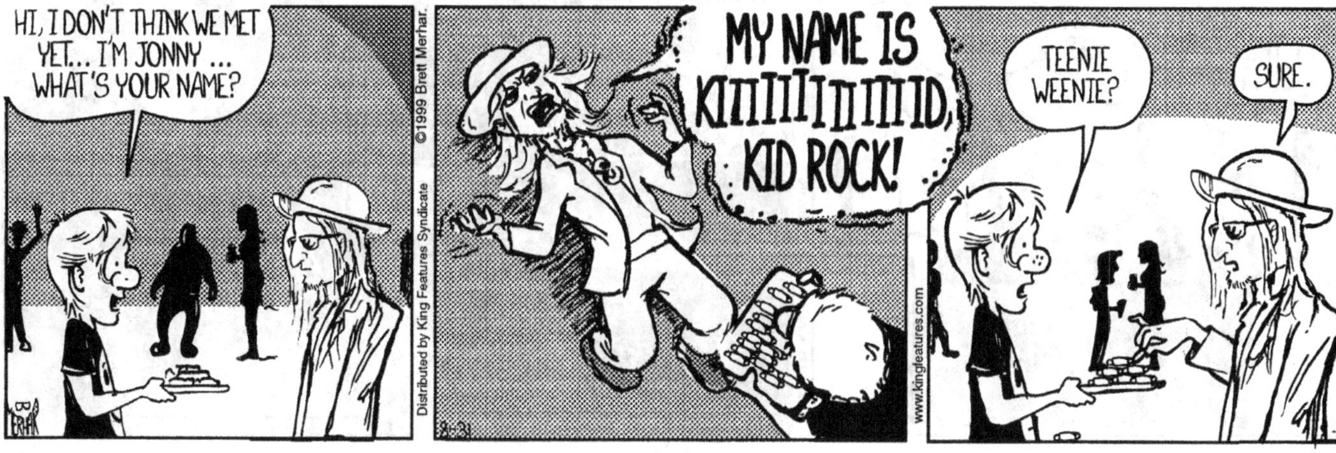
HI, I DON'T THINK WE MET YET... I'M JONNY ... WHAT'S YOUR NAME?
MY NAME IS KIIIIIIIIIIID, KID ROCK!
TEENIE WEENIE?
SURE.
©1999 Brett Merhar.
Distributed by King Features Syndicate
www.kingfeatures.com

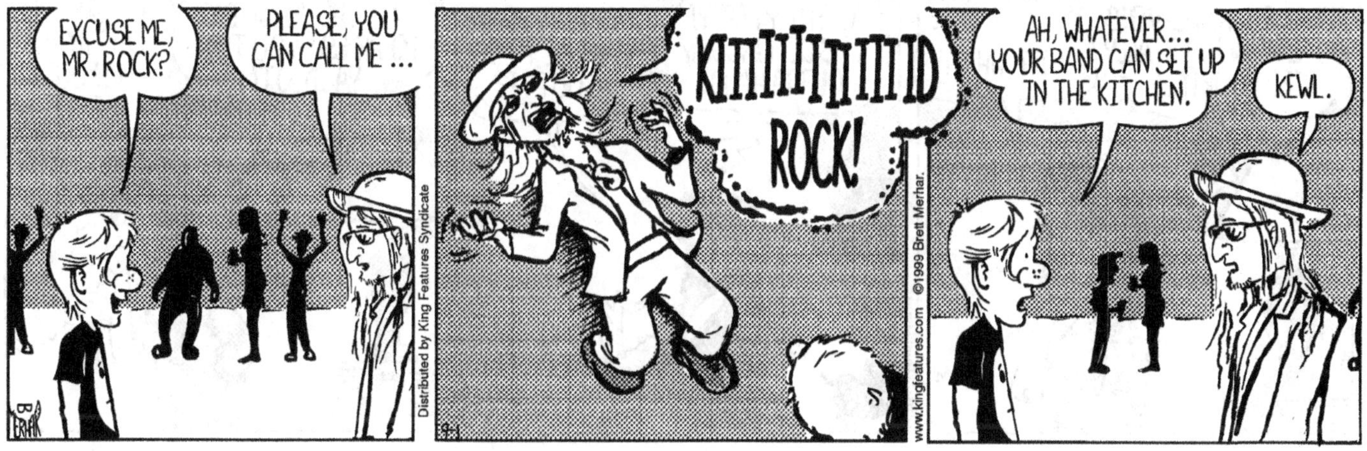
EXCUSE ME, MR. ROCK?
PLEASE, YOU CAN CALL ME ...
KIIIIIIIIIIID ROCK!
AH, WHATEVER... YOUR BAND CAN SET UP IN THE KITCHEN.
KEWL.
Distributed by King Features Syndicate
www.kingfeatures.com
©1999 Brett Merhar.

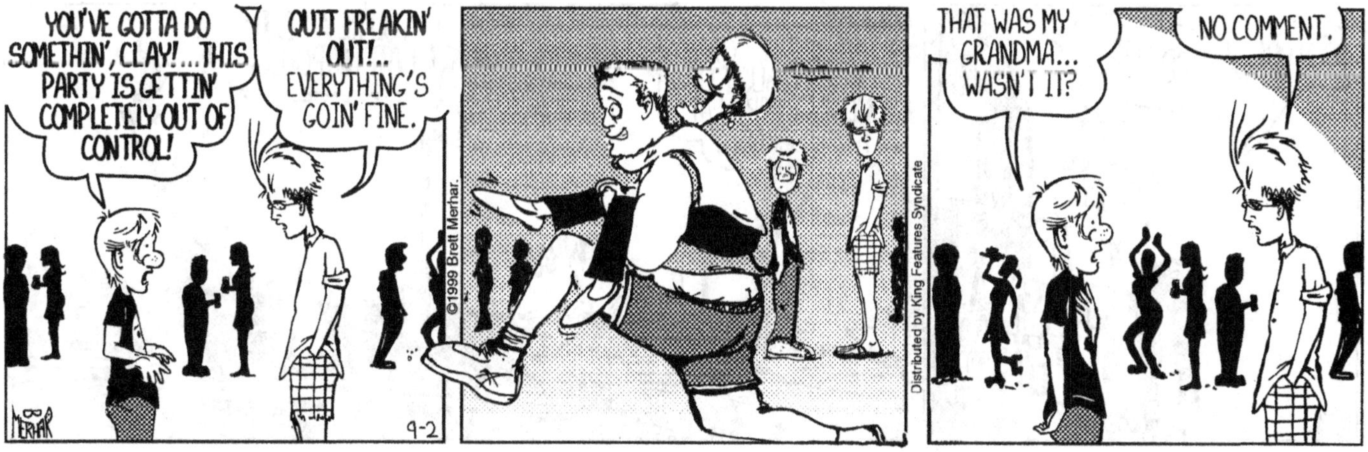
YOU'VE GOTTA DO SOMETHIN', CLAY!...THIS PARTY IS GETTIN' COMPLETELY OUT OF CONTROL!
QUIT FREAKIN' OUT!.. EVERYTHING'S GOIN' FINE.
MERHAR
9-2
©1999 Brett Merhar.
Distributed by King Features Syndicate
THAT WAS MY GRANDMA... WASN'T IT?
NO COMMENT.

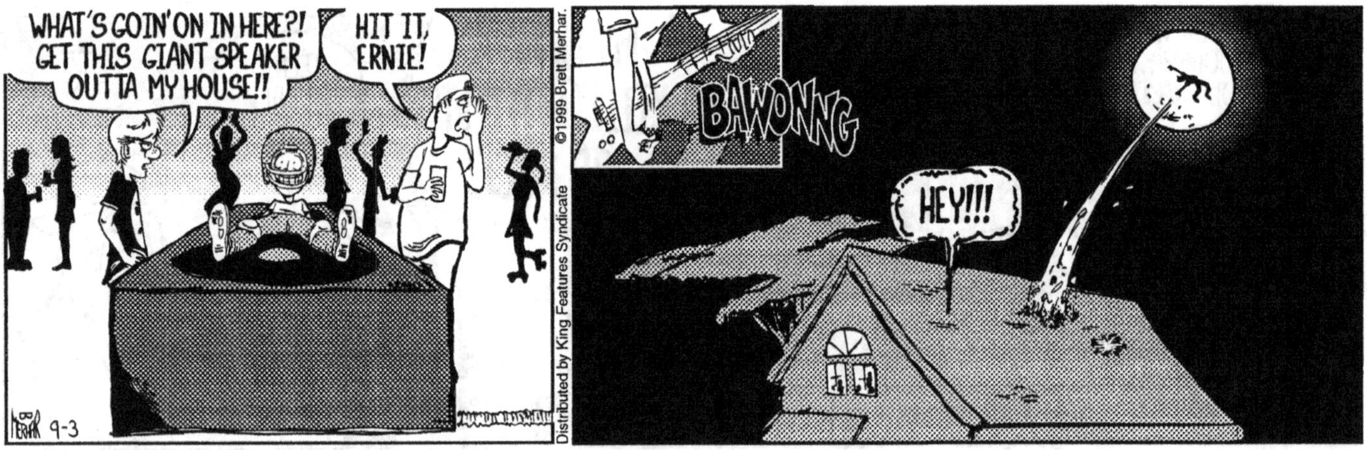
WHAT'S GOIN' ON IN HERE?! GET THIS GIANT SPEAKER OUTTA MY HOUSE!!
HIT IT, ERNIE!
MERHAR 9-3
©1999 Brett Merhar.
Distributed by King Features Syndicate
BAWONNG
HEY!!!

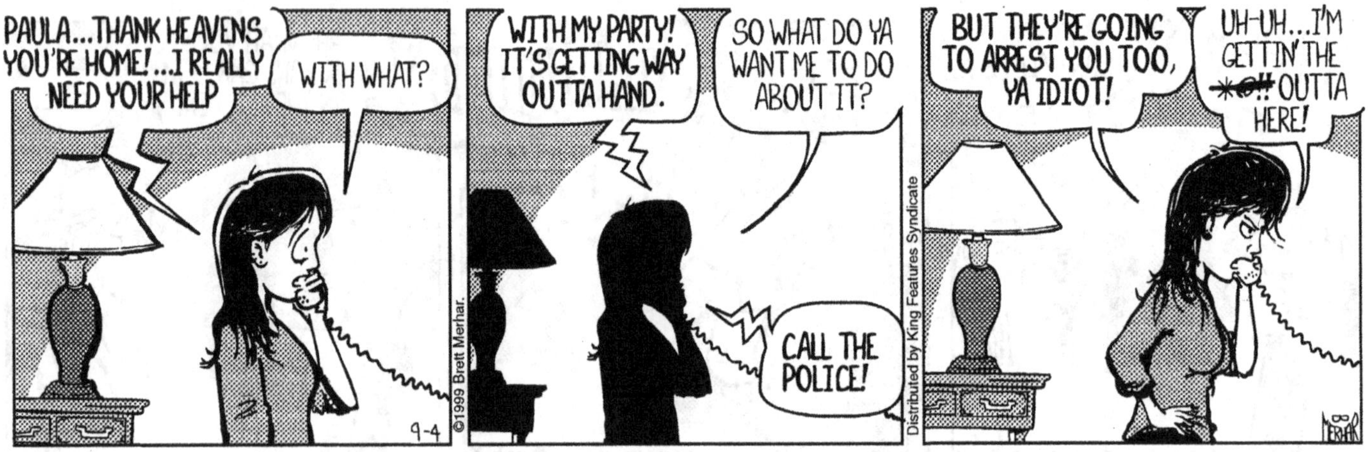
PAULA...THANK HEAVENS YOU'RE HOME!...I REALLY NEED YOUR HELP
WITH WHAT?
9-4
©1999 Brett Merhar.
WITH MY PARTY! IT'S GETTING WAY OUTTA HAND.
SO WHAT DO YA WANT ME TO DO ABOUT IT?
CALL THE POLICE!
Distributed by King Features Syndicate
BUT THEY'RE GOING TO ARREST YOU TOO, YA IDIOT!
UH-UH...I'M GETTIN' THE *@!! OUTTA HERE!
MERHAR

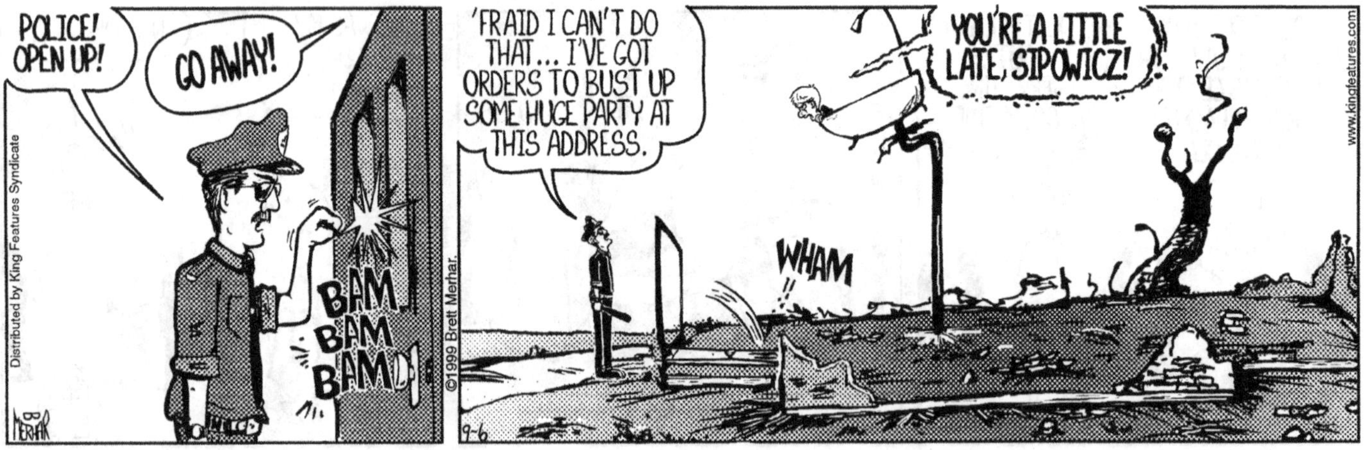
POLICE! OPEN UP!
GO AWAY!
BAM BAM BAM
Distributed by King Features Syndicate
MERHAR
©1999 Brett Merhar.
'FRAID I CAN'T DO THAT... I'VE GOT ORDERS TO BUST UP SOME HUGE PARTY AT THIS ADDRESS.
YOU'RE A LITTLE LATE, SIPOWICZ!
WHAM
9-6
www.kingfeatures.com

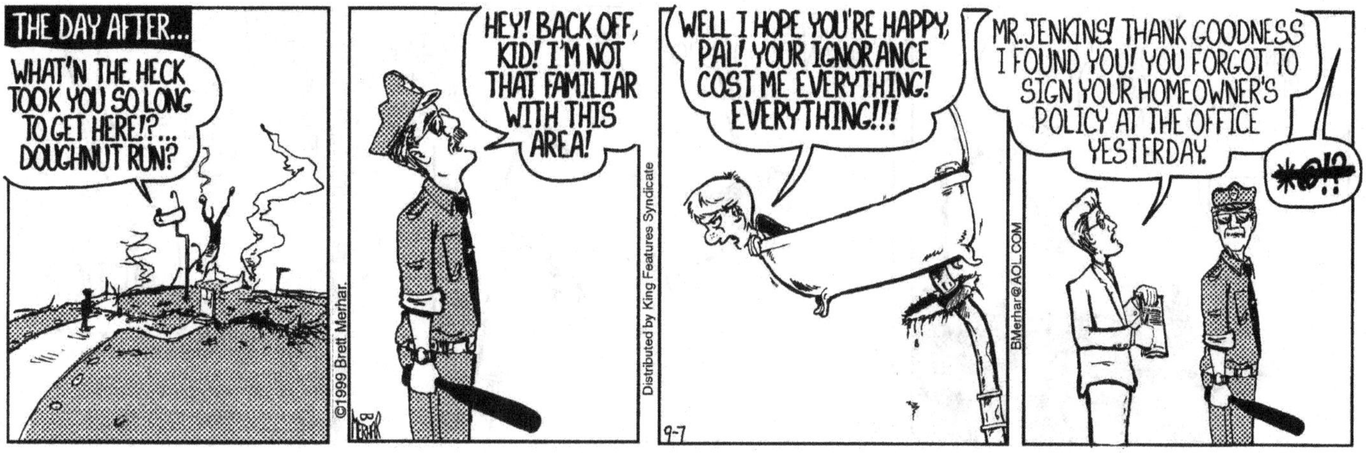
THE DAY AFTER...
WHAT'N THE HECK TOOK YOU SO LONG TO GET HERE!?... DOUGHNUT RUN?
HEY! BACK OFF, KID! I'M NOT THAT FAMILIAR WITH THIS AREA!
WELL I HOPE YOU'RE HAPPY, PAL! YOUR IGNORANCE COST ME EVERYTHING! EVERYTHING!!!
MR. JENKINS! THANK GOODNESS I FOUND YOU! YOU FORGOT TO SIGN YOUR HOMEOWNER'S POLICY AT THE OFFICE YESTERDAY.
*@!?
©1999 Brett Merhar.
Distributed by King Features Syndicate
BMerhar@AOL.COM
9-7

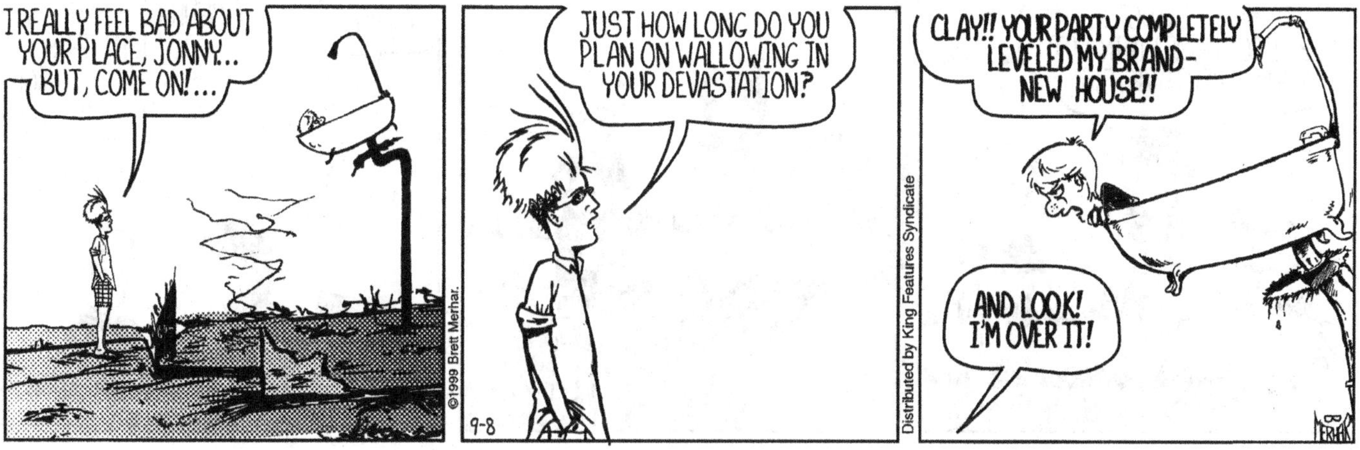
I REALLY FEEL BAD ABOUT YOUR PLACE, JONNY... BUT, COME ON!...
JUST HOW LONG DO YOU PLAN ON WALLOWING IN YOUR DEVASTATION?
CLAY!! YOUR PARTY COMPLETELY LEVELED MY BRAND-NEW HOUSE!!
AND LOOK! I'M OVER IT!
©1999 Brett Merhar.
Distributed by King Features Syndicate
9-8

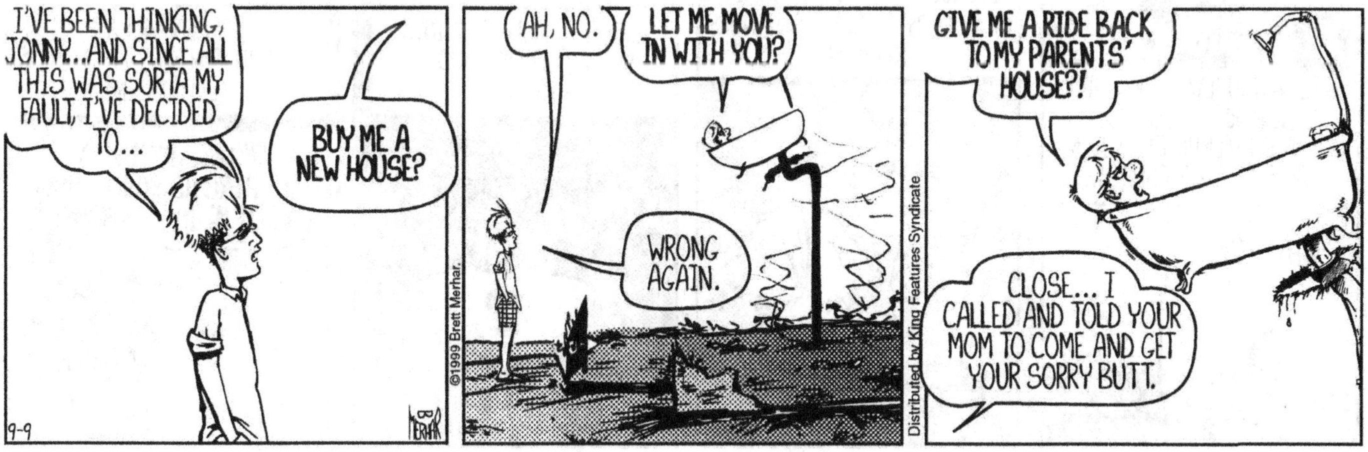
I'VE BEEN THINKING, JONNY...AND SINCE ALL THIS WAS SORTA MY FAULT, I'VE DECIDED TO...
BUY ME A NEW HOUSE?
AH, NO.
LET ME MOVE IN WITH YOU?
WRONG AGAIN.
GIVE ME A RIDE BACK TO MY PARENTS' HOUSE?!
CLOSE... I CALLED AND TOLD YOUR MOM TO COME AND GET YOUR SORRY BUTT.
©1999 Brett Merhar.
Distributed by King Features Syndicate
9-9

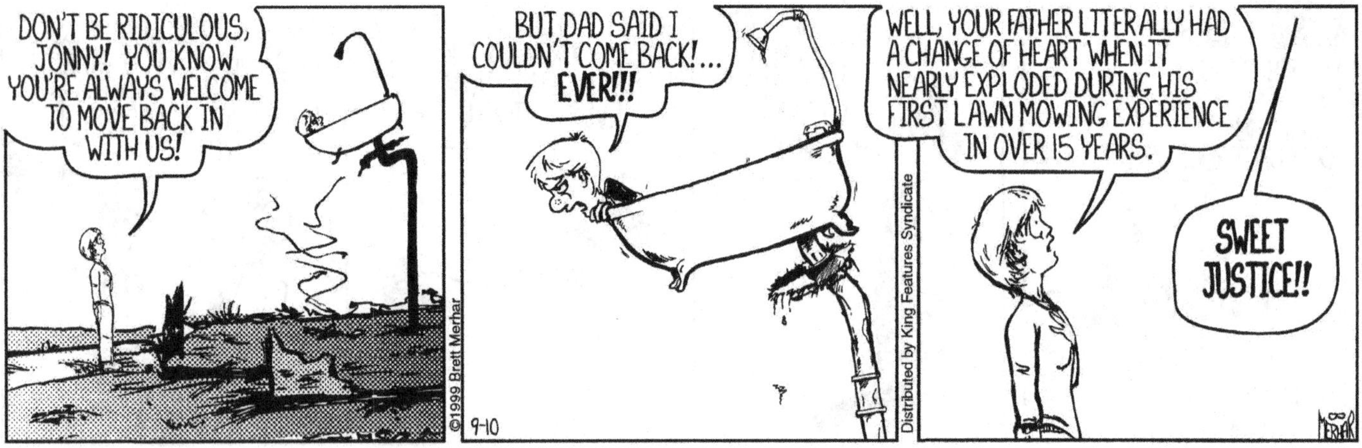
DON'T BE RIDICULOUS, JONNY! YOU KNOW YOU'RE ALWAYS WELCOME TO MOVE BACK IN WITH US!
©1999 Brett Merhar
9-10
BUT DAD SAID I COULDN'T COME BACK!... EVER!!!
Distributed by King Features Syndicate
WELL, YOUR FATHER LITERALLY HAD A CHANGE OF HEART WHEN IT NEARLY EXPLODED DURING HIS FIRST LAWN MOWING EXPERIENCE IN OVER 15 YEARS.
SWEET JUSTICE!!
MERHAR

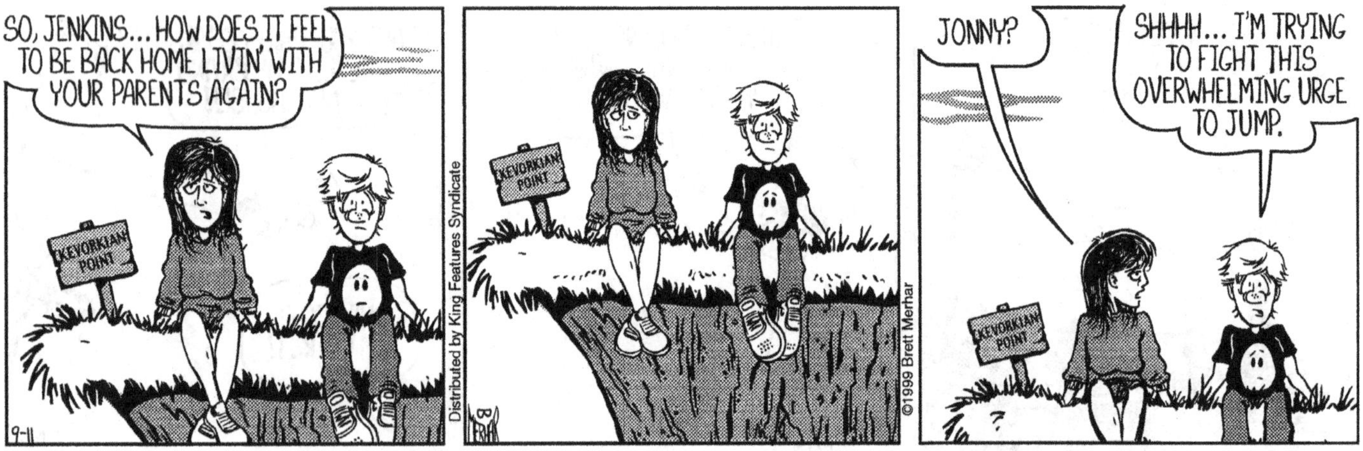
SO, JENKINS... HOW DOES IT FEEL TO BE BACK HOME LIVIN' WITH YOUR PARENTS AGAIN?
KEVORKIAN POINT
9-11
Distributed by King Features Syndicate
KEVORKIAN POINT
©1999 Brett Merhar
JONNY?
SHHHH... I'M TRYING TO FIGHT THIS OVERWHELMING URGE TO JUMP.
KEVORKIAN POINT

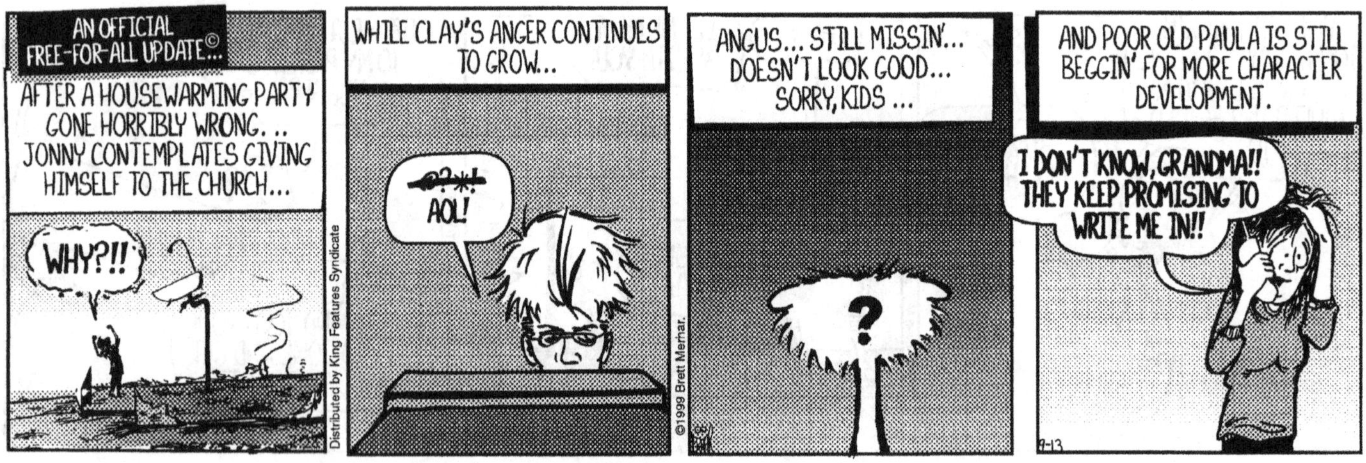
AN OFFICIAL FREE-FOR-ALL UPDATE©...
AFTER A HOUSEWARMING PARTY GONE HORRIBLY WRONG... JONNY CONTEMPLATES GIVING HIMSELF TO THE CHURCH...
WHY?!!
Distributed by King Features Syndicate
WHILE CLAY'S ANGER CONTINUES TO GROW...
AOL!
©1999 Brett Merhar.
ANGUS... STILL MISSIN'... DOESN'T LOOK GOOD... SORRY, KIDS ...
?
AND POOR OLD PAULA IS STILL BEGGIN' FOR MORE CHARACTER DEVELOPMENT.
I DON'T KNOW, GRANDMA!! THEY KEEP PROMISING TO WRITE ME IN!!
9-13

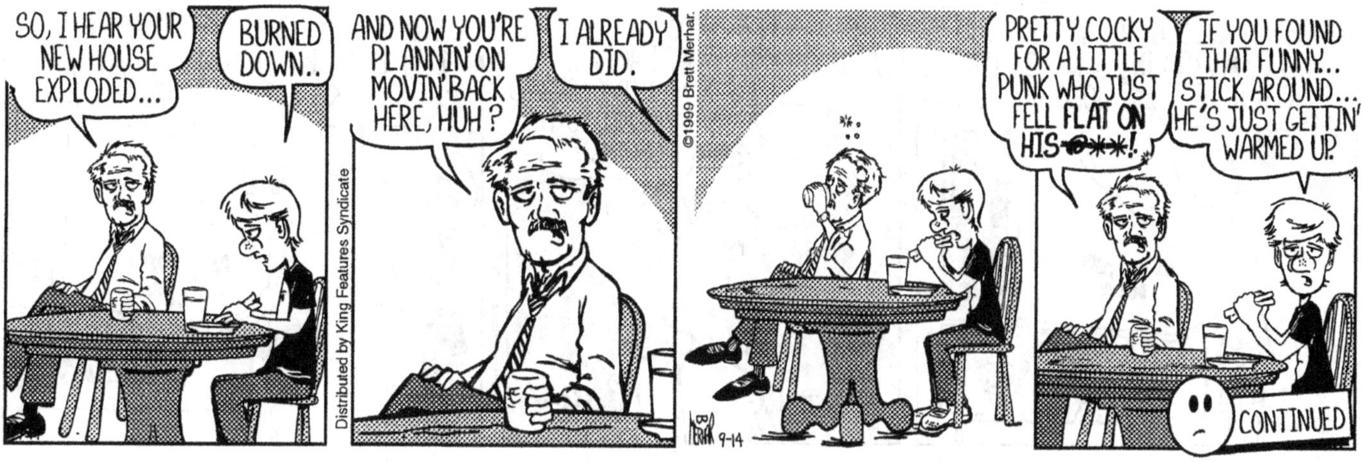
SO, I HEAR YOUR NEW HOUSE EXPLODED...
BURNED DOWN..
Distributed by King Features Syndicate
AND NOW YOU'RE PLANNIN' ON MOVIN' BACK HERE, HUH ?
I ALREADY DID.
©1999 Brett Merhar.
MERHAR 9-14
PRETTY COCKY FOR A LITTLE PUNK WHO JUST FELL FLAT ON HIS
IF YOU FOUND THAT FUNNY... STICK AROUND... HE'S JUST GETTIN' WARMED UP.
CONTINUED

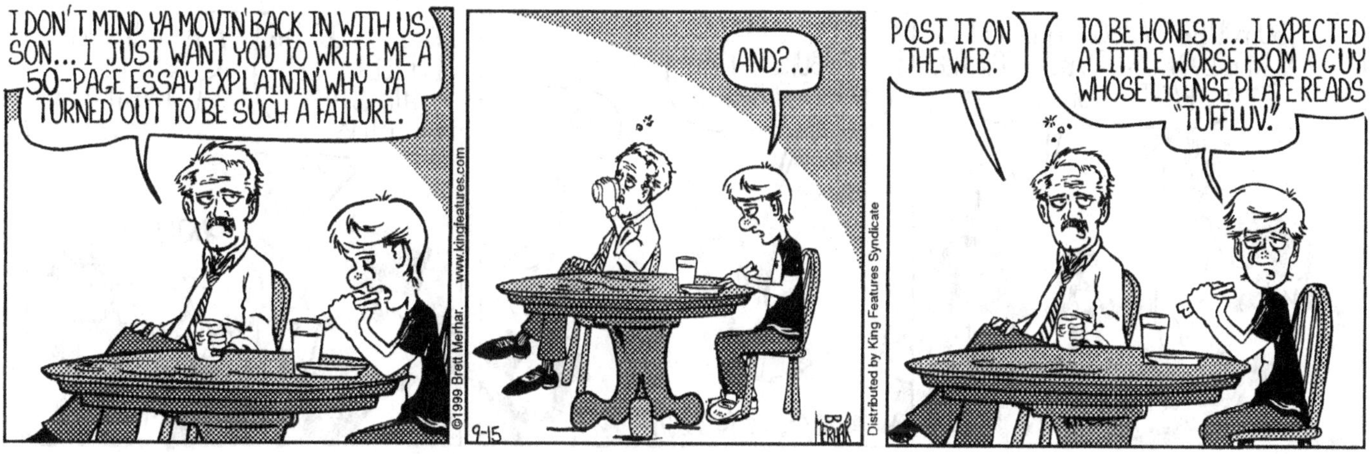
I DON'T MIND YA MOVIN' BACK IN WITH US, SON... I JUST WANT YOU TO WRITE ME A 50-PAGE ESSAY EXPLAININ' WHY YA TURNED OUT TO BE SUCH A FAILURE.
©1999 Brett Merhar. www.kingfeatures.com
9-15
AND?...
MERHAR
Distributed by King Features Syndicate
POST IT ON THE WEB.
TO BE HONEST... I EXPECTED A LITTLE WORSE FROM A GUY WHOSE LICENSE PLATE READS "TUFFLUV."

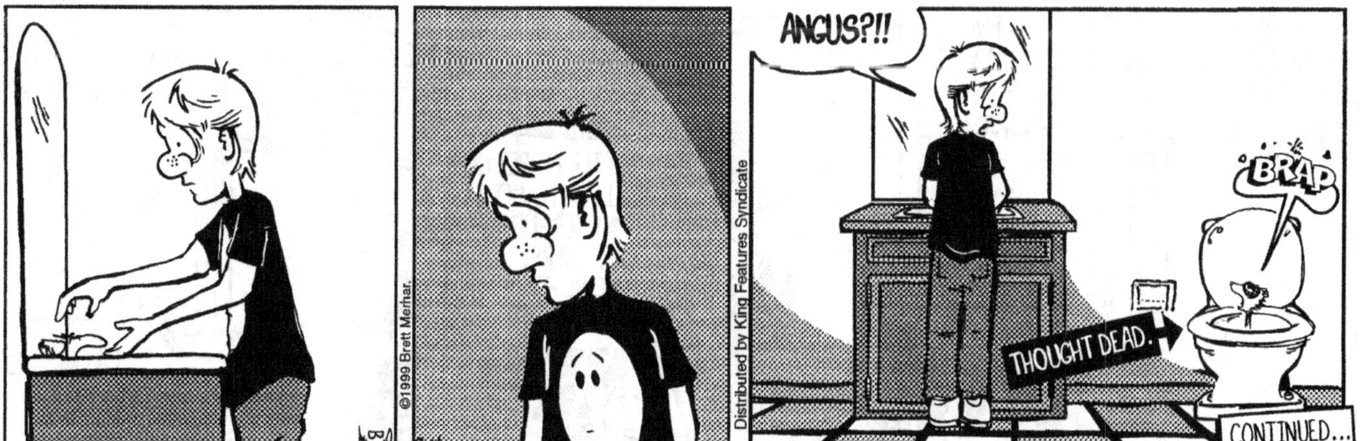
MERHAR
©1999 Brett Merhar.
9-16
Distributed by King Features Syndicate
ANGUS?!!
BRAP
THOUGHT DEAD.
CONTINUED...

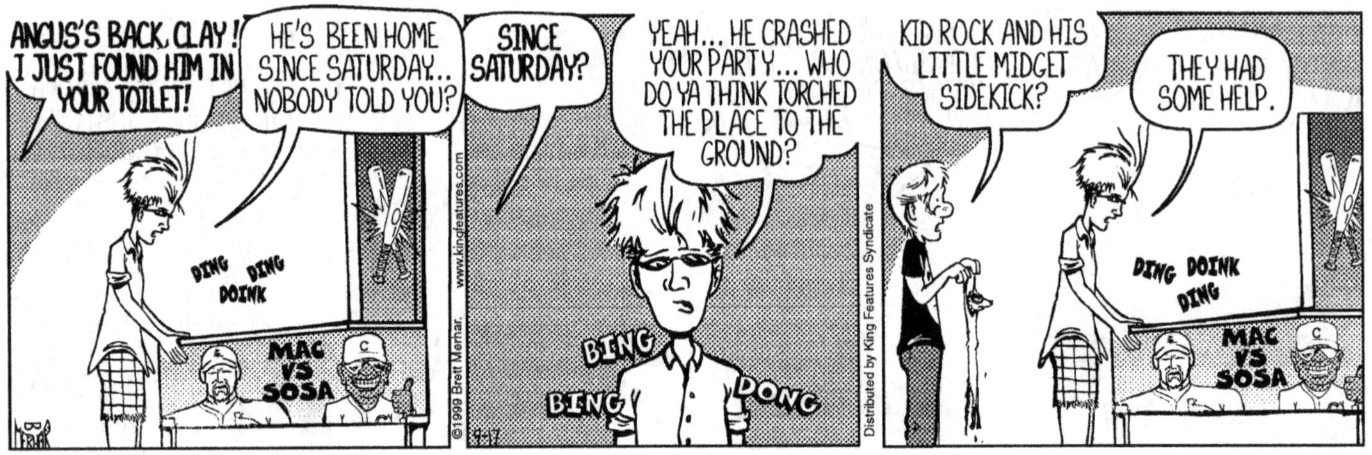
ANGUS'S BACK, CLAY! I JUST FOUND HIM IN YOUR TOILET!
HE'S BEEN HOME SINCE SATURDAY... NOBODY TOLD YOU?
DING DING DOINK
MAC VS SOSA
SINCE SATURDAY?
YEAH... HE CRASHED YOUR PARTY... WHO DO YA THINK TORCHED THE PLACE TO THE GROUND?
BING BING DONG
©1999 Brett Merhar. www.kingfeatures.com
KID ROCK AND HIS LITTLE MIDGET SIDEKICK?
THEY HAD SOME HELP.
DING DOINK DING
MAC VS SOSA
Distributed by King Features Syndicate

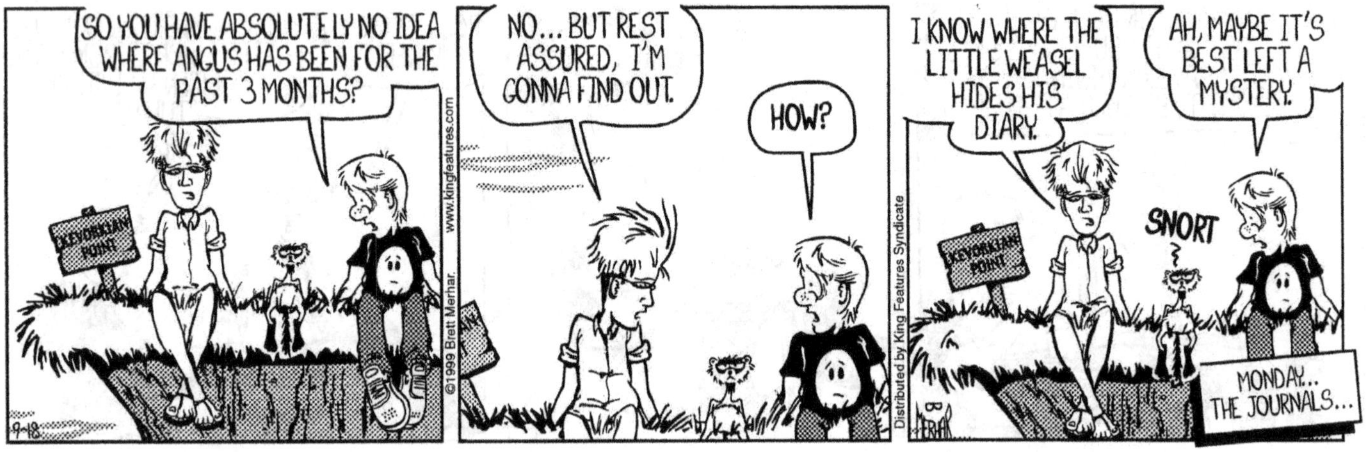
SO YOU HAVE ABSOLUTELY NO IDEA WHERE ANGUS HAS BEEN FOR THE PAST 3 MONTHS?
KEVORKIAN POINT
©1999 Brett Merhar. www.kingfeatures.com
NO... BUT REST ASSURED, I'M GONNA FIND OUT.
HOW?
I KNOW WHERE THE LITTLE WEASEL HIDES HIS DIARY.
AH, MAYBE IT'S BEST LEFT A MYSTERY.
KEVORKIAN POINT
SNORT
MONDAY... THE JOURNALS...
Distributed by King Features Syndicate

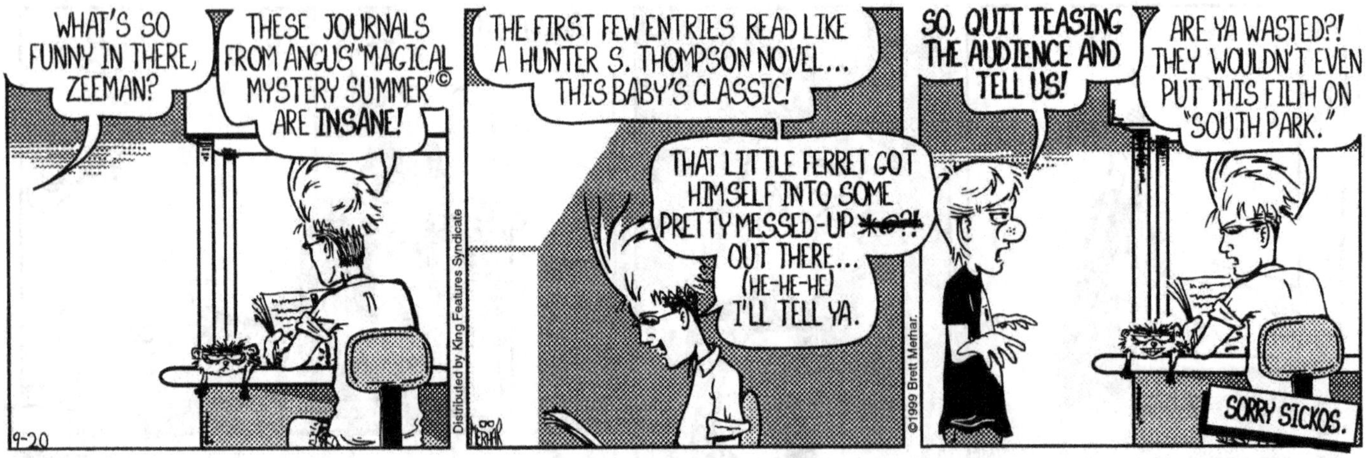
WHAT'S SO FUNNY IN THERE, ZEEMAN?
THESE JOURNALS FROM ANGUS' "MAGICAL MYSTERY SUMMER"© ARE INSANE!
Distributed by King Features Syndicate
THE FIRST FEW ENTRIES READ LIKE A HUNTER S. THOMPSON NOVEL... THIS BABY'S CLASSIC!
THAT LITTLE FERRET GOT HIMSELF INTO SOME PRETTY MESSED-UP *@?! OUT THERE... (HE-HE-HE) I'LL TELL YA.
©1999 Brett Merhar.
SO, QUIT TEASING THE AUDIENCE AND TELL US!
ARE YA WASTED?! THEY WOULDN'T EVEN PUT THIS FILTH ON "SOUTH PARK."
SORRY SICKOS.

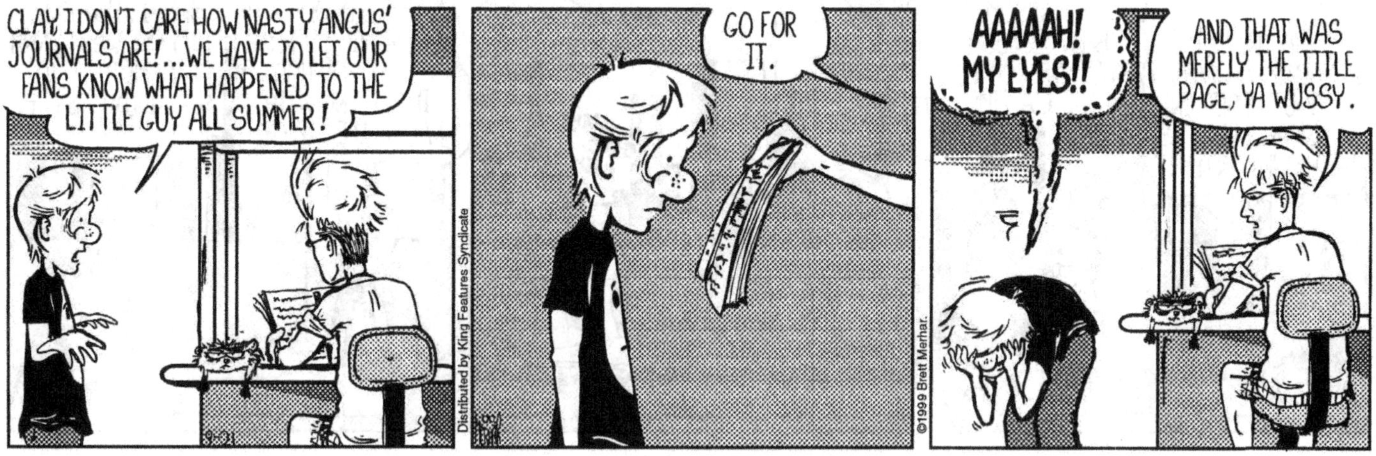
CLAY, I DON'T CARE HOW NASTY ANGUS' JOURNALS ARE!...WE HAVE TO LET OUR FANS KNOW WHAT HAPPENED TO THE LITTLE GUY ALL SUMMER!
9-21
Distributed by King Features Syndicate
GO FOR IT.
AAAAAH! MY EYES!!
AND THAT WAS MERELY THE TITLE PAGE, YA WUSSY.
©1999 Brett Merhar.

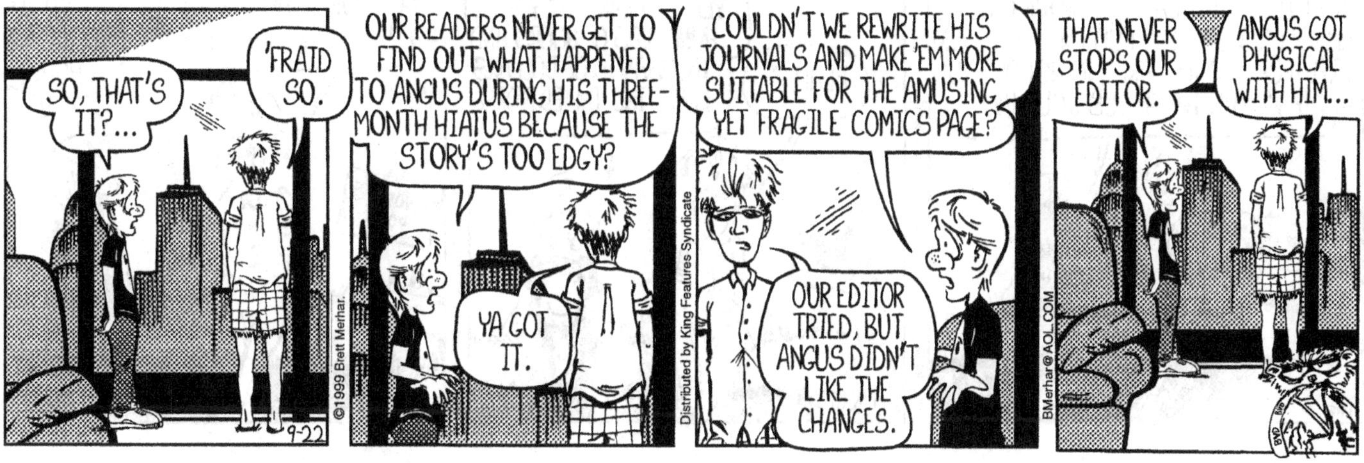
SO, THAT'S IT?...
'FRAID SO.
9-22
©1999 Brett Merhar.
OUR READERS NEVER GET TO FIND OUT WHAT HAPPENED TO ANGUS DURING HIS THREE-MONTH HIATUS BECAUSE THE STORY'S TOO EDGY?
YA GOT IT.
Distributed by King Features Syndicate
COULDN'T WE REWRITE HIS JOURNALS AND MAKE 'EM MORE SUITABLE FOR THE AMUSING YET FRAGILE COMICS PAGE?
OUR EDITOR TRIED, BUT ANGUS DIDN'T LIKE THE CHANGES.
BMerhar@AOL.COM
THAT NEVER STOPS OUR EDITOR.
ANGUS GOT PHYSICAL WITH HIM...

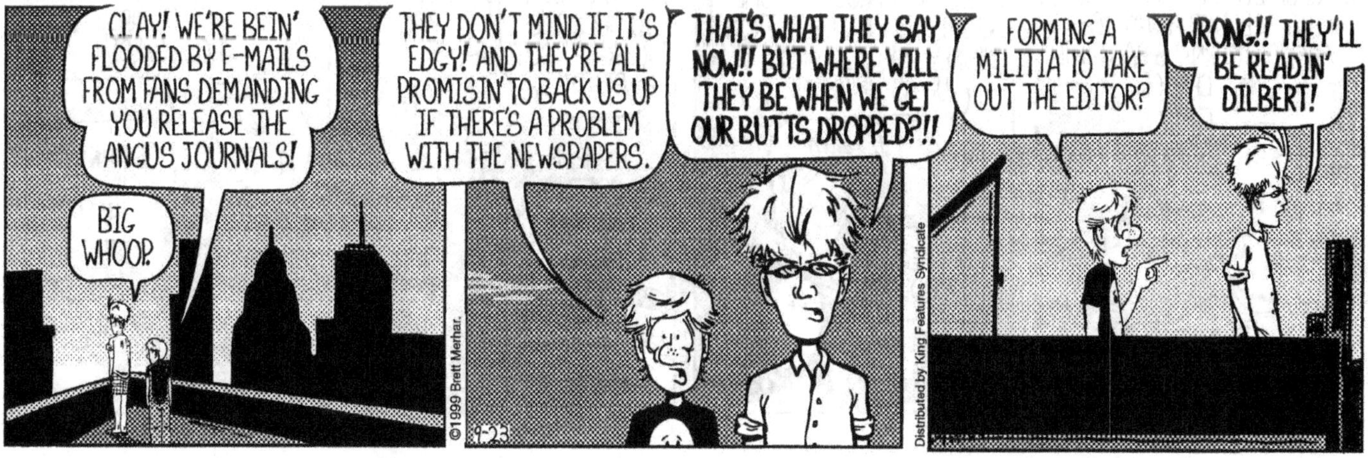
CLAY! WE'RE BEIN' FLOODED BY E-MAILS FROM FANS DEMANDING YOU RELEASE THE ANGUS JOURNALS!
BIG WHOOP.
©1999 Brett Merhar.
9-23
THEY DON'T MIND IF IT'S EDGY! AND THEY'RE ALL PROMISIN' TO BACK US UP IF THERE'S A PROBLEM WITH THE NEWSPAPERS.
THAT'S WHAT THEY SAY NOW!! BUT WHERE WILL THEY BE WHEN WE GET OUR BUTTS DROPPED?!!
Distributed by King Features Syndicate
FORMING A MILITIA TO TAKE OUT THE EDITOR?
WRONG!! THEY'LL BE READIN' DILBERT!

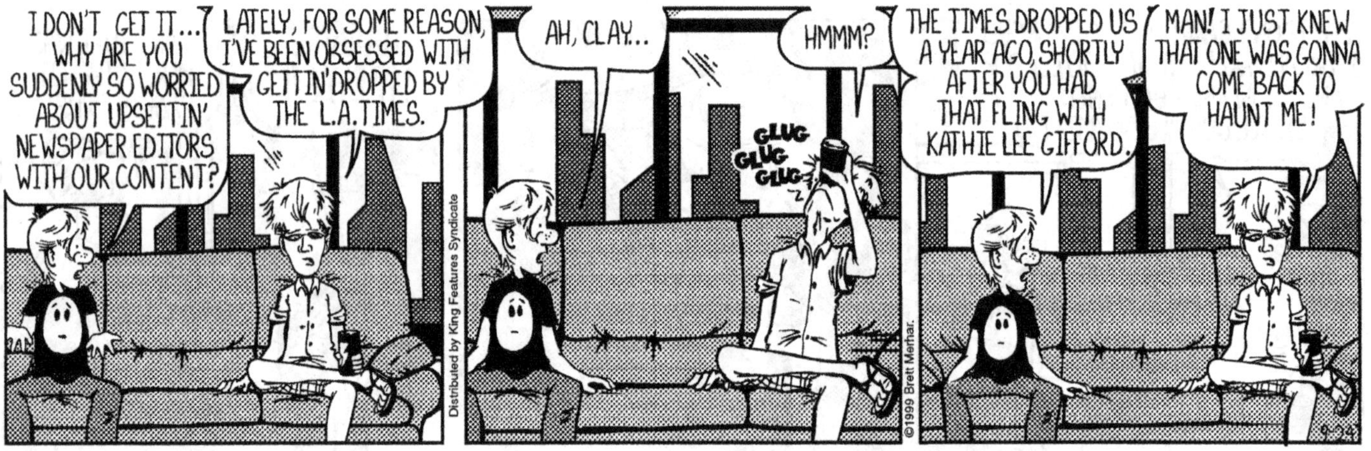
I DON'T GET IT... WHY ARE YOU SUDDENLY SO WORRIED ABOUT UPSETTIN' NEWSPAPER EDITORS WITH OUR CONTENT?
LATELY, FOR SOME REASON, I'VE BEEN OBSESSED WITH GETTIN' DROPPED BY THE L.A.TIMES.
AH, CLAY...
HMMM?
GLUG GLUG GLUG
THE TIMES DROPPED US A YEAR AGO, SHORTLY AFTER YOU HAD THAT FLING WITH KATHIE LEE GIFFORD.
MAN! I JUST KNEW THAT ONE WAS GONNA COME BACK TO HAUNT ME!
Distributed by King Features Syndicate
©1999 Brett Merhar.
9-24

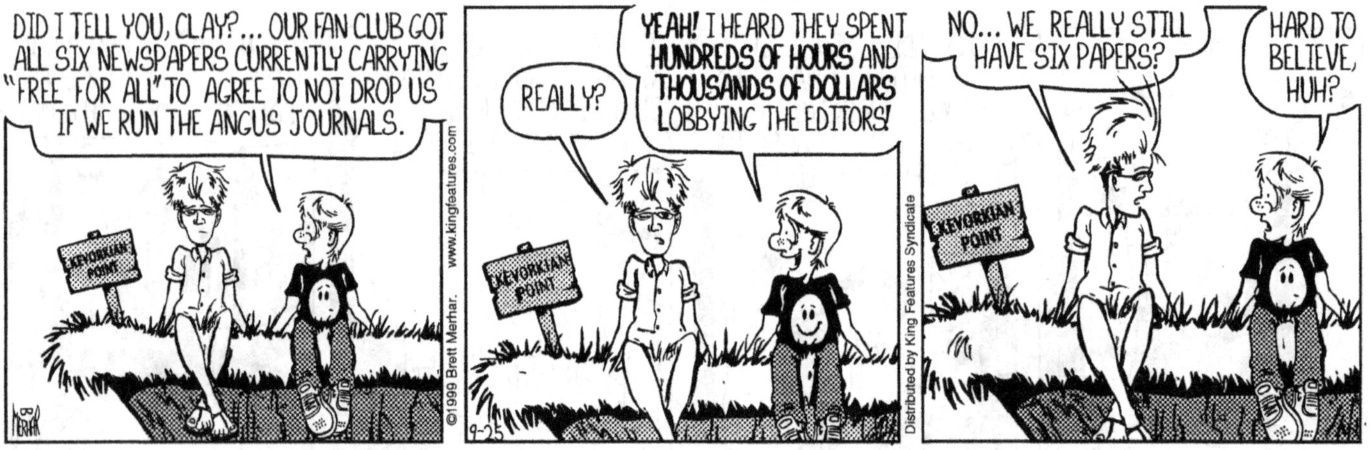
DID I TELL YOU, CLAY?... OUR FAN CLUB GOT ALL SIX NEWSPAPERS CURRENTLY CARRYING "FREE FOR ALL" TO AGREE TO NOT DROP US IF WE RUN THE ANGUS JOURNALS.
KEVORKIAN POINT
MERHAR
©1999 Brett Merhar.
www.kingfeatures.com
REALLY?
YEAH! I HEARD THEY SPENT HUNDREDS OF HOURS AND THOUSANDS OF DOLLARS LOBBYING THE EDITORS!
9-25
NO... WE REALLY STILL HAVE SIX PAPERS?
HARD TO BELIEVE, HUH?
Distributed by King Features Syndicate

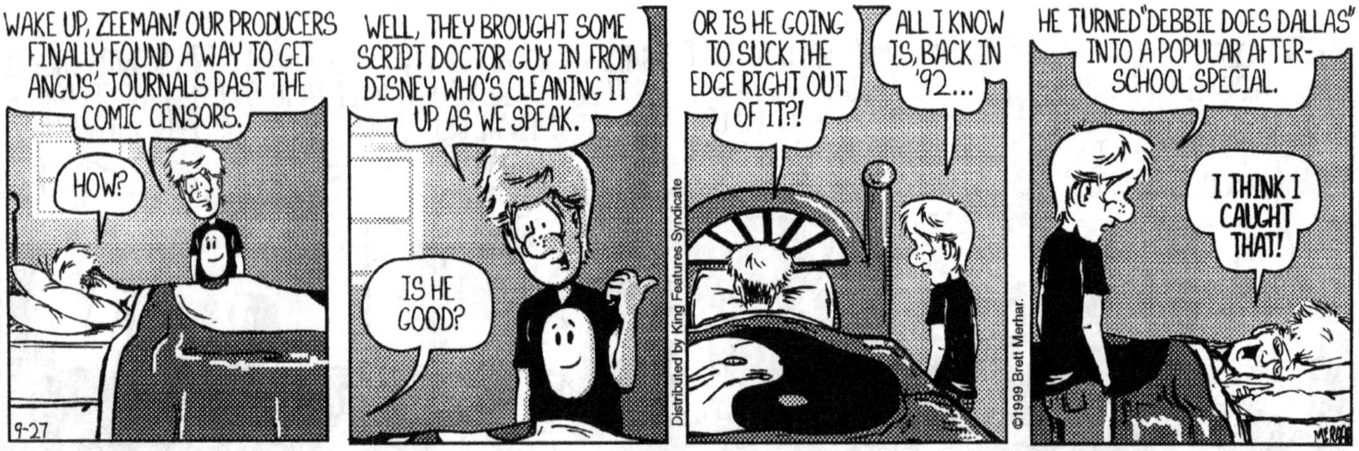
WAKE UP, ZEEMAN! OUR PRODUCERS FINALLY FOUND A WAY TO GET ANGUS' JOURNALS PAST THE COMIC CENSORS.
HOW?
9-27
WELL, THEY BROUGHT SOME SCRIPT DOCTOR GUY IN FROM DISNEY WHO'S CLEANING IT UP AS WE SPEAK.
IS HE GOOD?
Distributed by King Features Syndicate
OR IS HE GOING TO SUCK THE EDGE RIGHT OUT OF IT?!
ALL I KNOW IS, BACK IN '92...
©1999 Brett Merhar.
HE TURNED "DEBBIE DOES DALLAS" INTO A POPULAR AFTER-SCHOOL SPECIAL.
I THINK I CAUGHT THAT!

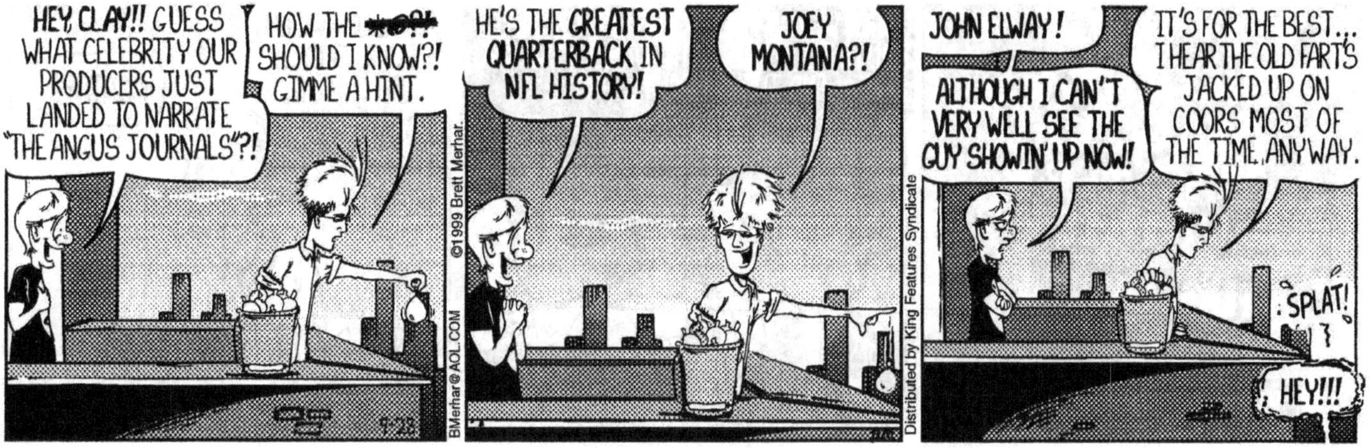
HEY, CLAY!! GUESS WHAT CELEBRITY OUR PRODUCERS JUST LANDED TO NARRATE "THE ANGUS JOURNALS"?!
HOW THE #@?! SHOULD I KNOW?! GIMME A HINT.
HE'S THE GREATEST QUARTERBACK IN NFL HISTORY!
JOEY MONTANA?!
JOHN ELWAY!
ALTHOUGH I CAN'T VERY WELL SEE THE GUY SHOWIN' UP NOW!
IT'S FOR THE BEST... I HEAR THE OLD FART'S JACKED UP ON COORS MOST OF THE TIME, ANYWAY.
SPLAT!
HEY!!!
9-28
BMerhar@AOL.COM
©1999 Brett Merhar.
Distributed by King Features Syndicate

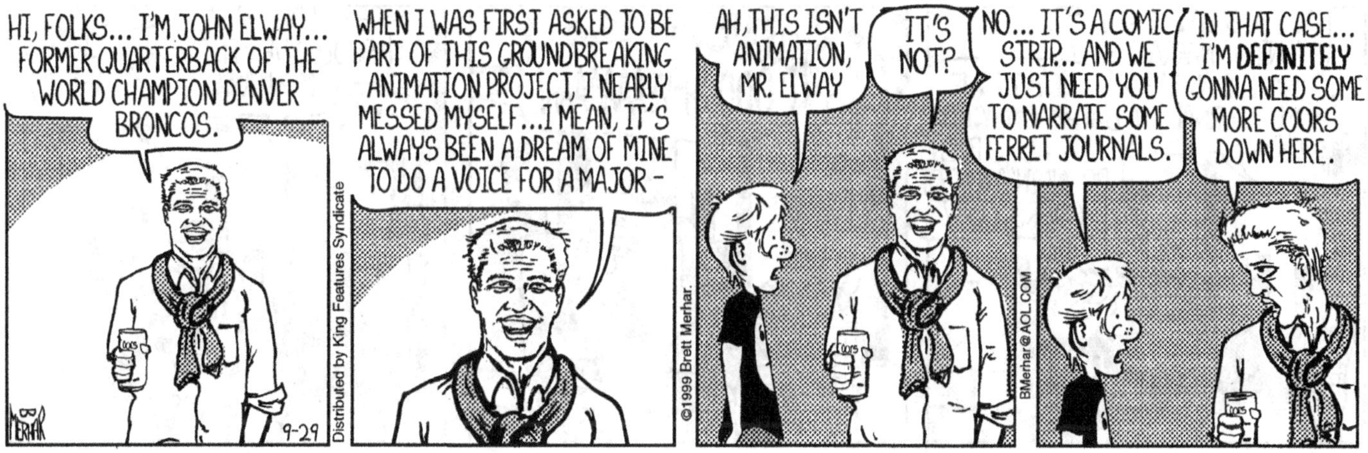
HI, FOLKS... I'M JOHN ELWAY... FORMER QUARTERBACK OF THE WORLD CHAMPION DENVER BRONCOS.
MERHAR
9-29
Distributed by King Features Syndicate
WHEN I WAS FIRST ASKED TO BE PART OF THIS GROUNDBREAKING ANIMATION PROJECT, I NEARLY MESSED MYSELF... I MEAN, IT'S ALWAYS BEEN A DREAM OF MINE TO DO A VOICE FOR A MAJOR -
©1999 Brett Merhar.
AH, THIS ISN'T ANIMATION, MR. ELWAY
IT'S NOT?
BMerhar@AOL.COM
NO... IT'S A COMIC STRIP.. AND WE JUST NEED YOU TO NARRATE SOME FERRET JOURNALS.
IN THAT CASE... I'M DEFINITELY GONNA NEED SOME MORE COORS DOWN HERE.

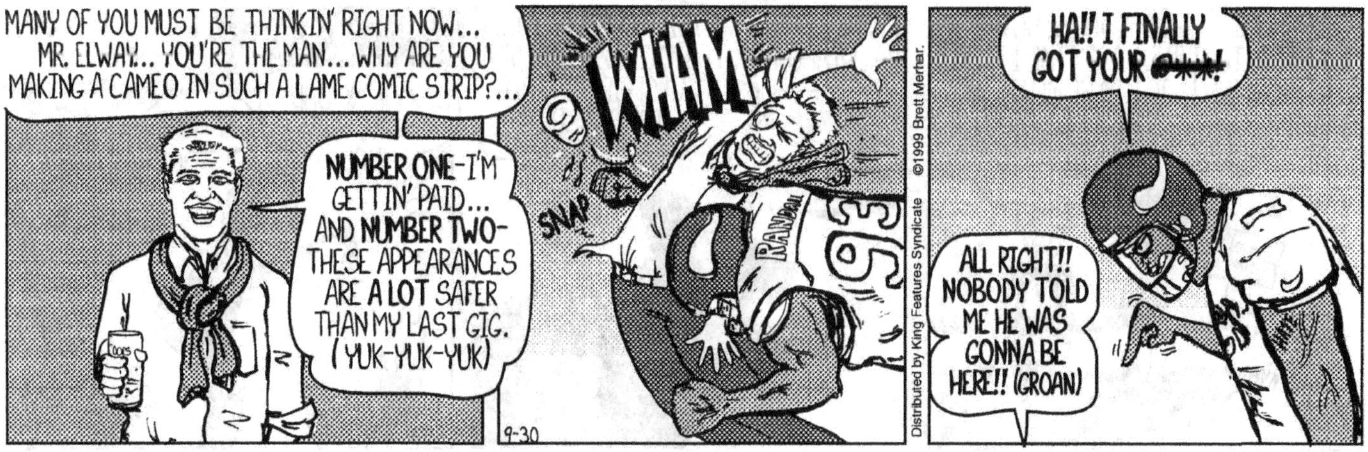
MANY OF YOU MUST BE THINKIN' RIGHT NOW... MR. ELWAY.. YOU'RE THE MAN... WHY ARE YOU MAKING A CAMEO IN SUCH A LAME COMIC STRIP?...
NUMBER ONE-I'M GETTIN' PAID... AND NUMBER TWO-THESE APPEARANCES ARE A LOT SAFER THAN MY LAST GIG. (YUK-YUK-YUK)
WHAM
SNAP
9-30
©1999 Brett Merhar.
Distributed by King Features Syndicate
HA!! I FINALLY GOT YOUR #@*!
ALL RIGHT!! NOBODY TOLD ME HE WAS GONNA BE HERE!! (GROAN)

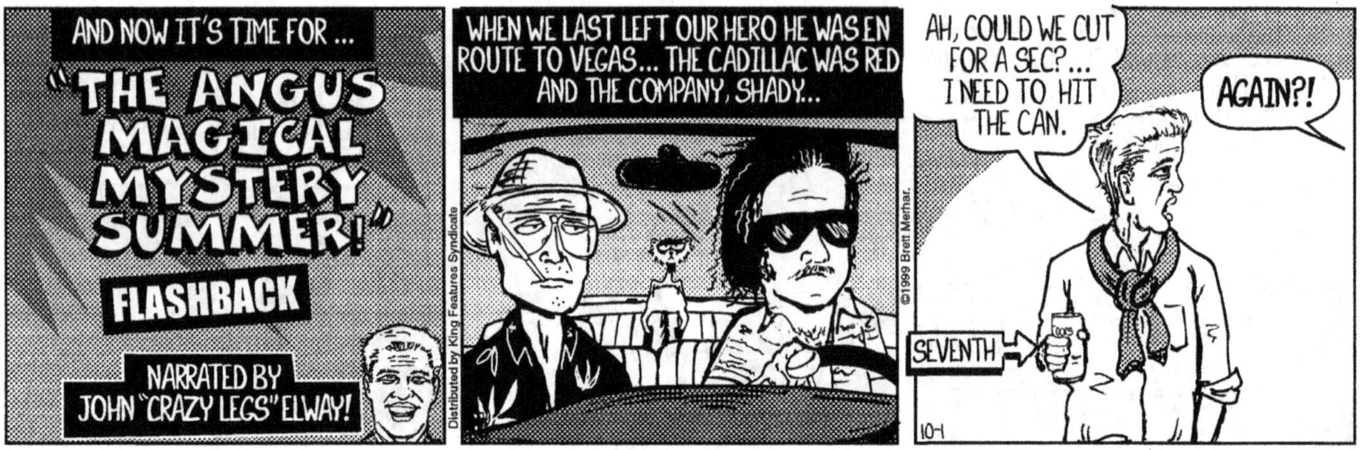
AND NOW IT'S TIME FOR ...
"THE ANGUS MAGICAL MYSTERY SUMMER!"
FLASHBACK
NARRATED BY JOHN "CRAZY LEGS" ELWAY!
WHEN WE LAST LEFT OUR HERO HE WAS EN ROUTE TO VEGAS... THE CADILLAC WAS RED AND THE COMPANY, SHADY...
Distributed by King Features Syndicate
AH, COULD WE CUT FOR A SEC?... I NEED TO HIT THE CAN.
AGAIN?!
SEVENTH
©1999 Brett Merhar.
10-1

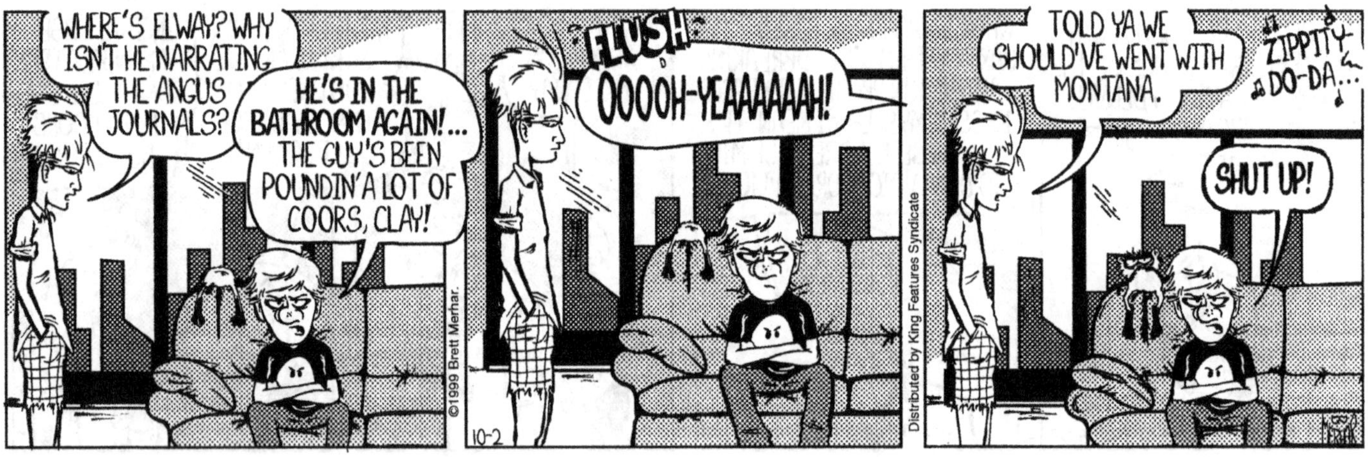
WHERE'S ELWAY? WHY ISN'T HE NARRATING THE ANGUS JOURNALS?
HE'S IN THE BATHROOM AGAIN!... THE GUY'S BEEN POUNDIN' A LOT OF COORS, CLAY!
©1999 Brett Merhar.
FLUSH
OOOOH-YEAAAAAAH!
10-2
Distributed by King Features Syndicate
TOLD YA WE SHOULD'VE WENT WITH MONTANA.
ZIPPITY DO-DA...
SHUT UP!

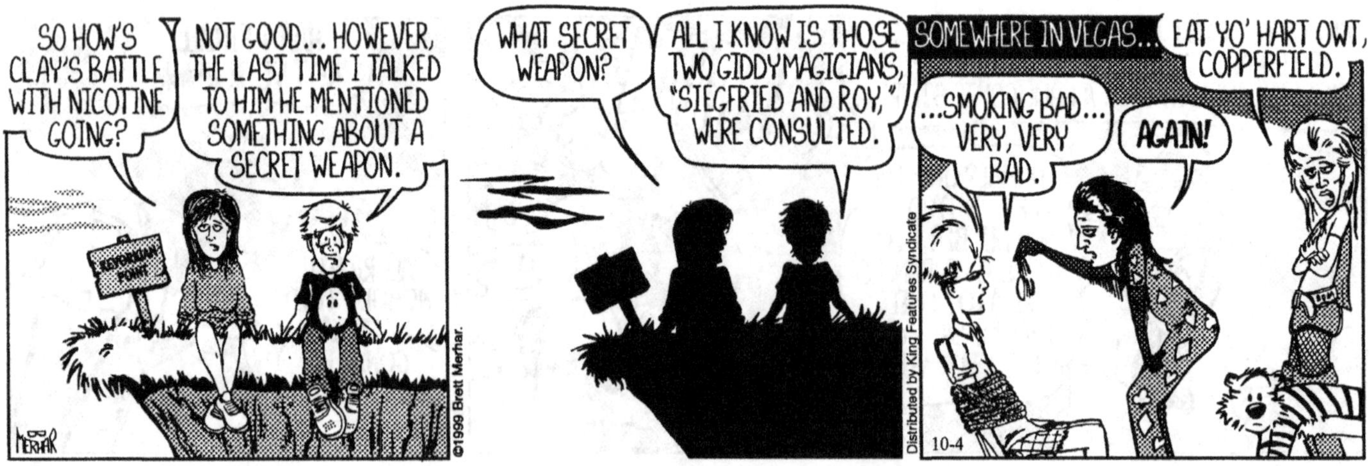
SO HOW'S CLAY'S BATTLE WITH NICOTINE GOING?
NOT GOOD... HOWEVER, THE LAST TIME I TALKED TO HIM HE MENTIONED SOMETHING ABOUT A SECRET WEAPON.
MERHAR
©1999 Brett Merhar.
WHAT SECRET WEAPON?
ALL I KNOW IS THOSE TWO GIDDY MAGICIANS, "SIEGFRIED AND ROY," WERE CONSULTED.
SOMEWHERE IN VEGAS...
EAT YO' HART OWT, COPPERFIELD.
...SMOKING BAD... VERY, VERY BAD.
AGAIN!
Distributed by King Features Syndicate
10-4

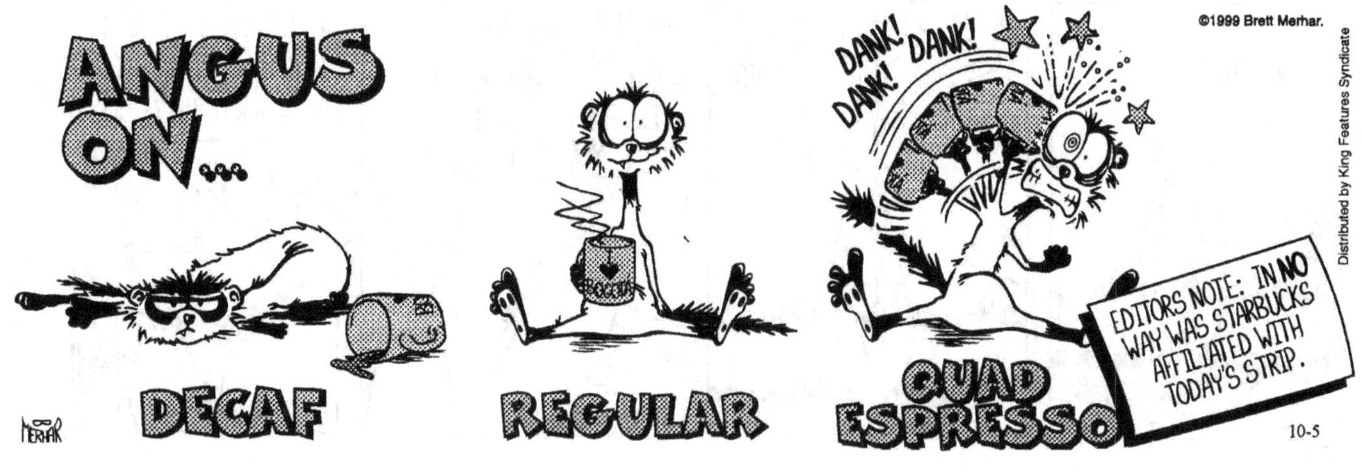
ANGUS ON...
DECAF
REGULAR
DANK! DANK! DANK!
QUAD ESPRESSO
EDITORS NOTE: IN NO WAY WAS STARBUCKS AFFILIATED WITH TODAY'S STRIP.
©1999 Brett Merhar.
Distributed by King Features Syndicate
MERHAR
10-5

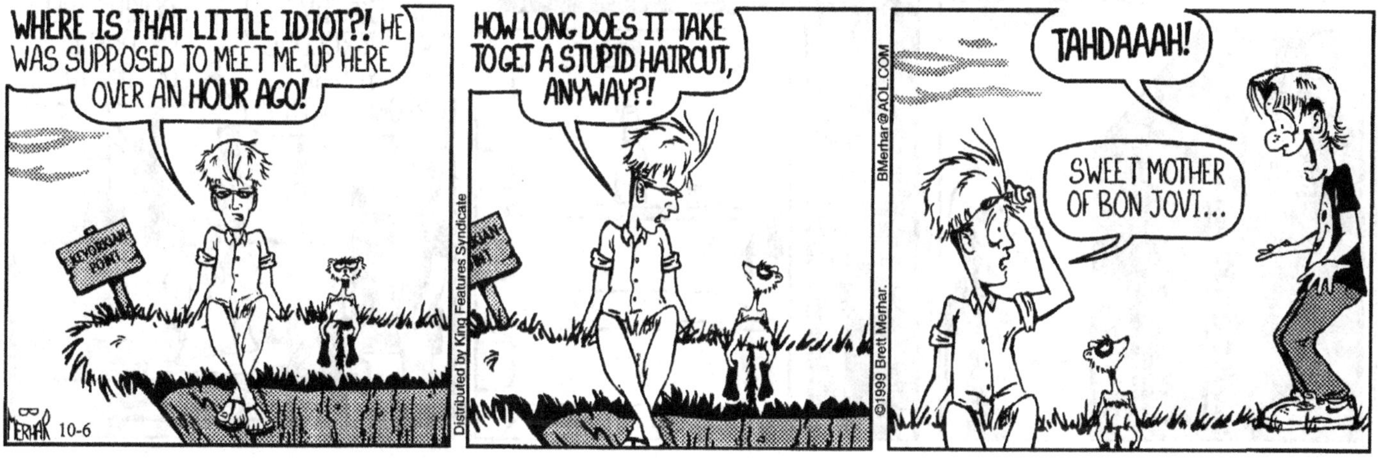
WHERE IS THAT LITTLE IDIOT?! HE WAS SUPPOSED TO MEET ME UP HERE OVER AN HOUR AGO!
KEVORKIAN POINT
MERHAR 10-6
Distributed by King Features Syndicate
HOW LONG DOES IT TAKE TO GET A STUPID HAIRCUT, ANYWAY?!
©1999 Brett Merhar. BMerhar@AOL.COM
TAHDAAAH!
SWEET MOTHER OF BON JOVI...

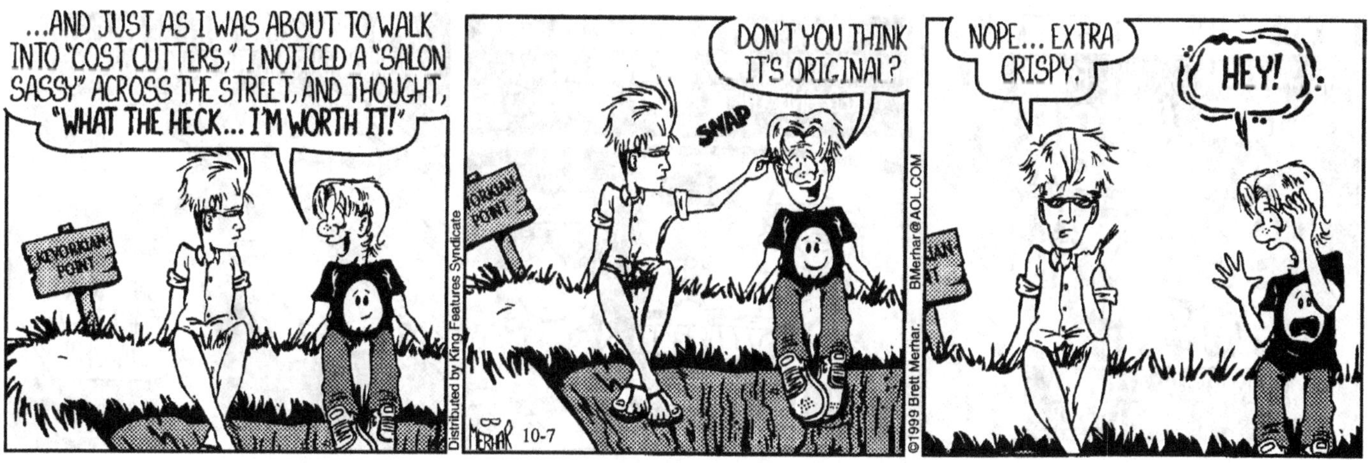
...AND JUST AS I WAS ABOUT TO WALK INTO "COST CUTTERS," I NOTICED A "SALON SASSY" ACROSS THE STREET, AND THOUGHT, "WHAT THE HECK... I'M WORTH IT!"
KEVORKIAN POINT
Distributed by King Features Syndicate
DON'T YOU THINK IT'S ORIGINAL?
SNAP
MERHAR 10-7
©1999 Brett Merhar. BMerhar@AOL.COM
NOPE... EXTRA CRISPY.
HEY!

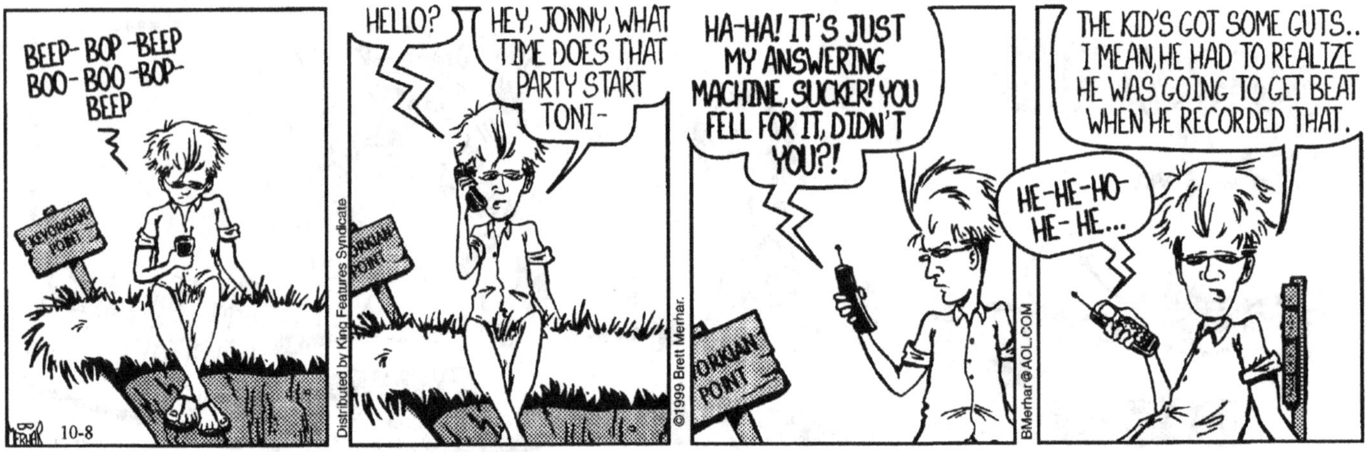
BEEP- BOP -BEEP
BOO- BOO -BOP-
BEEP
KEVORKIAN POINT
10-8
Distributed by King Features Syndicate
HELLO?
HEY, JONNY, WHAT TIME DOES THAT PARTY START TONI-
©1999 Brett Merhar.
HA-HA! IT'S JUST MY ANSWERING MACHINE, SUCKER! YOU FELL FOR IT, DIDN'T YOU?!
BMerhar@AOL.COM
HE-HE-HO-HE-HE...
THE KID'S GOT SOME GUTS.. I MEAN, HE HAD TO REALIZE HE WAS GOING TO GET BEAT WHEN HE RECORDED THAT.

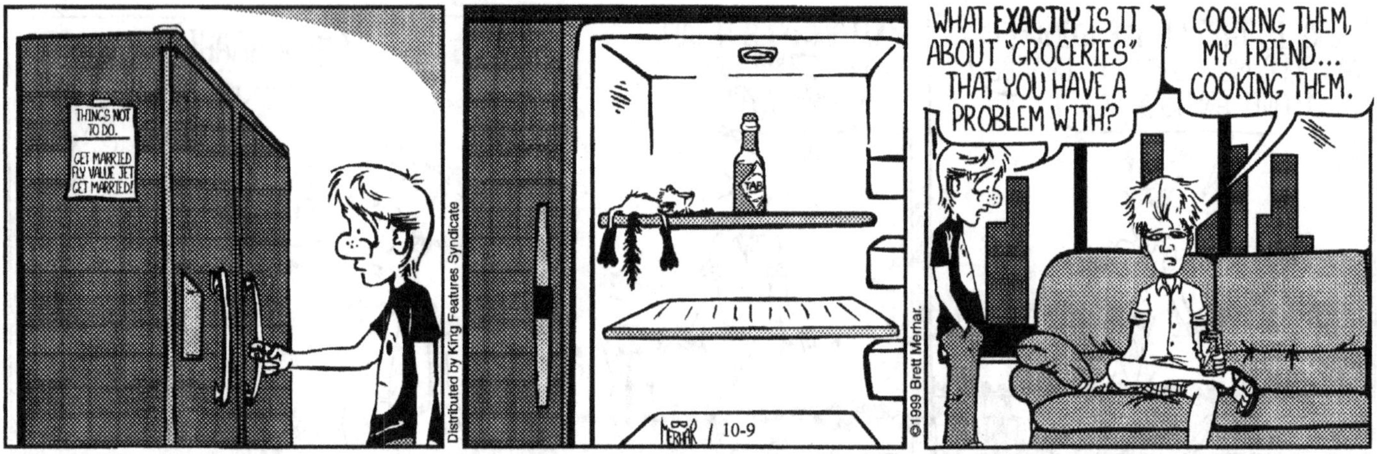
THINGS NOT TO DO.
GET MARRIED
FLY VALUE JET
GET MARRIED!
Distributed by King Features Syndicate
TAB
10-9
©1999 Brett Merhar.
WHAT EXACTLY IS IT ABOUT "GROCERIES" THAT YOU HAVE A PROBLEM WITH?
COOKING THEM, MY FRIEND... COOKING THEM.

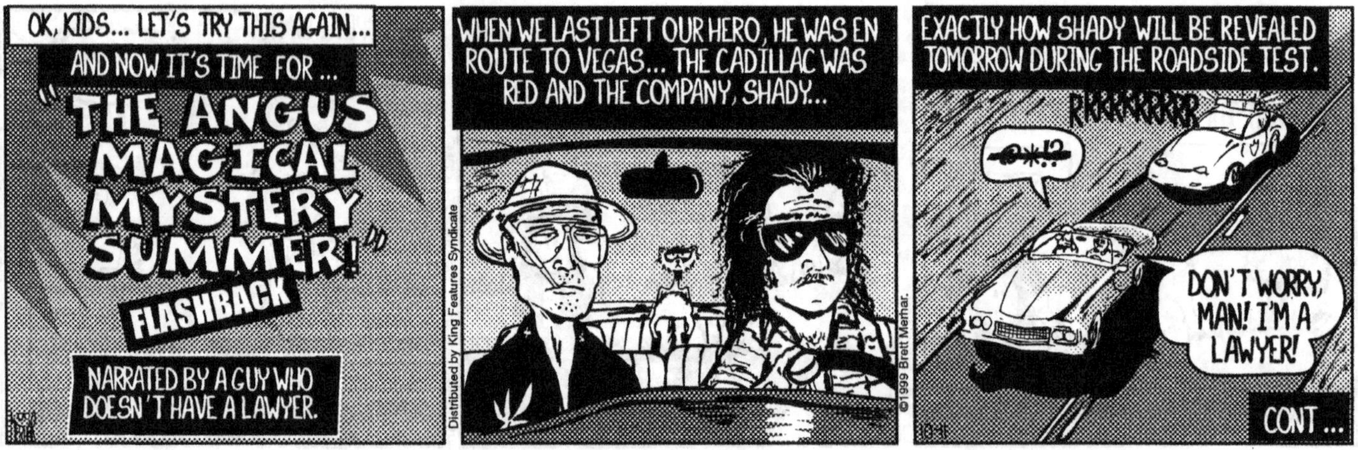
OK, KIDS... LET'S TRY THIS AGAIN...
AND NOW IT'S TIME FOR ...
"THE ANGUS MAGICAL MYSTERY SUMMER!"
FLASHBACK
NARRATED BY A GUY WHO DOESN'T HAVE A LAWYER.
Distributed by King Features Syndicate
WHEN WE LAST LEFT OUR HERO, HE WAS EN ROUTE TO VEGAS... THE CADILLAC WAS RED AND THE COMPANY, SHADY...
©1999 Brett Merhar.
EXACTLY HOW SHADY WILL BE REVEALED TOMORROW DURING THE ROADSIDE TEST.
RRRRRRRRR
DON'T WORRY, MAN! I'M A LAWYER!
CONT...

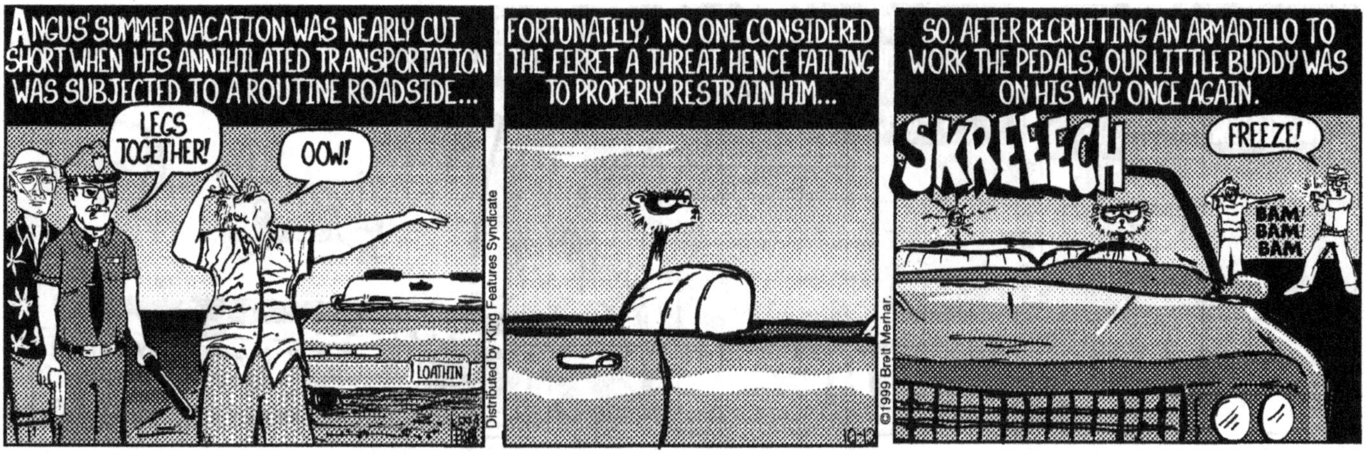
ANGUS' SUMMER VACATION WAS NEARLY CUT SHORT WHEN HIS ANNIHILATED TRANSPORTATION WAS SUBJECTED TO A ROUTINE ROADSIDE...
LEGS TOGETHER!
OOW!
LOATHIN
Distributed by King Features Syndicate
FORTUNATELY, NO ONE CONSIDERED THE FERRET A THREAT, HENCE FAILING TO PROPERLY RESTRAIN HIM...
10-13
©1999 Brett Merhar.
SO, AFTER RECRUITING AN ARMADILLO TO WORK THE PEDALS, OUR LITTLE BUDDY WAS ON HIS WAY ONCE AGAIN.
SKREEECH
FREEZE!
BAM BAM BAM

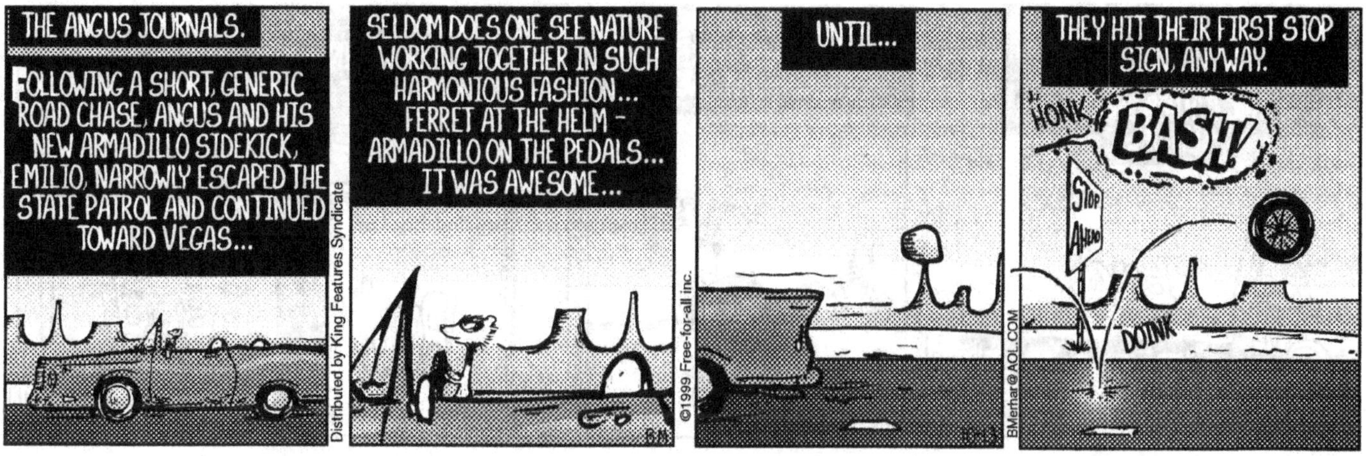
THE ANGUS JOURNALS.
FOLLOWING A SHORT, GENERIC ROAD CHASE, ANGUS AND HIS NEW ARMADILLO SIDEKICK, EMILIO, NARROWLY ESCAPED THE STATE PATROL AND CONTINUED TOWARD VEGAS...
Distributed by King Features Syndicate
SELDOM DOES ONE SEE NATURE WORKING TOGETHER IN SUCH HARMONIOUS FASHION... FERRET AT THE HELM - ARMADILLO ON THE PEDALS... IT WAS AWESOME...
©1999 Free-for-all inc.
UNTIL...
BMerhar@AOL.COM
THEY HIT THEIR FIRST STOP SIGN, ANYWAY.
HONK
BASH!
STOP AHEAD
DOINK

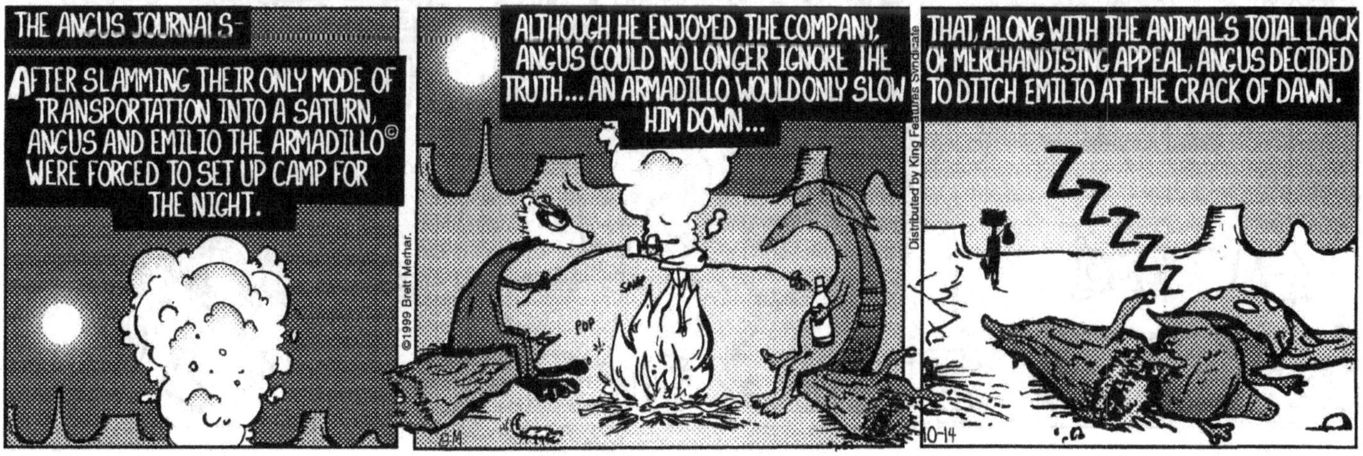
THE ANGUS JOURNALS-
AFTER SLAMMING THEIR ONLY MODE OF TRANSPORTATION INTO A SATURN, ANGUS AND EMILIO THE ARMADILLO© WERE FORCED TO SET UP CAMP FOR THE NIGHT.
©1999 Brett Merhar.
ALTHOUGH HE ENJOYED THE COMPANY, ANGUS COULD NO LONGER IGNORE THE TRUTH... AN ARMADILLO WOULD ONLY SLOW HIM DOWN...
POP
Distributed by King Features Syndicate
THAT, ALONG WITH THE ANIMAL'S TOTAL LACK OF MERCHANDISING APPEAL, ANGUS DECIDED TO DITCH EMILIO AT THE CRACK OF DAWN.
ZZZZZ
10-14

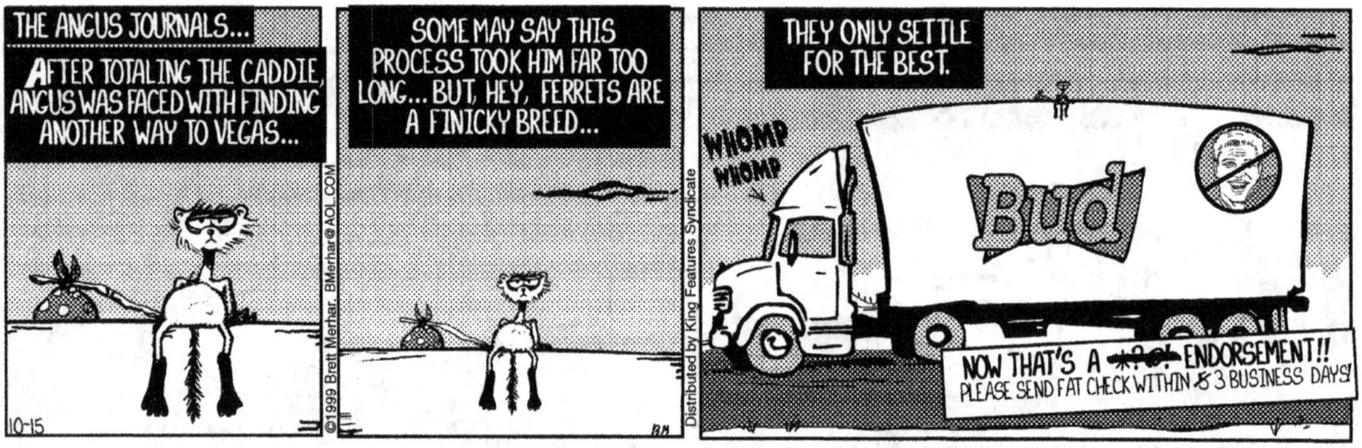
THE ANGUS JOURNALS...
AFTER TOTALING THE CADDIE, ANGUS WAS FACED WITH FINDING ANOTHER WAY TO VEGAS...
10-15
©1999 Brett Merhar. BMerhar@AOL.COM
SOME MAY SAY THIS PROCESS TOOK HIM FAR TOO LONG... BUT, HEY, FERRETS ARE A FINICKY BREED...
BM
Distributed by King Features Syndicate
THEY ONLY SETTLE FOR THE BEST.
WHOMP WHOMP
Bud
NOW THAT'S A *?@! ENDORSEMENT!!
PLEASE SEND FAT CHECK WITHIN 5 3 BUSINESS DAYS!

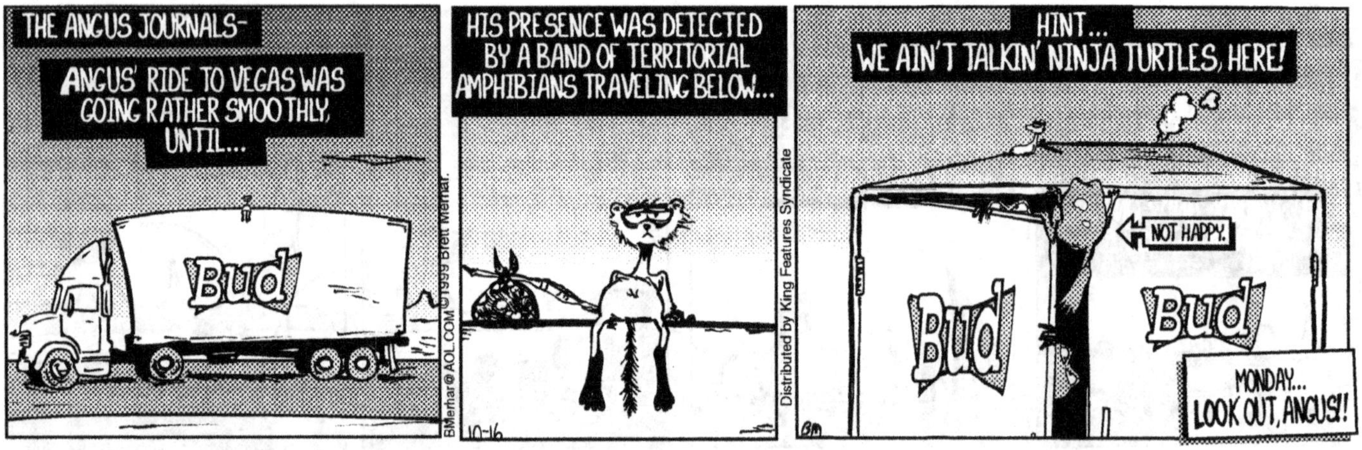
THE ANGUS JOURNALS-
ANGUS' RIDE TO VEGAS WAS GOING RATHER SMOOTHLY, UNTIL...
Bud
BMerhar@AOL.COM ©1999 Brett Merhar.
HIS PRESENCE WAS DETECTED BY A BAND OF TERRITORIAL AMPHIBIANS TRAVELING BELOW...
10-16
Distributed by King Features Syndicate
HINT...
WE AIN'T TALKIN' NINJA TURTLES, HERE!
NOT HAPPY.
Bud
Bud
MONDAY... LOOK OUT, ANGUS!!
BM

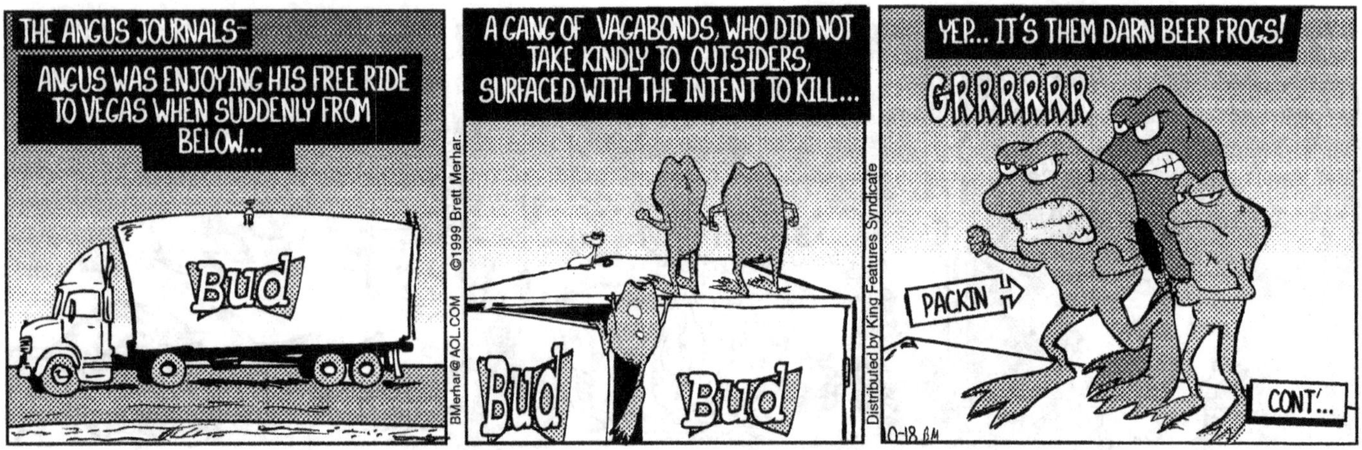
THE ANGUS JOURNALS-
ANGUS WAS ENJOYING HIS FREE RIDE TO VEGAS WHEN SUDDENLY FROM BELOW...
Bud
BMerhar@AOL.COM ©1999 Brett Merhar.
A GANG OF VAGABONDS, WHO DID NOT TAKE KINDLY TO OUTSIDERS, SURFACED WITH THE INTENT TO KILL...
Bud
Bud
Distributed by King Features Syndicate
YEP... IT'S THEM DARN BEER FROGS!
GRRRRRR
PACKIN
CONT'...
10-18 BM

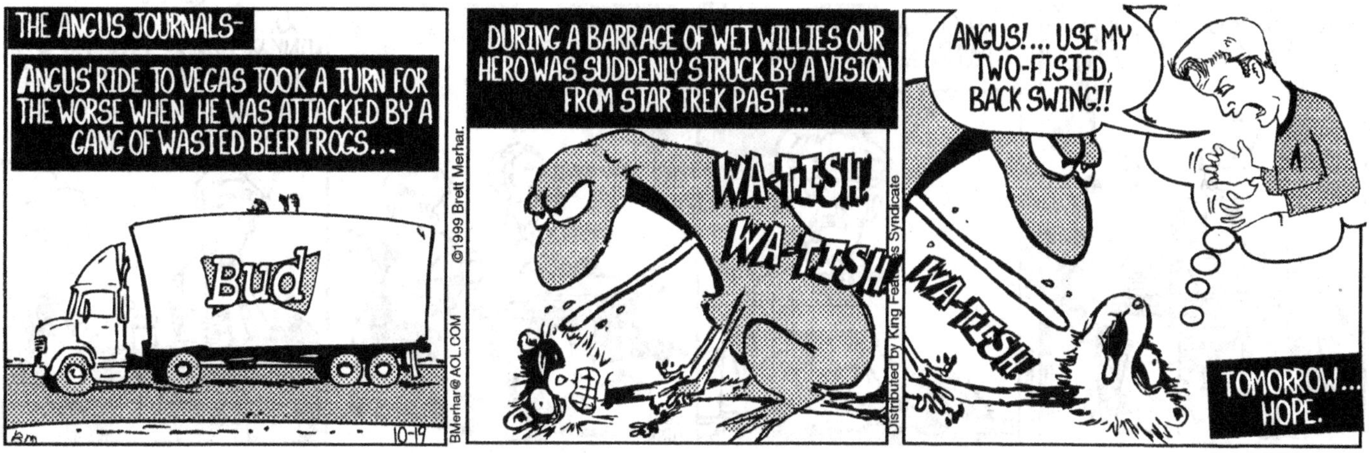
THE ANGUS JOURNALS-
ANGUS' RIDE TO VEGAS TOOK A TURN FOR THE WORSE WHEN HE WAS ATTACKED BY A GANG OF WASTED BEER FROGS...
Bud
10-19
BMerhar@AOL.COM ©1999 Brett Merhar.
DURING A BARRAGE OF WET WILLIES OUR HERO WAS SUDDENLY STRUCK BY A VISION FROM STAR TREK PAST...
WA-TISH!
WA-TISH!
Distributed by King Features Syndicate
ANGUS!... USE MY TWO-FISTED, BACK SWING!!
WA-TISH!
TOMORROW... HOPE.

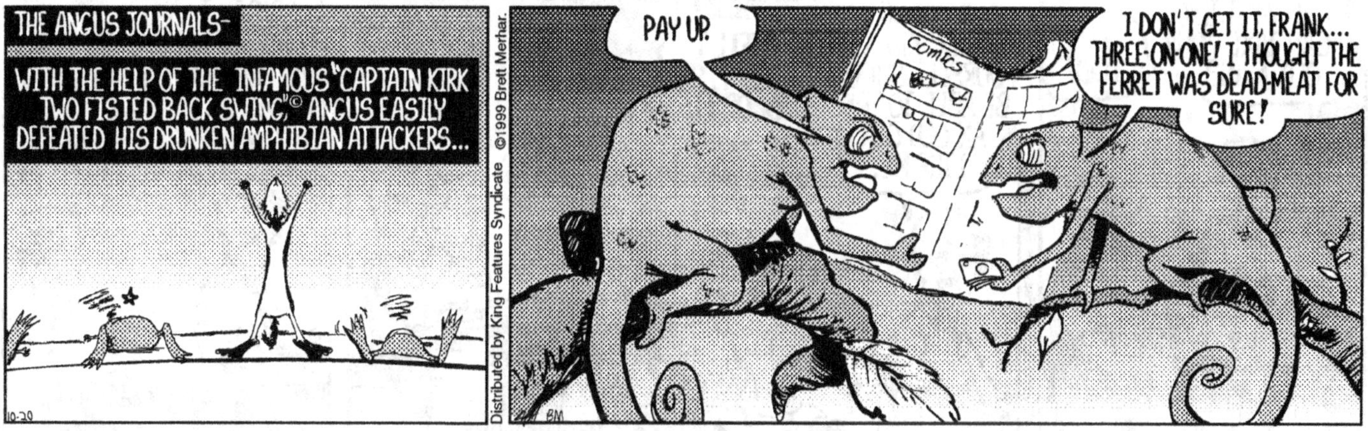
THE ANGUS JOURNALS-
WITH THE HELP OF THE INFAMOUS "CAPTAIN KIRK TWO FISTED BACK SWING,"© ANGUS EASILY DEFEATED HIS DRUNKEN AMPHIBIAN ATTACKERS...
10-20
Distributed by King Features Syndicate ©1999 Brett Merhar.
PAY UP.
COMICS
I DON'T GET IT, FRANK... THREE-ON-ONE! I THOUGHT THE FERRET WAS DEAD-MEAT FOR SURE!

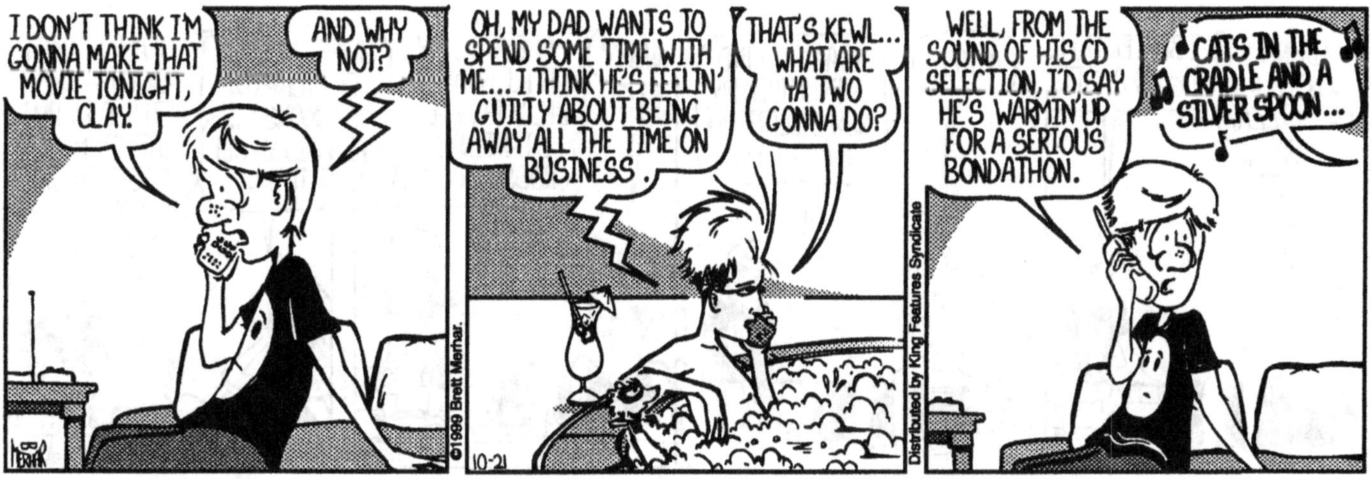
I DON'T THINK I'M GONNA MAKE THAT MOVIE TONIGHT, CLAY.
AND WHY NOT?
MERHAR
©1999 Brett Merhar.
OH, MY DAD WANTS TO SPEND SOME TIME WITH ME... I THINK HE'S FEELIN' GUILTY ABOUT BEING AWAY ALL THE TIME ON BUSINESS.
THAT'S KEWL... WHAT ARE YA TWO GONNA DO?
10-21
Distributed by King Features Syndicate
WELL, FROM THE SOUND OF HIS CD SELECTION, I'D SAY HE'S WARMIN' UP FOR A SERIOUS BONDATHON.
CATS IN THE CRADLE AND A SILVER SPOON...

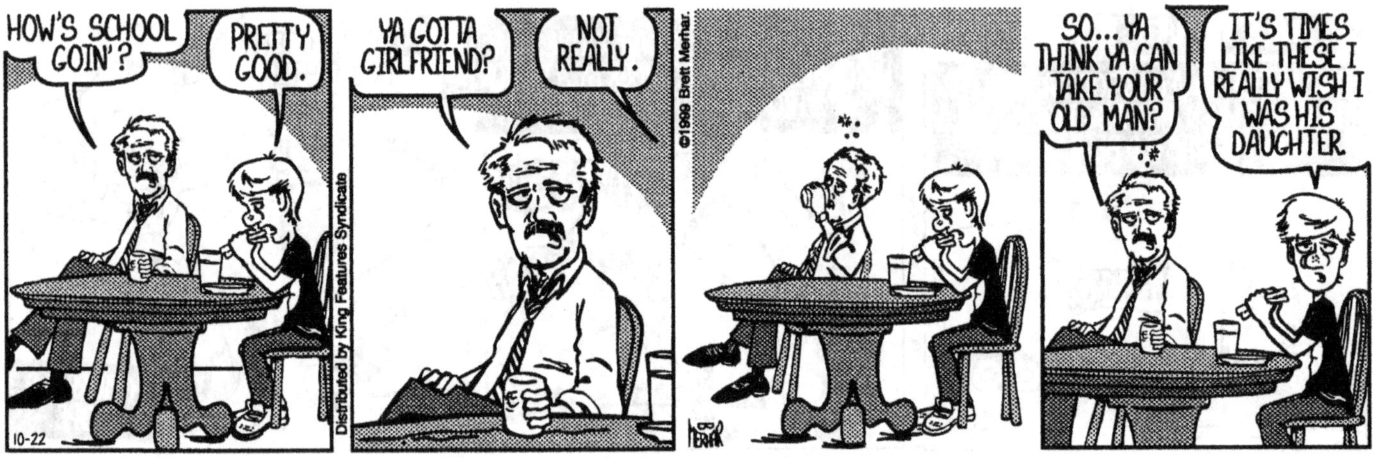
HOW'S SCHOOL GOIN'?
PRETTY GOOD.
10-22
Distributed by King Features Syndicate
YA GOTTA GIRLFRIEND?
NOT REALLY.
©1999 Brett Merhar.
MERHAR
SO... YA THINK YA CAN TAKE YOUR OLD MAN?
IT'S TIMES LIKE THESE I REALLY WISH I WAS HIS DAUGHTER.

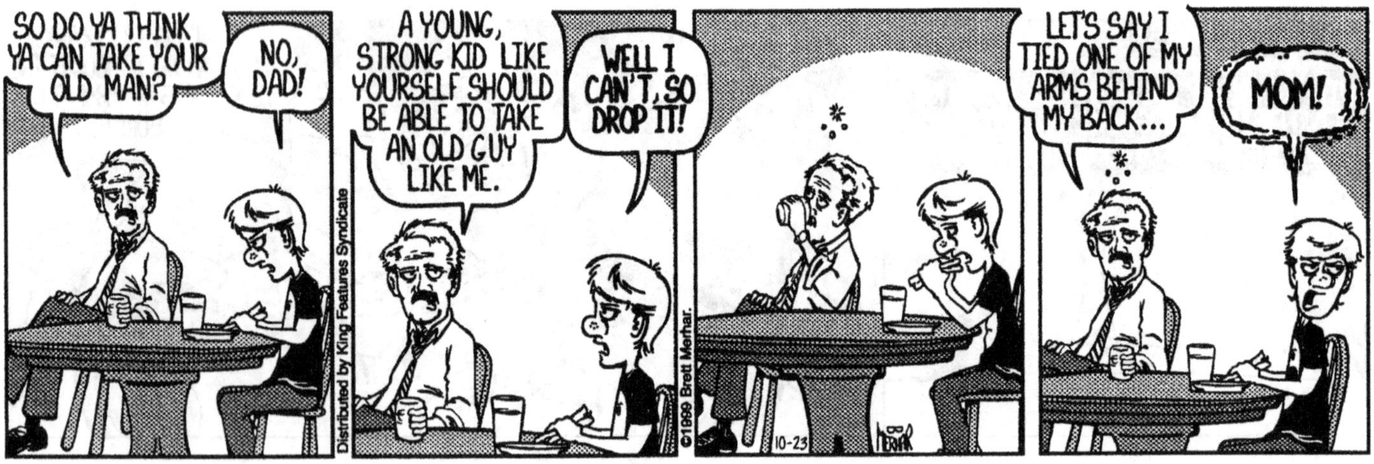
SO DO YA THINK YA CAN TAKE YOUR OLD MAN?
NO, DAD!
Distributed by King Features Syndicate
A YOUNG, STRONG KID LIKE YOURSELF SHOULD BE ABLE TO TAKE AN OLD GUY LIKE ME.
WELL I CAN'T, SO DROP IT!
©1999 Brett Merhar.
10-23
MERHAR
LET'S SAY I TIED ONE OF MY ARMS BEHIND MY BACK...
MOM!

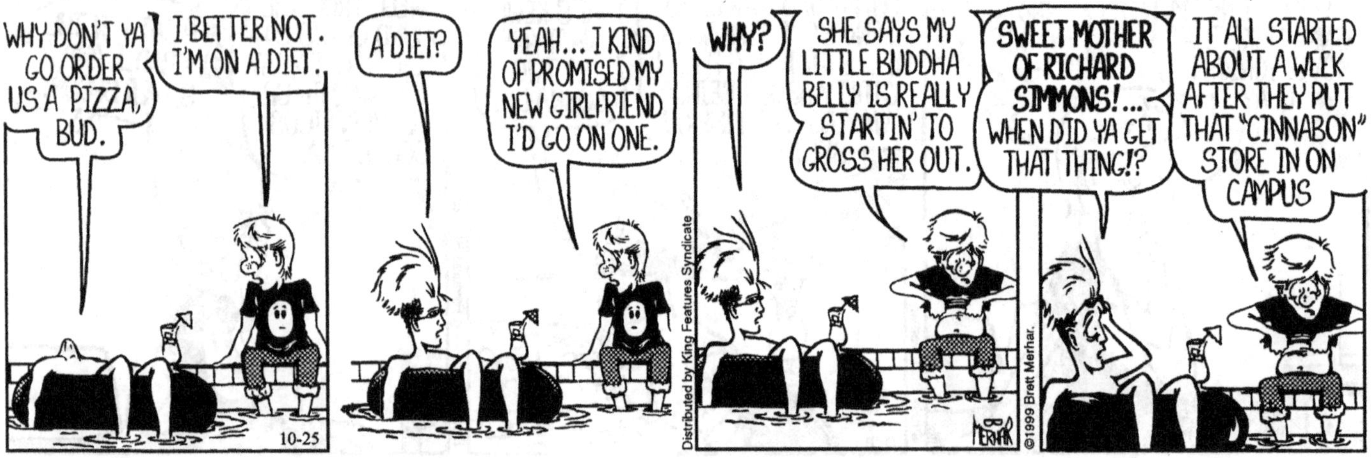
WHY DON'T YA GO ORDER US A PIZZA, BUD.
I BETTER NOT. I'M ON A DIET.
10-25
A DIET?
YEAH... I KIND OF PROMISED MY NEW GIRLFRIEND I'D GO ON ONE.
Distributed by King Features Syndicate
WHY?
SHE SAYS MY LITTLE BUDDHA BELLY IS REALLY STARTIN' TO GROSS HER OUT.
MERHAR
©1999 Brett Merhar.
SWEET MOTHER OF RICHARD SIMMONS!... WHEN DID YA GET THAT THING!?
IT ALL STARTED ABOUT A WEEK AFTER THEY PUT THAT "CINNABON" STORE IN ON CAMPUS

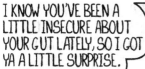

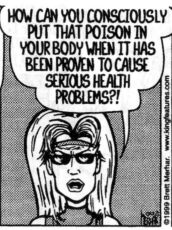

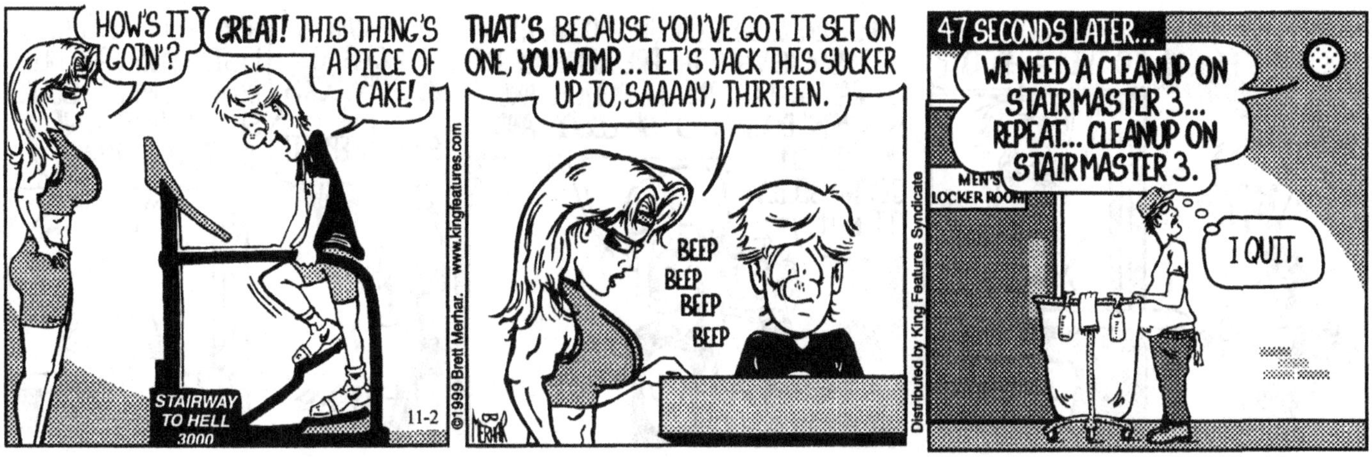
HOW'S IT GOIN'?
GREAT! THIS THING'S A PIECE OF CAKE!
STAIRWAY TO HELL 3000
11-2
THAT'S BECAUSE YOU'VE GOT IT SET ON ONE, YOU WIMP... LET'S JACK THIS SUCKER UP TO, SAAAAY, THIRTEEN.
BEEP BEEP BEEP BEEP
©1999 Brett Merhar. www.kingfeatures.com
MERHAR
47 SECONDS LATER...
WE NEED A CLEANUP ON STAIRMASTER 3... REPEAT... CLEANUP ON STAIRMASTER 3.
MEN'S LOCKER ROOM
I QUIT.
Distributed by King Features Syndicate

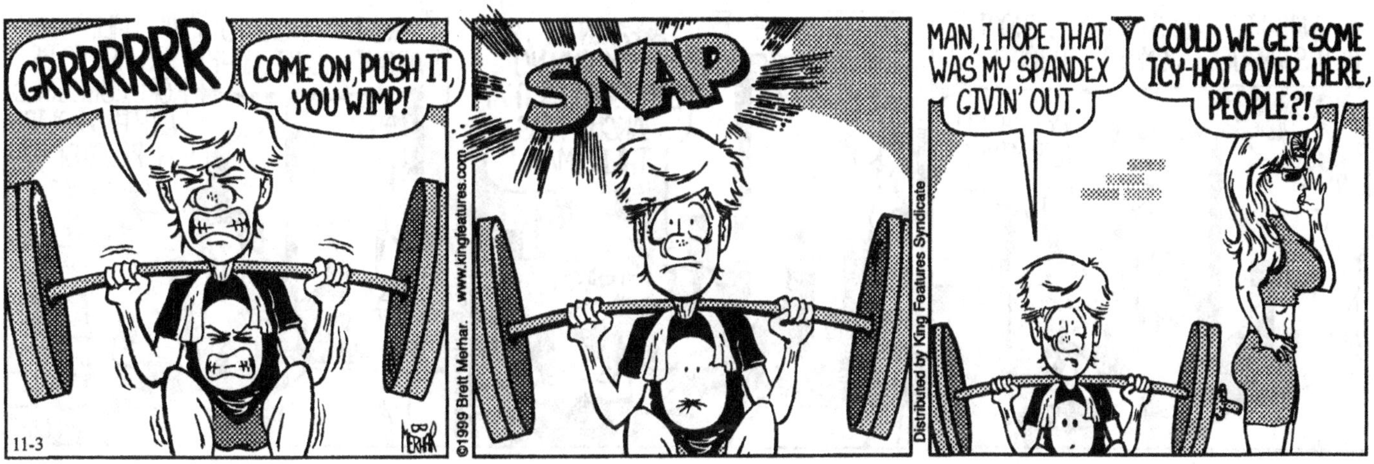
GRRRRRRR
COME ON, PUSH IT, YOU WIMP!
11-3
MERHAR
SNAP
©1999 Brett Merhar. www.kingfeatures.com
MAN, I HOPE THAT WAS MY SPANDEX GIVIN' OUT.
COULD WE GET SOME ICY-HOT OVER HERE, PEOPLE?!
Distributed by King Features Syndicate

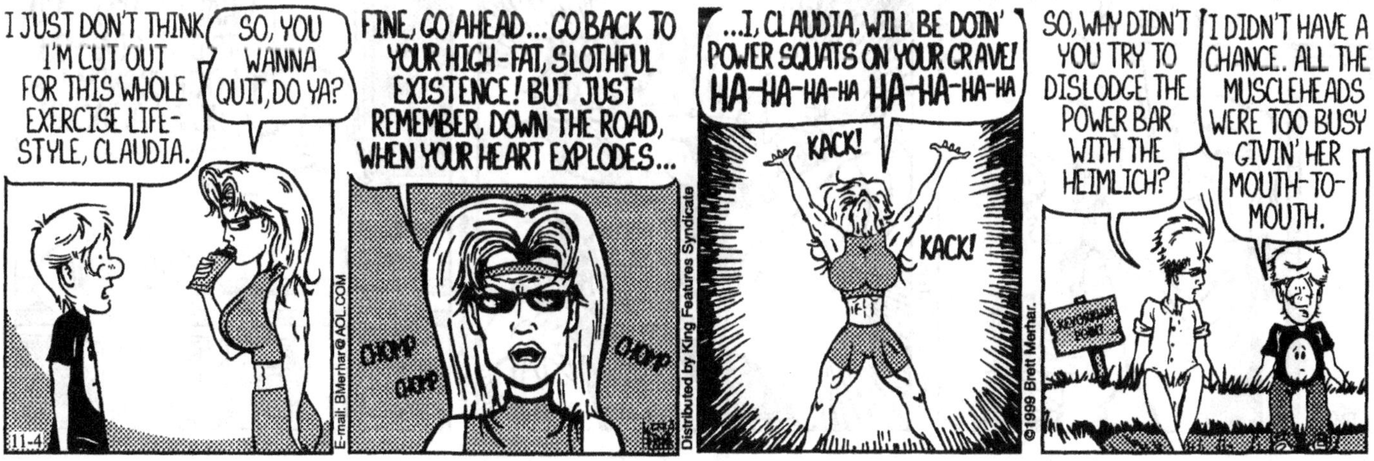
I JUST DON'T THINK I'M CUT OUT FOR THIS WHOLE EXERCISE LIFE-STYLE, CLAUDIA.
SO, YOU WANNA QUIT, DO YA?
11-4
E-mail: BMerhar@AOL.COM
FINE, GO AHEAD... GO BACK TO YOUR HIGH-FAT, SLOTHFUL EXISTENCE! BUT JUST REMEMBER, DOWN THE ROAD, WHEN YOUR HEART EXPLODES...
CHOMP CHOMP CHOMP
Distributed by King Features Syndicate
...I, CLAUDIA, WILL BE DOIN' POWER SQUATS ON YOUR GRAVE! HA-HA-HA-HA HA-HA-HA-HA
KACK! KACK!
SO, WHY DIDN'T YOU TRY TO DISLODGE THE POWER BAR WITH THE HEIMLICH?
I DIDN'T HAVE A CHANCE. ALL THE MUSCLEHEADS WERE TOO BUSY GIVIN' HER MOUTH-TO-MOUTH.
©1999 Brett Merhar.

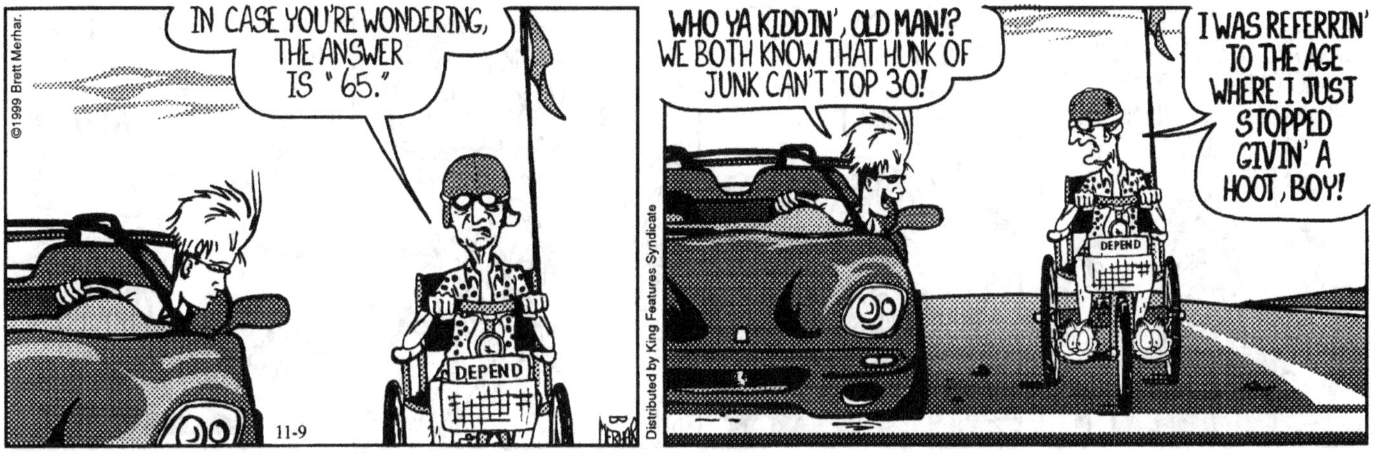
IN CASE YOU'RE WONDERING, THE ANSWER IS "65."
WHO YA KIDDIN', OLD MAN!? WE BOTH KNOW THAT HUNK OF JUNK CAN'T TOP 30!
I WAS REFERRIN' TO THE AGE WHERE I JUST STOPPED GIVIN' A HOOT, BOY!
DEPEND
©1999 Brett Merhar.
Distributed by King Features Syndicate
11-9

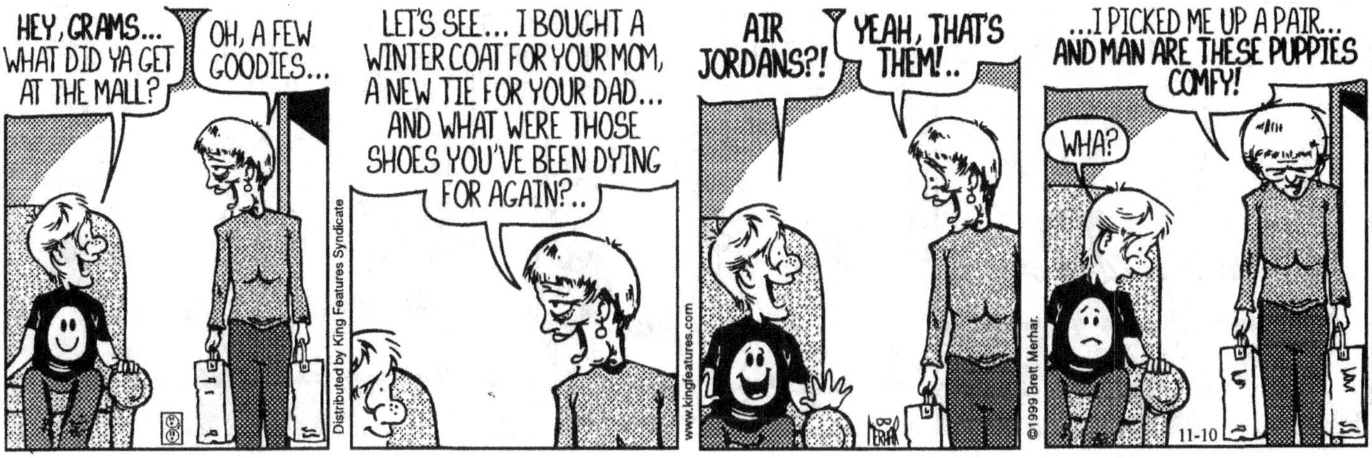
HEY, GRAMS... WHAT DID YA GET AT THE MALL?
OH, A FEW GOODIES...
LET'S SEE... I BOUGHT A WINTER COAT FOR YOUR MOM, A NEW TIE FOR YOUR DAD... AND WHAT WERE THOSE SHOES YOU'VE BEEN DYING FOR AGAIN?..
AIR JORDANS?!
YEAH, THAT'S THEM!..
...I PICKED ME UP A PAIR... AND MAN ARE THESE PUPPIES COMFY!
WHA?
Distributed by King Features Syndicate
www.kingfeatures.com
©1999 Brett Merhar.
11-10

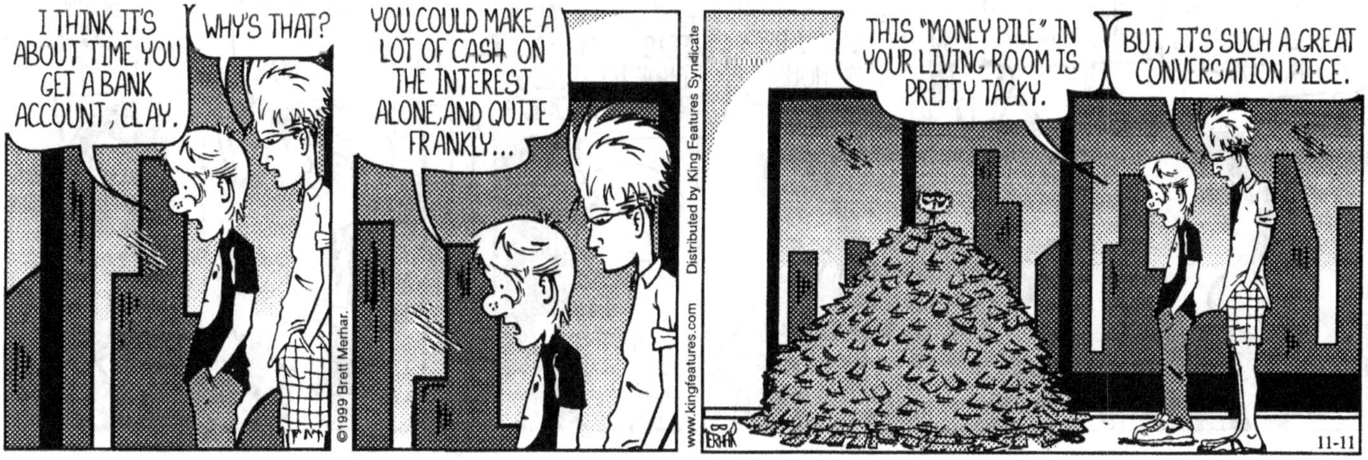
I THINK IT'S ABOUT TIME YOU GET A BANK ACCOUNT, CLAY.
WHY'S THAT?
YOU COULD MAKE A LOT OF CASH ON THE INTEREST ALONE, AND QUITE FRANKLY...
THIS "MONEY PILE" IN YOUR LIVING ROOM IS PRETTY TACKY.
BUT, IT'S SUCH A GREAT CONVERSATION PIECE.
©1999 Brett Merhar.
Distributed by King Features Syndicate
www.kingfeatures.com
11-11

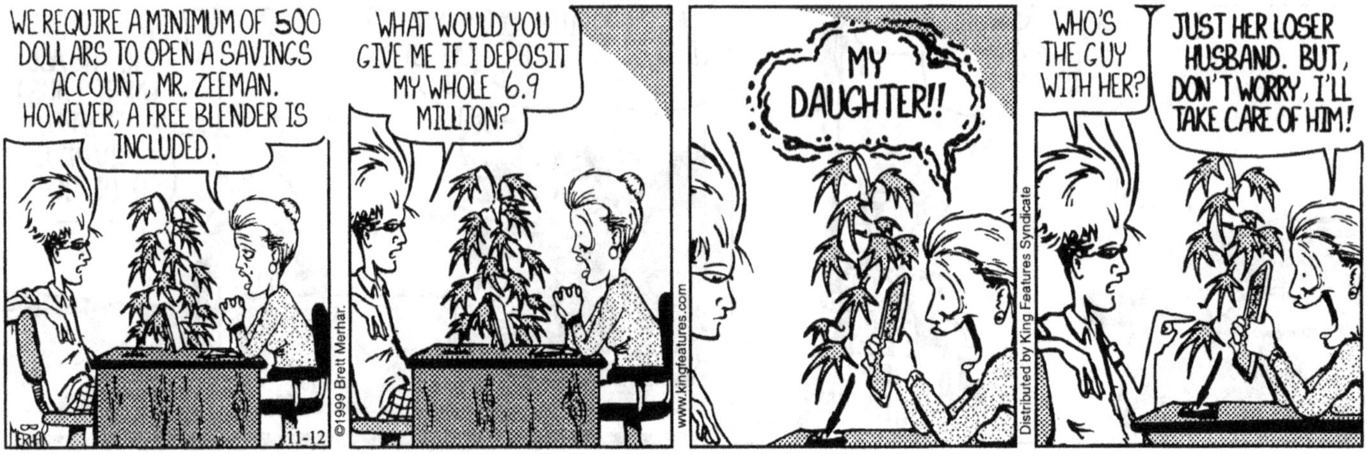
WE REQUIRE A MINIMUM OF 500 DOLLARS TO OPEN A SAVINGS ACCOUNT, MR. ZEEMAN. HOWEVER, A FREE BLENDER IS INCLUDED.
WHAT WOULD YOU GIVE ME IF I DEPOSIT MY WHOLE 6.9 MILLION?
MY DAUGHTER!!
WHO'S THE GUY WITH HER?
JUST HER LOSER HUSBAND. BUT, DON'T WORRY, I'LL TAKE CARE OF HIM!
MERHAR
11-12
©1999 Brett Merhar.
www.kingfeatures.com
Distributed by King Features Syndicate

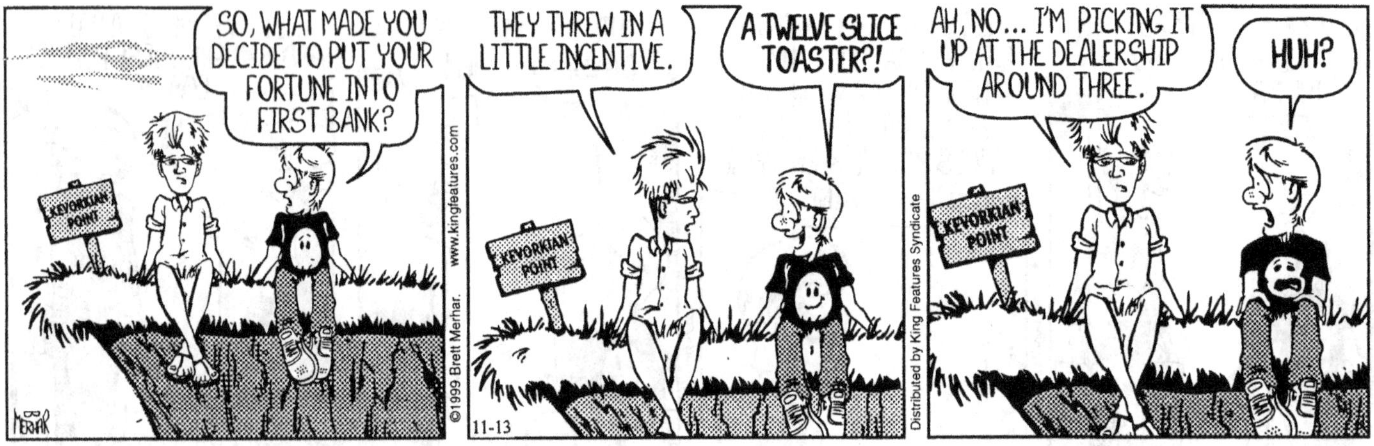
SO, WHAT MADE YOU DECIDE TO PUT YOUR FORTUNE INTO FIRST BANK?
KEVORKIAN POINT
THEY THREW IN A LITTLE INCENTIVE.
A TWELVE SLICE TOASTER?!
AH, NO... I'M PICKING IT UP AT THE DEALERSHIP AROUND THREE.
HUH?
MERHAR
11-13
©1999 Brett Merhar.
www.kingfeatures.com
Distributed by King Features Syndicate

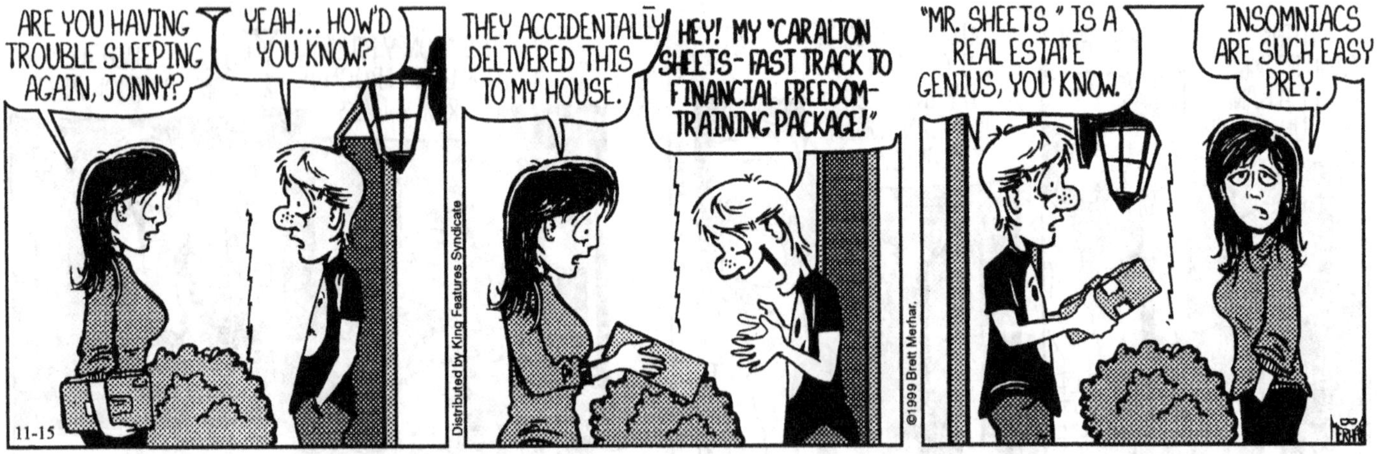
ARE YOU HAVING TROUBLE SLEEPING AGAIN, JONNY?
YEAH... HOW'D YOU KNOW?
THEY ACCIDENTALLY DELIVERED THIS TO MY HOUSE.
HEY! MY "CARALTON SHEETS- FAST TRACK TO FINANCIAL FREEDOM- TRAINING PACKAGE!"
"MR. SHEETS" IS A REAL ESTATE GENIUS, YOU KNOW.
INSOMNIACS ARE SUCH EASY PREY.
11-15
Distributed by King Features Syndicate
©1999 Brett Merhar.
MERHAR

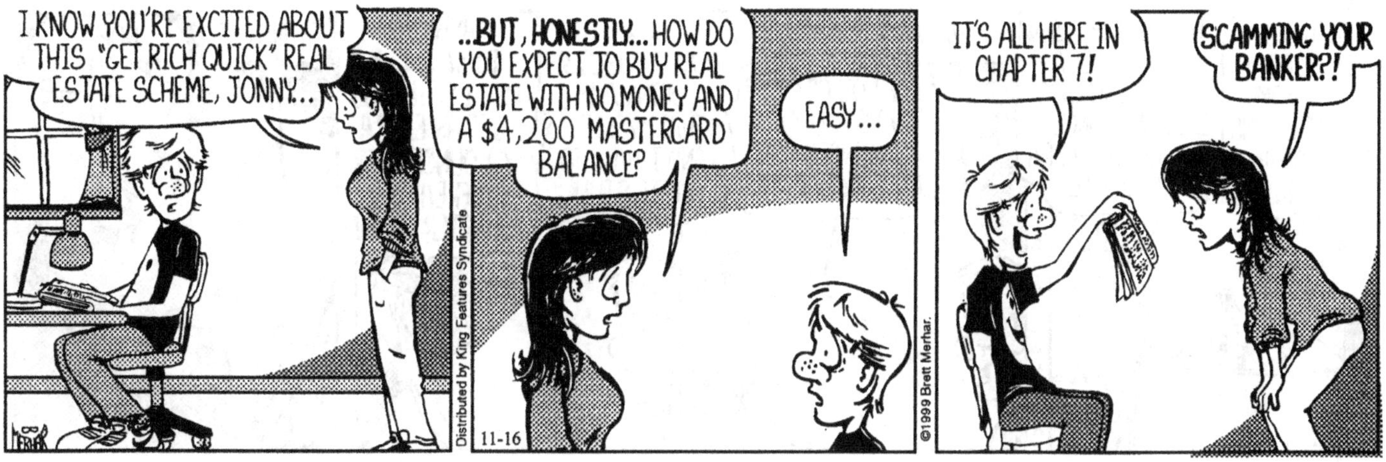
I KNOW YOU'RE EXCITED ABOUT THIS "GET RICH QUICK" REAL ESTATE SCHEME, JONNY...
...BUT, HONESTLY... HOW DO YOU EXPECT TO BUY REAL ESTATE WITH NO MONEY AND A $4,200 MASTERCARD BALANCE?
EASY...
IT'S ALL HERE IN CHAPTER 7!
SCAMMING YOUR BANKER?!
Distributed by King Features Syndicate
11-16
©1999 Brett Merhar.

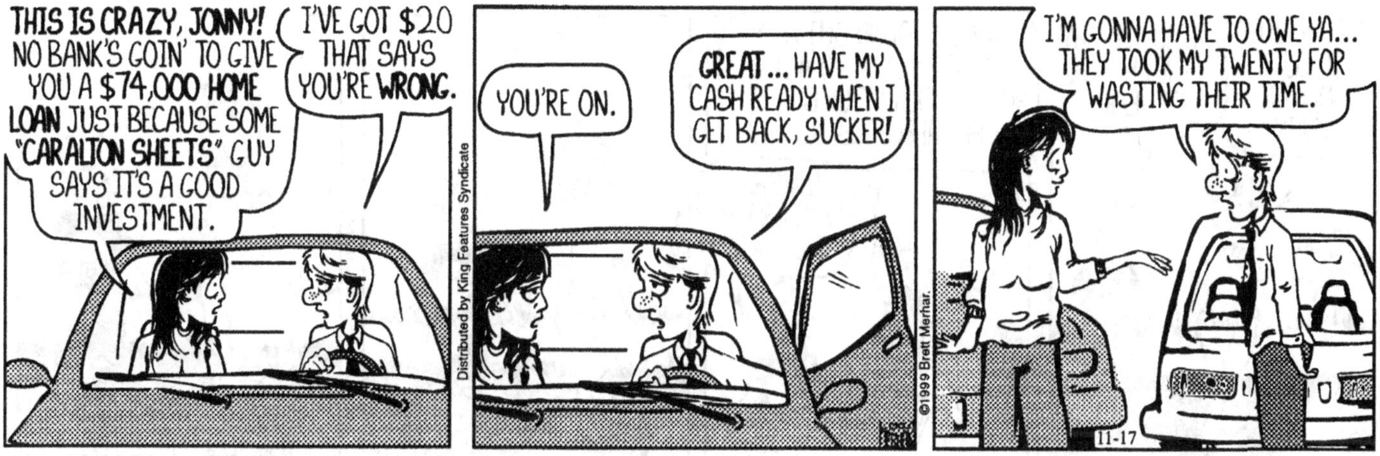
THIS IS CRAZY, JONNY! NO BANK'S GOIN' TO GIVE YOU A $74,000 HOME LOAN JUST BECAUSE SOME "CARALTON SHEETS" GUY SAYS IT'S A GOOD INVESTMENT.
I'VE GOT $20 THAT SAYS YOU'RE WRONG.
YOU'RE ON.
GREAT... HAVE MY CASH READY WHEN I GET BACK, SUCKER!
I'M GONNA HAVE TO OWE YA... THEY TOOK MY TWENTY FOR WASTING THEIR TIME.
Distributed by King Features Syndicate
©1999 Brett Merhar.
11-17

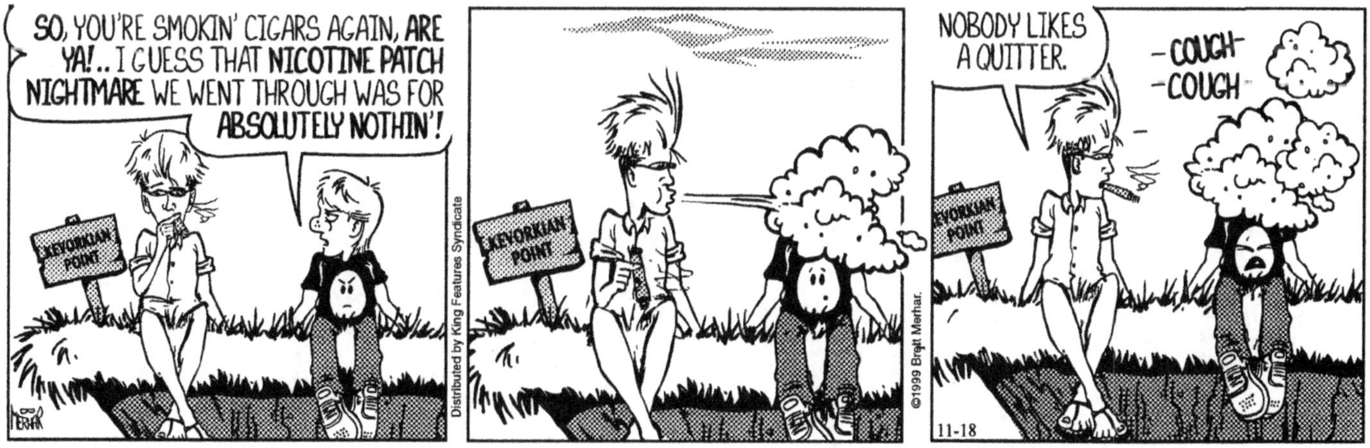
SO, YOU'RE SMOKIN' CIGARS AGAIN, ARE YA!.. I GUESS THAT NICOTINE PATCH NIGHTMARE WE WENT THROUGH WAS FOR ABSOLUTELY NOTHIN'!
KEVORKIAN POINT
NOBODY LIKES A QUITTER.
-COUGH-
-COUGH
Distributed by King Features Syndicate
©1999 Brett Merhar.
11-18

I'LL HAVE A SMALL POPCORN, SOME WHOPPERS, AND A MEDIUM COKE.
FOR AN EXTRA 25¢ YOU CAN GET A LARGE, WHICH HAS 24 MORE OUNCES. AND YOU ALSO GET A FREE REFILL.
MERHAR 11-19
Distributed by King Features Syndicate
NO THANKS.
ARE YOU **CRAZY?** THAT'S AN EXTRA 72 OUNCES FOR ONLY A **QUARTER!**
©1999 Brett Merhar.
I KNOW, BUT I CAN'T **POSSIBLY** DRINK ALL THAT MYSELF... AND I HATE TO WASTE STUFF.
MAYBE YOU DIDN'T HEAR ME! I SAID, YOU GET AN EXTRA 72 OUNCES FOR A FREAKIN' QUARTER, MAN!
THIRSTY?
NOPE... SPINELESS.

I'VE DECIDED TO QUIT SMOKING AGAIN.
REALLY?! WHY THE CHANGE OF HEART?
KEVORKIAN POINT
MERHAR
©1999 Brett Merhar.
MY MOM FOUND OUT AND THREATENED ME TO A 24 HOUR INTERVENTION BACKED BY HER AEROBICS SQUAD.
HARSH! I WONDER WHO TOLD HER?
11-20
Distributed by King Features Syndicate

ABOUT THE AUTHOR

Brett Merhar grew up in Rapid City, Fargo, Pittsburgh, and Denver. While majoring in fine arts and minoring in English at Colorado State University, he fashioned his observations on pop culture into an edgy comic strip he dubbed "Free For All," which was later picked up by King Features Syndicate. Brett passed away July 28, 2016.

Printed in the United States
By Bookmasters